AF663545

Developments in Meditation and States of Consciousness

Zen-Brain Reflections

Developments in Meditation and States of Consciousness

Zen-Brain Reflections

James H. Austin, M.D.

MOTILAL BANARSIDASS PUBLISHERS
PRIVATE LIMITED • DELHI

First Indian Edition : Delhi, 2009
Original edition published by the MIT Press, Cambridge, MA, U.S.A.
with the title 'Zen-Brain Reflections'

ISBN: 978-81-208-3348-7

MOTILAL BANARSIDASS
41 U.A. Bungalow Road, Jawahar Nagar, Delhi 110 007
8 Mahalaxmi Chamber, 22 Bhulabhai Desai Road, Mumbai 400 026
203 Royapettah High Road, Mylapore, Chennai 600 004
236, 9th Main III Block, Jayanagar, Bangalore 560 011
Sanas Plaza, 1302 Baji Rao Road, Pune 411 002
8 Camac Street, Kolkata 700 017
Ashok Rajpath, Patna 800 004
Chowk, Varanasi 221 001

PRINTED IN INDIA

By Jainendra Prakash Jain at Shri Jainendra Press,
A-45 Naraina, Phase-I, New Delhi 110 028
and Published by Narendra Prakash Jain for
Motilal Banarsidass Publishers Private Limited,
Bungalow Road, Delhi 110 007

To my early teachers Nanrei Kobori-Roshi, Myokyo-ni, and Joshu Sasaki-Roshi, for inspiration; to my wife Judy for her support; and to all those whose contributions to Zen, and to the brain, are reviewed in this book.

The test of a religion or philosophy
is the number of things it can explain.

Ralph Waldo Emerson (1803–1882)

Contents in Brief

Contents in Detail

Part III Neurologizing

Chapters Containing Testable Hypotheses

It is a good morning exercise for a research scientist to discard a pet hypothesis every day before breakfast.

Konrad Lorenz (1903–1989)

These chapters suggest potential correlates between brain functions, meditative training, and the phenomena of alternate states of consciousness. Discard any that do not pass critical testing (at any time of day or night).

List of Figures

List of Tables

Preface

> More wisdom is latent in things-as-they-are than in all the words men use.
>
> Antoine de Saint-Exupéry (1900–1944)

Over a century ago, William James chose "Religion and Neurology" for the title of his first Edinburgh lecture, a series that evolved into his classic work, *The Varieties of Religious Experience*.[1] As this millennium began, Koenig and colleagues published their *Handbook of Religion and Health*. Its 768 pages cite evidence suggesting that a person's religious orientation could benefit both brain and body.[2] Skeptics still wonder: can religion help our brains and bodies, and if so, how?

In late 1997, I sent off my manuscript of the earlier book that ventured to integrate Zen with the brain. Since then, countless books and journal articles have been published on separate aspects of neuroscience, Buddhism, and consciousness. For the present book I have selected pivotal areas in which to integrate these huge, separate topics.

This volume is no rehash. It takes up where the earlier book left off. Its new chapters address such questions as: How does acupuncture work? Can neuroimaging localize where our notions of self arise? How can brain imaging during meditation become more informative? Is there more than one kind of experience of "Oneness?" How do decades of meditative training and momentary enlightened states transform the physiology of the brain?

Requests for a less bulky sequel have been met by including far fewer source notes and references than were included in the 113 pages of reference citations of its 1998 predecessor.

Reflections occurs in the latest title for two reasons. First, "Reflections" represents a major update of the chapter in the first book entitled "Reflections on Kensho, Personal and Neurological." Second, the new title serves also to introduce a major new section, part IX. These final chapters do more than explore ancient literary and artistic traditions that had linked Zen enlightenment with moonlight. They present novel interpretations. These arose when I rethought earlier personal experiences and reviewed the latest research. These are new reflections, based on data new and old. They envision links that I could never before have imagined between four diverse topics: migraine, metaphors, moonlight, and mysticism.

In the past, Zen has also had more than a fair share of unimaginably dense riddles. Herein, I try to clarify matters and demystify the subject. Do not be surprised when you encounter chapters uneven in texture which set old lines of historical evidence right next to new research data out at the very frontiers of neuroscience. I integrate topics when possible, but offer no final pat answers. As before, a few testable hypotheses are ventured. Page xvi lists the chapters that contain them.

Part I revisits a major Zen theme: our personal interior *self*. I ask: How do we relate our private self, both to other people and to other things that we think lie "outside" our self/other boundary? Part II highlights several preliminary studies of meditation. I examine both the limitations inherent in their design and those of neuroimaging methods in general.

Part III updates information about the brain, including the amygdala and other parts of the "old" limbic system. Here, I comment on recent research that clarifies its "paralimbic" extensions. Do not get bogged down in these 31 chapters. Lay readers are encouraged to skim them and move on to part IV, which explores states of consciousness. Part V considers some elementary expressions of these states and comments on how appropriate it is to use drugs to simulate them.

Part VI pays a brief visit to the superficial states called absorptions, leaving more room for part VII to revisit the later states that confer crucial insights. Zen refers to such insightful "peak experiences" as *kensho* and *satori*. Part VIII comments on still more advanced states of awakening that realize "Being," then moves beyond to the rare ongoing *stage*. Only very few persons manifest this stage of "sage wisdom."

Part IX is the new section just referred to. It reviews the old history of how "moonlight" came to be linked with kensho. Its personal reflections begin by focusing on an unusual *late phase* of "kensho." This delayed "moonlight" phase has implications for the neurosciences, for Zen Buddhism, and for steering clear of the confusion caused by misidentifying genuine visual *illusions* as mere literary *allusions*.

Meditation, enlightenment, and consciousness are complex topics. The Path of Zen and its intricate interrelationships with the neurosciences call out for some temporary oversimplifications. Cast in this secular role, your author/guide invites you to peruse the simplified figures, tables, four (mondo) summaries, and glossary.

Also for the reader's convenience, many topics here have been cross-referenced to pages in the earlier book. For example, when you come across a citation in brackets like [Z: –], it points you to relevant pages in *Zen and the Brain* that can serve as an introduction.

Why are samples of Zen poetry included? Because their verses often express meaning more accurately than do my words of prose.

Even so, the reader will find not only that the essence of Zen continues to elude words but that crucial facts in the neurosciences still remain to be discovered. We are still very early on that path toward which James was pointing, still straining to integrate the potentials latent in "religion and neurology" into that singular unification which Saint-Exupéry distilled into the phrase, *things-as-they-are*.

Acknowledgments

Professor Nick Gier kindly invited me to give several lectures in his course on Buddhism. Fortunately, this led to an invitation to teach an entire course entitled "Zen and the Brain," and to my becoming formally affiliated with the University of Idaho. I am most grateful to him and to the Department of Philosophy for the opportunity this provided to access the library and interlibrary loan facilities of the university.

I also thank the many editors and program directors, now too numerous to list, who—because they invited me to write or speak at conferences—stimulated me to update and simplify the subject matter for the general audience.

This sequel is the direct result of my being invited by MIT Press to write a *slender* update of the first book. I now take this opportunity to thank Barbara Murphy, the neuroscience editor, for her constant encouragement, to thank Katherine Arnoldi Almeida for her skilled editorial assistance, and to thank Yasuyo Iguchi for her artistry in novel cover designs and illustrations.

I am especially grateful to Kathy Mallory for her ongoing patience and skill both in deciphering my handwritten revisions of her excellent typing, and in bringing the drafts of the manuscript to completion. Many thanks also to James W. Austin, Scott Austin, and Lynn Austin Manning for reviewing and commenting on the manuscript.

In recent years, as a member of Mountain Lamp Idaho, I have been privileged to share in the inestimable bounties of regular Zen practice with our local sangha, as well as in the retreats led by Eileen Kiera and Jack Duffy.

By Way of Introduction

Zen lies beyond the details of words and letters, outside mental conditions, in the inconceivable, in what ultimately cannot be grasped.

Eisai (1141–1215)[1]

This is the second book in a quest for the inconceivable. Its author has been attempting to repair his ignorance in three major areas: (1) Zen—What *is* it? (2) The human brain—How does it *actually* function? (3) Meditation and enlightened states—What *really* goes on? And there is a fourth area we still need to know more about: How has the brain been transformed in the rare sage who has entered the late *stage* of ongoing enlightened traits?

Most chapters in this book are expressed as essays, yet some require the form of a personal narrative. All chapters reflect the personal biases of someone raised as a Unitarian, trained to solve neurological problems at the bedside, who then pursued clinical questions into the research laboratory.

By 1967, I had become fascinated with the psychology of the underlying creative process in biomedical research. So much so that I started to write about it.[2] I soon realized how little I knew about the basic physiology of creative intuition. When I began Zen training in Kyoto 7 years later, my ignorance was compounded. I knew nothing about what caused another flashing form of insight: the flash of enlightenment known as *kensho* or *satori*.

What else happens that steers an otherwise conventional academic neurologist in the direction of Zen? It may help to revisit an interview conducted in 1998. It addresses this and other questions related to the earlier book, entitled *Zen and the Brain*.

You came to Zen both as a medical doctor and as a practicing scientist. What attracted you to it?

Well, I encountered Zen by chance during my first sabbatical in Japan. I was first attracted to it by the aesthetic qualities of the Zen temples and gardens in Kyoto. I was also drawn to it because I had seen that Zen had shaped the cultural life of Japan in many influential ways. There was one final crucial factor: the opportunity to learn from Kobori-Roshi. He was a remarkable Zen master. His presence communicated the essence of Zen, and I could converse with him in English.

Did Zen largely challenge, or corroborate, what you knew from science?

It did both, at different times. At the outset, nothing in my previous medical or neuroscience training had prepared me for Zen. The challenge stimulated me to learn more—both about Zen and about the rapidly expanding frontiers of brain research. I soon saw that whenever I could interrelate Zen and the brain, each field was capable of illuminating the other. So the challenge then became: *which* few facts in this explosive field of the neurosciences are relevant to Zen, and vice versa?

What is a mystical experience? Is it necessarily religious?

Large surveys show that it's not rare. About one out of three persons has experienced some kind of "mystical" or "religious" event at some time in their life. When that person takes up the spiritual path in a more formal manner, there occurs a sense of engagement in an ongoing quest. The quest is for practical steps that can help the person reestablish, by the deepest of insights, a sense of more direct relationships with the Ultimate Reality principle (however each person may choose to define this).

For many centuries, people who commit themselves to follow such a path have reported a wide variety of experiences. William James described some of these events, as have many others. Most experiences at one end of the spectrum tend to be brief and superficial; they "quicken" mostly the sensibilities and the emotions. Other events tap our much deeper levels of comprehension. Most cultures would regard the more advanced of these deeper states as being at least semi-"religious." Zen emphasizes the more profound insightful experiences that have existential overtones. They confer insight-wisdom. This is a special refinement of the other kinds of intuition we're more familiar with in relation to the creative process in general.

Isn't ordinary consciousness itself something of a mystery? Or, do you believe that consciousness is a physical phenomenon of the brain, one that science is increasingly demystifying?

Yes, "ordinary" consciousness has always been a source of mystery. Trying to demystify it, philosophers and scientists have succeeded in attaching relatively drab names to many of its ingredients. Yet consciousness slips through any net one might cast with words. It remains a vital emergent property, a result of the brain's seemingly countless interactive functions.

Do you believe that a meaningful distinction exists between the mind and brain?

Our words keep presenting problems. Brain and mind *are* different topics. However, I can hold a human brain in my hand and feel its weight. And I can also count, almost as "real," that feeling of mental cobwebs that arises whenever too heavy a burden of thoughts "weighs on my mind."

As a neurobiologist, I'm led to believe that our human brain is the organ of our mind. Indeed, before brains came to exist on this planet, there were no minds either. I also begin with the humanist bias and imperative. I'm immensely awed by the creative forces in the current universe. I just can't find much personal motivation in the notion that some kind of purposive, but incomprehensible, "Big Mind" is out there "in the ether."

What about the body and spirit?

The life-support systems of our bodies are essential. Otherwise our fragile brain functions wouldn't survive and flourish. As for the other word, my Webster's Third Unabridged gives twenty-five definitions of "spirit" (along with 11 definitions of "spiritual"). Zen is very leery of the pitfalls in words, for good reasons.

How do you view the current explosion of scientific work on consciousness, and the many books which now attempt to explain it?

Your question underlines our current dilemma. We already suffer from too many things to do, to read, to listen to, and to see. Part of the problem begins with the fact that the many writers in the field define consciousness differently. (The same Webster's dictionary lists five definitions.) One outcome is our present information overload. Gosta Ehrensvard anticipated this confusing situation when he said: "Consciousness will always be one degree above comprehensibility."

A Zen perspective has been available for centuries. But until recent decades, the scientific community did not understand the message, or it chose to ignore it. How can Zen make its age-old contribution to the study of consciousness? By inviting us to ask the naive and seemingly incredible question: what is this world *really* like without our intrusive self-referent self in the picture? Putting it another way, let's suppose a brain drops off all its subjective veils of *self*-consciousness. What, then, does the rest of its awareness—its pure, objective consciousness—perceive?

How does Zen meditation affect the brain physiologically?

There's still no short answer. Meditation creates a series of complex psychophysiological changes. To begin with a loose generalization, one might say that Zen meditation does involve a kind of *not* thinking, *clearly*. And it then proceeds to carry this clear awareness into everyday living. At the entry level are the simpler forms of meditation. They adopt a passive attitude and help to generate a "relaxation response," a term Herbert Benson introduced to summarize the early steps in a long process.

Several additional techniques help people further cultivate the art of concentrating while they meditate. Some of these approaches evoke calibrated levels of added stress responses within the brain itself. Thereafter, gradual transformations take place in the brain when meditators commit themselves to a very long-range process of mindful self-discipline, introspection, and meditative retreats.

What is the most important thing to understand about Zen and the brain?

I'd sum up briefly in the following way: Zen training is an agency of character change. It's a program designed to point the whole personality in the direction of increasing selflessness and enhanced awareness. To this end, the Path of Zen implies a long-range program of systematic training. It proceeds within a restrained and culturally acceptable established meditative tradition. The whole setting encourages each aspirant to engage in a series of meditative retreats. There, one shares their rigor and discomforts with other like-minded seekers in a supportive social framework.

Buddhism has become popular in the West. Do you regard this as a fad? To what would you attribute it?

This interest in Buddhism is a complex cultural phenomenon. Tapping many genuine sources, it has been on the rise, especially in the last four decades. Exemplars like the Dalai Lama and Thich Nhat Hanh have helped. Sixteen years ago, Joseph Campbell viewed Buddhism as the closest, most valid mythology for this planet. He also noted the big practical problem: it was hard for anyone to awaken to the realization that he or she was really an integral part of the larger whole.

One other associated cultural phenomenon gave a lift to the Buddhist approaches to meditation. Pundits call our era "The Information Age." But, in fact, we struggle to live in an artificial "Age of Information Overload." Our Cro-Magnon brains were not designed to process this blizzard of unwanted junk mail and email, or to be stimulated into so many trivial pursuits. Accordingly, human beings have begun to rediscover their deep, instinctual yearning for quiet, extended moments and hours of information UN-load. Many are now turning away from secondhand, so-called virtual reality TV and video games. They are reaching out toward more meaningful value systems—call some of their paths spiritual if you wish.

What is the most striking practical benefit you attribute to Zen practice?

One discovers a sense of increasing calmness and clarity while beginning to walk the Zen meditative Path. This evolves over the years, because the practice points one increasingly in the direction of simplicity, stability, efficient action, and compassion.

What's unique about your book?

Its author has personally experienced several different alternate states of consciousness. I went on to examine in detail both these brief phenomena and also the more gradual transformations that evolved during long-range meditative training. My background is that of a clinical neurologist and researcher. So, I've correlated my personal observations with the latest plausible explanations I could find in the neuroscience and Zen literature. The result is a series of testable working hypotheses. They tap psychophysiological and neurochemical levels of analysis. I don't pretend to understand Zen as a complex cultural phenomenon, but I have been willing to oversimplify the neurobiological correlates of its teachings and its experiential phenomena.

Part I

Starting to Point toward Zen

One does not discover new lands without consenting to lose sight of the shore for a very long time.

André Gide (1869–1951)

1

Is There Some Common Ground between Zen Experience and the Brain?

> The coming of Buddhism to the West may well prove to be the most important event in the twentieth century.
>
> Arnold Toynbee (1889–1975)

> Experience never errs. Only your judgment errs by promising itself results which your experiments didn't produce.
>
> Leonardo da Vinci (1452–1519)[1]

Toynbee believed that religion exerted a major regenerative influence in human affairs. Da Vinci warned us not to expect too much from our experiments. Some of the common ground we now seek between religion and neuroscience begins when we set sail toward that experimental domain often called psychophysiology.

Psychophysiology has become a formal discipline during the last half century. Its mainstream adherents are now wary of its earlier alluring promises. Researchers now conduct rigorous experiments and are increasingly exacting in critiquing their own results. When we use the term *psychophysiology* in the context of Zen and the brain, its basic physiological mechanisms may be condensed in three deceptively simple words. They involve excitation, inhibition, and disinhibition. The words describe the way impulses from one neuronal module go on to increase or decrease the firing rates of other cell assemblies.

Few of the resulting configurations actually filter up into consciousness, let alone into accurate first-person reports. This is only one of several reasons why readers and authors must be wary when researchers report so-called correlations and associations which seem to "link" physiological data with psychological events.

A promising step forward is the 2002 electroencephalography (EEG) study by Lutz and colleagues.[2] It is based on first-person reports by four astute observers. Their task was to resolve many random dots into a 3-dimensional (3D) geometric shape, one that they could recognize. Prior training had helped them both to recognize *and specify* their own *individual* categories of psychological experience. For example, they had become skilled at rendering this delicate judgment: Was I really prepared ("psychologically") *immediately before* I performed the required task? When these four trained subjects each did feel especially poised and ready *just before their task*, what did their EEG show? Characteristic *individual* patterns of fast, synchronized gamma wave activity in the frontal region.

The recent *Handbook of Psychophysiology* highlights the ever-present explanatory gap between such psychological events and the associated physiological data. These two domains may be very tightly linked, more loosely correlated, or completely unrelated.[3] And so we begin the present book with the following caveat: Most other psychophysiological data and theories are cited here to serve as working hypotheses. All are subject to revision. Some may be of heuristic value in narrowing the gap between Zen experience and neuroscience.

2

A Brief Outline of Zen History

> With its tolerance, its principle of nonviolence, its universal compassion extended to all living creatures, its high morality and humanity, Buddhism had and still has a great message for the world.
>
> Henry Sigerist (1891–1957)[1]

The Man and His Times

Our narrative might begin two and half millennia ago. Near the borders of present-day Nepal, young Siddhartha (563–483 B.C.E.) first saw life's harsh realities: a sick man, an old man, and a dead man. Deeply shaken, he later set out, at age 29, on the quest to find meaning in life.

Others shared his distress. The anguish of his sorely troubled contemporaries to the west still echoes in Job's lament, voiced by an author of the Old Testament, around 400 B.C.E. "One thing alone I feared, and it befell me—the very thing I dreaded. No peace had I, no calm, no rest; but torments came."

And, at about the same time, Greek choruses were expressing their varieties of angst in these lines by Sophocles (496–406 B.C.E.) in his *Oedipus Rex*: "What is unwisdom but the lusting after longevity: that urge to grow older, and full of days! But this tide of years, so vast and unremitting, casts up to our view only sorrowful and joyless things. For once we've aged beyond our prime, our pleasures drift beyond reach, all washed away."

Not until Siddhartha was 35 years old and then living in the north of India did he finally become fully enlightened. Worth noting is the fact that his legendary awakening occurred only after a rigorous 6-year spiritual quest. Suddenly, after he had meditated intensively through a very "dark night," *he saw with deep insight into the existential suffering of human beings*. He realized (1) what caused their anguish; and (2) how to prevent and relieve it. Indeed, after he died at the age of 80, his followers could distill his central message into these few words:

"Suffering I teach, and the Way out of suffering."

The Prescription

Soon, they would call this man the Buddha, meaning the enlightened or awakened one. The Buddha was both an insightful teacher and a healer. Having diagnosed the cause of his own distress, he went on to develop a prescription that others could use when they sought *inner* peace in their world of constant outer turmoil.

His remedy was a course of action. This Buddhist ethical approach is still in use down to the present day. It means following a sensible eightfold path: a combination of right understanding, thought, speech, conduct, vocation, effort, mindfulness, and meditation.

The Subsequent Buddhist Movement

In that ancient era, the Sanskrit word for meditation was *dhyana*. As Buddhist monks traveled north, dhyana would change into the Chinese word *Ch'an*. In China, this meditation school of Mahayana Buddhism absorbed strong cultural infusions from Taoism and Confucianism. Its influence peaked during the Tang dynasty (618–907). Later, when Buddhist monks transplanted this Ch'an school to Japan, the Japanese would pronounce it Zen. The very word, Zen, exemplifies this rich historical tapestry.

There are two major Zen schools. The *Soto* school emphasizes "just sitting" and a more incremental enlightenment. The *Rinzai* school is more austere, rigorous, and places more emphasis on sudden enlightenment.

The Nature of Siddhartha's Awakening

But what happened in Siddhartha's *brain* during that long night? Which insight into the basic cause and relief of suffering was pivotal in his sudden "enlightenment?" No witness was there; the actual details are lost in the mist of history. Only much later would his followers invent words he never uttered, develop legends about what transpired, compose "songs" he never sang. Now, 2500 years later, we are left to speculate.

The resonances from two short verses in the *Dhammapada* echo in speculation below. Not until around the third century C.E. were these verses compiled within the southern, Theravada branch of Buddhism. The passages suggest that his latter-day followers had also realized what was the root cause of human suffering: our self-centered personality *structure*.

The adapted verses below pass no test for historical accuracy as the words of the man widely regarded as "The Light of Asia." They simply highlight the fact—

as will other chapters in part I—that self-inflicted delusions are the central, structural cause of our suffering.

The Song of the Buddha, Upon the Occasion of His Enlightenment[2]

> In many a house of life have my senses imprisoned me, left me suffering, wearied by strife.
> But you, the builder of my every habitation,
> *Now* I know you.
> Never again will you erect these walls of pain.
> Never again will you raise up that ridgepole of self-deception.
> Nor lay fresh rafters against it.
> For now your house has collapsed.
> That ridgepole has shattered.
> Released from its every delusion, I now go serenely on my way!

3

Western Perspectives on Mystical Experiences

> You must understand that a perspective on life that is derived from an inner experience is different from one that is arrived at intellectually.
>
> Kobori-Roshi (1918–1992)[1]

> Taste as much of this as you can. Swallow what you need and spit out the rest.
>
> Taizan Maezumi-Roshi (1931–1995) (To his disciples, with regard to importing Japanese Zen teachings into the West.)[2]

Alexander Hardy surveyed three thousand contemporary Western religious experiences.[3] Their major phenomena (reported by 15% or more of his subjects) included a feeling of security, protection, and peace (25%); a sense of joy, happiness, and well-being (21%); a sense of "presence" (nonhuman) (20%); a sense of certainty, clarity, and enlightenment (20%); a sudden change to a new sense of awareness (18%).

A prelude of depression or despair ushered in 18% of the experiences. After their experiences, 19% of the subjects developed a sense of purpose or new meaning. What was the initiative for this religious experience? Some 32% of the subjects felt the source was "internal," but it appeared to represent an "answer" from "elsewhere."

Only rarely (2%) was the episode reported to be a *unitive* experience, the kind that merges the self into the all. We discuss this quality of "Oneness" in part

VII. In Zen, the orientation is twofold: toward the Path of unitive experiences, and toward actualizing them in one's everyday life. What are the ingredients in this Path of Everyday Zen, of Living Zen?

4

An Outline of the Path of Zen

> Wisdom can be divided into two: the original wisdom, and the wisdom gained after satori. Original wisdom is the Great Wisdom of Equality, and is inborn; but the wisdom gained after satori is the wonderful Wisdom of Differentiation.
>
> Master Daibi of Unkan (1881–19—)[1]

The Path of Zen emphasizes the Buddha's original teachings: human suffering is rooted in our longings, loathings, and ignorance. Most ingredients of the Path are not unique to Zen, yet when fully integrated they tend to take on a special flavor.

Formal Zen training evolves during years of an ethical, restrained lifestyle. It includes regular meditation, close relations with both an authentic teacher[2] and a support group, and regular meditative retreats.

When Zen Buddhists meditate, their practices begin with a foundation of calmness and clarity, then evolve into mixtures of receptive and concentrative styles. Regular, daily meditation cultivates feelings of calm awareness and emotional stability.[3]

Longer meditative retreats are crucial. They enhance the inherent tendencies of the Path to evolve through the earlier, more superficial "quickenings" and absorptions. Later still may arrive the more advanced, extraordinary alternate states of consciousness. These brief experiences convey successively deeper levels of insight-wisdom. They are moments of "awakening," of profound realization.

What is realized? A special kind of existential insight-wisdom. It comprehends "the way all things *really are.*" These advanced states are described (imperfectly) using such terms as *kensho, satori,* and Ultimate Pure Being. Only rarely, and usually in a monastic context, do the deepest transformations evolve into the stage of genuine "sage wisdom." This may be conceptualized as a late ongoing *stage* of enlightened traits.

Figure 1 ventures to outline the long process of Zen training in very schematic form. Please note: the whole approach emphasizes the *daily practical aspects of living Zen,* not the brief "experiences" which tend to draw undue attention.

Zen training evolves during a simplified ethical lifestyle (*sila*) that avoids indulging in unfruitful behavior. The practice centers on an authentic teacher (the *roshi*) and on a support group of like-minded practitioners (the *sangha*). The path

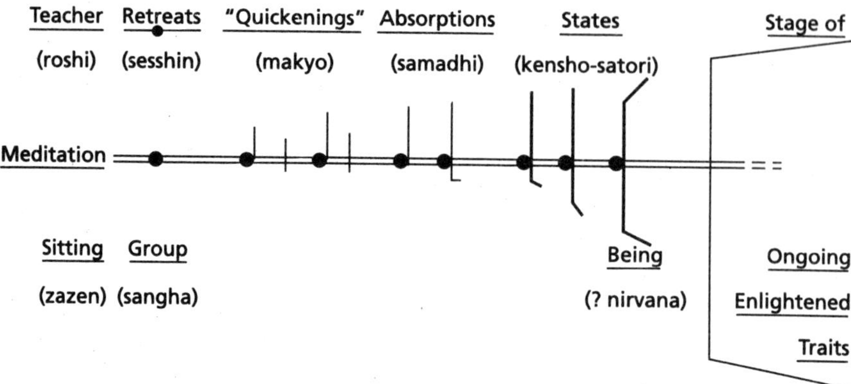

Figure 1 An outline of the Path of Zen

is endless. It involves regular meditation (*zazen*) and repeated meditative retreats (*sesshin*).

These initial steps are illustrated on the left side of the figure. The central emphasis remains on meditation and on carrying the meditative mode into the activities of daily living. The several round black dots along this central axis point to the importance of meditative retreats. In fact, only during intensive retreats do meditators usually arrive at levels of self-emptying sufficient to access more advanced extraordinary alternate states of consciousness.

Retreats, like Outward Bound experiences, are opportunities to find the "inner" self. Retreats become effective agencies of personal change, to the degree that they (1) evoke in the brain a calibrated series of physiological instabilities and stress responses, and (2) develop meditators' capacities to endure different kinds of anguish and to learn how much *they are the source of* their own discomforts, resistances, and boredom.

Five large topic areas are included off to the right side of the figure.

Quickenings

"Side effects" occur during the early months and years of meditation. They include emotional swings from vacant feelings to bliss, unusual body sensations, misperceptions (illusions), and hallucinations. These epiphenomena intrigue beginners. In formal Zen training, however, such "quickenings" (called *makyo*) are viewed as "by-products" of no spiritual significance. They are regarded as merely signs that one is moving along the path.

This book views quickenings as expressions of a variety of surges in the activities of messenger molecules in the brain. Some of these varied phenomena tend to occur at the advancing tidal edges of conventional arousals. They arise either as part of circadian (daily) or ultradian rhythms (every 90 minutes or so). Quickenings also seem to enter during the dynamic transitions between waking/drowsiness and sleep/REM (rapid eye movement) sleep. Quickenings arise especially when the brain's own stress responses—releasing biogenic amines, peptides, acetylcholine (ACH), glutamate, and γ-aminobutyric acid (GABA)—have gone on to destabilize and disrupt the person's ordinary sleep cycles and biorhythms.

Absorptions

Absorptions tend to arise in settings where concentrative meditative techniques are practiced intensively, as they are during a retreat. The several states of absorption often manifest a process of heightened attention that becomes sustained; the sense that one's physical self has faded; an impression of merging. Sometimes attention becomes focused on an actual object in the environment. At other times, one becomes aware that active behaviors are liberated from all sense of volition. In either case the senses remain open to the outside world. This is the reason for the term *external absorption*.

In contrast, other (less common) states turn inward (*internal absorption*). This mental field is one of a greatly amplified internalized awareness. A vacuum of enchantment opens up with no physical self inside, a vast space infused with a plenum of rapture and bliss [Z:467–518]. It contains neither thoughts, external sights, nor sounds.

States of Insight-Wisdom

Zen training is oriented both toward the slow, introspective development of character, and the rare later brief states of insight. Whether the pejorative roots of the old *I-Me-Mine* are trimmed slowly or are cut off quickly, the entire process allows the person's innate affirmative potentials to come to the fore.[4] This is the reason why, in the epigraph, Master Daibi speaks of that original, inborn wisdom in which we share equally with everyone and everything.

The term *prajna* refers to the swift sword cut of existential insights that severs the sense of the psychic self. The cut subtracts not only the conceptual and affective roots of the self but also their dysfunctional extensions into all other dualities.

What happens when this flash of deep insight illuminates an awareness shorn of all prior subjective conditionings? The experiant sees and comprehends all "things as they really are." The salient impressions during this "awakening" include *ultimate reality*, *eternity*, *unity*, *fearlessness*, and an unparalleled sense of *release*. One reason that Buddhist "awakening" experiences differ from other forms is that they are often preceded by long periods of emptying, calming, "no-thought" meditation.

By convention, the initial insight experiences tend to be called kensho. The term *satori* is reserved for awakenings that plumb deeper levels and are more transformative. Zen monks who have experienced such states do not say that they have "acquired" them or "attained" them. Rather do they refer to them in terms that hint at their arriving at a full grasp of reality.[5] Although these two states of "enlightenment" are momentary openings, they greatly stimulate the spiritual quest. They also tend to exert a positive transforming influence on the personality in enduring ways [Z:519–624]. So do those even rarer states in this next category.

States of Ultimate Pure Being

These very rare states tap into primordial incomprehensibilities [Z:625–636]. Experiential paradoxes abound. No word descriptions suffice when groundlessness coexists with an impression of infinite potential, nor when form and emptiness simultaneously coincide and equate.[6]

The Exceptional Stage of Ongoing Enlightened Traits

Notice that this long descriptive phrase refers to a *stage*, not to a brief state. It is applicable to that rare sage who—like the Buddha—continues to live selflessly, directly in touch with what goes on in the present moment [Z:636–697]. Liberated from prior dysfunctional overconditioning, this sage now leads a simplified life, yet adapts skillfully and compassionately to each new social complexity. The genuine sage becomes free to navigate evenhandedly—and ethically—between such opposites as might previously have been labeled "good" and "bad." Transformations at such depths reflect an amalgam of changes in traits, attitudes, awareness, thoughts, and behaviors. The person's nervous system has undergone a series of fundamental changes.

Elsewhere in the neurosciences, we keep asking how our system of cells, synapses, receptors, and networks continues to modify its own structure and function. It is time to ask these same questions of long-range meditative training, and to do so in controlled studies, *longitudinally*.

A Distinction between the Earlier Insight-Wisdoms and Those of Advanced Practice

Zen traditions hold that the brief states of insight-wisdom, and those beyond, are "nothing special." What remains crucial are the personal transformations that develop *after* these states, as a result of advanced, continuous daily-life practice. In part VIII we consider these issues further.

5

The Semantics of Self

> I know that I exist; the question is, What is this "I" that "I" know?
>
> René Descartes (1596–1650)

The conscious self begins with an elementary sense of awareness,[1] yet there is more to the core of our subjectivity than the "I." It is useful to look into three other terms that are used in connection with the self.

Amour-Propre

Dictionaries define *amour-propre* as "love of one's self." In its French and Latin roots, *propre* also hints at property rights. Do I somehow feel that I "own" myself as "property," and that I belong only to my very own self? Then these attachments to self stop me from giving myself freely to other persons. Furthermore, excessive degrees of self-love extend themselves beyond vanity and narcissism into conceit.

Proprioceptive is not a pejorative term. When proprioceptive is used in the neurosciences, it refers to vital internal sensory signals, the ones that help establish our *physical* sense of self. These signals arise chiefly from special receptors in our muscles, joints, and tendons. When stretched, these receptors help us generate a sense of our body's position and movement within external space. Proprioceptive impulses join other somatosensory messages up in the parietal cortex.

Narcissism

The fictions of narcissism afflict every one of us. Only very slowly can long-range authentic Zen training dissolve these fictions. Since childhood each word of praise from parents and teachers, and each glimpse of self in the mirror, had convinced us that we were indeed a very special self. Doesn't anyone so special deserve the very best?

To Ken Wilber, "Boomeritis Buddhism" is the "biggest internal threat to the dharma in the west."[2] What is wrong with today's "baby-boomer" generation? Wilber calls it "Boomeritis." Think of it as an unusually virulent, endemic, postmodern psychological affliction. It is a disorder that combines the extremes of pluralism ("all realities are equally valid") with those of narcissism ("don't challenge *my* convictions about *my* reality").

The ingredients of narcissism are a major barrier to genuine, deep, spiritual transformation. Until introspection and insights begin to soften the hard soil of one's old narcissistic attitudes, it is difficult for the seeds of transformation to take root and to grow. This is a long process of *de*conditioning. It requires a supportive environment. One slowly learns about oneself and starts to apply this new understanding every day, in subtle actionable deeds. This process of reshaping our old attitudes and behaviors is what is meant by *living* Zen.

6

Developing Our Conscious Levels of Self

> While the clear mind listens to a bird singing, the Stuffed-Full-of-Knowledge-and-Cleverness mind wonders what *kind* of bird is singing . . . tends to go chasing off after things that don't matter, or that don't even exist . . .
>
> B. Hoff, *The Tao of Pooh*[1]

When you were a baby and first heard a bird sing, your mind was relatively simple and reasonably clear. But now you realize how an older mind starts to chase after things and becomes cluttered. You have watched children, as we say, "go through stages." During their first 5 years they become clever, and run down long halls of self-reflecting mirrors. You have observed how their levels of consciousness proliferate, linking self, time, space, and trivial things into one huge amalgam of functions and dysfunctions.

A newborn baby might be characterized as engaged in the very elementary stage of *minimal consciousness*.[2] Panksepp's perspective as an experimental biologist leads him to believe that most neural underpinnings of this newborn's primitive self begin in certain deep midline regions. These circuits extend from the midbrain up into the diencephalon.[3] Observing your own baby's basic approach/avoidance responses to either pleasure or pain, you see that neither one requires elaborate higher constructs of self.

Then, by the end of the first year, you become overjoyed. Now you see your child pointing to objects, and hear his or her first intelligible words. This stage corresponds to the next level of consciousness: *recursive consciousness*. The term signifies that level of behavior which simply refers *back* to fragments of its own self's history. When this 12-month-old looks at you and says "Daddy" or "Mommy," your child is now perceiving, recognizing, and labeling in accord with his or her early autobiographical mode of experience.

A more obvious self-consciousness emerges between 18 months and 2 years. Piaget attributed this dramatic transition to the arrival of *symbolic* thought. Now your child uses personal pronouns, recognizes his or her own self in a mirror, displays shame and other self-conscious emotions. (Could there be a message in the observation that soon the "terrible twos" will arrive?)

Thankfully, by 3 years of age, a more advanced level of consciousness evolves. It is termed *reflective consciousness I*. Now your child can use two arbitrary rules flexibly, and may consider that one rule stands in contrast to the other.

Around 4 to 5 years of age, *reflective consciousness II* emerges. Children begin to reflect back on their own mental state and project outward into the mind of other persons. Observation suggests that they are developing a "theory of the mind." They also learn that two sets of rules which do not apply to one situation can still be integrated into one higher system of behavior.

Consider how this next higher, second level of reflective consciousness helps each of us to develop our concepts of time (see chapter 83). To illustrate: Children learn that time right *now* will—at sometime in the future—become time *past*. Why does this form of self-reflective consciousness help them personally? Because now they are able to conceptualize their own selves as existing in contexts that provide for both continuity and change over time.[4] Having arrived at this level, the child can hold on to the realization that "*I am* the *same one* who is *now* remembering what I *then* experienced."

This brief survey indicates that as we develop our notions about time they are intimately linked with our physical and psychic constructs of self. From this perspective we can better appreciate the major destructuring of consciousness that occurs during kensho-satori. For then, both the sense of self and the sense of time vanish simultaneously [Z:37–43, 562–567].

7

Some ABCs of the I-Me-Mine

We have met the enemy, and it is us.

Pogo

For purposes of discussion, we can visualize three main interactive components of selfhood:

the *I-Me-Mine*.

The *I-Me-Mine* operates within certain premises. The *I* exists physically, feels, is aware, acts, knows, thinks, and personifies various roles.

Things happen to the *Me*, both physically and mentally. With regard to the *Mine*, all private thoughts, opinions, and body parts are "*Mine*." All these possessions are *Mine*. *My* self is the sole axis around which the rest of the world revolves.

The triad obviously serves useful, constructive, and adaptive ends, Pogo reminds us—as if we didn't know—that it also has a covert, dysfunctional side. Zen tries to liberate, transform, and redirect these habitual unfruitful energies along more constructive lines.

But can our very own sovereign *I* create problems? You bet it can. Let us begin by expressing its range of problems in simple a-b-c terms. Our *I* is also *a*rrogant and *a*ggressive. Even so, it has a vulnerable partner: the fearful *Me*. This *Me* feels *b*eseiged. It can get *b*attered.

Finally, our *Mine* is readily *c*aptured by its "own" greedy longings. It *c*lutches at other people, it *c*ovets and *c*lasps onto material goods. Moreover, this *Mine* has another very bad habit. It *c*herishes and *c*lings to each of its biased opinions.

The *I-Me-Mine* has been described above in operational terms. This is how it feels and acts. The self becomes harder to acknowledge if we choose to view its three components only as words in the abstract.[1] Self, person, and I are not synonymous, as Galin points out.[2] He adds that much of our confusion about these terms arises because we use them in different ways in our ordinary metaphors.

Later, in part VII, we will observe how the sense of one's "truest, original self" emerges. It is liberated only when long-term training and insightful awakenings dissolve these constructs and concepts of the pejorative self. Meanwhile, let us summarize the overall direction of these transformations in table 1.

We observe that the capital letters and italics of the old *I-Me-Mine* have finally become eroded. The resulting i-me-mine has a lower profile. What happened to those former energies that had been previously diverted to unfruitful ends? They are now channeled toward modes that are more ACTUALIZED, BUOYANT, AND COMPASSIONATE. This is what Zen has been pointing toward all along. In the next chapters, we will point toward some ways our notions of self are represented in our brain's functional anatomy.

Table 1
The Pejorative Self and the Direction of Its Transformation

The Problem Self	*The Transformed Self*
An arrogant *I*	An ACTUALIZED i
A besieged *ME*	A BUOYANT me
A clutching *MINE*	A COMPASSIONATE mine

8

Constructing Our Self, Inside and Outwardly

> I related everything to my own person. Although I knew perfectly well what mine, yours and his meant, I couldn't get away from myself. Everything was a part of my world, my own universe, and I thought that everything was inside me.
>
> Complaints of patient 8[1]

We will gradually be saying much more about the physical and psychic aspects of self. Meanwhile, as chapter 6 noted, it is likely that some elementary forms of affective consciousness arise far down in the brainstem [Z:37–43].[2] Why so low? Because the stem contains both a basic motor system and a corresponding sensory mapping system, and each is registered to represent the same parts of the body. Where in the brainstem? Distributed among circuits that link its central gray matter with the overlying colliculi [Z:232–235, 241–242].*

This convergence is inherently self-referential. Here, in the midbrain, somatic information from the colliculi is already joining emotional response systems from the central gray to form a primitive scaffolding [Z:217–218]. Within such a framework, the rest of our dynamic primal constructs of self can rise up and begin to take shape. Then, after we refine these into concepts at higher cerebral levels, we can even attach words to them to describe the way it seems that our inside self is separate from the world outside.

Let us now reexamine the words at the beginning of this chapter. This neurology patient is expressing some overly self-referent symptoms. An infarct had destroyed a part of his association cortex at the back of his brain, on the left side. Where? At a key confluence: at the junction between his posterior parietal, temporal, and occipital lobes. (The same bookmark serves to locate figure 3, which we will also continue to refer to.)

His description is apt. His neurological examination showed much more. He could not *point* to items outside his own body. (Nor could the other patients in this report, all of whom had similar posterior parietal junctional lesions on the left.) A general term, *allotopagnosia*, describes this inability to point. The word *hetero*topagnosia describes a more specific disorder: a person's inability to point to other people in outside space.

Especially noteworthy in all nine patients was their persistent "self-referencing." For example, when asked to point outward, to the body parts of their examining neurologist, they pointed precisely to the corresponding part

*At this point, it could help the reader to insert a bookmark by figure 4 on page 74 in chapter 23. It shows these structures.

of *their own physical self.* Their "frame" of reference was "turned around" 180 degrees.

Why did they not only blur but reverse such self/other distinctions? Was it simply because they could not recognize that particular body part itself? No. They could point readily to another person's body parts in a photograph, or even to the appropriate parts of a doll. Therefore, theirs was not some general inability either to identify, or to locate, or to point.

Instead, *they seemed to have lost the normal frame of reference that we use to define, and cross over, a particular conceptual boundary, the barrier that separates our own construct of self from that of another living person.* It seemed almost as though they could not reach beyond the usual concept of "*My* turf," toward "*your* turf." Why not? Patient 8 defined his problem with precision: "I couldn't place you outside myself, you were in me."

As we examine his words and behavior, it is as though "I" and "mine" had taken over his perception. "You" and "yours," having now been *incorporated* in the patient's self, no longer seemed to exist solely *out there* anymore.

This disorder constitutes a loss of the usual, normal distinction: self-in-here/other-out-there. It was doubly manifest: (1) This patient's subjective report described "everything" as "a part of *my* world" ... "everything was *inside* me." (2) In their behaviors, none of the patients could *express* the normal self/other boundary concept using the standard motoric gestures of pointing elsewhere (either indicating by hand or by the direction of the movements of their eyes).

***Who* Points Where? At What?**

As Degos and colleagues went on to explain, normal pointing "involves the 'what' and 'where' systems simultaneously in a language-like gesture." ("What" refers to our occipital → temporal pathways. They recognize what an object is by its *pattern.* "Where" refers to our occipital → parietal pathways. They establish where an object is by its *position* in space.) A preliminary interpretation of their patients' findings might suggest that these normal links between the "what" and "where" systems appeared to have been disconnected.

But, there is also a "who" in the center of this behavioral task. We must not lose sight of patient 8's striking complaints. His behavior and his words were pointing to an *overly* self-referent self. Normally, we accept without complaint this natural, implicit role. After all, we are normally the sovereign *I*-person inside, the one *who* never has to think before we point automatically into that "what-where" of meaningful objects that exist in outside space.

What caused these patients' symptoms? When the authors began to speculate, they used the phrase "object centered" space to refer to our normal external space. In what way had this "space" become diminished in their patients? In the sense that some of its contents (its "objects") had lost their own separate identity. These objects had become abnormally coextensive *inside* that private space occupied by their patients' self-referent selves.*

As Degos and colleagues note, our normal object-centered spatial functions accomplish *two* things. First, they represent the items as detached out there in external space. Second, they also attribute a *separate* identity to each such object. This process of separate identification is deceptively obvious. It is easy to overlook. However, it does enable these external objects to exist "independent of the observer, thereby allowing them to be pointed out." Why couldn't their patients perform this particular normal pointing function?

We start to clarify a few of the subtle mechanisms involved in chapters 41 and 42.[3] Here, we will simply note that these *normal* sensorimotor functions do enable us to extend a part of our own body, *across* the self/other boundary, into that space beyond our skin.

How casually we accept such skillful acts each time *we* blend our physical self-image, seamlessly, into the external world! To do so, we normally engage the posterior parietal cortex and the adjacent posterior superior temporal sulcus.[4] Unfortunately, the lesions in these nine patients had severed the circuits that would otherwise have allowed these two regions (and their several allied regions) to interconnect.

When we normally reach out into the space beyond the self/other interface, hand outstretched, and grasp an apple, we do not conceptualize it as "extrapersonal space." Indeed, it becomes *jointly occupied instantly*. It now contains both our live hand *and* the apple in its immediate context [Z:244–247]. What kinds of words might describe the experiential aspects of such a merger? To Degos and colleagues the unification becomes "an integral part of self, in a visual-proprioceptive continuum." We might also describe such an event as the "embodied self-image in action."

But what causes someone like patient 8 to complain so openly about his referring his subjective feelings now *back to himself*? Degos and colleagues attribute such a complaint to their patients' failure at *object*-centered processing. They refer to this spatial dysfunction as an "objectivization disorder." Thus, when a person's *object*-centered functions fail, their subjective (*self*-centered) processing modes will then predominate by default. Note that this disorder represents an imbalance of two major functions. Such an imbalance can help to explain the curious excesses of *subjective* self-referencing that patient 8 describes.

---

*Our preference in this book is to discuss such spatial distinctions using two other words. Allocentric means with reference to *other* locations outside the person. In contrast, egocentric means with reference back to the central axis of the personal *self*. (See also parts VI and IX.)

Does his symptom of incorporating "everything inside *me*" resemble any other normal condition we're familiar with? In a sense, it resembles the common garden-variety of exaggerated inturning. Like what? It resembles those *normal subconscious, intrusive attachment functions attributable to our* "Mine" (see chapters 5 and 7). These operate automatically each time we look out into the external world to grasp an apple out there, and claim it as our "own" [Z:43–47]. My apple. On my turf.

So more than a simple failure of normal object representation may be occurring in these patients. Something more than just one keenly observant patient who finds he had lost his normal ability separately to identify an external target as an "independent" object. There is also a symptom and a finding that resembles an overacting, *overincorporating* "Mine." This aspect of the triad of self is overfunctioning to a degree that we rarely see. Indeed, the "Mine" is nakedly on display. This overt "Mine-like" function, perhaps *released* by a left posterior lesion, seems to have shifted toward an enhanced frame of reference, one that now reaches out and relates "everything to my own person."

Could there be a hidden message here? Does such an imbalance suggest what can happen after the opposite, *right* posterior parietal region becomes "liberated" (disinhibited)? Our two hemispheres normally exert a restraining, inhibiting influence on each other (see chapter 96, reference 13). Therefore, *left* posterior parietal damage could remove the normal prior tonic braking action it had on the right side. If so, then these patients' findings may be added to several other lines of evidence that tend to lateralize certain incorporating functions of our normal "attaching" selves more to the right hemisphere.

However, one cannot reach into the dynamic dysfunctions of all nine patients and grasp a single discrete mechanism that caused their normal embodying interface functions to go so far awry. Localizing a reaching *dys*function in a patient is never the same as localizing a normal function. Moreover, these patients had multiple signs of left posterior parietal lobe and adjacent cerebral dysfunction.[5]

Subsequent chapters will return us many times to this same, intriguing temporo-parieto-occipital junction. We will explore ways that this region—on the right and left sides—normally contributes to our self/other interface. We will glimpse how its models of the self can be displaced or dissolve, discover that other things outside it can also vanish from consciousness. All these will be found to occur in ways germane to the neurosciences and to Zen experience.

Object Consciousness

It is of more than passing interest that Degos and colleagues employ the term "objectivization." They use it to refer to those normal perceptual processes that imprint a separate identity onto an *object* which is out there in other-centered (allocentric) space. A century earlier, another neurologist, Hughlings Jackson, had referred to that same awareness. Because it could perceive a separate external *object*—a brick in his example—he called it "Object Consciousness." In contrast, he used "Subject Consciousness" to describe those human processes which made us *personally* aware not only of *our self* but of its manifold extensions [Z:380].

Exploring this normal subject/object distinction, and this boundary between them, will later help us appreciate many aspects of Zen. For example, the perceptual field during kensho will turn out to lack subjective, sentimental qualities and to be inherently objective in tone (see chapters 77, 92, 93).

9

Two Interpreters: One Articulate, the Other Silent

> "The Interpreter" is a glue that keeps our story unified and creates our sense of being, a coherent, rational agent.
>
> Michael Gazzaniga[1]

> We should not pretend to understand the world only by intellect; we apprehend it just as much by feeling.
>
> Carl Jung (1875–1961)

Some interpret the evidence from split-brain studies to suggest that the left hemisphere contains an "interpreter." This word refers to a questioning self prone to seek explanations and to construct imaginative theories to explain why events occur. Thus, each new "why?" seems to prompt a theoretical "because."

Yet the networks in each hemisphere are specialized for their own brand of "interpretation." Each side is dominant in ways that are complementary to the other [Z:358–367]. Why do interpretive processes seem more obvious to us when they arise from the left side? Because our impressive linguistic resources reside there. They readily verbalize our left hemisphere's many other functions.

To generalize: our left side is especially gifted at keeping online the impulse to sequence a set of facts into particular *cognitive* patterns. True, these patterns often imply coherent cause-and-effect relationships, but sometimes they also note *exceptions* to the general rules of our prior experience.

In contrast, our right hemisphere is no less alert to creating fresh interpretations once the incoming facts convey *affective* meaning. The right side begins with the greater gift for maintaining a keen, bilateral, ongoing awareness. Moreover, it remains poised to convey appropriate degrees of emotional response.

In our brain, the corpus callosum and other connections normally bridge the gap between the two sides. Their rapid, two-way, nonverbal dialogue is coded with preconscious nuances. Even so, the left hemisphere may be better able to interpret the emotional basis of some coded responses it receives from the right hemisphere than is the right hemisphere able to guess which cognitive messages are coming over in coded form from its partner on the left [Z:362–363].

In chapters 5 and 7, we defined the *I-Me-Mine* attributes of the self. Doing so, we assigned certain operational properties to the "*I.*" Together, they combine to establish its sense of being a separate independent identity. We do think of ourselves as unique individual persons. We clearly exist, feel, are aware, act, know, think, and personify roles. To this degree, a number of lines of experimental evidence can sometimes be interpreted to suggest that many coherent self-related functions of the rational "*I*" are represented more on the left side. Of course, if one side of the brain keeps postulating an explanation for why "I" had responded as "I" did to some outside event, this habitual tendency will reinforce the subconscious notions of selfhood represented on that side.

Gazzaniga can, therefore, with some reason, say this further about the "interpreter": "To our bag of individual instincts, it brings theories about our life. These narratives of our past behavior seep into our awareness; they give us an autobiography."[2] Yet, each self has many facets. It turns out that many other lines of neuroimaging evidence cited in part III will point to an "autobiographical" self whose circuits tap into multiple modules distributed throughout *both* hemispheres.

Moreover, as soon as we begin to localize the two other vulnerable premises of the self—the "*Me*" and the "*Mine*"—we discover how their many levels of anxious affect *feel tightly linked* to these "autobiographical" constructs. This comes as no surprise.

- When "bad" things happen to "*Me*" they are harming "*Me*" both physically and mentally. This harmed soma and this wounded psyche are both "*Mine*."
- Someone can rob "*Me*" of valued possessions "owned" by the "*Mine*." I can even be "disowned" of an inheritance I think is "Mine."
- Someone can challenge and overturn every prized thought, and opinion, and attitude that I consider "*Mine*."

Current evidence tips the balance more toward the right hemisphere for the emotionally loaded origins of many attitudes and behaviors. Some of these can be included under Daniel Goleman's phrase, "emotional intelligence."

To Summarize

Interpretations are dynamic processes. Some can be articulated, others remain silent but very influential. Many operations of the *"I"* are relatively accessible to our cognitively based tools of language, and they proceed under the direction of constructs often represented more in the left hemisphere. However, two other key constructs of the self are represented by the *"Me"* and the *"Mine."* They begin with different premises, arrive with different codes, resonate with important emotional interpretations. They reflect contributions from within the right hemisphere.

Selfhood arises out of interactive processes. They combine the multiple talents and interpretive capacities of both hemispheres.

10

Dissolving the Psychic Self and Its Veils of Interpretation

> Everything comes down to this: having sensations and reading nature. . . . To read nature is to see it beneath the veil of interpretation.
>
> Paul Cézanne (1839–1906)[1]

We have now observed that our psychic self is a higher-level, *bilateral* interpretive process. It links the cortex with many lower regions of the limbic system and their connections.

These vast circuitries resonate with countless instinctual and acquired emotional overtones. They help us condition not only the psychic responses of our whole brain but especially those associations reverberating between our big frontal and temporal lobes. One result is that rich admixture that we accept as "normal" everyday consciousness: swirling thought-streams, quasi-cognitive concepts, emotion-laden memories, and biased interpretations.

Valenced messages arising from these networks do more than polarize our interpretations and attitudes. *They also mobilize our behaviors.* Some positive messages leave us feeling attracted toward an event, longing to approach and connect with it. Negative messages fuel fear, causing us to withdraw, or perhaps to boil with anger, and to take aggressive action. Still others make us recoil with separate feelings of disgust and loathing.[2] These network biases have been pulling and pushing each of us since birth. They generate our unfruitful longings, anxieties, hostile behaviors, and loathings in countless unsuspected, overconditioned ways.

Zen views such personal prejudices (and our legacy of cultural distortions) as layers of subjective veils. They obscure our view, shut us off from a more

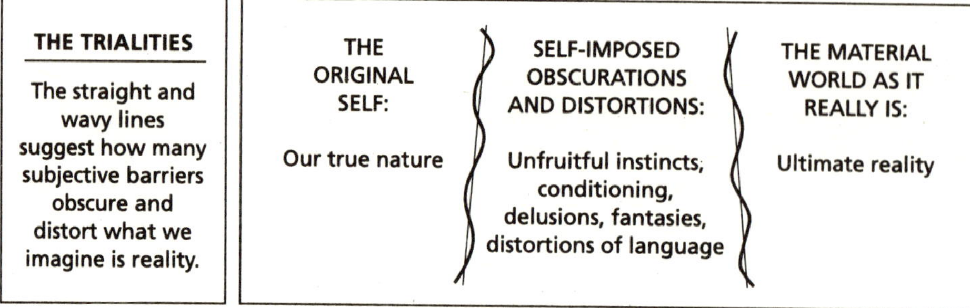

Figure 2 The trialities

objective view of reality, prevent us from reaching our mature potentials. Why does that often-used term, *dualities*, understate the basic problem? Because the world we inhabit is less a world of so-called self/other dualities than one obscured and distorted by a barrier of self-imposed "trialities" (as shown in figure 2). So, can our usual perceptions provide an accurate portrait of the objective reality of the OTHER world, in capital letters? No. Once we insert our own overinflated, subjective SELF, we distort all our percepts. We register only a very jumbled landscape. It looks like this:

S-o-ELF-ther.

"Other" hides in there, but SELF dominates. It obscures, distorts, and filters the message. From the Zen Buddhist perspective, this is the fundamental delusion. What do we resemble, instead? Just one tiny wave rising in a vast ocean, an ever so transient phenomenon in that whole vast universe of unconditioned unity. In such a domain, self is simply one other expression of OTHER.

Cezanne, whose words introduce this chapter, was trying to "read" nature by penetrating his own veils of interpretation. As we read between all the lines of part I, let us now try to condense and rephrase what occurs during long-term meditative training on what is often called the spiritual Path. Only when the veils of the *old*, overconditioned personal self drop away do we liberate the innate capacities of our "original self" to see deeply into the reality of this outside world. Only at the deeper levels of such an emancipation can our true nature register *objectively*. The result is an extraordinary, fresh impression: things as THEY are, not what they had always seemed to be in our overconditioned imagination.

What we see then are the ways individual things complement one another, as do yin and yang. But these words, like other language functions of the left side, are then no longer in the picture. Indeed, as Paul Valery phrased it, "Seeing begins when you forget the name of the thing you see."

11

Further Commentary on the Several Meanings of Zen-Brain "Reflections"

> As long as our brain is a mystery, the universe—the reflection of the structure of the brain—will also be a mystery.
>
> Santiago Ramón y Cajal (1852–1934)

One meaning of the hyphenated word "Zen-Brain," seems straightforward. From the preface, a reader can anticipate that the author will be reflecting on Zen topics from a brain-bound perspective. But chapter 6 used "reflective consciousness" to refer to the ways children develop through stages. And we now find Ramón y Cajal alluding to the mysteries of the universe as a metaphor reflecting the mysteries of the brain.

We have grown so comfortable, using metaphors and similes every day, that we overlook how much ambiguity lies in their wake (see chapter 54). Parts IV and IX explore these semantic issues further. Meanwhile, further explanations are surely in order, even now, because we have already seen "reflections" take on several meanings.

Zen holds up a mirror of dispassionate analysis to any who might try to mystify mysticism. Cajal and others in the brain sciences have also—for centuries—held up similar "mirrors," reflecting their own high goals for scientific objectivity. In their laboratories, and at the bedside, neuroscientists do not try to mystify the brain. They are studying the brain in the hope that they can *de*mystify some of its elusive phenomena, mirror neurons included (see chapter 65).

Zen and the brain sciences are two unsentimental areas. At the start of this new millennium, one can hope that progress in each of them will soon complement and be "reflected" in the other.

Item: Trainees in Zen and in the related meditative traditions undergo unusual mental quickenings, and they sometimes drop into extraordinary states of consciousness. You cannot probe deeply into the phenomena of such states without uncovering properties of fundamental neurobiological significance. Indeed, one finds that meditative experiences not only are "reflected" in the findings of neuroscience but that these two fields are so intimately interrelated that each *illuminates* the other.

My earlier book used the word "reflection" in several other ways [Z:593–613]. Reflection I described the first selfless phase of kensho. It was a term accurately conveying kensho's instantaneous (direct-like-a-mirror), flash of insight into nondual consciousness.

Reflections II, the next phase, observed multiple other experiential insights and impressions. These also turned over automatically. Reflections III became slightly more interactive; it began to hint that a minute self might be starting to return. Now the most elementary form of a "reflective" consciousness seemed back in position. Only then could the selfless oneness be appreciated that had just unfolded in the first two phases.

Reflections IV referred to the late period of enriched intellectual stimulation. These active thought processes extended themselves initially during the course of the next several days. Moreover, during the next three decades, a series of other "reflective interpretations" evolved into a long *contemplative* process.

The second book before you now, bearing this hyphenated word in the title, represents the further unfolding of these natural processes of reflection. In the pages that follow, I hope you will find that the phenomena of Zen experience enrich our understanding of the neurosciences. Beyond that lies the hope that the research cited herein might also encourage some neuroscientists to investigate and clarify the age-old meditative Path now to be discussed in part II. We shall need all the help we can get from neurobiologists to live mindfully in the present moments of this next millennium.

12

First Mondo

In casual conversations, people often ask me: "What did you learn as a neurologist, during your practice of Zen?" The following questions and answers sum up a few things I never appreciated before.

Why do you place so much emphasis on the self?

Because our *self* is so central a topic. Much of the Buddhist literature and most of the neuroscience literature are ill informed about the core functions and layers of the self. Our notions of selfhood start from the way the brain represents our body image—our *physical* self—as its implicit main physical axis. This body image represents our *soma*.

Infants soon begin to develop their representations of an implicit *psychic* self (their *psyche*) at many covert levels along the framework of this physical core. Only from within this overconditioned psyche do we look out later into the world, and behave accordingly for better and for worse.

So what?

Once you pass beyond this simple distinction of the self into soma and psyche, it then becomes easier to understand some differences between states of consciousness. For example, the early, superficial states of absorption drop out the sense of the physical self.

On the other hand, the later states of kensho not only drop out the psychic self but their insights transform the rest of one's prior existential concepts about what constitutes reality.

Kensho made it easier for me to envision the separate *"I-Me-Mine"* operations within my own self with greater objectivity and to recognize how deeply I had been overconditioned.

Part II

Meditating

Sit all together in meditation. Become peacefully calm and quiet, without motion, without stillness, without birth, without destruction, without coming or going, with no judgments of right or wrong, neither staying nor going. This, then, is the Great Way.

Hui-neng (638–713) (Final words of the Sixth Zen Patriarch)

13

The Attentive Art of Meditation

> I like the silent church before the service begins, better than the preaching.
>
> Ralph Waldo Emerson (1803–1882)

> All human evil comes from this: man's being unable to sit still in a room.
>
> Blaise Pascal (1623–1662)

Emerson and Pascal express the general idea. But if you relied on standard dictionary definitions, you'd believe that to meditate always means you are thinking and engaging in active contemplation.

Not so in Zen Buddhist meditation. Dainin Katagiri-Roshi (1928–1990) put it succinctly, "In Zen, you let your frontal lobes rest."[1] One basic approach to the Great Way is a calm, silent, no-thought style of attending to the present moment. Moreover, since at least the early seventh century, it has also been stated that no one arrives at enlightenment itself by either the processes of thought or of imagination [Z:700–701].

Emerson favored silence over preaching. Zen masters have long been comfortable with intervals of silence and no movements. Sitting quietly is ideal. It is a setting favorable both for the spontaneous expression of intuitions and for translating them into action. Can sitting still, in silence, enhance attentiveness itself? It can, if meditation is performed correctly. Yes, we do live fast-paced, complicated lives. Yes it *is* hard to shift from distracting circumstances, slow down, and train oneself to attend. But meditation does offer a quiet opportunity to settle down, a welcome interlude in which to begin to focus attention on just one thing at a time. Becoming fully aware of something relatively simple—this inbreath, this outbreath—is a good place to start.

True, whole trains of thoughts soon intrude. So, this "simple" task does require persistent self-discipline. (You may wonder: does Zen *really* involve *self*-discipline? Yes, this is another Zen paradox) With practice, the chatter of internal thoughts starts to drop away. Slowly, the benefits of introspection and restraint cut down on the sources of distraction [Z:72–73]. Gradually, one's interior life itself becomes more simplified. Wants become less urgent. Needs become fewer. Now it is easier to stay concentrated on the real essentials.

What other benefits accrue to meditators who learn gently to harness and focus their energies of attention? William James observed that the very root of our judgment, character, and will resided in our "faculty of voluntarily bringing back a wandering attention, over and over again." Bringing it back to what?

Table 2
The Attentive Art of Meditation*

Receptive Meditation	*Concentrative Meditation*
Sustained attention, *un*focused and inclusive	Sustained attention, focused and exclusive, aided by intention
An open, universal awareness; more formless	A more one-pointed attention; more formed
Gentle, employing a light touch	More forced, deliberate
Notices when attention strays	Holds attention fixed
Not cultivated by struggle	Requires willpower
A simple noticing of anything, distracting or otherwise	Works best in an environment free from distractions, physical and mental
Can shift into introspection and comprehension	Comprehension is not a necessary accompaniment
Several approaches, translated as bare attention, mindfulness, insight, just sitting, Vipashyana, etc.	Several approaches, translated as the path of the absorptions, samadhi, the "vision quest," etc.

* Meditation begins on a solid foundation of calmness. (*Shamatha* implies dwelling in tranquility.)

Approaches to Meditation

Shamatha is the Sanskrit term for the basic foundation of calm, relaxed bare attention. Its original meaning implies dwelling in tranquility. In general, such calm abiding is the essential preliminary step, a "letting go" that allows the meditator to access the next stages.

Then, as meditation evolves, the various Buddhist practices address *attention* in two basically different ways. EEGs readily differentiate these two forms of meditation and show that they both differ from control states of ordinary calm relaxation.[2] Table 2 outlines the major contrasts between two of the main generic categories of attention. These differences distinguish the more open forms of receptive meditation from those which shift toward a more focused concentration. Note that receptive meditation is open to examine *any* event—good, bad, or indifferent—in an even-handed, matter-of-fact manner.

Despite one's best efforts, the mind wanders. Meditators describe this jumping from thought to thought with the apt phrase, "monkey mind." However, we cannot pawn this restless habit off on primate relatives who leap around in a zoo. It begins internally. Who filled our own mailbox with self-addressed junk mail?

In practice, Zen students often find themselves trying out different styles at different times, not only while meditating on a cushion but also while attending to each present moment anywhere else. Paying bare attention to what is going on NOW is the essence of mindfulness. *It continues off the cushion.*

Daily-Life Practice

"Daily-life practice" involves the simple act of "being here now," during one's everyday garden-variety of activities.

- Do you ruminate mindlessly while washing the dishes? Look attentively at this next dish. Then remind yourself: "Each dish washed is a baby Buddha bathed."
- Is getting up every morning just another routine chore? Stop to consider how fortunate you are to be *alive*, still able to move, to hear, blessed with vision!

Yet, *living Zen* evolves beyond everyday degrees of mindful attentiveness and focused concentration. It also shifts into a spontaneous introspective process. During moments of solitude, little pauses then insert themselves. Quiet settings nurture small insights. They emerge spontaneously from a deeper ongoing, mulling-over, reflective awareness. How is this possible? Somehow, being more aware of things in the present moment enables us to pause, then to suddenly see situations in a fresh perspective. Holding on to these intuitive understandings (often writing them down) enables us later to make the appropriate creative changes. Sometimes it seems that meditation also enables us to maintain more deliberate kinds of protracted introspection online.

Attention strays. It always does. But little cues can bring us back to the present moment. Thich Nhat Hanh recommends letting the telephone's ring remind us to snap back to the present. Follow the breath, wait until just after the third ring. Then pick up the receiver, refreshed. When driving, do the same at a red (stop) light.

In his *Principles of Psychology*, William James addressed the issue of how to develop greater willpower.[3] His counsel applies equally to the daily-life practice of living Zen. Every day, he advised, engage your "faculty of effort" (in what we would later refer to as a kind of "setting-up" exercise). He suggested that we set out, systematically, to apply ourselves to the "little heroic things." *Things we'd really rather not do. To do them, anyway.* Later, he continued, when you really need your willpower, you'll then be better trained for the bigger tests, and no longer "unnerved" by their challenges.

Some Functions of Sitting Meditation (*Zazen*)

We tend to forget how remarkable a process meditation really is. In broad perspective, the meditative practices train attention in the service of multiple functions. Listed below are some obvious processes that evolved during the course of my practice. You can probably think of several others that you have observed during your own practice. Meditation

- Exercises our capacities to make an ongoing commitment: to set aside a block of time.
- Distances us from the usual world of distractions. Otherwise, this world rushes past mindlessly.
- Slows the flow, and calms. By sponsoring more detached pauses, meditation creates a quieter setting in which triggers can have greater effect when they finally strike.
- Lays bare the constant buzz of proliferating thoughts which block our becoming clearly aware.
- Demonstrates, convincingly, that we don't always need to be "*doing* things."
- Introduces elements of sensorimotor deprivation and stress responses (especially during the course of rigorous retreats). Some of these stress responses will later enable the brain to shift into the kinds of alternate states which help transform consciousness.
- Sponsors many kinds and levels of intuition and introspection. Some of these glimpses will expose our sources of resistance. Examining these episodes with greater objectivity, we find that we are overreacting, and gradually discover why.
- Demonstrates, convincingly, that we can still practice self-discipline, even while we are also taking steps to dissolve those self-centered constructs of our *I-Me-Mine*.
- Sponsors mindful acts of bare, sensitized attention. These focus on the present moment. This moment is *real*. The more deeply, and habitually, we appreciate this reality, the closer we may be to those rare major awakenings that realize "the way things *really* are."
- Becomes a way to celebrate just being alive *now* in this incredible universe.

* * *

If the Zen approach does allow a meditator's frontal lobes the opportunity to "rest," as Katagiri-Roshi phrased it, then would many years of meditation confer any structural and functional benefits on the brain? To answer this will require a longitudinal study of several different styles of meditation. Though concentrative styles of meditation do not "rest" the frontal lobes, preliminary structural MRI studies suggest the possibility that the frontal poles of some meditators might resist the atrophic changes of aging better than those of controls.[4] Time will tell . . .

14

Just This

In zazen, leave your front door and your back door open. Let thoughts come and go. Just don't serve them tea.

Master Shunryu Suzuki (1905–1971)[1]

Beginners soon learn that meditation is an art. One problem is that it takes such a long time to become art*less*. Meanwhile, how can one escape from that restless "monkey-mind," let go of discursive thoughts, settle down into clear, bare, awareness? It takes patience to continue. Meditation trains patience.

Through trial and error, each person finds ways to help relax the body and to let thoughts drop out of the mental field. Yes, various systems do work for a while, especially when practiced regularly. But soon one forgets to count each breath by the numbers, from one to ten. Thoughts intrude and overwhelm these numbers.

The following approach became a kind of temporary "home remedy" for my own mindlessness and distractibility. It provided just enough novelty to keep me from becoming bored, and just enough structure to enable my thought processes to subside by themselves. Other meditators report that the system also helps them ease into meditation.

Its five simple-minded stages disappear off in the distance toward some meaningful destination. Each stage is flexible. You can vary them endlessly to suit your individual needs. Their operational principles are straightforward:

- Focus on breathing *in* mindfully, and on breathing *out* mindfully. Allow each breath to fully occupy the foreground of the mental field.
- Loosen attention from all other random thoughts.
- Pay increasing attention to one physical sensation: the in- and outmovements of the lower abdomen.

The five stages evolve as follows:

1. First, take a deep breath. As you breathe in and out, pay very close attention to the rising and falling *sensations* way down in your lower abdomen. Then, during your next breath *in*, you say—silently—the word "JUST." A *prolonged* JUST. Your usual brief "just" won't do. This word expands to become J-U-S-T. You stretch the word out, so that it fully occupies the entire duration of each successive inbreath.

JUST serves as the prelude to your next *out*breath. In this setting it means something specific. JUST signifies that your attention is now going to focus on "Just" (on *only*) a single silent *number*, from one to ten, during each of your next ten expirations. You'll focus on *only* that particular numbered outbreath. Nothing else enters.

You are also prolonging each of these numbers throughout its entire outbreath. So the cycles become.

J-U-S-T W-O-O-N-N; J-U-S-T T-O-O-O, etc.

You repeat these one-to-ten counting cycles one or more times. Then you ease into the next stage.

2. Now, during each inbreath, you change your silent first word to "THIS." The word, also prolonged, becomes T-H-I-S.

THIS also takes on a specific meaning as a prelude to your next outbreath. THIS signifies that you will now focus *only* on THIS next particular *number* all during each of your next outbreaths. *This* particular number also stretches out to fully occupy its own prolonged moment: T-H-I-S W-O-O-O-N-N, etc. Each successive number then vanishes in ongoing time.

By now, you have left no mental space in which to develop any extraneous, discursive thoughts. Your breathing cycle is fully occupied.

3. You now have in place a temporary, artificial structure of words and numbers. It fully occupies your mental foreground. Meanwhile, what else is happening, in the *background* of your awareness? You also have been focusing more and more of your attention on that set of soft sensations down in your lower abdomen, the ones that you identified during your first deep breath. They are the ordinary rising and falling movements during each inbreath and outbreath. These rising and falling sensations are both tactile and proprioceptive. They become increasingly evident as your random thought energies recede.

4. By now, you've gone through one or more silent rounds of *"JUST* (one through ten)," and one or more rounds of *"THIS* (one through ten)." Many discursive thoughts have begun to drop off. *Thoughts leave by themselves*, as the underlying drive of their habit-energy fades. So, too, do all numbers (you don't have to force either of them to leave).

   At this point, you return to the same word that you used initially. Once again, you use JUST to fully occupy your whole *in*breath.

   But at this stage, when you reclaim the other word, THIS, it shifts over to occupy the second position. It replaces the former numbers. Now it fully occupies each *out*breath. The result: "J U S T T H I S" fully occupies each in-and-out cycle of breathing.

   Give *JUST THIS* a specific meaning. Let it signify that *only this* precious moment exists, right NOW, within the whole world of awareness.[2] Your mental field is now wide open, and all its contents have been reduced to this exquisite simplicity. Likewise, awareness of your physical self has faded. It is also reduced to one single focus: on just each rising and falling movement down in your lower abdomen.

5. After a few rounds of JUST THIS, both words also tend to drop out by themselves, leaving your mental field thought-free. Now a simplified bare awareness remains. It can clearly register those in-and-out breathing movements down there in the lower abdomen. Each movement is both your body's innate rhythm and its expression of the fundamental living, breathing, life force. You allow this natural rhythm to enter into your one-pointed mental foreground. All other temporary stuff has now gone.

Finally, after a while, during deep meditation, awareness exists, all by itself. Just awareness . . .

*   *   *

Practicing

Having read about these stages, try them out. By reviewing the simple diagrams,[3] you can observe how JUST (one through ten) gives way to THIS (one through ten), how all numbers then drop out, how JUST THIS replaces them, and finally how this phrase also disappears. All that remains is that bare awareness of the living, breathing rhythm in your lower abdomen:

And then awareness alone remains. . . .

Commentary

JUST THIS is a simple-minded mantra. It signifies an open, full acceptance of things just as they are, in *this* here-and-now. In such an open setting, you remain all too aware of two things: uninvited thoughts and sensations always stream in; they soon flow out through the backdoor. They are simply an expression of impermanence. Once you accept that they come and go, you'll never feel obliged to serve them tea.

Don't allow this sequence of "five" steps to leave the wrong impression. Above all, this whole approach is flexible. No magic numbers are carved in stone. Experiment to find what works for you!

For example, sometimes when you're about to start meditating, you'll be pleasantly surprised to find that *no* thoughts are pressuring you. At this point, you can dispense with all earlier stages (of what can seem mere ritual). Even if you then start with a token JUST THIS, you might discover that the phrase soon drops out. Other monosyllables can serve individual needs. I've used "Let Go," "Born Free," "Here, Now" as alternative words during a prolonged retreat.

Flexible self-discipline is at the heart of zazen. Your habitual practice of this art of "soft discipline" will become one of the most significant (if less appreciated) attributes of your meditative training. Awareness, honed and skillfully applied, recognizes that attention has wandered, and gently escorts it back.

Regular practice enables you to keep returning your attentiveness nonjudgmentally, with no sense of failure—*time after time*—to the words, to the numbers, to these faint in-and-out breathing movements down in the lower abdomen.

The Lower Abdominal Region

Why focus your awareness on this lower region, the *tanden*? For at least two simple reasons.[4]

First, the lower abdomen is far removed from your nasal passages. What happens when you focus your attention high up, on the flow of air as it stimulates the nerve endings in your nostrils and sinuses? You emphasize those to-and-fro sensations that enter your brain through your large fifth cranial nerve. This is a big nerve. It is already a major source of that pervasive sense of self-identity referable to your head [Z:37–43, 93–99, 178]. Do you need more sensations that center you in your own head than you already have?[5]

Second, tight sensations from the upper chest during breathing are another source of the physiological tensions that we link with feelings of anxiety. A focus on *lower* abdominal sensations helps distract one's attention away from any chest tightness.

In short, the flexible steps outlined above provide a temporary distraction for discursive mental activity. They enable you to *let go,* and to focus your attention on a vital rhythm far removed from other head and chest sensations.

15

Meditative Attention: Accessing Deeper Avenues of Seeing and Hearing

> When you practice correctly, the sounds of the valley streams, the colors of the valley streams, the colors of the mountains, the sounds of the mountains, freely release eighty-four thousand verses in concert.
>
> Master Dogen (1200–1253)[1]

> Look! Look! Who is this master that is seeing and hearing right now?
>
> Master Bassui (1326–1387)[2]

These days, people are paying more attention to attention. It has become almost a popular commodity. Countless children and adults are thought to have an "attention" deficit disorder. (Drugs tend to be over prescribed; a hasty diagnosis of "ADD" is open often to question.) It is essential to remember the prerequisites of staying attentive. Normal people must first be aroused, then awake (not sleep-deprived), also alert, and well motivated (not bored). Meditators have the same requirements.

Attention is awareness stretched *toward* something. Attention reaches out. We attend *to* things, orient toward them, face them. Our goal is to focus on them and perceive them clearly. While attention does include these executive motoric implications, it also stays in touch with its subtler origins in mindful awareness.

In ancient calligraphy, the earliest ideogram for this basic mindfulness began with two characters. The top one signified the present moment, right *now*. The bottom character stood for heart-mind.[3] In every century, to pay mindful attention meant going beyond merely registering data subliminally. It meant the capacity to focus on certain items, to incorporate them, and to appreciate them as percepts, in this *here-and-now*.

Zen practice first trains your attention to follow the movements of breathing. Then it trains attention to come to enhanced degrees of focusing—*spontaneously*. Later on, these capacities will finally enable one to open up one's sensitivities: to *hear*, not merely to listen. To *see*, not merely to look. To *feel*, not just to touch. Later still, on rare occasions, such refined attentive capacities may open up into many long seconds of salient perception during which you may begin to comprehend things "as they really are" [Z:69–71].

Some early Yoga practices, and those advocated by the Buddha himself, involved paying close attention to the "ordinary" everyday activities of life. This still means being mindfully aware of sensory experiences, including the actual moment-by-moment proprioceptive, tactile, and other sensations involved in walking, eating, drinking water, working, and so on.

However, it is still only a gross beginning to remain mindfully aware that one is, say, now reaching for an apple. At more advanced levels, there can evolve the simplest, selfless, artless *reaching for the apple*. This outstrips intention. Why do such actions now flow spontaneously? Because they are tapping *pre*attentional resources, and are shorn of all traces of the *I-Me-Mine* [Z:279–281]. During such behaviors, the *action* itself occupies the person's whole mental field. No thoughtful deliberations occur. Am I grasping that apple? No. *Apple grasped*.

Beginners are always puzzled. What does Zen mean by such terms as "no-thought," "no-mind," and "non-action." How can I be mindful, yet later arrive at a state called "no-mind?" Can I be active, yet later "let go" into a spontaneous "non-action?" Yes, to each paradoxical phrase. Yes, because when you first start to train attention by focusing on your body parts, on the way they move, on external items and events, this is only a *prelude*. Later, your attention will shift spontaneously. At this moment the self *lets go*, drops off. This "no-mind" refers to the natural flow of mental states and actions when they are free from all egocentric intrusions.

No-mind does not mean coma. It means that no self-centered thoughts interrupt the flow. Similarly, "non-action," implies that your old *I-Me-Mine* isn't intervening. It does not mean that all motor behavior stops.

Seeing

Meditators have been advised for centuries to seek out a quiet setting, free from all distracting sights and sounds. Taoist China was at home in the natural world. For Dogen, a natural outdoor setting of mountains, valleys, and streams was ideal. Dogen was deeply into seeing and hearing. Of seeing, he would say: "Open the eye, directly transmit through the eye, and receive the Dharma through the eye."[4] We do have a large visual brain [Z:240–244]. It is remarkably engaged in those extraordinary states of consciousness which yield the impression that all things are being *seen* "as they *really* are."

Hearing

Like other Zen monks, the 31-year-old Bassui (1327–1387) had chosen to meditate through the night. Suddenly, at dawn, the sound of the mountain stream "penetrated his whole body," and he came to his first realization. Bassui associated this event with Kannon, the Bodhisattva who hears the anguished cries of ordinary people and acts to save them.[5] The Zen tradition has a saying attributed to another Bodhisattva, Manjusuri: "Turn your function of hearing back toward your self and listen to the nature of the listener."[6]

Sheng-yen is a contemporary Ch'an master. He advises training one's hearing capacities in the following manner. The basic practice is to reach out—beyond mere listening—so that now you can really *hear the raindrops falling* in their regular continuous, unified rhythm. Another recommended hearing practice is to focus on the gurgle of water as it flows in a small stream. "Immerse yourself in the sound and lose yourself in it, forgetting the environment, to the point that the sound itself is dropped. Then the mind will slowly merge with the sound of the water, and enter into a state of unification, calm and quiescent both inwardly and outwardly."[7]

"Hearing the Dawn"

Hearing sometimes enhances seeing. As Bassui noted, sometimes when you hear a particular word or phrase—a so-called *turning* phrase—you find that your act of seeing then takes on remarkable new dimensions. Said he, on this subject of the turning phrase, "There are those who have had a great awakening—that is, their eyes have been opened to Buddha knowledge after hearing one word."[8]

Triggers strike unpredictably. When you are not expecting it, hearing can serve as the avenue of access to kensho's transforming vision. (See chapter 72.) In this regard, Richard Hunn, a disciple of Charles Luk, mentions a technique favored by some earlier masters. Suddenly, the master calls out to the student.

Then, just as the student's head and body starts *turning* automatically in response, the master quickly voices an urgent, "*What is it?*"

During such open moments, the student's mind may become briefly empty of what it had been thinking about a second before. In a sense, the student may then be thrust more than halfway into a state of no-self and "no-mind." What does the master's quick question accomplish at this very instant? In the language of the past, it serves to snatch the "pearl from under the dragon's chin."[9]

So, as a word, "turning" now seems to have taken on at least four applications. It can refer (1) more to the *sound or meaning* of a triggering word; (2) to that instant of *movement* when a person is turning their *head and body* to orient toward a sudden sensory event; (3) to an instant when that person is *shifting their attentional set* externally, toward the source of the sensory stimulus; (4) to the fact that if kensho were then to occur, it will *overturn* all of that person's prior conditioning. This sudden turning outward, both mentally and physically, will become an important topic later in chapters 50, 51, and 72.

Recent Research in Visual Attention

Positron emission tomography (PET) studies show that visual processing becomes activated when greater degrees of emotion invest attention. This occurs not only in vision's earlier stages back in the right visual association cortex but also in its later stages when its elaborations move forward into the right anterior temporal cortex.[10]

Attention wanes. Senior meditators find they have to "pay more attention."[11] Normal older people (ages 65–80) do attend more slowly to visual targets. During visual tasks, they are more distracted by extraneous items than are younger subjects (ages 18–34).[12]

16

Interpreting Synchronized Brain Waves

> When used with the appropriate methods and cautions, scalp-recorded EEG spectral activity will continue to provide noninvasive useful information on integrative brain function for many years to come.
>
> Richard Davidson[1]

Three quarters of a century ago, recording from simple scalp electrodes, Hans Berger detected spontaneous electrical potentials arising from his son's brain. The technique has come a long way since Berger coined the term *electroencephalogram*. Most EEG activities are still sampled by electrodes on the surface of the scalp.

They represent the pooling of huge numbers of faint dendritic potentials. These currents arise within each nerve cell's luxuriant tree of dendrites. A few others are gathered up from countless cell bodies.

Once all these various potentials are pooled and amplified, they then assume the form of much larger waves. These "brain waves" cycle up and down at several different frequencies each second (cps means cycles per second). Summated waves of excitation create their crests; waves of inhibition, their troughs. The thalamus acts as the dynamic, interactive pacemaker for much of this rhythmic excitatory/inhibitory activity up in the cortex.

EEG research during the past decade has focused on the possible significance of alpha rhythms (8–12 cps), theta rhythms (4–7 cps), beta rhythms (13–29 cps), and especially the faster gamma rhythms (30–70+ cps).

Magnetoencephalography (MEG) has also made noteworthy contributions. MEG amplifies the minute *magnetic* fields that our brain activity also generates. The interpretations of MEG data are not confused (as are those of the EEG) by the big differences in conductance between the dense skull and the fluid covering the surface of the brain. This fact makes MEG a more reliable way to compute the original neural source of the components of a particular field. At present, MEG (like EEG) still does not accurately localize field sources *deep* in the brain.[2]

Alpha Rhythms

The phrase *alpha activity* is often shortened to alpha. Alpha is seen most readily over the occipital cortex, yet it varies remarkably from person to person. Alpha is not regarded as an "idling rhythm," because persistent attention can facilitate alpha. You can also enhance alpha by *voluntarily* deciding to shift your attention into a more alert, but untroubled mode.

By the early 1970s, two findings became clear: (1) alpha activity decreased over the left hemisphere when mental activity involved verbalization; (2) alpha activity decreased over the right hemisphere during mental activity that involved spatial tasks. What was the meaning of this *inverse* relationship between alpha EEG activity and mental activity? It suggested that *reduced* alpha activity could serve to indicate a lateralized *increase* of cortical function.

It was then found that human subjects could show *less* EEG alpha power (consistent with their *greater* cortical activity) at a time when brain imaging showed that their thalamus was also *more* active metabolically.[3] This finding may reflect the ways the thalamus and cortex are often jointly engaged in complementary resonating, oscillatory activities [Z:263–271].

Special computations make it easier to recognize and to interpret this *inverse* relationship between localized alpha EEG activity and the actual degrees of activity in the underlying brain. These methods calculate the total power in the alpha bands over the two cerebral hemispheres, then compare them with alpha from a given electrode at a more localized site. Research based on this approach has pointed to interesting lateralized differences between alpha activity on the right and left sides of the brain.[4]

In recent years, the Wisconsin Center for Affective Science in Madison has correlated such alpha EEG amplitude asymmetries—especially from the right and left frontal regions—with a variety of psychological states and relevant laboratory findings.[5] In individual subjects, the differences are often striking, not only in selected adults but also in certain children. Moreover, rhesus monkeys also show similar individual differences in prefrontal asymmetry. These findings confirm the trends shown in their human counterparts. Monkeys who show greater relative *right*-sided prefrontal activation also show higher blood cortisol levels in their early-morning baseline samples. Overall, the data suggest that when we and our fellow primates show this right frontal preponderance of alpha activity, it tends to be correlated with higher levels of stress responses.

Theta Rhythms

Earlier EEG reports linked theta waves over the midfrontal region with states of focused attention during problem-solving tasks. These distinctive trains of rhythmic 6 to 7 cps activity tended to wax and wane. They were often called "frontal *midline* theta" or "mental theta." Later MEG studies show that "mental theta" has deeper origins. Its source is farther down within the medial prefrontal and anterior cingulate regions.[6] One MEG report briefly notes that frontal midline theta waves can occur during zazen and Yoga meditation. This informal study lacks subjective reports. It needs to be fully documented.[7]

Because our frontal lobes do keep monitoring and updating our responses, they help us maintain a given task "online." A different phrase, "working memory," is used to describe related frontal lobe functions. These are the kinds that help us keep certain recent items actionably "in mind" for brief periods. Intracranial EEGs have been recorded from patients. They show that theta increases more when the patients rely on their memory alone to navigate through a virtual maze as opposed to being guided by visual arrow cues.[8]

Standard EEG studies suggest that our short-term working-memory tasks are associated not only with coherent prefrontal theta activities (4–7 cps) but also with theta in the posterior association cortex.[9] These joint findings seem to correlate with the actual functional links joining the frontoparietal regions. (Though coherent synchronized gamma activities increase in a similar fashion, they are thought to be referable more to the earlier steps involved in initial sensory processing.)

The International Affective Picture System contains a wide range of affect-laden pictures. Whether viewers find the emotional *content* of each picture to be pleasant or unpleasant, their slower theta frequencies (4–5 cps) are often first to respond. These early responses are noteworthy in view of theta's widespread functional anatomical representations in the limbic system (see chapter 29). Synchronizations arise slightly later among the faster theta, alpha, and gamma frequencies.[10]

In rodents, theta activities are prominent in the hippocampus. Here, theta rhythms correlate with the more slowly responding GABA receptors, whereas the faster gamma EEG activities are associated with the faster responding class of GABA receptors.[11]

Beta Rhythms

It used to be thought that arousal and activation were always strongly correlated with low-voltage, fast, beta activities. It was also believed that in regions where more beta power occurred, alpha wave activity would therefore be reduced. Exceptions to this inverse beta/alpha relationship emerged when EEGs were studied during many different cognitive processes.[12] Indeed, beta power asymmetries on tasks often paralleled similar asymmetries of alpha power. Sometimes, both activities were *reduced* when the underlying cortex was being activated.

Recent research disclosed that beta waves and much faster frequencies were not so irregular and *de*synchronized as their gross appearance on the early EEG paper recordings had once suggested. In fact, both theta and gamma activities often took the form of rhythmic waves that were *synchronized*. This distinction is physiologically important. "Synchronized" refers to smooth waveforms that recur in a regular rhythm at a given electrode site. The term *coherence* is used when many of these same EEG peaks and valleys are all in synchrony at *many different* electrode sites.

Slower beta rhythms (15–18 cps) are associated with slow wave sleep. Beta activities at frequencies faster than 18 usually occur during active waking states and states of rapid eye movement (REM) sleep.[13]

In a major technical advance, both EEG *and* functional MRI (fMRI) can now be recorded *simultaneously*.[14] One such recent study of fifteen subjects[15] emphasizes the faster beta-2 activity which cycles 17 to 23 times per second. It accompanies an important kind of relaxed "spontaneous cognitive operations." These occur during "conscious rest" in "the absence of a task."

This sounds like a state meditators might enter. Suppose we were to enter, and remain, in this state of "resting wakefulness." Which regions would show this beta-2 activity? It turns out that they are the same cortical regions in which PET and fMRI signals *decrease* when some new task would require us to shift into explicit action or perception. In chapter 50, we will find that these sites include the medial cortex of the retrosplenial and dorsomedial prefrontal regions, as well as the lateral temporoparietal region.

On the other hand, suppose the solution to a new task requires acts of attention and the cognitive processes related to attention. Then the fMRI signals *increase* (and the alpha power *decreases*) in those other *lateral* regions of the fronto-parietal convexity.

Therefore, this particular (*non*task) beta-2 activity appears to be linked with processes in the more medial regions that may support our usual "resting wakefulness." It will be essential to determine which precise mechanisms and pathways cause this beta-2 activity to fade when a person first develops the impulse to engage in a new, active task (see chapter 51).

Gamma Rhythms

Our environment bombards us with data from countless sources. How does each new perceptual and conceptual piece of such an immense jigsaw puzzle fit into a larger coherent construct, one that we can use, consciously or unconsciously? Studies of gamma EEG activities have helped theorists wrestle with at least one aspect of this so-called binding problem. The problem has many facets.

Gamma rhythms cycle faster than 30 times per second. Some researchers place their upper limit at an arbitrary 80 cps. Often, gamma is simply measured at 40 cps. It can be hard to pin down precisely "where" gamma arises and what it "means," because gamma rhythms are ubiquitous. They can be detected both in single nerve cells and from larger constellations of neurons. Here, it suffices to begin by mentioning three caveats.

- Large muscles underlie the scalp electrodes that record the EEG from the frontal and temporal lobes. These muscles contract when you become emotionally tense. Their contractions create a broadband signal that contaminates the EEG. These peripheral muscle artifacts must be eliminated. Not until then can gamma band power be attributed to your brain itself. Electromyograms (EMGs) can detect these muscle activities, and various filtering techniques can be used to minimize their interference.
- In the brain, gamma activities appear to subserve not one but several different functions.[16] For example, sensory stimulation prompts brief, *phasic* gamma responses to occur. In evoked potential studies, these evoked components arrive reflexly some 100 milliseconds after the stimulus. A second phase occurs later on. These delayed, so-called cognitive gamma responses arise in association with the delayed P300 waveforms.

- An important point is often lost sight of: each time we achieve mental coherence, *focused attention also plays a pivotal role.* MEG studies show that gamma responses increase during the first 50 to 250 ms after we have been stimulated by a visual or auditory event. But suppose our attention has been *distracted* elsewhere? Now, *no such gamma increase occurs.*[17]

Current theories suggest that our brain's functional signaling is complex. Its "building blocks" could involve not only synchronized gamma activities but also some alpha, theta, and even delta oscillations. How, precisely, might multiple, distributed brain networks meld different functions into one meaningful event that could be described as "binding?" Could at least some aspects of *mental* coherence arrive at times when faster gamma activities "nestle" their peaks neatly into the "room" available in the spaces between the slower theta firing rates? Could oscillations represent processes that combine to form intimate, *physiological* phase relationships?

Bear with one current theoretical approach to this "nestling" question. It is so imaginative that it can serve several functions simultaneously.[18] It can become both an illustration of how hard-pressed neuroscientists are by the vast dimensions of the "binding" problem, and an example of gross speculations that may still have some heuristic potential. The theory begins with some numbers: when gamma waves cycle, say at the "magic number" of 40 times per second, then their successive peaks will be some 25 ms apart. Forty peaks can nestle into 1000 ms (1 second) if each gamma wave lasts 25 ms.

Next, the theory builds on two other observations: (1) We hear two distinct auditory clicks only when these two stimuli are separated by a critical interval of time. They must arrive *more* than 25 ms apart. However, if the two clicks occur *less* than 25 ms apart, we cannot discriminate them. We fuse the two, and hear only one sound. (2) Our short-term memory is limited. It remains accurate only if we burden it with no more than seven items at any one time. (It used to be a lot easier when our telephone numbers were limited to seven numbers, before area codes added the mental burden of three extra numbers to remember.)

Frank speculation leads on from here: perhaps a single, separate stimulus event (as defined by some 5 to 7 distinctive features) could constitute one coded "package." Then we might "bundle" each such event up inside five to seven of these successive gamma waves. If so, each gamma-clustered event would now last for around 125 to 175 ms (5 waves times 25 = 125; 7 waves times 25 = 175).

The features coded within various gamma event clusters might then go on to "nestle" inside one theta cycle. How so? Because a single theta cycle also lasts for a reasonably comparable period: some 143 to 250 ms. Perhaps then, one such theta wave could provide a "frame of reference" that might serve as a kind of "index function." Theoretically, processes of this kind might allow the brain to "bundle/nestle/index" several sets of stimulus features into their correct temporal sequence. In practice, such a scheme might help the brain perceive, encode, store, and then recall a single event.

During one form of meditation, at least, source analysis indicates that the gamma activity does not represent some artificial technical harmonic of the beta-2 wave activity discussed earlier. Instead, it arises from separate neuronal populations.[19]

In the laboratory, human subjects prepare mentally, anticipating the task ahead. ("Ready, set, go!") Gamma frequencies change within your frontal regions as soon as you start to prepare mentally for a visual task. For example, one well-trained subject consistently increased his frontal 36 cps gamma power during the 7-second interval before his visual task. Simultaneously, he *decreased* his 44 to 64 cps gamma power.[20] This trained subject provided a noteworthy introspective report: he felt "globally" more "focused" just during those particular seconds when his 36 cps gamma activity had become most well developed.

Zen meditative training emphasizes *clarity and immediacy of perception*. Clarity has both qualitative and quantitative aspects. It refers chiefly to that sharpness of perception which enables a percept to be fully and completely attended to. In physiological terms, it suggests that average signal-to-noise ratios are being enhanced globally or focally. This occurs in brief periods during the earlier years, is enhanced during retreats, and may later occur much more frequently in association with advanced degrees of monastic practice. When long-term meditators are also highly trained, will their reports of greater perceptual clarity correlate with particular gamma frequencies in certain regions? This hypothesis is testable.

Intracranial electrodes have recorded gamma activities from the human cortex directly. Individual human subjects do differ slightly in their gamma frequencies around 40 cps even when they perform standardized visual and motor tasks.[21]

We are tuned in to gamma at 40 cps. Humans have an innate physiological preference for stimuli that arrive at this particular frequency.[22] Thus, the optimal rate for delivering auditory stimulation is precisely 40 cps. This frequency prompts a steady-state EEG response, recorded from scalp electrodes, that peaks in amplitude at 40 cps. Stimulations of 40 cps also give the maximum regional blood flow increase in PET scans. This rate also selectively activates an auditory region in the pons and cerebellum. Gamma band activity is enhanced over the frontoparietal network when normal subjects anticipate a visual stimulus. This distribution of gamma correlates with their faster reaction times when they perform a simple visual motor task.[23]

Various lines of evidence converge to suggest that much of our "binding" of sensory features hinges not just on gamma activity per se *but on the way the stimulus goes on to induce gamma activity which becomes synchronized and in phase*.[24] Recent evidence suggests that our implicit attentional focus involves a similarly induced gamma activity, as well as gamma oscillations that then evolve further during the whole sequential process. The early gamma oscillations peak at 100 ms after the onset of a visual stimulus. They correlate with the coarse visual properties of this stimulus *and* with selective attention. The later gamma oscillations peak at around 250 ms. They occupy a broader band (55–85 cps) than does the earlier response (30–45 cps). These later oscillations correlate with the way the perceivers integrate their internal representations with their prior experience during subsequent cognitive processing.[25]

Recordings from intracranial electrodes show that we develop more coupling of gamma coherence between the cortex and hippocampus during the waking hours than during sleep. Moreover, this greater gamma coherence occurs both locally (within a cortical region) and transcortically.[26]

Intracranial electrodes at other sites have sampled gamma oscillations over a wide range from 30 to 130 cps.[27] The waves increase while visual stimuli are being encoded. In the fusiform gyrus, gamma oscillations increase when the patients focus their attention on a visual stimulus, but decrease later when they habituate to the stimulus. In contrast, gamma increases in the lateral occipital region during the anticipatory phase of visual attention, and before the visual stimulus actually arrives.

Very Fast and Slower Frequencies

Intracranial electrodes disclose rhythms cycling as high as 300 times per second in the subthalamic nucleus deep in the brain. These fast rhythms increase during movement and during dopamine stimulation, and are much reduced at rest.[28] Intracerebral electrodes also reveal that cats show fast "rippling" activity between 80 and 200 cps during their natural states of vigilance.[29]

Delta waves (0.7–4.0 cps) correlate with areas of brain damage in neurological patients. However, in normals, these slow waveforms are characteristic of slow wave sleep. The normal cortex has an intrinsic slow oscillation as low as 0.7 cps. This slow activity can be suppressed during waking states by the release of either acetylcholine or norepinephrine.[30] This finding of an intrinsic slow rhythm is of note in relation to the observation that certain kinds of internal mental processing sometimes reveal delta activities.[31]

In Summary

The brain's multiple rhythms express a basic fact: its many interacting modules are constantly shifting into complex physiological configurations. What does this imply in terms of a single emotion and a single thought? Firing rates of cells in one region do not explain these distinct experiences. They represent widespread, transient physiological linkages that are being "mediated by synchrony over multiple frequency bands."[32]

17

Some Gamma EEG and Heart Rate Changes during *Meditation*

> Questioner: How many years do I have to practice zazen?
>
> Taisen Deshimaru: Until you die.
>
> Taisen Deshimaru (1914–1982)[1]

> Long-time Buddhist practitioners self-induce sustained electroencephalographic high-amplitude gamma-based oscillations and phase-synchrony during meditation.
>
> Antoine Lutz and colleagues[2]

It probably takes a long time for regular meditative training to cause a persistent major change in the EEG. This chapter addresses the latest research on gamma EEG activities during certain Tibetan styles of meditation. The next chapter describes the EEG changes in alpha and theta activities in *Zen* meditation.

Recent Studies of Self-Induced, High-Amplitude Synchronized Gamma Activity

Please note: the subjects in these studies were long-term Tibetan meditators. First we need to describe the different nature of the practice these eight mature Tibetan Buddhists had engaged in before they were studied.[3] They had undergone prior training for some 15 to 40 years, and had spent an estimated ten to fifty thousand *hours* (!) meditating. Their average age was 49. The controls were 10 naive student volunteers who averaged 21 years of age. They underwent 1 week of meditative training, an hour a day.

The two groups had practiced a particular mental state for very different lengths of time: "a non-referential state of loving kindness and compassion." This state is not easy to classify into the usual concentrative or receptive categories. It is self-described as "unconditional loving kindness and compassion"; as an "unrestricted readiness and availability to help living beings"; as "pure compassion"; and as "non-referential compassion."

Furthermore, it is a state which has *no* specific point object on which the meditator concentrates, nor does it specifically involve memories or images. Instead, it "cultivates a receptivity or openness" to experience. After the meditator decides to enter this state, any volitional aspects are said to dissipate. Thus, the meditator allows his feelings of loving kindness and compassion to "permeate" his mental field, in a way that then becomes reminiscent more of a subtle mode of affect than of attention per se. Chapter 89 serves as another reminder that the development of selfless compassion is an implicit part of the spiritual path worldwide [Z:648–653]. Therefore, the research being described has a significance confined neither to Zen nor to Buddhism.

The EEGs that monitored this state were recorded using a 128-channel net of sensors. Gamma band activity was sampled at 25 to 42 cps. Slower wave activities were recorded at 4 to 13 cps. Various manual and other techniques were applied to remove muscle artifacts. The findings may be summarized as follows:

- At baseline, during the neutral, nonmeditative, relaxed state, the Buddhist practitioners had much more gamma band activity per given amount of slower wave activity than did the novice controls. This higher ratio of gamma to slower wave activity was especially evident over the *medial frontoparietal electrodes*.
- Some 5 to 15 seconds after the neutral period ended, the meditators began to enter their "pure compassion" stage of meditation. Now they gradually developed a robust and extraordinarily high degree of *synchronized* gamma activity.
- The amplitudes of this induced gamma activity were some three or more times higher than those achieved when they tried to mimic the ordinary contractions of muscles around the head that might occur during meditation.
- The more hours each meditator had practiced during prior years, the higher was their absolute gamma activity.
- Two meditators had the highest amplitude of self-induced gamma activity. A separate study was done of their *evoked* responses to auditory stimuli during a different style of meditation. The higher their gamma amplitudes were *before* the stimulation, the more their gamma amplitudes increased during these separate tests of *evoked* gamma activity. The different style of "open presence" meditation used for this later study requires a total relaxation of all muscles, including those of the head. It is said to resemble "pure compassion," but lacks its affective components.
- *Long-distance*, transcortical synchronizations were evident between the frontal and parietal leads. In one subject, the degree of synchronization between the two hemispheres increased some 30% during meditation. These synchronization effects were also greater in the long-term practitioners.
- Parallel fMRI studies showed enhanced signals in the caudate and putamen, thalamus, right insula, anterior cingulate, and left midfrontal regions. In contrast, signals were reduced in the right midfrontal regions.[4]

Comment and Interpretations

This study highlights the way long-term advanced meditators can induce synchronized high-amplitude gamma activity during a special state that resembles an induced, global version of compassion. In design and execution, the study sets a high standard for research on gamma activities in other styles of meditation.

What is the significance of the synchronized gamma activity that involves both frontal and parietal lobes? A conventional view is that the two lobes are operating hand in glove when we carry out behavioral acts. In one sense, the body image representations back in our parietal region might be conceptualized as providing the sensorimotor framework from which our frontal executive functions can proceed.

So, to the degree that such notions are valid, then this frontoparietal gamma pattern, when accompanied by caudate and putamen activations, might possibly be consistent with some generic "preparation" for an unusual version of what the meditators call "compassion." However, they also call it "nonreferential." Perhaps it has more in common with empathy, considering that it has yet to be directed toward an external object.

What does it mean when trained meditators activate their caudate and putamen? These two nuclei in the neostriatum are viewed as acting in concert with our frontal motor, premotor, and prefrontal cortex. To what end? To help us form *habits* at successively higher-level *behavioral and cognitive* levels. In this regard, it is important to realize that some mechanisms represented within these two nuclei serve goals that are excitatory; others are inhibitory.

What significance attaches to synchronized waveforms? In the previous chapter we defined these as waveforms that recur regularly and rhythmically. When these individually smooth wave peaks from adjacent regions all arrive at precisely the same time, this is called phase-locking. When phase-locked activities attain high amplitudes, it suggests that more nerve cells are synchronizing their firing into integrated activities. Greater degrees of long-distance synchronizing effects suggest that more transcortical or thalamocortical firings are being integrated. When these multiple synchronies involve much of the brain, the term *coherence* describes this uniformity of EEG activity.

Recent Studies of Changes in Heart Rate Oscillations Associated with Slowed Breathing

An increase in parasympathetic tone from the vagus nerve has long been known to slow the heart rate temporarily during each breathing cycle. The technical term for this is *sinus arrhythmia*. Many young athletes vary their pulse rates for this reason.

Highly complicated heart rate fluctuations occur in healthy young adults during Chinese Chi or Kundalini Yoga meditative techniques.[5] These oscillations are closely related to slow rates of breathing. However, the rate fluctuations are significantly greater than those which occur in the usual forms of sinus arrhythmia.

Recent studies have tested whether such variations in vagal tone clarify in a significant way the basic central nervous system mechanisms of meditation. When breathing slows to less than seven breaths per minute, it is associated with greater amplitudes of sinus arrhythmia. In transcendental meditation (TM) practice, during episodes of so-called transcending, slower breath rates do occur. They are accompanied by increased skin conductance responses to a bell ring, and by increased amplitude and coherence of alpha activity in the frontoparietal regions. In addition, there occurs a "significantly higher vagal tone during transcending."[6] In this condition, the tendency toward enhanced sinus arrhythmia during transcending is reported to be largely independent of the changes in the rates of breathing per se.

This study emphasized a fact long known: a variety of substates occur, at different times, during one individual meditation session. Indeed, these substates are so distinct, physiologically and phenomenologically, that they require separate, individual analysis. How are individual episodes of "pure consciousness" to be interpreted in relation to the more *general* aspects of consciousness when they are accompanied by breath suppression? This is discussed further in chapter 87 of part VIII.

18

EEG and Heart Rate Changes in Zen *Meditation*

> When one goes into Zen meditation, one passes, as a usual process, through a psychic field, from the surface down to the depth, as if one were plummeting into a lake in a diving bell.
>
> Nanrei Kobori-Roshi (1914–1992)[1]

> Worldly ideas or irrelevant thoughts pass through the mind even in time of meditation. In this case I simply wait and allow these things to go through my mind until they naturally disappear in an instant. I do not dwell upon these experiences that pass through my mind.
>
> A Zen monk[2]

In Hirai's series, Zen monks who had trained for many years often progressed through the following sequence of EEG changes when they meditated: (1) organized alpha waves appeared initially, even though the monks' eyes were open;

(2) alpha increased in amplitude; (3) alpha frequency slowed; (4) rhythmic theta trains occurred even though the monks were not particularly sleepy at that time.[3]

Hirai studied twenty-three Rinzai monks during a 1-week intensive retreat. Based on the number of years they had been in training, they could be classified into three groups: (1) less than 5 years; (2) 5 to 20 years; (3) more than 20 years. Rhythmic theta trains occurred only in those three monks who had trained for more than 20 years. Of the thirteen monks who had trained 5 years or less, the majority (eight monks) only showed prominent alpha waves initially. The remaining five monks either reduced their alpha frequency or increased their alpha amplitude or both.

The same Rinzai Zen master also ranked his twenty-three Zen monks independently on the basis of how proficient they were in meditation. Only four monks received his high-proficiency rating. Of these, three had rhythmic theta trains.

Hirai was well aware that when normal subjects become drowsy they also show similar EEG changes. He pointed, however, to the results in the larger series of Zen monks that he had also studied. During meditation, repeated auditory clicks tended repeatedly to block (desynchronize) their alpha rhythms. It remains to be seen whether this latter finding—reduced habituation to external stimuli—can be replicated in a contemporary EEG and polygraph study of equally well-trained Zen monks in a retreat setting [Z:104–107]. For reasons discussed in the last two chapters, the detailed responses of different gamma frequencies will be of particular interest, though changes in the alpha, beta, and theta range will still be informative.

Meanwhile, two recent studies of Zen meditation have been reported from Japan. In one, the subjects (six men, six women) sustained their attention and controlled their breath during a standard technique of Zen meditation. Their electrocardiograms (ECGs) were taken both during meditation and during control periods.[4] Half of the subjects developed frontal midline theta activity. Calculations based on their heart rate variability suggested that they developed greater degrees of frontal midline theta activities when their sympathetic nervous system was *less* engaged.

Multiple factors at many levels of the neuraxis can shift the functional balance between the sympathetic and parasympathetic divisions of the autonomic nervous system. Measurements at multiple levels will be required before we understand which mechanisms at which levels cause such heart rate variability. The caveat seems relevant to certain kinds of meditation procedures, which—though they may be described as "attention demanding"—also involve varying degrees of drowsiness or "relief from the anxiety."[5]

Some people are more anxious. Some people find it easy to meditate. If you're a more anxious person, does this trait influence either how deeply you can relax, *or* how much internalized attention you can develop? These issues were studied in twenty-two beginning Zen meditators. Their psychological state was first assessed by Spielberger's State-Trait Anxiety Inventory. Their meditation was then monitored with EEG and heart rate variability techniques.[6] During meditation, they developed increased alpha EEG coherence between the two frontal regions. The more relaxed subjects showed more bifrontal alpha coherence. Their greater degrees of relaxation appeared to correlate with their high-frequency heart rate variability, a *parasympathetic* index. However, higher scores for trait anxiety also correlated with the greater percent change in this high-frequency parasympathetic index. Subjects who showed lower trait anxiety were more likely to engage in greater degrees of internalized attention when they meditated.

In summary, Zen meditators tend to develop more alpha and theta activities bifrontally in association with a shift toward vagal influences in their autonomic nervous system. We need to know more about the basic psychological differences among persons who meditate.

Relevant Changes in Other Styles of Meditation

Meditators who undergo a mindfulness training program can develop lateralized changes in their alpha EEG activity, as discussed in the next chapter. Long-term meditators in the TM program also show patterns of EEG activities that are more enduring and coherent.[7]

Twenty experienced meditators in the Sahaja Yoga tradition were studied during rest and meditation using a sixty-two-channel EEG.[8] When assessed by conventional linear analysis, EEG power increased over the midline frontal and central regions in the theta-1 (4–6 cps), theta-2 (6–8 cps), and alpha-1 (8–10 cps) frequency bands. When other calculations were used for *non*linear complexity, the data suggested that these theta-2 and alpha-1 activities reflected less complex neuronal dynamics. In contrast, the faster beta-3 frequencies (22–30 cps) were associated with more complex neuronal dynamics. The authors suggested that when we focus attention *internally,* our "irrelevant networks" are being "switched off."

When positive "blissful" episodes arise during meditation, some EEG studies report that prominent theta activities become more coherent in the front and the back of the brain. Theta activities can also become more synchronized over the anterior and midline frontal regions, predominately on the left side.[9] This finding serves to introduce one of the themes to be developed in the next chapter: a general tendency for left frontal activities to correlate with our more "positive" emotions.

19

Delayed Physiological Responses to Meditation

> A robust cortisol response to acute stressors is beneficial in preventing stress-activated defense mechanisms from overshooting and damaging the organism. Chronically elevated baseline or average cortisol, on the other hand, appears to increase risk for a variety of diseases.
>
> C. MacLean and colleagues[1]

> The mindfulness group displayed a larger response to the flu vaccine, and—most interesting—the larger the leftward tilt in a person's brain activity, the greater the beneficial response to the flu vaccine.
>
> Daniel Goleman[2]

Life presents one stressful situation after another. We respond both acutely and chronically. Converging lines of evidence indicate that regular meditative practice does help one respond more appropriately to stressful conditions. Several different programs lay claim to beneficial results, including TM,[3] mindfulness meditation,[4] and other approaches known collectively as "mind-body medicine."[5]

Psychoneuroimmunology has also developed into a new specialty field.[6] Early research results established that immunological responses fell after dramatic events such as bereavement when one's spouse died, or 2 days of sleep deprivation. Final examinations—a common short-lived stressful situation—were recently found to have immunological consequences. Negative emotions and stressful experiences generate molecules known as proinflammatory cytokines. One such molecule, interleukin-6, enhances the production of C-reactive protein, a risk factor for heart attacks.

Cortisol: Pros and Cons

Cortisol is a glucocorticoid hormone. Cortisol levels in the blood normally start to rise at dawn and reach their lowest levels in the early evening. Adrenocorticotropic hormone (ACTH) from the pituitary gland stimulates the additional release of cortisone from our adrenal cortex as a normal part of our stress responses.

Cortisol has interesting effects on the brain, in addition to its effect on the body. It

- increases long-term potentiation in the hippocampus;
- increases serotonin (ST) turnover in the hypothalamus and midbrain;

- upregulates ST_2 receptors in the cerebral cortex;
- increases excitotoxic cell death in the hippocampus, and contributes to the memory loss associated with aging.

Theory: If stress responses release more cortisol from the adrenal cortex, and if regular meditation does reduce these responses to stress, then perhaps regular meditators would develop lower cortisol blood levels. Perhaps such lower cortisol levels would not interfere with the normal lymphocyte production of antibodies. Fact: one group of TM practitioners showed a normal pattern of blood cortisol levels.[7]

A standardized stress test was then designed to test a second group of male TM subjects. These men enlist our sympathy, because this task lasted an hour, and wasn't easy.[8] It included 6 minutes of sustained mental arithmetic, the need to use a mirror to trace a star, and maintaining a constant degree of hand grip tension. This stress test was repeated after the volunteers had then practiced in the TM program for the next 4 months.

After their 4 months of practice, these TM subjects did show a decline in their baseline cortisol measurements. They also showed an *increased* cortisol response to the standard laboratory stressors. Whether this particular pattern of cortisol responses reflects an entirely "adaptive" series of mechanisms could be open to several interpretations.

In another cortisol study, fifty-two male college students entered into a Thai Buddhist practice of concentrative meditation. Thirty nonmeditating male students served as their controls.[9] Baseline blood samples were drawn before the students began their 2-month training program. They were repeated at 3 weeks and at 6 weeks into the program. The way the students responded to a questionnaire at the end of the program helped classify them into two groups: (1) those who could meditate successfully and arrive at a state of tranquility; and (2) those who could not.

Both groups of meditators significantly lowered their serum cortisol to levels below those in the nonmeditating controls. The successful group reduced their cortisol levels significantly below their baseline levels, both at 3 weeks and at 6 weeks. In the *un*successful meditators, cortisol levels at 6 weeks did *not* differ from baseline levels.

A related question might be directed toward the sympathetic division of the autonomic nervous system: Do meditators who practice regularly also have lower blood levels of catecholamines, perhaps reflecting lesser degrees of activation of their sympathetic–adrenal medulla system?[10] In a different group of nineteen TM subjects, their 9:00 A.M. and 8:00 P.M. norepinephrine (NE) levels were significantly lower than controls. Their morning epinephrine levels were also significantly lower. Their response to stress was not tested. In summary, the results suggest that regular meditative practice can reduce blood cortisone and NE levels.

A Biotechnology "Stress Test" of Mindfulness Training

The recent economic downturn proved especially difficult for biotechnology companies. Under these stressful circumstances, employee anxieties would pose a rigorous challenge to the potential benefits of any kind of meditative training. It was to these employees in this difficult setting that Jon Kabat-Zinn chose to deliver personally his 8-week training program of mindfulness training.[11]

Kabat-Zinn's course includes training in a calming meditation that focuses on the breath, together with a scan of meditative awareness directed to sensations arising throughout the body.[12] His class of 25 employees met for 2 to 3 hours each week for 8 weeks. A silent 7-hour retreat was held during the sixth week. The employees were also expected to practice meditation at home for 1 hour a day, 6 days a week, using guided audiotapes. The control group consisted of sixteen interested subjects who had been placed on a temporary waiting-list.

The meditation class was conducted during daily work hours. Was this the optimal time? Not unless one were to view this corporate work environment as a challenging "stress test." Still, even this short program was associated with a subtle increase in the subjects' degrees of relative left-sided *anterior* EEG activation.[13] This increase was correlated with psychological tests that showed reductions in negative affect and increases in positive affect.

Contrary to expectations, the meditators showed significant EEG changes in the *mid-prefrontal* (F4–F3) electrode locations. Instead, their most consistent evidence of other, more lateralized, anterior cerebral activations was limited to leads farther back on the left side. These were at central and anterior temporal sites.

The meditators did develop a rise in their influenza antibody titers (significantly greater than controls). The rises occurred in response to receiving a vaccination against influenza at the close of their 8-week course.[14] The greatest increase in antibody titers occurred in subjects who increased their left-sided anterior activation the most. The antibody titers were measured in two subsequent blood drawings, after 3 to 5 weeks and 8 to 9 weeks respectively.

Neither the frequency and duration of the employees' practice at home nor the subjective changes (both items were estimated from self-reports) could be correlated with either the EEG findings or with the antibody titers.[15]

This relatively more rapid peak rise in antibody titers can be added to an already long list of reported physiological and biochemical changes. The data suggest that even short periods of mindfulness training can be of practical value in helping people relieve those natural responses of brain and body which are well-known to be adversely influenced by stressful situations.[16]

Other Studies of the Relationships between Personality Types and Immunological Responses

Several other psychophysiological studies link temperament with humoral and cellular immune responses. A subsequent study of fifty-two men and women in their sixth decade confirmed that persons who evidenced a "negative affective style" also mounted a weaker influenza antibody response.[17] What was meant by a "negative style?" The evidence was apparent in the way these people described in writing the happiest and saddest events in their lives.

Negative affective styles were correlated with three other laboratory tests: a greater relative *right* prefrontal EEG activation at baseline; a greater subsequent degree of relative *right* prefrontal EEG activation; *and* a greater relative tendency to blink the eyes during a test of the startle response.

Another study was conducted in healthy college students of both sexes. Those whose baseline EEG showed a greater relative *left*-sided activation began with higher lytic activities in their natural killer cells. They also showed a further increase of these cells' activities above baseline in response to viewing a "happy" (positive) film clip.[18]

Cancer: Another Kind of Challenging "Stress Test" of the Benefits of Mindfulness Training

Patients diagnosed with cancer undergo major stress responses. Various "psychological" interventions have been tried. Their effects on measures of humoral and cellular immunity often vary. The result is "a confusing overall picture."[19]

However, after the same kind of 8-week mindfulness meditation program, forty-two breast or prostate cancer patients were considered to have shown significant improvement in their overall quality of life, in their stress symptoms, and in the quality of their sleep. Their T cell production of interleukin-4 increased more than threefold. Interferon gamma decreased, as did their natural killer cell production of interleukin-10. This latter immune profile was thought to resemble the pattern shown by persons who shift up *from* symptoms of depression toward a more normal (and potentially anti-inflammatory) profile. It is relevant to note that during depression, patients often tend to show elevated levels of ACTH and cortisol.

In summary, meditation appears to help reduce stress responses, though the precise mechanisms responsible for its benefits are still being studied.

20

Breathing In; Breathing Out

> Thoracic respiration gradually shifts to the abdominal and turns into a predominance of abdominal respiration with the progress of the meditation.
>
> T. Hirai[1]

Where does our normal spontaneous respiratory rhythm come from? Researchers are still pursuing its pacemakers and intricate circuitry.[2] A particular small cluster of nerve cells down in the medulla does generate the basic rhythm of breathing.[3] Acetylcholine (ACH) receptors are now known to increase this breathing rate.[4] In contrast, an area in the dorsolateral pons can suppress respiration.[5] It lies between the main sensory and motor nuclei of the trigeminal nerve.

In her comprehensive review of the literature, Bouin cites a variety of ways that meditation influences respiration.[6] In the resting state, meditators usually breathe more slowly than controls, and each breath has a larger tidal volume. They also breathe more vigorously in response to carbon dioxide than do controls. However, *while* meditating, the meditators reduce their breathing rate even further, and then show a substantial *decrease* in their ventilatory response to carbon dioxide. During meditation, the carbon dioxide pressure (referable to the alveoli of the lungs) rises more than during relaxation. It seems unlikely that retained carbon dioxide alone would be the primary mechanism for all of the experiential phenomena during meditation.

Lower Abdominal Movements during Breathing

Like other practiced meditators, Zen monks breathe more slowly during meditation (*zazen*), and tend increasingly to spend more time breathing out than breathing in. Moreover, the more relaxed they become, the less the intercostal muscles of their chest contract, and the more evident become their movements down in the abdomen.

At this stage, the piston-like contractions and relaxations of the diaphragm become an increasingly significant cause of the *passive* movements outward and inward of the lower abdominal wall. Note that a more relaxed abdominal wall would enable its passive movements to become more apparent. But if you elect to *squeeze* out the very last of your inspired air, you can still feel your lower abdominal muscles *actively* contracting. Electromyograms would help distinguish between the two factors.

In this regard, a pathway was recently discovered in animals that does generate active lower abdominal contractions during breathing.[7] This path starts in the upper medulla in its ventral lateral portion. Its terminals descend to a second neuron, which then sends its axons far down into the spinal cord. These fibers end on spinal motor neurons, the ones whose synapses will finally lead to the contractions of the *lower* abdominal muscles. In experiments on lower animals, even after opioids stop all other breathing movements, only these particular lower abdominal muscles still contract rhythmically during the late expiratory phase.

Why Pay Attention to the Tanden?

It is not clear during which century the ancients first emphasized the benefits of focusing attention on the breathing movements down in the lower abdomen (the tanden). Zen teachers have commonly advocated the technique. It begs to be studied carefully, longitudinally, using modern psychophysiological and neuroimaging methods, especially in meditators already expert in its use.

The technique first requires arriving at a certain level of calm, undistracted relaxation. It also requires a degree of skillful one-pointed focusing on a faint rhythmic movement far distant from one's head. Because several mechanisms overlap and reinforce each other, teasing out their individual contributions will not be easy. Guided imagery techniques have also been successful in relaxing patients and in slowing their respirations to as few as 3–5 breaths per minute. Therefore, focusing attention on breathing is to be regarded as neither specific to Zen nor as mysterious.[8]

Subsequent chapters suggest that a person who can focus attention on a fundamental breathing rhythm might gradually calm the firing activities of such limbic sites as the amygdala (and possibly of such paralimbic sites as the insula). But ideally, the way the several general mechanisms evolve needs to be monitored by faster recording methods, including fMRI, rather than by slower PET techniques [Z:281–283].

Breath Suspensions during Shallow Meditative Absorptions

The basic animal research is relevant because we still don't know why benign breath suspensions occur during shallow meditative absorptions. Are the mechanisms that stop breathing opioid in nature or nonopioid? Or could both types be involved? [Z:96–98]. Further studies are indicated to confirm that primates also have comparable opioid-*resistant* pathways leading to their lower abdominal muscles. If so, then faint lower abdominal muscle contractions might still occur (and be detected, if looked for) in meditators even though most of their other movements associated with breathing at higher thoracic levels might seem to have been suspended.

The pons and its connections become of interest for several reasons:

- Its parabrachial complex of nuclei is a major source of ACH. [Z:164–169]. Patients develop apneustic breathing after lesions damage their dorsolateral pons at and below this complex of ACH cells.[9] Apneustic breathing means that breathing slows markedly. The term *apnea* refers to breathing that stops completely or permanently. In neurological patients who have pontine damage, breathing pauses at the end of inspiration, or expiration, or both. In meditators, careful studies have revealed that some meditators do first breathe in normal tidal volumes of air (between 500 and 800 mL). But then a "continual slight inspiration of another 25–100 mL" of air can actually occur, despite the fact that their breathing might appear to have "stopped."[10]
- The parabrachial region, and its connections, also plays an essential role in various conditioning processes. These lead to food preferences and to food aversions.[11] Similar longings and loathings are relevant targets of Zen training.
- The sensory and motor nuclei of the trigeminal (fifth cranial) nerve also lie in this dorsolateral pontine region. In between these two nuclei is the sensitive area that can produce apneic responses.[12] This sensory nucleus of the trigeminal nucleus is a major recipient of information about how much air flows in and out through the nasal passages (see chapters 14 and 73).

Benign breath suspensions imply that the meditator's respiratory drive is being inhibited. How? Where? Presumably by the release of GABA—and possibly also by opioids released during some phases of deep internal absorption. Do such *major* inhibitions arise at levels in or near the dorsolateral pons, and extend their influence into adjacent nuclei? If so, then other discrete corresponding inhibitory effects might possibly be detected. It would be of interest to test for changes in motor activity in muscles supplied by the fifth cranial nerve. This would be evident in electromyograms (EMGs) from the masseter and temporal muscles of the head; and for signs of any reduced sensory responses, apparent in evoked potentials elicited from lower parts of the face.

As a practical matter, neuroimaging researchers need to be aware that subjects who hold the breath for periods even as short as 3 seconds can generate confusing signals in fMRI recordings.[13]

Vigorous Acts while Breathing Out

A taut abdomen supports our trunk movements. A lax belly does not. This is one reason why the boatman times the end of his "Yo-oh heave *ho*!" cry to coincide with his strongest pull. Professional tennis has become increasingly noisy as grunting exhalations coincide with each stroke. In Japan, martial arts trainees have long been advised: "any attack must take place while breathing out (*yang*), if possible while the adversary is breathing in (*yin*), because he is then at his most vulnerable."[14]

In summary, the way we breathe in and out provides researchers with an intimate window into our brain function. That window has yet to be fully utilized.

21

A Quest for "No" Answers: Koan, Huatou, Jakugo, Mondo

> Koan study is essentially a skillful means to really make us question what this life is, until we fully resolve the question.
>
> Bernie Glassman-Roshi[1]

> Kobori-Roshi asks me: "Do you know why Zen methods are strict?" (I don't, so I say "No.") He continues: "When the Zen master says NO!, this is his direct way to gradually condition away years upon years of his students' unfruitful thinking and behavior." [Z: 61]

"No" does several things. "No!" jolts you out of your complacency. Negation encourages you to take a fresh look at what you're doing. It can also help you trace your resistances back to their source. In the process, you begin to discover how much your responses have been conditioned.

Negation itself has a long history, its source dating to ancient times. As far back as the Vedic Age (c. 1500–500 B.C.E.) negation entered into the ineffable mystery of that Ultimate Reality referred to in the Upanishads (*neti, neti*, "not this, not this").[2]

The "eight negations" attributed to Nagarjuna arrived in Buddhist India during the second or third century.[3] They argue for a conventional world of manifold phenomena, but devoid of any final definitive truth. To follow this self-annihilating logic is to reach the conclusion that all propositions are inherently invalid.

The Koan

Among the several negations used later in China, one in particular would become immortalized. It evolved into this koan often given to beginning students. A monk asked Chao-chou (778–897) "Does a dog have Buddha nature?" Chao-chou answered "No!" (*Wu* in Chinese; *Mu* in Japanese).

Who is prepared for this negation (so grossly unfair to every wonderful dog one has known)? Can such illogic add anything to one's spiritual quest?

It can, for several reasons [Z:107–119]. To review only a few:

- After you contemplate the larger issues for a very long while, it may dawn on you that this "No!," this *Mu*, can serve as a useful training device. *Not* necessarily because of what *it* alone adds, but because your whole mental posture of questioning can be turned around to help you cut through your own conditioning, your fixed opinions, your rigid attitudes [Z:110–119].

  Will you always remain sentimentally attached to dogs? Will you stay offended by a mere word? Little intuitions will help you recognize these and other fixed opinions—your longings and loathings. Resistances center not just on our old attitudes, but also on the way we elaborate them into expectations and fantasies. Examined during mindful introspection, these problem areas can be worked through more dispassionately [Z:125–129].

- A koan spins off further questions. It requires further work in depth. In this respect, it does not operate the same way as does passively repeating a mantra.

- Of course, "No" and *Mu* can serve more pragmatic everyday functions. Each is a single syllable, easy to remember. Repeating *Mu*, keeping it on line, incorporating the word sound into your lower abdomen—these techniques allow you to insert *Mu* whenever you find your "monkey-mind" transporting you off into self-indulgent daydreams. When said *very* gently, in the form of a soft nudge, "No" can help you return to the present moment and become realigned.

  Not that thinking is "bad." Thoughts are as natural as clouds in the sky. It's just that it is preferable to live mindfully right here, right now, rather than being carried away.

  At this basic practical level, then, a koan is useful during all kinds of situations as soon as you recall it and focus on its keyword or topic area. This becomes a simple exercise in reapplying your attention to the present moment.[4]

- Recalling a koan can guide one toward certain fluid modes of perception and perspectives. The approach here involves mulling over the koan at progressively deeper levels, both while one is resting or active. "No" enters once again, in the sense that *no logical guidelines* exist for this kind of open-minded investigative practice. Therefore, one byproduct is an increasing capacity to allow your attention the freedom to roam autonomously.

- The koan helps a busy roshi determine the student's level of progress. The trainee makes a presentation of his or her understanding of the koan during a formal interview. During this demonstration and the rapid interchange, actions speak louder than words. Body language helps the roshi determine how flexible is the student's state of mind. Immediate spontaneous responses to the koan are valued. They are one measure of the student's freedom to access more intuitive, unconditioned modes of experience, beyond reach of conventional forms of logic. What about the student's thoughts and perceptions? Are they free from culturally conditioned prejudices? Rigidities are grist for the mill of koan training.

- A koan is frustrating. Carefully calibrated degrees of emotional frustration can help "stir the pot."

Types of Koans

Koans are used in Soto Zen practice (Dogen collected 300), not only in Rinzai Zen. The first group of so-called entry koans is said to facilitate the initial opening into kensho. The trainee goes beyond this initial glimpse of reality during further rigorous, advanced practice with an authentic teacher. This means following an approach to "the matter beyond" (as suggested by table 10 in chapter 88).

The next group of koans is used in formal study to help comprehend the world of Oneness.[5] The third group of koans focuses on the unique diversity of all things, building on this earlier perspective of Oneness. Later koans teach students how to use living words, not dead words, to express the inexpressible. Subsequent stages of training often address the so-called five ranks of Tozan and various aspects of the major Buddhist precepts. The one-on-one confrontations involved in such a prolonged course of study go beyond mere intellectual knowledge, testing the student's faith in the system and the endurance of both parties.

Huatou

During his 6-year solitary retreat as a young monk, Ch'an Master Sheng-yen improvised several techniques similar to those just discussed above, but he did not use the word *koan* to label them. Thus, whenever he found his thoughts wandering, he would recall the phrase "put down." This had been shouted at him earlier by a senior monk. It was the equivalent of "drop it!" or "let go!"[6]

When his concentration skills had improved, he would ask himself, "What is it?" This question, like "Who am I?" is short, penetrating, and can be mulled over. Such questions are referred to as *huatou* (Chin.) or *wato* (J.). Some phrases also serve as a kind of punch line when they are condensed from a longer koan. For example, I have used "original face," or "where is one?" to recall the core of each of the two koans I have worked on in years past.

Koans are not for everyone. For me, a koan has served as a useful concentration device. It has helped me to become more attentive, aware, and questioning. Yet, in candor, when I compare them with all the other benefits of Zen practice in general, koans have played only a minor role.

My spontaneous intuitive functions seem to have been enhanced more by the total atmosphere during sustained meditative retreats. Smaller intuitions then progressed toward deeper insights of various sizes. These subliminal processes seemed to help me "realize" the hints underlying a koan in ways that I could then go on to apply to practical, everyday existential issues. These insightful appreciations seemed much more enduring than any understandings that might have arisen at intellectual levels from something I read or heard someone else say.

Jakugo

Jakugo are short capping phrases. They sometimes serve as a way for trainees to express something of the essence of a koan. However, they are regarded as lesser accessories to koan practice. They not only lack the sheer power of a koan—being "something of a cross between a koan and a footnote"—but run the risk of being used intellectually.[7] Master Daito (the founding abbot of Daitokuji) quoted or composed some 2271 capping phrases, but finally settled on a core group of some 24 of them. The Zenrinkushu is one of the two capping phrase collections, and some Rinzai schools still use it today.[8] In appendix A, the reader will find examples of these phrases quoted from earlier versions of this anthology.

Mondo

The *mondo* is a form of question and answer. Often, a junior monk asks a reasonably meaningful question, only to receive a tangential response from his master. Many old questions and "answers" simply illustrate both the limitations of logic and the Zen master's freedom to respond with free-floating spontaneity. The four "Mondo" chapters in this book serve a different purpose: the questions are answered as directly as possible.

22

The Roshi

> I would have all the teachers in schools of every kind, including those in Sunday schools, agree that they would teach only what they know, that they would not palm off guesses as demonstrated truths.
>
> Robert Ingersoll (1833–1899)[1]

> Avoid, like the plague, a clergyman who is also a man of business.
>
> Saint Jerome (c. 342–420)

In this new millennium, few students seem to understand what total transformation means. Who in the West knows at the beginning how much commitment it requires? Worldwide, relatively few genuine spiritual authorities are available, and they are stretched thin. Far too many "spiritual guides" exist who are soon caught up in commercial enterprises.

The pioneering Japanese Zen masters who first resided in the United States have almost all passed on. Their first- and second-generation trainees now face mounting obstacles in bringing authentic Zen principles to the West. The essence of Zen is gender neutral, and many of these effective teachers are now women.

In ancient China many old Zen masters were, in their own way, at least as iconoclastic as Ingersoll. All too often now, contemporary Zen teachers are being swept up into endless multitasking activities as entrepreneurs. Laski noted, as had Jerome, that commercialism was a major impediment to mystical experience [Z:453–454].

Nowadays, only the fortunate few find one authentic teacher with whom they can share close ties for several decades, overcome the mutual unease of parent-child transference reactions, and grow to mature levels of spiritual understanding [Z:119–125].

Mariana Caplan recently explored the dynamic subtleties that enter into the relationship between disciple and teacher. Her book is entitled *Do You Need a Guru? Understanding the Student-Teacher Relationship in an Era of False Prophets.*[2] Clearly, fruitful affinities require honest, reciprocal commitments.

Roshi in Action

A genuine roshi continues to serve as the living exemplar of that basic Zen principle: *actions* speak louder than words. Kobori-Roshi demonstrated Zen principles to me personally. I remember vividly the time he invited me to join in a tea ceremony with his parishioners. This ceremony, at which he presided, was held in a small classic thatched roof hut measuring only 10 ft. × 10 ft. or so. I'm back in Kyoto again . . .

* * *

> We are nearing the hut, and I now see that it has a very low door. Before entering, he makes the point: he, I, and everyone else first need to lower ourselves and sink humbly to the very same level in order to enter it.
>
> Inside, men and women are huddled close together. We hear the soft whistle of the boiling water, "like wind in the pines." We examine handsome gnarled wooden antique treasures, shaped by expert craftsmen long gone. It was during this quiet careful observation of antiques that I then began to understand, firsthand, the breathtaking cultural aesthetic principle of *wabi*, that spare beauty expressed by a poverty of materials. Awe-inspired breath makes the point. It is there, too, that I see demonstrated, and absorb, the elements of *sabi*, that deep pleasure in things that are well aged.

* * *

Decades later, Kobori-Roshi's own, hand-fashioned tea bowl now sits before me. It is of the ultimate simplicity in form. The impressions left in clay by his fingers create a living presence. At first, the bowl might look unfinished, because on one side the thin layer of rice hull glaze may seem carelessly thrown. Looking further, you discover his glaze accomplished something else: it spread beyond to soften the hard edge along the whole rim.

Presence

Great teachers make lasting impressions by their *presence*. What we can observe these days in Thich Nhat Hanh or the Dalai Lama, I saw earlier in Kobori-Roshi's demeanor, posture, and graceful actions. As an observer, I believe such presence expresses at the neurological level an extraordinary way of *being at home within the immediate space and time of one's surroundings*: *composure, readiness, grace*.

Kobori-Roshi said this, in turn, about his own revered teacher, Shonen-Roshi. "One of the most important things I learned from Shonen-Roshi was the warmth that radiated from his entire body. His smiling face was filled with an eternally optimistic light. This illumination emanating from truly religious persons is conveyed not by words but by their very being. Their entire body—just sitting there—conveys depths of meaning."[3]

Zen Education

Education implies the leading out of capacities that are already there. I have learned the most from Zen educators. They expressed Zen at the simplest practical, ground level of daily living. They were leaders who kept reminding me: I am my own "artist-potter." My job is to mold my own clay, develop the right habits, educate myself in how best to dissolve my selfish preoccupations. I am still a decades-long work in progress.

A roshi needn't tell you everything about Zen—just enough to pique your curiosity. Nor must he or she necessarily prescribe an ancient koan. What *is* Zen? *This becomes your implicit koan.* No roshi can answer this for you verbally or in writing. You'll struggle to resolve this question on your own. Over time, you'll be graced by intuitions and insights of varying sizes. They will offer you glimpses of what Zen "is." You will also learn "about" Zen by observing how your earlier overconditioned responses have evolved.

A good roshi, like a good track-and-field coach, attends not only to your warm-up rituals and general metaphysical fitness for the low hurdles but motivates you to train for more advanced goals, the kinds that build long-distance endurance and traits of character. On the other hand, should you ever imagine that the Path has a set of permanent goalposts, you'll find that they keep on moving.

In Zen, the expression is "mountains after mountains." Or, in Japanese: *Mi zai. Mi zai* ("Not yet. Not yet"). Or, in Sanscrit: *neti, neti.*

A roshi's behavioral repertoire varies. The messages are tailored to fit who that student is and what his or her level of understanding is at that particular moment. Your own need and tolerance for a kinder or more rigorous approach also vary from time to time.

On retreat, I liked being reminded that we were not in the presence of one teacher, but of four teachers.[4] True, this person up front was now our group leader in self-education. Yet, the whole group itself was another teacher, because we were all in this together. Our third source of education was the natural sensate world of sounds and sights, the birds, the leaves, the wind ... Finally we were being educated by silence. It would be in silence that we learned to listen deeply so we could really hear, to observe carefully so we could really see ...

The Grasping Self: A Zen Lesson in Letting Go

In addition to Kobori-Roshi, I have shared in private informal interviews with two other Japanese roshis and one esteemed teacher (Myokyo-ni). Each of them represented the Kyoto school of Rinzai Zen. Among their many virtues as teachers, one attribute stands out. Each one regarded the self as a major focus of Zen Buddhist training.

Over the decades, I have concluded that not until *self*-centered, "psychological" issues receive *top priority* in the teaching, do students participate in authentic Zen, at least of the kind I have learned to value. Self-negation is at the core of the Zen Way. *Annatta* is the technical term for the state of non-*I*. No-I is a useful yardstick with which to measure both the words and the actions of Zen teachers.

One of these Kyoto-trained Zen teachers taught me a basic lesson about myself. A simple, dramatic demonstration showed me how strong was my own *I-Me-Mine.* It happened during an informal private interview before our retreat began.

We had conversed for a while. Then, he took a short, dark, wooden stick from his lap and placed it down on the low table in front of us. It caught my eye immediately. No ordinary wood was this, but a wonderfully aged, irregularly shaped stick, obviously an antique object. This work of art, about a foot long and perhaps an inch and a half in diameter, exemplified *wabi-sabi.* Its mellow patina conveyed associations with long use and advanced age. No word was spoken, yet the roshi's nod obviously invited me to pick it up.

I did. Turning it over and around in both hands, I then held it horizontally with my right hand at one end, slowly admiring it as I had the other antique objects during that earlier ceremony in Kyoto.

Surprise! In one swift act, the Roshi reached across and suddenly grabbed the free end, eyes twinkling as he did so. And almost as fast, without thinking, as my grasp reflex tightened, I found myself locked into a semi-mock tussle with the rightful owner of this antique treasure!

It was an impromptu tug of war, neither of us moving that stick very far in either direction. The strength of his pull just sufficed to neutralize mine. So there we were, like two boys at play, tugging on his beautiful stick!

Soon enough, it dawned on me: How could I possibly dispute his ownership!? Yielding, and relinquishing my grasp, I found we were both smiling when our brief mock play session ended.

A simple unexpected demonstration: Yes, *I* had longed to go on admiring his beautiful stick. He had (playfully) thwarted *Me* from doing so. *I* had behaved like it was *Mine*, and had grasped the stick reflexly. The greedy grasp of the *I-Me-Mine* was nakedly on display.

Words were unnecessary. I had been *educated*. I had done more than observe the full extent of my own instinctual tendency to *grasp* things.[5] I had *felt* the strength of my attachment in my muscles, joints, and sinews.

Ours is a high-tech culture. Media-driven, it preaches instant gratification, virtual reality, and conspicuous consumption. Wordlessly, a simple stick had taught me this proprioceptive lesson. The message about myself still tugs at my bones.

An Ancient Way of Giving up the Self: Bowing and Adapting to Circumstances

One part of the long spiritual path involves engaging adversity, learning how to endure suffering, and emerging from the experience feeling both instructed and relieved [Z:355–358]. Many Zen teachers become adept at structuring various situations that enable you to experience adversity and embrace its anguish first-hand. To swallow one's pride, bow humbly, adapt to unfair circumstances, *and do so without reservation* is an ancient, time-honored way to trim back the roots of the egocentric self.

One early record of this long, rigorous, approach to transforming one's character dates to an era as far back as the dawn of Ch'an in the sixth century C.E. It is contained in the "Outline of Practice," the teachings attributed to Bodhidharma and his followers.[6]

This first semi-legendary Ch'an patriarch drew a distinction between: (a) those fruitful transformations that arose out of one's difficult hands-on practical experiences in daily life, and (b) conceptual benefits derived from merely reorganizing one's pattern of thoughts. Focusing on the former, the teachings prescribed a course of action. It began with two dynamic ingredients: (1) the practice of suffering through unjust situations, and enduring them without complaint even though they arose from circumstances beyond one's control; (2) going on to adapt one's behavior in an even-tempered manner to such unfair events.

Twelve centuries later in Japan, similar advice would echo from a Dharma heir of Master Hakuin. In his "Bodhisattva Vow," Torei Enji (1721–1792) pointed to a related form of Rinzai practice. It also enabled one to find release from delusive beliefs even if they had grown from ancient events for which one was not responsible. The practice involved openly accepting one's lot, "knuckling under" as it were, and relinquishing self-centeredness, even while undergoing harsh, unfair abuse.

Do any aspects of such adverse situations seem familiar? Could they be a shrewd part of some carefully calibrated training methods? What about the authoritarian posture assumed by some Rinzai masters who having subjected their students to an impenetrable ("unfair") koan, also insist that they resolve it at each interview?

And, in our own era, what about this remarkable capacity that we can observe in a selfless, evolved person, one who has learned the lessons of how to bow humbly and to adapt to unjust circumstances? Would this not be an important attribute that distinguished the Dalai Lama when his name came up for consideration as a candidate for the Nobel Peace Prize?

Part III

Neurologizing

Anatomy is destiny.

Sigmund Freud (1856–1939)

23

Landmarks. Brain in Overview

> The average adult brain weighs about 1400 grams (3 pounds), or approximately 2 percent of the total body weight.
>
> C. Noback and R. Demarest[1]

The brain weighs about the same as the liver. But, *information* is what it's designed to digest and resynthesize, not meals. Keep referring to this chapter as the rest of the book unfolds.

The simplified version of the brain in figure 3 shows major landmarks on the outer surface as viewed from the left side. At left, the prefrontal cortex occupies most of the convex portion of the *frontal lobe*. Just behind it is the primary motor cortex, the central fissure, and the primary somatosensory cortex. Within the *parietal lobe*, the superior parietal lobule is that small uppermost portion. The intraparietal sulcus is the boundary separating it from the larger inferior parietal lobule beneath. The *occipital lobe* is at the far right. The long *temporal lobe* extends from it.

Below the cerebrum lie the *cerebellum* and the *brainstem*. The pons appears as a small bulge in the uppermost portion of the brainstem. Below it, the oblique line points to the medulla, from which the spinal cord descends. The midbrain is hidden beneath the temporal lobe. The letters *A* and *H* refer to the much deeper locations of the amygdala and hippocampus in the medial temporal lobe.

In figure 4 we look up at the medial surface of the right hemisphere from below. The cerebellum has been removed from above and behind the brainstem. Now, the whole (shaded) undersurface of the inferotemporal and occipital region can be seen.

Two frontal lobe gyri are identified. The *gyrus rectus* lies along its lower medial surface. The *orbital gyri* are shaded to indicate that they lie along its undersurface. In back, the *precuneus, cuneus*, and *retrosplenial region* are identified, because they are three of the most metabolically active regions of the resting brain.

Note that major parts of the limbic system lie disposed in the form of a large oval around the brain's inner surface. By convention, the limbic system includes the *cingulate gyrus* and *parahippocampal gyrus*, the *hippocampus* and *amygdala*, and the *hypothalamus*. The *mammillary body* and *arcuate nucleus* are parts of the hypothalamus.

Longer dashed lines suggest the position of the right *thalamus*. In front, the large dotted stippling emphasizes how extensively the medial dorsal nucleus of the thalamus interacts, reciprocally, with the whole prefrontal cortex. In back, the faint stippling emphasizes that the pulvinar interacts with the cuneus. The

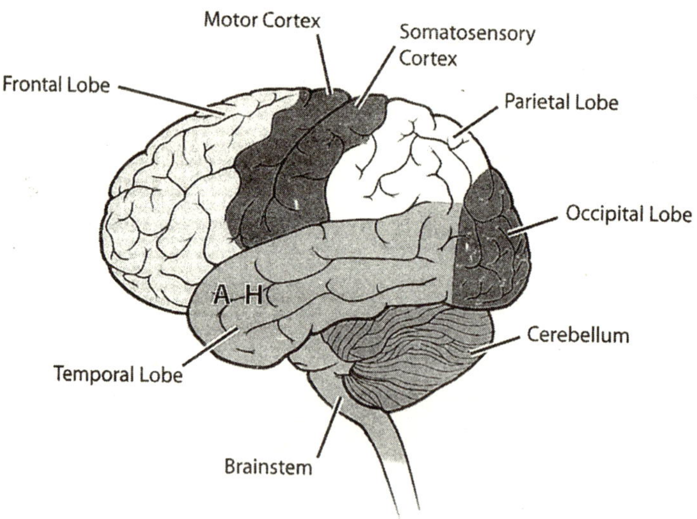

Figure 3 The left cerebral hemisphere

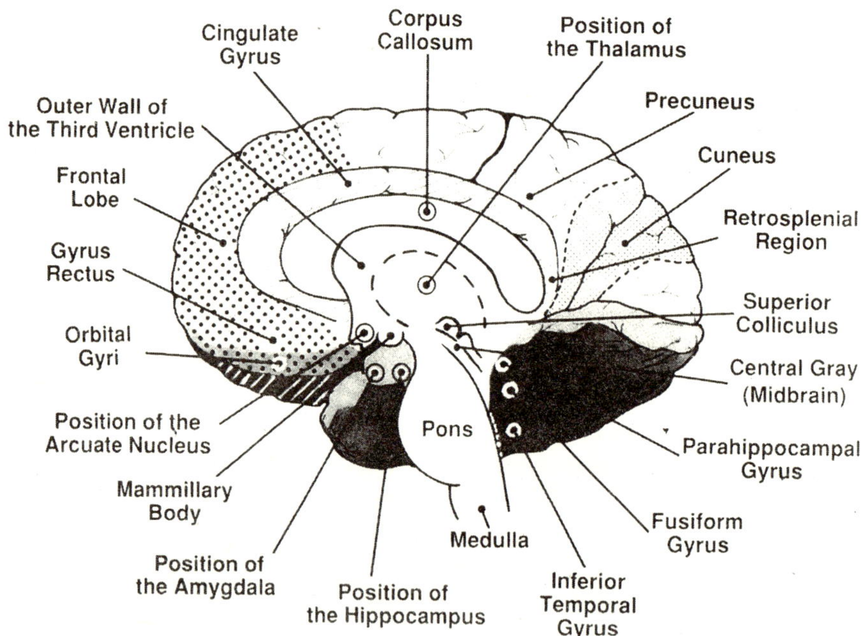

Figure 4 The right cerebral hemisphere, viewed from its inner surface

diagonal lines on the long cingulate gyrus suggest its extensive reciprocal interactions with the anterior thalamic nucleus.

The *fusiform gyrus* in the inferior temporo-occipital cortex includes a major color-sensitive region. This will become important to the discussion in part IX. In the rest of part III, we take up the *functional* anatomy of the landmark regions shown in these figures.

24

Messenger Molecules: Some New Data

> Yin and yang ... in the harmonious brain, excitatory and inhibitory synaptic signals coexist in a purposeful balance.
>
> Richard Miles[1]

This chapter highlights new research on our brain's neuromessenger systems. The shorthand word "systems" refers here to the sequence of mechanisms which bring a messenger in touch with its specific receptors.

Acetylcholine Systems

It was the Monday after Easter, 1920. In the middle of the night, Otto Loewi had awakened with the design for his experiment. In his laboratory he would soon prove that when the vagus nerve was stimulated, it released a chemical messenger that slowed the beating heart. That messenger turned out to be acetylcholine [Z:164–169]. It remains the most appropriate transmitter with which to begin our discussion.

ACH pathways inside the brainstem follow two major routes. One leads from a major cluster of ACH cells in the pons up toward the thalamus. The more ventral pathway ascends from the large ACH cells farther down in the medulla.

ACH acts on two major classes of its ACH receptors (nicotinic and muscarinic). Nicotinic ACH receptors respond quickly. High concentrations of nicotine receptors are evident in the medial dorsal and lateral nuclei of the human thalamus. When ACH cell bodies are stimulated down in the pons, thalamic nerve cells that have nicotinic receptors fire only 140 ms later. Nicotine has major reinforcing properties on behavior, and has long been identified as the primary molecule in cigarette smoke causing the addiction to tobacco. Nicotine receptors also enhance some dopamine functions in the limbic system and some functions of endogenous opioid systems. This may be one reason why nicotine creates the impression of being a desirable stimulant. Nicotinic receptors, widespread in the brain, play roles not only in reinforcement but in sensitization, locomotion, working memory, fear-associated learning, anxiety, and depression.[2]

In humans, nicotine dependence shows an intriguing association with high-hostility traits.[3] During an aggression test, only the high-hostility subjects who did not smoke showed an enhanced metabolic sensitivity to a skin patch containing a low dose of nicotine (3.5 mg). In contrast, the high-hostility subjects who were smokers also showed an enhanced response, but this occurred only when the patch contained a high dose of nicotine (21 mg).

The subjects' responses were monitored by PET scans. Those enhanced metabolic activities which did occur were distributed throughout the brain on both sides. However, subjects who scored *low* on hostility traits were not sensitive to nicotine, nor did a nicotine patch change their brain metabolic responses.

Five different types of muscarinic ACH receptors are currently recognized. Certain inbred strains of mice lack the important muscarinic M_1 receptor. Theta bursts produce only weak long-term potentiation in their hippocampus, and they show impaired working memory and memory consolidation.[4]

The next three neuromessengers are the biogenic amines. Their receptor systems play vital roles in *modulating* the brain's more potent responses to such fast transmitters as ACH and glutamate.

Dopamine Systems

For his research on dopamine, Arvid Carlsson was a co-winner of the Nobel Prize for Medicine or Physiology in 2000. His studies showed that dopamine (DA) plays a prominent role in energizing the functions of the basal ganglia, and that these DA functions are enhanced by giving its precursor, L-dopa.

Dopamine cell bodies reside in the midbrain, both in the substantia nigra and the ventral tegmental area [Z:197–201]. Dopamine from their terminals energizes both the dorsal and the ventral striatum, thereby enhancing the motoric effects of the caudate and putamen and the motivational properties of the nucleus accumbens. Dopamine also influences our mechanisms of attention at several levels. This occurs in subtle ways that enhance the impact of sensory stimuli.

Some five different dopamine receptor types are recognized. Dopamine DA_5 receptors tend to cover the large ACH nerve cells.[5] The outer shell of the nucleus accumbens contains more DA_1 receptors.

In primates, a DA_3 receptor *agonist* reduces blood flow in the orbitofrontal cortex, thalamus, and cingulate regions, among other sites.[6]

In the lateral amygdala, dopamine enhances long-term potentiation. It acts by inhibiting the local actions of GABA (see chapter 30).[7]

Dopamine nerve cells in the midbrain fire more when a monkey judges that there is a greater *potential* value to a particular anticipated reward.[8] Situations judged to be uncertain prompt an additional DA response. Similar adaptive properties of the DA system could motivate monkeys and mobilize their search for more data that could resolve an impasse.

Dopamine binding sites have been assessed by PET techniques in healthy normal subjects.[9] Subjects who were more aloof and personally detached tended to show more DA_2 receptors.

Given to normal healthy humans, methylphenidate (Ritalin) increases the release of dopamine.[10] How was this determined? Methylphenidate was given to subjects while they were performing a mathematical problem that was reinforced with a monetary reward. The task was monitored with PET scans after injection of a radiolabeled molecule that competes with dopamine for binding at DA_2 receptors. Methylphenidate helped the subjects become more interested and motivated while doing the math test. It also increased the extracellular levels of dopamine in the striatum. The subjects' enhanced degrees of interest, motivation, and attention suggest that methylphenidate's release of dopamine is one reason why it has helped certain patients who have authentic attention-deficit disorder.

Norepinephrine Systems

The human pons and midbrain contain only some 13,000 to 23,000 nerve cells in the locus ceruleus. However, the distant terminals of these norepinephrine (NE) cells have the most extensive axonal arborizations in the central nervous system [Z:201–205]. In primates, NE densely intervates the pulvinar and lateral posterior nuclei of the thalamus (not the lateral geniculate nucleus). Moreover, norepinephrine more densely innervates the brain's dorsal visual stream of spatial analysis than its ventral stream of pattern analysis [Z:245]. NE inhibits glutamate transmission through the extended amygdala at a very important junction: the bed nucleus of the stria terminalis.[11] Alpha-1 and beta NE receptors are located exclusively on postsynaptic cells. Alpha-2 receptors are located mostly on presynaptic terminals.

It is possible to make a few more tentative generalizations about the function of NE systems:

- NE increases the efficiency of signal transmission through many sensory networks.[12]
- Beta receptors mediate a particular human memory phenomenon: Memory for emotional words is enhanced at the same time that memory is impaired just for those items that precede the emotional stimulus.[13]
- Ascending NE systems contribute to arousal and attention during the waking state. They also modulate the collection and processing of salient sensory information.[14]
- The release of NE in pathways descending from the brainstem plays a role in reducing pain perception (analgesia).

Serotonin Systems

The third group of biogenic amine nerve cells releases serotonin (ST). Serotonin nerve cells are buried deep along the midline core of the brainstem. Here, they cluster into the several *raphe nuclei* [Z:205, 208; figure 7, 198]. The human brain contains only some 235,000 ST nerve cells, but each terminal network also ramifies extensively.[15]

Most interest in these pages focuses on the dorsal raphe nucleus because its slender axons rise up to innervate various parts of the cerebrum. Recent research suggests that a subgroup of ST nerve cells in this dorsal nucleus can release not only serotonin into the central nucleus of the amygdala but can also release corticotropin-releasing factor (CRF) there.

Most serotonin nerve cells fire actively during waking arousal, are less active during quiet waking, slow down during slow wave sleep, and cease firing during REM sleep.

ST functions do enter into sleep, vision, mood, social behavior, pain, and the response to stress. Beyond that, the multiple ST receptor subtypes and the different kinds of serotonin nerve cells make it difficult to correlate a specific receptor with a particular behavioral function of serotonin.[16]

Of the fourteen ST receptor subtypes, the levels of ST_{1A} receptors were recently studied with PET scans in the brains of fifteen healthy Swedish men whose personality traits were assessed with a battery of psychological tests. Their levels of ST_{1A} receptors varied markedly from subject to subject over a 3- to 5-fold range. *Low* receptor levels correlated with only one personality trait. This was their tendency to endorse modes of extrasensory perception and spiritual ideation, in contrast to having a more reductionistic, empirical view of the world.[17]

Why don't receptor data alone suffice to correlate a particular personality trait with levels of a neuromessenger? Because ST_{1A} receptors are *presynaptic autoreceptors* on ST nerve cells. Suppose one were to speculate that these 1A receptors might serve to index the *numbers* of ST nerve cells. Then low autoreceptor levels might suggest that the person had a relatively low number of ST nerve cells, and therefore released relatively *less* serotonin.

On the other hand, note what presynaptic autoreceptors do. They *reduce* the firing of their own nerve cells. Following this interpretation, the low ST_{1A} receptor levels in this study might translate into an increased firing tendency, into the release of *more* serotonin, and into enhanced serotonin functions. Even so, ST_{2A} receptor levels in the human cortex are being linked with personality traits that tend to avoid danger[18] and with tendencies to experience spiritual ideas.[19]

Inbred mice that lack the ST_{1B} receptor are more likely to self-administer cocaine. The hypothesis is that these receptors serve normally within the ventral tegmental area and the nucleus accumbens to hold in check any excessive expressions of the brain's motivational system.[20]

Human serotonin functions undergo interesting seasonal variations. Spring shows an overall trend toward a *lower* ST tone. Higher ST functions develop during the summer and at times in the fall. These interpretations are based on spinal fluid levels of a breakdown product of serotonin. In male monkeys the levels of ST breakdown products decrease with age.[21]

Selective serotonin reuptake inhibitors (SSRIs) are commonly prescribed worldwide for depression and various forms of anxiety. Why are some now being prescribed as "antishyness" drugs for "social phobia?" The rationale is that by inhibiting the *reuptake* of serotonin, after it had first been released into the synapse, the serotonin level in that synapse will then remain high, and will keep acting on its receptors on the next cell. How do SSRI drugs act acutely?

Recently, seventeen healthy human subjects were studied 2 hours after receiving citalopram (20 mg) or a placebo. Their visual evoked potentials showed intriguing, mixed responses. The drug weakened the degree of *electrophysiological* activation to *unpleasant* visual stimuli in the frontal and occipital regions. However, it enhanced the amplitude of the evoked responses to *pleasant* images in the parietal and occipital regions. Clearly, this SSRI drug could modulate the *processing* of emotionally valenced stimuli. In contrast, the subjects' own reports did *not* indicate that they were aware of having experienced corresponding emotional changes.[22]

When depressed patients receive SSRI drugs, it may take several weeks for beneficial effects on mood to be evident. This long delay suggests that slow, metabolic messengers are being influenced beyond the initial ST receptor sites. Chapter 37 discusses how important these "second messenger" mechanisms are in changing brain functions.

The next six chapters are devoted to an update on regions of the brain whose functions influence our emotional life in ways that are of major importance to Zen. By way of a preamble, it helps to recall that *yin* and *yang* are the fundamental principles in Chinese cosmology, and it is their harmonious *balance* that is crucial, not any single factor in isolation.

25

The Septal Region and the Nucleus Accumbens

> The nucleus accumbens, a forebrain structure critical for reward and motivation, has a key role in reinforcing properties of drugs of abuse.
>
> M. Barrot and colleagues[1]

Front and center in the limbic system are the septal nuclei. They lie just above and in front of the anterior commissure and third ventricle. Byzantine connections link the several septal nuclei with the rest of the brain. This makes their functions difficult to sort out [Z:169–172, 234, 236, 608, 620, 821]. Because the nucleus accumbens is an active part of the *ventral* striatum, it still helps to distinguish its functions from those of the lateral septal nucleus nearby.

The Nucleus Accumbens

The term *accumbens* (Latin, "to recline at table") comes from the way it seems to "lean" against the septum in the midline. Exaggerated "leaning" functions can incline us to move beyond impulses of mere longing and topple into habitually driven approach behaviors. Unfruitful habits become legitimate targets for long-range meditative training [Z:608].

The Role of Dopamine

Dopamine helps the accumbens serve as a dynamic motivational interface, relaying impulses to and fro between the limbic system and the prefrontal cortex.

The nucleus accumbens receives much of its energizing supply of DA from the ventral tegmental area of the midbrain. The outer shell of the accumbens projects back to the hypothalamus, the extended amygdala, and down to the tegmentum of the midbrain. This outer shell has more DA_3 receptors and more opioid receptors than does the inner core.[2] Damage to the core impairs conditioned approach behavior. So, too, do lesions that block input to the core from the anterior cingulate gyrus.[3]

The amygdala helps stimulate the midbrain to release more DA into the nucleus accumbens. This occurs in two different ways.[4] One path leads from the amygdala's *central* nucleus. It stimulates midbrain DA nerve cells to fire at a steady (tonic) level. This DA enhances the general sensory incentive properties of food. It also contributes to the appropriate appetitive tone that motivates the animal's behavior.

The second path descends from the amygdala's *basolateral* nucleus. It generates *transient* releases of DA into the nucleus accumbens (and also into the medial prefrontal cortex). These quick, phasic releases of DA help to select and coordinate the particular actions that become the specific, appropriate response to an incentive stimulus out in the environment.

Note how the frontal lobe exercises its veto on this process. Even while this basal lateral amygdala is being stimulated, the prefrontal cortex can still actively *suppress* the release of DA into the nucleus accumbens.[5]

Though approach behaviors predominate when DA energizes the nucleus accumbens, affiliative behaviors are linked to its supply of oxytocin and vasopressin (see chapter 33). On the other hand, the accumbens' many opioid and GABA receptors lean its functional options toward behavioral inertia and inaction.

Effects of Drugs

The public is learning that drugs and food can each be abused. As a general rule, any substance that is "abused" will release more dopamine into the nucleus accumbens and enhance its functional activity. Drugs of abuse have other effects on laboratory mice. They enhance both the rewarding effects of morphine and increase the mice's preference for a sugar solution.[6] On the other hand, many antipsychotic drugs act by *reducing* the functional activity of DA. When this occurs, certain local GABA nerve cells in the shell of the accumbens increase their inhibitory activity,[7] suggesting that DA had previously held them in check.

Responses of the Nucleus Accumbens in Human Subjects

It has been said that the nucleus accumbens behaves as though it "doesn't like to be disappointed." Indeed, more fMRI signals develop in your ventral striatum if your "rewarding" drink of fruit juice doesn't arrive on time.[8] This suggests that the accumbens is one part of a responsive system that signals when predictable rewards are late.

Signals increase in the *ventral* striatum while subjects are anticipating the arrival of unpleasant electrical stimuli delivered to the skin, irrespective of whether or not they also have the opportunity to avoid being shocked.[9] In the *dorsal* striatum by contrast, caudate nucleus signals increase only when distracting stimuli become very relevant to behavior.[10]

One recent study describes an *increase* in DA in the *ventral* striatum during Yoga Nidra meditation.[11] This occurred in association with increased theta EEG activity and with subjective reports of a decreased desire for action. How are such findings to be interpreted? This is not clear when you consider how intricate the connections are between the ventral and dorsal striatum, the frontal cortex, amygdala, and thalamus, as well as the reports of the other human studies just cited above. In a separate study, subjects who received unexpected monetary rewards during an effortful task also released more DA into the ventral striatum.[12]

The Lateral Septal Nucleus

The lateral septal nucleus receives its excitatory glutamate input from the CA3 nerve cells of the hippocampus. Serotonin influences its responsiveness to this hippocampal input, and lateral septal activities can be reduced in states of depression.[13] The lateral septum then projects to the medial dorsal nucleus of the thalamus. The path from there can lead messages on to the orbitofrontal cortex [Z:183, 236, 656; figure 6]. This circuit provides one way for items that have first registered in memory circuits to be relayed up to the orbitofrontal cortex. Experiments in voles and mice suggest that increased levels of vasopressin and oxytocin in the lateral septal nucleus help to promote affiliative behaviors and enhance bonding in a social context (see chapter 43).

26

The Wide Variety of Cingulate Gyrus Functions

> Why the anterior cingulate cortex is active in such a wide variety of cognitive and emotional tasks has become an important issue in recent research.
>
> P. Luu and M. Posner[1]

Each cingulate gyrus lies next to the midline, just above the corpus callosum. It then extends down beyond it at both ends like the curves on a long, horizontal letter C (see figure 4, chapter 23).

A glance at the numbered areas in figure 7 (see chapter 40) suggests why some cingulate functions are diverse. Some five to seven different cytoarchitectural zones might be included within its boundaries, depending on how they are drawn.[2] Moreover, the cingulate contributes to multiple larger integrated networks by virtue of its many interconnections with the rest of the cortex and the limbic system [Z:172–174].

If one were to attempt a brief preamble to this complex topic, it might be said that (1) the cingulate's roles in affect can be ascribed to its more anterior areas, whereas regions for selecting responses tend to be represented farther back; (2) in the midcingulate subdivision an overlap occurs between several motor control mechanisms, goal orientation functions, and a role in responding to unpleasant stimuli; (3) visuospatial processing can be attributed to the posterior cingulate region; (4) farther back still in the retrosplenial area, an access to memories seems likely. Why? Because this area has many connections with the anterior and lateral dorsal thalamic nuclei as well as with the subiculum of the hippocampus.

But recent research now has much more to say about this big, long gyrus. The next paragraphs provide a sampler.

The Anterior Cingulate Region

The anterior cingulate gyrus integrates multiple higher functions and also helps express them in distant activities of the autonomic nervous system. Two pivotal higher functions among the several it attends to are: (1) the way we pursue a given task while responding subconsciously to its potentials for either good or bad outcomes; and (2) the way we monitor and express our responses to situations that involve physical pain, suffering, and conflict.

fMRI studies show that subjects who adjust to conflict with fast reaction times have greater capacities to activate their anterior cingulate, especially its more dorsal regions.[3]

The cingulate responds not only to actual physical pain stimuli but also, in a similar way, to the *emotional* pain of social rejection.[4] Do people "lose face" only in the Orient? No. It happens all over the planet, and we know how unpleasant it feels. Let's say you have just been snubbed in public by a dear friend or loved one. When your egocentric "Me" is hurt, what happens inside your brain? To study similar situations, college students were monitored by fMRI while they played a computer game. When one student felt snubbed by the others, the increase in anterior cingulate signals was commensurate with that person's own report of being distressed.

How might meditative training reduce the pain of rejection and social exclusion? Consider some of the factors involved in the anguish you feel when you've been hurt socially. The "hurt" depends on how sensitive you are, and on how you've been conditioned to react each time you have been snubbed. Have you had experience in remaining more objective in such situations? Or, is your fuse so short that you've even considered reprisals against that person who damaged your self-esteem? If so, wouldn't you be better off if you could dampen your reflexive response patterns on both the sensory and the motor sides?

Meditative training is oriented toward quenching the fires of these several aspects of your responses. For example, on the sensory side, you could (1) choose to ignore such situations (turn a blind eye); (2) start to develop a "count-to-ten" attitude. This can provide a longer fuse and help delay an explosive charge; (3) begin to develop a thicker skin (in the right spots). On the behavioral side, greater degrees of insight can help you "wise up," enabling you to respond to such situations more creatively or learn to sidestep them entirely.

In fMRI studies, the anterior cingulate responds early when subjects must choose between a visual stimulus in either their right or left field. The more effort the subjects expend in carrying out this task, the greater the increase in signals.[5] Another fMRI study suggests that, once conflict is already expected, the anterior cingulate becomes involved in monitoring which competing attentional set might best be allocated to reconcile the conflict.[6]

The effects of relaxation were monitored in another imaging study. It asked the question: What are the fMRI correlates of biofeedback-induced relaxation? The study also assessed the degree of sympathetic nervous system relaxation with the aid of skin conductance measurements. One answer was that the relaxation induced by biofeedback was associated with significant *increases* in signals both in the left anterior cingulate gyrus and in the globus pallidus.[7]

Subsequent fMRI studies suggested that activity in the dorsal anterior cingulate cortex correlated with changes in the heart rate that were attributable to the *sympathetic* nervous system.[8] This aspect of anterior cingulate function could help integrate bodily states of arousal into appropriate responses, both to effortful cognitive and motor tasks *and* to painful sensory stimuli. Parallel studies were conducted in three patients who had focal damage to the anterior cingulate cortex on both sides. Their sympathetic arousal responses were impaired to mental stress.

In normal subjects, fMRI signals increase in the *left* dorsal anterior cingulate when their task requires them occasionally to inhibit their behavioral responses. In this instance, however, the heart rate changes appeared attributable to the *parasympathetic* nervous system and were correlated more with signals arising in the *ventral* anterior cingulate gyrus of this *left* side.[9]

The anterior cingulate gyrus is closely linked with excessive activity in three other brain areas in patients who have an obsessive-compulsive disorder.[10] PET studies suggest that, along with the anterior cingulate, the caudate nucleus, orbitofrontal cortex, and thalamus are "locked" together into a large reverberating circuit.

PET scans monitored heavy smokers who were experiencing strong cravings for cigarettes. Their findings resembled the data in other persons who are addicted to other substances and who respond readily to cues for cocaine, opiates, or alcohol (see chapter 61). In each instance, when the cue *first* arrives, the anterior cingulate gyrus is activated around the genu on *both* sides.[11] But thereafter, the dependent smokers' craving for cigarettes is related to increased activity elsewhere: in the orbitofrontal cortex, dorsolateral prefrontal cortex, and anterior insula, again on *both* sides (as occurs during cravings for other substances). One of the first steps in therapy, therefore, is to blunt the dependent persons' anterior cingulate responses *to the very first cues* that go on to sponsor subsequent addictive craving behavior.

If you're a worrywart and worry more than is warranted, you'll pick up more of your minor errors and show increased fMRI signals in both your anterior cingulate and medial prefrontal cortex.[12] Trial-and-error testing suggests that the dorsal anterior cingulate is sensitive to both internal and external sources of information about errors.[13]

Higher primates and humans have distinctive, large spindle-shaped nerve cells in their anterior cingulate and fronto-insular cortex.[14] Here, they are in position to sample emotion-tinged messages relating to past experiences and then to relay them forward into the frontopolar cortex of area 10. Perhaps spindle cells are part of that larger interactive circuitry that helps us recognize when we have just committed some error, thus permitting other prefrontal regions to develop adaptive responses that anticipate or compensate for our shortcomings.

In an fMRI study of fourteen subjects, signals increased in the *right* dorsal anterior cingulate region when they either felt pinprick pain themselves *or* watched another person's hand be pricked (vicarious pain)[15] (see chapter 65).

Chapter 36 discusses another role of the anterior cingulate cortex. It emphasizes how the placebo response to pain correlates with the presence of opioid receptors in the cingulate gyrus. Chapter 66 reviews the evidence that the anterior cingulate enters into some of the steps of ordinary insight.

The Posterior Cingulate and Retrosplenial Region

fMRI signals increase in the posterior cingulate cortex when subjects are evaluating emotional words. But this is only part of the picture, because both pleasant and unpleasant words generate their strongest signals from the left anterior cingulate cortex under the front of the corpus callosum (the genu).[16]

When subjects focus on pictures of either objects or scenes, the particular pictures with which they are personally familiar generate increased fMRI signals in the posterior cingulate gyrus in its mid-dorsal portion, the posterior precuneus, and the retrosplenial cortex.[17]

The term *splenium* refers to the other curved end at the *back* of the corpus callosum. Behind it, the exact boundaries and functions of the *retrosplenial cortex* (see figure 4, chapter 23) are still under discussion.[18] Most evidence suggests that at least the back part of the posterior cingulate does become activated during emotions. This region can overlap with some of the retrosplenial cortex, but is not limited to it. It is worth emphasizing that the precuneus and the cuneus, which show prominent PET activity at rest, are not themselves part of either the retrosplenial or posterior cingulate cortex.

27

The Amygdala as a Gateway to Our Fears

> Teach me to live, that I may dread
> The grave as little as my bed.
>
> Bishop Thomas Ken (1637–1711)

> To conquer fear is the beginning of wisdom.
>
> Bertrand Russell (1872–1970)

The name *amygdala* (Latin, almond) comes from its shape. Each amygdala is buried near the inside tip of the temporal lobe. As research on the amygdala has exploded during the past decade, so has its relevance to Zen. Even the amygdala's anatomical boundaries seem to have expanded. This more sizable "extended" amygdala might seem in keeping with our greater interest in understanding its complex physiological roles.

Item 1: The landmarks used in some human neuroimaging studies now refer to coordinates not only for the conventional amygdala (proper) but also for what is now referred to as the "extended amygdala." The extended amygdala describes those corridors of nerve cells that do in fact extend out from its central and medial nuclei into the basal forebrain. There they include the bed nucleus of the stria terminalis.

Item 2: Some thirteen different subdivisions of the amygdala have now been identified in monkeys. Their wiring patterns are sophisticated, and are served both by a full complement of standard neuromessengers and many neuropeptides. We are still groping to understand how, and when, all these different parts function in the human amygdala.

Meanwhile, recent neuroimaging studies in humans present strong hints about how the amygdala contributes to our emotional and social life. Even so, Zald's comprehensive review in 2003 indicates that the interpretations from such data are often provisional.[1]

With regard to Zen, it seems obvious that knowing how the amygdala functions can help us better understand some mechanisms of meditation. Moreover, recent research suggests that circuits involving the amygdala could help explain why a person's sense of fear might dissolve in kensho and in a near-death experience [Z:175–179, 567–570].

But it seems best to introduce this review of the amygdala with a short, bland summary: let's just say that it codes for the potential emotional, social, and survival value of an arousing stimulus, then relays this information elsewhere where it can serve matching responses appropriately and be consolidated into potentially useful memories.[2]

Studies in Nonhuman Primates

A monkey's amygdala has many reciprocal connections with the orbital and medial prefrontal cortex. It also declares a strong visual bias in extensive connections with the visual cortex. Its large basal-lateral complex of nuclei is oriented toward action. Each of its subnuclei projects both to the ventral striatum and to the medial dorsal nucleus of the thalamus.

The central nucleus of the amygdala is smaller. It projects forward to the basal forebrain and medially to the lateral hypothalamus. A descending pathway leads down to excite the norepinephrine nerve cells of the locus ceruleus and other brainstem sites [Z:175–178] (see chapter 33).

The early literature reported that after large lesions had been made surgically the *high*-ranking, dominant monkeys became submissive and fell in their troop's social dominance hierarchy. This pioneering research could not distinguish between functions referable to the amygdala itself as opposed to those conveyed by other nerve fibers that were merely passing through it (the "fiber of passage problem"). Now, preliminary MRI scans guide discrete chemical injections, and precise experimental lesions can be made that are limited to amygdala nerve cells.

One such recent study began with twelve *mid*-ranking male monkeys.[3] Their normal behaviors conformed to the usual monkey "social rule system." For example, they were not only (appropriately) "apprehensive in initiating social interactions" but also "more frequently displayed indicators of anxiety and tension." Then they received localized, MRI-guided, bilateral, excitotoxic lesions of the amygdala made with ibotenic acid.

Their subsequent social interactions became less apprehensive and less aggressive, but also more impulsive and uninhibited. Their sexual behaviors were enhanced. The authors concluded that the normal intact male amygdala was serving as a kind of "inhibitory brake" on social interactions.

A few young monkeys, only 1 year old, are already constitutionally inclined to be more anxious. These anxious monkeys exhibit relatively more right frontal EEG asymmetry, have higher blood cortisol levels, and they also display more intense defensive responses.[4] What does this cluster of EEG, hormonal, and behavioral indices of anxiety mean? Are they receiving more input from their amygdala on that *right* side?

To study this important question, extensive bilateral amygdala lesions were made selectively using ibotenic acid.[5] However, these amygdala lesions did not change the monkeys' preexisting frontal EEG asymmetry or reduce their *unconditioned* anxiety-fear responses. Indeed, the monkeys still continued to freeze when they saw a human intruder. Freezing expresses a basic, innate *trait*like component of an individual monkey's anxious temperament.

Which behaviors, then, were reduced? Each monkey's *acute un*conditioned fear responses were reduced *if* the lesions had removed more than 70% of the amygdala. These lesioned monkeys displayed less fear when they viewed a snake for the *first* time, and less fear when they were confronted for the *first* time by an adult male monkey whom they had never seen before.

The total pattern of these results supported the following theories: (1) the primate amygdala helps to mediate the *initial* responses to a threatening stimulus, but (2) other regions enable the brain normally to express its stable, traitlike responses. Trait responses are *present very early in life* and underlie individual differences in temperament.

But *which* other regions are they? The frontal cortex? Perhaps part of the extended amygdala that had escaped damage because its nerve cells extend outward toward the bed nucleus? The medial dorsal nucleus of the thalamus? Other sites?

Experiments in Rodents

Certain "downstream" modules and pathways might also need to be considered. The amygdala interacts with other regions lower down that can indirectly influence trait behavior. The classic study by Caldji and colleagues studied stable young rats who displayed few anxious behaviors.[6] When they were adults, these calmer rats later had more inhibitory $GABA_A$ receptors poised to calm excess firing in the amygdala than did their anxious cohorts (see chapter 33). Moreover, they also had fewer CRF receptors down in their brainstem. Fewer CRF receptors there would make it less likely that the terminals from CRF cells up in the central nucleus of the amygdala could release CRF and excite the locus ceruleus. This could reduce the anxiety-inducing effects of the norepinephrine that would otherwise be released each time the locus ceruleus became stimulated.

Research in freely moving rats demonstrates how intricate the amygdala's interactions are with several other regions.[7] Mild microstimulation of the basolateral amygdala did produce the expected mild activation of the rats' behavior. Then, however, the researchers inhibited the prefrontal cortex. Only under these conditions could amygdala stimulation release more dopamine into the nucleus accumbens. This result suggests that one important normal function of the prefrontal cortex is to inhibit the amygdala. This *blocks* its descending relays from going on to release enough dopamine to energize the ventral striatum.

When rats are conditioned to respond to threatening stimuli, their lateral amygdala nerve cells undergo two different types of rapid firing activity. The firing in one group of its cells serves the rat's immediate needs. These cells respond quickly, but only transiently. Cells in the second group respond more slowly to each stimulus, but their enhanced discharges last much longer, not only in episodes during training but also on much later occasions.[8] Nerve cells of this second type could serve a rat's needs for very long-term memory.

The Roles of the Human Amygdala in Emotion and Behavior

Animal research may provide simpler models for human behavior, but it cannot predict its nuanced complexity. Humans know acute, heart-pounding fear when they jam on the brakes to avoid hitting a pedestrian. Thereafter, their feelings of chronic anxiety related to injuring a pedestrian are set at a much lesser level of risk than at that moment of acute fear. Zald's critical review of the human amygdala cites 332 references and is organized under fourteen major topic headings.[9] In the scope of this review, we can only summarize selected topics, comment on the loss of fear during kensho, and add pertinent results from the most recent neuroimaging and neuropsychological research not in his review.

- The amygdala becomes activated when we see fearful facial expressions, hear fear-producing sounds, and smell unpleasant odors. Some of these aversive stimuli induce feelings of disgust. Other stimuli prove so threatening that they evoke fear-related responses.

  A caveat: humans are suggestible. Some persons develop more active placebo responses than others. When subjects react to ongoing painful stimuli, their differences can mislead or complicate researchers' interpretations of how the amygdala responds. (Related issues are discussed in chapter 35.)
- The amygdala does respond to pleasant, positively valenced stimuli. These "positive" emotional responses are not as marked or as consistent as are the responses to unpleasant "negative" stimuli.
- Sometimes our amygdala becomes *less* active during *extremely* pleasant experiences. Item: I have long been aware that certain musical sequences affect me profoundly. They produce both an emotional feeling of deep pleasure and "gooseflesh" extending from the back of my head down to my calves.[10] PET scan studies in other subjects show that blood flow to the amygdala is *reduced* during such "chill" phenomena to music. We need to identify all the pathways that can reduce the influence of the amygdala.
- From within kensho's total loss of self arises the impression of total fearlessness [Z:567–570]. This acute fearlessness seems attributable to temporary inhibitions within the several circuitries of fear that interconnect with the amygdala in both directions. For example, fMRI studies indicate that our amygdala is activated not only in the acquisition phase of conditioned fear responses but also *early* in the extinction phase. Delayed extinction of fear conditioning also involves the ventral medial and orbitofrontal prefrontal cortex.[11] The more primitive circuits of *self-preservation* connect the amygdala with the hypothalamus and with the central gray of the midbrain [Z:657–658].

  Other qualities of interest occur during kensho. For example, (a) more profoundly blissful experiences can occur, perhaps to the degree that endogenous opioids contribute to inhibition of the amygdala itself and its circuits [Z:619–620]; (b) if oxytocin or vasopressin were among the peptides released, an episode of kensho might be permeated by greater "affiliative" resonances (see chapter 34); (c) to the degree that GABA mediated inhibition within the amygdala and its closely related circuits, then a more clear-eyed unsentimental awakening might ensue.

- Regional blood flow to the amygdala can *decrease* when subjects leave their condition of passive rest and enter into more active visual tasks. Chapter 50 discusses the important implications of this general phenomenon of how the brain changes when a person moves into activity.
- The amygdala becomes more activated when stimuli increase our general arousal level, are unusually pleasant or unpleasant, or rank high on the motivational scale of approach/withdrawal.
- Our amygdala responds to novelty per se. However, its brisk responses to repeated novel stimuli are subject to rapid habituation. Because fMRI allows researchers to make repeated, fast measurements, fMRI can detect the amygdala's brief and transient responses. In contrast, PET studies involve longer measurement times. PET is more suited to the detection of the amygdala's more delayed and sustained responses.
- The amygdala can process emotionally valenced stimuli that we are not *consciously* aware of. This subliminal processing may reflect deep connections linking the sensory relay nuclei in the thalamus with the amygdala.
- The amygdala is not activated each time we consciously judge whether an ordinary stimulus is pleasant or unpleasant. However, emotional states of extreme anger and fear almost always activate the normal amygdala.
- The amygdala also becomes more activated during the readiness to act, psychological conditioning, autonomic arousal, release of "stress" hormones, and when our attention is heightened.
- Does the amygdala always lateralize its activations in ways that conform to earlier speculations about how emotions lateralize to the right or left side? No. Many discrepancies hinge on how the experiment is designed, on whether the subjects were studied by (slower) PET scans or more recently by (faster-responding) fMRI, and often on the basic personality of the individual subject. Thus, one fMRI study of fifteen subjects (men and women) found that the more extraverted they were (as an innate personality trait), the more they activated their *left* amygdala in response to happy faces (but not to fearful faces).[12]

  In another preliminary PET scan report, thirteen women (who did *not* have a snake phobia) viewed a video of moving snakes.[13] The degree of their amygdala activation correlated with their basic level of pessimism (dispositional negative affect).
- Our amygdala plays a more complex role in recognizing which emotion is expressed on another person's face than has been thought previously.[14] Early research showed that amygdala damage had reduced patients' abilities to recognize fear and other highly arousing emotions in other persons. Several optional hypoth-

eses have since been raised: the normal amygdala may function to help resolve acute ambiguities related to the safety of the environment; it may enter into the processing of emotions that are negatively valenced and of high arousal value; it may help recognize emotions that mediate behavioral withdrawal, and so on.

More recent functional imaging studies indicate that the amygdala processes facial emotions only transiently. Again, whether the right or left amygdala tends to be activated can hinge on the experimental design. Further studies are required to confirm the suggestion that the right amygdala might be more activated by *subliminal* emotional facial expressions, and that it might habituate more readily than the left.

The amygdala is clearly only one part of a large network that decodes the facial expressions and body language of another person. Included in this network's cortical representations are the temporo-occipital and orbitofrontal regions. When we view an emotional face, and hear at the same time an emotional voice, the amygdala modulates the responses of the fusiform gyrus accordingly.[15]

- Men and women seem to lateralize their amygdala activity differently. In one PET study of 11 men and 11 women, the task was to respond to an emotional event that was presented visually. The films that first provoked negative emotions were remembered better 3 weeks later by men in association with enhanced activity of their *right* amygdala, but the corresponding task in women was correlated with their activating the *left* amygdala.[16]

  Similar results occurred in an fMRI study. Here, the so-called cognitive style of twelve men seemed to differ from the style used by twelve women. Indeed, even when the negative pictures' emotional intensity was equated equally for men and women, the women enlisted significantly more brain regions when their *left* amygdala activation was linked with their ongoing evaluation of emotional experience.[17] In contrast, though the men activated significantly more brain regions during encoding than did the women, this larger association network included their *right* amygdala.

  As girls mature into adolescence, fMRI studies show that their left prefrontal region becomes relatively more activated in response to facial photographs expressing acute fear. It has been speculated that this may be an index of their greater potential self-control over the kinds of emotional behavior that might be mediated by the left amygdala.[18]

- The amygdala is reported to enter into normal fear conditioning in some, but not all studies. Subjects can be conditioned to develop fear responses to a particular face (face A) in the laboratory, by presenting this face just before they hear an unpleasant voice.[19] As a result of this prior conditioning, face A alone (but *not* face B) causes fMRI signals to increase in the amygdala on both sides. Later, the researchers make face B the new conditioned stimulus. Now, increased signals occur in the *orbitofrontal* cortex on the right, but these responses tend to fade. At this time, however, in contrast to earlier, the previous conditioned stimulus (face A) evokes increased signals only from the *right* ventral *amygdala*. This earlier "memory" for the early fearful conditioning by face A tends to persist. In most studies, the psychological deficits of patients who have chronic, selective lesions of the amygdala tend to support the theory that our normal amygdala participates in aversive conditioning.

- That said, the mechanisms through which humans become *socially* conditioned are much more complex. The amygdala is but one early gateway into much more intricate conditioning processes [Z:327–334]. We humans, too, not only conform to hierarchical rules, but seem to employ several different circuits at different times in our lives. Damage to the human amygdala during childhood interferes with reasoning about other persons, whereas damage in adult life does not necessarily do so in many studies.[20]
- Important among the amygdala's close "partners" is the orbitofrontal cortex. This is clear from research on our sense of smell. One advantage of studying olfaction is that its pathway leads straight into the amygdala. Another is that in the process of responding to odors our two dimensions of emotional experience—*intensity* and *valence*—can each be analyzed independently.[21]

  For example, a *strong* odor generates more fMRI signals in almost all subregions of the right and left amygdala. These signals increase no matter whether the odor is perceived as pleasant or unpleasant. But the emotional *valence* of the odor, whether its quality is pleasant or unpleasant, correlates with signals from different parts of the *orbitofrontal cortex*.
- An intact amygdala helps recognize the expressions of sadness in others. Patients who had previously sustained bilateral damage to the amygdala cannot accurately recognize sad expressions in pictures of other persons' faces.[22] Damage to the right amygdala caused a greater deficit in judging sadness than did damage to the left. However, chronic lesions of the right or left amygdala or both did not stop the patients from recognizing happy expressions. Overall, this pattern of results fits in with other lines of evidence: *frontal* lobe functions are more likely to be correlated with *positive* emotions in the happy-pleasant range than are functions referable to our amygdala.
- Enhanced activity of the amygdala is reported in patients suffering from a variety of kinds of depression. The degrees of activation tend to return toward normal as the depression lifts. Similar degrees of amygdala activation could certainly bias the way depressed patients evaluate and respond to incoming information. Does such a mechanism hinge on an accompanying increase in CRF and norepinephrine tone? This needs to be clarified.[23]

- The amygdala does more than react to external stimuli. *Our own internal thought processes shape its responses.* The way positive or negative thought processes shape the emotional responses of our amygdala is highly relevant to programs of meditative/spiritual training. For example, "positive" thinking approaches might afford a partial remedy for the kinds of "negative" ruminations that lead to anguish and other adverse emotional consequences.

  The negative effects of emotional preoccupations were clear in an fMRI study. The subjects chose *deliberately* to maintain their negative emotion *after* they viewed a disturbing "negative" picture. Signals increased in their amygdala. In which subjects did amygdala signals increase the most? In those whose self-reports indicated that they had already been temperamentally disposed to maintain a more negative affect.[24]

- Cognitive-behavioral therapy has access to the amygdala. Twelve subjects, chronically and severely afraid of spiders, were enrolled in cognitive-behavioral therapy. Before they began therapy, they were shown film excerpts of spiders. Their spider phobia resulted in increased fMRI signals in two sites in particular: (1) The right dorsolateral prefrontal cortex. How was this frontal activation interpreted? As representing "metacognitive strategies," the kinds a person might develop (secondarily) when attempting to *cope* with the fear triggered by the film. (2) The parahippocampal gyrus. Increased signals in this region were thought to represent the reactivation of those temporal lobe memory sites which had long served to maintain the patients' chronic spider phobia.

  The good news was that, after the patients underwent and responded to cognitive therapy, their subsequent exposure to spider pictures activated neither their frontal nor their parahippocampal regions.[25]

  Similar results were reported in another fMRI study. Again, cognitive strategies were employed to dampen the emotional responses of these subjects to aversive events.[26] As a result, the patients assumed a more "objective" mental stance while they were viewing highly negatively valenced scenes. As a result, they did feel that they became less involved in negative emotions. Changes in fMRI signals after treatment could be correlated with the patients' newly acquired efforts to "rethink their feelings." Among such changes were *decreased* signals not only in the amygdala but also in the *medial* orbitofrontal cortex, a site where other research also suggests that some of our fear responses are represented. We await similar rigorously conducted *longitudinal* studies of reduced fear responses in accomplished meditators.

- The amygdala and its relation to fearlessness. "The great death" is a phrase often applied to the total loss of self that occurs acutely during kensho-satori. A lesser loss of self occurs during sexual orgasm. It is sometimes called "the little death" (Fr. *le petit mort*). PET scans recently monitored human subjects during orgasm.[27]

One relevant finding was decreased activation in the right amygdala. This reduction was correlated with the "letting go" of fear and anxiety. The decreased activation was more evident in women than in their male partners. This partial, unilateral decrease lends support to the proposal that a deactivation of the amygdala and its fear-linked circuits on *both* sides could be responsible for the total loss of fear during kensho-satori [Z:175–180; 531–532; 620].

Perhaps in the future it may be possible to test the hypothesis that the amygdala and its connections are inhibited during the brief moments of genuine kensho at a time when fear is totally extinguished. If so, it might be postulated that this person would not then generate his or her former level of skin conductance responses either to reward or punishment. Nor would a new conditioned skin conductance response then be easily acquired by pairing a fresh visual stimulus with an aversive sound.[28]

- Each of the different nuclei in the amygdala need to be scrutinized during kensho. Why? Because the profound loss of fear may plumb different levels. It can also be expressed differently among individual persons who are high or low in trait anxiety. Subjects who test high in levels of trait anxiety develop more fMRI signals in their basolateral amygdala when they respond *unconsciously* to fearful faces that are shown for only a few milliseconds.[29] However, when fearful faces are processed through subjects' more *conscious* relays, signals tend to increase elsewhere: in the dorsal amygdala and in its central nucleus. In these nuclei, the local increases are said to occur irrespective of that person's existing level of trait anxiety.
- In summary, the amygdala serves as a gateway. The longer an acquired, emotionally valenced response has been in effect, the more it seems to have relayed beyond the amygdala itself into other circuits. In this respect, the amygdala resembles some memory functions of its neighbor, the hippocampus.

Do the foregoing lines of research help us understand Zen? Only if we appreciate how central to the age-old Zen Buddhist approach are such key issues as nonattachment, clinical objectivity, and the deconditioning of unfruitful emotional responses.

At the end of part I, we referred to the use of short "capping" phrases as one way to encapsulate Zen teachings. One of these ancient verses says:

Everything is true
just as it is.
Why dislike it?
Why hate?[30]

28

Expanded Roles for the Insula

> The right anterior insula supports a representation of visceral responses accessible to awareness, providing a substrate for subjective feeling states.
>
> Hugo Critchley and colleagues[1]

The insula is a hidden island. Only after you peel back the overlying gyri of the adjacent temporal, frontal, and parietal lobes do you expose the insula. Now you see this mound of cortex bulging outward, buried in the depths of the lateral Sylvian fissure.

Vesalius had mentioned the insula as long ago as 1543. At one time its central location and size had even led to its being called the central lobe. Only recently did it became part of the so-called paralimbic system. Various lines of evidence now hint that its anterior, middle, and posterior regions play distinctive (if not always "central") roles in several human emotions.[2]

The Insula and Disgust

Zen invites us to look deeply into the roots of our loathings and disgusts. The insular cortex qualifies for some of these introspections. When Penfield and Faulk stimulated the insula during brain operations, their patients reported unpleasant tastes and sensations of nausea referred to the stomach.[3] Later it was found that rats cannot develop their usual, easily conditioned aversion to noxious tastes after the insula has been destroyed by ibotenic acid.

Imaging studies show that we activate the insula when we view faces expressing disgust or when we look at disgusting pictures, such as cockroaches or decaying food. Moreover, we also activate the insula when we recall events out of our own lives that make us feel guilty (perhaps, in one sense, such guilt faintly resembles a version of disgust that is being referred back to oneself).[4]

The Insula and the Sense of Smell

One fMRI study monitored subjects who were inhaling odorants that generated intense feelings of disgust. On a later occasion, they viewed video clips which showed *other* persons' faces evidencing disgust. The evidence suggested that our anterior insula is processing (envisoning, mirroring) *both* our own disgust *and* our recognizing another person's expression of disgust.[5]

Subjects in a different fMRI study were responding either to very disgusting odors (animal feces) or to merely unpleasant odors (cat urine). (Aren't researchers carrying matters a bit too far in the name of science? That faint negative response you just experienced may have arrived via your insula.) Disgusting odors activated only the subject's *right* anterior insula and the right ventral striatum. Both types of unwelcome odors activated the *left* anterior insula. The left may play more of a generic role in olfactory perception per se.[6]

The Insula in Various Emotions, Including Empathy

PET studies of 41 selected subjects showed that a wide variety of brain regions responded when they recalled a personal episode that was "emotionally powerful."[7] Among the many changes noted, sadness and anger activated the anterior insula on both the right and left sides. In contrast, happiness and fear activated the insula on the *right* side only.

Empathy is an "affective" response. It means that you feel the same way that another person does (see chapter 65). Pain has both affective and sensory components.[8] When merged, these two factors make pain difficult to define and to study. It touches our sentiments and resonates there in subtly different ways. Subjects who themselves receive a painful stimulus include increased fMRI signals in the anterior and posterior insula on both sides among their responses. However, they only develop signals in the anterior insula (and anterior cingulate) when they empathize with their loved one, having been led to believe that this other person at a distance was then actually being subjected to a pain stimulus similar to the one they had felt earlier.

The anterior insula becomes more activated when emotions are imitated than when they are only observed. It has been speculated that the kinds of circuits that are oriented toward such simulated levels of affect become a step in the direction toward the processing of empathy.[9] It will require additional longitudinal studies to confirm and to clarify the basis for the structural MRI finding that long-term meditators have a larger right anterior insular cortex.[10]

The Middle Insula Stays "in Touch" during Maternal Attachment and Romantic Love

The *middle* insula is one part of the constellation of regions involved in certain positive emotions. Signals from this middle region increase when mothers look at pictures of their 2-year-olds, and when lovers of either sex look at pictures of their beloved[11] (see chapter 62).

Moreover, other recent lines of evidence suggest that this middle part has a supporting role in *exteroceptive* sensations of a rather special kind. It turns out that thin unmyelinated fibers convey slower touch sensations from the surface of the skin. These messages are directed *first* to the middle insula rather than being relayed there only indirectly by way of the somatosensory cortex. This pathway appears to mediate some of the pleasant feelings we associate with "caress-like, skin-to-skin contact." Have you ever wondered why you like to snuggle close, or why you like to "stay in touch" with family and friends? Perhaps some nuances of so-called skin-hunger might correlate with similar processes involving your insula.

The Posterior Insula: "Our Vestibular Cortex"

PET studies show that when you stimulate the semicircular canals on one side it activates the posterior insula on both sides, the right more so than the left.[12] Sensations of disequilibration are unpleasant, and vertigo has decidedly negative overtones. (The right hypothalamus also enters into this disconcerting vertiginous response.)

Other Visceral Signals to the Insula

The insula has been linked with changes in heart rate, blood pressure, and with the perceptions of pain and temperature. Critchley and colleagues' recent multidisciplinary study follows up on this prior research.[13] First, the subjects were rated in terms of their underlying degrees of anxiety. The more anxious subjects proved to be more accurate at tasks that required them to judge the explicit timing of their own heartbeats. (Not a skill most people are normally aware of.) Anxious subjects showed correspondingly greater activity in their right anterior insula and in the overlying rim of the nearby frontal cortex. Signals also increased in their right insula when they attempted to integrate their interoceptive awareness with external sounds. This led to the suggestion that the anterior insula might be able to serve a kind of interoceptive "comparator" role.

Neural Pathways to and from the Insula

The insula does more than help process smell, taste, touch, emotional and vestibular information. By following the course of various paths leading up to the insula we can understand how some of its functions are derived from messages relayed up by other *small autonomic* sensory fibers that ascend from different *internal* parts of our body.[14]

Several modest caveats apply to what most such small fiber pathways can accomplish: (1) They conduct their messages relatively slowly. (2) The information they convey is often relatively undifferentiated and poorly localized. (3) These slender afferent (sensory) fibers of the autonomic nervous system can influence emotional responses first by entering the hypothalamus directly, not just by relaying up through the thalamus to the insula.[15] (4) Their "softer" interoceptive messages do not necessarily leap to the forefront of our explicit cognitive processing. However, specific tasks can be assigned that focus a person's attention on them.[16]

Slowly, such small fiber *interoceptive* messages do relay up to the *ventral medial nucleus* of the thalamus. Once there, two of its subnuclei then send very different kinds of sensory messages up to the insula.

- The *posterior* subnucleus receives sensory information from *sympathetic* afferents arising from the head and body.
- The *basal* subnucleus processes different sensations rising from *para*sympathetic afferents. This basal subnucleus receives (and relays) a variety of other messages rising up from the brainstem (via the solitary tract nucleus and its gustatory extension) [Z:165, figure 5].

  An intriguing trend develops within such relays and crossings: sympathetic afferents become represented more in the right hemisphere, and parasympathetic afferents more in the left.[17]

What other implications follow from the interesting anatomical observation that much of the small autonomic fiber input to the insula comes up through this one specific *ventral* medial relay nucleus in the thalamus? The fact further emphasizes that this lower part of the thalamus is a bottleneck for almost every sensation (except olfaction) (see figure 8, chapter 44). Therefore, a local inhibitory process that caps this ventral region as a whole could block both kinds of sensory impulses, fast and slow, simultaneously. The fast somatosensory path normally relays larger fiber messages from the head and body. All along their way up to the cortex these messages contribute the most to our normal body image and to our implicit sense of existing as a physical self.[18]

The reticular nucleus of the thalamus is poised to provide the local cap that can inhibit, simultaneously, both these small fiber and large fiber pathways (see chapter 46). Its local inhibitory functions can block all major ingredients that form the framework of our physical self-image, along with their covert visceral and emotional attachments. This means that all of the above aspects of the physical self—superficial and deep—can drop out of conscious awareness at the same time (see chapters 74 and 75).

Commentary

When something tastes really bad, we spit it out immediately. Distaste → disgust → revulsion. As we recoil, no observer can mistake our body language or that of our face and tongue. Graded responses from the ventral striatum blend into such lower-level motor reflex systems. Simultaneously, we are also laying down new avoidance memories, because we do learn, as we say, from each bitter experience. The words hint at the ways our cortex and caudate nucleus enter into, and elaborate upon, our conditioned responses at more primitive visceral and affective levels.

How does this relate to Zen? Long-term Zen training helps a person drop off some deeper conditioned *loathings*, not just unfruitful desires and longings. In the neuroimaging studies cited above, researchers began by focusing on simpler, shallower issues: on disgusting smells and sights. Thus far, the research has yet to hone in on deep psychic interpersonal antipathies, ones that might be categorized as "loathings." Loathings in this category lie beyond a person's simple short-term responses to unpleasant stimuli or the simpler quick emotions of fear. Loathings and "revulsions" are often hidden in the more complex layers of what we call the "subconscious."

In their extreme manifestations, loathings tap hostile attitudes and chronic hatreds. Some can be carried to the point of obsessions. Like other emotionally charged attitudes, loathings move us, motivate us to act. The grave events of 9/11/2001 emphasized how essential it is for societies worldwide to study, understand, relieve, and avoid deep human responses that have become aversive to this degree.

Meanwhile, with regard to the insula, its right anterior region can be viewed as representing one cortical module in a larger network of emotionalized associations. *Collectively*, these all help us evaluate and respond to a variety of stimuli that memory tells us are negatively valenced. Negative signals from the anterior insula that represent our deep visceral feelings of disgust may weigh particularly heavily on some vital networking functions that enter into everyday decisions.[19]

29

Remembrances and the Hippocampus

> We don't know how the peak experience is achieved; it has no simple one-to-one relation with any deliberated procedure; we know only that it is somehow *earned*. It is like the promise of the rainbow. It comes and it goes and it cannot be forgotten. .
>
> H. Geiger[1]

> I can't say I was ever lost, but I was bewildered once for three days.
>
> Daniel Boone (1734–1820)

The hippocampus curls up in the medial temporal lobe. It helps us process some memories and forget others. It also functions as a kind of subconscious compass that helps us navigate a path through difficult terrain (Z:180–189). But to the degree that the hippocampus enters into a "peak experience," it would seem that this happens more as a kind of fortuitous grace than as something a person must always "earn."

This chapter samples recent reports that suggest how our mental states could change along with variations in our hippocampal functions.

Neuromessengers in the Hippocampal Circuitry

The medial septal nerve cells are pacemakers, releasing their acetylcholine into the hippocampus [Z:figure 6, 183]. Septal cells, in turn, have been driven chiefly by impulses rising up from the midbrain reticular formation. ACH activates its muscarinic ACH receptors, setting off gamma waves within the hippocampal CA3 area.[2] These then spread to CA1, in keeping with the normal direction of impulse flow. Once stimulated, local gamma oscillations can continue for prolonged periods of up to 3 hours, often seeming to nestle inside theta wave activities.

Preprocessed sensory information first enters through the parahippocampal gyrus. It then flows through its entorhinal cortex (along the perforant path) into the dentate gyrus. The so-called hippocampal *formation* includes not only this dentate gyrus but also its next relays onto CA3 and CA1 cells, and the path that leads on from CA1 cells to the subiculum.

Small interneurons release their GABA on $GABA_A$ receptors in ways that pace the rhythmic activity of this hippocampal network. Glutamate contributes to the oscillations, acting on its fast, non-NMDA (*N*-methyl-D-aspartate) type of receptors. However, long-term potentiation in the hippocampus involves a cascade of metabolic changes that modify local excitabilities more slowly.[3]

When dentate gyrus cells stimulate cells in the CA3 region, the excitatory effects at this next synapse increase dramatically from the first to the second of two closely timed stimuli (40 ms). And when these dentate cells suddenly shift toward even higher rates of firing, this effect creates a big increase in CA3 cell firing rates.[4]

On the *presynaptic* end of this curious synapse, adenosine A1 receptors confer a remarkably steady, tonic inhibitory property. Here, local *extra*cellular levels of adenosine serve to check overfiring in the hippocampus.

These four mechanisms—involving ACH, GABA, glutamate, and adenosine—provide only a brief sample of events that cause major increases or decreases in the timing and flow of impulses within our hippocampal formation.

Hippocampal "Place Cells": Their Role in Spatial Mapping

In roadless terrain, Daniel Boone would soon get lost without hippocampal place cells. Why are they called *place* cells? Because they fire chiefly when their incoming sensory data are being processed in a special way. They decode all this to mean that they are "in" a certain "place." Then, once they discharge, they probably contribute to the brain's widely distributed constellation of highly coded spatial coordinates. The brain then proceeds to use this silent "internal compass" to develop its own biological version of a global positioning system (GPS). What do these operations mean to us personally? They provide us access to our private map of 3D space.

Suppose a hungry monkey sees an apple, and keeps track of where this visual stimulus is positioned in space. In the process, it fires one out of every eight of its hippocampal cells. Most of these cells (69%) are coded to respond to that *particular external location* where this apple stimulus originated. Because cells with these external sensitivities are *other*-centered, they are called *allo*centric (Greek *allos*, other).

But another 10% of monkey place cells provide a very different frame of reference. They fire only if that visual stimulus in that location *refers back first to the position of the head and long axis of the monkey's body*. These cells use head-body coordinates for their frame of reference. Because they are *self*-centered, they are called *ego*centric.

What does it feel like when we merge large networks of such egocentric and allocentric functions? It feels "normal," as though *we are* in *this* world. We have our usual normal sense of inhabiting a distinct personal *place* within a matrix of "nonpersonal" space. And so we are poised to remember: "I was in *this* spot when *that* defining event occurred." Or, putting it another way, we say: "This was where I was when that event took *place*." Events take *their place* in ways that help us remember them.

Such a memory can persist for months, even though it took only a second or so for the whole process to code this event in space. Lacking this capacity, we would be forever bewildered. Much of this normal mapping process hinges on those same NMDA glutamate receptors which also contribute to long-term potentiation.[5] Some cells in the parahippocampus are already equipped to decode incoming sensory information and to provide coarse sensory data about location.[6]

Remembering and Forgetting

The different sets of hippocampal place cells just described help subserve two different frames of reference. These egocentric and allocentric modes of perception are fundamental to our basic self/other distinctions. But if we are going to encode spatial distinctions into memories we can *use*, we must classify and categorize them in many other ways. When monkeys perform delayed visual matching tasks, it turns out that their hippocampal cells are quite sensitive to separate categories of stimulus features. Not only that, but different monkeys employ individual classification strategies. They are unique, in ways reminiscent of those used by their distant human relations.[7]

Monkeys don't need to hang every association on the framework of some physical place localized by their GPS constructs. Sometimes their hippocampus enters into different kinds of abstract, visual stimulus-response associations, kinds which require no *spatial* reference frame.[8] However, this capacity to learn novel abstractions depends on the functional integrity of the rest of the limbic system. It is impaired when the fornix is cut. Why?

The fornix is a major overarching pathway. It normally conveys impulses down to the hypothalamus that began in the hippocampal formation, the cingulate gyrus, and the parahippocampal gyrus. Then, by way of completing this limbic circuit, the hypothalamus sends *its* major projection bundle, the *mammillothalamic tract*, up to inform the anterior thalamic nucleus. This key memory circuit links the lower limbic system with this anterior nucleus. In return, the anterior nucleus then has reciprocal connections with the cingulate gyrus, the orbitofrontal region, and the subiculum.

Novelty

Think this is trivial information? Consider how much data the hippocampus receives. Only a minute fraction is truly novel and really significant. How does a rat handle all this junk mail? Test the rat in a new spatial environment. Deliver salient events, but do so *unpredictably*. Only at these special moments does long-term potentiation increase at its CA1 synapses. During these times the rat also activates its local dopamine DA1 and DA5 receptors.[9]

In this new open field test environment, the rat's CA1 region is also stimulated to produce more CREB (the *c*yclic adenosine monophosphate [AMP] *re*sponse *e*lement-*b*inding protein).[10]

At some later time, it could be to a rodent's advantage to have some irrelevant memories fade, and also to have mechanisms on line that can *actively erase* memories. Enter protein phosphatase 1. When this enzyme removes just a few phosphate groups from proteins, it limits the laying down of new memories. But when it removes more phosphate groups, memory actually *declines*. If you wonder whether one such enzyme can affect the processes of memory, consider what happens in inbred mice born with *low* levels of phosphatase 1. Not only do these mutant mice readily lay down new memories, but even when they grow old they still hang on to their memories.[11] (A potential glimmer of hope for avoiding "senior moments"?)

PET scans have monitored human subjects while they were performing a visual and auditory task. The task required them to encode words. Some words were new to them, others were very familiar. The two different types of words served to activate a potential bottleneck in the *same region* of the hippocampus, even though they activated very different large-scale networks elsewhere in the brain.[12]

Implications for Meditation and for Kensho

Kensho and satori are brief, transforming moments. Fresh ongoing perceptions are registered accurately, and they often remain indelible. In contrast, old maladaptive memory associations drop out instantly. So do all prior personal constructs and concepts of the self. This psychophysiological pattern is very distinctive. It does not suggest that one's hippocampal CA1 cells per se are malfunctioning. Nor does it imply that one's usual stream of messages must have stopped on their way to CA1 cells from CA3 cells [Z:182–184].

Normally, we start to encode new memories with the aid of our hippocampus and adjacent temporal cortex. Next, we engage a widely distributed network in order to lay down, store, and retrieve memories.[13] The term *consolidation* describes the way memory traces soon pass beyond, then gradually become independent of, the first steps in this processing chain, both in the hippocampus and its nearby entorhinal, perirhinal, and parahippocampal cortex. In chapter 27, we observed that the amygdala also responds quickly, and then disperses its information elsewhere.

We consolidate memories mostly when we are either at rest or asleep, because these are the quieter times when we are not processing any *new* external events. What evidence suggests that such consolidation does occur at rest? Electrodes implanted widely throughout cortex have monitored monkeys' brain functions for many hours. The firing patterns are distinctive. They confirm that those same nerve cells which had previously fired *together* cooperatively during tasks, later *reenacted their responsivities. When? During the next rest period.* Yet at this time, no such task was being overtly performed. Without moving, the resting monkeys appeared to be "replaying" their previous task activity *spontaneously*.

Are such replaying data relevant to a period of open, relaxed meditation, an interval of quiet that seems reasonably close to an actual state of rest? This plausible hypothesis remains to be tested. If so, then perhaps actual "no-thought" mediation periods do offer a meditator the chance to consolidate—*spontaneously and subconsciously*—what had just been learned during the course of some experience that had immediately preceded it. For example, such an event could be in the form of information heard during a lecture or encountered while reading.

Spontaneous replaying tendencies at rest have a second set of implications. Both our ordinary leaps of creative intuition and extraordinary peak experiences usually occur *during pauses*. Each requires an extra, dynamic ingredient, not just the mere replaying of a problem long incubated but still unsolved. Novel closures often mean that some new item or motive source of energy has closed the information gap. Instantly, large networks shift into brand-new configurations.

What about the usual processes that enable us to *recall* ordinary memories? Functional brain imaging studies identify three *left* frontal regions that become coactivated when we *retrieve* memories: the polar cortex, the mid ventrolateral cortex, and the mid dorsolateral cortex. All contribute, whether the kinds of memory being tested involve events of personal experience (episodic memory), working memory, or factual items (semantic memory). The dorsal anterior cingulate cortex also shares in these coactivations.[14]

One basic function of Zen meditation is to calm the habit energies that drive these four sources of memory retrieval into endless strings of discursive thoughts. In short, the regular practice of zazen helps to dampen the ordinary "leaps" of one's monkey mind (see chapter 13). It is rare for kensho to occur while a person is actually seated and engaged in zazen meditation.

The self that will drop out during kensho had a very long prior autobiographical history. It was fearful. It had major impulses and motivations to *do* things. It possessed an acute sense of time. To the degree that these older memory formations had long since "passed through the hippocampus" and been represented beyond it, then kensho might seem to have dissolved their functional representations, at hierarchical levels *above* and beyond the hippocampus. Yet we still need to explain kensho's influence on immediate memory mechanisms, for these hippocampal functions might seem to be registering ongoing events clearly and at considerable speed. Does any recent research support such a process?

Recent fMRI studies confirm that patients who have medial temporal lobe damage don't need their hippocampus to recall their older, well-consolidated, personal memories.[15] Indeed, they accurately recall such prior experiences when prompted by such simple cue words as "river" or "nail." However, other patients had damage to their frontal lobes and to the *lateral* aspects of their temporal lobes. They did lose their remote autobiographical memories for time and place. These findings suggest that kensho blocks the links of early egocentric functions at frontotemporal levels beyond the hippocampus.

The Right Hippocampus during the Resolution of Ordinary Japanese Riddles

The Japanese are among the many who enjoy puzzles. One puzzle goes: "What can move heavy logs, but can't move a small nail?" Suppose you were a subject being monitored by fMRI when you saw this riddle. You had already been stumped by it at an earlier presentation. You still didn't know the answer this second time.

Eight seconds later, still puzzled, you finally saw the correct word answer. It flashed forth on a screen for 2 seconds: "river." During the next 8 seconds, with regard just to your two hippocampi, what would your fMRI show? Only your right hippocampus would participate in this particular moment of "insight."[16]

The Zen koan is also a riddle. It sometimes helps a person arrive at comprehensive, existential levels of insight. Insight is a big crucial topic. The hippocampus is only one part of it. We consider how ordinary insight can transform consciousness in part IV, and explore the qualities of a major flash of insight-wisdom (prajna) once again in parts VII and IX.

A "Born-Again" Hippocampus?

Major religious transformations in every culture are said to leave the person feeling "born again." It used to be believed that nerve cells could not regenerate. We now know that nerve cells *can* be formed anew in the dentate gyrus, even in older human beings.[17]

Relatively few "new" nerve cells are produced. No one has yet proved that they insert themselves into the normal functions of those several hippocampal cells whose synaptic sequences we described earlier in this chapter. If we assume that the human neocortex alone contains 20 to 25 *billion* nerve cells in normal, young adult male brains, and make an educated guess that this corresponds to some 164,000 billion synapses, then this many billion synapses is already equal to the number of stars in some 1400 Milky Ways![18] So a lot more conditioning and consolidation will have taken place up in all these cortical synapses than can ever be set straight by the efforts of a few new nerve cells down in a person's dentate gyrus. Human beings will not be "born again" simply because they have "newly born" nerve cells in their hippocampus, however well-intentioned and placed they may be.

Still, contributions of the subiculum to certain *sequences* of phenomena during kensho may be another matter (see part IX). For example, as noted above, the subiculum is one part at the far end of the hippocampal formation that soon enters into major *reciprocal* connections with the anterior nucleus of the thalamus [Z:figure 6, 183].

This means that the GABA cap of the reticular nucleus could modulate the functions—in *either* direction—of this upper limb through which the hippocampus contributes to memory. The GABA cap can close and open, acting sometimes as a shield, sometimes as a sieve. Its shifting modes could briefly interrupt, or enhance, the flow of impulses along the next two major reciprocal paths that issue from the anterior thalamic nucleus. These pathways in the limbic system engage the anterior nucleus with both the cingulate gyrus and the orbitofrontal cortex.[19]

These limbic avenues are vitally important in the reverberations that merge our limbic and cortical networks into complex functions that can either rise into consciousness or remain at subconscious levels.

Novel Implications to Orientation of Some Theta Rhythms in Hippocampal and Closely Related Circuits

Surface EEGs show that theta rhythms increase as meditation deepens (see chapters 16 and 18). Does this trend toward slower (4–7 cps) wave forms mean that our whole brain is slowing down and simply becoming more relaxed? Probably not, for several reasons.

First, because theta activities also arise in deeper brain regions. Several of these sites are now being linked with active human memory functions. Indeed, we could not remember either spatial or nonspatial events without the subcortical network that helps encode and retrieve our memories.[20] Moreover, when the brain is stimulated at theta frequencies it becomes especially capable of generating long-term potentiation in the hippocampus. This process greatly enhances the working memory functions that hinge on spatial relationships.

A brief survey of functional anatomy helps clarify how theta rhythms in the hippocampus and in other limbic circuits could participate in these and other vital orienting activities.[21]

The oral nucleus down in the pons is one source for theta activities. Then, higher in the hypothalamus, the supramammillary nucleus helps drive theta bursts at faster frequencies. Discharges from this nucleus then rise up to stimulate various "pacemaker" cells, chiefly in the medial septal nucleus. Their discharges prompt high amplitude theta rhythms in the hippocampal formation. These theta waves arise in hippocampal CA2–3 cells and in the dentate gyrus.

Other cells back in the posterior hypothalamus generate the more tonic theta discharges. These impulses take a different course, relaying up through the midline of the thalamus. From here, in its nucleus reuniens, stimulation can also develop theta rhythms in several other regions, such as the hippocampal CA1 cells, the subiculum, entorhinal cortex, and the orbitomedial prefrontal cortex.

Finally, the theta rhythms that emerge from the hippocampus can relay down to the mammillary nucleus of the hypothalamus. From here they speed up to the anterior thalamic nucleus through the mammillothalamic tract (the well-myelinated bundle of Vicq d'Azyr). From this anterior nucleus, messages take only a short step up to reach the cingulate cortex (the whole lengthy trip will complete the so-called Papez circuit).

Point of Interest: Different Kinds of Head Directional Systems Parallel These Same Theta Pathways

We *point* at important things. The moon, for example. When pointing our finger at the moon, our head and eyes swivel in that direction. This helps to orient our attention straight along that line of sight. Can a laboratory rat teach us anything about this lining-up process?

Even though none of its immediate ancestors were born in the wild, this rat does more than face forward and move its head from side to side as it explores a strange new laboratory maze in the dark. It also *remembers* how to find its way back through all these passages to its own nest. How does this tame inbred rat not only navigate but also create a dynamic, working "map" constructed from each new twist and turn of spatial remembrances?

In which direction are *you* facing right now? It is easy to overlook so elementary an attribute. Yet, every animal needs an exquisite sense of *where its head is pointing*, especially at the particular moment when it occupies each successive new *place* in a maze. Why? Because a creature's egocentric actions hinge on having more than just a long central spinal axis. Such a simple axial "center" would remain behaviorally neutral *if* it were to define only a hub to which all "place" stimuli from sites around the whole circumference were assigned equal value.

Instead, what do dynamic outgoing behaviors require? A physiological commitment to *one particular direction*. This is an *implicit, subconscious, orientation*. Out in *front* is where most action is—food, mate, potential threats. Eyes and ears are biased to face *forward*. One's behavioral compass has a need akin to that of a magnetized needle. It seeks a *north*.

The pointed nose establishes the pivotal compass heading. It reflects our forward orientation, not our occiput. Inside, in the brain, specialized kinds of multimodal nerve cells possess several kinds of direction-sensitive properties. What automatic functions do such directional cells serve? Some convey *a sense of an optimal direction*, the one in which you'd like to *be headed*.

We come next to some remarkable convergences. Many head directional cells are conveniently dispersed right next door to those very same theta-generating memory cells described in the section just above.[22] Indeed, in the rat, the theta rhythms that relay throughout these nuclei and subnuclei seem to comprise one ascending anatomical system. This particular grouping of "theta rhythm" cells has been called the "*medial* mammillary system." The term *medial* becomes easier to remember because this system includes cells restricted to the *medial* part of its two major limbic nuclei: the mammillary nucleus and the anterior thalamic nucleus. In the *medial* mammillary nucleus, a third of the cells fire only when the head *turns* in a precise clockwise or counterclockwise direction. Moreover, almost all such *angular* motion cells vary their firing rates at the theta frequency.[23]

Now, what about other adjacent clusters of directional cells? They are disposed nearby, just slightly more *laterally and dorsally*. For example, one lateral system sensitive to head direction includes nerve cells of the *lateral* mammillary nucleus. Other cells in this directional category are located in the same anterior thalamic nucleus except in its dorsal subdivision.

The hippocampal formation now turns out to contain a distinct set of cells. Each one codes for *both* location (place) *and* head direction (directional heading).[24] Their firing correlates with the arrival of each local theta wave. Firing rates indicate that their "sense of direction" tends to remain consistant, whereas their "sense of place" varies as the rat moves from one location to another.

So what? Prominent theta activity develops when animals engage in normal spatial exploration behavior, not only when human beings meditate. It is possible that some of the memories that animals have for successive events are based on the ways their medial (theta) system continually stays in touch with cells that also convey information about their place, heading, and angular head motion.[25] Such consultations could serve dual purposes. They might both help focus externally oriented spatial attention and later become part of the foundation for remembering which movements would next have been made into the immediate environment. Turning has interesting implications (page 40).

Of course, human theta wave systems are certain to be much more varied in their functional complexity than are these found in the rat. Still, one might speculate that when our brain shifts toward certain kinds of theta rhythms in the hippocampus and allied circuits, such a shift there might evidence a more open receptivity for registering the arrival of new signals, not simply a descent toward drowsiness and slow wave sleep.

30

The Well-Concealed Hypothalamus

> Here in this well-concealed spot, almost to be covered with a thumbnail, lies the very mainspring of primitive existence—vegetative, emotional, reproductive—on which, with more or less success, man has come to superimpose a cortex of inhibitions.
>
> Harvey Cushing (1869–1939)[1]

The hypothalamus is well concealed deep down at the base of the brain. Harvey Cushing, a pioneering neurosurgeon, was careful to avoid damaging the hypothalamus when he operated on the pituitary gland just beneath. The slightest slip here, and his patient might never regain consciousness. Space permits only a thumbnail sketch of this tiny, crucial region, citing three of its major subdivisions: lateral, periventricular, and medial [Z:189–196].

Lateral Hypothalamus

The hypothalamus lies in the midline just above the pituitary, that master endocrine gland with which it enjoys an intimate relationship. The multiple, essential, survival functions of the hypothalamus have been outlined previously [Z:189–196, 162–163, 232–233, 237, 238]. Then, in 1998, came the discovery by two laboratory groups of nerve cells that normally make a novel excitatory peptide. This peptide, called hypocretin (or orexin), is missing in both the hypothalamus and spinal fluid of patients who have narcolepsy.[2] Because hypocretin nerve cells normally supply this excitatory peptide to the basal forebrain and upper brainstem, and are continuously active, this deficiency explains much of the excessive sleepiness that characterizes narcolepsy.[3]

Ventral Periventricular Area

Nerve cells here, in the arcuate nucleus, make a wide variety of other important peptides. Among them are two smaller opioid peptides, enkephalin and dynorphin, and two pivotal stress-activated peptides, the endogenous opioid, beta-endorphin, and ACTH[4] (see chapter 32). Glutamate receptors in the hypothalamus serve as its major source of excitatory input. This finding helps explain why excess glutamate has such a selective excitotoxic effect on cells in this arcuate nucleus [Z:654, 665].

Medial and Posterior Hypothalamus

The medial hypothalamic nuclei are also essential for our innate reproductive, defensive, and ingestive behaviors[5] (see chapter 34). The paired mammillary nuclei protrude from the back of the hypothalamus, cleaved along the midline. Their limbic messages relay quickly up to the anterior thalamic nucleus and down to the midbrain. In cells of their medial subdivision, angular motions of the head are linked with theta rhythms. Other directional cells reside in the lateral mammillary nucleus (as discussed in the previous chapter). They contribute to head direction functions by virtue of the impulses relayed up to them from the vestibular and related brainstem nuclei.[6]

Age-Related and Seasonal-Related Changes

The hypothalamus varies its neuroendocrine repertoire. Its output depends on what kinds of messages it receives from the rest of the brain and body. More nerve cells in the periventricular nucleus express CRF in people over the age of 40 years, and more cells can also express vasopressin with advancing age.[7] In people under the age of 50, peaks occur in the number of vasopressin cells in the suprachiasmatic nucleus both in the spring and fall. Chapter 34 considers how this vasopressin may be related to their so-called affiliative behaviors.

31

GABA Inhibits; Glutamate Excites

The opposites are beneficial; the fairest harmonies arise from things that differ.

Heraclitus (540–c.480 B.C.E.)

GABA is the brain's inhibitory workhorse. It is the pharmacological opposite of glutamate. Its acronym stands for gamma(γ)-aminobutyric acid. The brain applies fast-acting GABA circuits at all hierarchical levels to check its local processes of excitation. A remarkable fact: the brain makes its GABA from glutamate. This places inhibition just one chemical reaction step behind excitation [Z:208, 210].

GABA Systems

We begin with GABA, even though most GABA nerve cells are small inconspicuous interneurons. Inside the thalamic relay nuclei of primates, where some 20% to 25% of the neurons are GABAergic, these local-circuit GABA nerve cells have highly branched dendrites.[1]

Draped all over the *outer* surface of the thalamus are the long dendrites of yet another layer of inhibitory nerve cells. They belong to the GABA "cap" of the reticular nucleus. These dendrites monitor impulses passing into and out of the rest of the thalamus. They enable the reticular nucleus to serve as a "gate" which can open wide or close down on this traffic. GABA nerve cells in the zona incerta and midbrain can also inhibit important nuclei of the thalamus (see chapter 46).

Another important cluster of GABA nerve cells resides down in the ventrolateral preoptic area. GABA from their terminals inhibits the firing of both the histamine cells of the tuberomammillary nucleus of the hypothalamus and the serotonin and norepinephrine nerve cells down in the brainstem.[2] Normally, when the tuberomammillary nerve cells do fire in the posterior hypothalamus, they help to drive our wakeful states. In contrast, GABA cells farther forward in the preoptic cluster are more active in slow wave and REM sleep. And when $GABA_A$ receptor agonists are injected directly into the tuberomammillary nucleus, they inhibit its functions and produce sedation.[3]

Most GABA nerve cells in this preoptic cluster also contain a peptide, galanin. This adds robust and long-lasting inhibitory effects when it is coreleased on its postsynaptic receptors.

GABA circuits enter into a feedback loop system with other sleep/wakeful systems. The whole system takes on stable physiological properties. It resembles, in engineering terms, the operations of a flip-flop circuit. Though such a flip-flop switch does stabilize our separate waking and sleeping states, it can also give way quickly during transition phases. This property is relevant to the way the brain can shift into novel states of consciousness.

GABA is also important down in the midbrain central gray region.[4] Here, when opioids are released on mu opioid receptors, the inhibitory actions at $GABA_A$ receptors are enhanced.

One hypothesis has proposed that meditation (1) creates increased ketone production in the body; and (2) this ketosis increases the amount of GABA that is converted from its glutamate precursor.[5] Multiple other mechanisms for the phenomena of meditation exist in the brain. These would seem a more likely way for meditation to increase GABA tone in the brain other than as a secondary result of some general metabolic acidosis that arose in the body. We turn next to consider how else GABA contributes to brain functions.

GABA Inhibition and the Silent Suppressive Surround

To ease into this discussion, it could help first to visualize a big doughnut, then the small hole in its center. The doughnut image serves to introduce a surprising finding. Half a century ago, Stephen Kuffler noticed that certain retinal nerve cells did fire (as he expected) when he shined a tiny spot of light in the *center* of their field.[6] But then he also directed a second small beam of light at the wider outer zone of cells that *surrounded* them. Now these cells in the center *stopped* firing in response to light. That outer "ring" of surrounding cells had strongly inhibited them.

Why is that outer doughnut-shaped ring called the *silent* suppressive surround? Because its potent inhibitory capacities remain silent. You do not realize they exist until you also stimulate the field of the cell in their center.

Two other items: (1) Both the outer rim of surrounding cells, and those cells in their center, interact in mutually inhibitory ways. (2) Yet, after a cell of either type has been inhibited for the first half second or so, it rebounds quickly. Now it fires in *much faster* bursts than before.

In brief, the "light-on" (excitatory) responses first evoke "light-off" (inhibitory) responses from the surrounding zone. But next, even brighter light-on responses occur.

Researchers then discovered that many other sensory systems *back within the brain itself* also respond with similar excitatory/inhibitory reversals. For example, suppressive inhibitory responses are typical of the brain's V4 nerve cells and characterize many other visual circuits.[7]

Moreover, related GABA inhibitory mechanisms come into play elsewhere in the visual association cortex. In a region called the "lateral occipital complex," the gross, elementary shape of objects begins to filter into consciousness.[8] Signal activity increases in this region as soon as we perceive that random visual elements are forming a distinct object or becoming a scene that is visually coherent [Z:601–602].

What else happens, back in the primary visual cortex (V1), at the same moment that this coherent "visual grasp" is developing at sites farther on in the associative cortex? V1 is *inhibited*. fMRI is fast enough to detect this *reciprocal* change. The evidence points to circuits that instantly create *feedback inhibition* within widely different areas of the visual cortex. These dynamic feedback inhibitory mechanisms operate over longer distances than do our localized center/surround inhibitions. Some visual feedback circuits are transcortical. Others are thalamocortical, and can be traced to the pivotal inhibitory functions of the reticular nucleus of the thalamus.

Later, we will have occasion to consider both brief antagonistic, center/surround mechanisms and the longer-range inhibitory processes. For we need to clarify how it happens that brief light-dark pattern reversals occur at the close of *kensho* during a phase of afterimages (see table 11, chapter 95).

Meanwhile, GABA mechanisms relevant to triggering phenomena can be studied in circuits seemingly as mundane as those that register the movements of a rat's whisker. When these long, highly sensitive whiskers contact anything, touch messages speed back through the rat's trigeminal nerve, then relay up through the thalamus to excite its cortex. Normally, however, a rat's GABA nerve cells inhibit this process. GABA reduces the amplitude of the firing in several thalamic nuclei and slows the rate of sensory transmission. But suppose these GABA inhibitory actions are reduced. What happens? The sensory gates open. The sensory relay nuclei are disinhibited. They now respond to the slightest whisker touch with very short latencies and much higher amplitudes[9] [Z:462].

Meditative training uncovers a wide variety of unusual epiphenomena. They may be intriguing to neuroscience, but in Zen they are nothing special. They simply mean that the brain's neuromessenger systems are readjusting their dynamic balance between inhibition and excitation.

Glutamate Systems

Glutamate is the brain's major excitatory amino acid transmitter. Many lines of evidence show that glutamate and aspartate accomplish the bulk of our everyday *fast*, point-to-point neural transmission [Z:654–659]. A few samples follow.

Glutamate, like acetylcholine, exerts a strong influence on functions at several levels. Its mechanisms act both directly and indirectly. For example, glutamate quickly excites most cells down in the reticular nucleus of the thalamus. Yet, at the same time, it can also inhibit other reticular neurons, and for a longer interval.[10] Moreover, deep down in the hypothalamus, glutamate can act to phase-advance the circadian clock. How? By stimulating the synthesis of nitric oxide in the pivotal suprachiasmatic nucleus.[11]

One subtype of glutamate receptor is the NMDA receptor. When glutamate activates these NMDA receptors in the hippocampus, they play a key role in creating the synaptic changes that lead to long-term potentiation and to long-term depression.[12] But when these NMDA receptors are blocked, the hippocampus can no longer enter into normal learning tasks. Similarly, when glutamate transmission is inhibited in the amygdala, it can no longer contribute to the pathways serving fear conditioning.[13]

Glutamate Toxicity

Overfiring by glutamate nerve cells creates an extra release of calcium ions. This creates more of the side effects caused by a local release of nitric oxide. A sequence of neurotoxic changes then unfolds. The next postsynaptic cells die [Z:654–657]. However, this process stops if the NMDA receptor on the postsynaptic cell is blocked.

You might think at first that to block glutamate excitation would profoundly inhibit most of the brain. However, ketamine is also an NMDA antagonist. In less than anesthetic doses, ketamine produces not sedation, but a highly disorganized schizophreniform state (see chapter 71).

Memantine is another drug that is an antagonist at NMDA receptors. Having already said that so many nerve cells normally depend on glutamate transmission, you might not think, at first, that it would benefit patients with Alzheimer's disease. However, memantine now appears to help these patients. Why? The current theory is that it acts by reducing the degree of excitotoxic neuronal damage that had been caused by glutamate overstimulation.[14]

32

Stress Responses within the Brain

> When you suffer an attack of nerves, you're being attacked by the nervous system. What chance has a man against a system?
>
> Russell Hoban (b.1925)

Not much, unless you make the commitment to change the way your own nervous system responds. It was the previous century that introduced the terms "rat race," "hassle," "24/7," "corporate jungle," and "soccer moms." Stressful events in stressful times set off a long sequence of adjustments. These changes in our brains and bodies are called stress responses.

The traditional way to think about the brain's stress responses was that they activated a now-familiar hormonal system. It started in the pituitary gland, then released steroids from the adrenal cortex. The second, neural, system was faster. It released norepinephrine and epinephrine into the bloodstream. They came from nerve endings of the sympathetic nervous system and from the adrenal medulla.

Only in recent decades did research begin to clarify a third route. Through this avenue, stress responses *directly* change our brain itself, not only our body.

You may wonder why this chapter now links stress responses *with* meditation, whereas part II discussed evidence that meditative training *relieves* stress responses (see chapters 13 and 19). It's because meditators can elect to experience Zen meditation as a contact sport, especially during retreats, not simply as an esoteric form of Eastern philosophy.

The Corticotropin-Releasing Factor Response System

Corticotropin-releasing factor (CRF) is an excitatory polypeptide. It is the main regulator of the familiar descending, hypothalamic-pituitary-adrenal hormonal axis. But CRF also acts inside the brain. CRF fibers from the paraventricular nucleus release their CRF both in the arcuate nucleus of the hypothalamus and throughout many other medial regions in the cerebrum and brainstem. Various steps in the CRF response system are outlined in figure 5.

Stressful stimuli, both mental and physical, send their messages to the locus ceruleus. Its nerve cells, in turn, send their fibers up to release NE into the paraventricular nucleus. Here, they stimulate its cells to release CRF.[1] CRF also modulates learning and memory, even at dose levels so low that they do not directly go on to enhance the mechanisms of arousal, locomotion, or anxiety.[2] Little stressors help us learn.

CRF acts on two different types of receptors. In mice, CRF released into the lateral septum region stimulates its CRF-2 receptors. In the hippocampus, activating CRF-1 receptors enhances learning. Both CRF-1 and CRF-2 receptors help to mediate fear and anxiety behaviors. If you inhibit *both* receptor types, then stress-induced behaviors are reduced more than when either receptor is inhibited alone.[3]

Animals employ several optional coping strategies when they respond to stress. How do they decide which option is applicable? The fact that CRF also stimulates the release of serotonin by the dorsal raphe nucleus seems to play a role.[4] *Active* confrontation, fight, or flight are the three options *if* the animal judges that the stressor is controllable or escapable.[5] But suppose it is decided that the stressful situation is inescapable? (You might reach this conclusion during a long retreat, where you slowly learn the art of enduring the inescapable.) What then?

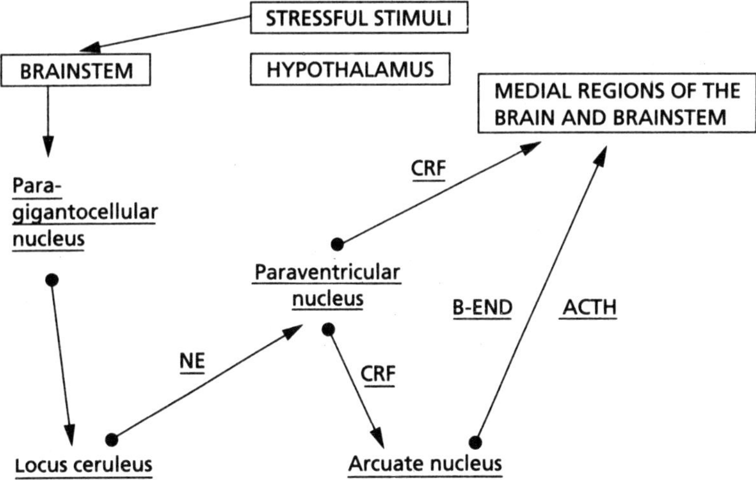

Figure 5 Stress responses within the brain
This figure diagrams the way stressful stimuli enter the brainstem, relay on to the hypothalamus, and then spread to involve the medial regions of the cerebrum and brainstem. A pivotal mechanism is the way norepinephrine from the locus ceruleus excites the paraventricular nucleus in the hypothalamus. This, in turn, leads to the release of corticotropin-releasing factor (CRF), an excitatory peptide. CRF goes on to excite a wide variety of other cells. Graded, well-calibrated levels of stress responses occur during retreats. Superimposed on these are the effects of abrupt triggering stimuli which can release additional norepinephrine.

Studies of animals show how they adopt *passive* coping strategies. Observation shows that animals then remain quiet, immobile, and reduce their responses to the environment. Though higher-level street-smarts may enter into such withdrawal-type judgments, other regions (such as the central gray) organize these two different coping strategies.

The Midbrain Central Gray

The central gray is shown in figure 4, chapter 23. It surrounds the long tubing (the aqueduct) that conducts fluid from the third cerebral ventricle down to the fourth. Active coping responses are evoked by stimulating the *dorsal* lateral columns of the central gray.[6] Flight reactions occur when excitatory amino acids are microinjected here. Some of these actions are correlated with a local increase in nitric oxide.[7] On the other hand, passive kinds of coping are triggered by activating the *ventral* lateral central gray. Although this region does have many CRF fibers, and even though the predominant role of CRF is excitatory, when CRF is injected separately into the central nucleus of the amygdala, this can *reduce* the animal's response to noxious stimuli.[8] (The next chapter helps explain how.)

Stress and GABA Receptor Function

Fortunately for animals and humans, the brain can invoke GABA and opioid systems to help it respond to stress. Although acute stress in rats first reduces $GABA_A$ receptor functions, it soon leads to a compensatory increase in the levels of neurosteroids in the brain. When these levels peak 30 minutes later, they act to enhance this GABA receptor's powerful inhibitory and antianxiety functions.[9]

Isolation is stressful for otherwise gregarious creatures. Rats have remained socially isolated in individual cages for 30 days. They show *decreased* functions of their $GABA_A$ receptors, and increase their anxiety-related behaviors. Plasma corticosterone increases to a modest degree, and neurosteroids like pregnenolone are reduced in the brain.

In summary, we can't avoid stress, but we can adapt to it.

33

Laid-Back Nurturing Promotes Laid-Back Limbic System Receptors

> I'm not frightened of the darkness outside, it's the darkness inside houses I don't like.
>
> Shelagh Delaney (b.1939)

> Maternal care during infancy serves to "program" behavioral responses to stress in the offspring by altering the development of the neural systems that mediate fearfulness.
>
> C. Caldji and colleagues[1]

Children's personalities are shaped by what happens in their early home environment. Researchers at McGill University asked: How does the *infant brain* respond when the circumstances are either stressful or more nurturing? In careful studies of a simple animal model, they showed that a calm, nurturing environment creates salutary changes in the brain.[2] Their important, *longitudinal* data in this model help us understand how meditative training could also exert similar long-range, beneficial calming effects. How? By influencing key receptors, and at levels as low as the brainstem and amygdala.

Suppose you wanted to replicate their research. How would you follow the way their experiment was designed? You would need to

- Select two kinds of rat mothers who show consistent differences in the way they nurture their offspring. Mothers in one group would be individually more nurturing; those in the other group would be less so.
- Observe and record how their offspring behave when they grew up and became adults.
- Examine the brains of these adult offspring at 100 days, using special light microscopic techniques. Verify which changes in key receptor levels correlate with each animal's *earlier* behavioral expressions of fear and anxiety.
- Screen for changes in the hippocampus, frontal cortex, and hypothalamus, but focus first on changes in the amygdala and locus ceruleus.

Why single out these two nuclei? Because, by interacting in mutually stimulating ways, they help sponsor primal anxieties and fearful responses to stress. Thus, norepinephrine from the locus ceruleus excites cells up in the amygdala. In turn, CRF cells in the amygdala's central nucleus release their CRF downstream. This peptide stimulates NE cells to fire in the locus ceruleus [Z:201–205].

Laid-Back Nurturing

How would you pick the rat mothers who were most nurturing? They display a distinctive, arched-back posture, and spend much more time in it. It might be summarized here with the phrase, "laid-back nurturing." In fact, these mothers often did lie on their back. From this position, they frequently engaged in licking and grooming behaviors, openly nursing their array of pups off on both sides.

In contrast, the less nurturing mothers tend to lie *prone*. They lie spread over their pups like a blanket, or lie on only one side while nursing.[3] It turns out that the laid-back, grooming mothers raise more laid-back (and less anxious) pups. The mothers who groom infrequently raise more anxious pups.

When the pups developed into adults, four sets of findings in their brains distinguished the laid-back rats from their less nurtured controls (figure 6).

- In the amygdala, more benzodiazepine-type receptors covered the central and lateral nucleus. Receptors of this type serve to index the site of GABA receptors. Enhanced inhibitory responses from these GABA receptors could reduce the tendency of the amygdala to fire excessively.
- The locus ceruleus also contained more of the same inhibitory receptors of this benzodiazepine type. (They were later identified as $GABA_A$ receptors.)[4]
- The locus ceruleus had fewer CRF receptors. Fewer CRF receptors here would reduce the excitatory effects of CRF peptides coming down from the amygdala. The locus ceruleus could remain less excitable, and release less NE.

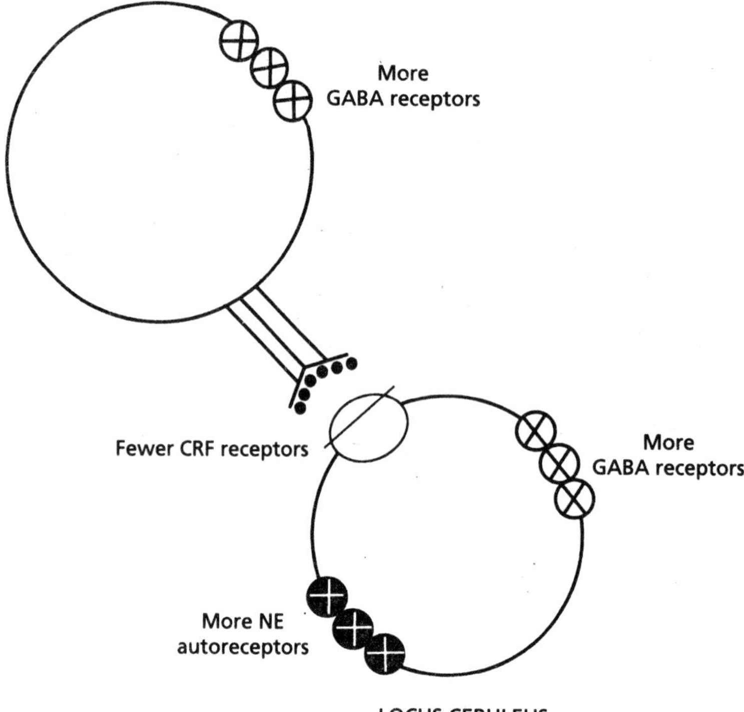

Figure 6 Neural correlates of reduced adult fearfulness: a response to early, laid-back nurturing The figure focuses on receptors which *limit* the excitability of the amygdala and the locus ceruleus. Laid-back nurturing reduces the degree to which the central nucleus of the amygdala (*top left*) can excite excessive firing of norepinephrine nerve cells in the locus ceruleus (*bottom right*). Subsequent studies showed that $GABA_A$ receptor levels were increased in other relevant regions. Their inhibitory effect could limit excessive firing in the central *and* lateral nuclei of the amygdala, the medial prefrontal cortex, the nucleus of the solitary tract, and the locus ceruleus.

- The locus ceruleus also had more autoreceptors for NE. Autoreceptors provide the negative feedback that reduces cell firing. Reduced firing in the locus ceruleus would also reduce its tendency to release excessive amounts of NE elsewhere in the brain. The net effect: fewer anxiety-related behaviors.

The four findings summarized above were the result of earlier preclinical research on pertinent receptor mechanisms. By implication, they suggest the potential ways that long-range meditative training could act *at the cellular level* to reduce our stress-related behaviors. How? By reducing the firing rates of certain anxiety-related nerve cells. Subsequent results, based on the same rat model, provide further support for this working hypothesis.[5]

The next five changes below suggest how long-range meditative training could also help reduce the firing rates in two other crucial sites in the limbic system: the hippocampus and the hypothalamus.

Several metabolic differences were also detectable in those calmer adult offspring who, as pups, had been nursed and nurtured by laid-back mothers.[6] For example, even though these adult rats had been subjected to acute restraint stress:

- Their plasma levels of pituitary ACTH remained lower than in their stressed controls.
- Their plasma levels of adrenal corticosterone were also lower than in their more anxious controls. Moreover, when a test dose of cortisone was injected 3 hours before restraint stress, it caused a greater reduction in their plasma ACTH response to this stress than occurred in the controls.

So:

- These adult offspring had become *more sensitive* to the way this cortisone feedback normally helps reduce the stress-induced ACTH responses of the hypothalamic-pituitary-adrenal axis.
- The laid-back offspring also showed an (appropriate and confirming) *increase* in the degree to which cortisone receptors were expressed in their hippocampus.
- They also showed a *decrease* in the expression of CRF in the paraventricular nucleus of the hypothalamus. This decrease could serve not only to *reduce* the release of anxiogenic CRF peptides elsewhere in the brain, it could also reduce the capacity of CRF to release more ACTH from the pituitary [Z:235–240].

The finding that more $GABA_A$ receptors developed in the laid-back offspring could translate into GABA having an enhanced capacity to stop excessive firing rates in many other systems.[7] Greater degrees of GABA inhibition, operating at multiple levels, could contribute in many important ways to the calming effects associated with meditative training.

This multilevel working hypothesis, at the cellular level, suggests how meditative training could calm the brain. It points to distinctive receptor changes in three limbic system nuclei, the locus ceruleus, and the anterior pituitary gland. The hypothesis needs to be tested in well-defined groups of human subjects. Ultimately, this will require controlled, neurohistochemical studies of human receptor systems at both light and electron microscopic levels.

In the interim, this kind of longitudinal, multidisciplinary research on an animal model exemplifies an important principle: one must include entire *messenger systems* in an experiment designed to clarify which crucial mechanisms modify stress responses and create enduring behavioral change. At a minimum, this means the following: baseline behavioral observations; neuromessenger levels, correlated with accurate receptor mapping techniques; and assays that can detect the delayed changes in *second* messenger systems. Neuromessenger levels alone might have sufficed five decades ago, but are no longer adequate to the task ahead.

34

Peptides in Social Affiliative Behaviors: Oxytocin and Vasopressin

> Oxytocin and vasopressin play a prominent role in modulating both affiliative behavior and the way the brain processes social information.
>
> Larry Young[1]

Social bonding and nurturing behaviors play essential roles in maintaining the social fabric. Yet, growing children and parents each need to let go at the right time. On the meditative path, you enter into a close relationship with your spiritual teacher. Yet *non*attachment has long been acknowledged as a useful attribute. How does each person in a dyadic relationship reconcile such paradoxes? [Z:678]. Only by delicate balancing acts.

Recent human and animal research has provided a glimpse of how the brain does integrate and reconcile special behaviors at certain times.[2] Two peptides are of interest: oxytocin and vasopressin.

Oxytocin

Oxytocin is a peptide composed of nine amino acids. Cells producing it are concentrated in the paraventricular and supraoptic nuclei of the hypothalamus. Oxytocin from the smaller nerve cells of the paraventricular nucleus is then released widely throughout the brain, to limbic regions in particular.

Norepinephrine enhances the firing of these oxytocin nerve cells,[3] but GABA and nitric oxide inhibit them,[4] thereby reducing the release of oxytocin during emotional stress.

In general, oxytocin helps promote maternal behavior, sexual receptivity, and affiliation behaviors. Affiliation behaviors bring individuals closer together into a positive social matrix.

Oxytocin also pulses from the posterior pituitary gland into the bloodstream. The oxytocin levels of recently delivered mothers correlate with these mothers' positive personality patterns of wishing to please, to give, and to interact socially.[5] More oxytocin is released into the brain and bloodstream, during birth, lactation, and suckling.

Infusing oxytocin into the brains of male *rats* increases their social interactions with other male rats.[6] When oxytocin is infused into the brains of prairie voles, it also increases the time they spend huddling, side by side (Vasopressin does the same.)

Differences in social behavior among different vole strains have generated much attention. Where I live, on the side of a mountain, all voles are the *montane* variety. They are small dark-gray rodents, dig burrows, look less like a mole and more like a field mouse. Their promiscuous behavior might seem reminiscent of the mountain men of the wild west in the nineteenth century. When compared with these loners, their human counterparts down on the plains were decidedly community oriented.

The voles that inhabit the flatlands are monogamous. What gives the brains of these *prairie* voles their major socializing edge on what we humans consider the "affiliation" scale of social values?

Consider the nucleus accumbens of monogamous male and female prairie voles (see chapter 25). The accumbens receives a very dense supply of oxytocin fibers from the hypothalamus.[7] Moreover, oxytocin receptors cover both the shell and core of the accumbens. And, in their basal lateral amygdala, the monogamous prairie voles also have more oxytocin receptors.[8]

Theories from the vole model have been tested in other animals. Mice can be genetically engineered to lack a functional oxytocin gene. These knockout mice neither recognize nor habituate to another mouse, even after they have been in repeated close contact with this potential friend and neighbor.[9] Histochemical studies confirm that such social exposures activate neither their medial amygdala nor other regions of their extended amygdala, in contrast to controls (see chapter 27).

When oxytocin is injected into the brain, a broad array of animal studies suggests that it reduces anxiety and has mildly sedative properties, especially in females.[10] Not only does injection of oxytocin into the cerebral ventricles of ewes stimulate their maternal behavior but in rats such oxytocin-induced calming may persist for several weeks. Taylor and colleagues suggest that such general calming and nurturing effects of oxytocin contribute to a brain's options to "tend and befriend." In contrast, its other primal stress responses tend in the directions of "fight or flight."[11]

Trust is an essential ingredient in any social compact, including that between Zen students and their roshi. People also tend to trust Swiss banks with their money. Trust has recently been studied in the laboratory under the auspices of a Swiss economic research institute. The findings suggest that oxytocin contributes to the way we trust another person.[12] Twenty-nine male subjects were cast in the role of "investors." They received a nasal spray of oxytocin 50 minutes before they engaged in a monetary game-playing task. Prior research had indicated that nasal oxytocin could be absorbed and reach the brain. Only these oxytocin investors became so trusting of their anonymous "trustees" that they kept giving them money to invest. Did an inert placebo spray make the control investors more trusting? No. Nor did the "trustees" who received the real oxytocin behave in a more trustworthy manner. The researchers concluded that oxytocin increased trust by virtue of its effect in promoting approach behavior in this particular social context.

Vasopressin

Vasopressin differs from oxytocin only in two amino acid residues. It, too, is made in the hypothalamus, released elsewhere into the brain, and is also released by the pituitary gland into the bloodstream.

Consider once again the brains of monogamous *prairie* voles. Dense coats of vasopressin receptors cover the ventral pallidum and medial amygdala. Moreover, male prairie voles have many more vasopressin fibers in their ventral pallidum than do the females.[13] When male prairie voles receive a minute amount of vasopressin in the cerebral ventricle, their social interactions greatly increase. This does not occur in montane voles.[14]

It is not a one-night stand when male prairie voles mate with their one female partner. The release of vasopressin helps to regulate their ongoing pair bonding.[15] This monogamous social behavior means more than an enduring affiliation with one particular partner. It also entails high levels of care for the offspring, as well as aggression toward unfamiliar animals.

In such behaviors, limbic system interactions are paramount. In male prairie voles, the lateral septum receives its vasopressin from nerve cells in the bed nucleus of the stria terminalis. Injections of vasopressin into this lateral septal nucleus induce pair bonding. Moreover, a vasopressin receptor blocker stops the pair bonding induced by mating.

Many vasopressin receptors cover nerve cells in the ventral pallidum of male prairie voles. More receptors can be added by injecting a virus that has been engineered to carry the gene for the vasopressin (VP-1) receptor. Afterward, these male prairie voles huddle and interact more with unfamiliar animals. They also develop a partner preference for a female. This occurs even after the two cohabit overnight but do not mate.[16]

Once again, theories from the vole model have been tested in other animals. Male *mice* who lack the vasopressin VP-1A receptor (vasopressin knockout mice) show not only a marked reduction in anxiety-like behavior but are also profoundly impaired in their capacity to relate socially to other animals.[17]

Adult rats who had been well nurtured as pups are both less fearful (more laid-back) and more maternal than their controls (see chapter 33). In these calmer rats, the males show more vasopressin VP-1A receptors in the calmer amygdala, whereas the females show more oxytocin receptors in the central nucleus of the amygdala and the bed nucleus of the stria terminalis.[18]

Other Messengers Contribute

Affiliation is not all due to these two peptides. Mesolimbic dopamine terminals from the ventral tegmental area richly supply both the nucleus accumbens and other parts of the ventral pallidum (see chapters 24 and 25). To us it comes as no surprise (but it probably was to her partner) to find that a dopamine DA_2 agonist, when infused into her nucleus accumbens, causes a female prairie vole to develop enhanced partner preference behavior, even though she and he had not engaged in mating. Dopamine also contributes to maternal behavior in rats.[19]

Recent human neuroimaging studies show that subjects diagnosed as having a generalized social phobia have less evidence of DA_2 receptors than do their healthy controls.[20]

Some sedative effects of oxytocin may relate to its ability to increase the activity of NE alpha-2 receptors.[21]

Studies of the social behavior of rhesus monkey mothers indicate that after they receive naloxone (the opioid inhibitor), they give their infants less attention, protection, and grooming.[22]

These simpler animal models have helped researchers develop new hypotheses about the mechanisms underlying our psychosocial and sexual behaviors. A little affiliation can go a long way to repair the frayed social fabric in a world where angst often prevails. Precisely how oxytocin, vasopressin, biogenic amines, opioids, and allied messengers interact in meditation and in the context of our more intricate human social equations remains to be established.

35

Our Brain's Own Opioids

Thou hast the keys of Paradise, oh just, subtle, and mighty opium!

Thomas De Quincey (1785–1859), *Confessions of an English Opium Eater*

Endogenous Opioids

Opiates have relieved suffering for ages when given by mouth or by injection. Yet researchers found that the brain made opiate-like substances only a few decades

Table 3
Opioids and Their Receptors

Endogenous Opioid[a]	*Acts Preferentially on This Receptor Type*[b]	*Comment on Actions*
Enkephalins	delta (δ)	Can increase the signal-to-noise ratio in the hippocampus[c]
Beta-endorphins	epsilon (Σ)	Are released, together with ACTH, into the brain
Endomorphins	mu (μ)	Have the most selective affinities of all endogenous opioids
Dynorphins	kappa (κ)	Have a variety of inhibitory, excitatory, and excitotoxic effects

ACTH, adrenocorticotropic hormone.
[a]The drug morphine is an *exogenous* opiate. It acts preferentially on mu_2 receptors, and slows breathing in particular.
[b]Opioids tend to act on more than one receptor type, except for the endomorphins.
[c]Met-enkephalin is unique in its antineurotropic effects (see chapter 38).
For further discussion of the opioids' signaling properties, see G. Stefano, Y. Goumon, F. Casares, et al. Endogenous morphine. *Trends In Neurosciences* 2000; 23:436–442.

ago. These molecules are now called the *endogenous opioids.* Four opioid systems within our nervous system are relevant to certain experiences that can occur on the path of meditative training (table 3) (see chapter 4) [Z:213–223, 506–508, 619–621].

Nerve cells in one opioid system make the *enkephalins*: leu-enkephalin and met-enkephalin. Both are short molecules, only five amino acids long. We release some enkephalins not only into the cingulate gyrus and other cortical regions but also into key subcortical nuclei that govern motor functions: the globus pallidus, the caudate nucleus, and the nucleus accumbens. Researchers are still working out all the organizing principles that promote their release.

The *beta-endorphin* system supplies our brain's deeper, more primitive regions close to the midline. This chapter reviews recent findings related to the third opioid system, which makes the *endomorphins,* and the fourth, which makes the *dynorphins.* Then, in the next chapter, we consider how opioids enter into the human response to acupuncture, the placebo response, and into the relief of suffering.

Endomorphins

The two endomorphins have extraordinary properties for molecules that are only four amino acids long. Of all the opioids, theirs is the greatest and most selective affinity for mu opioid receptors. The endomorphins' initial effects are further enhanced because a delayed metabolic cascade develops after mu receptors are activated[1] (see chapter 37).

Endomorphin-1 is more widely distributed in the cerebrum. Once it is injected into a rat's cerebral ventricles, the rat tends to go back to that particular place where it was at the time it received the injection. This "place preference" suggests that the endomorphin had conferred what was a kind of subliminal reward. When endomorphin-1 is injected into the midbrain (in the *posterior* part of the ventral tegmental area) it causes rats to repeatedly press a lever that enables them to be injected with more of the same. Once again these animals develop a conditioned place preference, and they also move about more actively.[2] These so-called rewarding effects of endomorphin-1 are separable from its pain-relieving (analgesic) effects. Moreover, even a very low dose will reduce pain, yet not depress respiration.[3]

Endomorphin-2 is distributed mostly in the brainstem and spinal cord.[4] Endomorphin-2 is the yang to the yin of endomorphin-1. It creates an *aversion* to that particular place where the rat was when it received the opioid. This place-avoidance effect is related to the way endomorphin-2 subsequently enters into other sequences that activate kappa opioid receptors. Surprisingly, down in the spinal cord, endomorphin-2 agonists can (secondarily) release two other opioids: dynorphin and met-enkephalin.[5]

Among their other complex secondary effects, each endomorphin can increase the local release of serotonin when infused into the dorsal raphe nucleus.[6]

Dynorphin

Dynorphin, discovered a quarter century ago, is a potent agonist at kappa opioid receptors. Human subjects develop unpleasant visual distortions, feelings of unreality, and depersonalization when given other highly selective kappa opioid agonists.[7]

Some human studies hint that dynorphin might have anticonvulsant properties. It is speculated that low dynorphin levels might be associated with an increased risk for temporal lobe epilepsy and with a greater tendency for seizures to spread from the temporal lobe.[8]

Dynorphin nerve cells have recently been found in parts of the human amygdala complex.[9] Dynorphin also coexists in the key orexin (hypocretin) nerve cells of the lateral hypothalamus which degenerate in narcolepsy.[10] Within the nucleus accumbens, CREB (*c*yclic AMP *r*esponse *e*lement *b*inding protein) regulates the expression of dynorphin.[11]

When young male rat pups are separated from their mothers for only 15 minutes each day, dynorphin B and met-enkephalin levels increase in the hypothalamus.[12] Dynorphin exerts a mixture of initial inhibitory and excitatory effects on CA1 and CA3 cells in the hippocampus [Z:223]. However, excessive levels of dynorphin are neurotoxic to cells not only in the hippocampus but also in the striatum[13] [Z:656].

The recent research surveyed briefly above suggests that dynorphin may be relevant to a few psychoactive drug experiences, including some that develop feelings of depersonalization and unpleasantness in general.

36

Opioids, Acupuncture, and the Placebo Response

> High placebo responders have a more efficient opioid system.
>
> P. Petrovic and colleagues[1]

This chapter sets ambitious goals. It examines how opioids, acupuncture, and the placebo response relate (1) to each other, (2) to Zen meditation in general, and (3) to phenomena sometimes experienced during meditation and alternate states of consciousness.

A Role for Opioids in Acupuncture

Everyone learns that needles hurt. How could a needle *relieve* pain? Few in the West were prepared to accept this preposterous notion. Then James Reston (a respected columnist for the *New York Times*) reported that acupuncture helped to relieve the severe pain he suffered after his emergency appendectomy in Beijing.

It now seems clear that opioid nerve cells in the spinal cord, the midbrain central gray, and the arcuate nucleus of the hypothalamus play essential roles in acupuncture analgesia.[2]

The earliest steps in pain relief depend on the way the thin needles influence certain sensory nerves: the very small type 2 and type 3 fibers. Many of these nerve fibers, lying inside muscle, normally convey our deep sensations of numbness and aching. Often enough to be interesting, some of these small sensory nerves lie under traditional acupuncture points.[3] Whirling the needle after it is inserted stimulates the nerve fibers. Nowadays, the effects of this *manual* acupuncture are often enhanced by passing a weak electrical current through the needle (*electro*-acupuncture).

Pathways Involved in Pain and Pain Relief

You might think that sensory nerves would only convey the *signal* of pain. Yet, our nervous systems are wired in ways that help us also relieve pain. One might summarize the early stages that produce our pain as follows: it begins as volleys of impulses that *ascend* from our peripheral nerves, and are then processed into "pain" percepts at successively higher levels in our central nervous system [Z:352–355].

However, these ascending impulses also stimulate other circuits at higher levels. Fortunately, some of these set off the secondary release of other neuromessengers which can *relieve pain*. These *descending* pathways release both endogenous opioids and *non*opioids (including serotonin and norepinephrine). They help to block pain impulses before they can rise up to reach conscious levels.

Pain Associated with Meditation

Meditators suffer many aching leg and back pains when they sit for long periods during retreats. Does this discomfort during zazen stimulate responses from these same small peripheral sensory fibers? *Could this lead to the subsequent release of relevant neuromessengers*? This plausible working hypothesis awaits a formal study. Meanwhile, it is very important to appreciate that certain time relationships are involved. The analgesic effects of acupuncture are *delayed*. Only after 20 to 30 minutes does the *subjective* pain relief occur.

This delay is relevant to the temporal profile of the phenomena that occurred during this writer's state of deep internal absorption [Z:478–479]. I did not drop into this state until 20 minutes *after* a significant series of untoward events. They began with a period of mental and physical distress prompted by severe numbness and tingling in my left leg. These sensory symptoms, in turn, had developed because my sciatic nerve was compressed while I sat in the half-lotus position with my left leg crossed. This 20-minute time lag lends support to the hypothesis that these several stressful events could have set off, after the usual delay, some potential endogenous opioid contributions that had entered later as a feeling of bliss.

Long retreats teach meditators important things about themselves. They learn what their pain threshold is. They discover their tolerance for suffering. They experience, firsthand, the way they respond to leg muscle compression, numbness, and varieties of prominent muscle aching. They learn, like other animals, to adapt.

Meditators may also be surprised to find that such pains sometimes melt away, say after the first 3 or 4 days of a retreat (Z:353). Observations such as these, both of pain responses and of pain relief, invite detailed serial investigations during retreats of how both our opioid and our other neuromessenger systems respond to unpleasant situations and aversive stimuli.

Effects of Electro-acupuncture on Opioids in Animal Experiments

Patients who attend pain clinics nowadays often receive electro-acupuncture. Acupuncture does seem to relieve nausea and vomiting, but how effective *is* it in treating various human pain syndromes?[4] Many questions still remain, despite the favorable nod given toward needle acupuncture by an expert panel assembled by the National Institutes of Health.

On the other hand, laboratory research in rats and mice already suggests that two different frequencies of electro-acupuncture stimulation can relieve their pain.[5] It can be easier to remember how these two separate sets of analgesic mechanisms differ if you pair "low" rates of stimulation with pain relief mechanisms at "high" anatomical sites. Conversely, "high" stimulation rates turn out to relieve pain by acting at "low" anatomical sites.

For example, *low*-frequency stimulation (at only 2 cps) enhances the release of met-enkephalin and beta-endorphin at higher levels in the central nervous system. Moreover, these effects can be blocked. How? By injecting antibodies against endomorphin-1 and -2 into the cerebral ventricles (higher up). These antibody results suggest that it is chiefly the *mu* opioid receptors which mediate the pain-relieving effects of this low-frequency electroacupuncture. In contrast, *high*-frequency rates of stimulation release more dynorphin A and B at lower sites down in the spinal cord.

Animal studies also suggest that messages from *low*-frequency acupuncture may relay up to stimulate the arcuate nucleus in the hypothalamus. When this nucleus then releases its beta-endorphin farther down in the central gray of the midbrain, it contributes further to the descending circuits that mediate the analgesic response. In contrast, high rates of stimulation may act on the parabrachial acetylcholine nucleus of the pons in ways that relieve pain by influencing other descending mechanisms.[6]

Sham-Controlled Studies in Humans

A recent study compared the fMRI responses to manual acupuncture, or electro-acupuncture with those to a "placebo-like" tactile (sham) stimulation.[7] Thirteen naive male subjects were stimulated at a standard site below the knee. Both modes of acupuncture *decreased* the signals in such limbic regions as the amygdala, anterior hippocampus, and cingulate gyrus (subgenual and retrosplenial portions) as well as in the ventromedial prefrontal area. What would such a decrease mean?

On balance, the data suggested that decreased functions in these circuitries might help diminish the several types of active pain responses that would be generated within other regions and enter experience. For example, though the needled subjects did not experience sharp pain, electroacupuncture (at either 2 cps or 100 cps) did increase fMRI signals both in their opposite anterior cingulate region (BA 24, 32), in the (appropriately opposite) leg area of their primary and secondary sensory cortex, and in the anterior insula on both sides.

In another study, fifteen human subjects received electro-acupuncture at a standard analgesic point. The results were monitored by fMRI. Authentic electro-acupuncture was especially effective in *increasing* the signal activity from the hypothalamus and sensorimotor cortex. It also *decreased* the signals from the front of the anterior cingulate cortex.[8] We shall see soon what such decreases might imply.

How Relevant to Zen Are Studies of the Placebo Response?

Skeptics contend that the response to acupuncture could be all "psychological." If the placebo response were "all in the mind," wouldn't this explain away all those patient reports that acupuncture had relieved their pain? And yet (by the way), if this "placebo response" does actually work on the "mind," couldn't the *brain* be changing too?

Price and Soerensen began their review of the placebo response by citing four of its potential mechanisms. "Placebo effects have been explained by Pavlovian conditioning, cognition (for example, expectancy), personality, and social learning, alone or in combination."[9]

Parenthetically, let us note that some skeptics hold similar views about how belief systems influence people who become involved with the "spiritual path." For example:

- Do these aspirants feel better simply because they *expect* this path will relieve them of mental anguish?
- Do they improve only because they trust their leaders and have faith in the path itself?
- Do belief, faith, and prayer help? In the scope of this chapter, we can approach such thorny issues only tangentially. A central question explored here is: Do opioid mechanisms help explain some aspects of the placebo response, and do they contribute to pain relief in other situations?

The human subjects in one study were asked to endure ischemic pain. It was caused by fully inflating a pressure cuff around the arm.[10] Under these conditions, *positive cognitive expectation* cues for pain relief did prove effective. Why did they appear to act via opioid mechanisms? Because naloxone (the opioid antagonist) completely blocked these cognitive cues from going on to influence the subjects' placebo response.

In another study, subcutaneous pain was caused by injecting capsaicin. Naloxone could reverse the placebo-induced analgesia in this experiment *if* the subjects had focused their own expectations of pain relief on very localized areas of their skin.[11]

People differ. Nature and nurture combine to make each of us different, anatomically and physiologically. Why do John and Jane respond much better to a placebo than do Joe and Mary? An early fMRI study of acupuncture provided some answers.[12]

First, let's be clear about what usually happens when a therapist inserts the thin needle into a relevant acupuncture site. The subject usually develops the so-called *deqi* sensation. Included in this sensation is a mixture of numbness, tingling, fullness, and a dull ache. It begins at the acupuncture site. Then, when the needle is manipulated, the *deqi* sensation spreads some distance away.

Eleven subjects did experience this *deqi* sensation after the needle was inserted (into the so-called L1 4 site) of the hand. And only these eleven subjects also went on to *decrease* their previous fMRI signals in *many* limbic, paralimbic, and subcortical regions bilaterally. For example, among those sites at which these signals were *reduced below* baseline levels were the nucleus accumbens, amygdala, hippocampus, parahippocampus, hypothalamus, ventral tegmental area of the midbrain, anterior cingulate gyrus (Brodmann area 24), caudate, putamen, temporal pole, and insula.

However, the way two other subjects responded to events was instructive. They experienced local *pain* at their needle site, *not* this expected *deqi* sensation of a numb, dull ache. Moreover, when their needle was manipulated, signals *increased* in many of the same brain regions just cited. Increased signals could be expected. Signals increase in many of these same regions when humans develop pain and unpleasant resonances of suffering in response to a variety of noxious stimuli (see chapters 25–28).

So, the *deqi* sensation is a special symptom produced by stimulation of small peripheral nerve fibers. *And it is not the same as a local pain.* Could this special numbness-tingling-ache also be regarded as a kind of early herald of pain-*relief* mechanisms soon to arrive? That is, could it be the *prelude* to the next sequences—20 to 30 minutes later—when we enlist *some* of our opioid pathways in the process of pain relief? And if so, could such delayed pain relief then be correlated with *reduced* signals in many of the same (higher-level) sites which would otherwise be activated during the actual production of pain?

Of course, these researchers were trying to conduct an fMRI study of the *deqi* sensation per se. They did not intend to *produce* pain at their subjects' needle sites. However, the next two PET studies did approach similar key questions. Each employed a different design. In the first study, pain was deliberately introduced. Then an opioid was given. Following this, PET scans monitored the steps through which the opioid relieved the pain. Finally, these individual opioid drug responses could be compared with the varying degrees of success that the same subjects had experienced when their placebo response was tested for its effectiveness in relieving pain.

Two PET Scan Studies of a Mu Opioid Agonist Drug

Agonist drugs activate receptors. Remifentinal is a synthetic opioid agonist that activates mu opioid receptors. It was given in clinically active dosages during two important pharmacological studies. The results of the first study suggest that *both* our higher-order endogenous opioid systems *and* our cognitive networks *each participate not only in the way opioids relieve pain but also in the processes through which a placebo relieves pain.*[13]

In this first controlled study, nine subjects received either a painfully hot stimulus (48°C) or merely a warm stimulus applied to the back of the left hand. During the painfully hot stimulus, the brain sites that responded included the insula bilaterally, the thalamus, and the *caudal* (*back*) portion of the anterior cingulate cortex.

The next step was to observe what happened in the brain when an active, *pharmacological* dose of opioid drug was given intravenously (not a mere tracer dose). In this instance, remifentinal was given in one single, rapid injection. Not until the pain-*relieving* effect of this opioid had reached its peak did the anterior cingulate cortex show its greatest *increase* in activation. During this phase of optimum pain relief, which part increased? The increased activity occurred more in the *rostral* (*front*) portion, not in the *caudal* portion of the cingulate. In humans, this rostral region is known to have a high concentration of opioid receptors. Interpretation: the opioid drug, acting on its receptors, had increased the activity of certain cells in the rostral anterior cingulate gyrus; this effect correlated with pain relief.

In parallel studies, tests were made of the same subjects' *innate* capacities to develop a placebo response. Some subjects derived much better pain relief from the inert placebo than did others. Which area became most active in their brains? Once again, the subjects who responded to the placebo with the best pain relief were those whose *rostral* part of the anterior cingulate gyrus became the most active site. In contrast, subjects who showed a low placebo response had lesser activity in this area.

What kind of local activity in this *rostral* anterior cingulate cortex might go on to help relieve pain? The authors suggested that activity in this particular region may have relayed some kind of pain *relief* message *down* to the central gray in the midbrain (see chapter 32) [Z:352–358].

One other region also increased its activity during the placebo response: the *lateral* part of the orbitofrontal cortex (see chapter 43). This finding raises another interesting possibility: perhaps we humans have access to a still higher collateral resource in the frontal lobe, one that would help to integrate several "coping" responses to relieve our sufferings and pain. In theory, when we develop such higher-level cognitive cues, they might act via relays from this *lateral* orbitofrontal region, which then go on down to reach those other descending pain-relief pathways that were outlined several sections above.

In greater detail, the theory would suggest that (1) by initiating a variety of "quasi-psychological" influences within parts of our frontal lobes, and (2) then by linking these cues with related activities arising in the front part of the anterior cingulate cortex, (3) we could next be able to relay messages downstream (to the thalamus or brainstem, or both), and (4) along the way, several endogenous opioids (and allied messengers) might be released which could finally help relieve pain and suffering [Z:352–354].

A caveat: these pioneering studies have resulted in intriguing interpretations that remain preliminary. We still need much more detailed information about the normal sequences and pathways that enable us to integrate and respond to pain signals.[14] These cautionary remarks are especially relevant to the intricate circuitry that also enables us to release opioids on mu receptors at the higher cerebral levels. This topic is discussed in the paragraphs below.

A second PET study had a different goal. It was designed to monitor just the responses to remifentinal, with *no* added pain. In this instance, two different pharmacologically active doses of remifentinal were given. Each dose was infused *slowly*. Under these conditions, the pattern of brain responses *to the opioid drug itself* could be observed. Activities increased in many different regions. The opioid was followed by significant *decreases* of PET activity in both the inferior parietal lobes and in the left fusiform gyrus.[15]

The two separate PET scan studies just cited above focused on the way the brain responded during active doses of an opioid agonist drug. However, in the research next to be described, the subjects received only minute *tracer* doses of a mu agonist molecule. This research was designed both to locate and to measure those mu *receptors* that could just *bind* this tracer molecule. These investigators wished to avoid the sedation and other extraneous symptoms that are caused whenever higher, *pharmacological* doses of an opioid drug are given and strongly activate many mu receptors. Instead, they asked the question, Does the brain respond to pain by releasing its own opioids on these receptors? (But, one wonders, is it possible to eliminate from an experiment all the types of placebo responses that were cited earlier by Price and Soerensen? (see note 9.))

PET Scans of Opioid Mu Receptors When Subjects Respond to Pain and to Aversive Pictures

The next studies illustrate the point made earlier: pain messages do more than activate several parts of the brain. They also lead to the delayed, secondary release of the brain's own opioids (and other messengers) which then help relieve pain.

Meditators already know from experience how their muscles can hurt. Pain researchers have devised other unpleasant ways to induce, and monitor, major degrees of muscle discomfort. One of these ways is to inject a concentrated salt solution into the large masseter muscle at the angle of the jaw.[16] Throughout the next 20 minutes, the subjects (who do volunteer for this) take on an additional mental task. Every 15 seconds, they rate how much pain they are feeling.

Carfentanil is a selective mu opioid agonist. When tagged with an isotope, and injected into the bloodstream, very small amounts of this radiolabeled opioid bind to mu receptors. Sensitive PET scan techniques then map the regions where these mu receptors are most concentrated.

First, a caveat about using PET scan techniques to calculate the *release* of neuromessengers *on* their receptors. When we respond to pain (or stressful situations) by releasing more of our own (*endogenous*) mu opioids, these *un*labeled opioids also move out to occupy their own natural receptor sites located on adjacent nerve cells. Here, our natural opioid molecules will *compete* with the injected (*exogenous*) tracer opioid molecule for the same binding sites available on these same mu receptors.

This means that *the baseline control study is critical.* Why must the conditions chosen for this baseline be as neutral and as standardized as possible (pain-free, stress-free, expectation-free, etc.)? So that as many mu receptor sites as possible will then remain *un*occupied. This leaves them still available to be measured by the tracer opioid during the next condition to be tested.

How does the investigator determine that the person's own *endogenous* opioid is being actively released during this next phase when the brain's response to pain is being tested? The crucial correlation relates to timing: the primary evidence is that the person's subjective relief from pain *corresponds at that particular time* with a *decrease* in local tracer binding below the original baseline. Why a decrease? This decreased binding suggests that those original opioid receptor sites are now no longer available to bind the tagged opioid. Why not? Because those receptors had just been freshly occupied by the subject's own, newly released (unlabeled) opioids.

Reduced to words, the method of measurement is indirect, because the equation reads like this: Baseline opioid receptor density minus receptor density at the peak of pain relief provides an index of receptors newly occupied by the subjects' own opioids that had just been released in response to pain.

Are all time relationships being reported accurately? Then it is reasonable to correlate the (subjective report of) relief from pain with the (calculated) release of that person's natural opioids.

Bearing these comments in mind, the subjects' muscle pain did relay back through the trigeminal nerve, into the brain stem to release endogenous opioids. Where? In both the right and left dorsal anterior cingulate and dorsal lateral prefrontal cortex. The induced muscle pain also went on to release mu opioids at certain lateralized sites: in the insula, the thalamus, and the hypothalamus on the side opposite the pain; in the amygdala on the same side as the pain.

A major point of emphasis in this book is that it is essential to listen with care when individual subjects report their personal experiences. The individual variations among the twenty normal men and women in this study proved instructive. They varied substantially both in how much muscle pain they perceived and in how they felt about their pain. Still, their subjective reports indicated that their pain was relieved at about the same time that their PET data provided the strongest evidence that they had released endogenous mu opioids.

Beyond that, the subjects varied widely in how *much* endogenous mu opioids they released. However, those subjects whose PET scans showed that they had released more opioids also tended to report more pain relief. Moreover, those who released more opioids also reported that less psychological suffering accompanied the pain they did perceive.

A second PET scan report from this same Michigan laboratory studied another group of twelve subjects.[17] This time their task was to respond to three kinds of pictures: (1) negatively valenced aversive images, (2) neutral images of common objects, and (3) blank images. All images were rendered in black and white. In one part of the study, PET scans monitored changes in regional brain activities as indexed by their blood flow. In parallel PET studies, radiolabeled tracer doses of carfentanil were again used. This part of the study provided a dynamic image of the change caused by the different kinds of pictures in the numbers of available mu receptor binding sites.

As expected, the first set of PET data showed that unpleasant pictures activated several limbic regions. In two regions the *relative* degrees of this activation were asymmetrical: (1) relatively more activation arose in the *left* amygdala and its extensions; (2) relatively less activation occurred in the *right* temporal lobe in its inferior pole. The greater opioid release also occurred in this same inferior pole of the *right* temporal lobe.

Can this lesser activity in the right temporal lobe be reconciled with the increased opioid release there? The authors suggest that when opioids are released on mu receptors, they reduce the "neural intensity of the response." What does this mean? It means that opioids *inhibit* local neuronal activity. Thus, the *relative* decrease of blood flow in the *right* inferotemporal region is interpretable as a decrease in the local neural activity there, an inhibition attributable to the local release of opioids. Physiological data from animal research supports this interpretation: mu receptor activation does slow the firing rate of some 50% of the nerve cells in the lateral amygdala.

fMRI Studies of Pain Responses

Some meditators (the "reducers") can tolerate the pain, suffering, and stress responses associated with prolonged sitting. Others (the "augmenters") cannot [Z:354–355]. Neuroimaging studies can clarify the ways that people respond differently. One hopes they will be applied to meditators along the lines discussed next.

In a recent fMRI study, seventeen normal men and women experienced a hot stimulus (as high as 49°C) delivered to the skin of their right lower leg. During a previous session they had been trained to use a visual analog scale. This enabled them to rate both the intensity and duration of their pain. Based on these preliminary subjective reports, the researchers divided their volunteers into two subgroups: most pain sensitive and least sensitive.[18]

The painfully hot stimulus activated the thalamus in both subgroups to about the same degree. But which part of the brain did the most sensitive individuals activate? They activated their cerebral *cortex* frequently, and to more robust degrees. For example, they increased their fMRI signals both in the anterior cingulate cortex, in the somatosensory cortex on the side opposite the painful leg, and in discrete regions of the prefrontal cortex near the frontal *pole* on the right side.

This study illustrates a crucial point. Yes, pain is always very difficult to evaluate. *But researchers can train their subjects, long before neuroimaging experiments begin, to provide accurate introspective first-person ratings of their experience.* Accurate first-person reports from well-trained observers provide the essential foundation for interpreting neuroimaging data.

Future Studies of Opioid Blockers in Alternate States of Consciousness

A single case report has been cited in evidence. This one meditator could increase his alpha wave frequency from 9.4 to 10.4 cps by repeatedly focusing his attention "on his breathing, and sight (eyes half closed) on the tip of his nose."[19]

Naloxone is a drug well known to block mu receptors. However, EEG techniques per se do not suffice to localize the site(s) where these opioid receptors are being blocked. Still, naloxone and two other drugs were tested because the authors hypothesized that the drugs would *reduce* this meditator's alpha activity. (In fact, the reverse occurred: naloxone tended to increase the magnitude of his alpha activity, though that result was not statistically significant.) The original report provides no subjective description of what this meditator was actually experiencing. Nor does it substantiate the notion that whatever shallow state he had dropped into was that distinctive state of deep internal absorption of the particular kind previously described (see chapter 74) [Z:469–518].

Two key questions remain untested. First, can an opioid blocker like naloxone reproducibly inhibit the special quality of that subjective *bliss* which occurs *late* in internal absorption? It is *this* singular affective experience that could be consistent with the release of opioids. No trial of naloxone, during a period of *ordinary* meditation, suffices as a relevant test for this particular question, as Horgan points out elsewhere.[20]

However, carefully controlled tests using specific opioid blockers are clearly indicated in the future. Because the second question is: Can opioid receptor blocking per se reverse any of the mechanisms underlying respiratory *suppression*? These major interruptions of breathing do recur frequently, even during the more ordinary, superficial levels of meditative absorption (see chapter 20) [Z:96–99]. (And they are of obvious interest, because morphine's distinctive suppression of respiration has long been known.) These recurrent moments of ordinary respiratory suppression are much more amenable to study than are the rare single episodes of deep internal absorption. The many cell bodies of and fibers of enkephalin nerve cells in the human brainstem suggest that it will be difficult to be certain where opioids might act.[21]

Comments with Regard to Future Measurements of Opioids in Biological Samples

Inside cells, beta-endorphin coexists with ACTH. (Both arise from one larger protein precursor molecule.) As a result, these two peptide molecules are released *together* from cells of the pituitary gland into our bloodstream. Both beta-endorphin and ACTH promptly rise to much higher blood levels in the morning, say around 9:00 A.M., than in the evening, around 8:00 P.M. During those evening hours, normal inhibitory mechanisms within the hypothalamus are thought to check the release of both peptides from the pituitary gland just beneath it. However, transcendental meditation meditators do *not* drop their blood levels of beta-endorphin and ACTH during the *evening*.[22] Why no drop?

GABA inhibitory mechanisms within the hypothalamus are the usual explanation for our normal lower levels in the evening. GABA provides the requisite "negative feedback" inhibition. So then, how could prior meditation *reduce* GABA's normal, and usual, inhibitory influence in the hypothalamus? The answers to this question are important, because surges occur at many steps along the meditative path. We need to know why, and how, the hypothalamus can become disinhibited and its responses become more labile [Z:189–196, 235–238, 318]. We also need to determine which other reductions in GABA inhibitory tone in different regions set the stage for later, unchecked surges of brain activity [Z:457–460]. To tease out the responsible mechanisms, detailed longitudinal studies of neuroendocrine responses will be required.

In such future studies, the *ventricular* fluid levels of beta-endorphin, ACTH, and of their releasing hormone (CRF) might be more informative than the levels of these peptides found in the fluid obtained from other sites farther downstream. (For example, such as in the more distant subarachnoid cisterns at the base of the brain.) Why? Because events that occur inside the medial hypothalamus might be more directly reflected in samples of nearby fluid obtained from its adjacent third ventricle. In contrast, beta-endorphin and ACTH levels found in the bloodstream, or obtained from subarachnoid cisterns closer to the pituitary, are more likely to have arisen from within the pituitary gland, and to be several more steps removed from their primary mechanisms, at sites upstream in the hypothalamus.[23]

Terminal Issues

In human research, delicate ethical and complex technical issues enter in, especially as life draws to a close. Some of these issues are illustrated in one study of dogs who died abruptly. When they were sacrificed, beta-endorphin levels were actually measured not only in tissue samples from their hypothalamus but also in samples of their cisternal fluid.[24]

The dogs' sudden cardiac arrest was induced by intravenous potassium chloride. The dogs in one group were awake at the very moment cardiac arrest occurred; the dogs in the second group had already been in deep anesthetic coma for the previous 15 minutes. The question was: would being awake *while dying* result in more of a stress response?

When dogs were still awake at the instant their heart stopped, their average beta-endorphin levels did rise (above the levels in their anesthetized controls) both in the hypothalamus and in the fluid samples taken from the major subarachnoid cistern at the base of the brain. However, it was only a twofold increase. This is a relatively minor opioid response, less than what one might anticipate could occur during many acute terminal conditions in human beings.[25]

In conclusion, thus far, the results with opioids have been intriguing, and detailed studies are clearly indicated.

37

Metabolic Cascades That Transform the Next Nerve Cell's Firing Responses

> Half of what you are taught as medical students will in ten years have been shown to be wrong . . . none of your teachers knows which half.
>
> C. Sidney Burwell (1893–1967)

> Calcium-signaling pathways in neurons can regulate transcription.
>
> Anne West and colleagues[1]

I was surprised to hear Dean Burwell say this. However, much information did change during the next decade. Our problem remained: some teachers identified which half was wrong, but other teachers knew differently. Few minds greet change with enthusiasm. The only person who really welcomes change, it's been said, is the baby with a wet diaper. Yet all things do change. Our bodies, too, change every day. But it is our nervous system that changes most dramatically from moment to moment, and Zen is only one of its agencies of transformation.

"Plasticity" is the term used loosely to describe the brain's vast capacities for change. Calcium ions are the signal for many early steps in this whole process. Calcium doesn't simply make our bones dense. In the nervous system, it plays dynamic roles.

Greenberg discovered one of calcium's important roles in change. He was exciting a nerve cell by stimulating its acetylcholine receptors. Afterward, he found that *the cell had changed the way it transcribed its DNA into messenger RNA*. It turned out that *in this very process of being stimulated, the neuron was changing its own excitability*. This and other lines of research showed that nerve cells, unlike light bulbs, had the special capacity to enhance their own "wattage." Indeed, in one sense, if you just turned on their "light" for a while, the light became even "brighter" [Z:223–225].

Imagine that one of your own ACH nerve cells is now in the act of firing. (Imagination can do just that.) This cell releases ACH at its distant terminals. This ACH is a "primary" messenger. It is also a *fast* neurotransmitter. Instantly these ACH molecules leap across the synaptic gap to activate their specific ACH receptors on the outside of your next cell. This event triggers the influx of calcium ions into this second nerve cell. Now excited, the second cell then fires off nerve impulses of its own.

However, those fresh calcium ions inside your second cell have not finished. Their signals now act as second messengers, setting off a long series of calcium-dependent steps. These trigger a delayed metabolic sequence of slower biochemical reactions that keep evolving after the next minutes, hours, or days. Paul Greengard was a co-winner of the Nobel Prize for Physiology or Medicine in 2000 for his studies on this cascade of effects. Many of these steps involve attaching phosphate groups to, or removing them from, crucial third messenger proteins.

Next, some of these messengers will even penetrate deeply inside the nerve cell's nucleus. From here on, an even later series of reactions can influence the transfer of genetic information. This proceeds both from DNA to RNA (transcription), and from messenger RNA into its next array of other protein molecules (translation). What do all these steps accomplish? Having reshaped the membrane structure of your second nerve cell, they have changed its excitability.

Neurochemists today are fortunate. Where would they be with no Arabic numerals, with no alphabet of Roman and Greek letters? They would be very hard-pressed indeed to name all the new receptors and other molecules that keep turning up almost weekly in such third messenger cascades. Most new factors seem poised to help our adult nerve cells *enhance* their "wattage," not to reduce it. Yet, a few are also essential, because they help hippocampal CA1 cells escape from certain memory functions they're better off without[2] (see chapter 29) [Z:182–184].

Avenues of Change: Two Model Examples at the Cellular Level

As adults, we know there are some old adaptive behaviors we would like to hold on to, and some new ones we would like to cultivate. On the other hand, it would certainly be an advantage to drop some primal fears that are at the core of our most unfruitful conditionings. Can a few calcium ions really initiate transformations in our behavior?

Calcium is pivotal in two recently discovered avenues of potential change. Note that each of the following calcium-sponsored processes can occur either quickly or slowly. The result can transform consciousness either acutely during brief states, or it can generate subtle long-term effects that can change behavioral *traits* incrementally.

One model of metabolic cascade starts as soon as a nerve cell releases its standard cast of messengers. When this ACH, glutamate, or biogenic amine activates its receptor on the next neuron, this event signals that second cell's calcium systems. They now start to generate a novel, versatile protein. It is called CREB.[3]

Current research indicates that certain CREB functions are relevant to many of the ways Zen training transforms consciousness. Let us sample a mere five of these many vital functions. CREB pathways can:

- influence the vital transcription functions that produce more neurotrophin and nitric oxide;
- target a separate factor that regulates the circadian sleep/waking cycle;
- enhance the effect of kinase IV, a different protein which sponsors certain of the fear memory functions linked to the amygdala[4];
- help to activate motivational drive in the nucleus accumbens[5];
- participate in other long-lasting forms of synaptic plasticity linked to learning and memory.[6]

The second model cascade employs a transcription factor called DREAM (*d*ownstream *r*esponse *e*lement *a*ntagonist *m*odulator).[7] It senses calcium levels inside the cell directly. DREAM then acts normally to *repress* certain transcription processes. If these were not reduced, dynorphin would reach excessively high levels. Thus, the more DREAM, the less of this opioid. In chapter 35, we noted that dynorphin not only helps reduce pain messages down in the spinal cord, it also influences limbic system functions at several higher levels.

Gene Products at Work

Inheritable gene products became the earliest building blocks of our nervous system. Gene products then went on to shape—and reshape—the nervous system's most vital functions. Less publicized research has uncovered "hidden" genes, working through "active RNA" species. These *non*-protein-coding RNAs help regulate separate ("epigenetic") layers of new information, molecules that seem to operate "underground," outside the conventional DNA sequence.[8]

Could such polygenic/RNA mixtures also help explain why different people report so many different "varieties of religious experience?" Surely, some original reasons for such variety start with those overt DNA and covert RNA differences which rendered each of us individually unique at conception. But soon each brain's awesome capacities for plasticity began to transform the way it responded to each next life experience.

Does a person's future have the potential to be brighter than the past? Meditative training provides one kind of setting in which affirmative experiences can reshape our responses in more adaptive ways. How? *Certain pivotal experiences—acting through metabolic cascades—could revise the ways our nerve cells transcribe our own DNA.*

So each of us is still a work in progress. Every present moment. Every day we have endless opportunities to transform our own stream of consciousness and modify our behavior. The kinds of novel metabolic sequences just now being discovered were unimaginable during that distant era in which Siddhartha lived and became the Buddha. Even now, at the beginning of this new millennium, the stunning implications of such research remain mind-boggling.

But other mechanisms have been known for many decades. They change the ways nerve cells grow.

38

Neurotrophins and Change

> In addition to their classic effects on neuronal cell survival, neurotrophins can also regulate axonal and dendritic growth and guidance, synaptic structure and connections, neuro-transmitter release, long-term potentiation (LTP) and synaptic plasticity.
>
> Moses Chao[1]

Zen training can transform a person. Transformation involves major changes. In the field of neurobiology, we have seen how "plasticity" refers to the way our nervous system changes. What changes during Zen "practice?" What happens when we keep returning to an affirmative thought, a better idea, a more appropriate behavior? If repetition does "strengthen" the functional links that integrate our networks, then how does this really take place at the level of individual neurons? Do cells that fire together *wire* together?

In 1986, Rita Levi-Montalcini and Stanley Cohen shared the Nobel Prize for Physiology or Medicine for their work on nerve growth factor. Research since then has shown that the neurotrophin family of protein molecules engages in a surprising number of interactions with many receptors and ion channels. For example, neurotrophins influence the function of serotonergic systems, and the construction of both new and long-enduring synaptic connections. A key enzyme serves as the target of the neurotrophic cascade in the brain. This signaling receptor is tyrosine kinase B.[2]

The basic operation seems straightforward: when a nerve cell fires actively it starts releasing more neurotrophins. Thereafter, neurotrophins play vital roles in enhancing the so-called synaptic strength that underlies long-term potentiation in the hippocampus. Precisely how this process relates to memory functions remains to be worked out. Chapter 41 describes how neurotrophins enter into the "plasticity" of the parietal cortex.

Recently, human subjects were studied whose neurotrophic factor had been rendered slightly dysfunctional. (This was caused by a genetic error involving only a single amino acid substitution.) They had a poor memory for recent or immediate episodic events.[3] It is noteworthy that rats reduce the expression of the neurotrophic factor in their hippocampus as part of their stress responses to unpleasant episodes of experimental restraint.[4]

During the early clinical trials, some patients noted unusually acute pain as a side effect when they were injected with neurotrophin. One potential mechanism for such pain has recently been discovered. It turns out that neurotrophins can enhance pain by activating those high-affinity tyrosine kinase B receptors just discussed. This process goes on to sensitize the responses of postsynaptic cells in the pain pathway to noxious stimulation by capsaicin or by noxious heat.[5]

Parenthetically, metenkephalin is unique among opioids. It acts as a *negative* growth factor. When its signals penetrate the nucleus of cells, they suppress the subsequent replicative activity of its DNA.[6] This unexpected negative effect of metenkephalin might serve to offset some of the positive trophic effects of neurotrophin and reverse some of its pain-producing side effects.

39

The Pineal and Melatonin

> ... there is a small gland in the brain called the pineal in which the soul exercises its function more particularly than in any other part.
>
> René Descartes (1596–1650)[1]

In the seventeenth century, it was plausible to suggest that the pineal gland was the "seat of the soul." Why? Look where it sat: right in the midline, just below the back end of the corpus callosum. From this central location, the pineal was flanked on either side by a bulging thalamus, and could look down on the superior colliculus.

Still, it seemed rather small to account for a soul—a mere 8 mm or so long. The fact that its glandular structure shrunk after puberty also contributed to its being viewed as a kind of vestigial structure, corresponding to the rudimentary third eye of some lower vertebrates.

Had Descartes known about melatonin, he might have been surprised. Indeed, its unusual hormonal properties have surprised many contemporary neurobiologists. First characterized by Aaron Lerner in 1958, melatonin has since been shown to be an important hormone that activates specific receptors both in brain and body.

After it was found that melatonin was made from serotonin, it was then discovered that the first step in this conversion involved a particular transferase enzyme. This enzyme was induced by norepinephrine (via cyclic AMP). Moreover, a different enzyme was involved in the second step. Its activity was markedly *reduced* by the amount of ambient light.

How is this relevant to current meditation research? These two steps in melatonin synthesis inform us that meditation's stress-relieving effects might reduce melatonin levels by reducing the release of norepinephrine. On the other hand, melatonin levels could increase if you closed your eyes during meditation and reduced the amount of light.

Eyes-Open vs. Eyes-Closed Meditation

Some patients are predisposed to develop a depression during the darker months of the year (a condition called seasonal affective disorder, or SAD). Sustained, closed-lid meditative practices can make such depressions worse, by reducing the amount of light energies that normally stimulate the brain.

The recommended Zen approach is to keep the eyes partially *open* during meditation. This traditional Zen approach, with the eyes hooded, has several beneficial roles [Z:table 19, 582]. Included among the benefits of open-eyed meditation:

- It can reduce or delay the hallucinations and other phenomena associated with inturned absorption.
- It helps extend awareness, delays drowsiness, and defers episodes of sleep.
- It allows more room in which to train various meditative skills.
- The meditator maintains contact with the outside visual world.

Meditation has well-known hormonal effects that can reduce the levels of ACTH and cortisone in the blood. Recently, it has been observed that a 1-hour period of meditation—at night—causes an acute *increase* in the release of melatonin from the pineal into the bloodstream.[2]

The ten experienced meditators in the study (10+ years of practice) followed the transcendental meditation (TM) tradition. (They had usually retired around 10:45 P.M., on average). During this study period, they meditated from midnight to 1 A.M. with their eyes closed. On the control night, they merely sat quietly between midnight and 1:00 A.M. with their eyes open. Subsequent interviews indicated that these meditators had not fallen asleep while meditating.

The subjects varied substantially, both in their original plasma levels of melatonin, and in how much these melatonin levels responded to eyes-closed meditation. However, all but one showed a significant acute rise in melatonin during the first hour *after* their nighttime meditation ended, in contrast to the values in controls. A second group of Yoga practitioners, who meditated for *only* one half of an hour starting at midnight, showed a lesser response.

A recent study of adult male meditators (n = 27; average age 46 years) reported that 1 hour of meditation *reduced* their plasma melatonin level slightly, from 4.9 pg to 3.4 pg. Three consecutive hours of meditation reduced the level even further. Controls who merely rested did not show such reductions.[3] Reduced norepinephrine tone is one plausible explanation.

It remains to be determined, in a suitably controlled study, how plasma melatonin levels will change during open-eyed Zen meditation and other styles of meditation performed at the customary specified times, and for the usual durations, during a 24-hour day.

Meanwhile, to know how to interpret such results, it helps to ask what the steps are through which meditation could affect the way the pineal releases melatonin.

The Normal Influence of Light

Once light strikes the retina, its signals pursue an indirect route to shift our light/dark, sleep/activity cycle. First, light signals stimulate the suprachiasmatic nucleus (SCN) back in the hypothalamus. Impulses from there relay far down into the upper thoracic cord. From there, they next *ascend* through peripheral sympathetic nerve fibers. Their nerve endings finally release norepinephrine onto the pineal cells, signaling them to turn on their synthesis of melatonin. Glutamate receptors also activate these same SCN neurons, helping them generate a cascade of light-responsive circadian rhythms.

Once melatonin is released, its signals modulate other basic sleep systems in the brain, both directly and indirectly. Melatonin's influence becomes especially clear in the sleep disturbances of patients who are totally blind. As the result of their retinal or optic nerve damage, their SCN does not receive its normal cyclic light and dark cues. However, when these blind patients receive only 5 mg of melatonin orally, 1 hour before bedtime, it sets off a major pharmacological response: they sleep much longer and more efficiently.[4] Stage II sleep accounts for most of their increase in sleep time. Rapid eye movement (REM) sleep also shows a slight tendency to increase.

When normal subjects receive pharmacological doses of melatonin, it can help reset their sleep/waking cycles. Travelers who take relatively small amounts can help "reset their biological clock." (I have observed that even 1 or 2 mg of melatonin usually promotes my falling asleep after flying to an East Coast time zone where clock time is 3 hours advanced.)

Meditation and the Delayed Promotion of Sleep

For over a decade, I have been consistently aware of another effect of meditation: its *delayed* sleep-promoting effects following one session of weekly formal, eyes-open meditation in the zendo (from 7:00 to 7:25 P.M., and from 7:30 to 7:55 P.M., with kinhin intervening). Later that night, after retiring at the usual time (10:00–10:30 P.M.), I sleep more soundly and awaken at the usual hour (6:30 A.M.) with a greater sense of mental clarity than on any of the other 6 days of the week.

It remains for future research to clarify to what degree the dim zendo light acting on the SCN contributes to these phenomena, and also to what degree additional mechanisms hinge on norepinephrine, on melatonin, and on the other intricate neuroendocrine influences on CRF, ACTH, and cortisone that are mediated via the hypothalamic-pituitary-adrenal axis.

As described in chapter 19, TM meditators who meditated twice a day on a *regular* basis appeared to change the way this hypothalamic-pituitary-adrenal axis released certain hormones.[5] These TM practitioners did *not* show the usual diurnal rhythm for ACTH and beta endorphin. Regular meditation seemed to be enhancing their hypothalamic sensitivity to cortisol. Possibly an enhanced GABA activity in the hypothalamus was causing an unusual suppression of the meditators' normal, expected morning *rise* in beta-endorphin and ACTH.

Blood Levels of Melatonin

Normally, our *daytime* melatonin levels are very low. In a milliliter of blood they often average less than 10 pg. A picogram is something on the order of a gnat's sneeze: one *trillionth* of a gram. The phrase serves simply to point out that melatonin acts as a *hormone*. Like other hormones, its biological activity depends on its activating exquisitely sensitive receptor systems.

Melatonin levels peak in early childhood, decline around puberty, then continue to decline substantially during each passing decade. Melatonin is a nighttime hormone. Normal adult levels don't start to rise until around 7:00 to 8:00 P.M. They peak—at levels five to ten times higher—around 3:00 A.M. By 7:00 A.M., melatonin has fallen to very low levels.

Melatonin Receptors Have Immunological Roles

When melatonin leaks out of the pineal gland and seeps into our bloodstream, it not only promotes sleep and tends to lower body temperature, it also influences our immune system. Sensitive melatonin-1 receptors cover the outer membranes of various cells, and some melatonin receptors act inside the cell's nucleus. Their messenger RNA correlates are found both in thymus and in spleen.

In contrast, the messenger RNA for melatonin-2 receptors is detected only in thymus.[6] One of the pivotal thymus (T) cells in this gland is called the T helper cell. These T cells help coordinate a large number of mechanisms in our immune response. They do so by releasing a variety of other signaling molecules called *cytokines*. Cytokines are glycoprotein hormones. They include the various interleukins, interferons, and so on. When melatonin promotes a good night's sleep it also confers immunological benefits.

Other Actions of Melatonin

In the brain, melatonin acts upon its receptors to provide both circadian and seasonal timing cues. Melatonin-1 receptors *inhibit* the inherently rhythmic firing rate of the SCN. In contrast, when melatonin-2 receptors are activated, they shift the phase of the circadian rhythm that is generated within this nucleus.[7] Therefore, melatonin itself is not a hypnotic agent that acts the same way as, say, the barbiturates do. Instead, it acts selectively. It can advance the time of sleep onset, because it *shifts the phase* of the daily (circadian) pacemaker.

Melatonin is a lipid-soluble molecule. Its potent actions as an antioxidant have drawn increasing attention to the potential *pharmacological* roles that higher doses might have in reducing the harmful effect of free radicals in the brain.

Implications for Future Melatonin Research

It remains for the future to establish the degree to which some immunological responses linked to mindfulness meditation (see chapter 19) are part of a cascade of reactions during which melatonin plays a significant role. Plasma melatonin levels will be only one part of this research. A practical clinical matter will be the degree to which the subjects close their eyes while meditating. Given the glutamate, norepinephrine, and GABA influences discussed above, future investigators would benefit from the active participation of specialists in their team to explore all the implications of melatonin. Consultants in psychoneuroendocrinology and sleep research could be essential in conducting meditation research at this level of complexity.

40

Cortical Anatomy by the Numbers

> There are, indeed, few textbooks of neurology, neurophysiology or neuroanatomy in which Brodmann is not cited, and his concepts pervade most research publications on systematic neurobiology.
>
> L. Garey[1]

Korbinian Brodmann (1868–1918) was an unusual neurologist. He became intrigued by the fact that different subdivisions of the cortex showed remarkable microscopic differences. To record all these cytoarchitectural differences, he devised a system which identified them by numbers.

The 1909 German edition of his book pictures Brodmann on its frontispiece: a goateed, prematurely balding man in a high white collar. But it's what those glinting eyes of his viewed under the microscope, and systematized, that we remember to this day.

Figure 7 presents a modern version of Brodmann's famous "maps."[2] Nowadays, the numbers are frequently referred to, in neuroimaging articles in particular. This explains why these pages often cite the now-common abbreviation, BA, for Brodmann area.

When you see BA in the chapters that follow, you may find it useful occasionally to return to figure 7 and also to compare its numbers with earlier gross anatomical landmarks for the lateral and medial aspects of the cerebral hemispheres (cf. figures 3 and 4, chapter 23).

In the course of these comparisons, one begins to appreciate what this map accomplished a century ago. Brodmann was no phrenologist. He had not casually numbered bumps on the skull. Using his microscope, he had systematically mapped the multiple unique ways nerve cells were arranged in different sites all over the convoluted cortex.

Note: The BA numbers do not define those CA3 and CA1 layers we referred to in the hippocampus. Nor do they directly apply to the direction that impulses flow in the visual system. By convention, these visual sequences have been numbered as V1, V2, V3, V4, and so on. Yet when Brodmann designated the primary visual cortex as area 17, the next visual association areas did become numbered areas 18 and 19, in sequence.

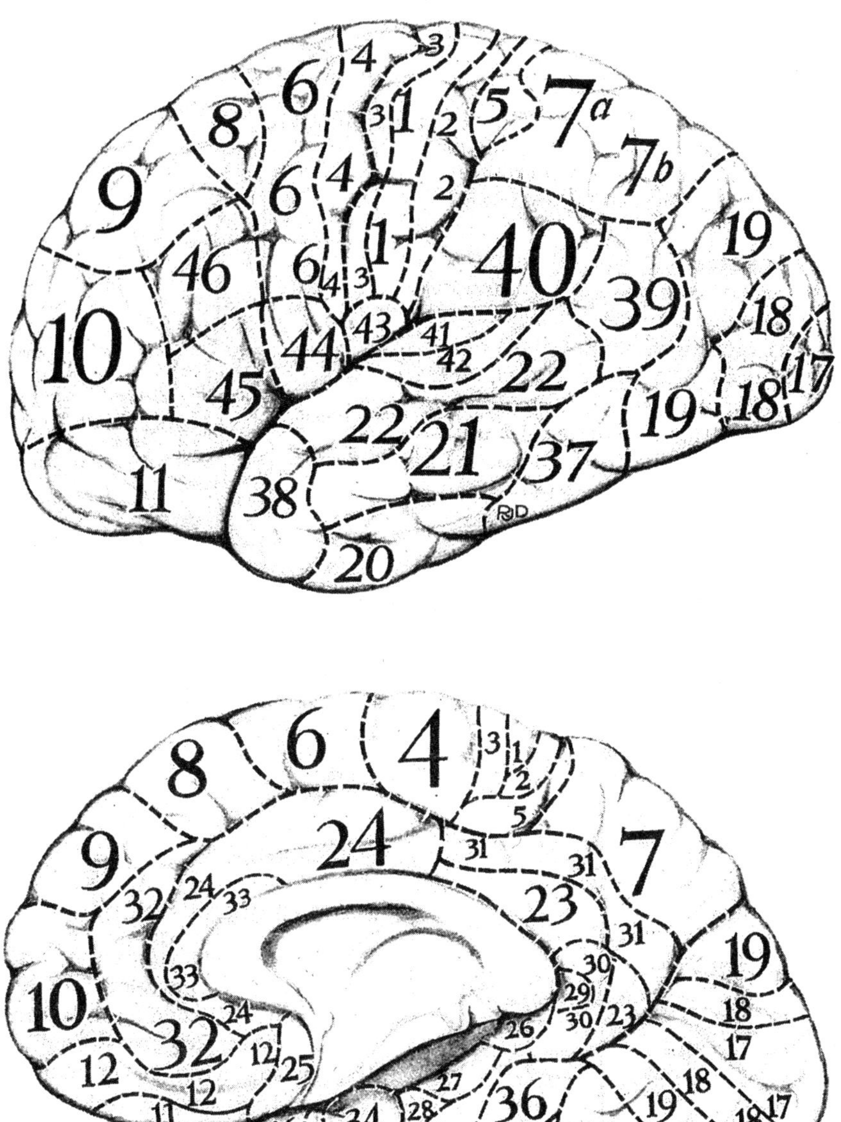

Figure 7 Brodmann's mapping by the numbers
These numbers refer to different regions of the *cerebral cortex*. *Sub*cortical regions such as the amygdala, and the thalamus and basal ganglia are not represented. (*Above*) The lateral surface of the cerebral cortex. (*Below*) The medial surface.

What distinctive functions does any numbered area serve? How does it interact with many others? Researchers will be puzzling for many more centuries over what *Homo sapiens* really "does" in each area.

It may help to recall that, for millions of years in the past—just in order to survive—the primitive counterparts of such numbers needed urgently to decode events in the outside world, asking: Where is it? What is it? Is it living or inanimate? Is it moving? What should I do about it?

In the next chapters we consider how the current human brain has evolved and continues to refine these questions.

41

Where Is It? A Prelude to My Action. The Parietal Lobe

> Every great advance in science has issued from a new audacity of imagination.
>
> John Dewey (1859–1952)

> We investigated whether and how neurotrophins are involved in neurite arborization and synaptic formation, or synaptic plasticity, or both.
>
> H. Ishibashi and colleagues[1]

The whole parietal lobe helps us to understand Zen. In chapter 8, we began pointing toward one source in the superior parietal lobule (BA 7) for the higher representations of our physical self (see figure 3, chapter 23). Other parietal lobe contributions to the self are reviewed in chapters 50, 51, and 52. Chapter 47 and part IX consider further the parietal lobe's active role in paying attention to the world of space outside ourselves.

Here, we invite the reader to imagine a parietal association cortex that enters into a dynamic, integrated, sensorimotor alliance. In order for us to locate an apple out there in the outside world, let's think of the brain as starting to ask the usual Where is it?–type questions [Z:244–247]. But now think of it as also asking Where is my hand?–type questions, for these are a necessary next step to actually grasping that apple.

3-D Representations of Our Own Physical Self-Image in Outside Space

Apple and hand start to come together, in a sense, in the parietal lobe. Anatomists split its posterior association cortex into two divisions: superior and inferior (see figure 3, chapter 23). The boundary line is the intraparietal sulcus. Yet we meld their physiological functions so seamlessly and unconsciously that we take them for granted. But suppose an acute stroke or a discrete penetrating brain injury is confined just to that uppermost region, also known as the superior parietal lobule (BA 7).

Let us first inquire: What functions do patients lose when their upper lobule is damaged only on the *right* side? They are no longer aware (a) of the left side of their own body, and (b) of items outside them in left extrapersonal space. Moreover, neurological examination reveals that these patients also lose other three-dimensional skills: (c) they can't tell where and how their own left body parts are articulated; (d) when they must rely on memory alone, they can't locate, reimage, and reconstruct familiar external objects that had once been located out in the left half of their external space.

Detailed neuropsychological tests were recently reported on a rare patient. Her slowly progressive focal damage was limited, on MRI scan, to both posterior superior parietal lobules.[2] Because both her right and left lobules were involved, she could reconstruct no accurate representation in three dimensions of *any* item off on either side of the visual or auditory space outside her body.

Bedside examination also disclosed a marked loss of proprioception. She could not position her own body in space. Nor could she tell where either arm or leg was. The authors concluded that she had suffered a primary loss of her egocentric "spatial representation system." She had lost her normal, private topographical "master map." This "map" had once informed her precisely where her body's physical parts were articulated. (It had been created long ago beginning with the raw sensory data that had been relayed up through her thalamus.)

The Inferior Parietal Lobule (Chiefly BA 39 and 40)

The brain elaborates upon at least two major additional categories of associations. These are represented among the diverse connections of its supramarginal and angular gyri. Each contributes to the ways we relate our inside self to the outside world.

1. *Symbolic functions*. Among the more obvious are not only our familiar, left-lateralized language-related skills, but also the topographical skills used to read Braille, and to navigate with visual reference to a map. We have no sense of expending much conscious effort while engaged in resolving many other similar polymodal and supramodal tasks. Our skills seem to proceed automatically. However, if these intricate functions are to remain effective during complex tasks, we must also keep them "on line" for many seconds. In such situations, the inferior lobule now takes on a crucial role.
2. *Attentive functions*. "Attention" is a shorthand word often used to summarize this second key category. The ways attention focuses on events in the present

moment is so central a topic in meditative practices that it is discussed in four chapters (13, 15, 47, and 75).

Neurochemical Correlates of the Embodied Self-Image in Action

As our brain develops new skills, how does it "strengthen" its synaptic contacts? (see chapter 38). Recent primate research focuses on nerve cells in the *intraparietal* cortex. Some cells here are versatile, *multimodal* neurons. They respond not only to visuospatial stimuli from the outside world but also to somatosensory messages that represent parts of the monkey's own body.[3]

Certain of these multimodal cells have been found to respond in intriguing ways. If we imagine that these findings can be extended to humans, it could help explain how we establish some kind of body image that serves as a sensory framework for our subsequent apple-grasping sensorimotor actions. But can nerve cells really insert vague notions corresponding to a self-image into the way a person *acts*? After all, "internal representations," and "body image" are mere words. Can the processes that these words substitute for leap across the next synapses, and become actualized in adaptive behaviors out there in *extra*personal space? And could they tentatively *personalize* this external space, as it were?

A quarter of a century ago, one could envision a naive model of how a chimpanzee might be monitored, both neurophysiologically and neurochemically, while it was engaged in an act of creative problem-solving.[4] In this new century, creative researchers do start with a hungry monkey, a long-handled rake, and they place a distant apple slice beyond the monkey's grasp. Gradually, only through trial and error, the monkey starts to use the rake to retrieve the apple slice. When you observe this process, you see the rake slowly becoming an "extension" of its hand.

Simultaneously, certain parietal nerve cells also develop a temporary "elongation" of their receptive fields. It seems almost as though these enlarging parietal sensory fields are enabling the monkey to make its "hand image" actionable. This postulated "working image" extends itself out toward the handle, and then toward the tines at the far end of the rake. In the whole process, one observes our primate relative developing and merging several functions reminiscent of imagination, intuition, and actualization.

Using special video monitor techniques, Japanese researchers have trained monkeys to redirect similar learning processes back onto themselves. The video findings suggest that monkeys (not only chimpanzees) slowly develop new "mental" constructs. These help them not only to establish a sense of their own unique physical self-image but also to go on to recognize their individual selves on the video screen.[5]

The self/other interface is critical in Zen. These two kinds of newly learned behaviors suggest that our primate relatives are transforming the ways their "body image" functions first participate at a simple self/other interface and then learn to reach out across it in their imagination. If so, what happens at the cellular level? What kinds of dynamic neural changes transform that old boundary, so that newer "inside" somatosensory representations can now mesh with "outside" visuospatial messages in creative ways?

Neurochemical Correlates

Starting with this same rake-apple model, Japanese investigators superimposed an ingenious neurochemical approach. At different times during the rake-learning process, they sampled the levels of key molecules in and around the *hand* area of the parietal cortex.[6]

They focused on the kinds of *neurotrophic* factors discussed in chapter 38. Why? Because these neurotrophin molecules have the capacity to promote the development of newly formed, transsynaptic functions, even during a learning period as short as 12 days. (The authors' assay system used ultrasensitive methods, similar to those used in forensic and medical DNA technology: reverse transcriptase and polymerase chain reactions.)

Indeed, the monkeys did increase their local expression of neurotrophin. When? Only while they were in the actual process of *learning how* to use a rake. These increases took place on the steep *ascending* limb of the monkeys' tool-learning curve, not during their later (more habitual) use of the tool. Rising levels of messenger RNA signaled that the monkey's own neurotrophic factor was undergoing its learning-associated increase.

The neurotrophin increases were sharply localized. Where? A key crossroads was at the anterior bank of the *left* intraparietal sulcus. This is the precise spot where, based on other physiological evidence, one expects that right-handed monkeys would be learning to integrate their visuospatial and somatosensory data in an effort to extend their reach by grasping the handle of a rake.

PET studies show that similar creative tool-using behaviors will also involve several other obvious regions, including the prefrontal cortex.[7]

These recent studies employed a relatively simple experimental design. Food served to motivate the monkeys. Their daily training exercises were monotonously repetitive. Do these and similar experiments bear any remote resemblance to Buddhist training approaches? Are they even vaguely related to such repetitive, daily-life practices as "loving kindness," or to visualization, or to any other aspects of persistent, mindful, long-term meditative training? Clearly, the transformations of behavior that occur on the Path are much deeper, more complex in nature, and are likely to evolve only on a very much longer time scale.

Preliminary reports using structural MRI suggest that long-term meditators in the mindfulness tradition have a thicker right prefrontal cortex than their controls.[8]

Meanwhile, these studies in monkeys illustrate the kinds of recent multidisciplinary research that may help clarify how we, too—by "strengthening" certain synapses—learn to reach out creatively in new directions. Further extensions and confirmations of these and other preliminary studies of neurotrophins will also be of interest because they have potential therapeutic implications for enhancing the way nerve cells function in human diseases.[9]

In the interim, with regard to Zen, this primate research is intriguing for one other reason. The monkeys are extending their physical selves out into their external environment. In part VII, we will be searching for some neural correlates of particular experiences called "Unity" or "Oneness." In such rare, extraordinary states of consciousness, self and other become experienced as "One" in a *variety of ways*. Could some categories of states represent a blending of various multimodal functions, such that they efface the old boundary between self and other in the process of their merging? If so, then one wonders: How do certain intraparietal cells, and other networks of multimodal cells that represent less obvious aspects of "self," enter into—or become excluded from—the total configuration?

42

What Is It? The Temporal Lobe Pathway

> Listen not to me, but to the nature of the Universe when it says: All is One.
>
> Heraclitus (540–c.480 B.C.E.)

> The truly free mind reaches a state in which opposites are seen as empty. This is the only freedom.
>
> Master Pai-chang Huai-hai (720–814)

Dynamic Temporal Lobe Interpretations

Our primary auditory cortex (BA 41) does occupy a small part of the temporal lobe.[1] But the large temporal lobe contributes much more to various mental states than simple listening and hearing [Z:247–253]. For example, along its top edge runs the plump superior temporal gyrus (including BA 22, 42). (See figure 3 in chapter 23, and figure 7 in chapter 40.) A long narrow valley serves as this gyrus's lower, limiting boundary. This superior temporal sulcus extends all the way back up into the inferior parietal lobule.

Both edges of this sulcal valley contribute intriguing functions. Toward its far end, along the *right* side, temporal nerve cells are coded to reconcile two aspects of visual movement in the outside world. One represents the path being pursued by the animated parts of any other live moving figure. The second becomes the "background" that serves to embrace the actions intended by this "figure" in its visual foreground.[2]

In chapter 8, we began to ponder the dual nature of such figure/ground interpretations. We might be reminded that visual motion *is* relative, just as Einstein's dictum points out. Take, for example, that strange realization that can happen when we are riding in a train. Glancing out the window at the adjacent track, we see the pale face of another passenger in another train looking across at us. It is a person, on a parallel track, who *does not seem* to be moving. Suddenly, we notice that the clouds and the surrounding landscape are moving backward. It is now clear: each of us, on our two separate train tracks, happen to be moving forward at just the same speed at the same time.

For that one special moment, we both seemed to inhabit the "same" parallel universe. Then, as our speeds diverged, the illusion collapsed (see chapter 77, figure 11).

So part of our own sense of *continuous* movement hinges on how much that visual environment outside us in the background seems to move *relative to us, as observers*. The temporal lobe helps us realize and reconcile these *self*-moving* vs. other-moving decisions.

Our Quest for Meaning: The Temporal Lobe as an Interpreter

When these and all other raw sensory percepts enter the brain, we must decode them in order to know *what they mean*. Only then do they make sense to us. The temporal lobe engages in very sophisticated *con*sensual interpretations when it integrates these multiple sensory modalities.

Consider one elementary decision: is this a new event, or did it happen before? We translate *déjà vu* to mean "yes, once before." But *jamais vu* translates as "no, never" [Z:247–253]. How do we separate the familiar from the unfamiliar? Only by consulting closely with other regions inside and outside the temporal lobes (see chapter 83). The following examples illustrate how—in the temporal lobe itself—five different regions can enter into such *comparative* interpretations. Note that the interpretations involve clear-cut either/or distinctions.

Kensho's interpretations are dramatically new, so let's begin with novelty decisions. When we respond to simpler novelty cues out in the environment, recent fMRI studies point to the *medial* temporal lobe (the hippocampus and

*Parenthetically, our vestibular cortex (farther forward in the posterior insula) and our head direction system inform us (at more subliminal levels) how our own head is moving acutely, and also where our head is positioned with reference to the Earth's *gravity*[3] (see chapters 28 and 29).

parahippocampus) as providing a basic memory context for the frontal lobe. But when we need more complex levels of meaningful (*semantic*) decoding, then it's the *lateral* temporal convexity that enters into frontotemporal processing.[4] Now both the superior (BA 22) and the middle (BA 21) temporal gyrus share in our efforts to bring *meaningful* interpretations *to words and objects*.

It is important to emphasize the vital contributions to *meaning* of the posterior temporal cortex. This becomes clear when we listen to jokes.[5] During the *semantic* portion of this auditory decoding, fMRI signals appear chiefly in the *posterior* parts of the middle (BA 21) and inferior temporal gyrus (BA 37).

Recent fMRI studies indicate that our early steps in the visual processing of external objects invariably activate the fusiform gyrus (BA 37) back at the temporo-occipital junction.[6] In contrast, signals increase in the anterior perirhinal cortex (BA 28/34) when visual patterns are more ambiguous and require fine-grained discrimination.[7]

Just by observing the expression of another person's *eyes*, how do we decode what that person has in mind? Evoked potentials have monitored such decisions, using a dense array of 128 channels. The resulting N270–400 waveforms suggest that the *right* superior frontal and anterior temporal regions help subserve this kind of intuitive processing.[8]

Unusual Symptoms in Patients Who Have Temporal Lobe Seizures

During states of insight-wisdom, two general categories of phenomena might seem referable to the temporal lobes: phenomena of addition (+), and phenomena of subtraction (−) [Z:605–615]. On rare occasions, certain neurological patients, during their focal temporal lobe seizures, can have additional "positive" symptoms of pleasure [Z:349, 405–407]. Some of these pleasurable symptoms during seizures are reminiscent of other feelings that may also occur in association with certain authentic "religious" experiences (a careful history should distinguish kensho-satori from a seizure episode) [Z:542–544].

It is noteworthy that three of the seizure patients cited briefly by Williams in 1956 reported feelings of pleasure in association with abnormal EEG discharges referable more to the *posterior* temporal regions.[9] One of his patients described an exhilaratingly pleasant feeling. It was accompanied by the sense that "I must get to the bottom of it," together with a hallucination and with depersonalization. Another patient developed a compulsion to look off to the left side, accompanied by a mood of pleasure and a feeling that space seemed to open up. A third patient reported the sudden feeling of being lifted up, of emotional elation, plus the feeling, "I am just about to find out knowledge no one else shares—something to do with the line between life and death."

When such very rare patients are studied in detail in the future, it will be of interest to test whether radiolabeled opioid receptors are, in fact, unusually increased—and whether benzodiazepine-GABA receptors are indeed decreased—in close relation to the focal site of origin and to the sites of spread of such a "pleasurable" seizure discharge.

Meanwhile, while we are still searching for the specific sites of origins of meaningful resonances, the circuits that involve certain of these more *posterior* parts of the temporal lobe would seem to be among the provisional candidates. Few other candidate circuits would seem to qualify so well, considering that they have also been associated with the phenomena of depersonalization, an "opening up" of space, and with the life-and-death issues of existence.[10] It is a remarkable finding that the left posterior temporal cortex continually increases in density until the age of 30 years, in contrast to the earlier declines noted in cortex elsewhere, as studied by MRI.[11]

An abstract summarizes preliminary data from patients who remained preoccupied with religious matters in between their occasional episodes of temporal lobe seizures. The abstract suggests that the patients responded more to religious words and icons—as indexed by their skin conductance responses—than did two control groups composed of "very religious" and of normal nonreligious subjects.[12]

Subjects who had previously undergone a genuine near-death experience tend to show more frequent left temporal lobe epileptiform EEG activity.[13] Whether such subjects would have had these tendencies before, or only after, their experiences requries further detailed study.

The Varieties of "Presence"

The particular "presence" associated with authentic teachers is an *ongoing* quality. Their followers recognize it readily (and distinguish it from lesser forms of mere charisma) (see chapter 22). The 1979 Hardy survey of religious experiences was based on subjects who grew up in our contemporary Western culture. 20% of them reported having experienced a different variety of presence. These were brief *episodes* that included a sense of "presence" (described as though something nonhuman in nature were present).[14] A brief sense of presence has also been reported by some 40% of subjects whose brains were being stimulated by weak artificial electromagnetic pulses. The issue of suggestibility has been raised considering that "15% of a control group" were said also to "sense a presence.")[15]

Most readers, and myself, have grown up in a pervasive Western monotheistic context. Suppose you or I were briefly to sense a presence during some kind of *spontaneous*, awesome, alternate-state experience. One obvious option would be to attribute the rest of that experience to some *divine presence*, to God. Several aspects of this epiphenomenon of presence now become germane to the temporal lobe issues under discussion. The scientific issues have cultural overtones, and have invited debates likely to continue.

- One issue has been overlooked. Presence serves subtly as a metric of *distance*. A spatial judgment is implicit when we sense that "something" important is "near" to (or "far" from) our central *witnessing awareness*.

  Early steps in such a normal global auditory 3D system take shape in the roof of the midbrain (Z:241–242). From the colliculi here, messages then relay up through the medial geniculate nuclei in the thalamus. Recent magnetoencephalography (MEG) research shows how we go on to localize sounds in 3D space at the cortical level. We channel the data from our two ears into the discriminative cortex of our *right* upper temporal region. This is where we "hear" distance.[16] Survival value is inherent in a 3D system that triangulates a threatening sound and *localizes* it as either nearby or far distant.

  But evolution refined our circuits. No longer does the whole system serve just a primitive early-warning function. Now it can mediate positive resonances that arise in more intimate social circumstances of "nearness." (As, for instance, when a loved one is not just present, but has snuggled close and is whispering softly in your ear.)

- A second issue: How are we to interpret the reports when brief episodes of presence arise naturally in a meditative/spiritual context? In this instance, presence often might represent a cluster of lesser phenomena, describable under the general category of "quickening" (see part V) [Z:371–465]. When such a sense of presence is infused with a positive affect, it might represent an *over*expression of phenomena vaguely similar to what has just been referred to above: something toward the normal, more intimate, "nearness" end of that *range* of abilities we use to localize events in *peripersonal* 3D space. Normally we seem to represent such a general sense of spatial "nearness" in or near the association cortex at our temporoparietal junction.

  As one working hypothesis, it would seem relatively easy for a person to develop a sense of presence when this region shares in the spread of an especially heightened sense of attention (see chapter 47). Other impressions might also reflect unusual constellations of spatial representations within this general network of associations. For example, sometimes a normal person may sense that the whole environment is drawing nearer. At other times, a person might sense that the physical "self" is tending to "fade" into the environment.

  However, a vague, spatial sense of presence is only one superficial issue. It is another matter to account for phenomena during which the self and the environment envelop each other and convey the impression of unification. (This discussion continues in chapters 78 and 79.)

- A third issue: What role, if any, does presence play in reports of Buddhist experience? Zen Buddhist icons do not resemble the kind of God figure, reaching out to touch Adam, that Michelangelo painted in the Sistine Chapel. Nor does authentic Zen pay attention to minor quickenings. Zen tends toward relatively quiet periods of no-thought meditation. Zen teachings do not focus intensively on theistic concepts or visual imagery.
- A fourth issue: Some persons refer to a variety of unusual experiences, often accompanied by a sense of presence, under the term "God experiences."[17] In our Judeo-Christian culture, many so-called God experiences are said to occur in "religious personalities." These persons are said to be characterized by egocentrism, chronic anxiety, and suggestibility. This interpretation of egocentrism would emphasize that it means the greater degree of "relative reliance placed on one's personal experience as a proof of reality."[18]

Although the Zen Buddhist experiences of kensho and satori are authoritative, they arrive on a foundation of selfless emptiness. They remain to be run through the gauntlet—at yet another layer of reality testing—by the roshi's rigorous criteria for proof. Moreover, in the orthodox Zen context, these brief states of enlightenment still tend to be regarded as nothing special. Such a hard-nosed, skeptical perspective tends to negate every pretense that a residual *I-Me-Mine* might attach its "own" supposed proof of reality.

- A fifth issue: Can earlier reports from the Persinger laboratory be confirmed that when weak, complex transcranial magnetic fields are directed toward the temporal lobes they induce "sensed presence" and other mystical experiences? No confirmation comes from investigators in Sweden.[19] They report that they had used the same or similar kinds of weak stimulation. Their carefully controlled double-blind study was based on 46 undergraduate theological students and 43 undergraduate psychology students. They assessed the psychological profile of these subjects using both a "temporal lobe inventory," an absorption scale, a "New Age Orientation Scale," and two other scales describing various relevant perceptual and emotional symptoms that are linked to mystical experiences.

  When the sham-fields were applied, their subjects "were just as likely to have marked sense presence experiences as those in the magnetic field condition." Whether their 89 subjects were religious or nonreligious, "personality characteristics indicative of suggestibility consistently predicted the mystical and somatosensory experiences."

43

What Should I Do about It? The Frontal Lobes

> Lateral, orbitofrontal, and medial prefrontal cortices are robustly interconnected, suggesting that they participate in concert in central executive functions.
>
> Helen Barbas[1]

When the symphony calls for deep throbbing resonances, the orchestra conductor points his baton at the kettle drummer. When it's time for high melodious notes, he points to the violins. Our frontal lobes perform similar executive functions. Knowing the score, they, too, rely on many other regions to start, and to stop, at precisely the right times [Z:253–259].

Functional Anatomy

In this higher executive and associative role, the prefrontal cortex leads a consortium. We depend on it to resolve practical matters "intelligently," and to socialize our instinctual drives. It has to "think" subconsciously, because many What should I do about it? questions demand instant go/no go answers. Yet it also must "think" slowly, and find time to reflect.

As the last century closed, it might have sufficed to divide the prefrontal cortex into three major parts. Now, to these we usually add a fourth. Please refer to figures 3 and 4 (in chapter 23) and figure 7 (in chapter 40).

- The *dorsolateral* convex portion (BA 46, 8, 9, 10, and 11)
- The *orbital* cortex, the slightly concave part which overlies the orbit (BA 13, 47, and the lower parts of BA 10 and 11)
- The *medial* cortex, that flat inner portion which faces the medial surface of the opposite frontal lobe (BA 12 and 32, plus the medial parts of BA 8, 9, 10, and 11)[2]
- The *anterior polar* cortex, on the front tip (BA 10 chiefly)

Recent research in patients and normal subjects has presented us with an embarrassment of functional anatomical riches. We are getting a better general understanding of how awesome is the reach of that baton when it acts in concert with the rest of the brain, of what might be involved when the conductor composes his own music, and even of how it feels when he imagines putting himself in the drummer's shoes.

The Dorsolateral Prefrontal Cortex

To summarize: this dorsolateral cortex helps select, manipulate, and monitor the kinds of incoming information that will shape the way we act, speak, write, and reason.[3] This is a tall order. Its more anterior extensions contribute increasingly to various processes and subgoals aided by reasoning. Its more ventral portions help update and maintain online a few items of information at any one time.

It's the novel and surprising ingredients in a task that activate this dorsolateral region the most.[4] After discrete damage to this region, patients can't pay the appropriate amount of visual attention to such novel events. The amplitude of one of their event-related potentials (ERP) is also markedly reduced. In normal persons, this "novelty P3 response" provides an index of how long they keep looking at a new stimulus. This particular response taps a wide "novelty network." It links the intentional and attentional resources of our dorsolateral cortex with the anterior cingulate gyrus and parahippocampus.[5]

Discrete dorsolateral lesions may also cause other symptoms: pronounced defects in working memory, in planning, in shifting attention, and impaired performance on a gambling task.[6] However, the lesions tend *not* to change either the patient's own subjective emotional state, social behavior, or the ability to identify the expression of emotion in another person's face or voice.[7]

Damage to the *right* inferior frontal gyrus causes problems in inhibiting task-related mental sets. *Left* middle frontal gyrus damage interferes with the patient's exercising top-down control of the task-switching process.[8]

While normal subjects are encoding semantic information, their fMRI signals increase both in the anterior and inferior prefrontal cortex as well as in their medial temporal lobes.[9] If more fMRI signals are generated while a novel stimulus is first being encoded, then this event is more likely to be remembered longer.

The Orbitofrontal Cortex

This lowest region is believed to participate actively in that larger orchestration which assigns to incoming messages their particular positive or negative "grade" on the emotional/motivational/survival scale of values. What correlates with a *reduction* in orbitofrontal functions in normal subjects? Highly trained monks have been monitored by fMRI while they were in a meditative state described as "open presence." Once they enter this state, outside events no longer distract them, nor do internally generated thoughts or emotions. Reduced signals have been observed in the orbitofrontal region in the six monks reported thus far.[10]

During a gaming task, patients who had prior surgical excisions of the orbitofrontal cortex on *both* sides could not monitor changes in the reward value of stimuli. Nor could they use this information to adjust their game behavior appropriately.[11]

After normal subjects were deprived of food and became hungry, they activated their superior temporal, anterior insular, and orbitofrontal cortex. PET scans showed that it was the increased activity in their *right* orbitofrontal cortex that correlated best with how hungry they felt and how urgently they felt they needed food.[12]

PET scans were also performed in other normal subjects while they ate chocolate—to, *and beyond*, a feeling of satiety.[13] Pleasant, positive associations with eating chocolate activated the *medial* and caudal orbitofrontal cortex. Unpleasant, negative associations with eating too much chocolate activated the more *lateral* and caudal parts.

Normal subjects were also studied by fMRI during a gaming task. It offered a positive monetary reward for a correct choice and a monetary punishment for an incorrect choice. Again, increased signals in the more *lateral* and caudal parts were linked with the possibility of punishing feedback. However, adjacent regions also participated when responses shifted in accord with the reward value of stimuli.[14] Current evidence suggests that unpleasant situations often register in the more lateral regions. However, this region might also help to provide resources for some coping strategies (see chapter 36).

The Medial Prefrontal Cortex

Research reveals this whole medial region to be crowded with intriguing functions. Among them: representing affectively tagged internal information that can be accessed by introspection; helping to regulate autonomic responses; contributing to a "default" state that represents a kind of real metabolic "baseline"; and processing actual monetary rewards.[15]

High-resolution fMRI studies monitored subjects while they engaged in a task of language comprehension.[16] Increased signals in the medial cortex suggested that it contributes to that overall coherent grasp we employ to draw successive sentences together into a logical form.

However, as Barbas's epigraph suggests, some networking functions of this medial region could extend into those of its several nearby neighbors (see figure 7, chapter 40). They include the anterior cingulate gyrus (behind), the orbitofrontal region (beneath and toward the outside), and the polar cap of the frontal lobe (in front). For example, many "theory of mind" tasks involve attributing mental states to other persons. Several reports suggest that these kinds of mental projections activate not only the more dorsomedial regions (e.g., BA 9) but also other regions more ventrally which are in or near the domain of the anterior cingulate gyrus.[17]

Normal subjects have been given other tasks which involve their monitoring their *own* internal mental state. Again, some overlap occurs between the activities of these medial frontal regions and the lowest (subgenual) parts of the anterior cingulate gyrus. Still, when normal subjects perform a sequence of expected tasks that are in accord with their own internal plans, fMRI signals do increase in their medial anterior prefrontal cortex (BA 32 and 10). And at such times they also increase in the ventral striatum.[18]

The medial frontal region enters into several other vital networking functions relevant to Zen. This discussion continues in the final section of this chapter and later in chapters 50 and 52.

The Anterior Frontal Polar Cortex

In general, we engage this frontal pole (BA 10) when we retrieve internally generated information from memory and manipulate it in more highly complex evaluative processes akin to "reasoning."[19] The lateral parts of BA 10 seem more involved when a person evaluates his or her own memories of having shared in particular events in the past. The medial parts seem to participate in the more general aspects of knowledge. They include the resources that subjects draw upon when they try to resolve test problems that pose emotionally charged moral and monetary dilemmas.[20]

In PET studies, normal subjects activate the medial and lateral aspects of this polar cortex when they engage in tasks of "prospective memory." These are planning tasks. *After an initial delay,* the subjects later carry out preplanned acts of intention. These tasks activate not only the more *lateral* polar areas but also their thalamic partner, the medial dorsal thalamus. Simultaneously, activity *decreases* in the more superior and medial frontal polar areas.[21] This mixed pattern suggests that the more lateral cortex (including the medial dorsal thalamus) may normally help to develop and *maintain* our internally generated planning scenarios. Perhaps also, the more medial polar cortex might normally play some kind of opposing role, one that could *suppress* such plans (a useful function but which therefore may need sometimes to be overcome).

Meditators know how hard it is to keep attention focused on a single topic. Awareness must be nudged back repeatedly—time after time—to their mainstream of mindful attention, both during a single meditation period and also during daily life practice. The study by Hunter and colleagues becomes of interest in this regard. They analyzed the time relationships involved in voluntary behavior. The findings suggest that increased fMRI signals in the polar cortex of BA 10 are associated with one particular facet of volition: a *self*-initiated, freshly remembered "intention" to act.[22]

Other fMRI studies show that signals also increase in the polar (and more lateral) prefrontal cortex (BA 10/46) when normal subjects use their hands in sequential tasks that are contingent on the arrival of unpredictable events.[23]

The "Self" as Represented in the Frontal Lobe: A Condensed Historical Sketch

It's been known for well over a century that damage to the front of the brain could change one's personality. The unfortunate case of Phineas Gage, transfixed by a tamping bar, dramatized this for generations of medical students after it was first reported in 1868. In 1934, Karl Kleist published his observations on almost 300 soldiers injured during World War I and on 106 other patients.[24] By then, it seemed possible to attribute something called the "self and social ego" to the medial and lateral orbitofrontal region of BA 11. Moreover, "Actions according to the personality" were then referable to BA 47. This region lay just beyond on the lower part of the lateral convexity.

In the past decade, several circuits (often showing a right-sided predominance) began to be linked with our more overt forms of private, "*self*-knowing" awareness. In contrast, other networks, more on the left side, were thought to contribute to different, more abstract kinds of knowing.[25]

As the 20th century closed, a reader could also find that a short list of the kinds of processing represented in the frontal lobes[26] would include such self-related normal categories as

- willed intentional actions;
- working memory in collaboration with one's own body image;
- events in autobiographical memory;
- social inferences based on "reading" another person's mind (theory of mind);
- "world modeling."

Even so, the hard neurosciences often tended to overlook the "softer" relationships between self and brain, as they neared an interface with religion. In 2003, it might still escape general notice[27] that key aspects of the phenomenology of enlightenment could be correlated with processes that change frontal lobe functions [Z:593–624], and that major dissolutions of the self could play an essential role in spiritual transformations.

Evidence reviewed in this chapter and discussed in chapters 50–54 also suggests that our frontotemporal networks play active roles in many functions of our omniself which have long been relevant to spiritual disciplines, both East and West.

Self-Directing the Brain toward Relaxation and Arousal

Meditators decide to meditate. After passing through an initial stage of calming, they often move toward stages broadly categorized as either receptive or concentrative meditation (see chapter 13). Recent fMRI studies have monitored the ways the brain "directs itself" as it participates in somewhat similar intentionally organized stages. However, in these studies, biofeedback techniques were used to induce either one of two goals: a state of relaxation or more intensified levels of arousal.[28]

Increased fMRI signals occurred in the ventromedial and orbitofrontal cortex. As intended, tonic skin conductance *levels* did change during various attempts at each of these types of intentional tasks. However, fMRI signals also increased in the left *mid*-orbitofrontal and right parietooccipital junction during the *successful* performance of either task. Thus, these signals increased whether the subjects had achieved their correct (intended) *decrease* in skin conductance levels while trying to relax or had achieved their correct (intended) *increase* in levels while trying to generate arousal. The results suggested an intriguing soft function for the left *mid*-orbitofrontal region: perhaps it contributes to a very subtle internal, *self*-generated reward, one that lends a subliminal positive sense (akin to satisfaction) when a task is successfully completed.

Frontal EEG Asymmetries: A Review of How They Relate to Our Temperament, Attitudes, and Behavior

Positive emotions can have constructive outcomes. Negative emotions can prove destructive. Each plays crucial roles in our lives. Among the frontal lobe's many interconnections, strong links occur with the amygdala on that same side. Are these amygdala ↔ frontal circuits the chief reason why certain personality types show more, or less, one-sided frontal activation during their EEG and neuroimaging studies?

Fox and colleagues did find that infants who show a *right* frontal EEG preponderance were more likely to be distressed by unfamiliar stimuli.[29] Moreover, those older children who had this same right frontal activation asymmetry were the ones more likely to withdraw, to be reticent in social situations with other children, and to develop "internalizing" types of behavior problems.

However, right frontal activations do not always correlate with a more "negative" affective response. Indeed, one particular subgroup of children that show this same right frontal EEG activation tend to be highly sociable, *not* withdrawn. Moreover, these children are also more likely to act out with "externalizing" behavior than are their other equally social cohorts whose EEGs fall into the "left frontal" activation category.

Table 4
Relationships between Frontal EEG Activities and Tendencies toward Different Patterns of Behavior

Behavioral Systems Expressing Greater Degrees of Activation	*Behavioral Systems Expressing Greater Degrees of Inhibition*
Strong correlations with relatively greater *left* frontal EEG activity	Weaker correlations with relatively greater *right* frontal EEG activity
Stronger correlations with motivational propensities to approach, to respond more intensely to *positive affective stimuli*, and to exhibit more positive affect as a *general* trait	More complex correlations with tendencies to withdraw, to arrest ongoing behavior, to exhibit increased arousal responses in association with anxiety, depending on the *specific* situation
Higher self-report scores for behavioral activation do tend to correlate with relatively less *right* frontal activity	Higher self-report scores for behavioral inhibitions do not necessarily correlate with relatively more *right* frontal EEG activity

Note: Condensed from the review by J. Coan and J. Allen. Frontal EEG asymmetry and the behavioral activation and inhibition systems. *Psychophysiology* 2003; 40:106–114. The tendencies toward "behavioral activations and inhibitions" have each been assessed on the basis of self-reports on questionnaires. "Greater frontal EEG activity" in one frontal region implies that alpha power is *lower* on that side than on the other side.

Several other hypotheses propose different explanations for the frontal EEG asymmetries. One interpretation suggests that the left frontal preponderance of activation in infants and children is associated not with the amygdala, but with greater *competencies* in verbal mediation skills and analytic abilities. These also lateralize more to the left frontal regions of our brain.[30]

On balance, the data suggest a multifactoral interpretation. During most social situations, each person's temperament or disposition reflects a *constellation of interacting modules*. These do not operate in only one single "amygdala-frontal" mode, or do they arise on only one side of the brain.

These various lines of EEG, psychological, and behavioral evidence are condensed in table 4.[31] The columns on the left describe left frontal EEG correlations. Those on the right summarize right frontal EEG correlations.

The table illustrates that our left frontal functions have two major associations. One is with our motoric tendencies to *approach*. The other is with a trend toward more "positive" emotional responses and attitudes. Right frontal functions are associated with different behavioral patterns. They lean in more "negative" directions. They also tend to vary in complex ways depending on the situation.

Recent fMRI studies support most of these earlier EEG-derived lateralized trends. Normal subjects tend to lateralize their *positive* (happy) emotional resonances more to the *left*. When they recall happy memories, fMRI signals increase in their *left* hippocampus, and in the *left* dorsolateral prefrontal region. Signals increase on both sides (right > left) in the *medial* orbitofrontal and adjacent anterior cingulate regions. In contrast, retrieving sad memories increases fMRI signals in both *lateral* orbitofrontal regions and in the adjacent ventrolateral prefrontal cortex.[32]

Verbal Humor and the Frontal Lobe

In societies worldwide, jokes are common currency. Jokes are like Zen in several respects. Jokes are to be *realized,* not explained at length. Then there's a joke's so-called punch line. Like kensho, it often hinges on surprise. Novelty triggers the collapse of old barriers. Gone are those rigid boundaries that had previously divided categories [Z:413–418].

Simple one-liners or two-liners appeal to children and grownups alike. Note how they shift our usual mental set:

> Why do hummingbirds hum? Because they can't remember the words.
>
> *　　*　　*
>
> A guy standing on one bank yells across the river, saying "Hey, how do you get to the other side of this river?" The guy on the other side yells back, "You *are* on the other side!"

In order to "get," and appreciate, a joke, it helps to be in an appropriate social setting, one in which a lighthearted element of playfulness prevails. (Perhaps this accounts for the tendency for pals to tell so many jokes in a bar.)

The more novelty that enters into the processing of words and meanings, the greater the increase of fMRI signals in the inferior prefrontal cortex and medial temporal lobe.[33]

In all languages, words often have double meanings. This makes it easier for puns to be thought of as the simplest and "lowest" form of humor. Even in French, which has its own specific term, *double-entendre,* the word *entendre* itself has several meanings, including to hear, to understand, and to mean.

Those who groan in response to a pun now have their opinions confirmed. fMRI studies show that puns are "inferior," at least in the sense of localization. Puns activate the left posterior inferior temporal gyrus (BA 37) and the left inferior frontal gyrus (BA 44 and 45).[34] In contrast, when semantic types of jokes are contrasted with mostly phonological jokes, jokes that decode *meaning* increase signals chiefly in the posterior parts of the temporal lobe, as noted in the previous chapter (e.g., in the right middle temporal gyrus [BA 21/37] and in the left inferior temporal gyrus [BA 20/37]).

Really funny jokes activate a secondary phase of pleasurable emotion. This is an interval of amused appreciation. It preferentially involves the ventral part of the medial prefrontal cortex (BA 10/11).

Derks reported the way his own brain waves responded while he listened to segments of radio comedy routines.[35] Within the first 120 ms a series of changes involved both hemispheres. Subsequent studies on 20 normals confirmed that the essential ingredient in humor was the recognition and evaluation of incongruity. This incongruity had to attain a certain salience to be effective. Its effectiveness also depended on the listener's underlying mental set and mood. Kensho also presents an incongruity so stark between the old view of the world and its novel view that can prompt laughter.

Visual Humor

A recent fMRI study monitored the responses of normal subjects to visual cartoons and to their verbal captions.[36] Signals peaked a mere 3 seconds after the cartoons appeared. The funnier cartoons increased signals in both *cortical and subcortical networks*. As expected, signals increased in the frontotemporal cortical network. Increases in the subcortical network occurred in the ventral striatum, nucleus accumbens, anterior thalamus, ventral tegmental area, hypothalamus, and amygdala. This subcortical cluster corresponds to the mesolimbic dopamine system. It serves as an index of the degree of both the emotional response, and of its potential knee-slapping behavioral counterpart.

What Else Does the Frontal Lobe Have to Do with Zen?

Zen involves decoding existential meanings. Sometimes the triggering stimuli are "turning words" (see chapters 21 and 72). Frontotemporal lobe connections are reciprocal and also cross over from one hemisphere to the other. It seems plausible that some triggering activations (which may have begun in or near the temporal lobe regions cited in the previous chapter) could develop further when a Zen trainee first decodes similar alternative and improbable word meanings, then shifts into deeply meaningful comprehensions during more global, integrative forms of coherence.[37]

With respect to zazen, we may be using some medial and orbitofrontal lobe regions to help nudge our early modes of relaxation and more intensified levels of concentration along the continuum from bare awareness to arousal and focused attention. The frontopolar cortex may help forgetful meditators return, time after time, to being more mindfully aware.

During this author's "taste of kensho," a sequence of phenomena unfolded (see chapter 93). In general, these appear to represent different processes of excitation, inhibition, and disinhibition in *selective* regions of the brain [Z:591, 604–606].

In broad brush strokes, the selective contributions from frontal lobe circuits and their allied connections would seem to provide a working hypothesis for the following seven phenomena of this state of kensho.

- The loss of the central *psychic* axis of self, and its self-referent notions of inhabiting a physical body
- The loss of personal planning for future scenarios
- The deep loss of all immediate impulses to engage in possessive, approach behavior
- The loss of the time relationships that had once served to link "logical" sequences in meaningful ways
- The loss of certain conditioned fear responses referred earlier via the amygdala
- The loss of other fixed categorical distinctions as soon as the prior boundaries dissolved which had once separated them
- A gain in the pleasurable, affirmative tone, possibly related to some degrees of left frontal preponderance

The frontal lobe could not be so changed—in an instant—unless its partnerships with the thalamus had also changed.

44

The Thalamus

> The thalamus has been referred to as the "Grand Central Station" of the brain, because virtually all incoming information relays through it en route to the cortex.
>
> K. Taber and colleagues[1]

All information except smell, that is. During that bad head cold when you lost your sense of smell, all higher conscious perception then hinged on messages that could first pass through potential obstructions in the thalamus on their way up to the cortex.

Normally, our thalamic gate opens widest when we're awake. Even then, messages get through only under certain conditions. These *vary*. Which messages get a free pass through this gate? *It depends on what else is going on that shapes our state of consciousness* [Z:263–274].

Recent research has clarified large gaps in our knowledge about how the thalamus functions (figure 8).

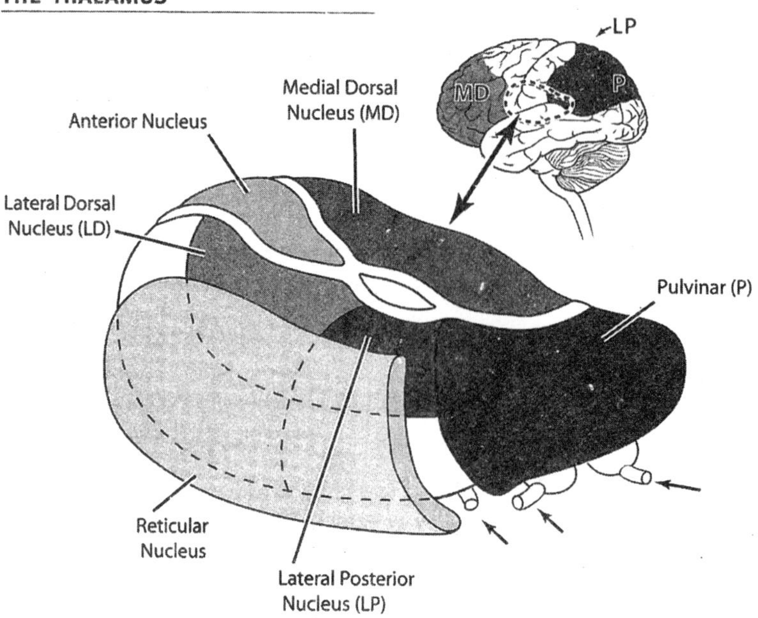

Figure 8 The thalamus

At the top right, that small version of the left cerebral hemisphere shows the general, deep central location of the thalamus by its ovoid of dashed lines. *MD* represents the major projection area of the *medial dorsal* thalamic nucleus over the prefrontal cortex. Farther back, the parieto-occipital association cortex is also covered by the major projection from the pulvinar nucleus of the thalamus (*P*). The small superior parietal lobule receives a lesser projection from the lateral posterior nucleus (*LP*).

Below is the much expanded view of the left thalamus looking down at it from behind. Three small arrows suggest the way most of our sensate information enters its sensory nuclei. The two arrows at the right represent the path the auditory messages take to the *medial geniculate nucleus*, and the path the visual messages take when they enter the *lateral geniculate nucleus* from the optic tract. Somatosensory and autonomic afferent messages from the head and body enter their respective ventral posterior and ventral median nuclei. The long, thin, curved cap is the *reticular nucleus*. It is shown artificially detached from all the other thalamic nuclei. However, its GABA nerve cells can inhibit all of them. Dotted lines suggest their borders. Not shown are the small intralaminar nuclei inside the thalamus or the parafascicular nucleus. The latter relays some pain messages up via the old medial spinothalamic pain system.

Recent Developments in the Anatomy of the Thalamus

A promising new technique called diffusion tensor imaging can now localize as many as fourteen thalamic nuclei in the living human brain.[2] Two important connections linking the thalamus with the temporal lobe have now been described. One path comes from the medial dorsal nucleus. The other arrives from the pulvinar in its medial and inferior regions.[3]

What makes this new pathway from the pulvinar *to* the temporal lobe so important? Because the temporal lobe was once regarded as "athalamic." That meant it would have no effective thalamic connection (aside from the obvious auditory relay it received from the medial geniculate nucleus). If this earlier view had not been corrected, one might have concluded that neither front nor back of the thalamus could influence the temporal cortex.

This recent evidence indicates that the medial and inferior pulvinar project to two important sites: the medial temporo-occipital and superior temporal regions.[4] Studies in monkeys show that pulvinar connections also include two crucial parts of the temporal lobe: its undersurface and its anterior regions.[5]

Biogenic Amines and the Thalamus

The thalamus has one of the brain's highest densities of norepinephrine alpha-1 receptors. This is in keeping with norepinephrine's relatively important modulatory role. Norepinephrine levels are higher than serotonin levels in the pulvinar-lateral posterior complex of primates.[6] In contrast, the thalamus receives "virtually no dopaminergic input."[7]

How Acetylcholine Projections from the Brainstem Influence the Thalamus and Cortex

Acetylcholine (ACH) plays a much more active, pivotal role in thalamic and thalamocortical functions. One vitally important cluster of ACH nerve cells lies in the parabrachial area of the dorsal pons (see figure 4, chapter 23) [Z:164–169]. When they discharge, and release ACH, this fast transmitter sets off a resonating sequence of biphasic responses. The results can influence thalamocortical functions for many seconds thereafter.[8] Consider four examples that have implications for kensho:

1. Nicotinic ACH receptors mediate the earliest excitation of thalamic nerve cells. Almost instantaneous, this firing is short-lasting.
2. The next sequence begins 1 second later. It is mediated by muscarinic ACH receptors and lasts for some 15 to 20 seconds. A prolonged depolarization of thalamic cells can last for up to 4 minutes, and the cortex can become activated all during this period.

Thalamocortical neurons tend to fire in *single spikes* during this period. This discharge pattern brings a sense of clarity to perception. In addition, cells in the anterior thalamic nuclei are now poised to fire more readily when stimulated.[9] Networks that include this anterior nucleus enter into the processes that consolidate memories. These observations provide one explanation for why some phases of alternate states of consciousness might register as both clear and memorable.

The firing rates of ACH cells can vary down in the pontine nuclei. However, even single-pulse trains here, at only 30 cps, produce up in the thalamus a "fivefold increase in synaptic responsiveness." This "develops slowly and reaches a peak after forty to sixty seconds."

Other mechanisms contribute to the prolonged increase in the excitability of the cortex which develops during this period. They include glutamate stimulation of the cortex *by* the thalamus; glutamate stimulation of the thalamus by glutamate nerve cells down in the brainstem; and ACH stimulation of the cortex by the other ACH nuclei in the basal forebrain.

3. GABA nerve cells of the reticular nucleus of the thalamus also have nicotinic receptors that excite them to fire. Their discharges set in motion a variety of potent inhibitory responses.
4. However, next there occurs a long-lasting ACH inhibition of this same reticular nucleus. This develops at muscarinic (M_2) receptors. This ACH effect is a *dis*inhibitory one. It releases thalamic nerve cells from GABA inhibition and further enhances the cholinergic activation of thalamocortical neurons.

Implications for Kensho

The four sequences and time relationships sketched above provide a working hypothesis for some events during kensho. Why are they not readily testable? Because they *could strike in a flash, unfold in less than a minute, and go on to have prolonged reverberations thereafter in second messenger (metabotropic) systems* (see chapter 37).

Nitric oxide can inhibit the oscillatory discharges of thalamic nerve cells, but the multiple other effects of nitric oxide could work synergistically within the sequences outlined above (see chapter 68). Nitric oxide release and glutamate release are closely related. The enzyme that synthesizes nitric oxide coexists in those same ACH nerve cells which project from the parabrachial area up into the thalamus.

Two Histochemical Categories of Thalamic Nerve Cells

In the past, one might cite the properties of the small intralaminar nuclei of the thalamus to account for many widespread, nonspecific discharges which synchronized the firings of nerve cells in both the thalamus and cortex. Recent immunologically based techniques suggest additional explanations. Under the microscope, these methods detect the presence of two different proteins in the primate brain. Each binds calcium ions.

One protein, *calbindin,* defines that category of thalamic nerve cells which project widely and diffusely to all areas of the cortex. These cells are the calbindin+ nerve cells of the thalamic *matrix*. All thalamic nuclei have them, especially the medial dorsal, lateral dorsal, pulvinar, lateral posterior, and intralaminar nuclei. Their global connections could help us integrate multiple resonances of sensate experience into a more unified frame of reference in one large field of consciousness.

In contrast, the larger *parvalbumin* nerve cells project up to a single cortical field in a localized area. These are the so-called *core* cells. They reside in the reticular nucleus, pulvinar, lateral posterior, and intralaminar nuclei. They project to the *middle* cortical layers, not to the superficial cortical layers.[10] Their input is also more selective. Normally, their activities would seem to best serve not only our more restricted needs for sensory perception but also our needs for multimodal sensory associative functions over the back of the brain.

These two patterns of circuits differ both in the thalamus and where they end in the cortex. Their networks help one envision a preliminary physiological basis for two of our normal properties of consciousness: (1) its discrete perceptual and cognitive phenomena; (2) its more coherent phenomena that are global in nature. Both sets of functions are the kinds that also express themselves, and overlap, during kensho.

The Limbic Thalamus

The term *limbic thalamus* includes three major thalamic nuclei that have close ties with the limbic system: the medial dorsal, lateral dorsal, and anterior nuclei.[11]

- The medial dorsal nucleus. Its major reciprocal connections are with all regions of the frontal lobe, as figure 8 suggests. Its large cells show its priorities. They are destined both for the orbitofrontal cortex *and* the anterior cingulate region. Its smaller cells interact with the dorsal lateral part of the prefrontal cortex.

  A glance at the major sources of input to this medial dorsal nucleus confirms why it plays such an important role in processing limbic functions. It is supplied by the anterior temporal cortex, amygdala, and entorhinal cortex.
- The lateral dorsal nucleus. It has major reciprocal connections with one medial part of the posterior parietal cortex. This part extends beyond into the neighboring posterior cingulate region (see figure 7, chapter 40). It is interconnected with the

subiculum portions of the hippocampal complex, and has additional links with the entorhinal complex (see chapter 29). These facts suggest that the lateral dorsal nucleus is in touch not just with hippocampal formation and parahippocampal gyrus circuits that contribute to memory but that it may be involved in attention and emotion in ways that researchers are now trying to define.

- The anterior thalamic nucleus. It has major reciprocal connections with the anterior and posterior cingulate cortex, and the subiculum of the hippocampal complex. Other interesting reciprocal connections are with the orbitofrontal cortex. Its major input from the limbic system comes via the fast pathway leading up from the mammillary complex of the hypothalamus.[12]

  Note: The reticular nucleus of the thalamus is poised to shape the responses of each of these three thalamic association nuclei. Together with its other GABA allies, it can exert a powerful influence on the way limbic functions relay up to the cortex (see chapter 46).

- The nucleus reuniens. This small nucleus of the midline thalamus contributes to "limbic" functions in ways not yet widely appreciated. Considering its many other inputs, why do the "massive" projections it receives from the medial prefrontal cortex qualify it to be added as a potential fourth candidate for our list?[13] Because no *direct* pathway leads from this orbitomedial cortex to the hippocampus. Therefore, the reuniens is the sole intermediary through which this important prefrontal region influences the hippocampus (see chapter 29). When impulses leave the reuniens, they then flow over to the CA1 cells and the subiculum of the hippocampal formation, on to the entorhinal cortex, and also back to the orbitomedial frontal cortex.

Head Direction Systems in Two Dorsal "Limbic" Nuclei: Anterior and Lateral

Daniel Boone's *stationary* "place cell" systems may not have been much different from ours. After all, when we remain in one spot, such systems help us to stay oriented and to recognize which particular place we are occupying in that immediate environment (see chapter 29). But Boone was no couch potato. He was out exploring the early frontier. Which skills besides a sense of place contributed to his "internal compass" and helped him navigate that maze of unfamiliar wilderness trails? Boone survived only because he had refined other kinds of basic subconscious skills.

To the early navigators on ships, this *dynamic* art used to be known as "dead reckoning." It helped you discover where you were right now on any voyage. To estimate this current position, you had to factor in two major considerations: (1) the several different directions in which you had been "heading"; (2) the distances you had just covered during each of those "legs." Why is "heading" still the operative word in this skill? Because the brain must know *where the head is pointed* in order to "head" in that direction. As chapter 29 observes, when your eyes, ears, and nose point the way, you "face" in that direction.

Rats too are survivors. Their innate skills at "dead reckoning" on land are also highly evolved. Specialized kinds of directional cells are not scattered at random. They reside in several key limbic system nuclei.[14] For example, many cells in the posterior subiculum track the current direction in which the rat's *head* is actually pointing. Such *head direction* cells can fire at rates that are independent of the place where the rest of the rat's body is positioned within the whole of external space.

A surprise: the *anterior nucleus of the thalamus* turns out to have the most head direction nerve cells (see figure 8). Indeed they comprise as many as 55% of the total number of cells in its *dorsal* subdivision. This many head direction cells represents a major commitment. What could they contribute to the activities of this anterior dorsal nucleus?

Their position alone suggests that they could help integrate the subtle notions of "heading" into higher functional levels. Which kinds of basic sensory information could they be relaying? Much of this sensory input that is vestibular in nature has been ascending from the brainstem. Here the vestibular system (aided by proprioceptive messages from neck muscles) has been intimately monitoring the posture of our head and its every dynamic movement with respect to gravity.

These anterior thalamic cells engage in sophisticated interactions. One striking finding: their firing *anticipates the next head direction* by some 25 msec. They plan ahead.

Another noteworthy item: 30% of the cells in the *lateral dorsal* thalamic nucleus are also sensitive to the direction of a rat's head. This lateral dorsal nucleus interacts with the precuneus and retrosplenial cortex, just as the anterior nucleus interacts with more rostral portions of the cingulate gyrus (see figure 4). So what?

In chapter 51 we will discuss an intriguing phenomenon that develops during certain physical movements of the head and trunk. *Early* in the process of beginning to move the physical self out toward "extrapersonal" space, our subjective sense of a self identity can fade.

How could so simple an intended movement, as (for example) that involved in the act of bowing, briefly diminish one's sense of self? One plausible mechanism may reside in the several interactive and anticipatory circuits that link sensory cues from the lower vestibular (and proprioceptive) systems with these two limbic nuclei up in the dorsal thalamus. It seems possible that relevant interoceptive messages from these anterior and lateral dorsal thalamic nuclei could help convey the current status of the person's self-image up to influence the vital functions of much of the cingulate gyrus and medial posterior parietal cortex. Chapters 50 and 52 consider how important these *medial* cortical regions are to the subtle underlying sense of our physical and psychic identity.[15]

A Caveat about "Locating" "Higher" Functions Only in the Cerebral Cortex

Later, in chapter 94, we describe "two" prototype visual pathways. Each passes through the lateral geniculate nucleus of the thalamus on its way back to the primary visual cortex. One (cone) path conveys color vision. While still discussing the thalamus, it is instructive to consider briefly an innate limitation of this path where it surfaces in its most color-sensitive region farther forward in the cortex.

This area centers on the fusiform gyrus. It occupies the undersurface of the temporo-occipital cortex (BA 37). This V4 color complex region is relatively low in the activity of a particular enzyme, the one that synthesizes GABA locally.[16] This observation could suggest that its *local* GABA cells (and its GABA terminals from elsewhere) are limited in their capacities to serve as the local sites for inhibiting color processing.

Let us now suppose that a normal person briefly loses all color vision, selectively. Would this mean that the color-sensitive cortex was being inhibited *locally*? Or could color processing be interrupted by events at some next *lower* level, say down in the thalamus, involving *sub*cortical circuits?

To my knowledge, no neurological precedent for this latter phenomenon has yet been described in humans. It is possible in animals, however, to separately block the rod and cone pathways down in the lateral geniculate nucleus of the thalamus (as will be discussed further in chapter 94).

But we now have a much better understanding of how the thalamus and cortex interact. The examples in this and the next three chapters illustrate that these microcircuits inside the lateral geniculate do not exist in isolation. From this perspective, a larger view is now emerging. It regards the lateral geniculate circuits as being engaged *at a complex physiological interface before* visual messages can pass through the "gate" up to the color-sensitive cortex. Contributing to the dynamic properties of this gate are *both* the reticular nucleus of the thalamus *and* the pulvinar.

Geniculate, reticular nucleus, pulvinar, cortex—these four elements become *one big processing unit*. How are we to conceptualize such an oscillating, interactive macrounit? Can one apply only what we had learned back in medical school about the simpler anatomy of serial relays? No. The tendency now is to think about such larger units as forming "a circuit, not a sequence."[17]

And this concept seems to fit in with the newer histochemical findings. They show that thalamic "core cells" do project up to discrete, selective areas of cortex. These parvalbumin cells reside not only in the lateral geniculate and reticular nuclei but also in subdivisions of the pulvinar. All three thalamic nuclei appear capable of making major contributions both to a wide range of our normal, discrete, perceptual functions and to others that are highly sophisticated.

In the past, the tendency was to think along serial, linear lines. Therefore, higher-order functions would somehow issue as "products" up there at "higher" levels in our cortex. At present, parallel processing and distributed functions offer a wider range of optional explanations for the properties of states of consciousness.

Nothing in this chapter can devalue the impressive functions of the parietotemporo-occipital cortex that will be surveyed later in part IX. Evolution has endowed this region with unparalleled associative functions. Rather, what is being suggested here is that some of its remarkable associations can be disrupted not only "up there in the cortex" but at several "lower" stages among the thalamocortical interactions just described. Trains do stop at Grand Central Station and scheduled arrivals from elsewhere can sometimes be long delayed.

In part IX, we further examine what might happen when trains of impulses also slow down and stop in the back of the brain. Even minor disruptions in the scheduled patterns of reciprocal oscillations could result in "imperfections" of perception. We shall see that such visual illusions can arise during kensho, but only at certain times.

45

The Pulvinar

> There is overwhelming evidence that the pulvinar has a role in visual salience.
>
> K. Grieve and colleagues[1]

"Salience" describes the automatic process that enables us to grasp a particular stimulus event, hold on to it, and transform it into a subject of special, meaningful interest. Covering the back of the thalamus is a large nucleus that plays a vital role in conferring salience. The pulvinar is the pivotal association nucleus for the back of the cortex. Its name means "cushion," suggested perhaps by its plump appearance as it spreads out over the small bundle of fibers that enters it from the colliculi.

Both the pulvinar and the superior colliculus are key parts of our "second" visual system. They enable us to make snap, reflexive, visual judgments (some blind patients use this second visual system, subconsciously, as the basis for their blindsight) [Z:241, 244, 271–274]. Through circuits that link the pulvinar with the amygdala, we process crude visual signals of low-spatial frequency. They signal us immediately when we glimpse fear on someone's face.[2] fMRI studies show that even though fearful faces are flashed for a mere 17 ms, they still generate subliminal signals that pass up through the pulvinar and stimulate the basolateral amygdala.[3]

Recent data confirm that the pulvinar is also part of a "second hearing system." It processes auditory reflex messages from the *inferior* colliculus. When normal subjects are suddenly aroused by a loud white noise, fMRI signals increase in their left medial pulvinar.[4] The pulvinar's newly discovered connections include not only those with the temporal lobe emphasized in the previous chapter but also a surprising link between its medial subdivision and the orbitofrontal cortex.[5] The connections from the human pulvinar to the fusiform gyrus (BA 37) have yet to be studied in specific, detailed ways that could help elaborate on the discussion in part IX.

The pulvinar plays not only a prominent role in assigning attentive value to a particular item that is being seen. It also enters into the processes of depth perception, and possibly also into higher-order egocentric frames of reference that are head- or body-centered.

What could happen when the reticular nucleus *lessens its prior inhibitory hold* on the pulvinar's input to the cortex? [Z:591–592]. Pulvinar functions could be enhanced. A preattentive type of parallel processing could confer a glimpse of direct, global perceptual import [Z:595–605]. This is the nature of the impression that arrives *early* in kensho (see table 11, chapter 95).

In contrast, the reticular nucleus can also interfere with visual cortical functions by inhibiting the pulvinar directly. When its GABA cap does disrupt the firing of pulvinar nerve cells, two things occur: (1) the amplitude of gamma oscillations up in the visual cortex is reduced; (2) gamma synchronizations are also reduced in the visual cortex.[6] This important evidence suggests that lesser degrees of misfiring in the pulvinar could contribute to the *late* visual illusions of kensho (see chapters 95 and 96).[7]

46

The Reticular Nucleus and Its Extrareticular Allies

> The GABAergic reticular nucleus: a preferential target of corticothalamic projections.
> Mircea Steriade[1]

We keep mentioning the reticular nucleus. Yet, when Kolliker described it over a century ago, it certainly looked like no other nucleus. It was just a thin inconspicuous sheet of nerve cells that capped the contours of the thalamus [Z:267–271]. But later, physiologists discovered that it served as a "gate" to the impulses streaming up from the thalamus and down from the cortex through its dendrites.

When physiologists stimulated the cortex directly, the impulses descended and excited the reticular nucleus. Its GABA nerve cells then fired and blocked incoming sensory impulses from relaying up past the thalamus. Stimulating the brainstem, on the other hand, inhibited these inhibitory functions. Now, when its GABA cells stopped discharging, more sensate messages could flow up through the thalamus into consciousness.

The first two sentences in the previous paragraph describe the way the GABA blockade of the reticular nucleus operates on sensory relay nuclei. This inhibition affords a condensed, plausible explanation for major phenomena that occur in internal absorption: its loss of vision and hearing; its loss of the sense of a physical body-self; its dearth of spatial referents within a vast open space (see chapter 75) [Z:589–590].

Complexities

Chapter 44 indicated that intricate reciprocal circuitries interconnect the thalamus and cortex. Though cortico → thalamic glutamate fibers greatly outnumber their thalamo → cortical counterparts, both kinds peel off collaterals that inform the reticular dendrites how fast their impulses are flowing.[2] And while it is true that glutamate nerve cells in the cortex (and norepinephrine) do excite reticular nerve cells, glutamate can act on various other thalamocortical nerve cells to create a series of rebound excitations.[3] Not only do some "wiring patterns" that involve the reticular nucleus seem almost as complex as those of the striatum,[4] but during normal waking behavior, the standard relay nuclei of the thalamus that we have been discussing can fire either steadily (tonically) or in bursts. Bursts are either rhythmic or arrhythmic.[5]

Our discussion up to now has considered three aspects of reticular nucleus function: (1) how it gates elementary sensory messages (they are the easiest to measure); (2) how its influence could extend, via the pulvinar, to the whole posterior sensory *association* cortex; (3) how it could also influence the *non*sensory nuclei of the limbic thalamus. But living Zen is not "merely experiential." It translates into action.

The Reticular Nucleus Influences Behavior

Thus far, we have discussed how the reticular nucleus influences the vertical, first-order, thalamocortical input starting to rise up *to* the cortex. It can also influence some kinds of higher-order *horizontal* transmission. These *trans*cortical relays help one cortical area interact with another. This is a fourth aspect of reticular nucleus functions. This influence has thus far been studied when it was brought to bear on messages in transit from the *motor* regions in the front of the brain.[6]

The mechanisms underlying anticipation are important (see chapters 50 and 51). It is when *a person is preparing for action* that "the reticular nucleus plays a crucial role" in influencing these *motor pathways*.[7] Recent research suggests that faster behavioral responses occur in association with the kinds of *anticipatory* gamma oscillations that arise within the frontoparietal network.[8] Consider how the executive functions that arise from our frontal lobe act normally to sponsor a "go," a "no-go," or a "stop" command. How could the reticular nucleus insert a discrete inhibitory message that would influence this high-level *motor* processing? Perhaps by reducing—selectively—the passage of other impulses that, if unchecked, could *interfere* with the timing of the person's optimum, anticipatory sensorimotor responses.

Hypothesis: To the degree that long-range meditative training reduces certain unproductive frontal lobe constraints and enhances other actions that are more fruitful, then a person's behavior could gradually become more efficient, liberated, and appropriate[9] [Z:668–677].

Various speculations in the interim have cast the reticular nucleus in several roles. Sometimes it may seem to operate like "a set of elementary searchlights." At other times it may act more like a "hub" that can marshal relevant thalamocortical channels for action, perhaps by sharpening the peaks of their firing patterns in accord with particular tasks.[10] Future investigators, aided by improved resolutions in neuroimaging techniques and by more sophisticated experimental designs, may be better able to monitor how the reticular nucleus influences our psyche. Perhaps then they will be able to clarify other ways it enters into the phenomena of Zen experience above and beyond the influence we now think it has on only sensorimotor functions.

The Extrareticular Inhibitory System

Two other regions also seemed inconspicuous in previous centuries. Today we are starting to appreciate that they too exert a potent, selective inhibitory influence on higher-order thalamic nuclei.

- One region is the *zona incerta*. This thin plate of gray matter occupies a section of the subthalamus just above the midbrain [Z:196]. Why did Auguste Forel, more than a century ago, coin the term *incerta* for this part of the diencephalon? Because then it was a site about which "nothing certain can be said."[11] Research in this new millennium suggests a few certainties.[12]

  Its GABA cells discriminate. They directly inhibit only the *higher*-order thalamic nuclei. Normally, what defines such a higher-order nucleus? Its excitatory input is of higher origin, and chiefly *descends* from the cerebral cortex. The medial dorsal nucleus is a typical example. In contrast, the *first*-order nuclei like the lateral geniculate nucleus receive their excitatory impulses from *peripheral* sensory receptors and lower levels, not from cortex.

The GABA terminals from the zona incerta are large, multiple, and end on dendrites close to the cell body of the thalamic nerve cells they are poised to inhibit.[13]

- The second region is the *anterior pretectal nucleus*. Its cells cluster on the roof of the midbrain near the colliculi. Their GABA terminals are also large, multiple, located proximally on $GABA_A$ receptors.[14] This nucleus also exerts a fast, potent, point-to-point inhibitory influence on higher-order thalamic nuclei. And not only on two key nuclei of the limbic thalamus (the medial dorsal and lateral dorsal nuclei), but also on a variety of somatosensory and intralaminar nuclei engaged in other complex corticothalamic functions.

So what? As we search for the mechanisms of kensho, both the more anterior parts of the reticular nucleus *and* these two new extrareticular allies are potential candidates for reshaping consciousness at higher levels. However, very different inhibitions of visual, auditory and other first-order functions occur in internal absorption. These seem attributable not to the extrareticular system, but rather to the posterior parts of the reticular nucleus itself (see chapter 74).

47

Higher Mechanisms of Attention

> Attention defines the ability to select stimuli and actions that are coherent with the behavioral goals of an organism.
>
> M. Corbetta and colleagues[1]

Upper and Lower Streams of Attention

Zen training emphasizes paying mindful attention to internal and external events. Why? Paying bare, mindful attention trains us to focus and isolate events that would otherwise be lost into the usual, blurred continuum between perception, emotion, cognition and intuition. Attention begins by sharpening the contours of ordinary perception *now*. This chapter discusses four cortical regions that become of special interest to events later on along the path. These are moments when "triggers" activate the brain and when attention may "turn" into kensho.

In the neurosciences, what does it mean when attention is said to be an "associative" function? It means that a consortium of distributed networks—high *and* low—collaborates in our "higher" attentive processes. Yet these consultations are almost instantaneous: it takes only 50 ms for our shift in attentive processing to enhance the color responses of the fusiform gyrus.[2]

Our cognitive goals and instincts direct attention out to focus on external things. Many of our quick, reflexive responses are organized in the midbrain. Here, in the colliculi and central gray, we represent the topographical map of our own body reasonably close to nerve cells that will be processing new sensory data entering from the outside environment.

For some practical cognitive operations, we often rely chiefly on the networks of our *upper* (occipital → parietal) stream. They attend to the many other kinds of top-down physical decisions that arise along the self/other interface. All these networks might seem to be asking naive rhetorical questions, but they are very action-oriented. Indeed, most responses to the Where is it? and the Where am *I* types of question are ready to be acted upon instantly.

Suppose you have already located that ripe apple in space, but you have observed that it is almost beyond your grasp. Why does it help to have your upper (occipital → parietal) stream of attention "online?" Because its visual metrics are coded to represent the *absolute* size of that apple,[3] and you will need very accurately guided hand-eye movements to reach around it with each curving finger.

In contrast, your lower (occipital → temporal) stream has been attending to different needs. Its codes represent objects in terms of their identity and *conceptual* relationships with one another. So, having already asked the *what* questions, it is sure that *this* red fruit is not only an apple but that it is the ripest of all and ready to eat. Its circuits can operate with messages that are more relative than absolute. Its interpretations also seem more accessible to consciousness.

Next, in order to bring that apple all the way up to your mouth, you will need to integrate those early, hand-eye representations with multiple other visuomotor functions. The more "sensory" these are, the more they draw on your inferior parietal regions on both sides.

But suppose your next task is to detect fruits of different kinds in rapid *succession*. For this, you will need to shift into more flexible modes of ongoing attention and quickly blend them into both working memory functions and pattern recognition functions. At this point, brief inhibitions must enter repeatedly into the equation. Not only will you now activate chiefly your right frontoparietal regions but also *de*activate some of your left temporolimbic regions.[4]

Parietal Lobe Contributions to Attention

One finding is relevant to the ways we *sustain* attention during meditation: we involve the posterior part of the intraparietal sulcus on the *left* when we try to maintain an ongoing state of continuous attention[5] (see chapter 41).

What if you already know a lot about *what* the object is that you are searching for, but do not know precisely *where* it is located in the environment? Now certain parts of your parietal lobe play a major role in orienting spatial attention.[6] Some fMRI data emphasize the right angular gyrus itself (BA 39). Other imaging data point toward modules a little higher up, again to the *intraparietal sulcus* and to parts of the superior parietal lobule on the bank just above this sulcus (BA 7). It is difficult to be certain, because this sulcus meanders. As it meanders, it serves as an arbitrary boundary line that divides the small superior parietal lobule above from the large inferior lobule lying below (BA 40 and 39). (In figure 3 (chapter 23), the line extending down to the left from the words "parietal lobe" points to this sulcus.)

A glance at the gyri and sulci in figures 3 and 7 (chapter 40) might lead you to conclude that other parietal lobe anatomical "landmarks" could also differ substantially from person to person. Therefore, in neuroimaging studies, the functional contribution to attention of one small spot in the intraparietal region must be determined in each person individually.[7]

Contributions of the Frontal Cortex to Attention

The frontal lobes have major interactions with both the upper and lower visual function streams [Z:table 6, 245]. This same intraparietal region carries on a monitoring dialogue with the frontal lobe. It matches each new stimulus with a fresh motor response when a person engages in a dynamic act, such as reaching out for an apple.[8]

Meditators may engage the more dorsal and lateral regions of their frontal lobe convexity in yet another role. These regions help us maintain our attentional set even when we are faced with major outside distractions.[9] This more sustained, willful, goal-directed process is called *intention*. During intention, especially important links connect the intraparietal sulcus with one particular region of the frontal convexity involved in directing eye movements (BA 8).

Parenthetically, three separate regions enter *normally* into the sensitivities that help place our mechanisms of attention on alert status. Moreover, they also have the potential to expand their bilateral alerting functions into triggering responses [Z:163–164, 452–457]. For example, Segundo noted half a century ago that when he stimulated either the inferior frontal region, the superior temporal gyrus, or the cingulate gyrus on only one side, this excited a *bilateral* arousal response from a monkey's reticular activating system.

Normally, a set of responsive relays link this same inferior frontal gyrus with the temporoparietal junction. Such a frontal connection could enter into bilateral alerting and generate a triggering response.

Contributions of the Cingulate to Attention

Some early models of attention postulated that the anterior cingulate region helps to nudge us motivationally, at an *early* stage of attention, toward particular stimuli that we feel drawn to. Recent interpretations suggest that this anterior cingulate region may contribute more during later stages, while we are still evaluating and monitoring activities that are already ongoing.[10]

Contributions of the Superior Temporal Gyrus to Attention

Recent models of attention include parts of the superior temporal gyrus.[11] The models further propose other properties relevant to triggering for a fourth region next to the superior temporal gyrus. This area lies just beyond, at the temporoparietal junction. Its complex mosaic of functions prove extrasensitive when *strong visual stimuli* arrive *unexpectedly*.

Recent magnetoencephalographic (MEG) research draws attention to special functions of our *right* superior temporal cortex.[12] This right side contributes to our quick 3D judgments of sound intensities. These have survival value, because they help us decide instantly: is this external object close to us or is it farther away? (This is convenient to have the next time when you're out driving your car toward a railroad crossing and suddenly hear a train whistle.)

The MEG data also hint that some response properties of this superior temporal region might enable an overflow of excitation from an *unexpected auditory* event to become the kind of trigger that could precipitate a meditator into kensho.

How Auditory-Induced Hypnosis Affects Attention

Hypnosis is used to distract and divert one's attention. Self-hypnosis and autosuggestion are also techniques used not only in "positive thinking" approaches but also in some versions of self-guided meditation [Z:352–355].

A very relaxed state was induced by hypnosis in eight subjects who had been selected for their high degree of hypnotizability. PET scan activity increased in both the inferior and middle occipital regions (BA 18 and 19). So too did the subjects' occipital *delta* EEG activity.[13] Why delta?

It was speculated that this increased occipital PET activity, associated with delta EEG activity, might be related to an innate tendency of the more highly hypnotizable subjects to develop higher levels of visual imagery, or to the unusually deep relaxation they could reach during hypnosis.

Other PET scan activities also increased: in the right superior temporal gyrus (BA 38 and 22), the caudal part of the right anterior cingulate sulcus (BA 24), and the left inferior frontal gyrus (BA 44). *Decreases* occurred in the precuneus on both sides (BA 7), the left posterior cingulate gyrus (BA 31), and the right inferior parietal lobule (BA 40/7).

In the early history of hypnosis, pain control often played a prominent role. Pain control was addressed in a second part of this same study. Painful stimuli were generated by immersing the subjects' left hands in hot water (47°C). Under hypnosis, verbal suggestions were made that this pain was going to become more severe or less severe. The hypnosis with suggestions of pain relief produced other widespread increases in PET activity. These occurred more in the left hemisphere.

How Does Visually Induced Hypnosis Affect Attention?

It has been speculated that hypnosis engages primarily those higher and more anterior networks of attention, the ones that are well supplied by dopamine, including the anterior cingulate gyrus.

In this regard, hypnosis can generate a so-called obstructive visual hallucination. If "obstructive" were a word to be taken literally, it might seem to refer to an "obstruction projected out there" that was somehow "blocking" a more distant object from being seen [Z:388–390]. However, when the whole process of hypnotic focusing becomes intensified, it heightens the person's attention on the imaginary image. Therefore, the mechanisms of this so-called obstruction are likely to be mediated by inhibitory functions of the reticular nucleus of the thalamus [Z:388–390]. This can explain why PET scans show a corresponding reduction of activity in the seemingly "blocked" area of the visual cortex, and why visual evoked potential amplitudes are also reduced.[14]

Other Aspects of Attention

In fact, much of our looking and seeing, our listening and hearing, occurs *pre*-attentively [Z:278–281]. It happens automatically, in networks that anticipate forthcoming events. Their expectations shape our perceptions, subconsciously, at multiple levels.[15] In these and other ways, Zen keeps returning the discussion in subsequent chapters to different aspects of attention.

Why continue to highlight the distinctions between attention out there into *extra*personal space vs. self-referent attention? Why distinguish *allo*centric attention (directed out to *extra*personal space) from *ego*centric attention (in which the frame of reference is back to our physical and psychic self)? Because these self/other distinctions help clarify the neural basis for many of the core events that will develop during kensho and transform consciousness in enduring ways thereafter.

48

Ever-Present Awareness

> Waking, non-REM-sleep, and REM-dreaming are not isolated states that interact, but are sequential expressions of an undifferentiated field underlying them . . . a fundamental unified field that gives rise to both the key characteristic physiology and the psychology of waking, sleeping, and dreaming.
>
> Frederick Travis[1]

Some ideas about "fields" draw on metaphysical traditions in ancient India. Hindu sages believed that an "absolute Witness" pervaded the whole universe. To Shankara (788–820), reality was an unwavering field of timeless awareness, "the constant Witness of all three states of consciousness—waking, dreaming, and dreamless sleep."[2]

I begin as a biologist. I am coming from the premise that the brain is the organ of the mind. This book addresses "fields" of consciousness that arise *inside* the human brain. From this biased, "brain-bound" perspective, if all brain functions truly stop, no "fields" remain to support our biological consciousness (or mind). This belief might seem to be challenged by some reports that a few patients, while "under general anesthesia," later describe having kept a persistent, active "awareness of awareness." For example, one large prospective Swedish study estimated that this kind of awareness during anesthesia might occur in 1 in 861 operations.[3]

Unfortunately, EEGs were not routinely used to monitor and establish the true depth of anesthesia in this study. Even if scalp EEG electrodes had been used, they would have been too far removed from the activity of those deep networks in the brain that help generate our most elementary "awareness of being aware." No surface EEG can provide more than the most superficial, indirect index of what goes on in such deep, midline regions as, for example, the nucleus accumbens, hypothalamus [Z:337–338], and brainstem [Z:311–136]. Meanwhile, a flat EEG (unlike a flat electrocardiogram) does not mean that all deeper functions have stopped.

Intrusions of Keen Awareness

Meditators keep rediscovering the many ways that their daytime awareness fluctuates. Polygraphs reveal that episodes of *awareness also tend to intrude themselves repeatedly into normal non-REM, slow wave sleep.*[4] Similar intrusions have a tendency to recur during many transitional phases as our consciousness shifts between normal waking, non-REM sleep, and REM dreaming.

An Electrophysiological Correlate of Coherent Visual Awareness

If you want to study awareness, how can you narrow the focus of your experiment to that particular instant when a person *first* becomes aware of a recognizable stimulus? One way is to measure event-related potentials (ERPs) (see chapter 49). You could record these below, near, and above the person's perceptual threshold.[5] In the research cited, the investigators' choice for brief visual stimuli were line drawings of either real objects (e.g., an airplane) or a scramble of comparable (unrecognizable) lines. Their subjects' critical finding was a prominent negative potential. It peaked 260 to 270 ms after the visual stimulus. This "visual awareness negativity" occurred *only* if the stimulus developed sufficient mental coherence to be recognized.

Researchers now have a useful tool to assess the threshold of awareness, and to see how the amplitude of this potential varies under different conditions, though the sources that generate it remain to be identified. Suitably modified for the modalities of touch and hearing, similar negative potentials could be used to assess the threshold of coherent awareness in *longitudinal* studies of meditators during their states of sleep and waking.

"Witnessing Sleep"

In 1994, Travis reviewed transcendental meditation (TM) reports describing a *different* condition. It was called "witnessing sleep." By definition, this nocturnal "witnessing" is not a brief intrusion during the daytime. Instead, the TM subjects notice it *as an ongoing impression of awareness while they are deeply asleep*. Sleeping, they still report continually experiencing "heightened self-awareness." Moreover, they recognize that this nocturnal awareness is also "similar to their experiences during daytime TM practice."[6]

Does witnessing sleep have an EEG correlate? The EEG shows, simultaneously, theta, alpha, and delta activity. These mixtures were seen both during stage IV (deep) sleep, as well as in earlier sleep stages. In fact, some normal, non-TM subjects may also show mixtures of alpha and delta wave sleep, as do patients who happen to be undergoing the experience of pain.

So does this kind of self-awareness called witnessing sleep have a specific surface EEG signature? It seems too early to say until detailed sleep studies of long-term TM and other meditators clarify a host of other obvious questions. These relate to the potential presence of gamma and beta EEG activities, electromyographic (EMG) data, and more specific details that clarify the various time relationships.

Meanwhile, one useful rule of thumb is that our faster surface EEG frequencies tend to be associated with being farther along on the awareness spectrum toward our normal wakeful, conscious states. These states begin with minimal arousal, bare awareness, and increasing attention. They then extend toward a full, global alerting and willful intentional response. Accordingly, we might expect that some faster activities (including at least some at the interface between theta and alpha) would be among those waveforms which could correlate in time with the sleeping meditators' sense of an ongoing "self-awareness."

In summary: One subjective component of consciousness appears to proceed on a "lighter" plane of awareness during "witnessing sleep." Mixtures of faster EEG surface activities are associated with this particular quality of witnessing awareness, and these faster activities are superimposed on the usual slower delta rhythms of normal slow wave sleep. The subjective evidence is believable: daytime meditative training does appear to help certain brain systems maintain a person's sense of awareness at this higher level, even after the person falls asleep. The EEG evidence is interesting but preliminary. The fact that several of the human stress responses that are linked with pain also produce similar EEG changes does not negate the findings (see also chapter 56).

Awareness during Other Mixtures of Conscious States

Some TM meditators also report that they can observe their dreams even while they still maintain their stable sense of selfhood. This is described as a "witnessing self." Such a word description does not appear to be the same as an "anonymous witness." It suggests that a silent subjective observer is aware of details actually taking place within the dream scene. As pointed out elsewhere, the term "lucid dream" has a very restricted meaning [Z:324–327]. It means that the subject develops sufficient self-awareness, at a particular moment, to conclude that this moment is actually a dream.

As might be expected, most lucid dreams occur when one aspect of the sleeper's level of consciousness is on a "lighter plane." This higher level often means that the sleeper is at, or near, the most wakeful transitional phases that occur either at the beginning or at the end of slow wave sleep. Indeed, when most lucid dreamers are studied in the sleep laboratory, their polygraphs display a conglomerate of features. The mixture is consistent with both dreaming and being awake.

Ken Wilber, an experienced meditator, describes his own ability during normal waking consciousness to enter a meditative state that shows alpha, beta, and delta EEG frequencies. He adds that he was also able to shift voluntarily into a state of mental cessation, at which time delta activity alone was prominent.[7] These preliminary accounts suggest that the latest advanced EEG, ERP, and imaging techniques—to be discussed in the next chapter—can add much more to clarify which activities, and which regions, can be correlated with our distinctive subsets of consciousness [Z:83–93].

Our brain can access a variety of potential sources to superimpose added discriminative functions on our basic level of awareness. For example, even when human subjects are sleeping, they can also "recognize" that certain external stimuli do have a special affective meaning. In this context, the stimuli still penetrate into their quiet non-REM sleep and activate the subjects' left amygdala and left prefrontal cortex.[8]

Faster EEG frequencies are not confined to the two major activity states of waking and REM sleep. Some cortical nerve cells stay active even during quiet slow wave sleep, confirming that the sleeping brain does not always stay in a state comparable with "total darkness."[9] Indeed, during this quiet, non-REM sleep the cortex can briefly develop fast, spontaneous oscillations at 20 to 60 cps.

49

Neuroimaging, EEG Tomography, Event-Related Potentials, and Caveats

> The complementary strengths and weaknesses of established functional brain imaging methods (high spatial, low temporal resolution) and EEG-based techniques (low spatial, high temporal resolution) make their combined use a promising avenue for studying brain processes at a more fine-grained level.
>
> Alex Gamma and colleagues[1]

The living human brain used to seem like a black box. Now, the brain scans in weekly news magazines and Sunday supplements show full-color images of our brains' innards. The field is rapidly expanding and confusing. A brief survey seems in order.

Computed Tomography

Like ordinary X-rays, computed tomography (CT) images render the different tissue densities in black-and-white tones. But unlike ordinary skull films, computers now enable huge amounts of X-ray data to be sectioned into slablike slices. These reveal internal details of the brain's anatomy. For instance, CT scans show the cortical gray matter as gray, render white matter as off-white, depict the brain's fluid-filled spaces as black, and still leave the bony skull as stark white.

Positron-Emission Tomography

Positron-emission tomography (PET) scans represent a major technological advance. They provide images of the *dynamic functional activity* in different brain regions. After certain radioisotope tracers are injected into the bloodstream, their presence in the brain is then used to estimate how much blood is flowing to, or how much glucose is being metabolized by, the brain's most active regions.

The principle is straightforward: the instant that the radioisotope-tagged molecule decays, it emits positrons. These fly off in opposite directions, 180 degrees apart. Outside the skull, a sophisticated array of recording devices now registers *where* and *when* these positrons arrive. When the data are analyzed both in space and in time, the original decay site inside the brain can be pinpointed and expressed as a 3D brain image.

When the isotope-tagged molecule is water, the recording time required (the *temporal* resolution) is around 1 minute, much slower than EEG-based or evoked potential techniques. The H_2O-based PET studies *estimate regional blood flow,* and this serves as an indirect index of local nerve cell activity. Newer radiomolecules make it possible to image the changes in receptor systems in the brain (see chapter 53). Because PET scans expose the person to radiation, repeated studies are limited.

The images from single *p*hoton *e*mission *c*omputed *t*omography (SPECT) scans reveal much less detail. Their *spatial* resolution is relatively low compared to PET. However, the technology is less expensive, and a subject can continue to meditate for many minutes in the upright posture, after the isotope has been injected, before entering the SPECT scanner.

Magnetic Resonance Imaging

In 2003, the Nobel Prize for Physiology or Medicine was awarded to Paul Lauterbur and Peter Mansfield for their contributions to MRI. The molecular *architecture* of the brain itself generates a natural, but weak, magnetic field. When researchers then place extrastrong magnets outside the skull, this creates brief changes in the resonating energy of the brain's own field. Sensitive detectors and computer technology transform these changes into a kind of 3D, static relief map that reveals the brain's anatomical structure. This "structural" MRI is superior to PET in both its spatial and temporal resolution. It is also less expensive and involves no radiation exposure.

The drawbacks: MRI is noisy; movement artifacts can interfere with signal measurements; and it is often difficult to image brain structures located near the nasal sinuses or large veins.

Functional MRI

Functional magnetic resonance imaging (fMRI) technique monitors the momentary changes in local blood oxygenation. Within a few seconds, these dynamic changes provide an *indirect* index of the brain's local neuronal activity, and can be used to generate 3D *functional* images. Based on these *b*lood *o*xygen *l*evel *d*ependent (BOLD) signals, refined methods can now localize signals even when they arise from smaller capillaries.[2]

Magnetoencephalography

Magnetoencephalography (MEG) captures the ongoing, serial changes in electromagnetic signals that arise when different brain regions become activated. Multiple sensors outside the head detect the weak magnetic fields from these physiological currents. Computers then transform these signals into images referable to brain anatomy. A signal's most likely source can be estimated (with the aid of other computerized techniques) often more accurately than is possible using current EEG methods. However, signals from deeper brain regions still remain beyond the capacities of MEG and EEG to localize.

A Commentary on Degrees of Resolution

Resolution poses a simple question: How well does a technique distinguish two sites in space, or two events in time, each of which is very close to the other? Though both MEG and EEG are limited by spatial resolutions of only around 10 mm, they do have superior temporal resolutions of only about 0.01 second. An array of multiple EEG electrodes has helped EEG improve its low spatial resolution. Researchers now have a promising dual approach: combining the high temporal resolution of EEG or MEG with the high spatial resolution of fMRI.

Each of the above imaging techniques has its own assets and liabilities. Investigators may request preliminary CT scans and structural MRI scans to reassure themselves that their "normal" subjects' brains are indeed *structurally* normal. Thereafter, PET scans, fMRI, and MEG imaging provide relatively detailed information about dynamic *functional* changes in local brain regions. PET scans process minute-by-minute changes, fMRI processes changes occurring over several seconds, and MEG data arrive essentially in real time.[3]

A Caveat about the Word "Magnet"

MEG is a *recording* system. It is not to be confused with transcranial magnetic *stimulation* (TCMS). In this technique, a coil placed over part of the scalp induces major changes in the local magnetic field that go on to stimulate superficial layers of the underlying brain. The result is a disorganized mixture of excitatory *and* inhibitory responses from the cortex beneath. In recent years, TCMS has been used as a research tool[4] and as a mode of treatment for depression.[5]

Low-Resolution Brain Electrotomography

Low-resolution brain electrotomography (LORETA) was based originally on detecting the distribution of the brain's raw electric field. The methodology has been improved over the past decade. To localize the source of modified activity, researchers now analyze and plot the data with reference to locations on a standard tomographic brain atlas.[6] In actual practice, even when H_2O-PET and LORETA monitor a person's brain activities simultaneously, surprisingly few correlations in the data prove to be statistically significant.[7] While these results point to the need for higher-resolution methods for electrical activity, they also remind one of an important point: local metabolic activity per se does not reveal whether a nerve cell's firing activity is serving an inhibitory role or an excitatory role.

Event-Related Potentials

How does long-range meditative training affect a person's physiological responses? Previous chapters suggest that this field is ripe for further investigation [Z:284–286]. One approach is to measure the way the brain responds physiologically to brief events: to flashes of light, to sounds, to coherent or incoherent pictures, and to other standardized stimuli. When many weak physiological responses are pooled and amplified, they yield waveforms that can be measured. ERP activity can also provide "proactive" information about how a person's brain first prepares to act, and then goes on to change in response to subsequent errors.[8]

Attention shapes responses. As soon as you pay attention to a visual stimulus it changes the way responses evolve in your visual cortex. This power of attention can show up in the visual association cortex between 50 to 100 ms after the stimulus.

Fearful faces and loud noises also exert conditioning effects. Though the brain begins to react at lower levels, ERP picks up the net changes from an aversive stimulus in the cortex of the fusiform gyrus (BA 37) as soon as 120 ms, and in the middle frontal gyrus shortly thereafter (at 176 ms).[9]

Chapter 96 will describe an unusual *spontaneous*, visual illusion. A black-white pattern switched once from a positive to a negative image, then reversed itself quickly. In the laboratory, the normal human posterior association cortex is quite capable of processing repeated black-and-white reversals from an external pattern. Indeed, the subjects view "checkerboard" patterns being rapidly reversed not once, but multiple times. This is a standard technique for inducing visual-evoked potential responses.

fMRI studies help localize the sequence of normal brain activations evoked by such visual reversals.[10] By 95 ms, the pattern reversals prompt a positive potential in the temporal region of area MT/V5. By 150 ms, a negative potential shows up in the transverse parietal sulcus. At 160 ms, the *ventral* temporo-occipital areas of V4 and V4/V8 then develop their negative potential. Not until 180 ms do the *dorsal* occipital areas of V3/V7 develop their negative potential.

Sensory "Triggers" and ERP Measurements

"Triggers" have long been known to precipitate alternate states of consciousness [Z:452–457]. Another variation on the ERP theme measures how we respond, automatically, to highly unusual and unexpected auditory stimuli. These so-called odd-ball stimuli generate a negative (downward-directed) response called the middle latency cognitive component. It arrives at 100 to 200 ms after the stimulus.

Late, positive, cognitive electrical potentials also occur. One other response to unusual stimuli is the classic P300. It occurs maximally over the parietal regions. This distinguishes it from the "frontal" P300, which occurs in response to more complex stimuli which are both novel and unrecognizable [Z:285–286].

On a retreat, meditators appreciate that their sensory responses become enhanced. Clearly, it is time to conduct carefully controlled longitudinal studies, preferably in more than one monastic context, of the ways individual meditators respond, over decades, to standardized stimuli in ERP experiments. This is not to be taken as an endorsement of so-called mind machines.

"Mind Machines"; Caveats and Controversy

Equipment is commercially available that delivers mild electrical stimuli or visual-auditory stimuli to the brain. The public has access to various kinds of this equipment and has already put some of it to so-called recreational use. Suggestibility plays an important role in the subjective results. For this reason, the authors of a 1998 report found that a sham period of application was a significant advantage when they tested the presumed effects that two such mind machines had on the responses of normal volunteers.[11] One can imagine how many futuristic mind gyms will soon be offered as the mental counterparts of the exercise equipment widely advertised today.

In previous reports, Laurentian University researchers in Canada suggested that stimulations from weak, complex magnetic fields do reach the temporal lobes and produce a sense of "presence" as well as other mystical experiences (a topic introduced in chapter 42).

Swedish researchers question the conclusions. In their hands, suggestibility affords an alternative explanation. They point out that such external equipment delivers *intra*cranial field strengths at levels estimated to be only some 3 to 10 micro tesla down in the temporal lobes.[12] In contrast, the standard clinical transcranial magnetic stimulations (TMS) employ much stronger fields in short pulses

(200–600 μs). These clearly induce intracranial currents that disorganize underlying brain functions.

The helmet currently used by the Canadian researchers uses a special computer-based technology to deliver complex magnetic fields in these low micro tesla ranges.[13] The subjects rest in a quiet chamber blindfolded. The authors now report that only some 10% of their subjects report a "sensed presence" when sham fields are applied. In contrast, some 80% of the volunteers in Canada are now said to experience a "sensed presence" after being exposed to the following conditions: (a) 15 minutes of a continuous, frequency-modulated field, when this is followed by (b) bilateral stimulations over the temporoparietal region which then deliver a burst-firing field every 3 to 4 seconds.

Given the controversy, it would seem prudent to monitor the subjects using EEG, event-related potential and fMRI measurements before and after such stimulations. The data could help determine whether or not, in each subject, these epiphenomena of the so-called induced "god experience" do correlate with localized, reproduceable brain changes that are precisely related to the prior intervals of weak field stimulation.

One hopes that these two research groups (and others not directly involved in this dispute) will address and resolve some core issues. For example: What is the basic functional anatomy underlying the normal variations in human suggestibility? Do the findings resemble some of those reported in persons who are suggestible to a placebo? (see chapter 36). Do persons who are more suggestible have stimulation thresholds much lower than average for responding to induced magnetic fields which vary in complexity and duration?

Do Subtle, Event-Related Changes Occur at a Distance?

This chapter invited the notion that functional MRI, EEG, and event-related potential techniques provide useful factual data about brain physiology even though the human brain is encased inside the skull. Indeed, two paragraphs above, it was also recommended that such techniques could be appropriate to use to help settle a recent transatlantic controversy: Does a relatively well-defined weak magnetic field actually stimulate the brain beneath the skull?

The scientific community is programmed to respond with skepticism to controversial ideas. Those who devote themselves to studying unexplained paranormal phenomena may tend to be viewed as engaged in far-out, almost subversive kinds of research. During the past four decades, seven different laboratories have published data suggesting that even though two people are separated in space, a few of them show event-related brain responses that they appear to share in time.

In this new millennium, researchers are trying to eliminate the most obvious kinds of artifacts and statistical flaws that might serve to explain away the earlier reports. Given the above recommendation to use newer techniques, it seems only fair to cite the following samples of how these methods can be applied to study such controversial claims.

The fMRI findings involving a single pair of subjects have recently been reported.[14] Subject 1 was a 51-year-old woman. Her fMRI signals did increase in the visual cortex (BA 18 and 19) at the same time that subject 2 was being stimulated—at a distance—by the rapid visual reversals of a standard checkerboard pattern. When their roles were reversed, subject 2 (a 54-year-old man) showed no fMRI changes.

A second report from the same laboratory was based on 30 pairs of subjects.[15] Again, during the "on" condition, each sender was being exposed to the flickering reversals of a checkerboard pattern. Each receiver's EEG potentials were measured during that same time window of 100 ms which corresponded with the P100 wave form evoked in each sender. Only 5 of the 60 subjects showed higher degrees of activation in their occipital EEG leads while they served as the receivers at a distance. One out of 12 may not seem to be a practical result. However, the data were considered statistically significant.

Clearly, you and I cannot assume that the newer equipment and statistical techniques will provide objective data that will immediately "settle" such controversies to everyone's satisfaction. Indeed, if subtle agencies somehow link the brains of distant persons it seems likely that their natures will remain elusive.

50

Self/Other Frames of Reference; Laboratory Correlates?

Explore thyself. Herein are demanded the eye and the nerve.

Henry David Thoreau (1817–1862), *Walden*

The true value of a human being can be found in the degree to which he has attained liberation from the self.

Albert Einstein (1879–1955)

Is thy psychic self a mere abstraction? A disembodied figment of thine imagination? Not if you believe some hard data turning up consistently in different laboratories. One early finding was especially intriguing: our brain metabolism stays unusually high, even when we are passive and feel completely at rest.[1] Why?

Most of this high resting activity, 80% or so, supplies the energy needs related in one way or another to glutamate, our brain's major excitatory transmitter. Our focus in this and the next chapter will be on three questions relevant to Zen:

Which parts of the brain use much of this energy? What functions do they use it for? How do these functions shift from one frame of reference to another?

For preliminary answers, we will cast a critical eye on neuroimaging data (based on PET, fMRI, and EEG techniques), as well as on the results of certain split-brain studies.

Do Any "Selfhood" Functions Correlate with This High Baseline Level of Brain Activity?

At rest, your brain already starts with this high metabolic activity. Suppose you now engage in a very "hard-thinking" exercise: try to decipher some difficult algebraic equations. Surprisingly little happens. PET studies reveal that rigorous mental tasks increase your local blood flow only a mere 5% or less above this original baseline.[2] From various lines of evidence two important proposals have now emerged. They draw a sharp distinction between your steady baseline *activity* and the brief *activations* that were then superimposed.

- First proposal: Let us consider that our brain is not "really at rest" until it *maintains a steady degree* of "tonic physiological *activity*" at this original baseline level.
- Second proposal: Let us use the phrase "further phasic *activations*" to describe those small increases that occur when we then superimpose some *new* cognitive or other brief task on this steady, ongoing state.[3]

It is a dusty old distinction to separate the brain's ongoing baseline *activity* from its being briefly activat*ed*. But it would gain major significance when researchers faced the puzzling question: What kind of "signal" was the brain giving off when it was monitored by fMRI techniques? The prior findings from PET imaging proved helpful. When some new task does activate a local brain region, the local blood flow first *briefly* supplies this region with *more* oxygen than it actually uses. Momentarily, the O_2 supply exceeds the O_2 demand. It turned out that this transient blood oxygen *disequilibrium* was the basis for the signal that fMRI then picked up.*

How do you know for sure when the brain has reached, and stays at, its *true* baseline level of normal resting activity? Gusnard and Raichle propose that the brain does not reach such a resting level until it maintains this physiological state at or near *equilibrium*. And equilibrium implies that, at *multiple* sites throughout the brain, the local ratios of oxygen supply to oxygen demand are *remaining at uniform levels*. So baseline means that the O_2 supply-demand ratios are uniform. It

*The fMRI data are then expressed in the form of this *b*lood *o*xygen *l*evel *d*ependent (BOLD) signal. The BOLD signal is believed to index the way a given local region has received and is *actively* processing neural information, not merely transmitting messages onto distant brain sites.[4]

means that the whole brain stays at its *steady level of activity* and is not engaged in extra "activation."

Baselines and Zen

At first, such proposals might seem more in line with economics than neurobiology. The reader may wonder: can a notion of "equilibrium" fit anywhere into our concepts of self and Zen? It can. In the laboratory, when you try to localize "self" (or any other complex brain functions), you encounter reams of data that are undergoing dynamic changes. You need a frame of reference for such rapid changes. Only the data you obtain first—under standardized, baseline conditions of equilibrium—provide you with this stable frame of reference.

When applied to the practice of Zen, equilibrium calls to mind a useful analogy. Equilibrium suggests a condition of readiness, of equipoise. Looking into the Latin roots of equipoise, we are led to envision an old-fashioned scale, one that already has equal weights occupying each of its two pans. This is not a scale with both pans empty. It is a scale poised in a state of *dynamic* balance. So, too, in the brain, does equipoise suggest a physiological state *poised* to tip quickly between its countless options. Equipoise describes the brain's potential to tip the scales in either direction toward excitation or inhibition, to shift functions quickly toward being activated *or* deactivated.

Neuroimaging Correlates of the Intact Self as a Prelude to Its Dissolution

When you wish to study the self, accurate baselines are essential. For two reasons:

1. Baselines help to evaluate self-*centered* situations. During our more self-related activities, we might expect certain brain regions to be functioning at relatively high levels.
2. Baselines help identify the opposite condition. When these aspects of one's egocentric self are *lost*, we would expect certain regions to show a corresponding *decrease* in their functional activity.

With this preamble, let us return to the questions raised at the start of this chapter. Do only certain regions in our resting cortex remain highly "active" even during *baseline* PET scans? Yes. Moreover, these particular areas stay highly active, not only when we simply close our eyes, rest, and let go of our obvious thoughts. Some of them also stay just as active even when we engage in relatively simple kinds of visual fixation and view external items passively. Which major *cortical* regions do remain highly active metabolically during these *tonic*, stable equilibrium conditions? There are four:

1. *The medial posterior parietal cortex*. These *medial* regions include the posterior cingulate gyrus, the precuneus, and the retrosplenial cortex (see figures 4 and 7). The early researchers were surprised to discover this unexpectedly high posterior metabolic activity in the PET scans of subjects who were relaxed and resting.

   I was one of these subjects. Back in 1988, I too was surprised. The color frontispiece of the hardcover edition of *Zen and the Brain* illustrates why. This recumbent meditator, whose eyes had been masked and whose ears were plugged, still showed a high level of metabolic activity. These same posterior medial regions still seemed to be actively processing some kinds of information, even though the subject was under the impression that he was maintaining some "resting" state near "baseline."

   Indeed, various other lines of evidence confirm that our posterior medial regions do stay tonically "involved" *at rest*. Researchers are still speculating at great length (and we will too) about how this active, ongoing "involvement" codes for all the subtle ways we monitor, register, and evaluate both the external world around us and conduct a silent internal dialogue in our own private world. Of course, *many of these processes are precognitive, automatic, and go on subconsciously*. This makes them difficult to specify and define in conventional psychological ways in the laboratory.

   However, the foregoing discussion does prepare us for the next set of crucial findings about our normal sources of selfhood. Suppose you take on a new task. You now shift from your baseline resting state of equilibrium toward some new *goal-directed* form of processing. What happens to that high ongoing activity back in this posterior medial cortex?

   Another surprise. *It decreases*. This new task does not activate your medial region. It *de*activates it. It *demands less than the prior average* amount of oxygen. After continuing to list the three other active regions that also share such decreases, we will return to consider what these observations imply.

2. *Posterior and lateral cortical areas*. These regions cover a broad area of our *convex* association cortex. We know a little more about what their normal functions are. In brief, they help us both *attend to and decode* many kinds of salient, novel, or familiar stimuli that enter from our environment (see chapters 41 and 42). These areas include the inferior parietal lobule (with its angular and supramarginal gyri) and the superior temporal gyrus (BA 39, 40, and 22, respectively).

3. *The ventral medial prefrontal cortex*. The complex functions of this region subserve many kinds of emotional processing. They involve online monitoring of our own internal and external responses (see chapter 43).

4. *The dorsomedial prefrontal cortex*. This region does normally become *more activated* at certain times: when we monitor or report our own mental state, generate self-related thoughts and emotions, and also when we imagine which kinds

of mental states other persons are experiencing. Present evidence suggests that this more dorsomedial frontal region may also play some kind of active role when we rehearse personal plans for the future. So this dorsal region also seems to be involved in many of our subtle representations of selfhood. Note, however: signals from this dorsomedial region also tend to be *reduced* when goal-directed behaviors do *not* directly refer back to the self.

In brief, what happens in these four cortical regions during our normal, ongoing spontaneous networking activities? Gusnard and Raichle propose that their high metabolic activities give rise to much of our almost continuous baseline functions. To which ones? To the *particular processes that subtly relate to self and are more internally self-oriented.* This important theory suggests that—*even at rest—these four regions may be helping to support a very substantial, but subliminal, degree of self-referent equipoise.*

Their early observations were updated and expanded in 2004 in a well-written review chapter.[5] The amygdala is an interesting new addition to the list. The visual association cortex is a qualified exception.

To Summarize: How Does the Brain Change When It Shifts toward External Goals?

Let us shift once more, away from our usual subtle forms of resting bare awareness and monitoring. The shift will be toward externalized tasks that can require different modes of *goal-directed* behaviors.[6] At this point, all four regions enumerated above as having potentially *self*-oriented functions become *de*activated. In addition, there can occur *a corresponding psychological change.* In the next chapter, we suggest an experiential quality to the change: it could include *a brief reduction in that vague prevailing subjective notion that we, ourselves, are the central axis to which all events are referable.*

Many other PET, fMRI, and psychological studies have tended to confirm the directions of the findings in the four areas cited. The observations are now generally accepted as an important new principle. The fact that parts of the medial prefrontal cortex already show more metabolic activity *at rest* than they do when attention shifts externally *or* internally has an important practical application. It means that the "resting" control conditions and the tasks chosen for imaging studies of selfhood must be designed and interpreted with extreme care.[7]

Other research groups are now studying similar "task-induced deactivations."[8] Could it be that the resting activity in these four regions reflects not a *mono*logue but our normal, private, subliminal *dia*logue? In a sense, does it resemble not one, *but both* ingredients—*self/other*—of the flowing, Jamesian "stream of consciousness?" If so, then we might consider the possibility that these four regions become partly deactivated each time they need to shift their *preattentional* resources along this *dual* interface from one form of basic equipoise toward a different set of parallel, distributed functions.

My current leanings would be to call attention to some less obvious automatic, *pre*attentive aspects of the functions that blend into this self/other interface. Why? Because it seems likely that immediate action by powerful *sub*cortical processes would need to occur in order for such pivotal shifts to change priorities in four regions simultaneously [Z:278–281].

What Causes the Widespread, Coordinated, Task-Induced Decreases in Signal Intensity?

Which mechanisms would our brain *normally* use to *de*activate (reduce) its activity in four widely separate regions of cortex *all* at the *same* time? GABA is our brain's inhibitory workhorse. This fast-acting transmitter has the option of quickly deactivating at three levels: thalamic, local cortical, and transcortical[9] (see chapter 46) [Z:208–210].

However, when imaging data show that a cluster of four large regions up in the cortex are consistently "deactivated," does this shift mean that only the small local cortical GABA interneurons are causing such localized *intracortical* inhibitions? This seems unlikely. True, GABA interneurons do consume energy when they fire, like all nerve cells. But their inhibitory functions contribute less to the net metabolic changes that shape glucose utilization locally than do all the other local excitatory glutamate activities.[10]

Recent fMRI studies suggest that signals increase in the frontopolar cortex at the instant a person makes a voluntary executive action. Simultaneously, the left dorsolateral prefrontal cortex becomes deactivated.[11]

Plausible intervening mechanisms for such larger scale operations may arise in the thalamus and neostriatum. Thalamic circuits are poised normally to link several cortical regions bilaterally into one simultaneous set of graded activations or *deactivations* [Z:267–274]. Two limbic nuclei of the dorsal thalamus assume particular interest. Nerve cells in the medial and lateral dorsal nuclei have special properties and pertinent interconnections (see chapter 44). It is easy to think that when our limbic system is functioning "emotionally" it can help to *motivate* us and nudge us into *motion*. But do we need restless, foot-tapping motion per se? No. Our most effective ongoing movements are economical. They are *directed* precisely from our extensions of self out toward their newly assigned targets of opportunity. Cells in the thalamus, sensitive to *head direction*, are among those which seem capable of helping a brain literally "face" up to each new task ahead and confront it in a forward-looking manner. Human neuroimaging data show that different deep *sub*cortical discrete stimulations can translate—several synapses later—into changes that shift cortical functions in one direction or another.[12]

Many issues remain to be settled. For example, why does beta-2 EEG activity seem to be correlated with the resting activity in several of these important medial regions?[13] It will be essential to define all the conditions under which deeper subcortical nuclei help generate—*and reduce*—beta-2 (and related) EEG rhythms.

Different tasks require different kinds of conscious semantic decoding and subconscious decoding. We also need to assess the way the processing varies during various kinds of shifts. Moreover, the observations in the next chapter will introduce a factor more difficult for imaging techniques to study: behavioral tasks involve movement. The quantity and quality of the actual motor implications of the task could also influence the task-induced deactivation.

Meanwhile, these pages keep pointing to a central issue. While we are normally meshing—seamlessly—our usual egocentric and allocentric frames of reference, how do we govern the networking among these and related regions? For all we now know, much of these four regions' normal high resting activity could represent their dual efforts of *integration*. We inhabit *two* frames of reference. It is not simple to mesh all the ingredients of both self and other into our "*one* subliminal stream of *sub*consciousness." It requires *work*. To this degree, then each shift toward externalized, allocentric tasks would seem to involve a *reduction* of those prior metabolic resources allocated to help integrate that personal side of the "balance pan" representing the egocentric frame of reference. Indeed, such a decrease from the condition at "rest" is consistent with the data.

We need to be very clear about how we normally accomplish this covert, overlooked feat that enables us to mesh our two frames of reference. Then we may be in a better position to specify which mechanisms govern major shifts into so novel a state as kensho. For then, throughout one field of clear consciousness, only an allocentric reference frame briefly prevails (see figure 11, chapter 77).

Split-Brain Studies of Self/Other Distinctions

Split-brain studies offer another perspective on the different assets and liabilities of the two hemispheres. For example, the left persists in trying to explain (aided by its language skills, of course) the rationale for whatever behavior it sees issuing from its disconnected partner over in the right hemisphere.[14] When one split-brain patient was shown various photographs of faces that had been artificially combined (morphed), his right hemisphere was better at recognizing the faces that included features of a familiar *other* person. In contrast, his left hemisphere was better at recognizing morphed faces that contained more of his *own* features.

Some mental tasks involve rotation of an image. These show that the *left* hemisphere of a split-brain patient is superior *if* these rotation functions employ an egocentric (internalized) frame of reference. In contrast, the *right* hemisphere is more competent when the tasks involve the kinds of special processing that are related to allocentric (externalized) frames of reference.

If we were to use *only* the evidence suggested by such visual tasks in these few split-brain patients, it might then lead to one provisional hypothesis: (1) the *egocentric* self might drop out during kensho because certain *left* hemispheric functions were preferentially inhibited; (2) *allocentric* functions might then predominate during kensho if it were also assumed that certain *right* hemispheric regions had remained relatively spared. Of course, a normal allocentric bias for some of these more right-lateralized processes could be aided by the fact that this right hemisphere's basic attentional domain embraces *both* sides of the external environment.

However, many other separate lines of evidence are reviewed in these pages, representing normals and other neurological patients. These data suggest that complementary aspects and modules of our self are distributed in both hemispheres. The selective nature of most phenomena of kensho tends to argue against an easy single hemisphere explanation [Z:358–367].

I never understood the fictions of the self through introspection alone. Then came the deep experience of abruptly losing the ordinary *I-Me-Mine* self in kensho. Only that loss made it possible to envision this normal self in terms of its basic operating principles. Viamontes, Beitman, and colleagues recently surveyed the many circuits contributing seamlessly to our ordinary sense of self-awareness.[15] Their interacting pathways confer functions that become refined into an integrated self whose general psychic properties fall into categories that are both emotional, automatic, appetitive, social, remembering, and observational in scope. What other descriptive words help us conceptualize our normal self-awareness? The authors conclude that it is "a harmonious blend of internal and external representations, central organizing principles, emotions, determinations of need, value, and risk, application of appropriate automatic movements, and visions of past and future." Experientially, these had all dropped out during kensho.

The next chapter reminds us how often Zen calls our attention to issues at the dynamic interface between self and the wide world outside our skin.

51

Moving Away from The Self; Embodied Teachings

> The fundamental delusion of humanity is to suppose that I am *here* (pointing to himself) and you are out there.
>
> Hakuun Yasutani-Roshi (1885–1973)[1]

> The motor command contributes to the objective perception of space: Observers are more likely to apply, consciously and unconsciously, spatial criteria relative to an allocentric frame of reference when they are executing voluntary head movements . . .
>
> Mark Wexler[2]

Why did I develop a sense of déjà vu as soon as I read that tasks which shifted the person toward *external* (allocentric) goals *reduced* the brain's metabolic activity? Because the neuroimaging data struck a familiar chord. My Zen notes from two decades earlier had recorded similar observations and relevant comments.

Back in 1981 and 1982, our Zen teacher had openly discussed the following information with our sangha and me.[3] It seems appropriate now to share this narrative with others. I would hope that some readers who are also investigators will test these working hypotheses. Let us see if they hold up under the rigorous challenges presented by future, sophisticated research techniques.

It was in July 1982, during our 2-day retreat, that Myokyo-ni (Irmgard Schloegl) invited us to observe what happens when we stood up from the sitting position. "At the instant that the actual *lift* takes place—*not* the whole process of standing up—are there any thoughts?" Whereupon we stood up, and many reported (as I did) having no self-centered thoughts during *that* brief moment. This first experience of *feeling less self-referent* would become more noticeable when she invited us to stand up once again, then spoke the word "What?," using it as a distraction (see chapter 15).

She went on to explain: "When you move forward, or bow into what is being done at this very *moment*, the loss of I occurs briefly. This loss happens by itself. It's not something you have to think about. In the same way, one 'learns' to drive a car by *doing* it. You no longer need to think about it or describe it to yourself; it's just 'being done.' From now on, the approach in your practice is always to keep widening this gap of no-I. Develop the attitude *of giving myself up to the practice*. So every time you bow or nod toward someone or something, you'll be acknowledging: 'I am *giving* myself *up*'.

"In your daily life practice, called *shugyo* in Japanese, keep *giving* of yourself gratefully. Do it unreservedly, wholeheartedly. Don't think about this in terms of *trying* to do it by some act of will in your head. Just *do* it. It's in the *doing*."

My notes even earlier in 1982 report her counseling: "Get down deeper into being *one with the action*, with no observer remaining. The environment is to be responded to quickly, not to be slowly manipulated. Move forward into the giving *up* of yourself. Zen is oriented toward training of the body in awareness, not endless thoughts."

Demonstrating the point with a slight forward lean at her hips, she continued: "*Giving myself*. It is a phrase you can apply to every situation in your daily-life practice. Give up yourself during your everyday activities: with shaving, tying your shoelaces, lifting a glass of water."

She made it very clear to her students that a person's sense of self tended to fall away *at the very initiation of action*. Moreover, she herself "embodied" the way this gap left behind self-related thoughts. Each time she bowed at the waist during these explanations, she gave it an explicit down-to-earth application. Her behavior exemplified the simple practical acts we too could take to promote a lessening of the sense of self *during our own daily-life practice*.

Here I was, reading neuroimaging articles over two decades later, again being reminded how often these two fields, Zen and the brain, could each illuminate the other. Then, in 2005, I stumbled across the following psychophysical research.

Voluntary Head Movements Enhance an Allocentric Frame of Reference

Move your own head. Visual experience confirms that near objects are displaced more than far objects. The visual world changes as each normal movement brings in new visual cues about the relative positions of objects in external space. When your brain decodes all this parallax data, it arrives at fresh visual judgments about objects' positions and distances.

In Mark Wexler's laboratory, the subject sits in a wheelchair. The subject's head moves voluntarily (or is moved passively) forward or back in the horizontal plane. The subject focuses on a target 40 inches distant. The task is to judge: did this object move *in 3D*—with respect to *its own* otherwise invisible background—and in the same forward or backward direction?

Several recent experiments verify that we apply *allocentric* spatial criteria each time we make active *voluntary* head movements.[4] In contrast, our usual *egocentric*, self-referent bias returns when our heads are displaced *passively* to the same degree.

Quasi-cognitive factors are involved as soon as a person begins to anticipate the execution of such a *willed* motor command. Even so, this seemingly self-directed process still allows the visual shift to take place into a more allocentric frame of reference. Some kinds of "commands" could be directed by seemingly lower, more reflexive mechanisms. Yet in fact, similar findings result whether a person shifts into the allocentric frame of reference consciously or (more or less) unconsciously. In either case, it would seem a biological advantage to have one's allocentric perceptions enhanced in 3D as one anticipates the next active move toward the food, or the hazards, that lie out there in extrapersonal space.

Working Hypotheses

Why else might it be useful, just as we start to move into a task, to *reduce* briefly the activity of certain cortical regions? Perhaps it contributes a twofold physiological advantage toward a more creative solution. For example, in a sense (1) it could help to clear the decks in preparation for the new action itself; (2) it could also help to wipe the slate clean for the ongoing processes that monitor each new bit of sensory feedback information that is about to return from the newly changed environment. Let us explore these options with the aid of three working hypotheses:

- The first is applicable to active Zen behavior because it focuses on both the motor and sensory aspects of novelty [Z:668–677]. It has these testable corollaries: (1) If leaning forward is integral to motor priming, then parts of the anticipatory motor system and parts of the vestibular-proprioceptive system could both contribute to the shifts involved in the early mechanisms of deactivations (see chapter 44) [Z:668–677]. (2) When some sense of actual motion is being processed at the temporal lobe level, then the MT/V5 region could also participate. (3) If the brain's array of novelty-detecting systems also has been judging that the anticipated task is a relatively more novel and important one, then the requisite deactivations might be even greater (see chapter 29) [Z:285–286].
- A second working hypothesis is applicable to long-term meditation. It relates to the self-referent parts of those four regions cited in the last chapter (and the amygdala). To the degree that they are also implicated in (and complicated by) the usual *pejorative* aspects of the *I-Me-Mine*, then *longitudinal* studies of Zen meditators could show a gradual *decrease* in this component of their regional cerebral baseline activity, in parallel with their gradual dissolution of selfhood *dys*functions [Z:141–145]. This hypothesis is more readily testable because it does not involve actual movement.
- A third working hypothesis is applicable to kensho. To the degree that parts of the four regions (and the amygdala) are implicated in (and complicated by) these usual pejorative egocentric aspects, then an acute future study, *during* kensho, could show a sudden, sizable *decrease* in their prior regional cerebral activity, in parallel with their acute loss of residual selfhood functions. Kensho evolves so quickly that this will be very difficult to test.

In the next chapter, we sample other recent neuroimaging studies that shed further light on the distributed systems which support our notions of self.

52

Neuroimaging Data from Different Studies of Self-Referent Functions

Having a sense of self is an explicit and high-level functional specialization of the human brain.

A. Reinders and colleagues[1]

Elaborate explanations have been marshaled to prove that—though we and all other things are "here" as transient phenomena—we have no lasting inherent, objective reality (see part VII). In the present chapters, we continue to explore the basis for our notions of the self and the way it relates to the world around it at the neurobiological level, not as doctrinal concepts.

PET Scanning while Thinking about One's Self

How do people turn back their lens of introspection so that it focuses *only* on themselves? Imagine you are the researcher who needs to design a study of this self-reflective mental process. You have already defined this process (in words), calling it a kind of "reflective self-awareness." Yet your human subjects have *feelings,* not only thoughts. Both feelings and thoughts will show up in your imaging data. But would *you* choose the queen of Denmark's personality traits and her physical appearance for your subjects to focus on during their thought-full reflection? Probably not.

These two queenly attributes did prove useful to Hans Lou and his colleagues.[2] This research team had theorized that the core of our "reflective self-awareness" hinges on the functional links between two of the medial regions (the precuneus and anterior cingulate cortex) and the angular gyri out on the inferior parietal convexity. (Their hypothesis was somewhat similar to that of Raichle and colleagues, just discussed in chapter 50.)

To test their theory, they gave seven normal subjects a sequence of four separate tasks. Each task in the series was to be thought about continuously.

1. They were to reflect on *their own* personality traits.
2. They were to reflect on *their own* physical appearance.
3. They were to reflect on the personality traits of the queen of Denmark.
4. They were to reflect on the physical appearance of the queen of Denmark.

Clearly, it is a *first*-person act of introspection to reflect back upon your very own personality traits and physical appearance. Then why would these Danish researchers select their own queen for the other tasks? Because none of their subjects (all Danes) knew this queen *personally*. Indeed, no subject had any strong feelings about her, say of the deeper kind they harbored toward their own parents, family members or some very close friend. So her subjects thought about this particular queen as someone "distanced" from their own self, more on a *third*-person basis. In this self/other study, her role was to serve more as a "neutral" control. She wasn't a mothering personality in this cultural context, but more of a "human other."

Each task required intentional, sustained, concentrated thought, but it did not require any movement (such as pressing a button to signal a response). The major finding of this study was that blood flow increased within the precuneus and angular gyri when the subjects reflected on their very *own* personality traits. As noted in chapter 50, the precuneus is one of the major "hot spots" that lies within the medial part of the posterior parietal cortex (see figure 4, chapter 23). (Only this precuneus result proved statistically significant when the PET scan data were corrected for multiple comparisons.)

In a separate study, Lou and colleagues recently monitored 13 Danish subjects with PET scans. Their tasks were to rate how well 75 adjectives described either their own psychological traits, those of a "best friend," or of someone distant (the queen).[3] All three types of tasks enlisted increased PET activities from a *medial* core of cortex. The increases included more of the prefrontal regions (BA 8, 9, 10) on the left, and the medial precuneus and posterior cingulate regions (BA 7, 31) on both sides.

What happened when the judgments focused more on their own personal self? More PET activity developed in the angular gyrus of the *right* inferior parietal convexity (BA 39) and in those same medial posterior parietal regions cited above. In contrast, during the more distant, semantic judgments about their queen, her Danish subjects developed greater activations in their left lateral temporal cortex (BA 21) and in their medial prefrontal cortex.

Taken as a whole, the findings emphasized the role of the precuneus and posterior cingulate region in directing the processes of memory *retrieval* and discrimination toward the self (chapter 44 has indicated that these cortical regions interact with the lateral dorsal nucleus in particular).

To test their hypothesis, the investigators then designed a separate experiment in New York City. Here, the tasks for their 25 American subjects were to process adjectives referable only to "self" or to "best friend." Sometimes, while the subjects were doing so, they also received transcranial magnetic stimulation (TMS; 2 tesla). This was delivered to that region of special interest: the medial posterior parietal cortex. This stimulation prolonged the subjects' response times.

It also reduced the efficiency of their judgments about themselves, but not about their "best friend." (A special stimulation coil was used, and different sites served as the control.)

Functional MRI Correlates of Selfhood

Kircher and colleagues conducted an fMRI study using a different design.[4] Each subject reviewed a series of words—all adjectives—that described psychological traits and physical features. The task seemed simple: judge which adjectives apply accurately to your own self. In one experiment, the subjects reached this judgment *intentionally*. What they did not know was that, in the second experiment, the researchers had covertly arranged various closely related adjectives. Why were these particular words still relevant for each person? Because they reflected the same high ratings that these same individuals had each given 6 weeks *earlier* to similar adjectives. On that occasion, they had also judged these similar adjectives as corresponding closely to their very own personality and physical attributes.

When the subjects rendered intentional judgments about their own selves, they did tend to activate the left precuneus (among various other areas activated). In contrast, the right middle temporal gyrus was more activated during those other self-related judgments that they were making *un*intentionally (i.e., that they were making without being aware of having made similar judgments 6 weeks earlier). In both instances the left superior parietal lobe and nearby regions of the frontal convexity were also activated.

Kelley and colleagues also used adjectives. They monitored the fMRI of 21 adults who were viewing a screen on which was projected various adjectives that described personality traits.[5] By the act of pressing a key with either their left or right hand, the subjects signaled their response to three kinds of questions: Does this adjective describe you? (self); Does this adjective describe the current President of United States, George W. Bush? (other); and, Is this adjective presented in uppercase or in lowercase letters? (a nonsemantic decision).

During judgments, the fMRI activities did increase over baseline in a number of regions. But such judgments (and the movements required) also caused significant *de*activations in the medial prefrontal cortex (BA 10), the posterior cingulate region (near the precuneus), and in the lateral frontal, parietal, and medial frontal cortex (on both sides).

The findings in the medial prefrontal cortex were distinctive. Here, both the semantic judgments about "other," and the nonsemantic judgments (about whether a word was in upper- or lowercase letters) produced equally robust *decreases* below baseline activity. "Self" judgment responses showed much weaker decreases. The greatest decreases developed farther back in the posterior cingulate region. These were associated with "other" judgments.

Johnson and colleagues monitored with fMRI 11 normals while they listened to descriptive statements. Their task was to render yes, or no, button-pressing judgments about their own abilities, attitudes, and traits.[6] These in-turned self-reflective thoughts activated the anterior part of the medial prefrontal cortex (BA 9 and 10) and the posterior cingulate gyrus (BA 23, 30, and 31).

A recent fMRI study of 19 normals also showed medial prefrontal activations during the "metacognitive evaluations" of self vs. other persons. In addition, a greater *right* dorsolateral frontal response was associated with rendering evaluations about the self.[7]

Wicker and colleagues recently analyzed the data from five previous studies with regard to tasks which had required combinations of externally focused attention, memory, general reasoning, mind reading, and self-referential functions.[8] The activity of the medial prefrontal cortex was maximal in the resting state. It was *reduced* more when the subjects had to focus attention out toward the external world than toward their internal world.

Fossati and colleagues found widely distributed fMRI signals responding to personality trait descriptions, including in the premotor cortex, caudate nucleus, and cerebellum.[9]

In a recent fMRI study, five right-handed adults were monitored while they looked at photographs of human faces.[10] One of their tasks was to (mentally) identify the picture as either their own face or the face of a famous person. Their other task was more complex: to "think about what the mental state was," given photographs showing just the expression around the eyes of the other person.

The self-identified faces increased signals in three gyri in the *right* frontal region: middle, superior, and inferior. During the second, so-called "mind-in-the-eyes" task, signals also increased on the right in the first two of these (BA 8 and BA 9, respectively). Moreover, increased signals also developed in the right medial superior frontal gyrus (BA 6); in the left middle frontal gyrus (BA 46); and out at the tip of the left superior temporal gyrus (BA 38).

Thus far, what can we conclude about the medial prefrontal cortex? The evidence suggests that it is active in the normal resting state, as Gusnard and Raichle have emphasized. This medial prefrontal cortex tends to be activated in some self-oriented conditions and deactivated in other-directed conditions. Farther back, the precuneus seems to be activated during self-reflection in some studies, and the posterior cingulate gyrus may be reduced during other-directed conditions. It is possible that tasks which require the subjects to actively move and tasks which recruit subtle emotional resonances will introduce unexpected variables.

The findings already surveyed in this chapter underline the caveat made earlier in chapter 50: researchers must design and interpret with extreme care *both* the resting control conditions *and* the tasks chosen for their imaging studies of selfhood.

EEG Studies of Gamma Activity during a Particular Kind of Meditation That Includes a Self-Induced, Dissolution of the Self

The EEG technique known as LORETA begins with the usual scalp electrode recordings (see chapter 49). Software then computes the data into a 3D functional image of electrical activity. The longer name for this multichannel technique is low-resolution electromagnetic tomography.

This EEG approach was used to study one experienced meditator, 59 years old. He was a long-time teacher/practitioner of a Tibetan form of meditation.[11] His gamma EEG activity was recorded in one frequency band (between 35 and 44 cps). He shifted his mental activity voluntarily among five different meditative states during the 7.4 minutes of total data that were analyzed.

During the first two states he visualized the Buddha; during the third he verbalized a long mantra. The fourth and fifth successive meditations are of special interest, because they relate to the "sources of self." During the fourth meditation, he concentrated on experiencing his self being dissolved into a "boundless unity" (the authors used the term "emptiness" to designate this state). However, during the fifth meditation he concentrated on experiencing the *reconstitution* of that usual self which had just been "dissolved" during the previous state.

As expected, LORETA analysis showed that a visualizing form of meditation was associated with gamma activities maximal in the right posterior temporal and occipital region. And during verbalizing meditation, gamma activity did lateralize appropriately to the left medial central area involved in speech. Intentional *self-dissolution* generated maximal gamma activity on the right in the region of the *right* superior frontal gyrus. This finding is in keeping with other evidence suggesting that our internally directed, *intentional* mental functions are correlated with frontal lobe activities [Z:253–259].

Intentional *reconstitution of the self* generated *left*-sided gamma activity. It was distributed over an area superior to that other left central area (cited above) which had represented the kinds of language functions involved in verbalizing meditation. In addition, this gamma activity also extended toward that other *right* posterior region (cited just above) which had represented the visualizing meditation.

Why were "self-reconstitution" functions distributed this way, on both the left and right sides? The authors attributed this to the fact that reconstitution was a mental process requiring effort. The willful intent to complete this task required the meditator to integrate components that were both linguistic and visual. Interestingly, as an index of how much intentional mental effort he put forth into this task, his efforts to reconstitute his former self showed a "stronger" gamma activity than did either his visualizing or his prior self-dissolution meditations.

A PET Study of Multiple Personality Disorder

The imaging data reviewed in this chapter thus far has been based on "normal" subjects, not on psychiatric patients. At first, it might seem that patients who have a multiple personality disorder would present a unique opportunity. If this is an accurate diagnosis, it could imply that one single patient has access to two different autobiographical selves at different times.[12]

This condition has recently been renamed dissociative identity disorder. It usually develops in a context of severe childhood psychic or physical trauma. In this disorder, one of the personalities can access the autobiographical memories of these traumatic experiences. Then, when the memories of these traumatic experiences are recreated (during a "traumatic personality state") the subject often exhibits the corresponding major emotional response.

In contrast, the patients also have a "neutral personality state." While in this neutral state they report that they do *not* remember these traumatic memories. They often respond as if these memories do not pertain to them. Over the extended course of their psychiatric treatment, the female patients in this study had become able to perform self-initiated and self-controlled switches back and forth (dissociations) between their neutral and their traumatic personality state.

In each patient, the task was to listen for 2 minutes to an autobiographical, audiotaped memory script. It recounted either a neutral experience or a trauma-related experience. Note that the patient experienced the trauma-related script *as personally relevant* only when she was—at that time—in the traumatic personality state. A ten-point scale rated the degree of the patient's subjective responses during the test procedure.

When the patient was in the traumatic personality state, and listening to the trauma-related script, regional cerebral blood flow *decreased* in the right medial superior prefrontal cortex (BA 10). Decreases were also found in the ventral-medial part of the middle frontal gyrus (BA 6). The major bilateral decreases (*de*activations) were found within the intraparietal sulcus (BA 7/40) (see chapter 41). Other decreases occurred in the parietooccipital sulcus (between BA 18 and the precuneus) and the left middle occipital gyrus (BA 19).

In contrast, the parietal operculum and the insula on the left showed the greatest *increase* in activation during the traumatic personality state (see chapter 28).

The evidence suggests that patients who are reliving psychic trauma decrease their activation in the medial prefrontal brain areas and in the posterior association cortex. On the other hand, the increases in activation in the left insula correlate with the associated feelings of psychic discomfort and disgust that are linked to especially traumatic memories.

A PET Study of Chronic Depersonalization Disorder

During genuine states of *acute* depersonalization, subjects lose their highly subjective personal sense of having a private, self-referent, affective center. Suddenly, much of the vibrant quality of their personality seems to have dropped out from the "inside" portion of their previous self/other boundary.

Chronic depersonalization is different. One might be (mis)led to think that patients who had been given the diagnosis of *chronic* depersonalization disorder would therefore show chronically *reduced* activity in the several candidate brain regions that seem to correlate with our normal self-related, "personalizing" functions.

Not so. This line of reasoning hinges on the assumption that (a) we are sure that these normal functions were the precise functions which the so-called chronically depersonalized patients had lost; (b) that dysfunctions in no other regions were responsible for this condition; and (c) we are certain we know which precise attributes of self correlate with resting activity, activation, and deactivation.

In fact, the situation is quite different in the study reported by Simeon and colleagues. Their patients did maintain their (chronic) depersonalization throughout the period that they were undergoing PET scanning.[13] But note how these patients described their condition. Do their own words match the singular quality and extent of the loss of self that occurs during kensho? Reading these patients' self-reports, we discover feelings that include "off base," "under water," "like a robot," "in a brain fog," "like my mind is a blank." None of these depersonalization symptoms are the same as the no-self (*anatta*) of kensho. Nor do they sound like the *reverse* of any subjective reports that had characterized the kinds of self-related tasks studied during the other neuroimaging reports reviewed earlier in this chapter.

During their PET scans, these eight patients and twenty-four controls performed a standardized task. It included reading, speaking, and memory recall. At this time, the patients did show slightly *lower* metabolic rates both in the lower part of the right superior temporal gyrus (BA 22, an association area) and farther down in the middle temporal gyrus (BA 21). However, their major findings were significantly *higher* activities in the parietal and occipital areas of the association cortex. These higher parietal activities involved both the superior lobule (BA 7B, somatosensory association area) and the inferior lobule (BA 39, multimodal sensory integration area). The higher occipital activity involved BA 19 (visual association area).

To the degree that data from other studies suggest that some aspects of selfhood may normally correlate with functions of the right superior and middle temporal region, the lower activities noted in this report still remain of interest. However, the study illustrates how valuable subjective reports are, and it emphasizes that we need to conduct imaging studies in authentic states of *acute* depersonalization in the future.

"Out-of-Body" Experiences; Self-Referent Functions Disorganized in Space

"Out-of-body" experiences help us understand how the sense of a physical self arises. During a classical, brief, "out-of-body" state, the experience includes: (1) the *displacement* of the center of self-awareness. It now looks *down* at a scene from a new reference point well above its usual earth-bound position; (2) the impression that the person's *own* body is still really "down there," even while this displaced awareness is observing it from this elevated perspective (*autoscopy*) [Z:445–446].

Perhaps as many as 10% of seemingly normal subjects may experience these illusory projections of the self. So, too, do a few patients who have focal neurological disorders.[14] Whether such temporary dislocations reflect local physiological dysfunctions, fixed disorders of structure, cortical stimulations by electrodes, or brief focal seizures, they most often disorganize the circuits localized to one key region: the temporoparietal junction. Normally, this junctional region helps us represent the kinds of *body image models* that serve as our own projections into the outside world. To do so, its networks link functions drawn from nearby association cortex (see chapter 95, section 8).

Several major factors combine to displace attention and to warp its self/other perspectives during a brief out-of-body state:

- An impairment of the usual way the person integrates the conventional forms of sensation that convey a personal sense of private *physical* identity. Often the proprioceptive disorder is prominent. Indeed, the person's actual body posture and movement at that very moment greatly influence the phenomena of the out-of-body illusion.
- An added impairment of several other covert constructs, the ones that normally help orient any person *in external space*. Some of these normal functions may be referable to the intraparietal sulcus which helps encode external space. When egocentric coordinates serve as its frame of reference, its activities are also influenced strongly by different positions of one's head.[15]

Other impairments could represent disorders of normal mechanisms more reminiscent of those that merge with one's vestibular sources of equilibrium. Under normal conditions, we are innocent of how many body-inside-space adjustments we are making. They can also be difficult to tease apart in the laboratory. Still, in daily life, a variety of mechanisms serve to stabilize our physical core of self in position within its changing spatial dimensions. Silently, they adjust each new model of our physical self with respect to what it sees, to the covert force of gravity, and they also anticipate our body's next moves out into *extra*personal space.

The few examples cited represent dysfunctions that disorganize a person's orientation in space. This brief mention of their multilayered mechanisms serves not only to introduce the later topic of overt physiological triggers (see chapter 72). It also serves to call attention to triggering stimuli that operate much more covertly. For example, consider what may be happening in the brain of a meditator who had been watching scenery move past, off to his right, through the window of a moving train. His train stops. He descends. He *turns*, to then stand quietly on the station platform. Abruptly, in kensho, all sense of self is lost completely, not simply displaced (see chapter 93).

Some neuroimaging research is beginning to hint how this might occur.

Comment on Neuroimaging Studies of Self-Related Functions

Gillihan and Farah question the existing evidence that certain brain regions process *self*-related information in a very special way.[16] True, with respect to our sense of the *physical* self, the *right* inferior parietal lobe does appear especially involved in our basic awareness of our left hand and arm when they remain *at rest*. Yes, the insula seems to contribute when we attribute personal "ownership" to the *actions* of our own hand and arm and start to believe that we are *the* active "agency" responsible for their behavior.

Yet, what about the other evidence referring to our *psychic* self? Do our personal traits, our personal (autobiographical) memories, our unique, *first*-person perspective on facts, beliefs and motives have specific localized and lateralized origins akin to those skills we use for language? The authors conclude that this area of research still needs to include many more carefully controlled studies of *non*self functions. Meanwhile, in their view, "the available data neither prove nor disprove that the psychological self is special."

Clearly, each article summarized in the foregoing sections addresses one small part of a large topic. Still, collectively, they exemplify the kinds of pioneering experimental paradigms currently used to seek out the higher-level regions that generate our self-related functions. The weight of the evidence is impressive.

Why do the regions vary? Why are they being regarded in these pages as "candidate" regions of the "omniself?" In part, because we do not all construct and conceptualize our "self" in the same way. These different experimental designs are currently tapping into multiple regions of widely distributed interconnected systems. We need more control data because these constellations vary from person to person.

It is true that first-generation neuroimaging studies were subject to "constraints that thereby weaken the models derived from them."[17] However, recent neuroimaging methods have become much more sophisticated. Future studies may show that the various layers of our selfhood are not limited to such widely distributed *cortical* systems as those specified above. The roots of selfhood could also be detectable among the deeper configurations which link the activities of multiple subcortical and upper brainstem modules with those up in the cortex.

Consider, for example, one next lower subcortical level, that of the thalamus (see chapters 44 and 45). Its medial dorsal, lateral dorsal, lateral posterior, and pulvinar nuclei interact with most of the anterior and posterior regions of the cortex that we have just seen are correlated with selfhood functions (see chapter 50). Moreover, these thalamic nuclei are subjected to the gating, inhibitory influences imposed by the reticular nucleus of the thalamus and its extrareticular allies (see chapter 46; figure 8, chapter 44).

A Comment on Some Lateralizing Aspects of Frontal-Temporal Lobe Interactions

Long axons, well insulated with myelin sheaths, speed impulses back and forth between the frontal lobe and all other lobes. Frontotemporal functions are doubly serviced. The uncinate fasciculus enters the front of the temporal lobe, and the major arcuate fasciculus curves around to enter it from the back.

Several preliminary studies suggest that certain of our higher-level modules of selfhood may be distributed asymmetrically. As children, we learn to recognize an image of our very own face using chiefly our right hemisphere. With respect to which higher associative functions enter into this task, some research points more to the right ventral prefrontal cortex; other data point more toward the right temporal lobe.[18]

When Miller and colleagues studied 72 patients with frontotemporal dementia, they identified a small subset who had suffered the most selective dysfunctions of the self.[19] In these seven patients, the greater damage was on the right side. In six of the patients, the right frontal lobe showed the greater abnormalities; in the seventh patient, the right temporal lobe was more affected.

Neuroimaging researchers have been assigning multiple self-referent psychophysiological functions to our cortex. Anatomically, these regions already seem overcrowded. This book suggests that many of their circuits are also so overworked that they create an excessive burden for our psyche. Can Zen training be of assistance, perhaps by offering the neurosciences new ways to test such theories of localization and lateralization? For example, if in fact the path of Zen enables its long-term trainees to let go of overly self-referent attitudes and behaviors, then overconditioned modes of grasping and rejecting can be tested for and be followed serially as they improve [Z:141–145].

A working hypothesis would propose that careful multidimensional longitudinal neuroimaging studies could reveal that the most highly accomplished meditators show a gradual decrease of activity—below their own, *earlier* baseline levels—in regions linked to their particular, individual self-referent longings and loathings.

Might such decreases occur more on the left or on the right side? Less important than a single answer is a more fundamental question: could researchers also design a sophisticated program of serial psychological and behavioral tests and of probing in-depth interviews? Only in this manner can we correlate future imaging and other data with measurable decreases in each subject's unfruitful, self-referent overconditioning.

53

Imaging a Meditating Brain: A Commentary

> In the present study, we compare the global and regional cerebral blood flow to the spectral analysis of EEG, and relate these to the subjective experience during the resting state of normal consciousness and the Yoga Nidra relaxation meditation.
>
> H. Lou and colleagues[1]

> In Zen, you let your frontal lobe rest.
>
> Dainin Katagiri-Roshi (1928–1990)[2]

Meditation is not monolithic. There are different styles of meditation, different stages and depths. Most results of meditation are subtle, few are dramatic. Some changes are immediate, others are delayed. Can brain imaging really clarify such complexity? Not unless researchers design, with care, each study. It must answer specific questions. A sample:

- What is the actual *content* of the meditator's *subjective* experience as each successive phase evolves?
- Which meditative techniques—focused and concentrative, or openly receptive—are being used? Are they being clearly described in detail?
- For how many years, in which tradition, has each meditator practiced, and with what degree of skill? Is the laboratory setting conducive?
- How hard was each meditator trying, and how well did each actually perform during the several phases of the testing period?
- Did each meditator have the opportunity to provide a later self-report that critiqued his or her performance?

- Is this a well-controlled, multidisciplinary program that monitors changes in respirations, brain waves, heart rates, and other physiological parameters?
- Do the data pass basic requirements for common sense and every appropriate test for statistical significance?

We were not expecting perfection in the pioneering imaging studies of meditation. Each preliminary report presents its own assets and liabilities. The goals in this chapter are to comment on neuroimaging during meditation in general, and to offer constructive suggestions about ways to design experiments that will help interpret future studies.

First, some remarks about how much *willed effort* enters into the task of meditating in a laboratory setting. Not only are there different alternative traditions of meditation, *even in a given tradition, meditation often evolves during the course of one session*. Many experienced meditators, after their early stage of concentration, have learned to "let go of self," and then to emerge into a more open, receptive mode of keen generalized awareness (see table 2, chapter 13).

The levels in this mode are often associated with, but are not limited to, a Soto Zen approach called *shikantaza*. It means *just sitting, not concentrating on a koan*. During this and similar kinds of receptive meditation, while our willful, focused attention is fading away, it is plausible to think that we are "letting go" of our major prior, driven, frontal lobe and anterior cingulate preoccupations with *intended* goals [Z:253–259]. It is in this sense that Katagiri-Roshi was referring to the "resting" of an *overworked* frontal lobe.

However, research on meditation is task-driven. Investigators set goals, and so do their meditating subjects. Expectations arise from both parties to this compact. Yet Zen meditation proceeds optimally in a setting that is much less goal-driven. Neuroimaging research faces a challenge. Can it provide an atmosphere as unobtrusive as possible?

Chapter 49 outlined various techniques of neuroimaging, including PET, fMRI, and SPECT. Chapters 50 and 52 discussed how researchers apply these methods when they search for the origins of selfhood. Let us examine reports illustrating how investigators apply neuroimaging when they study various kinds of meditation.

PET Imaging in Yoga Meditation

An early PET report in 1990 was based on eight subjects who had "at least one year" of experience in "Yoga meditative relaxation."[3] To reach their desired level of meditation, the subjects either repeated sentences or engaged in mental concentration on a "central point of power." Subjectively, the meditators described this level as a feeling of "relaxation, peace and detachment between body and soul."

Eyes and ears remained *open* during both meditative and control conditions. In the control period, the meditators continued to think about their daily affairs.

The most obvious general trend was toward *reduced* glucose metabolism in the *posterior* regions of the cortex on both sides. A ratio made this decrease more evident. It compared the greater reductions of metabolic rates in the posterior regions against the slight *increases* in the frontal regions. The authors attributed this greater posterior decrease of metabolism in the occipital and temporo-occipital regions to "reduced visual input during meditation, although the eyes remained open." (This issue was not enlarged upon.) The slight increase in frontal metabolism was not surprising. It appeared consistent with how much mental effort was involved in trying to concentrate and to repeat sentences. Metabolic activity was the same in the two hemispheres during the control and the meditation periods.

The epigraph to this chapter is taken from a different PET report by Lou and colleagues nine years later. They started to address some caveats cited in the chapter's opening paragraphs. Two important words opened their section headed "Results." The two words were "subjective experience." Clearly, the researchers made *first-person subjective experience* a priority. There, too, we find other significant statements: their meditators went on to enter "the experience of reduced conscious control" over their attention and behavior. It was stated that their subjects also developed a sense of "relaxation and 'loss of will.'" Yet, despite this loss of conscious control, their Yoga Nidra style of meditation was also associated with "an enhancement of sensory quality."

This phase, "loss of will," is a key psychological issue. Why? Because it relates to the way one's self is inserted when one is trying to attain a goal. It implies that the subjects' earlier mental effort of *intention* (associated with a prior sense of mental effort) was later lost. When did the self-reports indicate that this particular willful intention had dropped out completely from the meditators' basic impulse to act? Not during the earlier part of the study. Striving dropped out only during the *final* one or two stages of the four stages that were monitored.

This PET report was based on nine advanced Yoga teachers. Each had over 5 years of experience using related techniques. These subjects went through four successive stages of meditation while they listened to corresponding segments of a 45-minute audiotape.

Listening to a tape is, of course, unlike the silent, interior approach used in Zen. Although the audiotape technique is artificial, it does provide a framework. This kind of task structure tended to standardize the timing, duration, and content of the subjects' mental experience during each of their four separate meditative phases. It also served to bracket and identify an important later period. During this period, the subjects not only experienced a loss of will but also developed those distinctive PET findings which could be correlated with its loss.

The way we normally insert our *will*—into what we call *intention*—is an executive function linked to the frontal lobes. Thus, when the meditators say that their willful self-control drops out of the mental field, this subjective report serves to confirm the PET data: *no frontal lobe sites* played a significant active role during the last two corresponding stages of meditation (table I in the article makes this point clear).

Of course, other forms of receptive meditation also encourage mental efforts and discursive thoughts to drop off. In Zen meditation, for example, one allows them to drop off spontaneously, by themselves, but does not force them to leave (see chapter 14). This takes practice. It is a gentle, patient process of "settling down," of "letting go." It is a style not to be confused with any willed, forced, intensified attempts to deliberately "clear all thoughts."

Preliminary Preparation

Before these Yoga subjects entered the PET laboratory, they had already engaged in 2 hours of intensive *concentrative* meditation (*Kriya* Yoga). Why? Because they had learned from earlier experience that this preliminary high-intensity concentration would later help them to "let go" into the deeper levels of genuinely passive, will-less meditation. And these later, deeper, more passive levels were the primary objective of this study.

PET Stages 1 and 2

In confirmation of the points discussed above, the *first two* stages in this PET study showed major prefrontal *increases* in cerebral blood flow. These increases were referable to the right superior and inferior frontal gyri (stage 1), and to the left inferior frontal gyrus (stage 2). Contributing to such increased frontal activities, of course, might be the nonspecific effects of trying to focus on sensations in various body regions (stage 1), and on abstract feelings of joy (stage 2). Other increases occurred in other regions in keeping with the nature of such tasks (the association of "joy" with the *left* frontal region is of interest) (see chapter 43).

PET Stages 3 and 4

The effects of mental effort were also apparent during the third, "visual imagination" stage. Then, both inferior occipital gyri showed some of the highest cerebral blood flow increases recorded during the entire PET study. While the meditators were listening to the external audiotape, what particular kind of an induced internal visual image were they being instructed to envision? It was a summer landscape, outdoors, involving streams, trees, and meadows full of cattle. This style of meditative visualization is designed to evoke substantial increases in occipital and parahippocampal blood flow. Its soothing content can also contribute to other processes of relaxation that help lead to a sense of calmness.

What was the content of the taped message during the fourth, final stage? This message encouraged the meditators to enter into a "symbolic representation of the self." The suggested symbol for this "abstract perception of the self" was the internalized experience of a "golden egg."

The only significant PET scan *increases* during this fourth stage occurred in (a) the parietal lobules (inferior lobule on the left, superior lobule on the right), and (b) the left postcentral gyrus (the primary sensory cortex). In contrast, the authors commented on their subjects' "apparent lack of prefrontal and cingulate activity" during these later meditation stages. They suggested that the three psychological correlates consistent with this lack, and attributable to this "relaxation meditation," were "less volitional, motivational, and emotional control." Indeed, our ordinary experience confirms that these three distinctive aspects of our self do fade when we *fully* relax.

Word Problems

One must be careful about this word "relaxation." And extra careful about what it means in the phrase "relaxation meditation" or "relaxation response." The authors do say that their meditators were "passively following the instructions on tape." True, these subjects had already been accustomed to listening to a tape. But "passive" can also be a misleading word. The central issue focuses on the operational details. What actually takes place when a subject follows verbal, taped instructions? At first, these meditators were instructed to direct their sensory awareness toward their body, and then to experience "the weight of individual parts," one after the other. This soon becomes an *internally focused, active task* of some complexity.

Therefore, this first meditation stage evolves into a more *active* (and less relaxed) process than the word "passive" might suggest. Subjects have become active participants in a sequence of successive internal visualizations and proprioceptive imaginings. So it comes as no surprise to find that their stage 1 meditation also generated major *increases* in blood flow in such relevant regions as the left postcentral gyrus and both superior parietal lobules. EEG data were interpreted as suggesting that the subjects' theta wave power tended to increase in all EEG leads "in accordance with the subjective experience" of "reduced (conscious) control."

This tendency toward increased theta EEG activity and reduced desire for action during Yoga Nidra meditation was also found in the course of a recent report in 2002 by the same Danish group.[4]

SPECT Imaging

A SPECT study was performed during concentrative meditation. The meditators' task was to sit and maintain full concentration for some 70 minutes.[5] This particular Tibetan Buddhist style of meditation was carried to the point of *an induced "absorption."* Several demand characteristics inherent in this approach would seem to render it somewhat more strenuous than the usual "complex cognitive task."

This approach differs in other ways from standard Zen practice. In Zen, one usually stands up after sitting for 25 to 40 minutes or so. One then continues to meditate while walking (*Kinhin*). This physical activity becomes more than a refreshing physical and psychological respite—a kind of "seventh-inning stretch." It also embodies the *distinct practice of carrying one's open-eyed mode of meditative awareness into the dynamic, everyday activities of living Zen.*

Newberg and colleagues are to be congratulated both on their having enlisted eight seasoned meditators (each with 15 years or more of experience) and on the accomplishment of having studied them within the realities of a busy hospital environment. Their subjects' tasks were to "focus their attention on a visualized image and maintain that focus with increasing intensity" for 1 hour. At the end of this long, effortful 60 minutes, the meditators reached a "peak." This was self-defined as "absorption into this image." (Curiously, we are informed neither here, nor in an fMRI report to be discussed later, *what* the meditators were actually visualizing.)

The omission in the SPECT study leaves one wondering: What was in the "mind's eye" of these subjects during their long period of concentration? Whatever it was, we note that they were visualizing it with their eyes *closed*. Does the report also convey in words which kind of willfully induced absorption was said to have occurred? It was an absorption "into the visualized image associated with clarity of thought and a loss of the usual sense of space and time."[6]

Only when the meditators had reached what they considered to be their own desired level of "absorption," and then (still sitting) had signaled this decision to the researchers, did they receive their radioisotope. This was given unobtrusively, into the tubing of an existing intravenous line. Following this, their next task was to keep up their already intense mental focus during the next 10 to 15 minutes. SPECT scans, begun nearly 30 minutes after this injection, recorded the interim changes while they remained sitting.

Table I in Newberg et al.[5] indicates that the interim data, thus collected and averaged, represented only a 15-minute interval. This one aspect of their total meditative experience occurred between 60 and 75 minutes after meditation began.

Under these strenuous conditions, two *cortical regions* increased their blood flow (data from the deeper thalamus is discussed below). The two cortical regions were (a) the orbitofrontal cortex (+26%), and (b) the *body* of the cingulate gyrus (+25%). One wonders: what psychophysiological role(s), if any, would be attributed to these two substantial increases? The question arises because, in the sentences below this table, the reader encounters two curious exemptions: both the body of the cingulate and the orbitofrontal cortex were excluded from further statistical tests for significant correlations. Why?

The given explanation was that neither site "would most likely interact with other regions during the task of meditation." However, each of these two exclusions represents cortical regions that have intriguing and widespread interactive functions. So too does the occipital association cortex (also excluded). This visual region is of interest both because these meditators were engaged in a deliberate visualizing practice and because it had shown the greatest relative *decreases* during the visualizing meditation used in the early PET study by Herzog and colleagues. It seems questionable to exclude these regions when we still know so little about the whole process being studied, including all of the mechanisms that converge on events during the final critical 15 "peak" minutes.

Thalamic Considerations

The thalamus showed the highest of all cerebral blood flows in the baseline condition. Whatever influences might then have converged on the thalamus from multiple other sites during the next unmonitored hour of meditation, the thalamus did appear later to have responded to the intense concentration requirements during the visualization. In fact, the thalamus also became the third most active site during "absorption," showing a substantial *increase* in perfusion, averaging +14%.

Only the data referable to the right side of the thalamus became significant when it was subjected to statistical parametric analysis. (How this might relate to other evidence suggesting a greater participation of the right hemisphere in sympathetic functions and greater norepinephine levels on the right side of the thalamus remains to be explored.) [Z:263–267].

The normal thalamus is still governed by inhibitory mechanisms that enable it to cope with similar effortful and stressful circumstances (see chapter 44). In particular, its reticular nucleus can thwart any such unusual overactivity from spreading up from its other nuclei in ways that could overstimulate the cortex above. Unfortunately for neuroscientists, this inhibitory cap of GABA nerve cells in the reticular nucleus is much too thin to be measured by existing imaging techniques (see chapter 46). Hence, even though its impressive neural activity translates into vital inhibitory functions, its presence goes unspecified.

Table II does point out two sets of 3D (*x-y-z*) coordinates referable to the right thalamus. However, SPECT imaging lacks the resolution to be certain which thalamic nuclei are being assessed. Only refined techniques (like the diffusion tensor imaging discussed in chapter 44) have the potential to identify the more bulky thalamic nuclei.

Meanwhile, one may hope that the data from *future* higher-resolution studies might clarify how several larger nuclei in the thalamus are functioning during different styles of meditation. For example, the medial dorsal nucleus is a key association nucleus that could be involved in willful intensive effort. It cosponsors many interactions at the dynamic interface between the frontal lobes and the limbic system. One might hypothesize that some compartments of this medial dorsal nucleus could tend to increase their activity when meditators engage in intensive, stressful, concentrative meditative techniques that are permeated by affect and prolonged to the point of "absorption."

One hopes that in the future, measurements at other (more posterior) coordinates could help clarify the functional status of the large pulvinar and the small lateral posterior nucleus. Why? Because the pulvinar is our largest thalamic association nucleus (see chapter 45). It cosponsors most of the complex perceptual functions referable to the back half of our association cortex, including visualizations, one might suppose (see figure 8, chapter 44). In contrast, the small lateral posterior nucleus serves similar functions for just the small superior parietal lobule.

Theoretically, though the intrinsic activity of the thin reticular nucleus still escapes detection in current neuroimaging, it can have potent inhibitory effects on each of the three thalamic association nuclei that prevent them from transmitting their excessive levels of activity up to overstimulate these corresponding regions in the cortex.[7]

Regional Decreases in SPECT Signals in Parietal and Temporal Lobes

Statistical parametric analysis revealed significant *decreases* in several regions. Among them were noteworthy decreases in both superior parietal regions. As just discussed, reductions in blood flow in this (and other) regions are consistent with the way cortical functions can be *inhibited* by the reticular nucleus in the thalamus down below.

How does this reticular nucleus react to excessive (top-down) activation of the cortex or to excessive (bottom-up) activation of the midbrain reticular formation? In each situation, it can block sensory messages from being transmitted up through the lateral posterior (LP) thalamic nucleus [Z:503–506]. It is this inhibitory role of the reticular nucleus which prevents impulses from reaching the cortex of the superior parietal lobule.

Hence, the SPECT data showing superior parietal decreases are consistent with the proposal cited earlier: an extension of this deep GABA inhibitory blockade is the plausible cause for the loss of the physical self-image during the extraordinary state of deep internal absorption (see note 7). This novel state and its sensory loss represent a sharp break from normal perception, and occur *unintentionally*.

Transcortical pathways do connect the frontal lobe with the superior parietal region. However, it seems doubtful that a *direct* transcortical pathway from the frontal lobes per se could inhibit the superior parietal lobule to this degree.

The only other sites where SPECT signals were decreased were both in the temporal lobe. One site was the right lateral temporal gyrus; the other was the left inferior temporal gyrus. In their earlier PET scan report in 1996, Fink and colleagues found that this right lateral temporal gyrus was one small module in that larger configuration which appeared to contribute to our normal autobiographical sense of identity.[8]

Comment

The SPECT data represent an original contribution and lend support to independent proposals about how one's *physical* sense of self might dissolve. Further interpretations of this report are limited for several reasons. The evidence that blood flow increases in some areas and decreases in others occurs in isolation from other essential parameters of measurement. Especially limiting is the lack of first-person subjective ("psychological") descriptions of experience. We always need to know what meditators are actually *experiencing*. What is on their minds? Neuroimaging data during meditation must be closely correlated with both the form and the content of subjective experience. Psychological accounts are the essential framework for assigning meanings to the pixel counts.

Similar considerations apply not only to the relatively few "peak" minutes of a long-delayed absorption. They also hold true throughout the many intense minutes of induction that had gone on before. What was the form and content of the mental field during that long generative period leading up to the meditators' experience of "absorption?" And what emotions were they experiencing? We read only that the meditators' "subjective responses were impossible to quantify or analyze in a useful manner." Future imaging studies require more than a comment that "the subjects felt that they had an adequate meditation session."

Issues of timing are critical. Ideally, several sequences of neuroimaging and combined psychophysiological studies should be repeated (a) during one meditative session, at successive times during successive stages; and (b) during several meditative sessions, separated by days, weeks, months, and years.

In a critique of the 1999 PET study of Lou et al., it was stated that increases in blood flow were *not* noted in the frontal regions.[9] The original descriptions in that PET study indicate otherwise. That PET study was designed to measure four successive *stages* during one meditative session. In contrast, the SPECT study focused on one point at the culmination of meditation. It is not clear why a separate critique later considered that the 1999 PET study represented only "one time point."[10]

Functional MRI during Kundalini Meditation

Functional MRI is noisy. The sounds can be distracting. Lazar and colleagues hoped to minimize this disadvantage.[11] They asked their five subjects (each with over 4 years' experience) to listen to this noise on tape as "homework," so they could become accustomed to the noise in advance.

Later, inside the fMRI laboratory, during each breath cycle, the meditators concentrated on silently verbalizing one mantra during inhalation, another mantra on exhalation. As the authors noted, this is "a challenging task requiring constant vigilance." In their acknowledgments, the authors thanked their "intrepid subjects." No mention was made of whether the eyes and ears remained open. The earlier part of a meditation period was compared with the later part. Both meditation periods lasted 12 minutes. Thus, two separate time points were available for analysis.

Increased fMRI signals were detected bilaterally at sites within both frontoparietal-temporal and anterior cingulate regions. Increased signals were also found in the left superior parietal lobule (BA 7) when the final 2 minutes of the two meditation periods were contrasted with the first 2 minutes. Heart rate, respiratory rate, and ECG recordings were followed in two patients. The title of the article includes the phrase "relaxation response." Still, no statements from first-person subjective reports provide compelling evidence that genuine deep relaxation occurred. No subjective follow-up report records an individual meditator's success or failure to comply.

General Comments on Neuroimaging

Without timed, detailed accounts of meditators' internal experiences, readers are in no position to interpret with assurance the meaning of neuroimaging reports. In this millennium, the scientific community has every reason to insist on rigorous selection of subjects, prior training in the laboratory, and an equally rigorous program of refined, accurate psychological accounting. One hopes that future comprehensive studies of (Zen and other) meditators will be conducted with standards of excellence in psychological correlations that aspire to approach the technological sophistication of the neuroimaging instrumentation.

Ancillary Studies

The four neuroimaging reports described above suggest two other caveats for future studies: (1) "meditation" evolves during the course of each standardized period. To study the whole dynamic longitudinal process in Zen will require more than a single 12- or 15-minute interval of one-dimensional neuroimaging data; (2) "meditation" tends to evolve over much longer units of time in a graded manner. Indeed, the Path of Zen is a longitudinal process (see chapter 4). It evolves over decades. Only multidisciplinary approaches can help define precise, cause-and-effect sequential relationships in the whole brain/body human organism.

Several additional modes of psychophysiological monitoring were used in the studies cited. They included EEG and global cerebral blood flow;[12] polygraphic measurements of heart rate, breathing rate; and end-tidal CO_2 and oxygen saturation levels.[13] Additional data of current interest are gamma wave EEG recordings at various frequencies and heart rate variations during each breathing cycle.

Indirect indices of stress responses include plasma assays for catecholamines (norepinephrine, epinephrine), cortisol, thyroid hormones, and prolactin. Indirect indices of stress responses become more important when prolonged, stressful sitting is being carried to the extremes represented by intensive concentrative techniques for inducing absorptions.[14]

Other measurements of increasing relevance include blood levels of melatonin, antibodies, cytokines, and of white blood cells involved in the immune response. When practical, simultaneous assays of spinal fluid, cisternal fluid, or ventricular fluid can help distinguish between molecules released from the brain per se and the same molecules found in the bloodstream that can also arise from the pituitary gland, adrenal cortex, or adrenal medulla.

Future Neuroimaging Studies of Receptors: The Requisite Conceptual Framework

We still lack basic information about the functional anatomy of the normal human brain. We do not fully understand the psychophysiological sequences involved in the styles of Zen meditation and its related alternate states of consciousness. Advances in both of these projects hinge on defining how different regions interact physiologically within widely distributed networks.

What we need are model levels of analysis that have progressed so far beyond the preliminary (if imaginative) steps that they can define *successive sequences of exquisitely timed, direct, cause-and-effect relationships*. At the physiological level, the fundamental questions are relatively straightforward: *How does one module in one discrete region influence the next module? Is the net effect excitatory, inhibitory, or disinhibitory?*

Beyond that, it will not be enough to know, for example, that norepinephrine is released in "the thalamus." One also needs to know which kinds of NE receptors are there, and on which thalamic cells, in order to envision what the next physiological result might be. Once our conceptual framework at these levels is much further advanced, radio-receptor imaging data will begin to make more sense, at least in terms of the net changes that occur in the firing rates of the next nerve cells. In the interim, one hopes that researchers who plan to study how receptor imaging systems contribute to Zen meditation and to related alternate states of consciousness will have access to the latest authoritative reviews of the kind recently begun a decade ago by Torchilin.[15]

Since then, the report by Koepp and colleagues has pointed the way toward a much more refined dynamic neuroimaging approach to receptor binding.[16] These researchers studied a particular kind of psychophysiological activity, namely playing a video game. Their results suggested that subjects playing this game released more dopamine into the striatum. Their technique was based on a series of assumptions. How such assumptions work, in practice, in the context of opiate receptors is discussed in greater detail in chapters 35 and 36.

Here, in brief, the principle of competitive receptor binding assumes that fewer dopamine receptor sites will be available to bind an isotope-tagged dopamine molecule if these same receptors have already been occupied by the release of the brain's own natural dopamine molecules. Researchers are also assuming that their subjects' dopamine has just been released only during the specific task being assigned.

In the future, the challenge will be to apply the same principles of competitive receptor binding to estimate the release of many other pertinent messengers into key brain regions. A major problem: the dopamine systems of the striatum are relatively easy to study. The receptor populations and concentrations of other messengers are not.

Imaging the Brain of a Sage

Even now, however, one can envision the need to define which kinds of fine structural changes distinguish the brain of the advanced sage from his or her contemporary control subjects [Z:637–641]. The question is: which mechanisms underlie such very long-range attitudinal and ongoing trait changes as occur in the sage? Newer generations of selective receptor radioligands will contribute to this research, bringing higher levels of resolution than we imagined were possible in past decades. Even now, for example, PET imaging makes it possible to visualize not only the structural integrity of certain presynaptic terminals but also to assess the integrity of the membranes on the surface of their adjacent postsynaptic cells![17]

Do not think that the neuroimaging techniques described in these last five chapters provide "the answer" to Zen. Their data miss the consciousness of the person inside that machine. Zen is to be comprehended not through electronic wizardry, but through the seat of your pants, and perhaps in the intuitions you feel outdoors, or in some lines of poetry.

In this regard, we will be able later, in part IX, to sample some ancient Zen poetry, while closing out these present efforts to "neurologize" with this caveat by Vernon Rowe, a contemporary physician-poet.[18]

MRI of a Poet's Brain
In this image of your brain
I see each curve in the corpus callosum,
curlicues of gyri, folding of fissures, sinuous sulci,
mammillary bodies, arcuate fasciculus,
angular gyrus, tracts and nuclei . . .
but not even a single syllable
of one
tiny
poem.

It's time to put the book down, time to *let go* of all these facts about the brain, time to explore those states of consciousness that somehow create poetry.

Part IV

Exploring States of Consciousness

> I think of consciousness as a bottomless lake, whose waters seem transparent, yet into which we can clearly see but a little way.
>
> Charles S. Pierce (1839–1914)

Words and Metaphors in Religious Traditions

> The reference of the metaphor in religious traditions is to something transcendent that is not literally anything.
>
> Joseph Campbell (1904–1987)[1]

Words Create Problems

Consciousness is hard enough to understand without words getting in the way. "Neurotheology" has become a buzzword. Fashionable in some quarters, it has not entered my lexicon. So long as *theo-* usually implies God or some institutional monotheistic belief system, then this interpretation does not quite seem to fit into the topics covered in *Zen and the Brain* or in *Zen-Brain Reflections*.

This is not to embrace any movement that is "unplugged from its religious, spiritual, and moral roots and repackaged for secular, individualistic culture." Carter Phipps uses the phrase "enlightenment uncloaked" to describe this new antitheological posture.[2]

No, in these pages our focus remains on that age-old Zen approach to Buddhism. Among even its lay adherents, Zen has always emphasized a restrained, moral, ethical, and disciplined living in the world, with the aid of a support group of like-minded individuals (the sangha). The goal of this Buddhist approach is to refine one's traits of character, in keeping both with the traditions of the Buddha's sensible eightfold path and with the main Buddhist precepts as well (see chapter 4).

Metaphors

What sound did Basho actually hear at the old pond when that frog jumped in? Was it "the sound of water," as many earlier haiku translations would have us believe? Recalling our own experience by a pond, we know otherwise.

Basho heard no *figural* word image. He heard a unique *plop*! Only a frog enters the water with that plop! Headfirst. Legs trailing behind. Sometimes it's a *kerplop*, other times a *kerplunk*. It varies with the size of the frog and the angle of entry. Anyone who has been around ponds knows that no leaping fish, no stone, makes that special *plop*!

Our temporal lobe's pattern recognition circuits decode this plop instantly. Let us regard this special "plop" as consistent with a *primary* metaphor. The word's distinctive pattern of sound wave energies is very close to the sound a real frog makes when it enters the water. This is an example of onomatopoeia—a thing named in a way that *literally* approximates its sounds (e.g., bow-wow, hiss, bobwhite). This is *not* a figurative notion. It is not a sound that takes a long time to figure out. No maybes, qualifications, or calculations delay your instant decision "like" they do in a simile.

Later, in part IX, we will find that this writer, when pressed to describe a late visual experience in kensho, might have to employ as many as five words: a "visual misperception consistent with moonlight." Be assured then that this is simply an attempt to communicate something vaguely resembling such a primary metaphor, that leads to a more direct form of immediate shorthand recognition.

Most second-order and third-order literary metaphors are much more indirect. They arise from association links among networks farther on in the brain. They invoke the *poly*modal language functions of junctional regions, and integrate data from our special senses of vision, hearing, and touch. Now linked with memories and emotions, these processes become more elaborate abstractions. Finally—many synapses beyond—they leap into word thoughts and emerge into words that can be spoken. Some might find their way onto a page. Formal neuroimaging studies of how our metaphors evolve through such primary, secondary, and tertiary steps seem long overdue.

In the interim, a provisional working hypothesis might suggest that many of our earliest pattern recognition functions could be correlated with impulses racing along parallel pathways, first through the occipital, next the temporo-occipital, and then the more forward regions of the temporal lobe. So when visual stimuli evoke visual responses, their potentials peak first in the primary visual cortex (BA 17) some 90 ms after the stimulus. Their next peak occurs in the middle occipital gyrus, at around 104 ms. After that, the peak moves farther forward into the fusiform gyrus at 141 ms[3] (see figure 4, chapter 23). In and around this fusiform gyrus will arise much of our normal sense of color perception (see chapter 94).

Then, where will many of our abstract linguistic elaborations develop, in ways so utterly dependent on metaphors of one kind or another? A major candidate region is that sensory crossroad, with its nearby attentive focus: the inferior parietal lobule (BA 39 and 40) (see chapter 41). Thereafter, it seems likely that we might create further literary elaborations, or even yield to impulses for outrageous puns, within other circuits in the temporal and frontal lobes (see chapter 43).

But the central theme here is not figurative, discursive, or embroidered speech. The proposal under consideration is that much of the *immediacy* of Zen experience could arise in networks closer to our earlier percepts in the *back* of the brain. Here, sharpened by preattentive processing, events could be imbued with that special impression of salience. Its refinements inform us that we are now in the immediate lively presence of authentic, simple reality.

Joseph Campbell emphasized that every religious tradition employs metaphors. To Campbell, *a metaphor was an image that suggested something else.* It alleged that one thing corresponded with—or stood in for, or *was*—something else. In chapters 92 and 97 we will make a more explicit attempt to distinguish a visual illusion from a metaphor. Indeed, in its neurological context, no visual illusion in itself is a metaphor to the very person who is experiencing it at that moment. However, to some other person—someone who later hears about such an illusion or who only reads about it—it might be misinterpreted as a metaphor.[4]

Metaphors pose a major problem. They tend to become so abstract and indirect that we lose sight of an essential fact: their central truths often arose long ago in the direct, insightful experiences of individual human beings. It is plausible to think that the insight-wisdom the ancient worthies experienced in past millennia arose from a *pre*cognitive physiological core. Its *pre*linguistic origins contributed to the difficulties in expressing it in words.

Religious traditions worldwide went on to respond with fertile imaginations and complex mythologies in an effort to communicate their various ideas and doctrines. Campbell emphasized how heavily dependent religions became on their use of simile, analogy, and symbol, often to the point that these indirect, artificial modes of communication lost their moorings with the everyday facts of direct, literal, reality.

One less appreciated benefit of long-term Zen meditative training is the way it allows its practitioners to access longer intervals during which their left hemispheric language functions are diminished. The training enables word-thoughts to fade into the background [Z:283]. Suppose, at such times, that some physiological surge does develop into an alternate state of consciousness. Then, at onset, it can be relatively free from the discursive thought patterns that contaminate our ordinary lives.

This means that the state arrives—initially at least—*relatively* free from discursive mythological inventions including metaphors, similes, analogies, and related symbols. These, of course, may only be postponed. They do develop subsequently when the person later reflects on the experience in a cultural context, and tries to express in words the qualities of this novel state.

This is not to say that metaphors should be eliminated. Metaphors are not only essential, they are here to stay. The point is that unreined metaphors readily bolt and carry us away. To illustrate the hazards of such loose-reined associations, the old *New Yorker* magazine featured regular, tongue-in-cheek "Newsbreaks" preceded by the heading BLOCK THAT METAPHOR. There, unlucky writers found their extravagant use of clashing metaphors openly exposed. Zen training will not "block" all metaphors. It may enable them to become more literal, concrete and primary rather than more figurative abstract, and secondary.

Many useful figures of speech and other normal symbolic processes seem to arise in our posterior association cortex. Here, at the parietotemporo-occipital junction, our associations engage sight, hearing, touch, and proprioception in elaborate cross-modal transformations. Literary-minded readers and writers can appreciate that their similes and metaphors superficially resemble synesthesias.

People who have synesthesia find that when a stimulus enters one sensory modality it sets off a sensation in another. In its most common form, hearing certain words induces, involuntarily, sensations of color ("colored hearing"). Cytowic describes this phenomenon as an "allusion of the senses."[5] Synesthesia occurs in at least 1 in every 2000 persons, is more common in women, and tends to run in families. Synesthesias also develop acutely in other persons during the acute intoxications induced by amyl nitrite, LSD, or mescaline.[6]

Recently, 12 women were studied who experienced synesthetic colors while they heard spoken words.[7] Words increased fMRI signals in their most color-sensitive region in the left fusiform gyrus (BA 37), and also in V4 alpha, the region just anterior to this. Interestingly, color per se did *not* cause the normal increase in signals in these same areas. This evidence suggests that their normal visual avenues for color into this fusiform gyrus region are deficient, and that their auditory avenue is *over*active.

The synesthetes also showed increased signals in the right claustrum and the left posterior cingulate region. This claustrum finding is noteworthy because the right claustrum is activated normally when we transfer ordinary cross-modal messages between our *touch* and vision.[8]

Synesthesia is not the same as metaphor. It resembles metaphor only superficially. Metaphors are thought-contrived imaginative understandings. We invent them to link one thing with another. In literary English, we most commonly employ metaphoric elaborations of *tactile* sound.[9] In contrast, synesthesias are direct, immediate, and concrete systems of relationships. They enter automatically at a particular physiological level that is preliminary to language.

55

Multiple Meanings of "Taste"

To each his own taste.

Old Proverb

In the previous chapter we observed that metaphors take off around their edges and become hard to pin down. Taste is another avenue that brings sensory data into the brain. As these messages move forward, they, too, soon attach to words that become literary abstractions. Yet, in those early milliseconds of intimate sensory experience, taste remains our primordial, special, gustatory sense. To taste is to *know*, deeply, directly, viscerally.

Taste impulses first enter low in the brainstem, then compound with our sense of smell as they relay to higher levels. Buddhist teachings regard taste as one of the six varieties of consciousness (along with vision, hearing, olfaction, touch, and mentation).

During the last three decades, I have been discovering that very different meanings have become attached to the word "taste." The story of how my understanding of these meanings evolved provides an object lesson in the perilous art of cross-cultural, if not cross-modal, communication.

In the early 1980s, I had often used "taste" as a way to express the immediate way kensho's insights had penetrated consciousness [Z:536–539]. True, no interior self remained to which such insights could be assigned. Still, the messages arose instantly (from the depths, it seemed) with no intervening thoughts. The insights seemed "real," intimate, but were very difficult to communicate in words. In this sense, they resembled my usual sense of taste.

Then too, I had employed "the *taste* of kensho" as a qualifying phrase. It suggested that even these impressive insights were far from some ultimate "full meal." Instead, this initial "taste" was being viewed as merely the first hint of what the ancients said lies *beyond*. For by then, I understood more about the Path. What lay ahead was an endless path pointing toward more advanced levels of satori, of Being, and—especially—of entering into the daily-life practice of *living* Zen (see chapter 4).

Near the end of that century, in September 1999, I read that Charles Tart had a new website. Why was he calling it *TASTE*? Because, for one thing, this acronym stood for "*t*he *a*rchives of *s*cientists' *t*ranscendent *e*xperiences."[1] Tart hoped to enlist people whose background was in science to use this website as a repository for first-person descriptions of their mystical/religious experiences. A worthy goal![2]

Next, while glancing at a book review in 2000, I noticed that Ken Wilber had used the phrase "One Taste" as a way to convey the singular perceptual immediacy of non-dual unity.[3]

Late in 2002, I discovered that "taste" had enjoyed a centuries-old usage. In the Tibetan Buddhist tradition, "One Taste" described the third of the four Yogas on the Mahamudra path. (The first Yoga is training in one-pointedness; the second Yoga is training in simplicity at various levels.)[4] In this third Tibetan usage, "One Taste" refers to the way our usual duality of experience finally dissolves. No longer does it conform to two constructs: samsara on the one hand vs. nirvana on the other. Instead, only *one state* of nondual awareness is revealed.

I could certainly relate to this. Two decades earlier, during the direct insight of kensho, I had dissolved into this same "oneness." Not until I began to emerge from it could I start to appreciate, in retrospect, the sharp *contrast* between this novel state of oneness and my ordinary self/other notions of duality. (Chapters 76 and 77 explore this further.)

Subsequently, in 2002, I read an article by Thich Nhat Hanh. Here, he cited the way the Buddha had once described his own teaching as having only "one taste, the taste of liberation."[5] As Thich Nhat Hanh then went on to explain the origin of this phrase, the Buddha had said that "the water in the four oceans has only one taste, the taste of salt, just as [my] teaching has only one taste, the taste of liberation."

I could resonate with this usage of "one taste." It conveyed the total emancipation I had experienced late in kensho. *Moksha* is the technical term in Sanscrit for this profound feeling of complete physical and psychic liberation [Z:538, 611].

In January 2003, I stumbled across yet another resonance of taste. While perusing *A Dictionary of Japanese-Buddhist Terms*,[6] I found "taste" referring to the idea that the great ocean (of Universal Truth) has only "One Taste." In contrast, the rivers flowing into this ocean each have different tastes. One taste was now a phrase associated with ecumenical overtones: many religious paths could lead on up from different sides of the same mountain.

In May 2003, intrigued by the way the word had entered into its title, I now began to read *One Taste. The Journals of Ken Wilber*, published in 1999.[7] In its pages, Wilber explained that "the Tibetans call it One Taste because all things in all states have the same flavor, namely Divine." A further clarification arose in his statement, "One Taste is itself a peak experience, but it too will become, with further practice, a plateau experience, then a permanent adaptation.*

It is important to be clear about what Wilber includes in this two-word phrase. "One Taste" serves as a metaphor, used in three different ways. It can refer either to (1) a brief state of consciousness, (2) a more sustained quality of consciousness, or (3) the *"ever-present awareness* or *constant consciousness* or basic *wakefulness*, or *choice-less awareness* that transcends and includes all possible states, and is therefore confined to none." Let us begin by focusing on the advanced degrees of this third option, then come back and try to distinguish it from the first two.

Ever-Present Awareness

Chapter 48 introduced this topic and chapter 56 will continue to discuss it.

The *ultimate* development of this third category of ongoing conscious awareness would occur only in some extraordinary person who *continues to experience* this level of awareness, *and* to an extraordinary degree, throughout each 24-hour period. The Buddha serves as an exemplar, and more. He was said permanently to have maintained not only this same special quality but also to have gone beyond this to the unique level of "suchness" [Z:637–641]. One interpretation of his being called *Thathagata* is that the term described his having "gone beyond" ordinary dual levels of consciousness. Clearly, the furthest extent of this exceptional capacity for awareness per se will be manifested only by some (ideal) person who is very far along the Path into the advanced *stage* of *ongoing* enlightened traits.

We return now for some parenthetical comments about the first two options cited in the paragraph before last. Because similar varieties of awareness are probably also experienced (at least for *brief* periods of indefinite length) during and just after the earlier temporary, advanced *states* of satori or ultimate pure Being. Such transitory categories of enhanced awareness might be sustained, say, for hours or a few days, but are not likely to become permanent [Z:627–630].

What other words are used to describe the ineffable nature of these short-lasting, more advanced degrees of "One Taste?" They include the following: When "inside and outside are no longer two, when subject and object are nondual, when looker and looked at are One . . ." Within such nonduality, "Emptiness embraces all Form, nirvana and samsara are not-two, and the Witness is everything witnessed" (see chapter 78).

Now, to return to some more of the words Wilber employs to describe various aspects of the *third*, ongoing, category of "One Taste." It does feel "more like the simple feeling of Being," at least in the sense that it represents a more enhanced degree of that ordinary "present feeling of existence" which we can each already experience. However, this "One Taste" may become more pervasive in its more advanced manifestations. Then it can present as "a vast Openness in which all experiences come and go, an infinite Spaciousness in which all perceptions move."

Wilber continues: In our ordinary, simpler levels of awareness, we still retain "a primitive trace of subject/object duality." However, "with further development, the Witness disappears into everything that is witnessed, subject and object become One Taste, or simple-Suchness. . . . There is a crystal-clear awareness of everything that is arising, moment to moment, it's just not happening to anybody. . . . There is simply all of this, and I am that." At such levels, "One Taste" is experienced as "extraordinarily ordinary, and perfectly simple, *just this*."

Wilber says that only after 25 years of meditative practice did he begin to experience this level of "constant consciousness." Then it was an ongoing ever-present awareness, "a continuity of consciousness." When this kind of "unbroken witnessing" does arrive, "then the one condition and One Taste of all realms becomes shockingly, simply obvious." Then the person experiences the basic tone of "One Taste" as a "relentless ordinariness, nothing special. It is *just this*, nothing more."[8]

Wilber describes this kind of constant awareness as having extended throughout his waking, sleeping, and dreaming hours. Yet the quality of his dream consciousness remained at the level of an innocent witnessing. He had no desire to change anything. (This particular aspect is different from many lucid dreams. During lucid dreams, dreamers may retain their impulse to steer events[9] [Z:324–327].

* * *

From the foregoing steps in this narrative, the reader can appreciate that a simple five-letter word can take on a variety of nuanced implications. "Taste" can refer to a quality of kensho/satori; a qualification on kensho; the essential nature of "oneness"; an ecumenical understanding; an ever-present awareness; a profound sense of liberation; and so on.

This is one of the problems in understanding any spiritual path. Even simple words complicate cross-cultural communication. Imagine that you are a visitor who has just arrived from some other planetary system. Could you easily translate each of the above connotations of taste into your own preexisting frames of reference? Nor can we who reside on this planet assume that a given word means the same thing to us as it does to our neighbor.

Still, this phrase, *ever-present awareness*, is useful when it describes a certain sustained quality of consciousness, one which arrives only after long meditative training in mindful attention. No person reaches this quality of heightened ongoing awareness as the result of one single state per se, in the absence of such training.

Ordinary waking consciousness spends much of its time skipping from topic to topic, distracted by myriad preoccupations. The Path of Zen opens up fresh vistas, ways to live at levels of ongoing awareness, clarity, and effectiveness. Some readers may be intrigued by notions of attaining—or contacting—still higher levels of supernatural powers. However, our existing laws of physics limit our understanding to energies that are either gravitational, electromagnetic, or involve nuclear forces. These have not explained how such "vibes" might be emitted from a three-pound lump of tissue, let alone enable some external field of "global consciousness" to excite brain responses in a coherent fashion.

Meanwhile, brain-bound neurologists are constrained by more than their training that the brain is the organ of the mind. They face daily reminders of how vulnerable are its nerve cells. No patient recovers consciousness from that deepest coma caused by one small lesion, a transection just beyond the slender stalk of the midbrain.

Yet, chapters 13, 15, 47, and 48 did explore how ordinary consciousness might evolve into a 24-hour sense of awareness. Moreover, early in the next chapter we return to take a closer look at so-called witnessing sleep. Neither it nor its daytime expressions are viewed as esoteric or mysterious. Rather do they seem to be the refinements—through mindful, meditative *practices*—of the everyday intrinsic functions that monitor our basic sense of awareness. Those are what keep us attentive, and mindfully attuned to the fresh individuality of each present moment as it evolves into the next one, and then into the next one . . .

Meanwhile, be careful of words. Including the words on these pages . . .

56

Witnessing Awareness during Sleep (Continued)

> The flurry of waking activity comes and goes; the inertia of sleep comes and goes. Yet, throughout these changing values of waking and sleeping, there is a silent, unbounded continuum of awareness that is me; I am never lost to myself.
>
> Report by a TM meditator[1]

Experienced meditators have long realized something interesting: their everyday consciousness has become "clearer." Only more recently has it been widely appreciated that their daytime sense of this "witnessing awareness" does not necessarily stop. This sense of awareness may still continue *even during sleep* (see chapter 48).

Forman, for example, describes a kind of readiness during sleep using different words.[2] He had meditated twice a day since 1969, and then in January 1972 had an unusual "opening" episode. It was a "shift inside" that "now allows me to feel quiet inside, even while I think, act, whatever." Since then, he continues, "it is as if I do not quite go to sleep. I sleep with most of me, I feel, but this quiet part, this part that doesn't change, does not sleep . . . I am just ready for things, even at the depths of sleep."

TM meditators have also reported that they "witnessed" a "quiet" peaceful inner awareness or wakefulness during sleep. Another series of sleep EEG studies was commendably performed in these subjects' own homes.[3] While sleeping during the earlier portions of the night, the meditators developed the expected delta waves (1–3 cps), the EEG signature typical of slow wave sleep. However, *on these slow waves,* they also superimposed unusual degrees of faster theta-alpha activity. Moreover, during deep slow wave sleep, these advanced meditators now showed an unusual EMG finding: epochs during which the EMG activity of their chin muscle was *decreased.* Such a decrease usually accompanies the elevated levels of brain activity found during normal REM sleep [Z:316–322]. In addition, during their actual REM sleep, the density of their REM EEG changes was unusually increased.

These EEG and EMG findings provide further objective confirmation of the meditators' own subjective reports. Indeed, the evidence suggesting that they not only sleep at a "lighter level" but that they are also more "aware" is an important phenomenon of general neurobiological interest.

This greater "continuity of consciousness" has been studied subsequently in other TM meditators.[4] The 51 subjects were divided into three groups. Eight women and nine men were in each group. The first group had not yet been instructed how to meditate; the second group had practiced for some 7 years. They reported having "transcendental experiences" frequently during meditation practice, but only occasionally during other waking and sleeping hours. The third group of subjects had practiced for some 24 years. They reported the "continuous coexistence of the transcendent with waking and sleeping states."

Appropriate interviews and psychological tests were also performed. The basic question was, while they were *awake*, Did these long-term meditators (whom one might regard as having an "ever-present" variety of awareness) show consistent physiological differences from the other two groups? The answer was yes. Both their EEGs and contingent negative variation responses were different.

The EEG data suggested that when these "continuous co-existence" ("integrated") meditators were involved in task activities, they showed greater frontal coherence of those waveforms that cycled between 6 and 12 times per second. (This interval includes both alpha and theta frequencies.) Their extra 12 cps alpha activity also reached higher amplitudes in both frontal, central, and parietal EEG leads (see chapter 16).

First, a brief explanation of the *c*ontingent *n*egative *v*ariation response (CNV). This is an event-related potential of anticipation (see chapter 49). Subjects develop it during that interval of *waiting* between the first delivery of a warning stimulus and the moment when that second imperative stimulus arrives which signals them to make a motor response. The CNV potential has two aspects. The *early* negative potential peaks some 500 to 800 ms after the first stimulus. It reflects the kinds of highly automatic orienting responses that one's brain makes when it has just been "warned." The *late* negative potential peaks just before the second stimulus seems due to arrive. It reflects the brain's more immediate, proactive preparations during those 200 ms which serve to mobilize one's motor, perceptual, cognitive, and attentional resources.

When the third group of "continuous co-existence" subjects was given a *choice* of responses, their contingent negative variation potentials were *lower* in amplitude than in their controls. This finding was given a positive interpretation, in the direction perhaps of greater efficiency. The authors suggested that these subjects "did not initiate preparatory responses until they knew the correct response." This suggestion of improved "executive control," when coupled with the greater frontal EEG coherence, might be consistent with a more efficient level of frontal cortical functioning. As a practical matter, however, neither the reaction times nor the accuracy on tasks differed among the three groups.

Obviously, many further *longitudinal* studies are indicated to clarify exactly how, and why, long-term meditators differ from their nonmeditating cohorts. In the interim, the evidence suggests that when TM meditative practice continues for more than two decades, it can be associated with a subjective impression of being more aware while sleeping deeply that is supported by several EEG patterns. The semantic implication in the authors' wording that "a greater sense of self during activity" is present (and that this "sense of self" is perhaps a quality to be *desired*) would need to be checked against the findings in long-term Zen meditators. This may just be another problem involving words, because in Zen meditators a *lesser* "sense of self" during activity would be regarded as optimal [Z: 668–677].

57

Tilting the Emotional Set Point?

> There is no such thing as good and bad in an absolute sense. There is only the good and bad—the harm in terms of happiness or suffering—that our thoughts and actions do to ourselves or to others.
>
> Matthieu Ricard[1]

> A man who has not passed through the inferno of his passions has never overcome them.
>
> Carl Jung (1875–1961)

For over a decade, Richard Davidson and colleagues at the University of Wisconsin have studied asymmetrical EEG activities in the more frontal parts of the brain, correlating them both with differences in emotion and affective style[2] (see chapter 43). Converging lines of evidence have suggested that increased activity involving the left frontal cortex (and some decreases in activity in the amygdala) are linked with our everyday more positive emotions: vigor, enthusiasm, and buoyancy.[3]

These EEG asymmetries are exemplified in the "Happy Geshe" a Tibetan Buddhist monk who had practiced for over 30 years. His "life was his practice." Not only was he the abbot of one of the major monasteries in India, he was also considered to be both upbeat and laid-back, as well as spiritually advanced and scholarly. His frontal EEG asymmetry score was the point of interest. It was tilted three standard deviations toward the left side.

Many pages in this book raise inescapable questions about emotions. One such question is by which mechanisms could such a "leftward tilt in the emotional set point" represent a long term "fruit of spiritual practice?"[4]

58

The Roots of Our Emotions

> We boil at different degrees.
>
> Ralph Waldo Emerson (1803–1882)

> There is a road from the eye to the heart that does not go through the intellect.
>
> G. K. Chesterton (1874–1936)

Antidotes for the "Three Poisons"

Emotions get in the way of our seeing the world clearly. Buddhist meditative traditions regard human greed, hatred, and ignorance as the cause of much of our suffering. Daily meditation can reduce the habit energy that drives our superficial longings and loathings. But wisdom remains the only enduring remedy for existential ignorance. Deep insights into reality confer simplicity, stability, and provide the only lasting remedy for our major structural problem.

Siddhartha was the architect and builder of his own framework of self-deception. It was this that he shattered during his awakening, the deep delusion of a separate, enduring, egocentric self.

Gradually Calming the Emotions; Not Wanting; Nonattachment

In the chapter on witnessing awareness (chapter 56) we discussed the potential that very long-term meditative training has to bring into one's awareness an ongoing sense of greater readiness and clarity. Mindful, objective introspection also helps to generate little, acute intuitions. Intuitions identify one's unfruitful character traits and habitual misbehaviors.

Once you have identified your covetous behaviors, you can slowly reverse this trend toward greed with the aid of deliberate incremental acts of generosity. Employing similar, thought-out principles, you can slowly remedy some hatreds and loathings. How? By the deliberate long-term practice of loving kindness, plus

Table 5
The "Three Poisons" and Their Antidotes

For This Illness	*Apply This Remedy*
Greed (longing)	Generosity
Loathing (hatred)	Loving kindness, compassion, forgiveness
Ignorance	Mindful introspection

deliberate acts of forgiveness and tolerance (table 5). Cognitive psychology is not a new invention. The early Buddhists were well-versed in the practice of arousing in themselves affirmative states of mind. These included limitless kindness, selfless compassion, boundless delight in the joy of others, and unbounded equanimity toward friend and foe alike.

After mindful moments of introspection have first diagnosed some personal problematic issues, renunciation (*sila*) is an ancient word applicable to that wide range of behavioral responses useful in helping turn away from harmful situations and avoid unfruitful consequences.

After meditating for many months, I discovered that my former social "taste" for beer, wine, and other forms of liquor had begun to drop away. I had experienced what liquor could sometimes do to me, seen how it had severely affected other people. However, something else happened beyond these thought-provoking psychological factors. My "wanting" of alcohol seemed also to have dissolved. The level at which this vanished felt visceral, physiological.

The social problems caused by those who overindulge in alcohol are now being overtaken by the medical consequences linked to overeating and physical inactivity. Item: By the standards set by the World Health Organization, some 54% of our nation's adults and 25% of our children are overweight.

Another old term is *nibbida*.[1] The term translates best as a kind of *gradual* transformative comprehension. It is the kind of insightful ripening that matures eventually "into a deep understanding of the unsatisfactory nature of the conditioned world of constructed experience." As Andrew Olendzki explains, this kind of comprehension transforms chiefly the way one reconstructs one's own internal notions, "in *here*." It is not directed externally as a statement critical of what that other world has become "out there."

Objects "out there" will always be only "such as they are." What matters are our reactions to them. Our *internal* appetites are the real source of the problem. We get *attached* to attractive things out there. We then suffer the consequences for being so self-indulgent.

As a mental posture, nonattachment ripens and matures only very gradually. Slowly, we develop a better understanding of how we have allowed ourselves to become overconditioned by our culture, enabled ourselves to be entrapped into longings and loathings. At its most advanced levels, nonattachment is not a revulsion or a disgust. Rather is it a deep understanding: various attractions in the outside world have been tested *and found wanting*.

Recognizing Emotions in Others

Kobori-Roshi introduced me to the way the Japanese might invite a worried friend by asking: "How is your inner weather?" Some people can accurately judge what emotion is expressed on other peoples' faces. Paul Ekman measures their capacities to recognize emotions in the laboratory. His videotapes flash the microexpressions of a facial emotion for a mere one-fifth to one-thirtieth of a second.[2]

One highly experienced Tibetan-trained monk (Lama Öser) was exceptionally good at recognizing microemotions. His scores at recognizing the expressions of contempt, anger, and fear were two standard deviations above the norm. Another Western-born meditator (trained in the Tibetan tradition) was also exceptionally skillful in recognizing the expressions of happiness, sadness, and disgust.

Do such capacities represent enhanced processing speeds in general, special abilities to focus on key facial features, or some unusual attunement to emotions per se? These factors have yet to be measured separately. However, these enhanced abilities do seem to correlate with personality traits that evidence an interest in new experiences and an openness to them.

A separate study of Lama Öser tested his startle reflex to an extremely loud sound. This startle reflex begins some 200 ms after the sound, and lasts for about 300 ms. It is more intense in persons who harbor greater degrees of negative emotions—especially feelings of fear, anger, sadness, and disgust. Despite this extremely loud sound, Öser's *facial* muscles showed no startle response. His face did not twitch to the sound either while he was deliberately meditating in "the open state" or while he was meditating in a state of one-pointed concentration (as further described in chapter 89).

His comment was that "the explosive sound seemed softer, as if I was distanced from the sensations." In contrast, his heart rate, perspiration, and blood pressure still showed the usual responses to startle. The lama's social skills were also tested by confronting him with two persons who deliberately disagreed with him. He displayed more disarming smiles with the gentle disputant than with the aggressive one, yet he showed few of the polygraph changes that might have been expected to occur during such arguments.

59

Attributing Different Emotions to Various Brain Regions

> Anger is never without a Reason, but seldom with a good one.
>
> Benjamin Franklin (1706–1790)

> The "limbic system" has never been anything more than a high-order conceptual entity that helps us designate and discuss the general location of the families of functional neural systems that contribute most heavily to dynamic processes commonly placed under the conceptual umbrella of "emotions."
>
> Jaak Panksepp[1]

Our emotional roots run deep. Most simpler theories about emotions list their biphasic qualities along two scales. One scale is *valence*: pleasant/unpleasant; plus/minus; appetitive/aversive, and so on. A second scale is *intensity*, the amount of emotion. Personal experience teaches us that negative, unpleasant emotions not only acutely outweigh our positive emotions but also reverberate for longer periods.

Heilman emphasizes how emotional experiences arouse us and lead to behavioral activations.[2] Our emotions do *move* us. They prompt corresponding active muscle responses. Researchers can measure these approach/avoidance behaviors, along with their associated autonomic responses of arousal and activation. The immediate and delayed consequences of emotions can prove constructive or destructive, both for ourselves and for society.

Do these powerful affective states arise in our cortex? Panksepp notes that electrical stimulation delivered to the neocortex usually fails to evoke affective responses. Emotions are also difficult to elicit from most regions of the thalamus. However (using quite high levels of current), researchers can evoke fragments of emotional feelings from higher limbic and paralimbic areas (including the cortex of several cingulate, frontal, and temporal regions). But such strong stimuli may set off secondary epileptiform activities, which spread into lower brain systems. On the other hand, when stimuli are delivered directly to *subcortical* sites in the brainstem and lower limbic regions, they can quickly produce coherent, powerful, emotional behavioral responses together with corresponding affective states.[3]

Many different schemes have been devised to categorize emotions. A recent (2005) critical review of the emotions contends that solid data do not yet support many theoretical concepts in this field.[4] Panksepp (uncited in this review) has made a comprehensive survey of the sources of human and animal emotions. He identifies a series of basic emotional systems that result in obvious behavior, correlates them with *lower* brain modules and networks, then goes on to speculate about which neural modulators most likely play excitatory roles in these local systems.[5] (Interested readers are referred to this review. It predicts not only how our basic emotions originate but also how they become linked with the primitive core of our physical self.)

Panksepp classifies affective systems into three conceptual categories.[6] The first category includes our more reflexive *emotive responses*. They cause us to be startled, to spit out spoiled food (dis-gust), and to recoil from a painful stimulus.

In the second category are our "blue-ribbon," "grade-A" *emotions*. They are orchestrations, blending the higher zones of the limbic and paralimbic cortex with those deep midbrain regions which integrate sensorimotor emotional responses. A recent synopsis[7] lists the basic emotions in this second category as including

- seeking/expectancy (this basic system serves to support our positive, appetitive, motivational drives);
- the standard basic emotions: rage-anger, fear-anxiety, lust-sexuality, care-nurturance, panic-separation, play-joy.

Panksepp identifies the periaqueductal gray as a key region contributing to each of these emotional systems. Lying in the core of the midbrain, its technical name is the *central gray substance*, often shortened to the *central gray* (see figure 4, chapter 23) [Z:232–235]. Why single out the central gray? It is here that the several basic emotional systems cited above first begin to converge. Nearby in the colliculi of the midbrain are the polymodal sensory cells that first integrate our vision, hearing, and somatosensory information (Z:241–242). Also conveniently nearby is the midbrain region that begins to organize locomotion.

In the third category of emotions are our *higher sentiments*. These include shame, guilt, contempt, envy, humor, empathy, sympathy, and certain forms of jealousy. In any Buddhist formulation, at a bare minimum, one would also add: respect, gratitude, and humility. (The early phrenologists precisely localized the bumps for many sentiments, and could have added the emotion of sadness as well. However, contemporary neuroscience tends to regard these "sentimental" emotions as expressing complex mixtures of more primitive affects with our higher cognitive processes.)

Motivation and Approach Behavior

Emotion and *motivation* are two words that share the concept of motion. Positive motivation tends to correlate with forward motion, with approach behaviors. Those who classify behavior can find the two words very difficult to separate.[8] It will not do to suggest that emotions are what we human beings feel, whereas motivations are what move our pets and other animals.

One approach to this troublesome issue is to classify behaviors that express seeking/expectancy/interest in terms of a "basic emotional system," one that represents a generally positive motivation.[9] Some of the motivations that underlie a person's spiritual quest might fall into this classification, yet the strong instinct to *seek* is clearly a property that we humans share with animals.[10]

I can testify to one aspect of kensho that is relevant to this particular issue. It was the sudden *total dissolution of the motivation to act*. The impression was that the primitive motoric premise had been undermined far underground. A sense of nonintervention had replaced the whole motivational disposition to approach [Z:607–608, 220–222]. One cannot imagine so total a vacancy of approach behavior. Its absence can be fully appreciated only in retrospect.

In neuroimaging studies, many of our ordinary approach feelings and behaviors tend to correlate with *left*-sided activations.[11] Circuits involving the nucleus accumbens are among those contributing to our positive "forward-leaning" approach behaviors [Z:169–172, 620]. A key source for many of these activations of the accumbens are the dopamine nerve cells of the ventral tegmental area, another midbrain region near the central gray.

The instinct to seek out and approach is deeply rooted and exerts a powerful influence. No fence and no horizon line can contain the human quest. Three classic lines by John Masefield, evoke both its feverish quality and the way it empowers the brains of animals and humans alike:

> Go forth to seek; the quarry never found
> Is still a fever to the questing hound,
> The skyline is a promise, not a bound.

Frowning as an Index of Displeasure

We do not have to actually *move* backward to show displeasure. A simple frown suffices. The corrugator muscle lowers and contracts (knits) our brow. Bradley and Lang collected an International Affective Picture System (IAPS). Their series of pleasant pictures ranged from flowers to erotica. Unpleasant pictures ranged from a fork to a mutilated body. It was the unpleasant pictures that most contracted the frowning muscle, as shown by its EMG responses.[12] (Could long-term meditative training serve as a kind of long-acting "Botox," this time for the brain?)

Introductory Comments about the Lateralization of Emotional Functions

Emotions arise from many regions. Our individual brains are different, and our two hemispheres are also different. Still, *positive* affective states and traits do tend to correlate with more left frontal and other left-sided activations (see chapters 43, 50, and 52).

Some important clinical evidence supports this interpretation. The more the *left* hemisphere is acutely *in*activated by an amobarbital infusion, the more this allows the *right* hemisphere to be released from the prior tight inhibitory hold of its partner. Now *dis*inhibited, this liberated right hemisphere can express its own inherent tendencies toward more negative feelings.[13] This release of right hemispheric functions by an acute left-sided lesion serves as one explanation for the patients' unusual symptoms and pointing behavior described in chapter 8.

When music students listen to jazz, rock, or classical music, their EEG activation patterns indicate that *positive* emotional attributions correlate more with *left* temporal activations. In contrast, *negative* emotional responses correlate with more bilateral patterns that show a *right* frontotemporal distribution.[14]

MEG studies show that our brain reacts quickly to the expression on another person's face. In 150 ms, the right fusiform gyrus becomes activated in response to faces that are expressing emotion. Here, happy expressions evoke stronger responses than disgust.[15]

When subjects respond to pleasant or unpleasant words, their fMRI signals vary accordingly. Unpleasant words stimulate the *right* amygdala. Pleasant words activate the *left* frontal pole. Words of both types generate strong responses from the left anterior cingulate cortex under the curve of the corpus callosum (the genu).[16]

In general, responses to emotional pictures from the IAPS collection will increase fMRI signals on *both* sides in several regions: the medial frontal lobe and anterior cingulate gyrus, the dorsolateral frontal lobe, the amygdala and anterior temporal regions, and the cerebellum.[17] Unpleasant pictures activate the right hemisphere more; pleasant pictures activate the left hemisphere more.

Dynamic Sequences of Fear Responses

Fear is an adaptive response. Fear helps us survive, though we feel the cut of its two-edged sword. Which parts of our brain respond *first* to the repeated expressions of fear on another person's face? Our sense of fear also gathers momentum. Which other regions then participate during the next minute or so?

Consider what is involved. We gauge how much fear other persons' faces express by more than their "wide-eyed" appearance. Raised eyebrows and open mouths also signal that they are recoiling in fright. So at least three factors responsible for our impression can be identified: (1) we register the bare sensory facts; (2) we discern their particular pattern; (3) we guess which emotion this other person must be feeling, based on past experience.

When a recent experiment addressed these issues, it was aided by *simultaneous* fMRI monitoring *and* skin conductance responses. The 22 normal subjects were viewing the standard photographs of fearful or neutral faces.[18] The first segment of facial presentations lasted 30 seconds: four fearful faces alternated with four neutral faces. These first presentations of frightened faces prompted in the viewer the early increased *numbers* of skin conductance responses and a significant increase in fMRI signals localized in and around the left parietal operculum. This region included some of the secondary sensory cortex and the adjacent left insula (BA 43)[19] (see chapter 28).

The presentations of the next 16 faces occupied the next 60 seconds. Though fewer skin conductance responses occurred, they now coincided with a relative increase in fMRI signals in the *right* dorsomedial prefrontal cortex (BA 9), the left cuneus, (BA 18), and anterior cingulate regions on both sides, L > R, (BA 24/32). Perhaps, during this intermediate phase, the observer was now entering into more "top-down," semi-cognitive interpretations about what the frightened faces had just revealed.

The later presentation of eight faces occupied the final 30 seconds. The numbers of skin conductance responses again increased during this segment. This later phase coincided with a relative increase in *left*-sided signals. While these arose notably in the left amygdala, they also involved the anterior cingulate, superior temporal gyrus (BA 42) and orbitofrontal cortex (BA 11). These findings in the amygdala suggested that it might be becoming increasingly "vigilant" to a potential threatening situation, rather than becoming habituated to it. In general, responses tend to persist longer in this left amygdala than in its right-sided counterpart (see chapter 27).

Other Similarities and Differences

Neuroimaging studies show that men and women mostly activate the same regions when they process autobiographical memories.[20] During one recent fMRI study from Germany, men tended to show more signals in their left parahippocampal gyrus; women showed more signals in their right dorsolateral frontal cortex. Even so, the two genders showed no obvious differences either in the emotional intensity of their memories or in their memory performances.[21]

The two hemispheres differ in the ways they represent, and influence, the autonomic nervous system. For example, the left hemisphere tends predominantly to influence parasympathetic functions; the right is biased toward sympathetic functions. Subjects whose migraine headaches are only on the left side show enhanced parasympathetic responses (vasodilation, heart rate slowing) when "diluted soapy eye drops" are placed in either eye between attacks.[22] This local irritant stimulates the trigeminal nerve and the brain stem (see chapter 73).

60

Conditioning: Learning and Unlearning

> He who has broken the five fetters—lust, hate, delusion, pride, false views—is one who has crossed to the other shore.
>
> *Dhammapada*[1]

> There is nothing either good or bad, but thinking makes it so.
>
> *Hamlet*, 2.2

Kobori-Roshi emphasized how much prior conditioning we all had undergone. Yes, at birth, we were essentially *unconditioned*. Then, as life began to lure us, wound us, condition us, we learned not only to lust and hate but to take false pride in false views. We became deluded in many ways, and attached to our delusions.

In their unfruitful manifestations, *these emotions and delusions are precisely the conditionings which Zen would have us shed*. Long-range Zen training implies returning to the native virtues of our unconditioned self and thereby liberating its most fruitful expressions.

We accumulate bad habits, and they waste a lot of energy. But what *is* a habit and how can we change it? *A habit is a way of learned responding*. We establish good habits and bad habits. We form their synaptic connections gradually, both through trial and error and reinforcement.[2]

Monkeys integrate two kinds of functions when they develop their visual habits. On the sensory limb of their conditioning, their inferior temporal cortex helps them begin to discriminate and recognize *what* they see. Then, on the motor limb, the dorsal striatum, including the caudate nucleus and putamen, helps them develop their habitual behavioral responses. When these processes join, their links form stimulus-response associations.[3]

You can call this "learned habit formation" if you wish, but the message is clear. Once we establish a bad habit, it will not be easy to *un*learn. Unlearning means gradually enabling these sensorimotor and all their other allied circuits to become *less active* [Z:327–334].

The cerebellum also participates in conditioning. The way it contributes to motor learning in animals can be demonstrated as follows. A tone is delivered. The sound is followed—0.1 to 1.5 seconds later—by a puff of air directed to the eye.[4] After many trials, the animals become conditioned. They will close their eyelids just before the predicted arrival of the air puff. The interpositus nucleus, deep in the cerebellum, is one of several sites in the configuration that yields this conditioned response. It is relatively easy to extinguish such conditioning. Extinction occurs after the tone stimulus is delivered several times, but is not followed by the air puff.

Fear conditioning is different. Again, a tone serves as the conditioned stimulus. The animals soon learn that it will be followed by a more aversive (unconditioned) stimulus, namely a foot shock. Connections in the amygdala that engage its lateral and central nuclei play a prominent role in the circuitry for this form of conditioned learning. Other limbic and paralimbic regions are also involved in assessing the nature of this and other fearful stimuli that might lurk in the environment.[5]

Human Studies of Conditioning

If you happen to score higher on state and trait anxiety tests, you can be more easily conditioned in the laboratory. On the basis of their scores on such tests, five male subjects were preselected to be more neurotic and anxious than average.

PET scans then monitored these more anxious subjects during three phases of their responses: an initial phase of habituation to a tone; a conditioning phase in which the tone was paired with a brief shock to the wrist; and finally, during a phase of extinction. In this third phase, the tone was simply presented by itself once more.[6]

Given these experimental conditions, you might think that extinction could mean that the conditioned response was simply being allowed to dwindle, in a sense by default. However, the extinction phase was revealed to be one of activity, not passivity. During extinction, six regions of the *right* hemisphere showed *more* activation than occurred during the habituation phase: the orbitofrontal cortex, dorsolateral prefrontal cortex, inferior and superior frontal cortex, and inferior and middle temporal cortex. However, in the left hemisphere, only 2 regions were activated: BA 19 and the superior frontal cortex. No activation was apparent in the amygdala.

fMRI studies of conditioning were conducted on nine volunteers (seven male and two female).[7] The subjects looked at neutral-appearing faces, two male faces and two female. However, these faces were conditioned by being paired with an aversive tone. Skin conductance responses confirmed that the subjects did acquire conditioned autonomic responses. Conditioning increased signals in both the anterior cingulate and anterior insula regions, and in the medial parietal cortex. The anterior cingulate signals clearly appeared to anticipate the arrival of the aversive stimulus. This suggested that the subjects were linking unpleasant pain circuitry with memory.

Two subjects showed a rapid habituation in their amygdala signals just to the tone stimulus alone. This rapid habituation of the signals suggested that their amygdala was participating only in the *early* phase of the aversive conditioning (see chapter 27).

What about the motor limb of this conditioning response? It was evident in the enhanced signals from the supplementary motor area and in both premotor cortical regions, as well as in the red nucleus of the midbrain.

The neuroimaging data cited here tap only simpler forms of aversive conditioning. All the other ways that society conditions us have yet to be studied. Even so, it is already clear that our limbic and paralimbic systems, and those of our brainstem, enter into making us blush with shame, flush with anger, glow with pride, blanch with fear, and clutch with desire.

Conditioning and Extinction in Zen

Though major Zen insights acutely penetrate one's conscious experience, consciousness thereafter identifies mostly their surface expressions. Why? Because prajna cuts off the person's old visceral conditionings at deep, inexpressible levels. These silent subterranean processes might seem to have deprogrammed self-consciousness for only a few hours. However, their enduring changes set the stage for a redirection of the person's prior unfruitful personality traits.

Nirvana translates as extinction [Z:579–580]. Given the results cited above in the PET study of extinction,[8] a testable hypothesis would suggest that right hemisphere regions could play the more active role in the extinctions of the egocentric self during kensho-satori. However, these PET results first need to be confirmed by fMRI in normal subjects, under stringent conditions that firmly establish a true baseline of absolute data for the two hemispheres, thus avoiding *relative* comparisons between the two sides (see chapters 43, 50 and 59).

Buddhist practices involve other kinds of self-induced positive, affirmative conditioning. They enter into our developing "good habits." How can we cultivate them along the route toward genuine compassion? Chapter 89 discusses this important topic and its implications for ongoing and future neuroimaging research.

61

Addictions

> Every form of addiction is bad, no matter whether the narcotic be alcohol or morphine or idealism.
>
> Carl Jung (1875–1961)

> And what is grasping? There are four: grasping for sense-pleasures, for speculative views (about permanence), for rites and customs, and for delusions of selfhood.
>
> Majjhima-Nikaya I (49–54)[1]

People keep grasping for attractive things and, once grasped, grip them firmly. Drug addictions and obesity are now established as major problems in society. Reviewing drug addiction recently in the New England Journal of Medicine, Cami and Farre define it as "a chronic, relapsing disorder in which compulsive drug-seeking and drug-taking behavior persists despite serious negative consequences."[2] Some prefer the term "substance dependence," and find the words more comfortable than "addiction."

The ancient Buddhist teachings specify the "three fires" of longing, loathing, and delusion-ignorance. The teachings are applicable both to the problem of drug addiction and to less obvious forms of recurrent unfruitful behavior. In general, substances that lead to addiction tend either to induce pleasant states or to relieve distress, or both. For example, many drugs produce degrees of euphoria. Initially they act as "positive reinforcers." Later, they can act as "negative reinforcers." This means that they just postpone the unpleasant symptoms (dysphoria) that are sure to arise on that day of reckoning when these drugs are no longer available.

As a college student, I noticed that the smell of beer whetted my desire for a cigarette. Similar visual, auditory, or olfactory cues can induce a conditioned response. This can go on to create a craving for a drug, even though the actual "liking" for this drug might steadily decrease. When Pavlov's dogs became conditioned to salivate, an ordinary bell served as their cue. As their brains transformed this sound into a dinner bell, they recognized that this dependable signal would be followed by food.

Drug addiction in humans may begin as an "impulse control" disorder, a way of behaving that at first might seem to help the person cope with tense, stressful situations. Indeed, this impulsive act itself may lead to some temporary sense of pleasure or relief. A sense of regret may or may not follow.

Drug addiction gradually becomes reminiscent of well-known obsessive-compulsive psychiatric disorders in the sense that the addict develops both recurrent thoughts that cause anxiety and compulsive repetitive behaviors that appear briefly to reduce his or her distress.[3] Adding increasingly to the addict's problem are difficulties in making hard decisions and in judging consequences.

Animal Models of Addiction

Many lines of evidence from animal models are woven into our current theories of drug addiction.[4] What other factors enter into the sensory and motor aspects of conditioning that make addictive behaviors so difficult to break? A brief survey helps appreciate that multiple synapses are involved. Two major systems can be seen to underlie addiction: central and medial. Both systems involve the connections of the *extended amygdala* (see chapter 27).

- The *central* division. This network links the *central* nucleus of the amygdala, the central sublenticular extended amygdala, the *lateral* bed nucleus of the stria terminalis (BNST), and a transitional area in and around the shell of the nucleus accumbens. These regions interact with the *lateral* hypothalamus and with the *ventral* tegmental area. They also receive a prominent input from the basolateral amygdala, the insula, a part of the thalamus, and the medial frontal region. Many different terminals supply the lateral BNST with dopamine, norepinephrine, corticotropin-releasing factor (CRF), and neuropeptide Y. This nucleus also contains its own CRF and galanin nerve cells.
- The *medial* division. This network links the *medial* BNST, the medial nucleus of the amygdala, and the medial sublenticular extended amygdala. These regions have close interconnections with the *medial* hypothalamus. This medial division receives prominent inputs from the olfactory nuclei, the infralimbic cortex, the ventral subiculum, and the basomedial amygdala. Its output pathways lead to the ventral striatum, the ventral medial hypothalamus, and the midbrain central gray. The medial BNST contains high levels of vasopressin. Its morphology differs in males and females, both in humans and animals.

The Dopamine Pathway

Dopamine is crucial (see chapter 24). DA cells in the ventral tegmental area play a leading role in the reinforcing effects of drugs of abuse.[5] Two DA circuits are involved.

- The meso*limbic* DA circuit. These DA cells project to the nucleus accumbens, amygdala, and hippocampus. This limbic circuit is linked with the acute reinforcing effects of drugs, with the conditioned responses and remembrances that drive the craving for drugs, and with the unpleasant emotional and motivational syndrome that develops when addicting drugs are withdrawn.

- The meso*cortical* DA circuit. These DA cells project to all divisions of the prefrontal cortex, as well as to the anterior cingulate cortex. This circuit enters into the conscious experience of the immediate effects of drugs. It also is involved in drug cravings and in the compulsion to take drugs.

Not only do the circuits in these regions interconnect among themselves and with the extended amygdala, they sometimes inhibit and other times enhance the firing of ventral tegmental DA nerve cells.

The functions of the nucleus accumbens play a major role in the effects of psychostimulants (e.g. amphetamines and cocaine), as well as opioids, cannabinoids (marijuana), and phencyclidine ("angel dust"). In contrast, other effects of opioids, ethanol, barbiturates, and benzodiazepines are exerted through the DA cells in the ventral tegmental area.

The Opioid Pathway

Opiate receptors are widely distributed in the normal human brain (see chapter 35) [Z:213–223]. However, humans differ in the numbers and types of their receptors (see chapter 36). So do animals. Mice can be bred to lack the mu opiate receptor. These deficient mice are called knockout mice. Mu opiate knockout mice cannot develop analgesia when given opioids. They cannot be lured into self-administration of the opioid, nor can they undergo an opioid withdrawal syndrome. (Mice lacking kappa opiate receptors can develop analgesia; and they will express lesser degrees of the withdrawal syndrome.) Opiates, like other abused drugs, lead to the increased release of DA into the nucleus accumbens.

Long-Term Consequences of Drug Use

A person's acute impulse to take a psychoactive drug (it feels "good"; positive reinforcement) can evolve into a chronic compulsion to take the drug. Then, once addiction has been established, unpleasant feelings arise during any attempts at drug withdrawal (negative reinforcement). These symptoms continue to drive the drug-taking behavior.[6]

In the United States, despite many years of "recreational" abuse of cocaine, relatively few users became hooked into the compulsive use of cocaine, "only" some 5% to 18%.[7] What pushes the casual user into getting hooked? Animal experiments suggest two basic mechanisms that shape the progression to compulsive drug use. Rats can be trained to self-administer cocaine. When they have free access to cocaine for very short periods (1 hour) each day, their self-administration rates for cocaine remain relatively constant. In contrast, rats exposed to longer periods of continuous access (6 hours per day) develop escalating habits of self-administration.

Later, after cocaine had been withdrawn from both groups for 14 days, the short-access rats showed the more sensitized responses to a single infusion of cocaine. However, this late sensitization did not occur in the rats that earlier had access to cocaine for 6 hours each day.

Drug tolerance and drug withdrawal are each associated with complex long-term metabolic changes in second messenger systems (see chapter 37). Activation of CRF is one common mechanism underlying the development of drug dependence. Locus ceruleus nerve cells fire *more* during the dynamic, stressful phase of opioid withdrawal. This additional norepinephrine adds to the anguish of the withdrawal syndrome (see chapter 32).

In the short term, opioids lower the levels of cyclic AMP and of CREB (see chapter 37). Long-term administration of opioids activates CREB in the nucleus accumbens. Early during a period of withdrawal, increased dynorphin may contribute to the dysphoria. When dynorphin activates its kappa receptors in the ventral tegmental area, the resulting drop in DA in the nucleus accumbens can contribute to the craving for more drugs.[8]

Other Considerations in Substance Abuse Disorders

In the United States, some 45% of those who abuse alcohol turn out to have some other mental disorder during their lifetime. Some 72% of those who have another form of drug use disorder will also have a mental disorder at some time.[9] Therefore, once substance abuse has begun, it often complicates other psychiatric disorders and aggravates their symptoms.

Other Kinds of "Rewards" That Reinforce Human Behavior

There is still a tendency to talk about discrete "reward centers" in the human brain. The discussion above suggests, however, that both the positive and negative reinforcing aspects of drugs seem to act on intricate systems that engage multiple perceptual, motivational, and habitual motoric mechanisms.

Jung, like Buddha before him, realized how often we get locked into recurrent patterns of thinking and behavior. Consider, for instance, how quickly most humans respond to abstract *financial* rewards. The ways we set and reset our financial "values" have been monitored by fMRI. Normal subjects were studied while they were performing a gambling task, a game that carried financial penalties as well as rewards.[10]

Certain brain responses are linked with the *level* of the monetary reward per se. Greater financial reward levels correlate with greater increases in fMRI signals in the midbrain and the ventral striatum.[11] Other brain responses are associated with interactions between this actual reward level and shifts up or down from it.

Suppose financial rewards are both high and increasing. Only then do signals increase in those other key sites supplied by the ventral tegmental DA cells. The particular regions that respond in this context-sensitive way to reward levels include the globus pallidus, thalamus, and the anterior cingulate under the "knee" (genu) of the corpus callosum.

Suppose the financial penalty reaches high levels. Now fMRI signals increase in the hippocampus bilaterally. They increase further when the game players encounter a losing streak.

Addictions are excesses. They remind all consumers that value systems have practical bottom-line consequences. In an era of abundant instant gratifications, it becomes crucial to take a hard look at needs and longings. Jung knew that they include our loftiest, most idealistic impulses. It is easy to become trapped into "spiritual materialism" by habitual, overconditioned ways of thinking and behaving. An ounce of prevention always remains a useful option. For a few, it will mean a simpler lifestyle, and commitment to a program of long-term meditative training. These and other conservative measures can help a person avoid unfruitful overstimulation of those limbic and paralimbic nerve cells at the far end of the long DA pathways.

But now you might be wondering, What will this do to my love life?

62

Being in Love

> Our fMRI experiment on people in love supports this proposition: romantic love is an addictive drug.
>
> Helen Fisher[1]

> On the whole, our results suggest a push-pull mechanism of attachment that on one hand de-activates areas mediating negative emotions, avoidance behavior and social assessment, and on the other triggers mechanisms involved in reward.
>
> Andreas Bartels and Semir Zeki[2]

Readers of every age know that we feel romantic love at levels deeper than those of our ordinary states of consciousness. Romantic love actively takes over our lives. Fisher defines it as "a fundamental human drive ... a physiological *need*, a profound urge, an instinct to court and win a particular mating partner."[3]

If you can think back to when you have fallen *out* of love, you may also recall having suffered the anguished pangs of withdrawal. The similarities between romantic love and the topics in the previous chapter reflect the ways that both sometimes activate similar brain regions.

Neural Correlates of Romantic Love

John Z. Young (1907–1997) questioned whether there was any use for a neuroscience that could not tell us anything about love. Responding to the challenge, Bartels and Zeki conducted a pioneering study on romantic love. Their subjects were 11 women and 6 men between 21 and 37 years of age who considered themselves "madly in love," and who said their love had already lasted for more than 2 years.[4] The lovers were monitored by fMRI while they viewed pictures of their beloved. They also viewed control photographs of three persons of the opposite sex but of similar age with whom they had just been friends for as long as they had known their beloved.

Increased fMRI signals occurred bilaterally in the middle insula, the anterior cingulate cortex, and the *dorsal* striatum (caudate nucleus and putamen). The increased signals that developed in the pre-frontoparietal and middle temporal regions were more marked on the right. Did significant areas of *de*activation occur? Yes, in the posterior cingulate gyrus and in the amygdala.

Next, Bartels and Zeki studied 20 mothers whose average age was 34.[5] Each mother was viewing photographs of her own child, taken when the child was about 2 years old. Control photographs included another child the same age (with whom they had been familiar) and their own "best" female friend.

The authors compared these maternal fMRI findings with those of the women whom they had reported on 4 years earlier. These comparisons provide the best current data, from one team of investigators, about how the brain responds both romantically and maternally when women are actively contemplating their loved ones. Romantic and maternal love play an absolutely crucial role in our society. Accordingly, the major comparisons are summarized in table 6.

But first, an apology. In this book on Zen, one underlying theme points to ways we can diagnose the *origins* of our *unfruitful* longings and *over*conditioned attachments. The goal is to learn how, and when, to let go *when we carry such sentiments too far*. However, the two examples of love condensed in the table are presented because they show how defined visual stimuli and affective responses can be analyzed in a neuroimaging context. The fMRI data exist, but they are no substitute for the real thing. No love poetry is to be found in table 6.

Correlations and Interpretations of the Increased fMRI Signals

Correlations are hints. Associations are not proofs. Only many years of testing can establish firm cause-and-effect relationships. Meanwhile, their fMRI data invited the authors to venture a number of intriguing hypotheses. As chapter 28 notes, the middle insula has also been linked with active responses to caressing types of skin-to-skin contact. Activations in the vast anterior cingulate region have been linked with a variety of roles in emotive processing (see chapter 26). The lateral

Table 6
Some Neural Correlates of Maternal Attachment and Female Romantic Love

	Maternal Attachment	*Female Romantic Love*
Cortical activations	Middle insula (BA 14)	Middle insula (BA 14)
	Anterior cingulate, above and below the genu (BA 24)	Anterior cingulate, below the genu
	Lateral orbitofrontal region	None
Subcortical activations	Medial putamen and globus pallidus (less prominent in head of caudate nucleus and substantia nigra)	Medial putamen and globus pallidus; more in head of caudate, more in substantia nigra/ventral tegmental area
	Posterior-ventral thalamus	None
	Central gray	None
	None	Hypothalamus
	None	Dentate gyrus/hippocampus
	None in septal or preoptic regions	None in septal or preoptic regions

Note: The women are looking either at a picture of their own child or at a male beloved in a controlled experiment monitored by fMRI. The findings are bilateral, except as noted. The deactivations are discussed in the text.

orbitofrontal region also has subregions. At this writing, the fMRI evidence regarding their valence—whether pleasant or unpleasant—appears to vary among individual human subjects.

With respect to subcortical levels of activation, the striatum is increasingly linked both with our emotive consequences of reward, with our potential ability to modify our habits, and even with aspects of trust. Signals referable to the substantia nigra/ventral tegmental area could correlate with enhanced dopamine activation up in the dorsal striatum. However, several receptor populations cluster in this small midbrain area.

What do signals in the posterior ventral thalamus signify in mothers who are looking at their children? Perhaps they correlate with visual and auditory relays that are being enhanced by long, close attachments. Increased signals in the central gray region could correlate with maternal attachment, given the ways that both vasopressin and oxytocin are represented here (see chapter 34).

A significant omission distinguishes these two categories of attachment and romantic love from the forms of addiction discussed in the previous chapter. *No activation* is being reported in the septal and preoptic regions.

Correlations and Interpretations of the Decreased fMRI Signals

Some regions were *deactivated* when mothers and women in love looked at a photograph of their beloved. These remind us that—especially with respect to Zen—we still need to know much more about how these regions function. For example, what enters into the act of gazing at a loved one's photograph? Does it elicit a kind of bonding and merging between self and other that becomes socially useful? If so, then *some of these deactivated regions may be enabling that huge prior self/other barrier to dissolve*. Is this boundary dissolving in the direction of increasing selflessness?

But suppose, on the other hand, that the normal potential of some of these regions was such that when they were deactivated, the results would contribute to a kind of reckless oversentimentality. If so, such *under*functioning might be reflected in a love-is-blind category of responses that would prove disadvantageous. How does our brain normally insert the requisite checks and balances into such crucial functions? We need precise answers.

Earlier chapters suggested that some *right* hemisphere regions tend normally to contribute to a more negative emotional tone. In the data summarized below, the symbol R > L suggests an important conclusion: the regions deactivated were always reduced more on the *right* side.

The decreased signals occurred in these frontal, temporal, and parietooccipital regions:

- Medial superior frontal (BA 32/9) and lateral prefrontal (BA 9/46), R > L
- Middle temporal (BA 21), temporal poles, and amygdala, R > L
- Parietooccipital junction (BA 39/40) and retrosplenial region, R > L; medial cuneus and precuneus, R > L

To Bartels and Zeki, *deactivations* in these regions would serve to "overcome social distance." In their view, reduced signals in these regions represent reduced functions in networks that would otherwise mediate negative emotions, avoidance behaviors, and various other kinds of extracritical "social judgments" that would hinder bonding.

From a slightly different perspective, one might also interpret such right-sided deactivations as permitting a more porous boundary to open up between self and other. This would enable greater degrees of "closeness" and affiliative responses to develop with the rest of the world. Part VII considers related issues under the topic of "Oneness" (see chapters 77, 78, and 79).

Fisher's Results and Review of Romantic Love

Fisher and colleagues recently reported an fMRI study of 20 younger men and women who had been in love for an average of only 7 months.[6] While their subjects viewed a photograph of the beloved, signals increased in parts of the body and tail of the right caudate nucleus and in the (general) ventral tegmental area. Lovers who were in longer-lasting relationships also showed increased fMRI signals in the anterior cingulate and insula. Women tended to show more activity in the body of their caudate nuclei and in the septal region. Fisher interpreted this increase, including some of the more right-sided signals, as suggesting the possibility that "early stage romantic love is associated with underlying feelings of anxiety and craving, uncomfortable states of mind."[7]

In the previous chapter, a prominent role in the addictions was assigned to the dopamine that was released from the ventral tegmental area into the caudate, the extended amygdala, and related regions (see chapter 61). Fisher attributes to DA many of the feelings of "love sickness" that young lovers experience, together with their enhanced motivational drive to pursue the love relationship.

Desire Advances during Retreats: "Vipassana Romance"

Desire and anguish take many forms. During Zen training, both our urgent desires and our sufferings are grist for the mill of introspection. One form of acute romantic feeling can develop and has been given a name. The phenomenon is instructive, because when it arises in the course of a meditative retreat, its urgency can serve as the useful focus for self-analysis. If you can become sufficiently objective to do so, that is.

I am referring here to a kind of *short-term, powerful, affective experience, a kind of* schoolboy crush, *as it were*. My experience with this syndrome of desire-at-a-distance arose during two retreats more than two decades ago. The new fMRI findings just reviewed shed some light on the origins of this phenomenon of the so-called Vipassana romance.[8]

I came across this phrase in 2004. I had never heard it from any of my Zen teachers. Why not? Perhaps because Zen tends to simply allow the hothouse atmosphere of a retreat to encourage your own weeds to grow. Then, when the weeds flourish, you may be inclined to work with them, perhaps mention them to your roshi.

A working hypothesis for this syndrome might view its acute longings as but one expression of the generalized energizing responses to DA that surge to the surface during a retreat.[9] The syndrome seems to be common among meditators who share a retreat in mixed company for several days.

Chapter 13 listed "some functions of sitting meditation (zazen)." They included the way meditation "sponsors many kinds and levels of intuition and introspection." The fact is that *retreats soon confront you with an agenda of your own making*. Among the early issues that well up are these brief mental and physical romantic feelings for someone of the opposite sex. You are now confronted with one obvious desire. This intense longing illustrates one more attachment. On retreat, you have ample opportunity to acknowledge it and look deeply into it. This is your opportunity to work through your sexual nature, to learn from it, and to appreciate it. Indeed, once the syndrome is finally examined with clinical detachment, it provides an excellent example of the principle: "this too shall pass away."

Commentary

These fMRI studies provide an intriguing beginning. How does the slowly ripening, very long-term development of genuine spiritual compassion compare with these findings of maternal attachment and romantic love in younger adults? This area of research will be another project for *longitudinal studies* that future generations can await with great interest.

63

The Male Animal: Libido and Ex-Libido

> There it is, in us always, though it may be asleep. The male animal. The mate.... All the male animals fight for the female, from the land crab to the bird of paradise. They don't just sit and talk. They act.
>
> James Thurber (1894–1961) and Elliot Nugent (1900–1980), *The Male Animal*[1]

> Virtue consists, not in abstaining from vice, but in not desiring it.
>
> George Bernard Shaw (1856–1950)

Libido

There it is: that insatiable lusting to *act*. The instinctual drive to caress, to couple, to overcome any competition. Libido is not a male preserve. Readers of both sexes can recall how gonadal hormones took over, reshaped their anatomy, and still sponsor libidinous imperatives to satisfy "skin hunger."

An intricate web of mechanisms generates adult psychosexual behavior. Though the origins of this web are hard to untangle, many receptors for testosterone and estrogen swarm over the nerve cells in the medial hypothalamus and preoptic area. And pathways leading on from here release many neural and endocrine messengers, engaging both our body and brain in multiple dynamic interactions.

Beyond that, several deep medial and neighboring brain regions also employ a special enzyme. To endocrinologists, the enzyme presents a yin/yang paradox. Called aromatase, it converts testosterone molecules to estradiol. Estradiol does go on to activate *estrogen* receptors in such key regions as the medial preoptic area, the bed nucleus of the stria terminalis, and the anterior hypothalamic area. But this estradiol still promotes *male* sexual activity when it acts on these local nerve cells, even though it is still an estrogen derived from that earlier testosterone molecule.[2]

Opposites attract. Once their olfactory systems detect the faint signals of pherohormones, men and women go on to activate their hypothalamus differently. PET and fMRI scans have monitored these responses. They show that estrogen-like molecules (extracted from female urine) tend to activate the male hypothalamus. In contrast, testosterone-like molecules (extracted from male sweat) activate the female hypothalamus.[3] What will happen in the hypothalamus and related regions of meditators? Will carefully controlled studies show that their responses wane to such pherohormones over the course of several decades? Might some retreats even give rise to enhanced responses? The pherohormone research model could provide interesting data.

Hormones and Development

The first newborn son is always a surprise. His libido might seem poised for an early start. Why does that baby boy have such a large penis and scrotum? Because while he was still in utero, his mother's *placenta* secreted a stimulating hormone (chorionic gonadotropin). This gonadotropin drove her son's own gonads to produce temporarily high levels of testosterone.

A decade or so later, male and female bodies undergo further distinctive changes. Now, high levels of the gonadotropin hormone from the adolescents' own *pituitary* glands trigger their sexual maturation at puberty. Recent MRI studies reveal that women then go on to develop bigger frontal and medial paralimbic cortical regions in relation to the total size of the cerebrum. Men develop larger volumes of frontal-medial cortex, amygdala, and hypothalamus.[4]

Male and female brains also differ physiologically. The fact that Jack responds more than Jill does to erotic films occasions no surprise. During one recent fMRI study, the 20 men reported being more sexually aroused by the films than did the 20 women.[5] In the process, both men and women developed increased fMRI signals in many limbic regions. For example, increased signals occurred not only in the cortex of the anterior cingulate, medial prefrontal, orbital prefrontal, insula, and occipito-temporal regions but also in the amygdala and ventral striatum.

However, only the men also developed significant activations in two other regions: the thalamus and hypothalamus. The hypothalamus was more activated in the men who reported higher levels of sexual arousal.

Directly Experiencing Contrasts

Men tend to equate many of their notions of selfhood with their libido. But not until you *lose* your sense of self, not until you lose your libido, can you appreciate their true nature. Only then—in *retrospect*—can you understand how deeply each had influenced who you *are* and how you *act*.

Did I ever truly appreciate my intrusive "self?" Not until my *I-Me-Mine* had first dissolved, and then returned. Back in 1982, it would require this particular sequence—presence, sudden absence, then presence again—to truly awaken me to selfhood's immensely powerful intrusive energies. Fifteen years later, could I truly appreciate the prepotency of my libido? Not until *it* dropped out and then returned. The two episodes illustrate a simple experiential principle: once you lose something vital, you will finally appreciate it more.

Perhaps you are wondering: Does this preamble on libido relate to Zen? Zen emphasizes the primacy of direct experience, not layers of theological, doctrinal, and metaphysical abstractions. So the reasons for including the following first-person narrative are threefold. First, it represents an example of the basic Zen teaching: direct experience is crucial. Second, it illustrates the general principle: loss makes us more appreciative. Third, this story helps us focus on how our brain undergoes slow, deep, essential processes of change. Similar subtle mechanisms, operating during long-range meditative training, serve to transform a person's traits incrementally.

Ex-Libido

Seven years ago in 1997, having watched my prostate-specific antigen (PSA) levels climb for several years, I was found at biopsy to be harboring a low-grade prostate cancer. Prior to radiation, my urologist prescribed a 3-month course of antiendocrine therapy. The technical term is "combined androgen deprivation."[6] He said it was designed to shrink the prostate gland.

An understatement. The prostate was not the only thing that would shrink. Within 2 to 3 weeks, I learned firsthand how my brain and body felt when they were doubly deprived of both pituitary gonadotropin and testosterone. Another description of this treatment would be a course of "prescribed celibacy." It would shrink, to zero, every libidinous impulse and behavior I had felt and known deeply since adolescence.

Months later, this drug combination finally wore off. Now I could witness a very reassuring feeling: my libido was returning slowly to its former levels. Once again, this particular sequence—presence, absence, then presence again—*was teaching me directly, at visceral levels, how powerfully my deeper limbic nerve cell activity (and its inactivity) could shape my attitudes and behavior.*

Steroid Hormones Influence Gene Transcription

We think, constantly, in flurries. Brisk transitory changes in ions and neural messengers drive the "monkey mind." Their time course operates in milliseconds. Other mental processes evolve over seconds, hours, a few days. They are responding to slower metabolic cascades.

Steroid messengers act even more slowly. Once testosterone binds to its receptors on a target nerve cell, many days may pass before the results of the next metabolic cascades become obvious. First, the cascade of *intra*cellular signals needs to reach the DNA deep inside this cell's nucleus. Only later do the next chemical reactions emerge to modify the rest of the nerve cell (see chapter 37).

These sentences describe the kind of slow delayed "genomic" change that would reshape my gene *transcription*, cause my libido to gradually disappear, and only later give rise to its subsequent recovery. These words describe the slowly evolving neurochemical reactions that would transform my psychophysiology, undercutting my impulsive thoughts and my deeper instincts. This cascade of metabolic steps would slowly reset one major category of my brain functions at a dramatically lower operating level: Ex libido.

Subjective Feelings and Reflections

Words help me speak from experience. I do not recommend the experience. Experientially, this lost sexual drive affected me in two ways. It was both a deep vacancy of every sexual interest and desire plus a corresponding lack of all physical and behavioral manifestations. My urologist was considerate. Only when my libido returned did he comment that what he had prescribed during those months of androgen blockade was in fact, a "medical castration."

Fortunately, this metabolic deprivation was short-lived. Even though it had cut off the roots of all sexual longing, it was brief enough to produce no other changes obvious to me either in physical or mental energy, or in many other different motivational drives.

But in the interim, did I miss the old feelings and habits of behaving sexually? Yes. This reflected primarily a conscious mixture of concern for my understanding wife plus a sense of private regret. On the other hand, in one's 70s there is also some room to experience a subtle sense of liberation. Furthermore, as this chapter illustrates, I could view this brief eunuchoid experience with more than simple professional curiosity. Why? Because it served to confirm an earlier observation: "subtractions" of the psychic self play a key role in the phenomena experienced during kensho [Z:614, 653–659, 688].

Once again, the facts of actual direct experience—a loss of libido in my case—suggested an important conclusion: *Deep instinctual drives rise up from the depths of one's brain. Not until they become less excitable can one finally drop off greedy longings and attachments* [Z:650–663].

Implications for Our Understanding of Sage Wisdom

This conclusion is relevant to the long-range results of Zen training. The genomic changes just discussed act slowly. Nevertheless, they still transform the way vital messenger systems drive our behavioral functions in key regions. Similar slow changes seem pertinent to the mechanisms causing other major changes in traits and behavior during *decades-long* meditative training.

In this chapter, the waning of libido served as a clinical example. But later, in part VIII, we address different incremental changes that can dissolve other aspects of selfhood permanently. These will become manifest during the *late stage* of ongoing enlightened traits [Z:691–695].

Certain personal attributes are implicit in such late "sage wisdom." A genuine sage will live harmoniously, all unfruitful attachments having dropped off. Not the least of these is inappropriate sexual behavior. In this regard, the ethical restraints of *shila* remain the bedrock foundation for his or her daily-life practice, the guidelines so central to Buddhist and other religious disciplines [Z:73–74].

But the questions arise: What does enable sage monks and nuns to remain celibate? Is it accurate to think that it is only their strength of character? Does the red thread of sexuality still color their consciousness so much that they remain abstinent through *willpower* alone?

I doubt it. My "prescribed celibacy" taught me that celibacy need not depend on willed thought processes alone. It does not operate only at the level of imposed, top-down, psychological restraints. A more effective and spiritually authentic celibacy expresses a deep *attitudinal change at one's physiological core.* Former hard-edged drives soften, lose their urgent imperatives. Any earlier need to suppress obsessive behavior simply drops off. These deep psychophysiological reasons help explain why it is no longer necessary to impose higher-level cognitive restraints from above.

A narrative from the Theravada tradition illustrates how a young Buddhist monk's prior training in renunciation had influenced the way he behaved toward women.[7] One day, a group of attractive nursing students visited his monastery for several hours. These students, wearing beautiful Thai turquoise-and-white uniforms, sat near this monk (Ajahn Sumedho) all during a lengthy teaching session. After they had left, the monk's revered master, who had led the discussion, spoke to him about these attractive young women, and asked: "What did that do to your mind?"

The junior monk replied: "I like, but I can't want." His master was pleased with this response. For weeks thereafter, he continued to point out the basic principle: a trained monk turns away *from wanting to possess*. It is a basic lack of wanting. Attachments have been tested, and *found wanting* (see chapter 58). This attitudinal transformation develops in the absence of any notions of fear, repression, or aversion.[8] George Bernard Shaw, no angel, could see that a lack of desire was a crucial ingredient in such "virtues."

Thoughts are superficial. Zen aims deeper, at attitudes. How can long-term monastic training bring about the requisite psychophysiological subtractions *at depth*? One can envision processes at the neurochemical level that transform a nerve cell's excitability. These subtle changes start at the receptors out on the cell's surface, cascade down into the nucleus, then move back out again to change the way the cell fires (see chapter 33). In a similar manner can the kinds of slow changes that subtract a person's libidinous drives also dissolve, reshape, and redirect that person's various selfish impulses? Only deep subtractions can transform a person's traits of character.

The next chapter confronts the aberrant behavior of those few religious leaders who violate the centuries-old teachings of their traditions. At this distance, perhaps the most charitable way to view their failings is as immaturities. No matter how venerable such offenders may appear to be, they certainly lack the maturity of character expected of their station.

Did some other teachers in the older generations seem both wizened and more wise? Perhaps they benefited not only from the ways aging changes nerve cells but also (one may hope) from a more realistic, matter-of-fact approach. Perhaps they learned from hard experiences, and softer ones too, how libidinous impulses do tend to wane with each passing decade [Z:653–659, 660–663].

64

Cracks in the Bowl: The Broken Seal

> A bowl of morality, if not perfect, cannot hold the water of Zen.
>
> Zenrin Kushu[1]

Countless neuronal and hormonal interactions drive sexual behavior. Some complexities are built into our genes. By one estimate, 78 genes on the Y chromosome contribute to "maleness," serving to integrate male brain and body functions at multiple levels.

Blood testosterone levels contribute to male sexual behavior, but they do not explain its wide range, much of which is culturally determined. Item: an advertisement in *Time* magazine (special winter issue, December 2002).

Will a 3-page advertisement for testosterone alert only relatively few American men to consult their doctor—only those four to five million who (so this ad implies) already have their testosterone levels "running on empty"?

Hardly. Instead, what seems more likely is that such testosterone ads will tempt millions of other males to find ways to use this hormone to enhance their performance. Will our social fabric, already frayed, be strengthened by three-page ads that tend to encourage more problems with steroid abuse than we already have among athletes?[2]

Aggressive, inappropriate male behavior poses major cultural problems worldwide. Published evidence already documents major sexual transgressions by male teachers in several meditative communities. A few reports, involving Zen teachers, stand out as sobering reminders. As one sangha member recently observed: "If you put poison in one side of a lake, it doesn't stay there. It poisons the whole lake. What a teacher does affects the whole community."[3] Clearly, such teachers needed prompt, appropriate psychotherapy and rehabilitation before they could assume responsible positions as potential leaders.

In some Western forms of religion, the communion bowl used to be symbolic of near perfection. It has since begun to develop cracks in the rim. Publicity given to serious problems within the Boston diocese and elsewhere continues to expose the universal challenges that sexual drives and misbehaviors pose.

Charisma is no substitute for character, especially in spiritual matters. Rectitude does not need cogitation. It expresses deep attitudes of character. In Buddhism, the moral and ethical values of authentic practice are grounded in each person's exercise of restraint and renunciation (Skt. *shila*). This restrained behavior applies to *leaders and led* alike, to both men *and* women. No member who would remain true to the real spirit of a Buddhist sangha can enter into any "mutual complicity" that encourages sexual misconduct. Nor do legitimate Zen teachers need to indulge in so-called crazy wisdom or to pursue any "beat" or "zigzag" path that might lead their disciples astray.

During the past decade, several responsible senior leaders and their religious communities have confronted sexual transgressions within their institutions. Working together, they have removed from office subordinate teachers who could not live up to the trust once placed in them. The problem is not new. Societies have always needed to confront the moral imperfections of teachers and others in authority.

In the East, millennia-old evidence suggests that wise leaders understood an important principle. Though they delegated to subordinates the responsibility to act ethically and morally, they did *not* delegate their own final *authority* to judge the results. Ideograms still in use today illustrate this time-honored leadership principle.

Consider the word *inka*. In Zen, inka stands for a very high-level certification. This is no ordinary Good Housekeeping seal of approval. The Zen master reserves inka only for the few exemplary disciples who have proved themselves both as leaders and as qualified to teach.

The ideogram for inka has two parts: *in* is on one side, *ka* is on the other. The root meaning resides in the character for *in* (*yin* in Chinese). The right half of this *in* consists of an ancient character shaped like our modern letter *P*.[4] In ancient times this character represented an actual object. It stood for the image of just the right half (**P**) of the emperor's official seal (**¶P**), *after* the Emperor had broken in half the whole seal.

A broken seal—what did this old custom signify? The right half served as a token, and it was given to the recipient. It certified that this lesser official had indeed been granted permission to act *responsibly* on the emperor's behalf. However, the emperor always kept the left half (**¶**). This confirmed that no such token permission could weaken his own final authority.[5]

Religious communities worldwide could benefit from ensuring that no seal of approval, including inka, is granted in perpetuity. Wise spiritual leaders continually monitor their subordinates. They delegate responsibility, but never relinquish the final authority to judge the results and to act accordingly.

In Zen, it is a practical matter. After all, you are trying to simplify life. You wish to practice a *living* Zen, in ways that lead toward greater harmony and stability [Z:641–645]. This means setting priorities, remembering the precepts, and following them. You cannot arrive at "no-thought" levels of meditation with a head full of distractions.

65

Empathies, Mirror Neurons, and Prolonged Affirmative Attitudes

> Workers have often free-associated to "empathy," seizing on those aspects of the term that most engaged them, and then bringing the peculiar skills and vocabularies of their discipline to the task.
>
> H. Davis[1]

> Your imagination is your preview of life's coming attractions.
>
> Albert Einstein (1879–1955)

The Varieties of Empathy

Empathy seemed simpler a century ago. Then, the original German word—*einfühlung*—conveyed the meaning of "feeling into."[2] Various disciplines have since become preoccupied with the many facets of empathy. Like love, it remains an elusive topic hard to pin down. Empathy tends to expand if you pose such questions as: how do we learn vicariously from another person's experience? Why do some persons become psychopaths in society, whereas others become autistic? What generates altruism as opposed, say, to deception? And, yes, how do we really learn to *intuit* what is on someone else's mind?

Free associations multiplied a decade ago. Researchers discovered that so-called mirror neurons fire in the most anterior and inferior part (F5) of the *premotor* cortex of the monkey. These "mirror" cells do not discharge only when one monkey performs certain tasks by itself. They also fire when this first monkey *merely observes* a second (other) monkey that is performing this same motor act.[3]

In short, these mirror cells become active even when the witnessing monkey seems passive and does not move. Because mirrors reflect, the questions began something like this: were some local circuits somehow "reflecting" external events? Once again, we address that fertile interface where self and other meet. Zen-brain reflections arise along this interface.

Clearly, it was a whole *system* of *sensorimotor* cells in that first monkey which appeared to be mirroring the behavior of the second monkey. Indeed, the requisite minimal circuitry would include the superior temporal and posterior parietal regions (both of which normally relay messages to and from the inferior frontal cortex), plus the added "empathetic resonances" arising from limbic/paralimbic connections.[4] When human subjects were studied with PET scans and fMRI methods, thalamic and cerebellar modules were also found to be responsive partners in this vast perceptual-motor network.

Yes, those original *premotor* "mirror" cells per se did seem capable of contributing to at least a few elementary, automatic, *motoric* aspects of our social cognition. However, these cells were not deemed likely candidates for our other, high-level sensibilities of the kinds that could fall easily within the rubric of the elastic term "empathy."[5]

Indeed, in everyday life, how could one split such a continuum of simultaneously interacting components? A newer vocabulary was improvised to address this situation. Its phrases included a "perceptual-action model of empathy." "Embodied representations" were postulated, ones that could be modified by motor and emotional "contagion."[6]

Meanwhile, in theory at least, it was becoming increasingly plausible to contemplate highly sophisticated "mirror"-like nerve cell systems. Somehow these would enable us as individual human beings not only to mimic other persons, but also to anticipate (perhaps even to share in) their belief systems, attitudes, positive and negative emotions, perceptions, and intended actions. Self seemed to have "mirrors" that would reflect others, become sympathetic with them. *Inside had ways of experiencing outside.*

During studies of inferred pain, for example, subjects could be shown still photographs. Some of these pictures depicted other persons' hands and feet posed in situations highly likely to cause pain. Control scenes showed comparable extremities posed in different circumstances that seemed nonpainful. What parts of the subject's brain responded to situations assessed as painful? fMRI signals increased in the anterior cingulate, anterior insula, and cerebellum (as well as thalamus, to a lesser degree).[7]

Indeed, other recent experiments suggested that fMRI signals increase in the anterior paracingulate cortex when the observing subject concludes that a socially *inter*active situation is implied, beyond the simple notion of entering into an isolated, unilateral intention per se.[8]

Subtle functional distinctions have recently been attributed to the ventromedial and orbital prefrontal cortex (see chapters 43, 50, 52, 59). When lesions damage this area (especially on the right side), the patients do not readily understand another person's ironic utterances or recognize social faux pas.[9]

The few examples cited in this chapter and elsewhere[10] barely introduce the range of topics that might arise with relation to the "empathies" and "theories of mind." Worth noting in any book about Zen, however, is that brief isolated experiences of intense empathy are not *in themselves* to be regarded as "authentically religious" [Z:429]. And even if a person's regular meditative practices do cultivate a few more of the affective sensitivities underlying empathy, these responses are prone to relapse. Therefore, the early phenomena of empathy are many fragile steps removed from that later *selfless* reaching out implied in fully ripened compassion. We discuss this enduring *unself*conscious stage later, in chapter 89 [Z:650–652].

Meanwhile, let us close by improvising a kind of koan. It might serve as a preamble to part VII where different kinds of experiences of oneness will be discussed. The next paragraph contains the several "iffy" suppositions that lead up to its question. They are prompted by those same core concepts of self/other that become involved whenever we try to personalize words like "mirrors" and "reflections."

Let us suppose that the brain's "mirror" systems were to lose all sense that anything about their shiny reflecting surface might ever have imposed a *barrier*. Suppose further that all representations would open up and become free which had previously limited the personal self to concepts of only what went on inside its *own* skin. Now, whatever remained in awareness could coalesce—*in one experience*—with *each and every perceptual representation* of the world outside.

The question is: How would such a novel, nondual, unifying, identity be experienced? Chapters 77–79 consider such an extraordinary state of consciousness.

Cultivating Affirmative Attitudes

Imagination shapes consciousness. Positive thinking is a potent creative force. It influences our behavior and enters at several levels into our response to placebos.

Years ago, Norman Vincent Peale popularized the "power of positive thinking" in a book with the same title. Peale's preachings echoed the messages of countless predecessors. Ancient India was already well-versed in the transforming power of kindly thoughts. These millennia-old beliefs entered into the "sutra on kindness." Its verses today still offer these suggestions to a person who would wish to cultivate unlimited kindliness: "even as a mother watches over and protects her only child, so with a boundless mind should one cherish all living beings, radiating friendliness over the entire world, above, below, and all around without limit."[11]

The full text of this *Metta-sutta* is popular not only in the southern (Theravada) school of Buddhism. In the Tibetan Buddhist tradition, its contemporary practice is personified by the Dalai Lama who says, simply, "My religion is kindness."

Can skilled meditators learn to focus their *imagination* on a particular meditative state of loving kindness? Then, by internalizing this state and practicing it repeatedly, actually go on to change the way their brains function? Some of the early evidence suggested that one highly trained monk had changed his EEG by focusing intently on love and compassion to such a degree that it "soaked the mind." EEG activity in the left middle frontal gyrus shifted toward gamma frequencies during this mental focusing.[12] This intriguing finding stimulated widespread interest in the potential of practicing loving-kindness meditation repeatedly (see chapter 17).

Elsewhere, in a primate laboratory, it was found that monkeys changed the chemistry of the hand area of their brain while this hand was "learning" to reach out with a rake (see chapter 41). So it does seem reasonable to suppose that—over time—well-trained human beings might also learn to enhance their brain's capacity for compassion through the skillful, imaginative practice of *repeated* loving-kindness meditation.

After all, it was only a few decades ago that no one hesitated while singing that familiar song, the key words to which were: "accentuate the positive . . . latch on to the affirmative . . ." A few years later, Isen's reports presented simple, down-to-earth, confirming factual evidence. After people did feel positive about life events they became optimistic and developed affirmative behaviors [Z:350–352].

Clearly, given the right encouragement, we have many ways to put "the power of positive thinking" to work in harmonizing aspects of our attention, cognition, emotion, and behavior. Each one of these functions is crucial, both to our survival and well-being as individuals and to that of our society as a whole.

But through precisely what *mechanisms* does long-range meditative training create *enduring* affirmative states and traits of compassion? Chapter 89 reviews some preliminary findings. To clarify these steps will take many more decades of rigorous research. But already, some simpler models of insight are being investigated with the aid of sophisticated techniques.

66

Through What Steps Does Ordinary Insight Transform Consciousness?

> Insights are sporadic, unpredictable, short-lived moments of exceptional thinking, during which implicit assumptions about the relevance of common knowledge to a problem must be discarded before a solution can be revealed.
>
> J. Luo and colleagues[1]

Luo and colleagues recently monitored ordinary levels of insight using both high-resolution fMRI and evoked potential techniques. In chapter 29, we noted their finding that subjects who resolved ordinary Japanese riddles also activated their right hippocampus.[2] There is more to the story.

In the next study from the same laboratory, 13 healthy right-handed men and women were monitored with fMRI while they were presented visually with a series of 42 ambiguous sentences.[3] Half of these sentences were very difficult. For example (I cannot guess this one. Can you?): "The haystack was important because the cloth ripped."

After 8 seconds of (what would seem appropriate) incomprehension, the subjects then viewed the solution cue. This word was presented for the next 2 seconds. If this next association word fully resolved the ambiguity, they quickly pressed one key that acknowledged this so-called, Aha! reaction. But if they could not understand that this next cue word "solved" the ambiguous sentence, they quickly pressed a different key. This negative result was called a "non-Aha event."

They responded quickly in each instance: The Aha! event took only 1.87 seconds for key pressing to occur. The non-Aha! event took 1.09 seconds.

A parallel experiment was also conducted using evoked potential responses. The Aha! event response generated an obviously greater negative deflection 380 ms after the answer arrived. Source analysis localized this N380 waveform to the anterior cingulate gyrus.[4]

Now to return to that ambiguous sentence: "The haystack was important because the cloth ripped." We can all empathize with the subjects. Their cue to its solution was the word *parachute*.

When we resolve such a puzzle, we need to (1) let go of all our prior fixed notions about what "cloth" usually means; (2) regard "cloth" in a new way (as the canopy of a ripped parachute); (3) regard the haystack as something capable of cushioning the person's fall; (4) integrate all these ingredients into a novel meaningful "picture-narrative."

That is not all that can happen. To varying degrees, there can also occur (1) a "feeling-of-knowing," "the light bulb effect"; (2) a feeling of release from being puzzled; (3) maybe a delayed feeling of relief or accomplishment at having made the connection.

The Data and Their Interpretation

The fMRI data showed that two major cortical areas were associated with the Aha! reaction. First, signals increased in the anterior cingulate cortex on both sides. This was more evident on the *right* (BA 24 and 32) than on the left (BA 32). Signals increased in the cingulate even more when the sentences proved harder (and took longer) to solve.

Second, signals also increased in the *left* lateral prefrontal cortex (BA 6 and 9). It was most sensitive to the most difficult sentences and remained so throughout the three blocks of the experiment.

Given what we have observed about how many functions seem to tap into the anterior cingulate (see chapter 26), the data are open to several interpretations. The authors suggest that the anterior cingulate became activated as a part of the general mechanism of "conflict detection between different ways of thinking." This theory would focus on one dynamic, semantic interface, when incomprehension faces potential comprehension. This interpretation would emphasize that two divergent sets of data had now registered in the mental field, and that the conflict between their two points of view was being *detected*.

The authors then suggest that the left lateral prefrontal cortex became activated in the course of breaking this impasse and of *resolving* the conflict. This theory would be in keeping with other established executive functions of the frontal cortex, including its roles in selecting among alternatives and in shifting attentional sets.

In the authors' most recent fMRI study, they monitored the different ways that their subjects responded to two kinds of puzzles. One kind were intricate "cerebral gymnastic" word puzzles. The other kind were "homophone" word puzzles (resembling silent auditory puns) in which simpler task-solving principles were involved. As expected, signals increased more in the right anterior cingulate (BA 24 and 32) in responses to the more intricate task and also increased more in multiple other regions (their tables 2 and 3).[5]

Comment

These pioneering, high-resolution studies of ordinary insight represent an important first step on our very long path toward understanding extraordinary states of insight-wisdom. However, a glance back through the steps involved during that incomprehensible parachute sentence task, and through the sequences of what else can happen, illustrates that this is *not* a study of kensho-satori. Not yet. Not yet.

In brief, these are preliminary studies. Researchers are supplying their subjects with solutions to what are difficult problems involving language. This is not yet research into the kinds of *spontaneously* generated *major* shifts that resolve massive existential issues relating to the self. To cite several pertinent differences:

- An explicit word puzzle is being provided from the outside. It is followed seconds later by the supply, gratis, of a prepackaged *WORDY* solution. These artificial conditions do not reproduce the way a koan is presented, worked on for a very long time, incorporated, and then finally resolved by an internally generated shift into an alternate state of consciousness.
- Nor does it reproduce the way that a spontaneous flash of insight-wisdom, when it occurs in the absence of a word, illuminates not just one artificial riddle but a major existential domain, and does so in the *absence of the sense of self*.
- Nor does it resemble the way a sudden, nonspecific sensory stimulus—when *not* related to linguistics—triggers the entry into a state of kensho-satori.
- The experimental design is oriented toward what the authors refer to as a "high-level cognitive process." Kensho's shifts are likely to involve many lower-level functions as well.

Some remote similarities:

- Mental tension is being generated by an incomprehensible riddle. (One could anticipate that a Zen koan would generate somewhat similar kinds of mental tension with corresponding neuroimaging correlates.)
- There is an instant later in kensho when it is appreciated that both elements of a paradox had coexisted in one large mental field, elements which were formerly incompatible (see chapter 77). However, this juxtaposition of mundane reality and Ultimate Reality has already been reconciled into "Oneness." No sense of conflict is present during that prior instant.
- Kensho shifts automatically into a mode that lets go of prior fixed notions. Its integration of multiple percepts and concepts into a novel, meaningful, global impression occurs spontaneously and naturally as a kind of effortless "grace." It leaves no residue of being "task-related."
- Kensho leaves the experiant with a deep, long-lasting impression of release.

The epigraph accurately describes the fact that insights do discard all prior "implicit assumptions." Our implicit assumptions are represented in networks and modules in the brain. If they are suddenly discarded, then where in the studies cited are the data commensurate with the *de*activations reflecting their disappearance? (see chapter 50).

Thus far, only a single fMRI data point is being used to "average" all the milliseconds of those different mental steps required to resolve the experimental word puzzle. Researchers still have a long way to go before their techniques can monitor all the fast-moving, flashing insights and sequences of kensho (see part IX).

The techniques used in the studies discussed above are providing very high degrees of spatial and temporal resolution (see chapter 49). These methods are now applicable to experiments designed to study certain moments of ordinary creative problem solving and ordinary intuition.

Different Frontal Lobe Roles in Shifting Mental Sets

Suppose you need to solve a tough problem. Creative problem solving requires you not only to generate several hypotheses but also to *discriminate* among them. Moreover, you must also drop your prior mental set of assumptions, shift decisively into one correct configuration, and hold onto it.[6]

In most current neuroimaging studies, researchers pose mental tasks for their subjects to solve. The ordinary kinds of "matching" problems are among such tasks. These require the subjects to develop modes of divergent thinking, to sift among these latest options, and then to choose one of them.

During the earlier process of generating more potential solutions, fMRI signals increase in the *dorso*lateral frontal region (BA 46), more so on the *right* side.[7] This evidence is consistent with the possibility that the subjects are enlisting more of their attentional and other cognitive resources in their efforts to add and maintain these several new options "on line." In contrast, the *right* prefrontal cortex in its *ventral* lateral region tends to contribute to set-shifting per se. (This small area of BA 47 lies between area 45 and area 11 in figure 7). What about the later time of *closure*, the instant impression that such voluntary, thoughtful matching tasks have just been successfully completed? Now, in the subjects tested, the fMRI signals also increase in other frontal regions on their *left* side (BA 9, 10).

Why do people shift into kensho? Is it only because their right prefrontal convexity takes the lead, and actively points some kind of "baton," as it were? Does such a discrete quasi-executive, top-down signal direct the brain into a cascade of extraordinarily new configurations? That wasn't what it felt like. Kensho's flash of insight felt thought-*less*, spontaneous, *un*-self directed (see chapter 43).

Several lines of the research reviewed herein raise other interesting possibilities. Suppose a person were suddenly to *drop* into an extraordinary state, a *non-*striving state of preattentive parallel processing. This selfless state had "let go" of all egocentric functions represented chiefly in the deeper cortex along the midline (see chapters 50–52). At this instant, it could be a twofold advantage both to consolidate such a novel state and to continue to keep that old pejorative self out of the picture. To stay longer within this new state, it could help if its whole field of allocentric impressions remained relatively stable, *involuntarily on line,* during the next few moments. (This is no time to shift back into one's ordinary I-Me-Mine dual operating mode). Now the person's habitual practice of mindful attentiveness during many prior years becomes crucial. It is at this point that it could contribute to the relative stability of kensho.

67

Second Mondo

> Many persons nowadays seem to think that any conclusion must be very scientific if the arguments in favor of it are derived from twitching of frogs' legs—especially if the frogs are decapitated—and that—on the other hand—any doctrine chiefly vouched for by the feelings of human beings—with heads on their shoulders—must be benighted and superstitious.
>
> William James (1842–1910)

What's the bottom-line message about meditation?

This book looks into the heads of real people, and seeks the physiological basis for a few of their doctrines that James might call "overbeliefs." Zen suggests that regular mindful meditation can help us let go of discursive thoughts, become more aware of what is really going on in the present moment, and help put into practice the intuitions that will illuminate who we really are and how to simplify our life.

I thought Buddhism was mostly about a philosophy of religion. Why does this book go into so much neuroscience?

(You should see the *first* book!) This book is what you might expect from a neurologist who views Zen training as changing the psychophysiology of the human brain. The latest neuroscience articles reviewed here suggest how these transformations could occur as a result of regular daily-life meditative practice and occasional retreats. We have started at the gross anatomical level, then moved on to where the action really is: first in networks and nuclei, and then down at the level of single nerve cells and their receptors.

I have seen some neuroimaging pictures in color in the magazines. From what you are describing, it looks like these amazing new methods are finally getting us somewhere.

The technical progress has been amazing. Not everyone agrees how their results are to be interpreted. Still, the tendencies are for changes on both sides of the brain to underlie the ways it shifts toward more affiliative and allocentric responses.

You're emphasizing how our emotions interfere with our seeing reality clearly. Are you suggesting that our emotional life is bad for us?

No. The point is that life becomes both more efficient and inspired once we learn how to channel the energies fueling our consciousness into mindful avenues that become more creative and adaptive, not into trivial pursuits and unfruitful fantasies.

Wouldn't it be easier to become spiritually enlightened by taking some kind of a pill?

No. The next four chapters explain why.

Part V

Quickening

If you really want to reach this realm, do not vainly waste time day or night, or recklessly misuse your minds and bodies.

Master Keizan Jokin (1264–1325)

68

The Remarkable Properties of Nitric Oxide

> Nitric oxide is a gas that diffuses through all psychological barriers to act on neighboring cells across an extensive volume on a specific time scale. It, therefore, has the opportunity to control the processing of vision from the lowest level of retinal transduction to the control of neuronal excitability in the visual cortex.
>
> J. Cudeiro and C. Rivadula[1]

When we use the word "quickening" throughout part V it refers to brief surges in the brain's activities. In the next six chapters, we consider some mechanisms of surges and the phenomena that accompany them.

To the public, nitric oxide had long remained unknown. Then it became linked with the underlying mechanisms of penile erection. But nitric oxide had already received major attention in research laboratories worldwide—and still does. By 1998, the Nobel Prize would go to three pioneering researchers—Robert Furchgott, Louis Ignarro, and Ferid Murad—who codiscovered its effects on causing blood vessels to dilate. Both before then and since, nitric oxide has been implicated in an astonishing variety of actions in the body and in the brain. From the next few pages that briefly review its properties, readers can appreciate why its versatile functions could be so potentially important to Zen and the brain [Z:412–413] (see chapters 93, 95, and 96).

Basic Characteristics of Nitric Oxide

Nitric oxide ($NO^{\bullet}$) is a gas. The dot signifies that it is a highly reactive free radical. It diffuses readily through lipid membranes, and its half-life (estimated in the test tube) is around 6 seconds. Theoretical models suggest that a single point source of $NO^{\bullet}$ might extend its sphere of influence over a diameter of 200 microns. This would enable $NO^{\bullet}$ to act as more than a retrograde messenger at one synapse. A minute "puff" of the gas might be large enough to influence some two million adjacent synapses.[2]

Our other messenger molecules are stored in vesicles. Not $NO^{\bullet}$. It is synthesized on the spot by the enzyme nitric oxide synthase. Like other enzymes, *this synthase is best viewed as operating within a certain microenvironment*. In fact, this $NO^{\bullet}$ synthase is activated only in a total system that contains calcium ions and calmodulin. Calcium ions are released at particular cellular sites, especially where glutamate has just crossed its synapse to activate its NMDA receptors (see chapter 31). Already we can visualize a microenvironment where a close link exists between the release of glutamate and the synthesis of $NO^{\bullet}$.

The Neuroanatomy of Nitric Oxide Systems

Antibodies prepared against this NO• synthase bind to the local sites where this enzyme produces its NO•. In the human brain, two clusters of nerve cells show intense local staining for this enzyme.[3] An intriguing fact: both clusters *also make acetylcholine*. These two cholinergic nuclei in the dorsolateral pons are the pedunculopontine tegmental nucleus and the lateral parabrachial nucleus (see chapter 24) [Z:165]. The oral pontine nucleus (a source for theta activities) is also heavily stained (see chapter 29).

In contrast, the serotonin nerve cells in the dorsal raphe nucleus stain only moderately, and serotonin cells in the other raphe nuclei of the medulla stain weakly. Dopamine cells of the substantia nigra do not stain, nor do the norepinephrine cells of the locus ceruleus. However, in the cerebellum, Purkinje cells and basket cells are positively stained.

Higher up, scattered cells stain in the paraventricular nucleus of the hypothalamus and in the amygdala. In the hippocampus, only lightly stained cells are seen in the CA2, CA3, and CA4 regions. The striatum shows intensely stained nerve cells in the caudate nucleus, putamen, and nucleus accumbens. However, cells neither in the thalamus itself nor in its lateral geniculate nucleus are stained. (This lack in humans contrasts with findings in the cat and other animal species.) In the deeper layers of the cerebral cortex, a few large cells stain darkly.

Only certain *axonal fibers* also stain for the synthetic enzyme. High degrees of nerve fiber staining are seen within the striatum, the basal forebrain, the hypothalamus, and parts of the cerebellum. This staining of NO• synthase raises the possibility that NO• might diffuse out from these more distant axons to reach sites far removed from their cell bodies of origin. However, the microcircuitry of the striatum and other nuclei is so complex that this fiber staining cannot be attributed to any particular cell of origin.[4]

Neurochemical Sequelae of Nitric Oxide: Their Different Time Relationships

It was first thought that NO• stimulated only one major metabolic target. This target was *inside* certain adjacent cells. It was presumed to be a very different enzyme, the soluble enzyme that makes cyclic guanosine monophosphate (cGMP). Thus, when NO• increased, the net result would be to raise the levels of cGMP in other cells close by.

This NO•-cGMP system opens up intriguing avenues through which the brain could modify its old behavior patterns. Of obvious interest is the striatum. Why? Because the striatum contains especially high levels of this cyclase enzyme which is poised to synthesize more cGMP [Z:676]. And, as noted, the fiber network of the striatum also stains densely for the synthase that makes NO•.

Higher levels of cGMP have many crucial long-range effects. They far outlast a brief puff of NO˙. Second messengers like cGMP create major changes in the excitability of their nerve cells. For example, cGMP acts on protein kinase G to reshape the ion channels through which messenger molecules exert their immediate functions (see chapter 37).

Within seconds, NO˙ begins to initiate this cascade of reactions that affect protein kinase G.[5] Relatively low NO˙ levels promote these responses. The net result is an *increase* in the rate at which local nerve cells fire in bursts of activity. This increased burst firing is but one small part "of a richer chemistry through which NO˙ elicits biological signaling."[6]

Some "richer chemistry" requires higher concentrations. Now, NO˙ acts differently, targeting amino acids directly. One such chemical reaction, termed *S*-nitrosylation, transforms the properties of proteins that contain cysteine. It proceeds more slowly than do those metabolic effects of NO˙ which are mediated by cGMP and driven by enzymes. The time scales of such direct chemical effects of NO˙ vary. Some estimates suggest that they fall into the "2-minute range."

Whereas ordinary nitrogen (N_2) is an inert gas, NO˙ is highly reactive. How do its chemical reactions go on to alter nearby molecules? The basic preliminary steps are

$$NO^{\cdot} \longrightarrow O_2^{\cdot -} \longrightarrow ONOO^-$$

In this reaction sequence, $O_2^{\cdot -}$ represents the *superoxide* molecule. Formed in mitochondria, superoxide leads to the formation of *peroxynitrite* ($ONOO^-$). Peroxynitrite can penetrate lipid membranes. It is one of several species of reactive oxygen molecules which bind to cysteine and thereby *inhibit the functions* of various proteins.

The slower *S*-nitrosylation reactions that occur at higher NO˙ levels change nerve cell excitability in the direction *opposite* from those at low NO˙ levels. In fact, they *inhibit* nerve cell firing.[7] This particular biphasic quality—an initial excitation, a slower wave of inhibition—is of interest in relation to the way phenomena sometimes evolve through different phases during alternate states of consciousness (see parts VI and IX).

Nitric Oxide Signals and Their Relation to Local Increases in Brain Blood Flow

Buerk and colleagues recently reported an important insight into how NO˙ enters into brain signaling.[8] These researchers measured the levels of NO˙ electrochemically. They inserted gold-plated microelectrodes into the somatosensory cortex of the rat. NO˙ increased immediately when they stimulated the rat's opposite forepaw. NO˙ levels peaked within 0.4 seconds after stimulation, and returned to their baseline level after only 2 seconds. This NO˙ peak occurred *before* any local field potential changes, and *before* any local increase in cerebral blood flow.

Local blood flow did begin rising slightly later, after a 1-second delay. It finally reached its peak at the end of the 4-second period of paw stimulation. Researchers need to identify the precise mechanisms that lead to this early NO˙ release. The observation that NO˙ is a signaling molecule that can locally increase cerebral blood flow has crucial implications for how our brain is able to adjust its oxygen supply to its oxygen demand (see chapter 50).

Even this initial survey suggests that NO˙: appears rapidly in cortex after a forepaw is stimulated, has excitatory effects which appear within seconds, then inhibitory effects which might be delayed for a few minutes, and later has a broad range of prolonged second messenger consequences.

Clearly, we are in the presence of an embarrassment of riches when we try to correlate certain of these discrete NO˙ changes with particular events along the Path of Zen (see figure 1, chapter 4). The issue is not so much whether NO˙ "might" be involved in quickenings, absorptions, insightful awakenings, and later stages of the Path. The question is how its potential roles can be accurately tested, evaluated, accepted, or rejected.

The research selected below illustrates a few more of the mechanisms triggered by NO˙ that can change relevant brain functions phasically, tonically, and can operate on time scales that stretch from seconds out to many days.

Effects of Nitric Oxide during Waking and Sleep, and Its Immediate Effects on Synaptic Plasticity

In the thalamus, NO˙ levels rise 38% higher during active waking than during slow wave sleep. NO˙ levels are 6% higher during the active episodes of REM sleep than during the baseline state of active waking.[9] Acetylcholine nerve cells down in the pons provide a plausible source for this release of NO˙ into the thalamus. Once there in the thalamus, NO˙ changes the oscillatory bursts of thalamic relay cells toward more tonic modes of firing. The direct effect of NO˙ on some $GABA_A$ receptors is to reduce their activity.[10] However, in the hypothalamus, NO˙ may enhance the synaptic functions of $GABA_A$ in the paraventricular nucleus.[11]

More Immediate Pharmacological Effects of Nitric Oxide

Most NO˙ is synthesized in that particular site, rich in calcium ions, where glutamate has just activated its NMDA receptors. In cats, NO˙ also acts *selectively* to further increase these glutamate responses at their postsynaptic sites.[12] These localized NO˙ effects, measured in the lateral geniculate nucleus, do not depend on the corelease of ACH. Nor are they mediated by $GABA_A$ receptors, nonspecifically.

In the cat thalamus, NO˙ enhances the transmission of visual signals some 72% through the lateral geniculate nucleus to the cortex. Yet a dynamic balance exists in the visual system. It can shift the visual phenomena of alternate states in either direction. We have already noted that NO˙ mechanisms also include built-in provisions for negative feedback. These can block the subsequent responses that are mediated through the NMDA receptor.[13] On the other hand, down in the brainstem, NO˙ and glutamate can again magnify each other. Not only does glutamate increase NO˙ production, but NO˙ can then go on to increase glutamate release.[14]

Delayed Metabotrophic Effects of Nitric Oxide

When NO˙ increases a nerve cell's levels of cGMP, this cGMP then changes the cell's ion channels and transforms its subsequent excitability. For example, one glutamate pathway is important in modifying behavior. It runs from the orbitofrontal cortex back to the striatum. Here, NO˙ signals stimulate the local production of cGMP. The resulting "second messenger" cascade then strongly enhances the tonic firing of medium spiny nerve cells in the striatum.[15]

Nitric Oxide, Norepinephrine, and Lateralized Stress Responses

NO˙ enters into the delayed stress responses that evolve when animals are restrained. Starting 1 day *after* this acute stress, and continuing for the next 5 days, limbic nerve cells express more NO˙ synthesizing activity in the amygdala, hippocampal formation, and entorhinal cortex.[16]

Stress responses increase the release of NE into the brain [Z:235–240]. In the isolated hypothalamus of a rat, NE causes a "dramatic" enhancement of NO˙ synthase in the large cells of the supraoptic nuclei. A lesser increase is also evident in cells of the paraventricular nucleus.[17]

Earlier in this chapter, we observed how a sensory stimulus to a rat's forepaw caused an immediate increase in NO˙ in the opposite sensory cortex. Rodents have paw preferences. Like humans, some reach for food with their right paw, others with their left paw. Some are ambidextrous. It turns out that the cortical levels of NO˙ in the brains of mice are higher in the *right* hemisphere. Thereafter, the NO˙ levels also correlate with the paw preferences of individual mice.[18]

When normal right-handed humans focus attention on their *left* hand, they generate more MRI activation than when they focus attention on their right hand. In addition, focusing attention on the left hand at a time when both hands are being stimulated increases the activation in both cerebral hemispheres.[19] These recent findings support many lines of evidence indicating that our *right* hemisphere is dominant for externally directed mechanisms of attention, and that the left side of the human body is more sensitive in tests of tactile perception.

A testable working hypothesis is that at some levels along the sensory pathway to the somatosensory cortex, or along the networks of attention, NO˙ synthase levels could be higher in the right hemisphere of right-handed human subjects.

How this hypothesis might relate to a greater afferent sympathetic representation in the right hemisphere[20] and to the greater NE levels in some thalamic nuclei on this right side can be determined only by future research.

A plausible corollary is that when enhanced levels of stress during a meditative retreat release more NE in the right hemisphere, this might go on to prime the NO˙ synthesizing systems more in this right hemisphere. As these stress-related sequences unfold, episodes could develop that present first excitatory and then inhibitory phenomena, as discussed in part IX (see chapters 93, 95, and 96).

Interrelationships with Peptide and other Messenger Systems

Over several days time, NO˙ changes the function of the mu opioid receptor. NO˙ increases this mu receptor's binding capacities while decreasing its ability to go on to activate its G-protein coupled receptor.[21] NO˙ released from neighboring cells activates oxytocin nerve cells in the paraventricular nucleus. The next sequence of results relays on to levels far below where it generates penile erection by separate NO˙ mechanisms.[22]

NO˙ has the potential to increase the synaptic levels of NE and dopamine by inhibiting their reuptake.[23] It is not clear if such an increase might translate into significant physiological effects in human subjects.

Some neurotoxic effects of methamphetamine and MDMA are related to enhanced dopamine activity. These side effects may depend on the presence of NO˙, whereas other effects of MDMA that are mediated by serotonin do not depend on NO˙.[24] (See chapter 71.) Some behavioral effects of phencyclidine in the hippocampus may also be mediated by NO˙.[25]

Delayed Toxic and Metabolic Effects of Nitric Oxide

Glutamate has long been known to have undesirable excitotoxic effects (see chapter 31) [Z:654–656]. Many are now attributable to the way *glutamate increases the release of NO˙*. NO˙ goes on to damage DNA, lipids, RNA, and proteins through the basic, nonenzymic chemical reactions just described. These preliminary steps require both the superoxide anion *and* NO˙ in order to yield the toxic peroxynitrite molecule.[26] NO˙ could participate in "etching" of the brain.

Item: The ACH nerve cells in the brainstem are highly resistant to the toxic side effects of NO•. In fact, ACH nerve cells cultured from the parabrachial nuclei are some 300 *times* more resistant than are ACH cells from the medial septal region [Z:165].[27] During near-death states, when there is a terminal flurry of excitation/inhibition, when an extra release of NO• reaches levels that would prove toxic elsewhere, and when many anoxic regions of the brain have shut down, these surviving ACH nerve cells could still be contributing to the phenomena of near-death experiences [Z:164–169, 443, 452].

Unhappily for healthy seniors who could need help forming new memories, experiments suggest that NO• reduces the growth of new nerve cells (neurogenesis) in adult rat brain.[28] Various kinds of oxidative damage have been linked increasingly with degenerative diseases of the human nervous system. The evidence suggests that reactive oxygen species selectively nitrate a second amino acid, tyrosine. The result is that certain proteins will now have their properties changed by this new moiety, 3-nitrotyrosine. Antibodies which detect this altered tyrosine are now available. They can serve to target localized nerve cells that have had their proteins modified by an unusual local exposure to NO•.[29] This could be a useful chemical "fingerprint" for NO .

NO• has important implications with regard to neuronal plasticity. The influence that NO• has in changing the brain is not limited to certain forms of ("shorter") long-term potentiation in the hippocampus. NO• may also be involved in different, *very* long-term potentiation changes that also affect the brain [Z:181, 677]. For example, NO• can enhance the growth factor responses of a cell by virtue of its ability to increase both a moiety called $p21^{ras}$ and certain kinases. This effect that NO• has on gene transcription does not require cGMP.[30]

Commentary on Nitric Oxide

NO• has acquired a dual, reputation as a two-edged sword. It can play both a physiological *and* a potentially neurotoxic role in the brain.[31] Its synthetic enzyme—NO• synthase—coexists in different kinds of nerve cells. Their primary messenger can be glutamate, GABA, ACH, biogenic amines, or neuropeptides. Moreover, this NO• synthase is found in both short interneurons and in large cells with long axons. It can occur in their cell bodies, dendrites, axons, and nerve terminals.

For these multiple reasons, it is at least theoretically possible that when any one of these different nerve cells undergoes a calcium-related discharge, its firing activity might also include the discrete synthesis and quick release of NO•. The potential results could add intriguing new dimensions to the limited view we had a few decades ago. Back then, one nerve cell was believed to discharge only one chemical messenger at its synapse.

The heavy staining for NO' synthase in NO' nerve cells and fibers of the human hypothalamus, parabrachial region, and cerebellum suggests that NO' may play a more substantial role in their functions.

Is a "cloud" of NO' released in the brain? It is more likely to be a puff. And a tiny puff, at that, with a volume perhaps closer to 15 microns (twice the size of a red blood cell) than those 200 microns suggested in earlier estimates.

The section below, and chapter 73, discuss related aspects of an interesting observation: glycerol trinitrate—an NO' donor—can trigger migraine headaches in susceptible individuals.[32]

A general review of the biology of NO' systems is available. It presents many other details not covered in these pages.[33]

Saved for the end of the next chapter are the ways NO' is also being implicated in some of the myriad responses to a different gas. Do not be confused by its similar name. It is nitr*ous* oxide (N_2O), sometimes called "laughing gas."

Relevant Effects of Nitrates and Nitrites as Nitric Oxide Donors

Nitroglycerin (glyceryl trinitrate) was known as far back as 1847 to produce headaches.[34] A few years later, Alfred Nobel recognized its potential as an explosive agent. Amyl nitrite was soon discovered. Its vasodilating properties were used to relieve angina pectoris in 1867. Amyl nitrite "pearls," when crushed and inhaled, were often used in subsequent decades as a rapid treatment for angina pectoris.

Since then, amyl nitrite and other nitrites have been used for "recreational" purposes. They are known on the street as "poppers."[35] In this chapter, the point of interest is that amyl nitrite behaves like an NO' donor.

The psychosexual aspects of the volatile nitrites are reviewed up to 1982 in the *Journal of Psychoactive Drugs*.[36] Inhaling amyl nitrite in a sexual context may facilitate the process of "letting go." It ushers in a sensation of "timelessness mixed with immersion in the immediate moment." The resulting orgasm is described as "prolonged, intense and exalted." An accompanying visual percept is a bright yellow spot with purple "radiations."

Other symptoms of amyl nitrite inhalation include "withdrawal into the self, slowing of time sense such that music may seem more distant or slower, metamorphopsia, disinhibition, and heightening of emotions." When used in a sexual context, inhalation has also been described as leading to "an oceanic sense of oneness with the sexual partner" and with "heightened and prolonged orgasm."[37]

Studied by PET, out of the context of sexual arousal, amyl nitrite inhalation caused a global increase in cerebral blood flow, together with increased palpitation, breathing difficulty, dizziness, and headache. However, among the subjective reports were also significant *decreases* in anger, fatigue, and depression.[38]

Glyceryl trinitrate is also an NO˙ donor. When given intravenously by infusion it can induce migraine headaches (see chapter 73). Of the migraineurs whose responses were tested, 23 had the diagnosis of migraine without aura; 21 had the diagnosis of migraine with aura. In this whole group of 44 patients, nitroglycerin prompted a migraine headache in 33. In only one patient was the headache ushered in by a preliminary aura. This patient's visual aura was triggered each time the glyceryl trinitrate was given.[39] In a separate study, nitroglycerin was given by the sublingual route, again serving to trigger a migraine headache. Plasma levels of calcitonin gene–related peptide were shown to increase significantly during the migraine attack.[40]

In studies of these NO˙ donor actions in rats, nitroglycerin readily crossed the blood-brain barrier. It caused a noteworthy increase in cGMP in part of the trigeminal nucleus in the brainstem.[41] How NO˙ relates to cortical spreading depression (an important mechanism associated with migraine in humans) is currently under study.[42]

In summary, when NO˙ donors enter the systemic circulation, they reach the brain. Their subjective effects in the brain are clearly enhanced when human subjects are already excited. In persons who are already predisposed to migraine NO˙ donors can precipitate the headache phase and sometimes the visual aura.

A Preliminary Survey of Potential By-Products of NO˙ in the Venous Blood of Zen Meditators

The nitric oxide synthase discussed thus far is the enzyme made inside nerve cells. However, different forms of this enzyme also make NO˙. Some of their NO˙ arises in the endothelial lining of blood vessels and some from various other body tissues. Oxidation and nitrosylation soon form various chemical by-products of this NO˙. When these molecules leak into the bloodstream, their levels can be estimated in samples of peripheral venous blood. The levels of lipid peroxides and of nitrate/nitrite in the blood can serve as two *indirect* indices of the NO˙ that has arisen from multiple sources.

This total pool of potential by-products of NO˙ was assessed recently in a group of 20 adult Korean Zen meditators. They had practiced once or twice a week for 4 to 5 years.[43] The matched control group had not practiced any form of stress management. The Zen group showed lower levels of lipid peroxides (17 vs. 28 micromoles), but had higher baseline levels of serum nitrate/nitrite (4.6 vs 2.5 micromoles). Samples drawn before and after one hour of zazen meditation showed no change.

It would seem premature to comment on these findings. However, such a pioneering study draws attention to how much we need to know about the ways long-term meditative practice influences nitric oxide and its neurochemical sequences in the *central* nervous system. Studies of spinal fluid are awaited.

Our brain can synthesize NO˙ discretely and spontaneously. How do its remarkable properties enter into the phenomena of alternate states of consciousness? This seems likely to be a fertile field of research for decades to come.

A different gas, with a similar name, caused considerable attention centuries earlier. The next chapter discusses *nitrous* oxide.

69

The Nitrous Oxide Connection

> The atmosphere of the highest of all possible heavens must be composed of this gas.
>
> Robert Southey (1774–1843)[1]

High praise for another gas. Two centuries ago, *nitrous* oxide already had a reputation for prominent psychoactive effects. The British romantic poet Robert Southey certainly enjoyed getting high on nitrous oxide. His contemporary, Samuel Coleridge, while also under the influence of N_2O, felt "more unmingled pleasure than I had ever before experienced."[2] No less an observer than William James had also described, in 1882, its "tremendously exciting sense of an intense metaphysical illumination" [Z:407–413]. Because N_2O activated motoric systems and energized impulsive behaviors, it had already become known as "laughing gas."

Then it was noticed that N_2O had pain-relieving properties. This led to its use in dental surgery to produce analgesia and mild anesthesia. Recent preclinical studies have suggested that N_2O releases beta-endorphin and also influences several other neuromessenger systems.

Nitrous Oxide Effects on Endorphins

N_2O does increase the release of opioid peptides into the central gray of the midbrain. There, these opioids inhibit GABA nerve cells, which *had* been in the process of inhibiting the release of norepinephrine from its *descending* pathways. NE functions were then released as a result of this *dis*inhibition. These mechanisms could then be invoked to explain—at levels below the central gray—many of the analgesic and antinociceptive effects of N_2O.[3]

Other research in the mouse demonstrates that antibodies to dynorphin or met-enkephalin block the antinociceptive effect of N_2O.[4]

Nitrous Oxide Increases Corticotropin-Releasing Factor and Norepinephrine

N_2O also acts at a higher level to increase the release of NE. It activates CRF nerve cells in the paraventricular nucleus of the rat hypothalamus and enhances the rat's antinociceptive reflexes at lower levels. A CRF antagonist reduces the activity of locus ceruleus cells and also reduces this antinociceptive effect.[5]

Other Nitrous Oxide Effects on Glutamate and GABA Systems

In tissue culture, N_2O blocks glutamate receptors of the NMDA type on rat hippocampal nerve cells, and slightly enhances the actions of GABA on $GABA_A$ receptors.[6] These in vitro findings are curious, because certain nerve cells degenerate in the back of the brain when normal adult rats are exposed to N_2O for only a short period.

An important point: These neurotoxic changes in living animals localize to one particular spot: that region near the posterior cingulate gyrus and the retrosplenial cortex which stays *extraactive*—even at rest—in normal human subjects [Z:282-283] (see chapter 50). This localized N_2O toxicity resembles the effects caused by other drugs that block NMDA receptors. For example, the anesthetic drug ketamine also blocks NMDA receptors, and it causes the same distinctive localized neurotoxic side effects.[7] So too does the illicit psychoactive drug phencyclidine ("angel dust"). In contrast, GABAergic agents stop this toxic reaction.

It is true that N_2O has some NMDA receptor blocking properties, and that it may also weakly enhance GABA receptor activity. However, present evidence suggests that these particular retrosplenial and posterior cingulate cells are vulnerable to further overfiring when the brain is exposed to N_2O, ketamine, and phencyclidine. The responsible mechanisms, though very important, remain to be defined.[8]

Supporting this "overfiring toxicity" hypothesis is the finding that N_2O produces histological evidence of increased neuronal activity affecting *multiple* cells throughout the rat nervous system,[9] and that it can also block certain receptors.[10]

To the degree that some of our normal self/other functions are referable to this same active medial retrosplenial and posterior cingulate region and that they seem to drop off during long-term meditative training, then its vulnerabilities would seem to make it an interesting candidate for longitudinal neuroimaging research and postmortem histological studies [Z:653–659].

One PET study involved human volunteers who were responding to painful heat applied to the skin of their left forearm. Breathing even as little as 20% N_2O activated the paraolfactory area (BA 25) and the orbitofrontal cortex (BA 10 and

11). These two activated sites become of interest, because stimulations delivered to these two regions have been reported (in separate studies) to cause analgesia, presumably by interacting with other circuits that modulate pain[11] (see chapter 36).

As if this wide variety of N_2O effects were not enough, some actions of *nitrous* oxide have now been shown to depend on the way it increases the levels of *nitric* oxide (see the preceding chapter 68).

Nitric Oxide as a Mechanism Underlying Some Effects of Nitrous Oxide

N_2O has been shown to enhance the activity of the enzyme that makes $NO^{\bullet}$ ($NO^{\bullet}$ synthase). Mice breathing N_2O show fewer anxiety-like behaviors. Suppose, on the other hand, you now inhibit their $NO^{\bullet}$ synthase. After this, N_2O no longer stops their anxious behaviors.[12]

These findings suggest that some anxiety-relieving effects of N_2O may be related to its ability to increase the release of $NO^{\bullet}$.

A Caveat about Nitrous Oxide

N_2O has multiple mechanisms of action. It is not innocuous. Though William James once said that breathing N_2O induces a state wherein "truth lies open to the view," these are *fleeting* "truths." Indeed, as Peter Roget observed, "the nature of the sensations themselves ... bore greater resemblance to a half-delirious stream than to any distinct state of mind capable of being accurately remembered" [Z:407–413]. In short, inhaling N_2O yields an inchoate mixture of symptoms that range from delirium through brief expressions that might seem only partially to resemble absorptions or kensho.

Could certain of the quasi-kensho-like mental state phenomena of N_2O hinge on the release of $NO^{\bullet}$? If so, it will be important to determine *which* ones, and precisely *when* they arise in the whole fleeting sequence. Only when safe blockers of $NO^{\bullet}$ synthase become available for human use will it be feasible to even consider such a complex experiment.

Meanwhile, the myriad actions of N_2O and their rapidly shifting kaleidoscopic effects complicate its role as a potential agent for clarifying the mechanisms of alternate states of consciousness. The same reservations hold even truer for other currently available psychoactive molecules. Their rapidly evolving mental phenomena outstrip investigators' efforts to correlate their actions with fMRI signals, and challenge efforts to time their onset precisely with the aid of EEG, MEG, and ERP techniques.

On the other hand, the rapid pace of the new $NO^{\bullet}$ research that has just been reviewed and its suggestive relationship with N_2O suggest a promising future for preclinical investigations in this important area.

70

Self-Abuse by Drugs

Not a drop of alcohol is to be brought into this temple.

Master Bassui (1327–1387)[1]
(His dying instructions: first rule)

In swinging between liberal tolerance one moment and outraged repression the next, modern societies seem chronically incapable of reaching consistent attitudes about drugs.

Stephen Batchelor[2]

Drugs won't show you the truth. Drugs will only show you what it's like to be on drugs.

Brad Warner[3]

Implicit in the authentic Buddhist Path is *sila*. It is the time-honored practice of exercising sensible restraints [Z:73–74]. Sila's ethical guidelines provide the bedrock foundation for one's personal behavior in daily life. At the core of every religion are some self-disciplined renunciations corresponding to sila. Yet, a profound irony has been reshaping the human condition in most cultures during the last half century. It dates from the years when psychoactive drugs became readily available. During this era, many naturally curious persons could try psychedelic short-cuts and experience the way their consciousness might seem to "expand." A fortunate few of these experimenters would become motivated to follow the *non*-drug meditative route when they pursued various spiritual paths.

One fact is often overlooked. *Meditation itself has many mind-expanding, psychedelic properties* [Z:418–426]. These meditative experiences can also stimulate a drug-free spiritual quest.

Meanwhile, we live in a drug culture. It is increasingly a drugged culture, for which overprescribing physicians must shoulder part of the blame. Do drugs have any place along the spiritual path? This issue will always be hotly debated.[4]

In Zen, the central issue is not whether each spiritual aspirant has the "right" to exercise their own curiosity, or the "right" to experiment on their own brains in the name of freedom of religion. It is a free country. Drugs are out there. The real questions are:

- Can you exercise the requisite self-discipline to follow the Zen Buddhist Path?
- Do you already have enough common sense to ask that seemingly naive question, "What would Buddha do?" (WWBD).

- Can you avoid sharing in the herd mentality? Drug proponents will reassure you that it is OK to take drugs of unknown purity, drugs which are currently illegal, on grounds that you are only following examples set by friends, unlicensed gurus, and historical precedent.

The Precepts

Buddhism's five major precepts are designed to include the laity. They are rules of training, adopted voluntarily. They are not words to be played with, nor principles to be abandoned lightly. They anticipate serious practical matters.[5] In effect, these precepts say: I undertake to refrain from killing, stealing, lying, sexual misbehavior, and using intoxicants.

This chapter is not addressed to anyone who uses drugs and who believes that drugs have a place on the spiritual path.[6] Its pages are addressed to readers who might be interested in "trying" drugs for various reasons, including curiosity. I strongly believe in curiosity, but not when it conflicts with my other principles.[7]

The Challenge of the Three Fires

The Buddha identified three "fires" as the root cause of our anguish. This is the triad of longing, loathing, and ignorance. They are also known as the three "poisons": greed, hatred, and delusion. Two and a half millennia later, permissive societies find themselves ingesting herbal remedies of variable purity, with an unusually free access to psychoactive street drugs. Drugs *are* out there.

Language sugarcoats the issue, makes taking drugs easy to rationalize. People talk loosely about "drug abuse," "substance abuse." They are misnomers. It is as though the drug were an object, some distance away, a thing which was being acted *upon* harmfully by an *anonymous* person. This deceptive wording displaces abnormal human behavior, projects it somewhere else. Instead, the act amounts to *self*-abuse, not "substance" abuse. A real *person* is abusing his or her very own brain. "Substance" abuse shifts attention away from the actual, personal *brain abuse*.

So let us continue this line of questioning at the level of self, because it is ultimately for each individual person to decide how the questions will be answered.

- Will I allow into my body powerful chemicals of unknown purity, substances that could derange the fantastic neurochemical circuits of my brain?
- Do I have some subversive need to challenge authority figures, and to confront legal boundaries in general?

- Is the taking of a psychoactive drug truly in keeping with the authentic *spirit* of the precepts—the spirit of restraint that is at the core of a genuine spiritual quest?
- Do I understand that this spiritual path means looking deeply into my own appetitive drives? Do I clearly realize that thirsts, hungers, longings and graspings are *self*-indulgent symptoms? That they are to be confronted, acknowledged, and worked through? That ignorance is to be *repaired*—not winked at? That to confront one's curiosity and hunger for drugs *is an integral part of the training process itself*, grist for the mill?
- Am I so thirsty for new experiences (so incapable of adhering to that mature commitment, which meditative training requires) that I must seek a quick fix in some illicit chemical made by someone I do not know?
- Do I know how many risks are involved, how very rare is any outcome of true lasting religious import? Or am I in denial, ignoring evidence that might run counter to *my* opinion? [Z:418–439].

***Who* Needs Drugs? Who *Needs* Drugs? Who Needs *Drugs*?**

During their early meditative training, most meditators will encounter brief hallucinations, illusory phenomena, and other mental quickenings. These are impressive psychic events. To experience them, you do not need psychedelics. These nondrug "side effects" occur regularly on the meditative path, and are called "makyo." They demonstrate our brain's intrinsic, unsuspected, dynamic capacities at grabbing attention and sharpening it [Z:373–376]. These incidental *meditative* phenomena help stimulate many persons to continue on the Path, and did stimulate my own search to go further.

But my bias is that of a physician. I was trained to "first do no harm." My advice to others has always been "meditation, not medication."

I hope you are not expecting me to endorse any course of behavior called "beat Zen," "bent Zen," or "zig zag Zen." My inclination is to view them as cultural aberrations.

As for that alliterative term "zig zag Zen," each alteration in the jagged course of these three zs is accurate. It depicts how taking drugs departs from the otherwise straight course of authentic Zen Buddhism.

Counterfeit Words

Recent decades have seen several new words coined to soften the often carnival image of the earlier psychedelic era. That was a time when so-called recreational street drugs were not just a cottage industry. In some quarters, they were a rite of passage. "Entheogens" was a term later devised by a committee, meaning "God generated within you." Entheo serves to camouflage the many *un*godly hallucinations that can afflict the person who takes a "mind-manifesting" psychedelic drug.[8]

Next came "empathogen," a term devised to convey the empathy-promoting effects of the street drug "Ecstasy." Spin doctors might prefer that the public would overlook one other medical implication of "path," a term whose roots also imply abnormality. (e.g., *path*ogenic means capable of causing disease.)

A recent arrival is the term *entactogen* (Greek: "touching within"). This invention is designed to soften the public image of a drug like MDMA (3,4-methylenedioxymethamphetamine; Ecstasy). Though it is relatively free from major perceptual alterations, MDMA can indeed harm the human brain as is discussed in the next chapter.

Emergency room physicians still see patients on "a bad trip" acutely "freaked out" by LSD. Many health professionals have become so keenly aware of LSD's side effects (as an entheo*pathogen*) that they do not need to invent some new milder phrase for it.

Cautionary Tales

Most paeans to psychedelics were written by people outside the health professions who had not only "used" them but then survived.[9] Do their tales tell the *whole* story of their survival? Not often enough in ways that reach the printed page. Consider Rick Doblin's follow-up critique, published almost three decades after Pahnke's classic experiment in 1962 of twenty Christian theological students [Z:436–438].

Doblin points to a very significant omission in the original report. "Pahnke under-emphasized the difficult psychological struggles experienced by most of the psilocybin subjects"[10] [Z:436–439]. Only two of the seven subjects whom Doblin interviewed during his follow-up study said that their psychedelic experience had been a completely positive one. The other five all had moments during which "they feared they were either going crazy, dying, or were too weak for the ordeal they were experiencing."

The original report omitted another significant fact. One subject who received psilocybin became deluded, ran out onto Commonwealth Avenue, was chased down by Houston Smith, and had to be tranquilized by an injection of Thorazine (chlorpromazine).[11]

Readers discover Houston Smith speaking on both sides of the controversy during the past four decades.[12] He is certainly correct when he says: "The goal, it cannot be stressed too often, is not religious experiences: it is the religious life. And with respect to the latter, psychedelic 'theophanies' can abort a quest as readily as, perhaps more readily than, they further it."[13] Amen!

As Aitken-Roshi observes, "there is a qualitative difference between the ecstasy, that some people report from their drug experiences, and the understanding, the realization, that comes with Zen practice. We seek understanding, not ecstasy." Gassho![14]

Peter Matthiessen had used several psychedelic drugs regularly for 10 years. His comment was: "At no time did the 'I' dissolve into the miracle.... Lacking the temper of ascetic discipline, the drug vision remains a sort of dream that cannot be brought over into daily life."[15]

Eric Davis adds: "One does not need to be a genius, or even a psychologist, to understand how easily drugs can amplify delusion, dissociation, and spiritual materialism, let alone feed into patterns of behavior and consumption that lead ever further away from the Dharma."[16]

J. P. Barlow argues for both liberty and LSD. However, he does add that LSD "is dangerous because it promotes the idea that reality is something to be manipulated rather than accepted ... and of course, if you're lightly sprung, it can leave you nuts."[17]

Contrasts between Spontaneous and Drug-Induced Experiences

When Allen Smith was 31, he had an experience of what he regards as "cosmic consciousness."[18] He describes his mood elevation during this episode as constant, all-pervasive, and at the level of ecstasy. The "merging" that occurred during "cosmic consciousness" was "just *being*," and "the knowingness" extended beyond ordinary significance to "encompass everything." His only prior drug exposure was with marijuana in social settings. Subsequently, he took some twelve to fifteen "trips" with LSD, hoping to recapture the experience. While on LSD, his moods changed rapidly but infrequently. On LSD, there was "usually still a person present to whom something could happen." The "self" was never far away. The LSD episodes felt like "an experience."

In the Hardy anthology, one woman compared her subsequent drug experiences (of mescaline and hashish) as follows: "They seemed inferior, impermanent, working upon me; glossier."[19]

What Would Buddha Do? (WWBD)

Anyone can pose this question today. You need not be a person who professes to follow the Buddhist Path. When the moral and ethical restraints of *sila* are coupled with the support of the *sangha*, the blend often supplies the useful ounce of prevention that helps a vulnerable person avoid the later need to seek a pound of cure.

On one of my visits to Ryoko-in during the late 1970s, Kobori-Roshi went to a drawer, took out a small packet, and showed it to me. It was a drug that someone had given him "to try." He asked, "What is your opinion about taking drugs?"

I said, "Don't ever take it." He replied, "I agree; I won't."

That is still my advice. No drug studies cited anywhere on these pages would find me queuing up to be a volunteer subject.

Meanwhile, as this new millennium dawns, we find the venerable Houston Smith being invited to review his previous writings about the relationship between psychoactive drugs and religious/mystical experiences.[20] The main title selected for this book, *Cleansing the Doors of Perception*, is derived from William Blake. Blake wrote: "If the doors of perception were cleansed, everything would appear to man as it is, infinite." Blake's sentence starts with *If*. This is a very big *If*.

Following Rick Doblin's approach, let us consider some iffy issues that Smith's title leaves out. With all due respect, might it be viewed as leaning toward one side of the story? True, drugs can heighten attention. Yes, perceptual clarity can occur at the *beginning*. However, the drug-induced state soon takes the user on a roller coaster ride. The rest of the "trip" includes a barrage of hallucinatory and affective phenomena. It severely "alters" consciousness, clogs it unmercifully. The drug trip *distorts perception*. It does not cleanse it.

With a view toward a balanced perspective, it may be useful to recall the words Blake chose for *his* own title, under which the sentence quoted originally appeared. He entitled it "The Marriage of Heaven and Hell, a Memorable Fancy."

Houston Smith does provide his readers a cautionary tale in the personal comments he voiced to Timothy Leary (just after Leary had enabled him to ingest mescaline): "I feel like I'm in an operating room, having barely squeaked through an ordeal in which for two hours my life hung in the balance."[21]

Everyone today confronts the prospect of journeying to alluring destinations. Psychoactive drug trips are available. From the Zen perspective, the *ongoing daily-life practice of mindful living remains essential*. Brief experiences are "nothing special," whether they are induced artificially by a drug or arise spontaneously. As Michele McDonald-Smith says: "When a person feels that they need drugs to go deeper in their spiritual journey, they're just reinforcing the attachment to those particular states of consciousness and the need to get them back again."[22]

Who needs more needs? Who needs more attachments? The central question remains: *How can I perceive and realize with utmost clarity this wondrous world that I already inhabit*? This is not a question of LSD or MDMA.

The question remains: WWBD?

71

How Do Certain Drugs "Alter" Consciousness?

> A man's nature runs either to herbs or to weeds; therefore let him seasonably water the one, and destroy the other.
>
> Francis Bacon (1561–1626)

Word Options

Words change their meanings. Back in Bacon's era, herbal remedies were assumed to be good for what ails you. In our era, it may depend on which kind of compound-leaved plant you're cultivating in a hidden corner of your backyard herb garden.

From our pharmacology teacher in the mid-1940s, we learned—second-hand—that various drug intoxications could blur self/other distinctions. I still remember how Professor Otto Krayer illustrated the point, citing an opium smoker who had said: "Am I smoking this pipe, or is the pipe smoking me?"

The psychedelic 1960s introduced radical changes. Millions of people began to talk about, and use, major "mind-altering" drugs. These drugs did more than "alter" your state of consciousness. You could get so "stoned" on them that you would retain only a blurred memory of the episode. Years later, users who could still reminisce wistfully about such "mind-blowing" alterations might proclaim: "If you *remember* the '60s, you weren't really *there*!"

This book explores a different approach: a Zen that appreciates nature and rock gardens without getting stoned. Yet today, many still continue to use that era's phrase: "altered" state of consciousness. Nowdays, "altered" is often used as a general term to refer not only to a drug-induced change but to *any* kind of substantial change in consciousness (including those in *non*drug religious/mystical/spiritual categories).

I remember the 1960s clearly, not having used drugs. I prefer to believe that our normal, clear consciousness has many alternative options [Z:305–311]. So I speak of all these states on the Path—and in a *non*drug context—as *alternate* states of consciousness (see chapter 4).

Alternate is not a new invention. There is a historical precedent. Zinberg used it, also deliberately, back in 1977. He chose *Alternate States of Consciousness* for the title of his book on this large topic. In those days, "alternate" was an unusual choice of word.[1] Why choose "alternate?" Its novelty helped it stand out. It offered a clear contrast to "altered." That was the point. "Alternate" served as a counterweight against what had become by then a widespread misunderstanding:

Sure it was OK to *alter* your consciousness with drugs. Wasn't this the quick and easy way to gain enlightenment?

A quarter-century later, new books are now coming out with deceptive titles. Contributors extol the alleged virtues of psychedelics as "entheogens." Today, *alternate* still stands out, as it did in 1977. Its resonances convey an *anti*drug statement: Just say No. It's *not* OK. There is *no* easy way.

I do not object when someone wishes to talk about drug-induced "altered" states of consciousness (though "altered" still sounds like what can happen to your pet at a veterinary office). Nor do I object to those who may prefer the usual word, "alternative." It does sound more comfortable, at first. But to my ears, this longer word does not signal the requisite contrast with "altered," nor does it acknowledge the rationale for Zinberg's salient contribution.

As a substitute term, *alternate* is not without claim to historical accuracy. Before adopting alternate for use throughout my 1998 book, I first checked out the word in *Webster's Third New International Dictionary*. There I found that among its Latin roots is *alternus*, meaning "interchangeable." There, one also finds the option—still using *alternate* as an adjective—to specify "a choice between two, or among more than two objects or courses." The key phrases are "interchangeable" and "among more than two." Do they not describe the many optional ways our states of consciousness can shift when we are awake or asleep?

Moreover, farther down on the same page, the dictionary has a separate listing for "alternate consciousness." It is used in this instance as a noun meaning "a conscious state dissociated from a person's usual state." These several usages liberate us from the fixed notion that the word *alternate* must be defined solely in terms that imply "oscillating," to swing back and forth, at regularly recurring intervals, between each one of a pair, as might occur in the example of an "oscillating current."

In this sequel emphasizing a long-range Zen Buddhist meditative approach, there is no need to engage in any extensive review of psychedelic drugs [Z:418–443]. However, recent research indicates that several drugs have pertinent effects and side effects that relate to our discussion.

MDMA (3,4-Methylenedioxymethamphetamine)

Wouldn't it be great to feel, and to *be*, more loving? Don't we owe it to ourselves to *try* Ecstasy, just to see if it lives up to its street name? The two questions express deep, universal, instinctual longings—the drives to satisfy our*self* and our curiosity. *They also define the root of our problem.*

MDMA, also known as Ecstasy, exerts its major influence by enhancing the tone of the serotonin system[2] (see chapter 24). Its overall effects on the psyche hinge largely on increased levels of serotonin; its stimulant effects on mood may relate to some dopamine DA_2 receptor stimulation; its mild perceptual effects may be due to additional activation of serotonin-2 receptors.[3]

Unfortunately, MDMA has drawbacks. It has documented neurotoxic effects on those slender, vulnerable serotonin terminals which the dorsal raphe nucleus sends up to supply the cerebrum [Z:424]. Reports from Johns Hopkins and Harvard Medical schools link regular MDMA abuse with persistent mental impairment. In the 1998 study, MDMA users (averaging 60 times over 4 years) were impaired on verbal and visual memory tests even after they had been abstinent for a month or so.[4] In a 2004 study, heavy MDMA users (60–450 times) showed significantly slower mental processing and greater impulsivity.[5]

Single doses of MDMA have been administered to healthy volunteers who had not taken it before.[6] The subjects developed enhanced mood, became emotionally aroused and more extraverted. Low-resolution brain tomography (LORETA) translated their 31-channel scalp EEGs into 3D functional images. Fast frequencies were increased over the anterior temporal and posterior orbitofrontal cortex, consistent with their subjective symptoms (see chapter 49).

Other imaging studies have addressed the topic of MDMA toxicity.[7] The same major PET study has even been published twice (once in the psychiatry literature and again in the imaging literature), perhaps for reasons related to its social significance.[8] Thirty subjects were current MDMA users; 29 were former MDMA users. In current users, the study pointed to a significant reduction of serotonin transporter sites in the midbrain, thalamus, left caudate, hippocampus, occipital cortex, temporal lobes, and posterior cingulate gyrus. Female subjects showed more evident reductions in keeping with MDMA's greater perceptual effects in women. Longer periods of abstention were correlated with less severe decreases in the serotonin transporter site. This suggested that some abnormalities might be reversible.[9]

Psychological tests of regular MDMA users show significant evidence of depressiveness, inactivation, and emotional excitability.[10] When these users' eyes remain open, LORETA studies show a global increase in various frequency bands. Greater alpha-2 activity occurs chiefly in the right temporo-occipital regions (BA 37 and 19).

In subjects naive to MDMA, pretreatment with a dopamine DA_2 antagonist (haloperidol) reverses the expected pattern of pleasure, well-being, and euphoria. Instead, the subjects shift toward dysphoria, anxious derealization, inner tension, and difficulty concentrating. This shift in a negative direction suggests that the release of dopamine mediates some of the usual euphoriant effects of MDMA.[11]

Pretreatment with a selective serotonin reuptake inhibitor, citalopram, attenuates only a bare majority (about 60%) of the acute psychological effects of MDMA in healthy naive subjects.[12] This evidence supports the theory that dopaminergic actions (and perhaps others not yet defined) contribute to the remaining 40% of the effects of MDMA. Sobering evidence has recently been presented that MDMA can adversely affect not only the brain but also the developing fetus in some animal models.[13]

Ketamine

Ketamine is a dissociative anesthetic. Its major action is to block glutamate receptors at the NMDA* receptor complex (see chapter 69). Normal subjects develop an acute, highly disorganized, "altered" mental state when they are injected with even a subanesthetic dose of ketamine. One investigator likens their complicated symptoms to a "model near-death experience."[14] Vollenweider, in an excellent review, surveys the evidence that this drug state resembles a schizophreniform psychosis.[15] The evidence includes both the subjects' symptoms and PET scans revealing their "metabolic" evidence of frontal hyperactivity.

Ketamine is not unique in either respect. Psilocybin (a serotonin agonist at serotonin-2 receptors) also produces similar symptoms and PET scan findings.[16] Both drugs can prompt severe, life-threatening anxieties and major perceptual distortions. Subjects who experience such "mind-blowing" symptoms will soon generate other secondary, reactive symptoms in response to them. *Secondary* "psychic" manifestations then complicate how one is to interpret (as cause or effect) the PET scan activity patterns both in the frontal region and elsewhere. Future investigations (e.g., with fMRI) will need to specify the precise times of onset and sequences through which all such symptoms evolve [Z:439].

Ordeals

Extraordinary states of consciousness arise when several psychophysiological mechanisms converge. Many of these will be the major stress responses triggered inside the brain itself. These begin when the person first confronts acute life-threatening events (see chapter 32) [Z:235–240, 443–452]. Our fear of death is caused not only by actual external threatening events. Nowadays, such fears can represent the ordeals brought on by major psychoactive drugs.

Researchers have devised a useful questionnaire to characterize the complex mental symptoms caused by ketamine and psilocybin. A state called "oceanic boundlessness" is one primary dimension in this questionnaire. It indexes the person's levels of derealization and ego dissolution. These phenomena may evolve into several other feelings that include "merging with the cosmos" in association

* This is not MDMA. NMDA is the particular type of receptor sensitive to, and activated by, the brain's own excitatory amino acid, glutamate (see chapter 31).

with the loss of the sense of time.[17] Which PET scan findings correlate with this particular mixture of symptoms? They include activation of prefrontal–inferior parietal networks in parallel with *de*activation of a striatolimbic network centered in the left amygdala (see the discussion of "doing time" in chapter 83).

A second dimension in the questionnaire is "visionary restructuralization." This phrase softens the impact on the psyche of visual distortions and frank hallucinations. In fact, these two symptom complexes are accompanied by the "dread of ego-dissolution," and are associated with the subjects' feelings of paranoia at being in a life-threatening situation. PET scan correlates of this discomforting mixture include activations of the left dorsolateral prefrontal cortex, of both upper and lower visual streams, in parallel with *de*activations in the left globus pallidus and parahippocampus.

Subsequent PET studies of (*S*)-ketamine have revealed added layers of interacting mechanisms. Even though ketamine acts as a glutamate antagonist at NMDA receptors, some of its altered state symptoms may also be related to dopamine DA_2 receptors. The (indirect) evidence suggesting an *increased release* of dopamine appeared in the ventral striatum, the caudate nucleus, and the putamen. Moments of heightened mood occurred that ranged from euphoria to grandiosity. These moments coincided with an increased release of dopamine in the ventral striatum.[18]

Marijuana (Cannabis): A "Gateway Drug"

Marijuana is often the first "herb" to lure innocents through the gate and down the garden path toward major "theobotanicals." Almost half of all 18-year-olds in the United States and in most European countries admit to having tried it (*really* inhaling) one or more times. Some estimate that perhaps 10% of that teen age group become regular users.[19] Its main psychoactive molecule is THC (Δ^9-tetrahydrocannabinol). THC acts chiefly on the brain's abundant cannabinoid CB(1) receptors. The multiple interactions that occur next involve GABA, dopamine, opioid, and several other messenger systems. Similar CB receptors mediate multiple actions in tissues elsewhere in the body.[20]

A study of 311 grown twins has recently revealed some long-range consequences of using marijuana. Whether the twins were identical or fraternal, one of them had used marijuana before the age of 17 years; the other twin had not.[21] To collect these discordant sets is a feat remarkable in itself, given the widespread social use of marijuana. However, this Australian study appeared to have controlled for this and other shared environmental influences.

The twin who had used cannabis by 17 years of age was 2.1 to 5.2 times more likely to engage in other drug use, to develop alcohol dependence, and to develop drug abuse/dependence than was the co-twin. The identical and fraternal twins had just about the same vulnerabilities to abuse various other substances. But the most decisive factors in the use of cannabis were the local social contexts and the peer relationships within which it could be obtained and used. Thereafter, easy access to cannabis appeared to reduce the social barriers that might otherwise protect the twin from going on to use other illegal drugs.

The marijuana-induced euphoria usually appears between 7 and 15 minutes after smoking begins. EEG studies during this induced euphoria show that alpha power increases 70% over the parietal leads on both sides. Various other subjective aspects of intoxication persist for 60 to 70 minutes after smoking starts.[22]

In humans, marijuana's immediate actions seem to "mellow" the person. However, it also causes delayed exaggerated responses to stressful circumstances. Why? One important clue comes from mice. When mice are subjected first to restraint stress and then to THC, the two *combined* activate the central nucleus of the amygdala. However, neither factor alone is sufficient.[23]

In rats, THC (like cocaine, amphetamine, and ethanol) causes large increases in beta-endorphin levels in the ventral tegmental area, and lesser increases in the shell of the nucleus accumbens[24] (see chapter 25). Most of the other psychoactive properties of THC arise from its actions in the ventral tegmental area and the nucleus accumbens.[25]

In acute toxicity studies in humans, smoking marijuana disrupts both the transient attentional and the more sustained functions that the subjects require to solve working memory tasks. It also decreases theta EEG power globally, and reduces the amplitude of event-related potentials.[26]

Δ-THC itself, when given intravenously to 22 healthy subjects over a 2-minute period, produces schizophrenia-like positive and negative symptoms, alters perception, leads to both anxiety and to euphoria, and disrupts both immediate and delayed word recall.[27] Large doses of cannabis can also provoke an acute psychosis that resembles schizophrenia. Heavy users among young recruits in the Swedish army had a *six*fold greater incidence of schizophrenia on follow-up.[28]

Chronic toxic effects were evaluated in 31 subjects who had been "entered" *prenatally* (as fetuses) into a unique prospective study.[29] Now 18 to 22 years old, they were tested psychologically. One task, monitored by fMRI, required them to inhibit their responses. The subjects whose *prenatal* exposure to marijuana had been most marked showed greater degrees of increased fMRI signals in their prefrontal cortex on both sides, as well as in the right premotor cortex. Left cerebellar signals were reduced.

If the data in this chapter reflect what can happen to the brain on the garden path toward major "theobotanicals," it is one path I choose not to take.

72

Triggers

> When Heaven is about to confer a great office on you, it first exercises your mind with suffering and your sinews and bones with toil.
>
> Mencius (372–289 B.C.E.)

Daito Kokushi (1282–1338) was the founding abbot of the temple in Kyoto where I first began Zen practice. He entered monastic life at the age of 10. Later, having worked on the same koan for the previous 2 to 3 years, he happened to toss a key onto a desk. At that instant, he "attained a boundless satori of complete interpenetration . . . sweat covered his body."[1]

Meditators experience heightened epiphenomena, such as the feelings that their perceptions are energized, and that their emotions are swinging rapidly in cycles. One's perceptions are especially sharpened during retreats. They seem to enter consciousness faster than usual. The interval shortens between each stimulus and its instantly registered impact. A sense of immediacy arises. *Quickening* is a term that can be used to suggest at least one (of several) model mechanisms that help us appreciate why such surges occur.

Sometimes a triggering stimulus sets off a mystical or enlightenment experience. Meditation repeated often on a retreat seems to sensitize a person to triggers [Z:452–457]. In the Zen *meditative* context, triggers will be striking deep after a very long prelude and often in a setting involving some inner turmoil. It has been said that if awakening sometimes occurs more or less by accident, then meditation makes you more accident-prone.

In natural outdoor settings, subtle and sublime stimuli sometimes serve as triggers. Yet the historical record suggests that many triggering sensate events are not only sudden but also startling. Recent fMRI and EEG studies clarify how the brain responds to such external stimuli.

fMRI Responses to Visual Stimuli

Pavlov noticed the way his dogs pricked up their ears. He then went on to regard the whole behavioral orienting response as a what-*is*-it? reflex. Clearly his dogs' behavior helped focus their attention on a novel or significant stimulus in order to extract further information from it.

In a study of human subjects, fMRI signals differed depending on whether or not a visual stimulus was meaningful enough to evoke an arousal response in the autonomic nervous system.[2] When stimuli were significant and *did* increase the skin conductance response, the subjects' orienting response increased signals in the right anterior cingulate (BA 24), left hippocampus, and ventromedial prefrontal cortex (BA 32).

Another fMRI study examined the effect of unexpected visual stimuli. These odd stimuli prompt distinctive evoked potential responses, many of which arise in the prefrontal cortex.[3] Enhanced signals occurred consistently within the middle frontal gyrus on both sides only when the stimuli had an implicitly affective novel quality.

EEG Responses to Novel Auditory Stimuli

A previous study of hippocampal slices (in vitro) found that bursts of gamma oscillations were followed by slower beta wave oscillations. In the present EEG study of ten normal human subjects, loud, novel auditory stimuli also prompted a gamma-to-beta transition.[4] Both gamma and beta oscillations habituated markedly after the initial response (see chapter 16).

It was the slower beta-1 activity at 12 to 20 cps that trailed the gamma, not the faster beta-2 frequency of 20 to 30 cps. The earliest phase of the evoked gamma and beta oscillations was distributed more in the frontal and superior temporal regions. The later gamma and beta oscillations (peaking between 300 and 680 ms) tended to peak over the parietal association areas. Chapter 47 emphasized how the sensitivities of these regions contribute to our higher mechanisms of attention.

Alternative Ways of Stimulating the Human Brain

Blindfolded subjects report unusual experiences while swinging in a large pendulum in various directions over a 2- to 20-minute period.[5] They can lose their sense of orientation in space, lose their sense of time, pay "visits" to other worlds, and can experience a wide variety of "religious" and other mystical-type alternate-state phenomena. These reports suggest that different kinds of vestibular stimulation have "triggering" properties when subjects are deprived of their usual visual cues. Our vestibular system responds to movement in all dimensions of space, and sometimes to repeated to and fro movements of the eyes.

The human vestibular system can also be stimulated by irrigating the ear canals with a cold solution. The resulting nystagmus continues for at least 90 seconds after the stimulation stops. During such vestibular stimulation, fMRI signals increase *primarily on the right* side. The increase involves not only the temporoparietal junction discussed in chapter 52. It extends into the posterior insula, the anterior insula, the pre- and postcentral regions of the parietal lobe, the ventral lateral portion of the occipital lobe, and the posterior extension of the inferior frontal gyrus.[6]

We prefer to maintain our body image in a stable, undislocated place in space. Vertigo is unpleasant. The wide distribution of fMRI signals in the brain during excessive degrees of experimental vestibular stimulation is consistent with the variety of aversive secondary perceptual and emotional responses that can occur (see chapter 28).

Musings about Kensho

I have wondered for years why kensho happened at *that* particular place and time (see chapter 93) [Z:536–539]. Some of these recent vestibular findings might be relevant to more subtle precipitating causes, including the preponderance of the normal vestibular representation in the right hemisphere.

I had been practicing Zen for some 8 years. This was the start of the second day of a 2-day retreat. En route, I had been seated on the right side of a London underground train, facing forward, looking out the window to my right at the sequence of passing scenery. This repeated shifting of gaze and focusing of attention off to the right could have elicited subtle degrees of optokinetic nystagmus during a period of 15 minutes or so of traveling time.

On getting off the train and waiting for the next train to Victoria station, I *turned* to the right. There, as the train clatter faded, I looked away from the tracks and off into some ordinary London scenery where a bit of open sky was showing above and beyond. I had now faced up to the fact that I would be late for the first morning sitting. To be late for anything is not my style. This was especially true for sitting during a retreat.

I surrendered the last notion of that feeling of obligation. I *let go*. I *gave up*.

Several factors converged at that moment. The ways they came together could have served as a subtle impetus for initially right-sided responses, some involving the right temporoparietal junction. Note that one "heard distance" in the right superior temporal region (chapter 42).

Some Other Lateralized Sensitivities of the Right Cerebral Hemisphere

Our right cerebral hemisphere is dominant for various attentional mechanisms. These are directed externally toward extrapersonal space[7] (see chapters 15 and 47). A variety of tests also suggests that we have a central physiological asymmetry in the way we process *somatosensory* data. Meador and colleagues documented this in their study of 126 healthy adults of both sexes, 110 of whom were right-handed. Using a weak electric pulse, they tested the sensory thresholds of their subjects' right and left index fingers. Among their normal right-handed subjects, the *left* fingers were significantly more sensitive than were the right fingers in all age groups.

The right hemispheric functional dominance for processing somatic signals is supported by other kinds of evidence.[8] When unusual pains complicate cerebrovascular accidents (strokes) they are most likely to occur after *right* thalamic lesions. Norepinephrine levels are also higher in many right thalamic nuclei.

73

The Extraordinary Scope of Migraine: "The Hildegard Syndrome"

> Migraine is a multisystem disorder of neuronal hyperexcitability.
>
> Daniels Pietrobon and Jorg Striessnig[1]

> The awareness that migraine is an expression of the genetics, personality, and way of life of an individual is only very recently being proclaimed.
>
> William Goody[2]

Migraine is a common disorder, so common that everyone assumes doctors know all about it. I didn't. I had no lecture on migraine in medical school. I had to pick up my information about its brief quickenings later, at random, as I went along. However, even when I was a student, we did appreciate that it was a "psychosomatic" disorder. The way it occurred in families suggested a genetic component. This meant that migraine patients were "constitutionally predisposed" to have symptoms. (We even called this predisposition a "diathesis," which served to hide the lack of a more precise understanding.) But not until I was a resident in neurology did I begin to appreciate migraine's incredible scope.

The Early Symptoms of the Aura

My patients' wide range of symptoms soon taught me that migraine was an extraordinarily multifaceted disorder. The aura is the earliest (prodromal) phase of migraine. Oliver Sacks observes that its early phenomena include "single and complex affective states, deficits and disturbances of speech and ideation, dislocations of space-and-time perception, and a variety of dreamy, delirious, and trance-like states."[3]

Among the several classes of early symptoms, two are referable to various temporal, parietal, and occipital regions. Why are they noteworthy? Because they have implications for the phenomena of alternate states of consciousness in general, and also for my taste of kensho (see part IX). They are (1) the various visual illusions that occur during migraine auras, and (2) the particular interpretations—

déjà vu and jamais vu—that reshape time and memory (see chapter 42). When this second set of symptoms occurs early, they are not only more intense than the ordinary (nonmigrainous) variety but also last longer.[4]

A Personal Account

Until four decades ago, migraine remained someone else's illness. I then had a single, brief visual aura, my first and last. I was alone, walking outdoors, on an only partially sunny morning, around 10:00 A.M. The day before, I had flown across three time zones to the east, lost sleep, and also came under some unanticipated psychological stress. The brilliant aura was classic: a zigzag line of scintillating "fortification spectra" suddenly appeared way up to the right. At its lower edge a dark scotoma soon appeared. It expanded and gradually blocked all vision in my right upper visual fields (in the right superior quadrants of both eyes) during a period of perhaps 5 minutes. These visual symptoms cleared slowly over the next several minutes, as did a mild problem thinking clearly.

Even so, it was a simple matter to self-diagnose these bright and dark symptoms as an obvious migraine aura. I waited apprehensively for the severe headache, nausea, and vomiting I felt sure would arrive. Nothing happened. No other relevant symptoms attended this aura.*

While waiting, I recalled how my father had mentioned having "migraine" headaches as a young man, but he never spoke of having a prelude of visual symptoms, nor of nausea or vomiting. He attributed his headaches to being placed under stress at work. Father and son were alike: conscientious; "visual" personality types, keenly sensitive to the aesthetic resonances of color, line, form, and design. Both were Sunday painters: he highly talented in oils, I dabbling in watercolors.

Migraine in Physicians

Here I was that morning, having been board-certified 5 years earlier as a specialist in neurology, still not yet aware that a person could develop *only* a visual aura, and not progress beyond that to the other classic symptoms of migraine!

To Walter Alvarez at the Mayo Clinic, this fact was already well known. He had estimated that over 12% of his male migraine patients did not progress to the next headache phase (his survey included some 618 persons who had this same kind of visual scotomata).[5] Moreover, when a smaller *selected* sample of

*Chapter 94 will introduce a separate personal narrative. Chapters 95 and 96 will comment further on the relationship between the *late* onset of its very brief visual phenomena and the several kinds of visual symptoms that can develop in people who are susceptible to this syndrome we call migraine. The icon on page 277 understates such a scintillating scotoma.

physicians was interviewed at a medical convention, 38 out of 44 reported having experienced "many solitary scotomata with never a headache."

In 2003, another selected subgroup of physicians was surveyed. These were neurologists attending a review course on headache. Among these 220 respondents, 46.6% of the men and 62.8% of the women had diagnosed themselves as having migraine. In the subgroup consisting of headache *specialists*, 71.9% of the men and 81.5% of the women reported that they had migraine.[6] (This confirms the ancient suspicion, usually leveled at our psychiatric colleagues, that "To know one, you have to *be* one.")

Migraine in the Population at Large

Selection biases aside, we are in the presence of a very common disorder. In Western countries, one estimate suggested that 8% of the men and 25% of the women have migraine.[7]

A recent, well-designed study in Denmark surveyed 3000 men and 1500 women (averaging 40 years of age). The overall lifetime prevalence of migraine (of all types) was 12% in men and 28% in women. Among the Danish men, only 1% had migraine aura without headache, as compared with 3% of the women.[8]

Another large study focused on the prevalence of migraine in a survey of 3224 Japanese high-school students (age 13–15 years).[9] Of these, 8.8% of the boys and 9.4% of the girls reported having *several* visual illusions (of one or more kinds) during the previous 6 months. A history of unilateral migraine headaches could be obtained in 11% of the boys and in 13% of the girls (with nausea or vomiting, with or without relevant visual disorders).

Note that more than one type of *visual* illusion occurred in this subgroup of students who gave an obvious history of migraine. One of these visual illusions was *micropsia*, a reduction in the size of objects. It was slightly more common in boys than in girls.

Parenthetically, a *persistent* micropsia can occur secondary to chronic localized brain damage in adults. Postmortem studies have been reported in two rare adult patients. Their symptoms of *chronic* micropsia were caused by fixed structural damage in the lower lateral part of the visual association cortex (BA 18 and 19). This *hemi*micropsia affected one half of the visual field on the side opposite the damage.[10]

Studies of Images and Afterimages in Persons Who Are Predisposed to Migraine

I have always had prominent visual afterimages. I regarded both their black-and-white and complementary color versions as not worth mentioning. In addition, I often noted prominent negative afterimages, especially during repeated episodes of meditation while I was on retreat, or after paying attention to a lecturer who stood against a light background. My morning meditations are often still accompanied by small, round retinal phosphenes. These begin as dull light spots, then evolve into a dark black spot as local retinal inhibition then responds [Z:378–379].

What predisposes some persons (who have no other symptoms at the time) to develop prominent afterimage phenomena? (The general question will echo in chapters 95 and 96 where it becomes more specific: Why did a brief negative afterimage phase occur at the end of my illusion of "moonlight?")

De Silva made a pertinent observation in his outpatient clinic. He noticed that patients who had a *past* history of migraine (but who that day were not having any active migraine headache symptoms) kept reporting visual afterimages after he had just looked into their eyes with an ophthalmoscope.[11] Indeed, they reported bright-spot afterimages almost three times more frequently than did the nonmigraineurs. And the afterimages in these migraineurs lasted a long time: between 30 seconds and 2 minutes. Two minutes is a long time.

Many recent laboratory studies have confirmed that migraineurs develop visual phenomena easily. They also have a low threshold for seeing images of luminous phosphenes when subjected to transcranial magnetic stimulation. This evidence of hyperexcitability occurs whether the stimulation is delivered over their primary visual cortex (V1), or farther on over their visual association cortex (V5).[12] In addition, the migraineurs could later draw their phosphenes more accurately, and experienced them in a manner that was more direct, vivid, and sustained than did their controls.

Patients during an episode of active migraine show an evolving sequence of changes in the electrical activity of their brain. One patient, who had *only* the aura of a scintillating scotoma in the right fields, was studied recently by magnetoencephalography (MEG).[13] During the first scintillation phase itself, both the left visual association cortex and the left inferior temporal cortex showed desynchronization of alpha activity in the MEG. Then, after this bright aura ended, desynchronized gamma activity developed in the left inferior temporal lobe and lasted for the next 8 to 10 minutes.

This patient's aura resembled mine. The study confirms that the early aura is associated with a desynchronization of the previous local alpha wave frequencies in the *inferior* temporal and occipital regions. It also raises the possibility that a later inferior temporal lobe dysfunction, related to some form of "desynchronization" of gamma wave frequencies, might be responsible for the localized scotoma (visual defect) that often follows the early scintillations (as the scotoma did in my case). The site of this inferior temporal lobe abnormality lies reasonably close to that more medial and inferior region where we process colors: the V4 color complex in BA 37 (see figure 4, chapter 23).

But what accounts for the migraineurs general tendency to develop visual afterimages when they are having neither headaches nor any visual auras? Is excitation per se the sole physiological basis for these visual aftereffects? When researchers deliver transcranial magnetic stimulation at *low* frequencies, the data suggest that what fails (under these mixed conditions) are the requisite *inhibitory* circuits within the primary and visual association cortex.[14] Other recent theoretical models also suggest that the underlying dysfunctions in migraineurs involve an alteration in the usual *balance* between excitation and inhibition.[15] Even though negative afterimages do appear later, they can contribute a relatively strong wave of additional percepts in themselves.[16]

In most patients, their brief episodes of actual migraine headaches punctuate much longer intervals during which no headache symptoms occur. However, for a few days *just before* a person's migrainous symptoms do begin, a variety of neurophysiological changes often build up to their maximum. These enhanced tendencies are reflected in obvious dynamic changes in the person's evoked potentials, habituation, and EEG activities.[17] Why are the excitabilities of their nerve cells changing?

Recent Genetic Findings Related to Ion Channel Functions

Members of certain migraine families show genetically determined changes in their calcium channel functions, and also in functions referable to other ion channels (see chapter 37). These changes could help explain why localized zones of increased brain excitability occur at the advancing *margins* of what has long been called "the spreading depression of Leão." Clearly, both excitatory and inhibitory disorders of function contribute to the migraine aura.[18]

Nitric Oxide and Migraine

An intriguing link now exists between nitric oxide and migraine.[19] Sublingual nitroglycerin is an $NO^{\bullet}$ donor. It serves to trigger a subsequent genuine migraine episode in susceptible migraineurs. This evoked migraine headache can be correlated with a significant rise in the plasma levels of a particular peptide. This peptide is involved in the calcium systems which can be related, in turn, back to the gene for calcitonin.

PET scans monitored 24 persons subject to migraine while their headaches were being precipitated by the infusion of glyceryl trinitrate. The dorsolateral pons was activated during their induced headache phase. The pontine activations occurred on the right side when their headaches were lateralized to the right side. The pontine activations occurred on the left side when their headaches were induced on the left side. When the headaches were bilateral, the pontine activations were also bilateral, with a left-sided preponderance.[20] How might excessive activity in the dorsolateral pons translate into a lateralized migraine headache? One possibility is via steps that lead to an excessive release of the calcitonin gene peptide from the nearby trigeminal ganglion on that same side.

NO˙ also has protean manifestations (see chapter 68). It requires no leap of faith or imagination to propose that NO˙ is sufficiently versatile to be involved in several mechanisms and sequences underlying kensho [Z:412]. This speculation could be supported by the *late* arrival during kensho of the phase of visual illusions (see chapters 93–96). Is there a message in the *late* arrival of these illusions, namely that NO˙ may have played some earlier role in their genesis? Many of these same visual illusions, of course, also occur during the early aura phase of subjects susceptible to migraine, never to be followed by headache or other obvious later symptoms that would be easily recognized as "migraine."

Implications for Zen

Migraine is not just a form of headache per se. As the first epigraphs indicates, one of its basic mechanisms is a "disorder of neuronal hyperexcitability." When migraine is viewed from this psychophysiological perspective, then we can appreciate that *its net tendencies toward excessive excitation and inhibition can influence the brain's responses during alternate states of consciousness.*

It seems that Buddhist cultural traditions (and some researchers in the neurosciences) are not yet aware of this information. However, Christian mystical lore already has ample historical precedent for the influence of migraine. A documented case in point is the remarkable German abbess, Hildegard von Bingen (1098–1178). She had many episodes of visions. Sacks directs attention to the fact that Hildegard left exquisite accounts, and figures, illustrating how various components of her own migrainous auras contributed to the countless visions (religious/mystical) she had since childhood and which she continued to experience during her adult life.[21]

How much do we know today about the underlying mechanisms of migraine? It is barely the tip of the iceberg. Most of its intricate neurochemistry and psychophysiology remains to be discovered. Parts III and IV illustrate at how many points neuronal excitability and inhibition can change the phenomena of consciousness.

Problems of classification are sure to arise wherever these uncharted regions of migraine overlap the mechanisms causing other conditions, including the phenomena of alternate states of consciousness. For decades to come, confusion at these interfaces is likely to sow discord among the wary and unwary.

Current research suggests that a person's predilection for migraine can be reflected in enhanced degrees of excitation *and* inhibition (and probably of disinhibition as well). These basic physiological tendencies toward heightened responses can reshape the quality and quantity of our consciousness. This perspective can help explain why certain meditators are especially prone to experience unusual epiphenomena of unusual amplitude. While these are of considerable psychophysiological interest, they assume no spiritual significance.

More specifically, such physiological predilections may help us understand the genesis, magnitude, and duration of certain late perceptual illusions such as achromatopsia, negative afterimages, distancing, displacement, and micropsia (see part IX).

The second epigraph proclaims the fact that only recently have we become aware of migraine's multifaceted nature. How can one increase the general awareness that a potentially confusing interface exists between migraine and mysticism? A practical way would be to give it a label. "The Hildegard syndrome" comes to mind. The phrase could run the risk of being misunderstood. However, properly interpreted, the religious and neuroscience communities have much to learn from the historical record, and no disrespect is intended to any system of belief or to anyone.

So, to heighten the general awareness of this interface, let words try to define such a "Hildegard syndrome" as the brief coexistence of a mystical/spiritual/religious state of consciousness accompanied by other psychophysiological phenomena that express the person's predisposition to migraine, broadly defined. Much of the controversy that can develop around such a dual presentation could be tempered by the simple recognition, in the most matter-of-fact way, that two different conditions can overlap. As we were reminded in medical school: "A patient can have measles *and* a broken leg."

Meanwhile, a problem can arise for contemporary students and teachers of meditation. Current trainees cannot expect that their teachers will have been programmed to respond positively to unusual perceptual symptoms. In 1974, Kobori-Roshi certainly did not (see table 12, chapter 101) [Z:472]. Nor has it been my experience in this millennium that an objective reporting of brief, delayed late visual illusions evokes a welcoming response from Buddhist teachers, even after it is made very clear that such visual illusions came very late and had followed the much earlier (and much longer) phase of insights during a taste of kensho.[22]

However, in 2004, a neuroscience investigator concluded that unusual visual phenomena are "windows on the visual brain." In fact, unusual visual episodes can serve research as a "valuable route for studying the neural mechanisms of visual awareness."[23] One can envision an era when future generations of Buddhist teachers, East and West, perhaps inspired by the open example of the present Dalai Lama, will begin anew to appreciate the promise inherent in a judicious neuroscience approach. In the interim, the pioneering investigations by Kasamatsu, Hirai, and Akishige, begun in the mid-1960s in Japan, serve to illustrate how meditation can be openly studied in Zen monks in a monastic setting.

Part VI

The Absorptions

It is by undivided devotion that I can be known in such a form, truly seen, and entered into.

Bhagavad Gita 11: 154

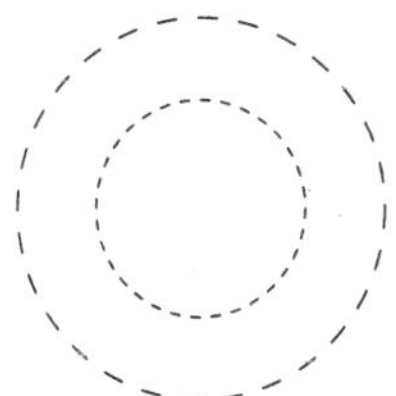

The Varieties of Absorption

Don't be swept off your feet by the vividness of the impression. Rather say: "Impression, wait for me a little. Let me see what you are and what you represent. Let me try you."

Epictetus (C.E. 55?–135?)

Let us try to see what absorptions are. Then we can better determine what they represent. The absorptions are hyperattentive states on the meditative path that change many sensory and affective impressions (see chapter 4). The old term, *samadhi*, can be used in so many different ways that it confuses the unwary. In ancient times, this Sanskrit term suggested that things were being "placed together," joined in the sense of a union [Z:473–478, 530–534].

Early Indian Buddhists conceived of some eight levels along the path to what they called "samadhi." The first four stages developed during the practice of what we referred to as *concentrative* meditation (see chapter 13). Within the contemporary Zen context, the word "samadhi" can still imply a bringing together, and a uniting, but only *if* we qualify the nature of such a "union." In these pages, it means that *awareness* moves toward, blends into, finds itself *held* onto, and becomes *absorbed into whatever is in its field*.

My preference is to use the general term *absorption* (not samadhi) for three reasons: (1) Absorption suggests the way one's attention becomes totally committed—often leaving the impression that it is being *held*—within one field to the exclusion of others. (2) Absorption implies that the sense of physical self fades at these moments when one's attention is focused or enhanced far beyond its ordinary limits. (3) *Samadhi* is an elastic term. It means different things in Indian and Sino-Japanese traditions.

A simplified classification of absorptions might begin with *where* the enhanced attention is being *directed*. Is it directed *externally*, or toward an *internal* mental field? At another level of classification (one that can overlap with the first) we might also divide experiences of absorption into (1) those that occur when the person is not moving; and (2) absorption during movement.

The motionless category includes the two extremes of directed attention mentioned above. One of them refers to those uncommon moments during seated meditation when the meditator's extraordinarily intense attention turns inward. This *internal absorption* witnesses a vast *internal* space. It lacks not only the sense of the bodily self but also all external sights and sounds. In contrast, the other extreme describes the meditator who focuses intense attention on an *external* object (such as a candle), and who then becomes "absorbed" into this narrow, concentrated, external field.

Yet absorption can also occur when a part or all of one's body is *moving*. Absorption into a very small movement can occur even during quiet, sitting meditation. Thus, attention can become focused into the simple rising-and-falling movements of abdominal breathing. Or, absorption can also occur during more complex behaviors, such as when the person is erect and has become fully engaged in walking meditation. The two instances recounted below took place during formal meditation practice. They illustrate the curious impression that develops: the person's former physical boundaries of self completely dissolve *into the action*.

* * *

In 1977, while meditating in the zendo one evening, all thoughts had finally vanished during the second round of sitting. Eyelids remained half-open. No unusual mental or physical stresses had occurred. Attention then began to focus just on the in-and-out breathing movements down in the lower abdomen. Suddenly, enhanced attention came to a very sharp point of focus, held on just the simple, physical up-and-down rhythm of each breathing movement itself. No sense remained of the rest of my body, nor of anything in the environment.

This episode lasted for perhaps 15 to 30 seconds. What made it memorable was the strength of its involuntary surge and its one-pointed, total fixation of attention. The very fact that rhythmic breathing movements continued serves to distinguish this variety of focused absorption from some other forms, during which breathing movements are suppressed (see chapter 20).

* * *

A slightly different episode occurred during the fifth day of the Rohatsu Seshin, in December 1998. It was mid-morning. I had finished that round of seated, quiet meditation and had been engaged for a minute or so in the usual, next slow-paced form of walking meditation (*kinhin*). Suddenly, while walking, every sense vanished that this *person* was *doing* the walking. *Walking was continuing by itself*. No body was doing it. Nobody.

Normal vision took in the ordinary zendo scenery; hearing noted the faint shuffling sounds of other feet; somasthetic sensibilities remained aware that walking was being performed automatically; motor functions serviced smoothly every coordinated act of ambulation. Yet no physical sense remained that any *I* or *Me* or *Mine* was inside, directing "My" walking. This complete absorption into the *act* had no physical axis of self in the center. It continued for perhaps 10 to 15 seconds before it faded. It refreshed the meditator temporarily, but had no other accompaniments.

* * *

The two episodes cited were superficial absorptions. Neither blocked out sensation as thoroughly as did that earlier, first deep internal absorption, during meditation [Z:469–472].[1]

The Ordinary Mental Field

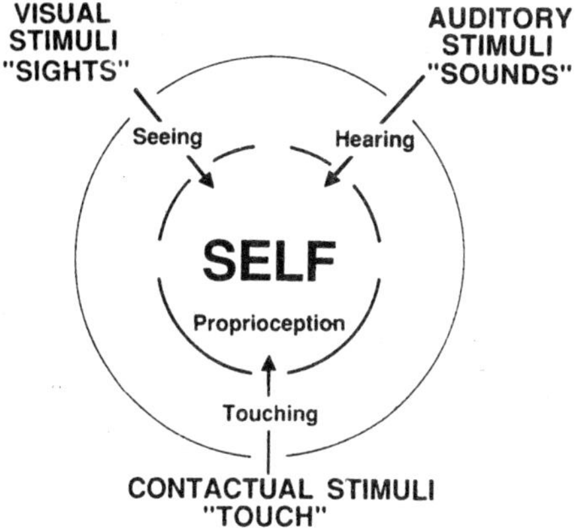

Figure 9 The ordinary mental field of the physical self
Self-referent stimuli enter the thalamus from the outside world and combine with stimuli from various internal proprioceptive events. The blend contributes to the physical axis of self, a structural framework onto which we refer our concepts and impressions of existing as a separate "self." Superimposed, we add a complex of *I-Me-Mine* attributes which relate this sensate physical self (our soma) to our other thoughts, emotions, and attitudes (our psyche).

It was that striking experience of internal absorption, back in 1974, coupled with my ignorance of what might have caused it, which first stimulated this neurologist to continue to pursue these investigations for the next three decades.

The ordinary mental field, diagrammed in figure 9, differs strikingly from the mental field during that deep level of internal absorption (figure 10).

Plausible Mechanisms for Internal Absorption

Which pivotal mechanisms could underlie a state of clear ambient hyperawareness—a state that also blocks seeing, hearing, touch, and proprioception? Suppose one were pressed to speculate. This state was precipitated in a setting of meditative concentration and stress responses. We could envision the resulting mechanisms of absorption then unfolding through the kinds of psychophysiological sequences outlined below. Note that these sequences involve multiple levels, in the limbic system, basal forebrain, thalamus, and brainstem (table 7).

The Mental Field of Internal Absorption

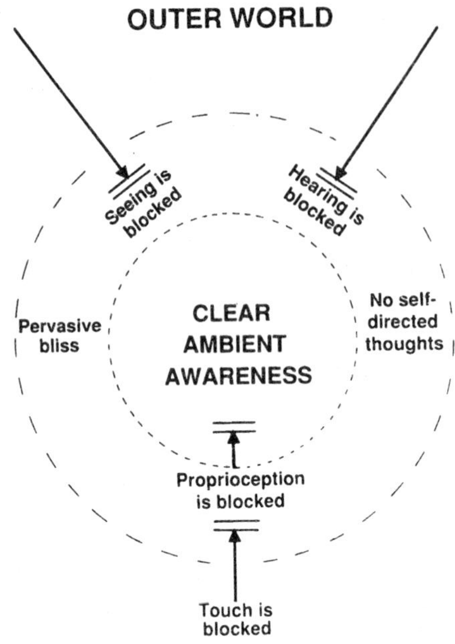

Figure 10 The mental field of internal absorption with sensate loss
A major internal absorption is an extraordinary state of consciousness. The physical sense of the body vanishes. The ordinary physical boundaries of the *I-Me-Mine* are effaced. Here, the dashed lines serve only to indicate its former boundaries. What remains is an anonymous witness to a silent, heightened, clear, ambient awareness. Note that sensations are blocked, shutting off not only the outer world but also proprioceptive information from the head and body. Aside from a pervasive enchantment and delayed bliss, most emotions do not register. In itself, this state lacks permanently transforming insights. See the legend to figure 8. Compare figure 10 with figure 9.

Table 7
Stress Responses Potentially Involved in an Episode of Internal Absorption

Category of Response	*Local Sites Involved in Excitation*	*Subsequent Changes*	*The Witness Experienced*
*Stress responses**	The lateral hypothalamus Parts of the basal nucleus of the forebrain	Increased hippocampal excitability Increased posterior cortical excitability	A visual hallucination of a leaf from memory: this was the discrete, local expression of a more generalized posterior cortical hyperexcitability and hyperawareness
	The back of the reticular nucleus of the thalamus	Closing of the thalamic "gate" on ascending visual, auditory, and somatosensory messages at the leve of the first order relay nuclei of the thalamus	A loss of the physical sense of self, inside a glistening black, unbounded, enchanting vacuum of space
	The arcuate and paraventricular nuclei of the hypothalamus next to the midline	Corelease of several key peptides in midline brain regions (CRF-enkephalin, and beta-endorphin-ACTH)	A delayed plenum of blissful affect

CRF, corticotropin-releasing factor; ACTH, adrenocorticotropic hormone.
* Stress responses can be prompted intentionally. This can occur during intensive, prolonged concentrative forms of meditation. Or they can arise more or less inadvertently. Stress responses can also activate receptors in the locus ceruleus, amygdala, paraventricular nucleus of the hypothalamus, and midline prefrontal cortex that mediate excitatory functions (see chapter 33).

Table 7 can represent only part of the phenomena of internal absorption[2] [Z:478–479]. How does it conceptualize the brain's unusual responses? As reactions sensitized by ongoing mental and physical stress [Z:235–240, 589–590]. It views these stress responses as arising from prolonged intensive concentrative meditation and from additional stressful events.

The basic physiological processes that become enhanced in internal absorption are both excitatory and inhibitory. For example, the early stress responses are viewed as mediated by the usual two fast transmitters, glutamate and acetylcholine. In this case, however, their net effects mediate *hyper*excitability, not only at cortical levels but at lower sites as well. When the reticular nucleus responds, with its fast-acting GABA, sensory transmission is inhibited from passing up through the thalamus. Only later does the delayed, blissful plenum arrive. It could be mediated by slower-acting opioid peptides.

The oversimplified version presented has yet to probe a more complex issue: the curious preliminary state change. This had first plunged the meditator through several sleep transition zones. First to occur was the *descent* toward sleep (to be commented on below). Next came a rapid *ascent* toward a hyperaware state of wakefulness.

Earlier speculative schemes have been presented that viewed meditation as a "top-down mechanism."[3] Single-pointed arrows were used to suggest the way an "attention association area" of the right frontal lobe might either cause deafferentation, or stimulation of, the right parietal lobe.

In table 7, internal absorption is viewed as a distinct, *major* meditative state. It is rare, and random in occurrence. It is not to be conflated with a deliberately induced, more superficial meditative state or with any more advanced state(s). Though it is set in motion by a variety of stressful responses, these seem to gather momentum in chiefly a "bottom-up" spontaneous *ascending* manner, rather than in a willed intentional "top-down," manner.

Table 7 places a high priority on pivotal events mediated by one particular inhibitory site: the reticular nucleus of the thalamus (see chapter 46). The proposal draws a sharp distinction between the functional connections of the *lateral* hypothalamus [Z:190–192] and two different hypothalamic nuclei located next to the *midline*. Why do these latter two midline paraventricular and arcuate nuclei become of special interest? Because they can corelease the opioid peptides, enkephalin and beta-endorphin, respectively, along with ACTH [Z:194, 514, 237–238]. These peptides might help explain some of the delayed plenum of blissful affect that can infuse consciousness in deeper absorptions (see chapters 35, 36).

Other Kinds of Absorption

So much, then, for the rare, special kinds of deep internal absorption that can block not only vision but also hearing and somatosensory messages. What about the mechanisms for more superficial varieties of open-eyed absorption, say of the more ordinary kinds, the first two brief examples that were cited above?

Recent neuroimaging research is of interest in this regard (see chapter 50). The data suggest that several more *medial* cortical regions *reduce* their activity as soon as our brain shifts *away* from its resting preoccupations with monitoring and integrating self/other issues and orients toward different goals.

The first two personal states of superficial absorption just described hint at a somewhat similar possibility. Perhaps some subtler *psychic* and *physical* codings for self (as might tentatively be represented in the precuneus and medial frontal regions) could dwindle if a person's usual subliminal proprioceptive awareness were suddenly taken over and referred to an *unusual* site. "Unusual" need not always mean "elsewhere," beyond one's own skin. It might just mean that awareness was displaced toward goals that were "different" from the ones that had been prevailing up to that moment.

For example, after awareness had been directed for a long while down on the simple in-and-out rhythmic movements of lower abdominal breathing, it might suddenly be taken over and "held captive" down there on the tanden, a site far removed from the person's usual *head*-centered self (see chapter 14).

Similarly, the notions of self might fade from view during the execution of the more complex act of walking, *if* proprioceptive attention had been directed away from this same head-centered self. And had been diverted where, instead? Even farther down toward a "different-from-usual" focus—namely into the feelings in the legs and the feet as they contacted the floor while walking.

Sleep States in Relation to Absorption?

Robert Forman interviewed a contemporary Soto Zen master, John Daido Loori, who described two unusual episodes. In each, there appeared to be zero mental content, and there was apparently also some lack of responsivity to events of the outside world.[4] During the first, he described sitting by a tree for 4 hours. The second occurred after severe physical pain. He sat for 6 hours, and afterward experienced a feeling of elation.

Only limited descriptions are available. At first glance, the two very long episodes do not fit the standard categories of absorption, as just outlined, in which attention is enhanced. They also sound more like a most unusual kind of sleep state than coma.

I had dropped into a somewhat similar condition of zero mental content *at the onset* of the episode of internal absorption. This first phase was a "sudden plunge" [Z:480–481] into an abrupt gap in consciousness, one which did not cause me to lose my erect sitting posture. This gap may have lasted less than a minute, but I cannot be sure.

Before this plunge into a zero mental state there had occurred a period of unusual physical and mental stress. The blank interval ended with a rapid, smooth ascent into hyperawareness. In retrospect, I attributed this plunge into blankness to "the clifflike onset of an unusually amplified, but basically sleeplike, state."

Animal studies suggest some potential answers. In the cat, a slight increase in serotonin tone in the deep medial thalamic nuclei creates 8-cps EEG rhythms. *Attention lapses* during this interval. Physical pain and stress responses also release more norepinephrine into the brain. During states of low arousal and light sleep, norepinephrine can then act more on its postsynaptic, alpha-2 receptors. Why, at this particular moment, does the way norepinephrine acts seem to present a paradox? Because it promotes slow wave synchronized *sleep* [Z:201–205].

I do not pretend to understand why an advanced Zen meditator might report blank periods lasting up to several hours. Yet, until we know everything about what precipitates sleeplike states, I would be reluctant to dismiss these first-person reports from a long-term meditator who had such credentials.[5] Moreover, a Zen anecdotal account cites the story of Master Hanshan in sixteenth-century China. He sat immobile on a bridge absorbed in samadhi for a day and a night, unaware of his surroundings.[6]

Effortlessness as a Prelude to Absorption

The quality of "effortlessness" has been emphasized as a prerequisite of a particular kind of absorption. This variety is described as occurring *during* meditation by subjects who practice in the style known as Advaita meditation.[7] Their tradition refers to this particular meditative state of consciousness as "transcendental," "Advaita," or "pure consciousness." It seems to resemble other, conventional, superficial forms of meditative absorption. In practice, it would not be confused with kensho or satori. It can be characterized by

- a subjective experience that the sense of space, time, and physical self are absent;
- a sense of peacefulness; of unboundedness.

Among its laboratory correlates are

- respiratory suspension (apneustic breathing); slowed rates of breathing; higher amplitudes of respiratory sinus arrhythmia; higher alpha EEG amplitudes; higher alpha EEG coherence; lower baseline skin conductance; larger skin conductance responses; greater skin conductance responses to external sounds at the onset of episodes of respiratory suppression[8] (see chapter 20) [Z:93–99].

Why is the quality of "effortlessness" relevant to our discussion? Once again, it directs our attention to a phase of "letting go" as a prerequisite of meditative absorption. I can verify from personal experience this role of "letting go." As a prelude to the plunge into internal absorption, my will dissolved. I lost all prior sense of striving, pressure, stress, or strain. Feeling released from purpose, I had settled into a phase of simple acceptance. All this happened *passively*.

I can also verify a similar goal-less interval in the later setting just prior to kensho (see chapter 72). In neither instance was this *my* volitional decision. The *whole situation* dictated "letting go," and that is what happened *to* me. It was not the result of my "doing." Giving up occurred *passively*.

75

Space

> When we started this research, more than three decades ago, no more than five papers were published in a year. Now, hundreds of important and exciting papers are published annually.
>
> K. Heilman and colleagues[1]

Representing Space

Usually, we think that "space" is something "empty." And, if we "neglect" something, it means we pay no attention to it. Who would want to pay attention to anything that was empty?

A lot of researchers would, and are doing so. They are intrigued by patients who "neglect space." Why? Because their patients' deficits illuminate one of our brain's greatest miracles: the way we *re*-present the world outside us. And we don't just register those items of this external world passively inside *our* "mental space." We *reach out into it,* confident that we have reconstructed all of its items in *their* correct 3D relationships! (see chapter 41) [Z:487–492, 521–522].

William James, a century ago, discussed "space" within a single chapter of his classic, *Principles of Psychology*. Even then, he devoted *148 pages* to space, more than he invested in any other topic. Maybe there is more to space than meets the eye.

A reader in 2002 had a simple yardstick with which to gauge how complex this large topic had become in the interim: a total of 55 different authors contributed to one 401-page text devoted to the *neglect* of space![2]

One fact complicates matters. It is often overlooked but crucial. First, we must pay *attention* to space. Only then can we define which items are out there, and *re*-present them inside our brain in their proper 3D relationships. Moreover, researchers have discovered that we code "near space" different from "far space." We also code space above the level of our eyes different from space below eye level.

What investigators have yet to pursue is one aspect of subliminal space that could help us understand internal absorption. The question is: precisely how do we represent the entire volume of *ambient* space, meaning space throughout that vast 360-degree envelope above, below, and to the front and back of us? This expanded space is what opens up in internal absorption [Z:495–499].

Interactions in 3D Space

Previc reviews in detail the four types of model, overlapping systems that help each person define 3D space and act within its successive layers.[3]

1. The *peripersonal system.* It helps us look *down* so that we can grasp objects that are within 2 m ($6\frac{1}{2}$ ft.) of our body. The posterior inferior parietal region is a major cortical module.

   We do not usually think about the way we are also coded to represent 3D auditory space this close to our head, but it too exists[4] (see chapter 42).
2. The *extrapersonal focal system.* It helps us search for objects *above* the horizontal and recognize faces at distances beyond 2 m. Dopamine pathways into the superior colliculus, lateral pulvinar, and caudate may play a role in enhancing this search. However, the inferotemporal region is a major cortical module.
3. The *extrapersonal action system.* It enables us to navigate, given that we have already established our individual sense of being physically "present" in the world. The superior and medial temporal regions are major cortical modules.
4. The *extrapersonal ambient system.* It helps to orient us in space in general, and to use automatic body-in-space coordinates. These help stabilize the way we perceive the larger outside world while we are actually moving through it. The parietooccipital region is one major cortical module.

Neglect of Space

Certain brain lesions cause a patient to neglect external space. Because overlappings exist among the four systems outlined above, it is sometimes difficult to decide at the bedside what is causing the patient's neglect. Are spatial mechanisms damaged at the perceptual, attentional, motor, or conceptual level?

Accordingly, when researchers begin to study "space" in normals, and spatial neglect in patients, they will need to understand how their subjects first attend to, and then decode, those objects and scenes inside that actual space "out there." They will also need to consider the rest of that imaginary *reconstruction of space,* the one with which their subjects are trying to "picture" things in their internal "mind's eye." Meanwhile, they will always need to remember that most such processing goes on subconsciously.

Allocentric Frames of Reference

Our brain circuits are attuned to basic self/other distinctions. We distinguish quickly between what is "inside" our own self (ego-) and all those "other" things that are outside (allo-). When we process items *ego*centrically, we ourselves are the central frame of reference. We refer the data back to internal spatial coordinates, to the position of our own eyes, head, or torso.

In contrast, when objects are processed *allo*centrically, an *impersonal, spatial* frame of reference comes into play. This system represents external objects as existing in *their* setting. It uses *their* coordinates, "out *there*." It acts almost as though it had no immediate need to inform our personal physical axis of self that these objects are present (see chapter 29).

The physiologies of these two systems normally merge. Before they do, which parts of the brain seem to be more involved in this direct, allocentric mode of processing incoming sensory messages?

Human PET data suggest that allocentric frames of reference are mostly attributable to the *back* of our brain. Thus, activity occurs in these following posterior regions when we process external objects as existing solely "out there" in space: visual association cortex, bilateral occipital cortex, lingual gyrus, right hippocampus, inferior occipitotemporal and inferior parietal cortex.[5] Recent studies in monkeys would add to this network some nerve cells up in the supplementary eye field of the frontal lobe and down in the superior colliculus.[6]

Human fMRI data suggest that the parietal (dorsal) visual pathway provides us with information about an object's spatial location while impulses are flowing up through the angular gyrus *and* the precuneus. These parietal signals begin earlier, peak later, and last longer than do those along the ventral pathway. This lower pathway (that helps to recognize the object's form) relays chiefly through the fusiform gyrus into the inferotemporal region.[7]

This PET and fMRI research evidence from normal human subjects becomes even more intriguing when it is correlated with the clinical findings in certain neurology patients. Their symptoms and signs are caused by lesions in these parietotemporo-occipital regions (see chapter 8). The damage to their allocentric circuits creates an imbalance in their frames of reference. This seems to tip them toward overactive egocentric modes of perception. They may even develop the impression that outside stimuli are "inside" themselves.

But then, how does our normal brain first *integrate* these two basic spatial reference frames? How does it *select* which one to weigh more heavily (allo- vs. ego-)? Up at the cortical level, these complex automatic networking decisions may require integrating frontal lobe functions with those of the other three lobes (chapter 47 considers the issues further). Yet, as Behrmann and Geng conclude: "Although we know that multiple spatial reference frames are used for coding spatial position, we do not know how these are coordinated to subserve integrated behavior."[8]

However, subcortical regions, including the thalamus, its reticular nucleus, and the striatum, will also be in that consortium of deeper regions which shape our own body's movements through space. Their networks contribute to the integrated behaviors that fit our physical self seamlessly into—and across—that dynamic interface of space "out there" where self begins to penetrate other. (See also chapters 8, 41, 42, and part VII.)

Part VII

Insightful Awakenings

My dear brothers and sisters, we are already one. But we imagine that we are not. And what we have to recover is our original unity. What we have to be is what we are.

Thomas Merton (1915–1968)
(Spoken in Calcutta shortly before he died.)

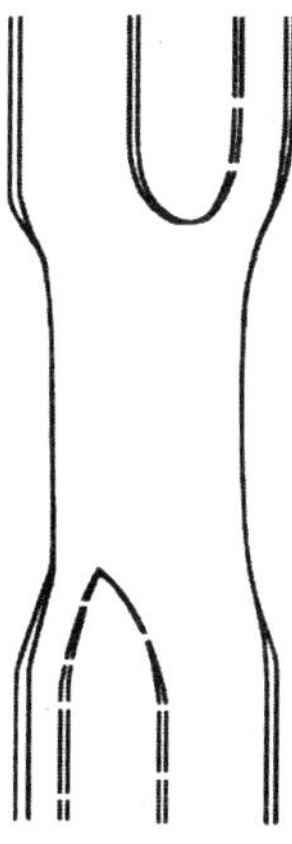

Affirming One Reality: A Commentary on the Sandokai

Questioner in audience: Dr. Suzuki, When you use the word reality, are you referring to the relative reality of the physical world or to the absolute reality of the transcendental world?

D. T. Suzuki: Yes.[1]

Forms do not *look* empty. They have shapes. So why does the Heart Sutra insist that form *is* emptiness, that form and emptiness are the *same*? [Z:698–699]. To begin to resolve this paradox, it may help first to reexamine the question.

To do so, let us begin now with the living reality of *this* world of form right in front of our eyes. Let form stand for our own everyday world—for its people, trees, rocks—all sorts of material phenomena that are individually different. Sure, it looks *real,* but this world is still only "temporary." For in the perspective of eternity, those rocks will crumble to sand. Why is it also a world of appearances? Because each of us views this "mundane" world only through our own egocentric veils (see figure 2, chapter 10). This intrinsic psychic conditioning creates *my* friends, *my* trees. Once again, all this is transitory. This, too, shall pass away.

As for emptiness, chapter 85 explores its subtleties. Meanwhile, let us begin to expand our mental horizon to consider those aspects of the "big picture" that were implicit in the second part of the question posed to D. T. Suzuki. Let us allow our conceptual imagination to open up to a vast endless domain of absolute Universal Reality. This concept embraces everything in a timeless cosmos. It stretches back eons beyond endless eons, vanishing long before stardust slowly gave birth to this planet on which all such human concepts have just arrived only very recently.

Is it possible to reconcile two mental concepts so very different as the form and emptiness in these two examples? "Yes," says Suzuki.

It is an eloquent "Yes." It invites us to drop all the dualities in such notions. "Yes" affirms that beyond all such categories *they are already the same.* His "Yes" reminds us that inherent in prajna's insight is this overarching, *nondiscriminative* profoundly affirmative message: all things—and each one of us—coexist as integral parts of this same eternal Oneness.

The historical issues surrounding this message of monism lead at least as far back as ancient India. When the early Buddhist patriarchs of India awakened to this same universal insight of nonduality, they knew that words could not express the truth of their realization. They tried anyway. One result was the Heart Sutra. Everyday, worldwide, members of the various branches of Buddhism chant its message: the coexistence, and identity, of form and emptiness.

When Buddhism then spread north to China, Master Shih-t'ou (700–790) would later become one of its most influential teachers. It was said that his great awakening was triggered when he read a certain old passage. Those words had been written over three centuries earlier by Seng-chao (378–414). That young scholarly monk had a difficult task. His challenge was to integrate the early Indian Buddhist beliefs about the absolute universal principle with the beliefs taught by the indigenous Chinese Taoists. Seng-chao had concluded that Ultimate Reality was not separate from the forms that made up our relative world of phenomena. Instead, *both were of one fabric.*[2]

Judeo-Christian traditions were expressing something similar. It comes down to us in the word we now call *immanence*. Its root, in Latin, is *immanere*, to remain in. It describes the ultimate reality principle as embedded within the whole material universe and throughout all its forms.

Which triggering passage, written long before, was said later to have inspired Shih-t'ou? It read:

> The ultimate self is empty, void and formless, yet the myriad things are all of its making. Is a sage someone who comprehends these myriad things as the self?[3]

This same penetrating question echoes down through every century. The next chapters explore some tentative answers.

Inspired by reading Seng-chao, Shih-t'ou then went on to compose his own verses. They live on today in Soto Zen centers worldwide, their rhythms still chanted daily in various tongues.

Back then, the literary customs of the Tang dynasty prevailed. Given these, we would not be surprised to find that Shih-t'ou may have transplanted a few phrases and ideas from much earlier centuries into his verses, then blended them into the insights he himself had just realized during his own recent flash of insight.[4]

The *Sandokai*: This is the way we in the West use Japanese-English to romanize the original title that Shih-t'ou had used for his own new verses. Its spelling might first appear very different from its Chinese-English counterpart: the *Ts'an-t'ung-ch'i*. Still, when pronounced, the two titles sound reasonably similar. However, any reader needs to be aware that current translations of this title and its verses often differ substantially. The reasons are several.

Can any translation today have the same meaning as did the original, a work composed of only 220 Chinese characters?[5] Suppose you were to insist on having only a direct, literal translation of each original Sino-Japanese ideogram. It would be a crude version in broken pidgin English. Professional translators can only be humbled by all the major compromises they have had to make. Beyond that basic problem, the casual Western reader may not yet suspect how many other major semantic compromises can enter in.

Begin with the title itself. One soon discovers that this same Sino-Japanese title has been translated into English in different ways. Some options from our own era are the "coincidence of difference and sameness"; "merging of difference and unity"; "inquiry into matching halves"[6]; "realizing unity"[7]; "the coincidence of opposites"[8]; "the harmony of difference and equality"[9]; "the identity of relative and absolute"[10], and so on.

The above examples suggest that different translators (perhaps not unlike Shih-t'ou himself) might have chosen to insert aspects of either their own *private* experience, or earlier personal opinions, or even some doctrinal belief system into a given phrase. Moreover, each translator can have several other subjective needs that determine why older versions differ from those of our present era.

Let us be more specific, citing only a few potential conflicts that a contemporary translator might need to resolve: Must I adhere rigidly to literal interpretations, to traditional doctrinal formulas (and often multiple footnotes) to remain within acceptable scholarly traditions? Or can I remain true to what experience tells me is the direct, immediate flash of Zen insight itself? Because surely this deepest experiential truth entails letting go of my own tendencies (*and* often those imposed by the Tang cultural ethos on the original author) to attach arcane, dated references that overburden a line and blur the central message.

Nor do the translator's conflicts and compromises end there: Can I still be true to those few old original ideograms, yet express their flowing spirit and intent in a readable *contemporary* literary style? Furthermore, must I conspire with the original author in old mystifications, thereby perpetuating the notion that everything about Zen is forever mysterious, if not unknowable?

The following verses of the Sandokai are a freely rendered composite. With a bow to the elegance of Dr. Suzuki's "Yes," they serve as a way to introduce the issues of "Oneness" to be discussed at greater length in the next six chapters. This writer, no translator, wishes fully to acknowledge how much the verses' content (if not always their form) stems from five versions of translations into English that have appeared during the last quarter-century (Compare with notes 3, 4, 7, 9, and 10).

One potentially confusing ambiguity stems from an ancient Chinese custom. Back then, "light" often signified our ordinary (daylight) material world, in which phenomena were readily perceived. This meant that "dark" would then stand for the other, noumenal world (which, to continue that interpretation, was a domain no *un*enlightened person was yet aware of).[11] Yet, no matter how the ancients might have interpreted these words in their own era, they still conceived of lightness and darkness as mutually interactive and interdependent, in full accord with Taoist principles of yin and yang.[12]

The following translation points toward the basis for Suzuki's "Yes." It is oriented not only to other chapters throughout this book but also toward the ecumenical needs of this new millennium.[13]

* * *

Affirming That the Relative and Absolute Are One Reality

The wisdom of India's Great Sage intimately inspired people everywhere. Whether this message of the Buddha's One True Path fell on wise or foolish ears, it reconciled whatever divergent views they might have heard from other teachers, some saying that the Way to awakening was always gradual, others declaring that it must occur suddenly.

Wisdom still flows from this one original wellspring of our true nature. Each of its pure branching streams flows on in the darkness of night, remaining clear in the light of day.

Our every attempt at grasping this realization is fundamentally deluded. Even though a person might seem to have briefly merged with the "absolute," genuine enlightenment remains altogether beyond such a state. And even though our many perceptions appear to interpenetrate one another, each item still retains its discrete, individual character.

Things may seem to be the same on the outside, but their internal compositions can differ markedly. Likewise, though sounds may at first seem pleasant or harsh, all such word distinctions vanish once you become illuminated. Only then do you finally comprehend how seeing clearly is so totally different from your former cloudy vision.

When this true nature of all things is finally unveiled, you realize it instinctively, the same way you turned toward your own mother the moment you were born.

Just as the essence of fire is heat, so is it in the nature of wind to blow, of water to be wet, of earth to be solid.

Similarly, your eyes were destined to see forms, your ears to hear sounds, your nose to smell, and your tongue to taste—sometimes sweet, sometimes sour.

And just as countless lofty leaves spring upward from one lowly taproot, so in turn does each and every thing arise from the One Fundamental Source. Note that lofty and lowly are like all similar discriminating phrases. They remain mere words.

So, too, were those wordy distinctions between light and dark, mentioned earlier. For such aspects of light and darkness are everywhere interdependent. Co-existing, each complements the other. Observe, when you are walking, how first your left foot leads, then your right. Similarly, in everyday life, one finds that each single thing goes on to contribute to the larger whole.

Therefore, how does our mundane world of myriad phenomena fit within the Universal? As seamlessly as the well-crafted lid fits into its matching box. All ordinary phenomena meet the unbounded Absolute head-on—two arrows, striking point to point in midair.

Always read between such lines. Then you can realize their deeper underlying principles. No quick, casual interpretations suffice.

Can you see right now what's directly in front of your eyes? If not, then how will your footsteps ever be correct when you're trying to walk the Path?

Travelers on this Path aren't making "progress" toward some final "destination." This Great Way is not a matter of "far or near." Do any mountains and rivers seem to be blocking your way? They are only in your imagination.

Listen carefully. If you truly wish to understand this mystery, I implore you:

Day and night, waste no time!

77

Varieties of "Oneness" and "Unity." Category I: A and B

Contemporary American Zen fable: The Asian-born monk travels to the United States. At his first baseball game, he's waiting in line at the hotdog stand. Each customer is being asked, "What'll you have?" They reply, in turn: "One with mustard," "One with catsup," "Three with relish," and so on. Finally, it's the Zen monk's turn to be served. When asked, "What'll you have?," he replies: "One With Everything."

There's always been a lot of loose talk about "oneness." I have not yet found any formal analysis, anywhere, that critically examines the dimensions of this topic from a neuroscience perspective. Now comes this light-hearted apocryphal tale. It is a fable that people can understand, and misunderstand, at several levels. Are we ready to take a closer, deeper, look? Can we imagine what it *is* to *be "One With Everything?"*

Not what such a Oneness is "like." Not what it might resemble. Not Oneness "as if" the word were just a literary allusion, another metaphor or simile. Rather, what *it is to be* Oneness. To "realize" it in your bones, to awaken to it, to *be* enlightened, if only for that moment. Of course, a deceptively simple reply to such a question might run as follows: Each of us is already "there," so we don't have to "think" about it or try to imagine it; it's only our deluded mindset that stands in the way of our realizing this implicit fact of "oneness."

Few can hold on to this intellectual truism. Overconditioned networks and biased attitudes stand in the way. Our discriminating brain quickly returns. Its subjectivities continually intrude. They separate our private "inside" self from that other vast domain "outside." This inside/outside split becomes more than one big physiological dichotomy. Its "trialities" make it hard to overcome (see chapter 10). But other psychic intrusions also compound the basic problem. Some of them are culturally imposed concepts: right/wrong, poor/rich, black/white, and so on. Others are self-inflicted at more basic physiological levels: I/you, mine/your.

One perspective for viewing such divisions--at least at an intellectual level—is to return to the familiar metaphor of the ocean. Only when each transient wave gives up the fiction that "IT" possesses its very own individual, enduring identity can it become One with all the rest of the water in the ocean. Similarly, each of us needs to jettison a boatload of our overly self-centered networks. Then we'll be in a position finally to realize our original, intrinsic "Oneness" with everything else in the universe. This need not happen all at once. We can *lighten* our load incrementally. To lighten up is one implicit meaning of en*lighten*ment.

Our feet tread this planet only briefly. Each of us, like the wave, is a "transient phenomenon." One wave form may appear and disappear, yet the whole ocean is not diminished. How do we, the waves, and all other temporary phenomena fit into the vast universal scope of (what we theorize is) an "absolute cosmic reality?" The previous chapter described how the early Taoist and other teachers in China later elaborated on the early Indian philosophical speculations about this "Absolute Oneness."

A century later, Ch'an master Tung-shan (807–869) would address such universal themes in "highly enigmatic" poetry.[1] Still, the fourth of his five "ranks" does seem to pull together the phenomenal and noumenal dichotomy into a "single" oneness. In translation today, this fourth stage would then become the mode of "mutual integration." What simple visual device did Buddhists use later to symbolize this "mutual integration?" Not just a linear circumference, not the kind of line we associate with an ordinary circle. It was a full disk, a bright, "solid white circle."[2] Like the full moon.

In chapter 97, we will observe that many people used a single circle to allude to a lot of things: the moon, the awakening of kensho-satori, the Dharmakaya, as well as to symbolize this particular mode of "mutual integration." Therefore, in any era, it proves useful to recall Joseph Campbell's caveat: All symbolic expressions of a mystical experience are faulty. Special care is required to distinguish the phenomena of the shallow absorptions from those insights which characterize the deeper awakenings.

The Shallow, Merging "Unities" of the Absorptions

It always seems necessary to clarify the important distinctions between absorptions and authentic states of insight-wisdom.[3] Hence another brief reminder, stressing that absorptions are relatively common, and chiefly change the *sensibilities* (see chapter 74). They do not convey this deeper, *insightful* awakening into oneness.

Absorption is well-named, because its hyperawareness soaks up, as it were, either the internalized world, or the external world, whichever field happens to be perceived at that moment. During the absorptions, the person tends to lose the usual sense of occupying the *physical* body-self inside the skin, which had always served as the barrier separating the *internal self* from the *external world*.

The Deeper "Unities" of Insight-Wisdom (Prajna)

These are rare. Recalling Hardy's series of contemporary Western religious experiences, we find that only rarely (2%) were the phenomena regarded as sufficiently "unitive" in nature to unify the self and the all.[4] *But* unitive *experiences are not all the same*. They differ because they arise at several levels.

The goal in this chapter is to come to grips with this thorny issue. We propose to define terms, and gradually to describe how a sense of "unity" does away with all conventional "dualities" and "trialities" implicit in our self/other relationship. Then, in the next chapters, we consider some physiological correlates that could underlie these different experiential qualities. Please note that this discussion regards unitive impressions as qualities of insight *within* states of consciousness, not as states in themselves.

Novel insights are central to the states of kensho and satori. Their deeper impressions on the psyche are profound. Moreover, their comprehensive illuminations resonate within the higher octaves of what seems to be a wide, "open" consciousness. Why does this sense of *openness* occur?

Consciousness has been vacated. It has shed not only all of its prior burdensome *psychic concepts* of self but also every discursive notion of their former links with a physical body-self. Consciousness feels liberated within such a vacancy. It is free to read between the lines. Now it discovers freshly minted, meaningful interrelationships in everything it perceives. Consciousness feels awakened, "reborn."

In these pages, we do not tread on soil alien to the Judeo-Christian past. In Christian meditative traditions, the ancient process that empties the personal self of rights and ambitions is called *kenosis*. One finds veiled in the following translations in the King James version of the Bible the same unconditioning that occurs during what our generations now call a "peak experience": "Whoever does not receive the kingdom of God like a child shall not enter it" (Mark 10:15). "Except a man be born again, he cannot see the kingdom of God" (John 3:3–6).

Pursuing Dictionary Definitions of Identity, Oneness, and Unity

Standard dictionaries define *identity* as sameness in all constituents (and also as oneness). *Unity* (also defined as oneness) refers to that quality of being made up of elements that are intimately associated. However, turning next to a Buddhist dictionary, one finds that the *selfless* experience of *oneness* is defined as "the experience of true reality."[5]

This Buddhist dictionary then provides a crisp operational definition of insight-wisdom: enlightenment makes clear, it says, that the absolute world of emptiness* and the relative world of phenomena are "entirely one," not separate domains. Thus, "the experience of true reality is precisely the experience of this oneness ... there are not two worlds."

Later on in this chapter we are going to discuss two distinct sequences that occur during kensho. That discussion will expand on this brief dictionary definition of enlightened oneness. It will propose that only during the second of these two phases can the implications of the first moment be comprehended. Only then will the essence of awakening dawn on the witness: the world of phenomena and the underlying noumenal world are indeed *one and the same*!

Categories of Oneness/Unity

A daunting task lies before any author who might be foolish enough to even think of *rushing* in where angels fear to tread. Subtleties abound in the whole topic. This is why we will proceed very slowly during the rest of this chapter and the next chapters. Moving back and forth—using words, a visual diagram, and a table—the plan is to develop several *advanced, insightful* categories of "Oneness." Readers will be invited to recall their moments of keen *intuition*, and to allow what they believe about ordinary "cognition" to fade into the background.

Several points need to be emphasized at the outset: (1) Each of the oversimplified categories of insight includes subtle qualities of an instant, *pre*cognitive flash of understanding. Insightful comprehension is not only wordless in itself, it also eludes ordinary later attempts to define it linguistically.† (2) Each such insightful understanding seems to arrive directly. It is not *thought* about until later. (3) Some insights appear to register their impressions at greater depths than others. (4) Deeper comprehensive insights tend to cluster. Each component reinforces the others (e.g., no self/no fear/no time/no doing). Their interactive nature tends to create a sense of authenticity that confirms the sense of reality. Long-range transformative potentials reside in such deeper, extraordinary, blendings of insightful consciousness. (5) Ambiguities of classification abound: people overvalue their "realer-than-real" experiences, tend to describe them imperfectly, and elaborate them into "overbeliefs." If mixtures and overlappings happen to occur, they cause further confusion.

---

* It bears reemphasis: In the cultural context of Buddhism, "emptiness" does not refer to an experience that remains "hollow" and devoid of *all* meaning (see chapter 85).

† Here, Roman numerals are being reserved for only the categories of *insight*. This is as part of an ongoing effort to distinguish them from other mental processes during the absorptions. Thus, "category I" refers to the kinds of insights into unification which the writer experienced during kensho. Those in the very first phase, "phase A," were present at kensho's onset. Those in "phase B" arrived a few seconds thereafter. The next chapters discuss other categories of insight. Why are they called "provisional?" I cannot be certain of their form and content, because I lack direct personal experience with them. Thus, all comments about categories II, III, and IV remain "provisional" and speculative.

Two Implications of the Word "Realization"

The alert reader may already be aware that "realize" and "realization" are elastic words. We often find them used in ways that could obscure the distinctions between the two different phases soon to be discussed. For example, at the start of kensho, the one world is being directly *experienced* as "the true Reality." In a flash, reality is being *made Real—realized,* in the form of a *verb*. In this phase, the self is absent. It is not there to comment, nor are any words or other discriminating functions at its command.

Sometime thereafter, a diminutive "i-person" begins to emerge. This later moment heralds the partial return of a slightly more discriminating, but still minute, self-consciousness. The thin edge of some vague concepts of time have also returned. Awareness, now looking back, glimpses that awesome event which had not only just been experienced but which obviously still prevails for the most part. Only at this second instant, in retrospect, can a now obvious set of facts finally be "realized." It is at this precise point that the same verb now implies recognized, appreciated, comprehended by insight.

The insightful message then is different: *This* profound, nondual Unity—now ongoing—is the Real Reality; it had just taken over the whole mental field and dominated it during the prior moment. Implicit in this second phase is a kind of automatic, precognitive, experiential *appreciation* of the first. Reality had just been made Real; now that ongoing fact is being recognized *and appreciated*, as well as realized.

The two phases in tandem exert a powerful net effect. Plumbing the depths of experience, they took over my belief system. For several days thereafter, no critical cognitive thought processes were ready to remove *all* of the weighty unifying impression left on my consciousness. Later, after a relatively long interval, and now aided by both language and the passage of time, I could look back and try to put into words a simple fact: this nondual world had been "realized" (made real) in two seamless, successive instants in two different ways. Only the second phase, with its nascent capacity for instant hindsight, is a "realization," the descriptive *noun* that language would later place on the unique comprehension involved in this experience.

After this preamble, it may be easier to see how these two phases might fit into the first category (I) of a general classification. Now let us continue this narrative discussion with the aid of a formula and a diagram.

Category I. Phase A. Perfection Unifying ALL Things as THEY Really Are (Unity among Diversity)

When selfhood vanished, it took along with it that limiting boundary which had once served as its former interface with the "other" world outside. In the pages up to now, we used a conventional symbol to represent this usual self/other barrier. It was an ordinary slash: "/".

But at this entry into kensho, only an allocentric world existed. It was no longer "that" world, something "*outside* myself." It was *this* newly unbounded world. Indeed, the kind of witnessing which then prevailed throughout this allocentric world contained no dualistic versions of *that* former outside world. Nor did this particular kind of witnessing notice that the prior boundary had vanished at that instant. Instead, this selfless field was registering one integrated set of *explicit* observations:

A simple formula might summarize the way this novel field of *unity among diversity* then appeared:

FIELD OF UNITY$^{(m)(R)(E)}$

Of the three superscripts, (m) stands for *multiple*. It symbolizes the fact that *into each, and among all*, of the myriad items witnessed in the world outside was infused an unparalleled refinement of aesthetic appreciation. Each individual one was seen in its *perfect total interrelationship* with every other part of the whole. All fit together perfectly.

(R) stands for another implicit global comprehension: everything manifested Ultimate Objective *Reality*. The sense was: All these things exist as they *Really* are.

Finally, (E) represents the awesome realization that this all-embracing Reality was the *Eternal state of affairs*. The sense was: all things exist *beyond any reference to time*, in themselves, just like *this* (in this "suchness").

Category I. Phase B. Full, Reflective Appreciation: This Prior Oneness Had Just Reconciled All Dualities*

When that initial phase (phase A) of total unification flashed in, it completely dominated the mental field. Not only was *no personal self inside, none of that person's previous criteria for comparison existed*. Hence, at that instant, in no way could any witnessing person then "appreciate" this first extraordinary phase for its unique qualities. It simply registered as a fact and was fully accepted as a fact.

Then, slightly later, after an indefinable interval, an elementary sense of "i" began to return. It was only this tiny version of an "i" that had the capacity to *reflect* back spontaneously—reflexly—on the events that had just transpired.

The facts then confronting this diminutive i-self posed an immense paradox (a paradox of such depth and scope could never before have been imagined): (a) an ordinary mundane world had *always* previously been existing out there; (b)

* (One-and-the-sameness, Which Had Just Been Witnessed Could Now Be Fully Appreciated in Retrospect), and Was Ongoing.

yet only just moments before, that old conventional material world had suddenly become transformed and vivified (at a level "realer than real") into objective "Reality" itself; (c) therefore, these two versions—that old perspective which had always *seemed* real, this newest realization that *was* absolute Reality itself—*were One and the Same.*

This was a stark awakening. The fact that they were absolutely One was impressive in its novelty. (It was certainly a new fact for the anonymous observer, but it was not a new insight that had never arisen elsewhere.) It simply expressed that ancient awesome truth many others had experienced during millennia past: *Samsara is none other than nirvana.*

Parallel Universes Reconciled

At present, you and I are still trapped inside our usual self/other mode. As long as we are, we cannot step out of our own skins and deeply realize that "this" individual self is an integral part of "that" whole vast "other" universe. Only during a supraordinate state of consciousness can two such "separate" self/other "entities" as samsara and nirvana unite into "Oneness."

Two events made possible this second, supraordinate unifying insight: (a) these two states (the ordinary and then the extraordinary) had presented their contrasts immediately, back to back; (b) a supracognitive syncretic process of insight had instantly reconciled their stark contrasts. This fresh insight did more than reconcile the awesome new Reality. *It held on to the comprehension* that these two domains (which might have seemed separate in space and time) were *ONE and the same.*[6] Figure 11 ventures to illustrate how two "parallel universes" can give way to One.

Start at the top. Here, we imagine that we live in the usual dual, self/other world. On the left, our "inside" self is the larger (and certainly seems more important). Off to the right side, the rest of the world lies "outside" us. The thick lines represent the imaginary boundaries which separate "this" dominant, sovereign self from the "that" "other" world. Each of the two separate tracks seems to run parallel to the other.

Suddenly—farther on down—during a timeless moment of "Oneness," the old egocentric self dissolves. Then, all things in the whole environment are perceived as *they really* are: *ONE*. How can such an insight of Eternal oneness first register as a fact (in phase A), yet not be *completely* appreciated at that very same instant? *Because no discriminating self remains during this first phase.* No analytic thought process exists which can contrast the nondual quality of this special *ONE moment* with any of the person's old memories.

Soon, however, a tiny *reflective* consciousness can begin to realize the awesome oneness of this moment (as the curved, dashed, pointed arrows suggest).

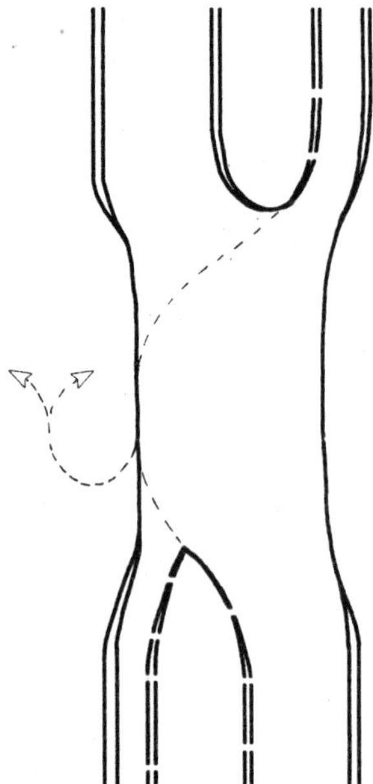

Figure 11 Parallel universes, transformed by insight into Oneness

What is that large arc of thin dashed lines curving to the left inside the moment of oneness? It suggests that only the allocentric perspective exists once the old egocentric self and its frame of reference is entirely absent.

The bottom of the figure depicts several transformations which developed during kensho: that former inflated self has now become "thinner." "Pores" appear in its boundary; they open up that newly awakened self to a fresh appreciation of the outside world. The two tracks also lie closer together. Their closeness is intended to suggest that now the person's sense of conceptual dualities is not so separate—and so opposing—as it had been initially.

If one were to regard the top and bottom of this diagram as analogous to two sets of railroad tracks, then the single lines during oneness could convey one other implication. It is that no conventional train of thought operates during kensho's *ONE* moment of expansive insight. Zen has always emphasized no-thought (*mushin*). Insight is its ultimate refinement. Indeed, no-thought prevails during insight. Not until later do those usual discriminating thought processes return. Slowly, they begin to reestablish the person's former dual "track" concepts of inhabiting "two parallel universes."

Thereafter, most of the egocentric self will gradually return during the next hours and days. Even so, small intuitive glimpses reenter awareness.[7] These fleeting insights reverify the earlier impression: Oneness is Reality; the self is *not* walled off on one side of two separate compartments.

This is the basis for the five discontinuities depicted from top to bottom in the "other" right-side track. These suggest that our whole environment (the supposed "other") *always exists in a relationship—more open and inclusive than we realize*—with each of its individual creatures: we and everything else are integral parts of this larger whole. No mental prism of self can split this Ultimate Reality into smaller fragments. We and the universe might seem to inhabit parallel tracks, but we are really ONE.

Consider, just as another visual analogy, what a person might experience if one of the standard figure/ground illusions were suddenly to be appreciated in a similar manner. When we usually look at a page showing this familiar picture, we will see *either* the two curves of that white vase in the center *or* those two dark facial profiles facing inward. In contrast, the kind of new overarching perspective we have been discussing would appear as black faces beholding a white vase [Z:380–381].

While the distinctions between phase A and phase B are still fresh in mind, let us now consider how and where they might have arisen in the brain.

Phases A and B. Possible Psychophysiological Correlates

Phase A. A Syncretic Inclusiveness: All-in-One; Unity among Diversity

The prefix *syn-* suggests that several things come together simultaneously. What does syncretism mean in terms of visual processing? It describes that special supraordinate capacity which integrates widely opposing details into one large meaningfully unified picture.

Many of our normal syncretic visual functions seem referable to the parietooccipital cortex. However, much of their salience also hinges on their pivotal interactions with the pulvinar and lateral posterior nucleus of the thalamus. The nearby cortex of the right posterior temporal lobe also contributes to our sense of visual closure. Its infusions help "fill in the gaps" and create meaning, even when some parts of the picture are still missing [Z:601–605].

Certain neurological patients lose their visual syncretic functions. This disorder is called *simultagnosia*. Their lesion damages the upper (more superior) portions of the visual association cortex. The patients cannot see the forest for the trees. If presented with the picture of a large forest, they process only one tree at a time, unable to grasp the sense of the *whole* big picture at once.

This first phase of kensho presented a totally unified vision. Moreover, its added degree of harmonious perfection was another important aspect. This attribute suggested two things: not only had the mental field lost all negative valences and affective dissonances but a novel affirmative tone was also infusing the whole scene.

Phase B. Unity Appreciated: A Retrospective Realization of the Implications of Nonduality

This second insight is different. Barely beginning to return are some of the most elementary notions about time and other faintly discriminative memory functions. Now it can be appreciated that the extraordinary nonduality which had just taken over a moment before constitutes the *real*, perfect sacred Reality. This Real domain *prevails* because it IS one and the same as the world of phenomena. This reconciliation of two highly complex sets of memory concepts, old and immediate, is extraordinarily authoritative. Disbelief is suspended. Supraordinate acts of this nature are likely to draw on the coherent functions of multiple regions on both sides of the brain.

Yet what I am able to describe in words is only the beginning. Other witnesses have found words to express their different kinds of insights into Oneness.

78

Varieties of "Oneness" and "Unity." Provisional Categories II and III

> The eye with which I see God is the same eye with which God sees me.
>
> Meister Eckhart (c.1260–c.1328)

The next three categories may come as a surprise. (Zen is full of surprises, and of paradoxes too.) Here is the problem: previous pages have all emphasized a Path that points in the direction of *selflessness*. This lack of self, or no self, is described by a particular technical term, *anatta*. However, traditions from both East and West do mention other kinds of "Oneness" that occur in advanced states *beyond* the absorptions. Though their individual accounts may lack precise details, they leave the distinct impression that one or more aspects of self somehow become identified as an *integral* part of the larger sense of identity that is equated with unification. What does this mean?

A general descriptive phrase for such a coexistence might read something like "All things are one, including aspects of myself." A recent account of awakening by a Zen laywoman phrased it this way: "The Universe and I are one body. I am the Buddha."[1] Table 8 outlines where and how such aspects of self might

Table 8
Varieties of "Oneness"

Category	*Descriptors*	*Summary of the Field of Consciousness*	*States of the Physical and Psychic Self*	*Transformation Potential**
I.Phase A: Unity among diversity; "All is one"	Allocentric immanence; integrated coherence; objective, nondual reality; eternal suchness	Perceptions are transfigured; mundane realities are perceived as "reality"; perfection is explicit	Absent	0–+
I.Phase B: Full appreciation of unity; in retrospect, "All is indeed one, in perpetuity"	An immediate, retrospective, appreciative "realization": "Samsara is none other than nirvana"	An insightful reflective reconciliation of what the first nondual phase has just implied and *continues* to imply	A diminutive, elementary "i" is emerging	+–++
Provisional category II: "All is one, including some quasi-physical aspects of myself"	May resemble those in phases A and B above, plus hints suggesting a different category	A literal recognition of some quasi-physical representations consistent with the self	Paradox: Internally empty of "self," yet some of its outer *physical* representations are included	+–+++
Provisional category III: "All is one, including some aspects of my psyche that are nonphysical"	?Less evidence of the qualities listed above	A figurative, more implicit identification with more refined "mental" concepts referable to subtle functions of the psychic self	Paradox: Internally empty of "self," yet some of its subtle *psychic* concepts and manifestations are included	+–+++
Provisional category IV: "All is one" at levels of comprehension that may evolve toward a more fundamental experience of "Being" the Ultimate Reality	Eludes description: A more profound "Oneness" coexisting with the depths of emptiness in the earlier phase . . . then, evolving beyond "Oneness" to a still deeper proprioceptive and psychic sense of identity at the level of "Being," *beyond* Oneness	Plumbs depths that are "altogether beyond"	Paradox: Internally empty of "self," yet some hints of its basic awareness coexist with their proprioceptive counterparts during the earlier Oneness, and this awareness later helps confirm the impression of "Being"	+++–++++

* "Oneness" blends several qualities of experience into a net impression. However, the depth of the accompanying insights can vary. So, too, may the degree of moist-eyed affect that coexists. A consensus over the centuries is that when more extraordinary states of greater insight occur in the more advanced states, and when they include the qualities in categories II, III, and IV, they may have a greater transforming potential. Whether, in fact, they *do* or not, varies depending on the individual person, the nature of the insights, the setting, and the social context.

begin to fit into a tentative taxonomy of states that include various qualities of Oneness-Unity among their phenomena. (It begins with category I, as discussed in the previous chapter.)

When "awakenings" contain major insights—and *only then*—they tend to be placed farther along on the kensho-satori spectrum of alternate states of consciousness. This uncharted wilderness of allied states begs to be explored. No fully detailed critical account of their phenomenology or of their potential neural correlates is available at present.

By way of a tentative conceptual framework, this chapter makes use of the ancient distinction between soma and psyche. Table 8 represents the next two major subtypes of phenomena, describing their qualities of oneness as category II and category III, respectively [Z:37–47].

- Category II is off at the "soma" end of the spectrum of possibilities. It could be thought of as more of a "quasi-physical" impression of "Oneness." Perhaps this subtype includes states that "incorporate" some (residual) *physical* constructs of self out into the larger open field of consciousness.[2]
- Category III is off at the other end of the spectrum. These impressions of "Oneness" could arise from the inclusive, intuitive, creative network of functions that we assign to the realm of our personal *psyche*.[3] In this subtype, the major existential insights would tap into precognitive levels of direct comprehension.

For purposes of clarity, we expand upon each category separately below. It remains possible that sometimes they might overlap or include elements of category I as well.

Provisional Category II: Oneness That Includes Aspects of "Myself" as a "Quasi-Physical" Representation

At times, the flavor of this subtype might suggest something more than the "simple" impression that parts of one's physical self had remained and were being externally displaced. An unusual quality of *self-recognition* might also enter into this autoscopic process of being projected outward, and merging into, the visual scenery of the world outside. This variety of "Oneness" appears to be associated sometimes with what we might describe as an "identity by self-recognition."

To recognize oneself is not an esoteric function. It is a normal physiological process in which vision plays a major part. We all develop the capacity to recognize our own self in a mirror between 18 months and 2 years of age (see chapter 6).

A Zen meditator recently used words in a narrative that suggested such a subtype.[4] He had just finished a summer retreat a week earlier, and was walking toward a small bridge on his way to work. Then

> The universe was me and I was it. I looked up at the sky and that experience was exactly like looking at a mirror. I don't mean that metaphorically either ... I got that same feeling no matter where I looked. I looked at the asphalt road and it was my face ... the bridge was me staring back at myself.... It was a physical sensation, as if the sky had my eyes and could see me staring up at it.... This state was "true" ... far more true than the state I had considered to be normal up until then.

The words describe a novel visual sense infused with the "truth" of real perception. Note that the words reject the idea that the "mirror" aspects of his state corresponded with the way we might commonly employ a "mirror vision" type of description as an ordinary literary metaphor. Such an explicit denial merits attention. This seems to be another author/witness who wishes us to be clear about what he is trying to communicate. He too cautions the reader: his words are an attempt to describe a curious change in direct perception; his words do not represent a contrived literary allusion.

His sentences describe a "physical sensation": his face literally *in* the asphalt road. A later sentence might sound less impossible to the general reader. For now, although his "eyes" are in the sky, when these eyes look back down at his own eyes he renders this only in the form of a softer, "as-if" simile.

These words are strange on the page. (Are those in Meister Eckhart's epigraph more comfortable?) They suggest that a very unusual kind of "self-"*recognition* is taking place. That old outer boundary of his skin is no longer a fixed barrier. His *physical* self-image is being displaced externally, turned around and merged into *inanimate* objects.

What happens in the brain when an asphalt road embodies the face of the witness, and when the sky embodies his eyes? Why does the poet Rumi say: "We are the mirror as well as the face in it. We are the taste that is tasting this minute of Eternity?" With regard to the complex origins of such phenomena, certain of their aspects almost seem reminiscent of a mixture of heightened allocentric perception and self-recognition, combined with an out-of-body (somatic) hallucination (see chapter 52).

An account from the Hardy Research Centre describes two somewhat similar episodes. They occurred, 3 years apart, in association with a sense of peace and no fear, as follows: "I am part of nature itself and it is a part of me—we are one. And all the scenery I am looking at is mine—a part of me."[5] (Some aspects of this incorporation resemble the symptoms reported by the patient in chapter 8.)

Provisional Category III: Oneness That Includes Some Aspects of My Psyche That Are Nonphysical Representations

We are venturing out onto exceedingly soft ground. However, that ancient distinction between soma and psyche does begin with some correlates in gross anatomy. To recap: we represent our physical body-self (our *soma*) mostly in circuits within the back of the brain, relying on relatively hard-wired sensory "constructs."

In contrast, the research reviewed in part III attributes many of the more complex "mental" aspects of our *psyche* to the frontotemporal, superior temporal, inferior parietal, and limbic regions. Their circuits are either in, or connect in significant ways with, the *front* of the brain. They draw heavily on mixtures of soft- and hard-wired associations. One result of their networking functions is a psychic triad, an interactive blend of cognitive, emotional, and instinctual components.

The many concepts and notions of our cognitive self seem to be relatively accessible to our consciousness and under our willful control. However, our psyche expresses its emotional roots and instinctual drives subconsciously at levels beyond our control. A state that chiefly expresses such emotional and instinctual circuits proves difficult to articulate and to classify.

Parenthetically, it was possible (in my experience) to undergo a softer comprehension of unification—one that plumbs sacramental depths—during a surge of raw emotionalized awareness. And to cry, and to feel greatly released from all tension. Yet not to conclude, in retrospect, that this event went beyond the level of a state of "quickening" [Z:373–376, 404]. (An "affiliative" surge?)

Still, keeping in mind this gross distinction between soma and psyche, we might wonder: could this third category of generic "Oneness" sometimes follow a pattern similar to that suggested by the second? That is, could it also displace (or project) certain aspects which that person attributed to themself *outward* into some external, allocentric domain? And could such projections represent subtle attributes of that person's *psychic* functions?

If so, then *which* psychic attributes? Could some first approximation begin with a developmental model? Consider the way our self-centered behaviors slowly became reoriented and turned *outward* when we were children. Again, we are referring to a normal physiological pattern of development. After all, once we had attained the age of 2 years, and mother pretended to be distressed, we could finally reach out to console her with our newly budding empathy (see chapter 65).

Consider another apocryphal tale, this one about the young child who first presents his mother with his *own* toy. It's a "gift!" (but one with no insight into what *she* herself might value). Then, at a later stage the gift might be his crude drawing of a flower, soon a better-drawn valentine. Later still comes the fragrant bouquet of real flowers (when he has matured sufficiently to remember what kind she likes).

What we have just outlined lies at the elementary end of our psychic "spectrum" of self-development. These are childish, outward-oriented notions. They represent the crudest of intentions. Farther off toward the adult end are the later refinements of attitudes now under discussion in category III. These code for more mature, socially oriented, acquired character traits and aspirations.

Let's be clear about how this preamble applies to the basic issue. *This developmental capacity to emerge from self-centeredness and to reach out beyond—with deep insight into larger meanings—is at the core of Zen awakening and mature behavior.*

From the Zen Buddhist perspective, this whole developmental spectrum of personal and interpersonal growth rests on a simple principle. The way it unfolds—like the lotus in the morning—represents the flowering of our innate, original nature. Gratitude and compassion toward others, for example, are regarded as "native virtues." Moreover, from this perspective, the "spiritual" quest itself is seen as an innate *instinctual* response. It is not an externally imposed "goal." Nor does it need to be acquired from our culture, from the "outside," in some top-down manner. The "fruits" of the practice arise spontaneously from this ongoing instinctual flowering of the personality.

We may never define every microcircuit that enables "native virtues" to express themselves as ethical behaviors, as a sense of gratitude, and as genuine compassion. But researchers now have new data about how mature brains function when they generate certain *intuitive* notions about other people and events in the outside world.

Intuitive Brains and "Mirroring" Minds

Intuitions help us guess what another person has in mind. It is not simple to intuit someone else's thoughts, motivations, and emotions. We must

- perceive that the other person is probably experiencing "something";
- scan our own internal data bank for the particular options that might match what this "something" might be;
- recognize which option fits all the circumstances;
- project this pattern of inferences back outside ourself and attribute it to that particular person's internal mental processes.

Note that this projection of a psychic inference resembles a counterpart of that externalization of the *somatic* self-image just discussed in category II.

To clarify the mechanisms underlying category III, it helps to return to the phrase "theory of mind." It is now being used to summarize this fourfold capacity to "read" another person's mind. The phrase refers to the operations involved in *my* mind guessing what's on *your* mind, or putting myself in the other person's shoes. True, such "theories of mind" do invoke many frontal lobe associative functions (see chapter 43). However, these frontal executive functions need to direct and coordinate a variety of other *interacting* networks and modules elsewhere.

Our primate cousins have been studied using implanted electrodes while they engaged in similar guessing games. Recall that the physiologists first found that certain nerve cells in the *premotor* cortex fired when a monkey performed a specific action. Then they noticed that the same premotor cells also fired the same way when the monkey merely *passively* observed a different monkey who was performing the identical act.[6] The first monkey only *seemed* passive. Its brain was actively engaged in the monkey business of *mimicry*.

The nerve cells that engage in such mimicry activities have since been called mirror neurons (see chapter 65). They reflect the way the whole brain operates as a sensorimotor unity. On the sensory side, they stay in touch with visual and other events in the outside world. On the motor side, they are poised to represent the larger circuits of a potentially active motoric self.

Premotor cells are versatile. They are also attuned to sound. They discharge when the first monkey *hears* the typical *sound* (say of a hammer on metal) that could only be the act of the second monkey—now out of sight—striking metal with his hammer.

How can single mirror neurons in one monkey be coded to simulate particular motoric (behavioral) acts of another monkey? By virtue of *cross-modal* memory links to sensory cues and associations that are both auditory and visual in nature.[7]

It is already being suggested, on the basis of fMRI studies, that human brains are likely to have analogous, though not identical, capacities to simulate. These could help one person predict the future motor actions of a different person.[8]

Further to clarify the mechanisms underlying category III, we turn next to other human research on functions of the psyche. The questions are: Which higher-level regions do humans use most when we monitor our own mental state? and, Which are involved when we attribute a particular *mental* state to another person?[9]

- *Self*-monitoring functions usually activate BA 9 and 10 in the *medial* prefrontal cortex (see figure 7, chapter 40).
- When guessing what another person's mental state is, we activate different medial areas. These are located *inferior* to these, residing around the anterior cortex near the cingulate gyrus. Recent studies also implicate the activity of a region farther

back in the temporoparietal junction when we're in the process of thinking about other people.[10]

What Relevance Does Such Research Have to Category III, "Oneness That Includes Some Aspects of My Psyche That Are Nonphysical?"

Clearly, it is a rare state of consciousness that in one single unbounded mental field, is (a) apparently experienced as "*non*dual," and (b) also includes some kinds of psychic resonances of the self. Do any other lines of evidence bear on such a singular phenomenon?

Years ago, after nonstressful meditating, I happened to experience an unusual minor, incidental, spontaneous "quickening" [Z:395–397]. It took the same familiar verses that I was then chanting, and recast them in the form of large fast-moving bytes. These lengthy auditions were both heard and known to be my own. Their sentences were projected out into peripersonal space directly in front of me. The agility and the scope of such released frontal lobe networking functions is astonishing and must be experienced to be believed.[11]

What would happen if a similar kind of hyperfluent activity selectively enhanced other functions in other parts of the frontal lobes? Suppose such networking functions had been excited, or disinhibited and released, by primary events sponsored by mechanisms elsewhere, say, within the thalamus. Could a different outward projection surge up from the *psyche*, as it were, not as *words*, but in a manner that distilled the essence of the normal developmental sequences of maturation discussed earlier in this chapter?

Clearly, the category III phenomena will differ from this early superficial "quickening" that I happened to experience while chanting. Category III phenomena seem more likely to occur later, and to be most well developed in only very few, mature, long-term practitioners. So the question then becomes: What changes have evolved in the brain functions of these advanced trainees? Why is it more likely that when *they* experience a state of Unity, certain of its qualities include *some* representations that they find are identifiable with aspects of their psychic self?

Let us begin with adepts who are training in a monastic setting. Let us proceed from the premise that over time they already will have developed a more appropriate, insightful sense of self-in-the-world. Their sense of self has been pruned and honed by ongoing mindful introspection. Suppose further that their brains had been "gentled" by this long training, that they had become more compassionate and insightful, and that their lower-profile "i-me-mine" self would then be less likely to relapse into its former overinflated version, the egocentric self of the *I-Me-Mine*. It could follow that when advanced states of kensho-satori *happen to occur*, these states will have immediate access to this more transformed and more mature psychic circuitry.

This is not a new idea. Zen has been engaged for centuries in developing this lower-profile self. It can help us now to consult some wordy evidence from the past, to see if it can clarify how self and oneness might—or might not—relate to each other.

However, by way of preamble, it is instructive to cite the words of the Polish-born British novelist Joseph Conrad (1857–1924). Conrad learned English as his second language. He could say, with authority, "Words, as is well known, are great foes of reality." Conrad's perspective no doubt echoes that of the early Zen masters who, if they returned today, might find that their original meanings (as represented in Sino-Japanese ideographs) had changed in the process of being passed down to us through multiple translations.

Dogen's Comments in the Thirteenth Century about "Self" and "Oneness"

How can anyone represent, in a mere picture, the content of the mental field of insight-wisdom? For *Zen and the Brain,* I employed a visual device. It showed impulses (representing data from the outer world) entering that core of awareness which the old *I-Me-Mine* self had just vacated [Z:610; figure 19]. The witnessing awareness to this extraordinary event (called the "experiant") was defined as whatever registers that experience in the *absence* of self.

In this context, I had turned to Master Dogen for one of his classic quotations. I preferred to use a particular translation for the epigraph. It read: "To study the Way of the Buddha is to learn about oneself. To learn about oneself is to forget oneself. To forget oneself is to experience the world as pure object."

Why this preference for the phrase, "the world as pure object?" This was the way it *was*. I could relate to a translation that described "the world as pure object." During kensho, when my subjective self vanished, the whole external world had then presented itself as totally "objective." In fact, "objective vision" soon leaped to mind as the phrase most appropriate to describe this awesomely novel perspective [Z:538, 573–577].

With respect to what Dogen himself really meant, centuries ago, that last sentence of his above becomes especially important. Contemporary translators since have arrived at different versions, as illustrated in the following examples:

- "To forget the self is to be actualized by myriad things."[12]
- "To forget the self is to be verified by myriad dharmas."[13]
- "To forget one's self is to be confirmed by all dharmas."[14]

The examples beg the question: when the self is forgotten during kensho, precisely *how* are all those details in the outside world being actualized, verified, confirmed? To Dogen, it may have been clear that forms are seen, sounds are heard, and all are being known intimately "with body and mind as one."[15] If we were to take this interpretation literally, then this too would seem to be consistent with a unification experience in which soma, sensations, and psyche, were all being integrated. (Such an experience might include further refinements of the qualities in *both* category II and category III.)

Can such a body-mind intimacy in the qualities of oneness be experienced at an even more profound level? Elsewhere, we pointed to the possibility that more advanced, extraordinary states (states in the category of "Ultimate Pure Being"), would seem to exist "altogether *beyond*" kensho-satori [Z:627–633]. If such a rare advanced category of states of awakening does plumb levels of "Being" in this very manner, then perhaps its existence might best be summarized by the statement: "to be enlightened by the ten thousand things is to *be* the ten thousand things."[16]

Do we have any accurate, detailed descriptors referable to an experience of "Being?" Not really. Why not? Because such states seem to have gone "altogether beyond" any of the earlier quasi-physical or metacognitive levels of abstract, self-referent identity [Z:698–699]. Words do not issue from the altogether beyond.

The next chapter provides further hints about how difficult it is to find accurate words. It continues the present discussion, to the point of proposing a fourth category of the varieties of "Oneness." In this variety, oneness can "open"—beyond *some* lingering representations of the psychic self—into "Being."

79

Varieties of "Oneness" And "Unity." Provisional Category IV

> To carry yourself forward and experience myriad things is delusion. That myriad things come forth and experience themselves is awakening.
>
> Master Dogen (1200–1253)[1]

> It's not that I as a separate self merged with everything. It was just a pure seeing that everything is one, and that I am that.
>
> Adyashanti (a.k.a. Steve Gray)[2]

Two Zen Masters' Instructive Commentaries on Oneness

In the first epigraph, Master Dogen was drawing a distinction: you are deluded if your egocentric self still remains "in there" trying to reach out to grab at some "experience" of being "enlightened." True awakening happens only when the things of the world advance and "experience themselves."

A contemporary master, Master Sheng-yen, added these recent comments on the experience of Universal Oneness: "When a person is at this stage, they recognize that the entire universe is the same as themselves."[3] However, Sheng-yen had also observed earlier that "To feel that everything in the universe is part of you is good, but it is not enlightenment."[4]

For Sheng-yen, such (universe-self) feelings are the "illusory expressions of a larger sense of self gained through hard practice."[5] He acknowledges that one result of such an experience might be a "tremendous power that would come from the idea that 'the universe is the same as me.'" And he also notes that some people who have had "this kind of realization can often become very great religious leaders." However, he cautions that their identification with the universe as a whole still represents one more overvalued ego attachment that they later will need to give up.[6]

The Big Problem

So the major question remains: What exactly is this variation on the theme of the "self," or the "ego," that is being identified as coexistent either with the universe as a whole, or even with divinity in some form? It is certainly not that former narrow, selfish ego from which the person had suffered earlier.

No aspect of that earlier inturned, selfish ego would have a place in sudden extraordinary awakenings. Then why would Sheng-yen say that a person gains "a larger sense of self" only as the result of rigorous practice?[7] What kind of "larger sense of self" could occur as a result of long "hard practice?" And finally, how does it relate to a state of "Being?"

Toward a Still Larger Psychic Sense of *self*-in-the-World

Let us interpret "a larger sense of self gained through hard practice" to signify what it did in this last chapter. There, it meant that certain aspirants' extensive training process enabled them to develop more mature attitudes and ongoing enlightened traits. By way of condensing what all these words signify, let us suggest that the trainees have evolved a *larger sense of self-in-the-world*. Some of this, as it relates to kensho, might be envisioned as corresponding to the bottom part of figure 11 (chapter 77). Here, we recall, the earlier inflated self had become "thinner," more porous, and more aware of its intimate interactive relationships with people, things, and events in the outside world. This is a *smaller* self.

New attitudes and transformed traits *are not mere abstract psychological descriptors*. They arise from functions redistributed among *actual nerve networks* within that more mature person's brain. We refer now to major new constellations of functions, ones that have traversed the steep learning curve between ordinary factual knowledge and deep understanding, between ordinary seeing and insightful living. This smaller self has a larger view of the world.

The previous chapter cited our normal capacity for self-recognition as developing between $1\frac{1}{2}$ to 2 years of age, and our capacity for empathy as beginning around the age of 2 years. Do any other relevant, nonesoteric precedents exist within normal human development for an adult aspirant who goes on to evolve and project even "larger" attitudes of self-in-the-world? Recent neuroimaging studies of children say yes. The data show that we go through two major early developmental passages in the externalizing of our personal selves. In the process, our intuitive functions evolve in ways that not only grasp new cause-and-effect relationships but then project these new understandings onto the outside world.[8]

The components in the first stage begin to ripen before the age of 2 years. Their elementary steps help us anticipate what our parents and siblings have "in mind": hinting at their simpler goals, perceptions, emotions, and actions.

The second stage does not start until later, around 4 years of age (see chapter 6). Why are its "conceptual" functions much more advanced? Because they enable us to attribute subtle *beliefs and attitudes* to others (and also have some inkling of them in ourselves). The neuronal components of this second system are more complex. Multiple chapters in part III and IV have prepared us to appreciate why so many frontotemporal regions contribute to it: the medial prefrontal cortex (BA 9), the temporal poles (BA 38), the superior temporal sulcus in its anterior portion (BA 22), and the temporoparietal junction (BA 39/40), as well as its posterior extention (BA 22) (see figure 7, chapter 40).

Both sides of the brain participate when we reach beyond the narrow confines of self into a better understanding of the outside world. When neuroimaging researchers first tested "theory of mind" functions, their intellectual tasks emphasized logic and powers of reasoning. Naturally, the brain responded to logic-based tasks that hinged on language by activating more networks in the left hemisphere.[9] Other "theory of mind" tasks that hinged on visuospatial skills and attention have since tended to activate corresponding regions more in the right hemisphere.

Note that we are postulating particular kinds of *insightful* functions as relevant to "a larger sense of self-in-the-world." These processes are more automatic, intuitive, and language-free. Depending on the setting, they may access many similar modules on *both* sides, and engage in fast parallel processing with deeper subcortical networks.

But notice also: such a slowly acquired "larger sense of self-in-the-world" is *not* "larger" because its functions are overinflated and *bigger*. In fact, it plays a very low-profile ecological role in society as a whole, one much less self-indulgent than ever before [Z:668–677]. Indeed, Sheng-yen has also pointed out that a person at this advanced stage is *not* self-conscious of being liberated: "When true wisdom arises it comes undetected and unannounced."[10] Moreover, these evolved attitudes and traits of the psyche will have stayed closely attuned to the subconscious sensorimotor functions of the physical self. The dual nature of such transformations can enable a *whole* brain—front and back, low and high—to express, *without thinking*, what that person has *become*.

What we have been trying to describe in words is a new, mature lifestyle. Its ongoing, flexible, adaptive behavior is expressed quickly by a stable, simplified, person—a smaller "self-in-The-Big-Picture" (a theme discussed further in part VIII).

A Contemporary Narrative of Oneness That Evolved into Emptiness at the Level of Being

The personal episodes narrated in the pages of this and my earlier book emphasize the distinct *sequences* through which kensho and internal absorption evolve. An advanced category of states was proposed earlier [Z:627–630]. It corresponded to states late on the Path of Zen that might be included under the term "Ultimate Pure Being" (see chapters 4 and 87).

A recent article in *Tricycle* is instructive because it describes the way a Zen meditator experienced the quality of "Oneness." The experience evolved through two phases. The earlier state evolved later into a sense of "being the universal reality." The subject was a 31-year-old man who had been in intensive Zen meditative training since the age of 19.[11] At age 25, while in zazen, he entered kensho, "penetrated to the emptiness of all things and realized that the Buddha I had been chasing was what I was."

Having then formulated his own koan as "What is this that I am?", he pursued this question independently. Six years later, at the age of 31, he sat down to meditate and heard a birdcall outside the window. Then, "from my gut, I felt a question arise that I had never heard before: Who hears this sound?" Immediately, he entered an extraordinary, *emotionless* state, during which "I was the bird and the sound and the hearing of the sound, the cushion, the room, everything. It was just a pure seeing that everything is one, and that I am that."

While in the middle of this "Oneness," he understood "that I was everything in manifestation" (both subtly and in a material sense), "and yet I was also total emptiness, empty of even the experience of emptiness, and suddenly everything was seen to be a dream." Accompanying this was "a deeply felt kinesthetic sense of being everything and at the same time nothing. I knew with my whole being that who I really was wasn't even the oneness, it was the emptiness prior to the oneness, forever awake to itself. This knowing has never changed or faded in any way.... Enlightenment is awakening from the dream of being a separate me to being the universal reality."

The words describing this extraordinary episode are of special interest to this chapter's theme. They clearly illustrate that oneness can (1) coexist with emptiness at a level of understanding that is deeply confirmed with reference to some physical notion of a body, and (2) then yield to an even deeper understanding ("with my whole being") of a more fundamental identity with emptiness. This level of comprehension has become intimate with the use of the word "being" and appreciates that its manifestation tends to be ongoing.

Another interesting aspect of this narrative is its trigger: the natural sound of a birdcall. The primary and secondary (association) auditory cortex lies in the superior temporal gyrus. This is one of the three cortical sites from which, when you stimulate it in a monkey on only *one* side, impulses descend to the upper brainstem, and are then rebroadcast back up in the form of widespread arousal responses that excite the cortex on both sides (see chapter 72).

Possible Psychophysiological Correlates of Provisional Categories II, III, and IV

We are continuing to ask two questions of the several advanced states along what seems to be a *spectrum* of qualities of unification: First, how do several aspects of the self—including the more evolved, low-profile psychic-self-in-The-World—become manifest as phenomena in the field of consciousness? Second, which networks could possibly give rise to this remarkable spectrum of impressions that culminate in a *dynamic, shared identity within the whole "Big Picture?"* (see table 8, chapter 78).

- Category II Oneness includes "quasi-physical" aspects of the self. The descriptions suggest that several threads of a distributed system are being woven together. In such a process (1) somatic representations of the subject's physical self seem to be enlisted into a moment of heightened attention, and projected out into an allocentric mode of external perception; (2) these body image representations appear to be linked with curious recognition themes reminiscent of the personalized decisions made instantly in *déjà vu* or *déjà vécu* episodes.

  The externalized somatic representations are termed autoscopic phenomena. *Autoscopy* means seeing parts or all of one's own body "out there" in extrapersonal space while still maintaining one's habitual, grounded sense of an egocentric frame of reference.[12] Many of the responsible lesions (and focal sites for seizures or stimulations) tend to cluster around the parietotemporal junction. It is plausible to correlate the heightened and sharpened attention with the activation of nearby parietal lobule attentional mechanisms. The sense of reality that infuses such themes might correlate with additional activations that include the medial temporal region and the back of the medial orbitofrontal cortex.[13]

- Category III Oneness includes functions of the psyche likely to be more widespread. These "quasi-psychic aspects" involve networks in functional configurations that are cognitive, emotional, and instinctual. The way we ourselves normally envision the outside world evolves in significant ways at around 2 to 4 years of age. Our long-range adult maturity also evolves over decades, incrementally. Only after we undergo "passages" during several decades do we discover how many ethical, ecological, and other-directed orientations rise spontaneously into the mental foreground when our self-centered preoccupations fade.

  Correlates of our psyche reflect whole-brain functions, interacting. How can an immature, SELF-preoccupied person become transformed into a low-profile sharing self, an intimate partner in the whole Universe? Interactions involving both the medial frontal and temporal lobes probably play significant roles in reorganizing our subconscious attitudes and belief systems.

  Our native virtues of gratitude, empathy, and compassion tap deeply ingrained instinctual functions. If such virtues are to become actualized, major reorganizations must occur in the prior functions of networks whose deep roots extend within more midline regions, including the thalamus, basal ganglia, hypothalamus, and brainstem (see chapters 34, 37, 38, 41, 89, 90, and 91).

- The category IV quality of Oneness is intrinsically more indefinable in terms of its phenomenology. Its underlying state does seem to have the potential to evolve "into Being." As the impression of "oneness" vanishes, and as all other discriminating higher functions also dissolve, this state of Being could be expressing the deep central core of the networks underlying consciousness. These arise within the upper brainstem and at diencephalic levels just beyond. Note that these regions serve not only excitatory functions but also mediate inhibitory functions on higher-order thalamic nuclei that could significantly reduce the discriminating aspects of consciousness (see chapter 46).

  Where do such qualities of "Oneness" fit in with respect to the other major sequences and states outlined earlier on the Path of Zen? (see chapter 4). The first kensho could include the two phases of category I Oneness, A and B, described in chapter 77. Subsequent states of kensho that progressed toward satori could include the provisional qualities of "Oneness" in categories II and III. Category IV could accompany a profound transformative episode which evolved in its second phase into the state of Being, at which point the impression of "oneness" could disappear.

  To oversimplify the Path thus far: How might we view the current human condition? Most human beings seem overwhelmed by their efforts to multitask their everyday world. From this perspective, novice meditators on their mats might seem to be at least trying to be *in* the world, but not *of* it. Then how could an experiant be described, during an extraordinary moment of Oneness? As feeling selflessly *IN THE WORLD AND OF IT.*

We turn next to a discussion of why such an insight is so special.

80

Prajna: Insight-Wisdom

The only medicine for suffering, crime, and all the other woes of mankind is wisdom.
Thomas H. Huxley (1825–1895)

Early at our very first meeting, Kobori-Roshi introduced me to the term *prajna.* It refers to an extraordinary flash of insight-wisdom. Prajna reaches depths far beyond one's ordinary generic levels of insight and minor "epiphanies." Its shift of consciousness unveils *existential* issues.

Prajna has also been likened to a "lightning strike," a "thunderbolt." My "taste" of kensho suggests that what evolves is not one bolt of insight, but a flashing sequence of branching strikes.

Like our more ordinary kinds of intuition, prajna unveils special comprehensions *wordlessly.* One of its many paradoxes is that, while it clarifies the vast unity of all things intimately, prajna usually begins to do so *selflessly* (see chapter 77) [Z:545–549].

When people first encounter Zen, they try hard to "think about" it, and to imagine what it is. Prajna's insight-wisdom is not a thought. Nor can you imagine it. However, it is possible to arrive at several conceptualizations "about" Zen. One of mine is that Zen is an ancient way to celebrate the lightning strike of creative intuition. Another concept reflects the effortless way prajna bypasses tortuous detours of formal analysis. This unique quality of insight-wisdom suggests that massive parallel processing systems have snapped into a novel configuration.

The early Indian Buddhists were well aware that this level of mental illumination had a "flashing" quality. Their *Diamond Sutra* was among the many that Kumarajiva (C.E. 344–413) went on to translate later into Chinese. While its verses do note prajna's lightning-like *quality,* they also present five other attributes in the form of airy similes. Could you guess what prajna is from these furtive images? They suggest prajna is *like* a "dream," an "illusion," a "bubble," a "shadow," and a "dewdrop."[1] Mystifications are a legacy from that cultural era. They were not intended to answer the question.

What *is* this special kind of wisdom? In Chinese cultural traditions, various ideograms for prajna began to suggest that it could imply the arrival of wisdom, a clear mind, the capacity for acute perception and flexibility.[2] Later, during the

Tang dynasty in China, the Hosso school of Mahayana Buddhism came to grips with four of its more basic attributes.[3]

1. The "great perfect mirror wisdom." It reflects—as does a clear mirror—all phenomenal things as they really are.
2. The wisdom that observes the ultimate, nondual, equality of all things.
3. The wisdom which discerns that all phenomenal things have distinctive individual features.
4. The wisdom intrinsic to all perceptions which enables them to become agencies of creative transformation.

Today, we might be just a little more specific about this last attribute, because there came to exist another apt Buddhist metaphor for prajna. It pointed to the dynamic basis for prajna's transforming property. Its symbol is a sword. This sword cut of insight-wisdom severs the egocentric roots of the person's deluded attachments. The Japanese have another phrase, *hannya no chika*. It translates as "the wisdom-fire of prajna that destroys delusions."

Can different ancient Sino-Japanese ideograms, when translated into contemporary English, help us define the qualities of other phenomena in states of consciousness that might seem indescribable?

81

Words for the Inexpressible

> Whenever ideas fail, men invent words.
>
> Martin Fischer (1879–1962)

> A word is needed to call forth a concept; a concept is necessary to portray a phenomenon. All three mirror one and the same reality.
>
> Antoine Lavoisier (1743–1794)

When William James drew up a short list of the characteristics of a religious/mystical experience, he placed ineffability first. Next came its noetic quality, transiency, and passivity. We can understand James's thesis. No words can *fully* express the inexpressible (the ineffable). Notwithstanding, old phrases from Asian cultures do shed light on the elusive qualities of kensho-satori.

The evidence is provisional, because words and idiomatic phrases evolve in the course of passing from one culture to the next. Countless Buddhist constructs passed from Sanskrit and Pali to Sino-Japanese over the course of many centuries before they were then translated into English. Ideograms compound the problem.

This narrative begins with the term *kensho,* the word we have used to represent the initial experiences of insight-wisdom. *Kensho* is derived from the Chinese *chien-hsing*. It means seeing into one's true nature. *Ken* is "seeing into something"; *sho* is "one's true nature."

Simple so far. But suppose you pursue other options for kensho in standard dictionaries. Then it gets confusing. Kenkyusha's *New Japanese English Dictionary* (4th edition, 1974) lists eight different definitions of the word *kensho*. (One of the nouns is "manifestation." Another is an "on-the-spot verification." Fortunately, their ideograms do differ.)

On the Trail of Satori

With respect to the word *satori,* this same standard dictionary begins to clarify the situation. Here one finds *satoru* (the verb) meaning "to realize," "to awaken to," to "comprehend," "to be spiritually enlightened." *Satori* (the noun) means "comprehension," "spiritual awakening," "enlightenment," "realization." This ideogram is the one kanji most often used to signify satori in both its verb and noun forms:

Perhaps a dictionary limited to Japanese-*Buddhist* terms would present fewer complications.[1] Here, we find *kensho-godo* defined as "seeing one's true nature and realizing the Buddhist Way." (However, among its four characters, the third is the very same ideogram as that already used to represent satori, as pictured above.)

But we are searching for English words that help to clarify the actual *form and content* of kensho-satori. So we now turn to a collection of old Zen sayings.[2] Here we find that Shigematsu has not only translated centuries-old classical Chinese sayings from Japanese into English but also provided their original ideograms.

Focusing on four ideograms that he translated as "satori," we find hints about its form and content:

1. *Shinyo*: true thusness; true unchanging reality
2. *Mushonin*: insight into the immutable reality of all existences
3. *Bodai*: Buddha nature; the intrinsic nature of all things
4. *Ryo*: total comprehension

A Phrase for the Inexpressible

But another phrase, *gongo dodan*, is noteworthy. Why? Because it refers to the inexpressible in a very interesting manner. Its literal meaning is *"the path of words has been cut."* As a descriptive phrase, it points toward a distinct "soft" insight, one that had entered kensho early in Reflections III (see table 11, chapter 95). Its message was clear: *there is no way to convey this* totally new understanding, this view of things as they *really are*.

You might ask: Why wasn't this "realization" just the same as any of your ordinary kinds of thought-filled ideas? First, it welled up spontaneously. It penetrated with none of the sense of mental "friction" as does an ordinary thought. Second, it "felt" like the earlier, deeper insights. Third, it arrived in a particular context, around the same time when there entered the first hint of a re-emergent, diminutive "i."

Much later, in retrospect, it would seem that this first soft realization of ineffability was a message arising from levels in the brain somewhere between those of an intuition and of a deeper insight. Perhaps its soft message was the only insightful commentary that diminutive "i" functions could make at that particular instant.[3]

More Useful Descriptions of the Other Qualities of Kensho-Satori

Over the centuries, different Buddhist schools have since found ways to articulate major qualities of kensho-satori. In their old Sino-Japanese phrases we can discover concepts like eternity, suchness, nonduality, liberation, and so on. When translated, the following words and short phrases can still help puzzled readers who may wonder what is so *special* about this state of insight-wisdom[4] [Z:542–544].

- *Bussho joju*: the eternal presence of Buddha Nature.
- *Byodo muni no chie*: the wisdom of realizing absolute, nondual reality.
- *Fusho fumetsu*: neither arising nor perishing. The ultimate reality of things is a static quality.
- *Gedatsu*: liberation, emancipation; freedom from all bonds.
- *Genryo mu funbetsu*: direct perception; no discriminating thoughts.
- *Hogen*: the so-called dharma eye—that aspect of insight-wisdom which sees deeply into the reality of things.
- *Honpusho*: originally not produced. In the inactivity of ultimate reality, nothing comes into existence and nothing disappears.

- *Muga*: nonself; egolessness.
- *Mui jinen*: the as-it-isness of absolute reality; things as they *really* are, beyond all change (*mui* is discussed in the next paragraph).
- *Shinyo*: true suchness; unchanging reality.
- *Taige*: deep understanding with the body.

* * *

Wu-wei and Its Relation to Satori

Mui receives a more detailed interpretation in Wood's *Zen Dictionary*.[5] Here we find the Japanese word *mui*, as one that could be associated with the Chinese term *Wu-wei*. Wu-wei usually implies nonaction or selfless action [Z:607–608]. In China, *wu* also came to imply the sudden enlightenment of satori. "Wu was identified with satori," Wood explains, in the particular sense "that when ... satori comes there is in it no action—not even the action of thought." In this centuries-old usage, satori evolved into an adjectival noun. It came to represent the distinctive experience that is *wu*, a state that was devoid of all form and action.

I could resonate with these interpretations for three reasons. This quality of stasis, this sense of nonaction, and this subtle impression of noninterference had all entered during the taste of kensho. *Wu*, a word that had originated in China as an old Taoist term, still carries the "implication that one is talking about the *Samyak sambuddhi* (real experience) or the Tao."

The many old words unearthed in this chapter were coined by those who were seeking to articulate the inexpressible. It seems fitting to close by citing this counsel from Shigematsu.

> A word is a finger that points at the moon. The goal of Zen students is the moon itself; not the pointing finger. Zen Masters, therefore, will never stop cursing words and letters.[6]

We who can only write "about" Zen are trying to practice a difficult art: finding which words to use and when to let them go.

82

Suchness and the Noumenon: An Allocentric Perspective

> I hold suchness to be the basis of all religious experience.
>
> D. T. Suzuki (1870–1966)[1]

If *suchness* were "the basis of all religious experience," then why doesn't everyone know what "suchness" means? The problem, as Suzuki noted, is that it must be experienced. Suchness "defies a clear-cut definition." It gets "lost" when you present it as an idea. "Strictly speaking ... any philosophy built on it will be a castle on the sand." So suchness begins beyond reach of our ordinary discursive intellect. It is a profound experience of realization, not some thought that you can conceive from the armchair.

His namesake, Zen master Shunryu Suzuki (1905–1971), once said that the true purpose of Zen "is to see things as they are."[2] But even if insight-wisdom illuminates such "seeing," how can it serve to enhance the basis of all religions? Could it be by "elevating" religions to the same status as everything else in the universe—that is, both matter-of-fact *and* sacred?

Shunryu Suzuki also had these profound words to say about selfless awareness: "Not to be attached to something is to be aware of its absolute value." Let us take this last sentence as a major theme throughout this chapter. For when does a human brain deeply comprehend those values it holds to be "absolute?" When it finally sees them from an *un*attached, selfless perspective.

As D. T. Suzuki explained, Asian languages had pointed toward suchness for countless centuries. The Japanese used *sono-mama*. The Chinese employed *chi-mo* or *chih che shih*. Much earlier, the Sanskrit term *tatatha* had become a core notion of Mayayana Buddhism. The word referred to the absolute Buddha nature of all things in the universe.[3]

Of course, a word like "suchness" soon becomes wielded as though it were only an abstract concept. Even so, its original "Buddha-nature" usage still points toward some kind of ultimate principle that human minds imagine must lie beyond all categorical distinctions. Hence, when used in this manner, "suchness" continued to suggest some basic reality residing behind and beyond the mere appearances of all things (and concepts) which are only temporary phenomena.

Gradually, a more explicit phrase entered common English usage: "seeing all things as they really are." In this chapter I will use italics to illustrate that each word in this phrase conveys subtleties of meaning. Together, they point to the profound qualities of the insights in kensho and satori that realize the *timeless, immanent, interrelated nature of all things*.

Let us suppose that you had never heard of Zen, and then you happened to undergo this major "peak experience" spontaneously. Would these insights of suchness themselves change simply because you once happened to have read what Immanuel Kant had written over two centuries before in his momentous *Critique of Pure Reason*?[4]

No, *they* would not. But after 1781, a thicket of logical constructs became available in the West that would turn out to have great heuristic value. For these constructs set up this seemingly impenetrable epistemological barrier: sharp limits constrain what you and I can *know* about the "real" world. Indeed, Kant claimed that we can truly know things *only* as they appear to our senses, as *phenomena*. But to us, he asserted, that other world of the thing-in-itself—the *noumenon*—will remain forever unknowable.

As Kant (1724–1804) explained: "The concept of a noumenon implies a thing that is not to be thought of as an object of the senses but rather as a thing in itself (solely through pure understanding)." And he then regarded this *Ding an sich* as "merely a boundary concept in order to limit the pretension of sensibility, and therefore only of negative use."[5]

Had Kant himself ever deeply experienced suchness during some unrecorded "peak" state of consciousness? Even sympathetic biographers advance no conclusive proof of this.[6] We may wonder: If Kant had truly experienced suchness before 1781, would he then have gone on to write the following unqualified assertion?

> It remains completely unknown to us what may be the nature of objects in themselves and apart from the receptivity of our senses. We know nothing except our own way of perceiving them, a way peculiar to us, and which does not necessarily pertain to every being, though it surely pertains to every human being.[7]

Each negation in these two sentences above rests on hidden subjective premises. They also exclude certain contingencies. Note that his first sentence ends with the possessive, "*our* senses." And that his second sentence also contains another possessive, "*our own* way of perceiving." Both statements assume that our ordinary ego-self is attached to what it knows and perceives. Both further assume that the *ordinary* self's claim to "owning" this attachment remains unbroken throughout time.

Yet, what if every ordinary possessive sense of "our" suddenly dropped out? What if "time" dissolved into eternity? Because *two* things vanish during *extra*ordinary "peak experiences": both the personal sense of "self" *and* time's cause-and-effect relationships.

Moreover, mystics would always doubt that initial Kantian assertion: "completely unknown" (*ganzlich unbekannt*). *Completely*? Even German contemporaries found this dogmatic stance too absolutist. "Kant's acceptance of the distinction between phenomena and things-in-themselves ... met with much criticism."[8] Kant's every ambiguity and inconsistency stimulated successive generations of philosophers to react, each in accord with its own ethos. It was a fertile notion indeed that some absolute iron curtain must split phenomena from noumena.

Schopenhauer (1788–1860) accused Kant of logical inconsistencies. He argued that no person could make any valid inference about the existence of things-in-themselves using phenomenal data while simultaneously defining such data as "things" that were not capable of being expressed.[9] Yet he and various phenomenologists would also be stimulated to construct semantically formidable interpretations of their own.[10]

Soon the radical empiricists would try to undermine the entire notion of any "boundary concept." Using more flexible criteria, pragmatist doctrines could be interpreted to suggest another conclusion: we could test the validity of a "truth" by its consequences. This utilitarian definition emphasized what each of us could learn through direct *living experience* and observation. We did not need to refer to idealized thought systems based on logically structured, wordy abstractions.

Neurophysiological issues began to surface. Bedside studies of neurological patients were being correlated with laboratory research in the neurosciences. To oversimplify one possible question: Could the brain of even a mental giant like Kant wield constructs in some artificial ways that could "completely" split, into two categories, our brain's normal, dynamic integrative functions? For these newer correlated research findings were lending support to at least four kinds of hierarchical generalizations:

(1) Our brain functions are widely distributed. (2) Even so, it is the associative fluency of regions in its more "executive" front part that sponsors and monitors our more insightful intuitive functions, whereas (3) our mostly "receptive, sensate" functions are being identified with our brain's back part. (4) Notwithstanding, many subcortical systems (e.g., limbic, thalamic, and brainstem) play early, decisive roles. These deeper regions do more than help generate our core of basic awareness; their networks also infuse emotional qualities and degrees of salience into all that we think and perceive.

Seemingly in line with such hierarchies of brain function, the Zen master Thich Nhat Hanh recently presented a further definition of noumenon. He described noumenon in terms of something "that can be intuited only by direct knowledge (intuition) and not perceived by the senses."[11]

So what about that old logic-tight construct of 1781, the noumenon? In practice, weren't its original premises becoming undermined? Hadn't those rigid Kantian architectonics (with which he tried to reject Locke's and Hume's ideas) erected only an *artificial* barrier to our "pretensions of sensibility?" And—by the way—didn't Thich Nhat Hanh's recent definition of noumenon sound rather similar to D. T. Suzuki's views about suchness?

How Crucial to This Issue Is the Brief Loss of Self during the Extraordinary State of Awakening?

Zen Buddhist traditions emphasize a key point: one's personal sense of self dissolves during kensho and satori. And yet, during this state of deep enlightenment, a keenly witnessing core of awareness persists, even though it lacks every egocentric trace of its old, possessive *I-Me-Mine*.

Table 9
Relationships among the Terms *Mundane, Suchness,* and *Noumenon*

Ordinary Experience	*Extraordinary States of Insight-Wisdom*	*?An Ontological* Unknown of Some Kind*
A term: *Mundane*	A term: *Suchness*	A term: *Noumenon*
Impression: "This is real"	Impression: "This is *really* real!"	Issue: Are we "really" certain this speculation is "really" valid?
A self-*referent* "working reality"	A self*less* "enhanced reality"	The question posed relates to whether there exists a domain of "Absolute Reality"
Lesser infusions of salience mark noteworthy events	Major infusions of salience emphasize rare, but memorable episodes	A speculative construct, as abstract as are concepts of "heaven" or "utopia"
Private, personal; having a subjective quality	Impersonal; having an objective quality	Personal and cultural belief systems vary

* Relating to metaphysical theories about the nature of being or existence.

This "awareness anonymous" is extraordinary. No conventional word adequately encompasses all of its qualities. I have found it useful to resort to the word *experiant* to refer to this "totally objective spectator in absentia."* Experiant suggests one astonishing fact: "experiences" do occur in this state, but they have a novel objective flavor. What lies at the core of this objective quality? An unimaginable fact: this unique awareness retains no personal subjectivities (see chapter 10). It is unattached, selfless, bodyless, completely *impersonal.*

Moreover, this state has dropped off not only our familiar surface "needs" and anxieties, such as those we normally access using conscious introspection. Its awareness has also become profoundly detached—as Shunryu Suzuki knew—from our *un*conscious longings and loathings. Because this awareness lacks our deepest covert visceral emotions, it covets nothing, dreads nothing.

In kensho, prajna's brief "flash" of insightful awakening simplifies multiple existential complexities. Yet, afterward, other contentious issues and questions may arise among both experiants and uninitiates: What constitutes ordinary "reality?" Are we really sure our concepts are correct when we think that other "realities" must lie beyond it? Table 9 represents an oversimplification.

By way of explanation, let the left column represent our familiar mundane terrain. In the middle column are states of consciousness that are uncommon. The column on the right reflects speculative thought processes. However, the concepts in this last category, both personal and cultural, might still be thought about in a relatively open, less artificial manner, especially by some persons *after* they

*In these pages, the variant spelling of "experiant," with an *a*, serves to suggest that some compartments within consciousness still go on experiencing, even though the ordinary foundations of selfhood are *a*bsent (empty) of all self-referent attachments.

had undergone a selfless "peak experience." Accordingly, open spaces between the three columns are in keeping with potential openings between the three categories.

The Sequence of Reflections after Kensho

Kensho is a momentary state. It starts abruptly, peaks, has a diminuendo, then sponsors various thoughtful probings after the fact. During kensho's earliest phases, no paradox is evident. No single sensation could convey its direct, global impression of "Reality" (nor is the scene being hallucinated). "Reality" is itself being *realized*. However, this insightful process is not your usual kind of "realization." Rather it reflects much deeper levels of reading between the lines than you ever experience during your shallower intuitions.

Instead, several aspects of kensho are more reminiscent of how you respond after you have been a student in an advanced art appreciation course. Later, when you stand in front of an old painting in a museum, you discover your new capacity to *see into* it. Now, seen afresh, various details in the painting as a whole reveal novel comprehensibilities.

Kensho's rare qualities go beyond this. Notably, each such grasp of large interrelationships impacts directly, immediately, wordlessly. Moreover, it infuses authoritative degrees and kinds of salience. These infusions "validate" and reinforce the deep impression made by each new understanding as it flashes in to "illuminate" the mental field.

While still *inside* kensho, the weighty imprimatur of salience helps verify the authenticity of the insights. But what about later? Would such a sense of conviction endure permanently? Say that someone's training and experience—*prior* to kensho—had been that of a hard-nosed neurologist, psychologist, or psychiatrist. Could this person ignore the likelihood that the episode had been but an extraordinarily powerful illusion? [Z:290].

During kensho itself (and during its transient reflections for several days thereafter), this neurologist regarded its total perspective as a genuine glimpse into the immanent perfection investing *everyday things as they really are*. In this manner had "nirvana" and samsara appeared to constitute "One Reality" (see figure 11, chapter 77). Nothing within this brief glimpse of "oneness" had suggested that such an identity had supernatural origins, or that it was artifactual.

Later that week, my views began to evolve. They continued to change during the following months while I read about various extraordinary states and uncovered new scientific facts. As I then analyzed some of the forms with which such events had impressed themselves on other persons, the evidence was also consistent with the impress of a most powerful illusion. At first, how could I resolve the issue? It was a simple matter. I could adopt a new context for my using the term "illusion."

Because what was the *basic* illusion? Kensho's insights had laid it bare. The *basic* illusion was my former, entirely self-referent way of looking intrusively at the world. In sharp contrast was that brief, penetrating view of the world through the open eyes of kensho. *This* was, so it seemed, the more accurate perception. More *Real*. Maybe it wasn't as perfect as it appeared to be. But on balance, it was not as gross a *mis*perception as my previous egocentric perception had been.

Did this evolving viewpoint seem to contradict the core of my professional beliefs? No. Was it in conflict with the central premise of my 1998 book? No. The kensho episode and the author-neurologist remained seamless aspects within the expanded experience of the very same person. The two perspectives seemed to be reconciled (as Maslow had once observed) within a kind of "single complex supraordinate unity" [Z:642]. I could be of two minds, as it were, with relative ease, "hedging my bets," untroubled by whatever misperceptions might be represented within either mundane "reality" or the "Reality" of suchness.

"Reality" and "reality"

Countless generations have speculated about what "Reality" might *really* be. And the questioning may intensify after a person emerges from kensho-satori: Does some kind of "Absolute Reality" exist? Or do these two words represent one more imaginary belief system that has been culturally transmitted? No ontological, epistemological, or neurological wordplay settles such questions. The pragmatic point remains: Major "peak experiences" can have salutary effects on the physiology of the brain. They can transform the person's later attitudes and behavior in society, because their deep impressions leave enduring memory traces.

It is noteworthy that Immanuel Kant, in his subsequent writings, would later soften, with more positive resonances, the impenetrably "negative" implications that he cast with his 1781 doctrine of the noumenon.[12] Once again he would be led to suggest that, *in practice*, our innate morality and "free will" were expressions of our behaving *as if* our systems of ethical belief were true. Still, in print, he would regard such constructs as unknowable and unprovable.[13]

Toward the Nature and Origins of Salience

This practical issue—how we each behave as responsible individuals within society—is of immense importance. We need to reach a better understanding of how each of our brains comes to "realize" what is its actual "ground" of "reality." With few exceptions, the neurosciences have not yet placed high on their agenda this vital need to clarify how human beings authenticate reality, either their seemingly "Absolute" notions about "Reality" or their ordinary levels of "working reality."

The issue goes far beyond those snap conclusions we reach because our pattern recognition functions close quickly on some incoming sensory data. It is the much subtler mechanisms that we must seek out and identify, the ones which infuse the deeper kinds of meaning that will reshape our everyday lives.

Daily, these brain mechanisms introduce nuances and differing magnitudes of significance that greatly reinforce our ordinary impressions. But once we invest certain events with special symbolic overtones, we can feel them resonate with enduring affirmative values. When we then lean forward and move to actualize such positive values, the practical results can become more fruitful for society in general. No longer must our actions remain limited to small individual responses that ring "true" only within our local, private working reality [Z:600].

Peak experiences are useful models to study. They call attention to a particular set of resonances that greatly enhance our sense of reality. The term "salience" can serve to categorize their meaningful perceptual attributes (see chapter 45; table 9, this chapter). When several distinctive properties resonate harmoniously in unison, they enhance meaning by imbuing it with significant import. At a minimum, these reality-enhancing properties of salience include a sense of memorable portent, a *direct* impression of coexisting within a universe of perfection free from affective dissonances, and an impression of certainty so profound that it tends to authenticate the presence of an ultimate "Truth."

Existing research suggests that the impress of salience could spring from several interacting hierarchical systems. For example, its deeper origins could include, again at a bare minimum, parts of the limbic system that, having been integrated with the posterior thalamus, go on to influence thalamocortical perceptual functions.[14]

Suchness Revisited

The foregoing discussion, and table 9, may help us reexamine the ancient topic of suchness from fresh perspectives. One of these approaches reflects the reductionist perspectives within neuropsychology. From this direction, researchers would be seeking precisely timed physiological and chemical data. They would hope their results might identify each of the several components of suchness that create its implicit "sense" of "reality."

But first let us reaffirm what kensho's suchness also implies. When kensho emphasizes "things as *THEY* really are," why does *THEY* stand out in the foreground? Because selfhood has dropped out of the mental field, and all of its "own" attachments to things have vanished.

A second approach to understanding suchness points us off in the direction of ontology (see the column on the right side of table 9). Christian Wolff (1679–1754) was an early contemporary of Kant. He introduced the term *ontology* into Western philosophy, using it to designate a field of speculative thought. *Ontology*, if we accept one of several representative definitions, is "a branch of metaphysics that deals with reality itself, as apart from the subjective impressions and thoughts of the person who experiences it."[15] (Logicians could object, on the grounds that Wolff could hardly have been "apart" from *his* concept.)

Let us recognize that words are linguistic concepts derived from human brains. Do we, *must* we, accord such concepts rigid boundaries? If so, then such quasi-barriers are fragile creatures imposed by our own imagination. A word like "ontology" remains vulnerable not only to the lesser indentations of mere thought but also to the spontaneous penetrations of major insights.

The questions being asked, then, are these: During kensho, can someone's brain take even the *first tentative step* toward comprehending the essential nature of "objects in themselves?" If so, what is this first step? Experiants feel certain their glimpse is authentic. Could *any small part* of this impression be genuine? Is there, as it were, some "porous interface" between the ways we humans interpret two words—suchness, as invoked by D. T. Suzuki; the noumenon, as imposed by Kant during his formal effort to limit our pretentions?

Let us inquire first: What kind of evidence might support the proposal that kensho's "peak" state of consciousness could provide at least a *partial* glimpse into some incredible domain that was previously "unknown?" This pivotal decision hinges on an elementary yes-or-no interpretation: Has such a "first step" revealed a certain kind of extraordinary new perspective? Even if the answer is yes, then this decision does not mean anything esoteric. It would imply *only* one thing: the "Big Picture" *is* capable of being perceived more accurately. Why? Because the person's previous self-referent veils and overconditioned barriers of thought no longer hide from view the true nature of such an inconceivable world (see chapter 10). Not that this world is being perfectly perceived, or universally comprehended. Just that it is perceived *a little more accurately* now that it is being seen in its unveiled state.

Suchness and the Noumenon

To help clarify the relationship—if any—between suchness and the noumenon, let us first employ some language that might be used at the levels of descriptive psychology. Next, a second perspective will be presented. It will draw on the data from psychophysiological research which distinguishes between our egocentric and allocentric forms of consciousness.

Each of these two perspectives—first, the psychological and then the psychophysiological—will voice admittedly personal opinions. Even so, the reader will find assembled a series of stilted sentences that do point toward the same tentative endpoint: a yes-or-no answer. A yes answer to the questions asked three paragraphs above might do more than help reconcile the statements of D. T. and Shunryu Suzuki with those of Kant. It might also begin to reconcile, at some practical supraordinate level comfortable to Maslow, the unresolvable dichotomies created by our own fixed ways of thinking.

1. *Descriptions in psychological terminology.* Kensho suddenly releases a brain from its previous overconditioning. Egocentric filters have dropped out of the picture. With the thick veils of self cast aside, consciousness now functions in an extraordinarily clear, impersonal mode. Gone are all those old intrusions of the *Mine* into every scene. Gone with it are those limiting constructs implicit in Kant's possessive phrases: "the receptivity of *our* senses," and "*our own* way of perceiving." Yes, an apple still registers as an apple. But now it registers with full awareness of *ITS* "absolute value," free from all subjective hungering.
2. *Descriptions in psychophysiological terminology.* It helps first to review the basis for the ego-/allo-distinctions we introduced earlier (see chapters 29 and 75). In brief, recent primate research shows that the two terms describe two fundamentally different ways that our normal brain is poised to process sensory data that are about to enter from the outside world.
    a. Emerging out of one of them—the brain's *egocentric* system—are constructs that are implicitly *self*-referent. In a monkey, how does this system process an external fruit like an apple? Registering the apple's coordinates, it uses lines of sight that relate the apple's visual percepts with reference to the head, eyes, and body of this observing monkey [Z:491].

        Similar "wiring" patterns are available early in the brain of a human infant. With these coordinates we have established our own self-centered *physical* axis. On this firm primal physiological basis we could soon go on to elaborate our own intricate *psychic* constructs of self. Before long, any apple seen also became *mine* to covet, grab, eat, hide ...

        Note how that original apple had been "lost" in the subsequent, elaborate synaptic shuffle.
    b. By contrast, the second network system is called *allocentric.* Its central pathways are coded to represent only a simpler, *selfless*, totally objective view. These circuits will first register an apple just as an "event." It is a round red thing in space "out there." Ordinarily, these two different systems work together, adding to the ways we establish such opposing pairs of concepts as self/other, this/that, subject/object, and so on.

With reference to these terms, what happens during kensho? Major deep physiological shifts occur. They seem capable of releasing the human brain into its freestanding *allocentric* mode. Allocentric networks have been liberated from the tight grasp of the old egocentric self. Now they appear to register within consciousness just that sense of "things" as *THEY are* out there.

It's not that simple. Could a shift that simply leaves out our egocentric frame of reference alone account for so novel a landscape and for so unique a state of consciousness? Can the usual allocentric frame of reference *in itself* explain how a state can instantly leave the impression that *all* items, in their detailed particulars, not only exist *"as they really are"* but are also integrated into a unified context that is vastly more meaningful?[16]

Not likely. For note what also happens: Within that vast field, it is deeply understood that all individual items and diverse events belong to the *same extended family*. They coinhabit the same dynamic Universe, in perpetuity. Interrelationships of this nature, impressive in their perfection of suchness, would seem to require both extra layers *and* magnitudes of the salient infusions discussed above.

Even so, for our brain to comprehend such universal meanings, so deeply affirmative in tone, would seem equivalent to taking that one small tentative step which is the issue under discussion. A step toward what? Toward that special kind of "awareness of absolute values," that seeing "things as they are," to which Shunryu Suzuki had referred.[17]

It remains for psychobiographers to ponder some covert historical issues: Had Kant's insightful brain ever penetrated partially (far beyond the great intricate thoughts of his ordinary "working reality") into his own *unbekannt*? Do we really know why his own early handwritten short lists could reduce all his a priori categories into these few prescient concepts: magnitude, reality, subject, ground, and parts in their interrelationships with the whole?[18]

At this distance at least, it would still seem possible that some of Kant's many to-and-fro evolutions of thought, evidenced throughout his lifelong writings, might reflect his introspective, ongoing attempts at *self*-critiques, his own private mindfully reflective quests to arrive at more advanced degrees of his own "pure understanding."

Meanwhile, in this new millennium, the rest of us have newer conceptual options. We can choose to regard prajna's first flashing insights within suchness as the perennial expressions of a human brain's basic physiological functions, not just as some layers of cultural add-ons imposed by the conditionings inherited from past centuries. Our generations need not believe that seemingly thick barriers of word-thoughts, however raised, can permanently curtain off the flashing illuminations cast by these first impressions of "Reality" and of "Immanent Perfection." For such prelinguistic messages arise selflessly, spontaneously, in *unconditioned* form. The natural truths that emerge are part of everyone's ancient, universal biological heritage.

83

The Construction of Time

> The now, the here, through which all future plunges to the past.
>
> James Joyce (1882–1941), *Ulysses*

Our Personal Sense of Time

Past ... here and now ... future. Our way of dividing time into three segments seems sound. Yet personal time is an abstraction, an elastic chronology that humans insert into an otherwise impersonal universe. On a 24-hour equivalent of the galactic time clock, it has been only during the past few seconds that human brains on planet Earth have tried to define what else "time" might be. Before that, no word label tried to represent this whole ageless Universal Reality (as far as we now know). It was here, only recently, that hominid cultures ventured to imagine what such a cosmic "Oneness" might be. Not until earthlings evolved a symbolic language would an inclusive Yahweh-God-Tao-Buddha nature have seemed anything other than nameless and undifferentiated.

We have come a long way. We now believe not only in a cosmos of near-infinite space (13 billion light years is a long way out there). We sense that it might stretch toward a fundamental perpetuity, an eternity if you will, beyond that currently observable edge. Nevertheless, at birth, each of our brains began to compound its own personal version of time. These private notions hinge on more than our estimations of intervals between events. As James Joyce hinted, each "now" of private "time" also involves our making implicit *spatial* associations with items that are already *here*. We relate those spatial coordinates of apples and other things out "there" in space back "here" toward our own self-referent body image in the center.

We don't have to search very far for examples of Joyce's other word, "now." Two common phenomena illustrate how our present *now* is but a fleeting moment, poised betwixt an imaginary future and a swiftly vanishing past.

The Temporal Lobe: Déjà Vu and Jamais Vu

It is normal to experience illusions of *déjà vu* (see chapter 42). What we see "now" seems so familiar that we conclude: "Yes, I've already seen this before." Ordinary déjà vu episodes are eloquent whispers, conveying a twofold message:

- Our brain does have circuits that help us respond to the nuances between an event in our present time and incidents in past time.

- Many potential instabilities reside within the medial temporal lobe. Just a minor cerebral event—a little loss of sleep, a fever, a predisposition to migraine—can break down that fragile barrier which had once walled off a previous incident inside its "earlier" memory compartment, and had stopped it from being linked with the immediate events of this present moment.

My temporal lobe used to be vulnerable to loss of sleep. Sleep loss unveiled its low threshold for déjà vu episodes. However, déjà vu experiences can also occur in patients whose focal seizures start in the medial temporal lobe. Moreover, stimulating the amygdala or hippocampus also prompts them. Sites over the outer temporal cortex are less productive.[1]

The "positive" (yes, I remember) resonances of déjà vu have a "negative" counterpart. This contrasting visual experience is termed *jamais vu*. Its literal meaning is "No, I've never seen this before." fMRI studies are still trying to untangle how we decide which events are familiar and which are not.[2]

Many of these complexities reside among the personal circuits of the omniself. Why? Because when we tag an event in time, we register more than the here-and-now details of its exterior context. We also inject *our own* interior premise: how *we* felt about where *we* were when it happened. So, into that Joycean here-and-now of an event, each implicit self-referent observer inserts his or her own particular autobiographical frame of reference. Early PET scan studies began to localize some modules of this personal omniself more within the right temporal lobe [Z:247–253].

Recent neuropsychological research also suggests that the right temporal lobe contributes long-term representations that help us estimate time.[3] All 18 patients in this study had previous surgical removal of their anterior and medial temporal lobes. Their task was to reproduce, spontaneously, various durations of time. The nine patients who had *right* temporal lobe resections *under*estimated the longer time durations (of 5, 14, and 38 seconds). In contrast, other data suggested that it was the *left* temporal lobe that would normally be processing the more instantaneous time perceptions (in the range between only 10 and 100 *milli*seconds). Millisecond durations are crucial when we process language and music.

The Parietal Lobe and Our Sense of Time

Time is a "judgment call." Several other regions of our brain help us distinguish "newer" events from "older" events. Recent fMRI studies suggest that the superior parietal lobule is also one region that helps us categorize some events as newer and others as older.[4] In contrast, the temporoparietal junction and the right intraparietal sulcus become involved when we first detect salient new items to which we are prepared to respond.

Single nerve cells in the monkey's inferior parietal association cortex often respond to more than one kind of stimulus.[5] These *multimodal* properties could help the monkey brain represent details of items in the environment *both in space and time simultaneously*. In trained monkeys, these nerve cells develop firing patterns that correlate with the monkeys' attempts to judge *elapsed* time. Indeed, the remarkable ways this parietal association cortex contributes to primate behavior led one reviewer to conclude that "any magnitude, be it a distance in space, time, or a quantity to be judged" would be grist for the mill of its spatial and motor transformations.[6]

Frontal Lobe Contributions to the Ways We Normally Sequence Recent Events

Both our working memory and our memory for episodic events also help us to judge time.[7] When we engage our frontal lobes in estimating time sequences they almost seem to be referring back to what is in a sense a kind of "internal clock."

For example, normal subjects have first been monitored by fMRI while they process the way items are sequenced within one list, and later while they compare the sequences of items (back and forth) between two different lists.[8] In general, both their right and left prefrontal activities support such different complex memory tasks. However, sequencing items *within* a list activates their *left* prefrontal lobe more, whereas signals increase more in the right prefrontal lobe when they judge how items are sequenced on the two different lists.

The "Direction" of Time: Frontal and Temporal Lobe Contributions to Past → Present → Future

Time passes all too swiftly. Whether it is milliseconds or decades, time seems to move in one direction. Hence that old term, "the arrow of time."

Physicists may still debate whether the cosmological arrow always agrees with this psychological arrow.[9] Here, however, let us adopt the standard arrow metaphor as a simple model for the issues to be discussed during this and the next chapter. Let us begin with the same kinds of memory functions that enter into the déjà vu/jamais vu decisions described above. Translated into English, the full question to be posed is: "Does this particular event, in this present moment, correspond with some prior instance in (*my*) time past?" Not until we first scan our own memory stores can we answer yes (déjà) or no (jamais).

So let us now return to that now/then interface of our conscious memory. If we follow the visual model of "time's arrow" illustrated above, we soon find ourselves directing our gaze off at an angle toward the *left*. Why? Because the left part of the arrow symbol is intended to represent the *older* historical events in our own retrograde memory. And normally, what small detail distinguishes the very back end of an arrow?

The arrow's notch. So let this notch serve as the farthest back in time any of us still retain our oldest childhood memories. From that remote horizon of our personal time on the far left, one could envision a chronology of new incidents. Each would occupy its own position on the timeline of our normal viewing. This succession of events would extend farther along the arrow shaft to the right, toward the ever-advancing edge of each new present moment. In animals, some of the earlier and simpler operations that enter into these kinds of ordering and sequencing appear to involve the temporal lobe's hippocampal formation.[10]

We are poised, next, to invoke human frontal lobe functions of the kinds just cited above. Can this arrow metaphor illustrate how the frontal lobes enable us to make special *recency* decisions involving time sequences? [Z:557–560]. What makes such recency judgments special? Suppose you needed to test your own skills at recency judgments. This is how you might proceed. Imagine that a long arrow is released gently, starting way off to your *left*. It flies slowly through that space in front of your usual 3-second "window of now," and then vanishes from sight off to your far *right*.

How would you respond if someone were now to ask you: "Which three parts of that arrow did you see last, most *recently*?" This isn't easy. You might have to change your mental set. For your task is to assign top priority to "most recently" (last seen), not to "earliest" (first seen).

Therefore, your correct responses would begin at that *back* end of time's arrow. They would unfold in the following sequence: notch, most recently (you've got sharp eyesight); feathers, recently; rest of shaft, earlier, and so on. Recency judgments are challenging. One must file each fresh detail not only into its correct position along some timeline but also make quick mental shifts into an overview mode. The frontal lobes specialize in this kind of working memory task.

Notice, in this imaginary arrow analogy, how recency ("time") decisions often equate subtly with spatial, distance decisions. In such instances, your frontal lobes must now enter into more complex supraordinate mental operations than had sufficed for those simpler hunches about then/now that were discussed at first. Nor can the rest of the brain be overlooked, because keen visual perceptions and fine attentive focusing are required to detect a small detail like an arrow's "notch" in flight!

Areas deep to the frontal lobe also help establish our autobiographical timeline. In one recent study, the patients were all asked to lay out a year-by-year and decade-by-decade timeline of events. Their task resembled that in the board game called Life.[11] The patients in one group had sustained prior damage to the basal parts of their forebrain. Even though they could recall various events, both personal and public, their particular *dates* for these events were far off the mark—off by an average of some 5.2 years. The patients in the other group had temporal lobe damage. They could not recall events as accurately, but their dates were off by only 2.9 years. In contrast, the normal subjects were reasonably accurate. There is hope for us in this fact: the normals mistimed their chronologies by only 1.9 years. The data also suggested that when we later recall an event, we use memory processes different from those we had used initially when we registered this event and then encoded it in "time."

Hospitalized patients whose strokes recently damaged their right hemisphere have the most problems accurately estimating the correct time ("clock time"). They are also more prone to overestimate the passage of time and to guess that it was later in the day.[12]

An earlier PET study of normal subjects had also suggested that the circuits we use to lay down memories are different from those we use later to retrieve them. Normals activated their *left* frontal brain regions during the initial encoding, whereas they activated their *right* superior frontal regions during retrieval.[13] The left fusiform region also became activated when the subjects first encoded information about time. On the other hand, when they later retrieved items related to time, they activated their anterior cingulate cortex.

Frontal Lobe Contributions to Action Scenarios, with Special Reference to Our Subconscious "Doing-Time"

Now we are getting to the point, and to whatever might lie beyond. Because it is our frontal lobes that help us project *prospective* scenarios. In so doing, they help to transform our parietal attentive functions into *intention*. The frontal lobe's potential action scenarios hint at where time's arrowhead might land far off to the right, in that "not-yet" dimension called future time.

Why are this arrow's outlines interrupted as they approach the tip? To suggest that any sense of "future time" is not real. It is still an imaginary realm. Notwithstanding, consider how hard-driven we can be when we make plans for this covert domain. It is a strange arena, one where instinctual urges contend with fearful fantasies, where foresights are not so common, and real insights are rare. But something else about this imaginary realm of the future is instructive, because of what it implies.

Future Time Implies "Doing-Time"

Future time has very practical, hidden applications. The phrase doing-time helps to appreciate these silent, implicit functions. Doing-time sums up some vital operations of a widely distributed personal clock. It reflects the ways our frontal and parietal lobes interact with subcortical striatal and cerebellar motor systems.

For example, during our lifetime, doing-time has made countless incidental notations. What do its files record? *I can do this much in a split second.* My goal is *do*able, actionable. Are we aware of this covert, future-oriented file? No. Not until it surfaces on the curb—survival value personified—instantly informing us: "Dash this fast across the next wide street, or you'll get run over. It's wide, but you can make it if you hurry!"

Few would still be alive today if we hadn't honed our instincts to consult doing-time. And if *all* personal time is to dissolve—as it does in kensho—then these deep circuits of subconscious doing-time will also need to drop out.

This is a tall order.

A Parable of Present Time

All private time comes to an end. In the interim, can we learn to spend "*quality* time" with all that life has to offer?

This is a tale the Buddha told, according to one of the old sutras.[14] Fleeing from a fierce tiger in hot pursuit, a man reached the edge of a precipice. Luckily, he caught hold of the root of a wild vine, and swung himself safely down over the edge. Trembling, he glanced far down to the base of the precipice. There he saw a second tiger also waiting to eat him if he fell. He knew that he was a goner, because two wild mice started gnawing away at the slender vine.

But suddenly he saw a luscious strawberry growing within easy reach. Realizing that the vine would soon part, he reached out with his free hand, picked the fruit, and placed it in his mouth. How sweet, how delicious the taste!

What does the parable mean? Is it useless to eat if you're soon going to die anyway? Or are we being encouraged to pay attention to every present moment, to savor it, no matter what the circumstances might be? Because every minute alive is surely a miracle in itself. The physical form of every physical body—like a wave in the ocean—is certain to disappear sooner or later. Realizing that each and every moment is truly precious, the issue is: Can we live it *fully*, right Now?

84

Disorders and Dissolutions of Time

> Each individual wave of self rises up, according to its own nature, plays for a while, then disappears. I remain the shoreless ocean.
>
> Ashtavakra-Samhita (2nd century B.C.E.)

Disorders of the Sense of Time; Splitting Internal and External Time

The time was January 2004. I sat up straight as soon as I came to that sentence in the article. It said that normal people experience episodes when "time" moves abnormally fast or slow.[1] This report carried me far back to my own childhood. I remembered vividly having such strange time distortions myself.

These episodes occurred only when my fever climbed above 101°F. Then, all events in the *exterior* world proceeded much too slowly, unpleasantly so. Simultaneously, all my *interior* mental processes seemed to be going extra fast. This dissociation of the passage of time seemed to be proceeding in both directions simultaneously. It could last for several hours, waxing and waning. The same distinct symptom complex recurred during some five or six childhood illnesses, never at any other time. I think I may have told my parents, but the time-warp episodes were too strange to mention to anyone else.

The article that caught my attention was by Abe and colleagues. They had surveyed adolescents, and found that 14% of them also had their illusions *only* when they had a fever. Another item caught my interest: migraine was reported (as a separate condition) three times more often among adolescents who had such illusions of time (and vision) than it was by their cohorts (see chapter 73).

Distortions of the sense of time (faster, slower) are not restricted to children who have febrile illnesses, or during the aura of actual migraine headache episodes themselves. Distortions of time also occur when the temporal lobes are stimulated directly in patients who have epilepsy.[2]

Within the temporal lobes reside two other functions closely linked with our sense of time (see chapter 42). For example, area MT has been associated with the ways we normally perceive both movement and distance. Time yields the vague impression of seeming to "move" and to "flow." Moreover, time also develops implicit associations with distance [Z:558–559].

So as I read further, I began to wonder about this curious, episodic childhood dissociation of time. Clearly, it had split my usual sense of time into two categories: "interior" and "exterior" time. Could any part of this phenomenon be useful? Could it help clarify the mechanisms underlying other interior/exterior processes, those functions that I use when I distinguish my interior self-referent self from other items in the world outside?

There are fundamental reasons why such questions about internal/external themes keep recurring in these pages. They address an issue basic to Zen and the brain: Which modules and networks serve the *internalized* functions of *this ego*centric self? And how do they differ from those other-referent functions, the ones which first register *externalized* events going on out in *that allo*centric world? (see chapter 29). Similar themes have also entered into the discussion of how our self-images and functions become projected out into external space (see chapters 78 and 79), and acted on (see chapter 41).

So is this febrile "time splitting" accessible to study? Not without appropriate lengthy explanations, detailed permissions from parents, and young patient-volunteers and preparations in advance. Careful EEG, MEG, and related neuroimaging studies during recurrent febrile episodes of time dissociation might contribute certain kinds of useful data to the internal (self) versus external (other) issues at hand.

Suppose, for example, that a "slow-motion time illusion" were *limited* to events perceived out in the external world. It is possible that changes in activities might lateralize more to the junctional association areas around one temporal lobe. These changes might correlate with the side (and sites) that contributed more to this individual's (allocentric) perceptions out in that external world. In any event, the most informative data would be that obtained from a young, reliable subject whose illusion that time was being warped seemed more absolute than relative, and was limited to only "one" of the two possible worlds at a given time: say either a slow flow "out there," or a fast flow "inside."

In medical terminology, the term *tachy-* refers to too fast; *brady-* means too slow. Why did I outgrow my "tachy/brady" split in time perception? (I've had higher fevers since.) Why is such an illusion most obvious during childhood? Perhaps this time-splitting phenomenon correlates with the relative patterns of immaturity of a child's frontal, temporal, and parietal lobes.

Recent structural MRI studies reveal that not until a child is about 11 or 12 years of age does the frontal and parietal lobe gray matter reach its maximum volume.[3] The adolescent temporal lobe gray matter lags. It does not attain its maximum volume until even later, at 16 years. It seems likely that a fever's rapid tempo serves to unveil some inherent physiological instabilities within, and among, these slowly maturing circuits.

Dissolutions of Self-in-Time

Brief physiological instabilities can do more than "warp" our normal time-tagging codes in either direction. Personal time can *dissolve* when it loses all of its customary categories of present and past and their projections into the future. What does this total dissolution of time "feel" like? Solely by way of illustration, let us imagine that you are now being invited to look "inside" this writer's mental field during kensho. There you will observe what happens when time "drops out" as a content of consciousness.

Recall that this state of consciousness had been "his" for the previous 49 years. He had "owned" it. Suddenly, it became *anonymous*. Be reassured that *your* own sense of self will not change. Your own normal consciousness will still be peering inside this scene through your usual semantic "window." You will simply be an impartial "outside witness." You will maintain your own personal sense of the "now," as you define it within your own normal "time frame." Which means, by the way, that your own sense of this "now" will be limited to that fleeting instant of the present which is perhaps only 3 seconds or so wide.[4]

As you begin to enter someone else's state of consciousness with your own time frame intact, why might you sense the need to move to a vantage point out on the leading edge of your own time frame? And why, once there, would you turn to take a slightly retrospective stance? Because you have already anticipated something: you will need to look *back, at an angle*, beyond the trailing edge of your time frame. Only from this oblique position can you glimpse that marginal region—at the trailing edge of those 3 seconds—where that other person's present events will be on the verge of "plunging" off (as James Joyce might say) into his or her own immediate historical past.

But there's still that important fact which you had recalled at first. The episode of kensho you are now about to witness is an *extra*ordinary state. Its previous occupant had just been rendered anonymous. Do any of "his" historical episodes remain, events that you could be witness to? Would anything belonging to "him" remain—far off to the left in that direction toward "then?" No. That former occupant's sense of "*his* time past" had vanished. This special state had no access to any personally tagged events in his remote past. You would be gazing off into an indefinable vacancy, an emptiness unoccupied by events.

Achronia. A "Shoreless Ocean"

Yet, *during* kensho, this experiant had no immediate sense of being disadvantaged. Time was not "lost," "lacking," or "subtracted." Instead, the impression was of being *beyond* (any conceivable personal notion or conventional constructs of) time. No concept of time existed. Neither this word nor this writer existed.

To consider what this really means, let us return briefly to the epigraph at the beginning of this chapter. It suggests how some ancients may have felt when faced with the inexpressibility of their awesome impressions. The apt phrase, "shoreless ocean," is instructive. Even landlubbers know that shorelines limit the ocean's vastness. Yet the last line of this verse envisions an extraordinary scene—the ocean which has no shores. Some unbounded infinity extends beyond any horizon, and there never existed a shore to stand on.

Just as shoreless takes metaphor beyond an "oceanic" experience, so does kensho feel beyond even time*less*ness. No prior concept of "time" remains to which "less" could be attached. Time hasn't been *less*ened. Nor is it "felt" to be "*missing*." It isn't "*felt*" at all.

Language faces a major hurdle to describe this extraordinary state. It is so far beyond the ordinary that no precise word exists in either my standard or medical dictionaries. I am wary when "new" words are introduced. Yet neuroscientists need to be aware of this total vacancy of personal "time"—its non-existence state. So let's call this zero state *achronia*.[5] It occurs not only in kensho-satori but in related extraordinary states, especially when the self is also absent.

Kensho Is Open at Both Ends, beyond Ordinary Time*less*ness

Could some other analogy help convey, in words, how all concepts dissolve that are related to one's sense of time?

The previous chapter discussed how we construct our *normal* sense of personal "time." Then too, there arose that same need to gaze back toward the *left* of time's so-called arrow in order to envision events on the cusp of their "plunging off" into the past. Now we return to the arrow, and specify the ways several factors converged to delete it during kensho.

The first of these factors was that total retrograde vacancy of his former *self*. "*Retro*grade" is a term that simply refers to time past (e.g., retrograde memory *loss* is the way the word is usually used). Continuing to employ an arrow as a visual metaphor, such an absence of time past during kensho is equivalent to losing the back portions of the arrow of time. So, during kensho, that arrow's *left* parts would simply disappear. No past time.

Now let us consider the three forward projections of time cited in chapter 83. They had included such normal time-related functions as (1) recency decisions that operate to shift time sequences to and fro; (2) imaginary scenarios that keep projecting our intentions far into the future; and (3) covert measures of doing-time. In that previous chapter, it had seemed reasonable to envision these and other *prospective* functions as extending off along the *right* side of the arrow of time.

Now you may be able to glimpse the scope of kensho's dissolution of time. For at each end, all prior limitations have lapsed. Only vacancies remain. At left, no archer, actual or implied. No notch at that back end during infancy. No feathered interval since then. Off to the right, no arrowhead points to some imaginary future. No willful compulsion *must* fire any arrows off toward some actionable, longed-for destination.

Instantly, the former subjective sense of "time" has opened out, at both ends, into a zero state beyond time*less*ness. Off to the left? Nothing *retro*spective. Off to the right? Nothing *pro*spective.

What happens within that (former) narrow "window of now?" It still registers, and encodes, the ongoing sequence of unique events.[6] Part IX stands as a testimony that certain basic immediate memory functions still continue to encode and record, even in the absence of self, at least in some parts and connections of the hippocampus.[7] But off in either direction a yawning gap opens out where the edges of that old time frame briefly vanished into perpetuity.

What impression remains when all these other dimensions of subjective time dissolve? Various languages substitute mere abstractions for these two openings out into a vacancy. Words such as beginningless past and endless future are not quite accurate. At least, not if you read "-less" to mean that the experiant was really noticing the fact that "time" had actually been subtracted at that very moment. No, that fact is not appreciated until later.

In English, the flavor of the experience points (imperfectly) above and beyond all words and time constraints, toward

...e...t...e...r...n...i...t...y...

"Altered" Temporality

Temporality refers to our normal sense of time. "Altered" is a useful way to convey what can happen to a person's sense of time on drugs (see chapter 71). Shanon's comments on this phenomenon are based on his having ingested an Amazonian brew called ayahuasca "about 130 times."[8]

Perhaps *the* main effect of what he refers to as "powerful" degrees of ayahuasca intoxication is the state experienced "as being outside of time." To Shanon, his discovery that time could be so dissolved was "intellectually most unsettling" (see chapter 70).

This drug intoxication–induced impression of "being outside of time" is described as entering "the realm of the eternal." It occurs along with a "distinct ambience," including a sense of serenity and sanctity. Here, also, can be encountered the "realm" of "ultimate meanings." The description includes "the experience that one is directly perceiving the real essences of things." This deep sense of "reality" conveys some distilled comprehension of an underlying "grand design" of things. (So, too, does the "suchness" of kensho; see chapter 82.)

How is the constellation of "altered" temporal phenomena described when it occurs during drug intoxication? It is described in terms of a drugged state that is still being "witnessed," not in terms of a state from which the self has totally dropped out. In this respect, the present writer's years of earlier meditative experience prior to kensho could be pertinent. During this episode of kensho, self and time had already dropped out early, and insightful events seemed to unfold in natural ways. Space had not been filled up with the kaleidoscopic rush of hallucinations that occurs in a drug-driven altered state, nor had there arisen any unpleasant rapid shifts in frames of reference.

85

Emptiness

> A questioner asked: "Lord, to what extent is the world called empty?" . . . The Buddha replied: "Because it is empty of self and what belongs to self."[1]
>
> Questioner: "And what is the freedom of mind that is empty?" The Buddha replied: "To be empty of self, or of what belongs to self . . . means being empty of passion, aversion, and confusion."
>
> From the old Pali sutras[2]

When the Buddha awakened and realized emptiness, he understood that his prior way of seeing the world had been deluded. His own self-constructed ridgepole of self-deception had been the basic structural problem (see chapter 2). This, he realized, was what had prevented him from truly appreciating the Oneness of Absolute Ultimate Reality. Indeed, this fresh open perspective of Reality was so unlimited as to be beyond all concepts either of form or of no form.[3]

But the Buddha was also a teacher. He needed to bring emptiness down to earth. In the old sutras, he anchored it there, and gave it a personal meaning, when he said: "You do not know emptiness if you like or dislike any dharma . . . or if you quarrel or dispute with anyone."[4]

As we now start to explore the way this term *emptiness* evolved, it is essential to recall what the old sutras proclaimed: not until the personal sense of self vanishes does emptiness begin. This means that the *I-Me-Mine* drops off *all* of its longings, loathings, and ignorance—the so-called three fires, or three poisons (see chapter 58). These passionate emotions—and confusions—are rooted in the delusions of being a separate self. Our likes and dislikes cause deep anguish. They continually distort the way we perceive the Ultimately Real domain of which we are a tiny integral part (see chapter 77).

Shunyata was the Sanskrit term that the early Mahayana Buddhists used for the basic emptiness we are discussing in this chapter. The later Zen formulation of emptiness would point to its wordless experiential core: no mental constructs, no abstractions, no voluntary thought processes. Gone was every last trace of that former psychic self, including what the Buddha had earlier identified as its "belongings": its tangled bundle of old feelings and other attachments (see chapters 57 and 60) [Z:570–572].

After the Buddha died, about 483 B.C.E., the concept of emptiness became more complicated. It came to be used in so many ways that the resulting ambiguities persist to this day. For example, Conze identifies some twenty different kinds of emptiness.[5] His list begins with what drops out on the subjective side (eye, ear, nose, tongue, body, mind). It ends with that essential emptiness ("altogether beyond") which prevails irrespective of any enlightened being's capacity to discover it.

Why have we inherited so many versions of emptiness? The Buddha's followers had tried to translate the basic primary *experience* of self-emptiness into a series of secondary, expansive philosophical and doctrinal overbeliefs. (It is not clear how often such literary attempts were based on direct, firsthand experience, aside from the liberating release of *moksha*.)

Some 350 years after this, various concepts coalesced into one sutra. In its later written form, it would often be called the "Perfection of Wisdoms Sutra." Over the centuries, some of its wordings would mislead the unwary to think that the sutra had implied a nihilist philosophy (e.g., nothing "really" exists because "everything is empty")[6]. Even today, though the condensed form of the *Heart Sutra* is chanted daily in different tongues all over the Buddhist world, some might think that it hints at such rarified metaphysical levels [Z:698–699].

When our cognition first struggles to understand the concept of emptiness, we might have vaguely in mind something concrete, say a glass with no water in it. Not so in the traditional Zen Buddhist sense. As Cook explains, Buddhist emptiness is "a term which negates the system of words and concepts with which we categorize that which is 'out there.'"[7] Buddhist emptiness knows no distinctions. It employs none of those separate categories that our thought systems have built up and hold so dear. Moreover, mere *words*—like glass and water—are not themselves actual entities. We have invented words as substitutes for real things as they *really* are out there. Words are artificial, psychologically conditioned linguistic constructs [Z:549–553].

During the fifth century C.E., the Indian *Avatamsaka* (flower ornament) *Sutra* began to be translated into Chinese. Thereafter, some of its ideas were absorbed into academic philosophical traditions. Indeed, within the Hua-yen school of Buddhism, emptiness evolved to include two additional constructs. The first was that all things coexist in a *dynamic interdependence* with all other things: they don't exist just in their own right.

The second was that all things are endlessly in flux; they do not endure. When we wish to illustrate similar concepts of impermanence, we might be inclined to philosophize by saying: "trees don't grow to the sky." But the Zen Way, beyond that, is to *translate words into action*. Immediate ecological action means you turn over that old pile of fallen leaves, creating the compost that nourishes next spring's seedlings. Actions speak louder than words.

Still, the later Sino-Japanese traditions continued to develop interpretations of emptiness that became more cosmic than down-to-earth in their implications. Why, in this emerging perspective, could emptiness never mean a vacuum, never imply "nonexistence," nor be necessarily tied down to any ordinary personal self-referent meanings? Because it also began to refer to the potential of the whole cosmos for inexhaustible, *creative change*. At this juncture, emptiness could now include the potential, *simultaneously*, to become manifest as optimum *fullness*.[8]

Expansive ideas do not germinate only in dreams or spring fully formed from one's imagination. Where did Buddhists get the ingredients of this later perspective? Perhaps some arose during different levels of extraordinary personal experiences. Consider, for example, even the early state of internal absorption. It presents the paradoxical impression of a vast spatial *vacuum* infused by blissful resonances, a *vacuum plenum* (see chapter 75) [Z:513–516]. Moreover, impressions of seemingly "cosmic" energies may infuse the more advanced states of Pure Being (see chapters 79 and 87) [Z:627–630].

Suppose one were pressed hard to condense into one paragraph some kind of logical correlate for this last "emptiness-fullness" construct. A word explanation might run something like this: Within vast emptiness is the unlimited creative potential to become manifest everywhere in Form. This "eternal noumenon" continues to express its creativity during each present moment *now*, in each millisecond of our ordinary world of actual phenomena. From this perspective, *an original Emptiness is already, and always was, manifestly immanent in Form.*

If this sounds vaguely familiar, it is because such conceptualizations happen to fit in reasonably well with most current theories about a 13 billion-year-old universe that started with a "big bang," and with that tiny planet derived from stardust, on which hominids evolved some 4.5 million years ago.

Everywhere we now gaze, emptiness is immanent in form. Everywhere, things are in transition, impermanent. When we chant the *Heart Sutra*, the interpretations above might help reconcile briefly its otherwise puzzling expression: "Form is Emptiness; Emptiness is Form." But to go deeper, as Kobori-Roshi taught me 30 years ago, "You have to *know* emptiness." He meant that only *direct experience* can realize this awesome, wordless, liberating message: Form and

Emptiness coexist; phenomena and noumenon coexist; samsara and nirvana coexist; Heaven and Earth coexist; *all is One.*

What did he mean by direct experience? He was referring to the operation of *prajna,* the insight-wisdom which, in a flash, comprehends that the myriad forms of everyday phenomena are each an integral part of the vast infinite whole (see chapter 80).

Kobori-Roshi also cut through the later doctrinaire metaphysical approaches. He, too, was a teacher who brought these complex abstract issues down to earth, because he continued to view "emptiness as Suchness, 'as-it-is-ness'" [Z:570–572]. In so doing, he remained grounded in the original insight of the ancient sutras. Phenomena *do* take many forms: stone, cloud, crow's *caw,* our feeling of joy. Each already exists in its own suchness, as *it* really is. Each is empty of every concept that we project onto it, free of any word we try to attach to it, try as we might to describe it.

Master Pai-Chang Huai-Hai (720–814) understood that emptiness liberated the person from every conflict that was self-inflicted by emotionally pointed likes and dislikes. This was why he said back in the Tang dynasty: "A truly free mind reaches a state in which opposites are seen as empty. This is the only freedom."[9]

Liberation is implicit in emptiness. Opposites stop fighting. The resulting freedom of action extends out into acts of compassion. Why is authentic compassion (*karuna*) so rare? Because its acts arise from those subconscious, instinctual levels in the brain which seem always to have been deeply informed (see chapter 89). Informed about what? About the BIG picture: about *identity,* about self=other. Liberated compassionate behaviors arise spontaneously from innate, actionable, conflict-free, intuitive levels. Compassion becomes increasingly actualized once one finally begins to appreciate that all Forms are the sacred expressions of the same, eternal, dynamic, creative Ultimate Reality.

86

Third Mondo

> Factual knowledge is not understanding.
>
> Heraclitus (540–c.480 B.C.E.)

Can you briefly summarize the major ways the brain differs at different steps along this Path of Zen?

Early in life, our brain circuits are already differentiating "self" from "other." Around the age of 4 years, our brain starts to become more sophisticated about the outside world and develops intuitions about the attitudes of other people in it. Zen meditation continues this innate developmental trend. In calmness and clarity, it begins to *re*train the adult aspirant's brain in the refined arts of paying more mindful attention. Longer meditative retreats will help develop attitudes of self-discipline and habits of mindful introspection. Slowly, one identifies the problems associated with self-centeredness.

More rigorous retreats and concentrative styles of meditation generate stress responses. They also create swings of greater amplitude in the brain's emotional and instinctual responses and in one's sleep/waking biorhythms.

"Quickenings" are physiological surges that tend to ride the tides of the next arousal cycle *or* sleep cycle. They are brief expressions of a wide variety of corresponding surges in the activities of the brain's messenger molecules.

Internal absorption is a relatively early state, a further surge in amplitude into hyperawareness. Simultaneously, it deletes vision, hearing, and the sense of one's *physical* self-image. These sensate losses seem referable to an inhibitory blockade down at the level of the ventral thalamus, mediated by the back of the thalamic reticular nucleus. Not so in kensho.

Kensho is an extraordinary state of insight-wisdom. It briefly cuts off all the egocentric networks that had overconditioned the *psychic* self. It not only spares the sensory messages entering through *allo*centric pathways, it imbues them with meaningful resonances of unparalleled significance.

Kensho's sense of fearlessness suggests that primal fear circuits have been inhibited within the amygdala and its connections. Its death of the psychic self and its sense of eternity seem referable more to thalamic interactions with their corresponding frontotemporoparietal networks.

Kensho's quality of nondual "Oneness" includes the realization that the old mundane version of reality is one and the same with the awesome new Ultimate, Objective Reality in all its diversity. A variety of networks on both sides would seem to be engaged, and disengaged, in such a syncretic act of integration.

Part VIII

Openings into Being; and Beyond to the Stage of Ongoing Enlightened Traits

In the Bible it is said that "In the Beginning, there was the Word," but in the deepest realm of Zen meditation there is no single word.

Nanrei Kobori-Roshi (1918–1992)

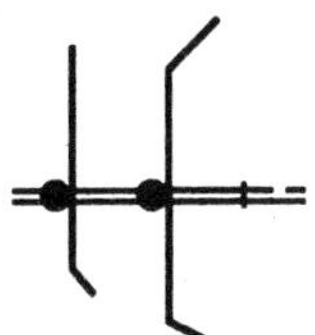

87

Problem Words: "Pure Consciousness"; "Being"; "Cosmic"

> The question really is not to define the fact—for we cannot do that—but to get at and experience it.
>
> Edward Carpenter (1844–1929)[1]

> A word is a word. An experience is an experience. Both are different.
>
> S. Shigematsu

Kobori-Roshi advised me early to beware of words that had multiple meanings. This chapter probes a few more of them.

The phrase "pure consciousness" continues to sow confusion more than a decade after Forman pointed to its semantic pitfalls.[2] When someone employs the term today, it remains unclear whether its usage describes an early moment, an intermediate step, or some ultimate stage among the several optional varieties of consciousness.[3]

When I started to meditate in Kyoto, it took several weeks before I stumbled into the early moments of thought-free awareness. That first episode was a surprise to a neurologist. I never expected my awareness could rest lightly on *nothing*! Later, when the quiet moments of open awareness had lasted longer, I could realize that my physical sense of self had been dropping out increasingly from the mental field.

Chang had written, back in 1959, that a "stopping" of the breath (Chin.: *chih shi*) was a common, natural phenomenon that occurred during periods of meditative absorption.[4] TM investigators went on to conduct a detailed study of these silent epochs of so-called pure consciousness that could occur *during meditation.* They confirmed that the episodes were often accompanied by a suspension of respiration[5] (see chapter 20) [Z:93–99].

However, these particular "pure" moments which do recur during meditation have thus far tended to be, in Forman's word, "rudimentary."[6] I agree. Most are interpretable as "shallow preludes" to the much deeper states of the major absorptions [Z:99]. It is their tendency to recur that makes them convenient to study in the laboratory.

Some deep *internal* absorptions convey further alluring impressions of a "pure qualityless consciousness."[7] Even so, this is only a *temporary* state of consciousness. It is subject to being interpreted (with reservations) as only the "supposed" ground of consciousness. In Forman's terminology, similar brief episodes could be classified simply as "pure consciousness events."[8] Such an "event" is transitory, and usually occurs during meditative absorption. It contains no intentional thoughts. It is remembered—in retrospect—as being a thought-free interval.

Others have expressed the view that "unmanifested, absolute, pure consciousness" is "easily experienced." Maybe so, if you are an adept. However, this word "easily" seems difficult to reconcile with the next statement which includes the following reference to what I have been used to thinking is a much later state of "Being": [when the meditator] is left without an object of experience, having transcended the subtlest state of the object, he steps out of the process of experiencing and arrives as the "state of Being."[9]

The Advanced State of "Being"

At this point, to avoid confusion, I need to point out that when I refer to the "state of Being" in these pages, it is to what I think of as a very rare and advanced state, not as one that is easily experienced (see chapter 4) [Z:627–630]. Sages in past centuries have hinted that—within this rare state—the essence of Being coexists with a zero condition of the personal psyche [Z:570–572]. More recently, Heidegger (1889–1976) ventured into this semantic arena. He began with the word "Being." Then he simply placed an X through it.[10]

Does this artificial X cancel the essential "isness" or suchness within a state of Being? No. Instead, each reader who views this crossed-out word symbol remains free to interpret what "Being" means. In these pages the deep issue goes beyond metaphysical wordplay. Our quest is to clarify the extraordinary mechanisms of Being—their *metaphysiological* origins, in one sense.

How can a literary work represent a very advanced state of consciousness that is *not* easily experienced? Elsewhere, we chose a blank, unnumbered page to express the lack of content of this advanced state of "Ultimate Pure Being." This was a feeble attempt. It could only hint at an experiential paradox so profound that form and emptiness both coincide and equate to the nth degree.

In such extraordinary alternate states of Being, every old physical and psychic boundary constraining the former self would seem to have dropped out. This could include a loss of that person's directional sense. Normally, the anterior nucleus of the thalamus helps to integrate head direction functions into higher levels of spatial processing (see chapters 29 and 44). To the degree that the GABA cap of the reticular nucleus interrupts the directional aspects of such anterior nucleus processing, it might contribute to the net impression of an unpointed, unbounded selfless state.

The Controversy

Semantic problems seem inevitable in this arena. Some observers choose to regard "pure consciousness" as at or near the so-called ground level of conscious experience. Others choose to view it as a rudimentary event during an earlier meditative state that is relatively shallow. "Ground level" is a phrase that can take on earth-bound connotations like "shorelines." Its premise of solidity can leave you unprepared for phenomena like "groundlessness," which can open up into a vast, shoreless ocean.

This advanced state of Being referred to on the Path of Zen (see chapter 4) seems very far removed from simple episodes of "pure consciousness." It appears to present itself, simultaneously, more as the *coexistence* of infinite potential and *groundlessness*. These are extraordinary qualities. They suggest that the phenomena of states in this category of Being correspond with the advanced degrees of "emptiness" that were discussed two chapters ago (see chapter 85).

No final list of properties seems easily to characterize the most advanced expressions of the states in this category of Ultimate Pure Being. Nor will rival philosophical theorists easily resolve their hard-argued intellectual question: What is Being-as-such? (Some may be under less pressure to argue the point after they themselves—following Edward Carpenter's lead—had been fortunate to undergo the actual, sequential experiences of suchness and Being.)

"Cosmic Consciousness"

This Edward Carpenter defined "cosmic consciousness" in 1892. He regarded it then as a "universal consciousness." It resembled, in those Hindu traditions he was aware of, the blissful deepest knowing of the all-pervading Reality.[11] His writings suggest that he sometimes used the term to refer to a state, and at other times to an ongoing attitudinal approach.

In 1894, Carpenter also spoke to some other key issues. We used the word "Oneness" to refer to their general qualities in chapters 77, 78 and 79. With particular regard to the perspective from which things were being *seen*, he began by using the following words: [a perspective] "as from some more universal standpoint" ... a sense that one *is* those objects and things and persons that one perceives (and the whole universe). He then went on to add: "—a sense in which sight and touch and hearing are all fused in identity."[12]

Moreover, Carpenter also referred to the issues discussed in chapter 78, ("Oneness," category III). There we addressed the more difficult problem: How does a brain slowly develop a mature attitude of selflessness-in-the world, *and* then express this maturity during an advanced state of consciousness? With regard to this issue, Carpenter appears to have referred obliquely to capacities of insight that go beyond our ordinary concepts of morality. It was these capacities that draw on instincts that D. T. Suzuki would later call our "native virtues." With respect to such qualities, Carpenter said: "the whole faculty is deeply and intimately rooted in the ultra-moral and emotional nature, and beyond the thought region of the brain."

The word "cosmic" has entered twice into another classification system. In that version, the state of consciousness after the absorptions is called "cosmic consciousness" (*Turiyaita*).[13] Beyond it, the next level is the sixth state called "Refined Cosmic Consciousness." This is followed by a seventh state called "Unity Consciousness."

Conclusion

Our different tribal disciplines do not yet seem ready to settle on the same "sign language." We need standardized terms to express both the different phenomenological levels of consciousness and their (more or less) "qualityless" qualities.

88

Are There Levels and Sequences of "Nonattainment?"

> Meditation at the most advanced level has been known since ancient times as "pure clear mediation arriving at being-as-is." It represents a mode of experience of the greatest degree of insight, at a level that approaches object consciousness.
>
> Thomas Cleary[1]

> When the time is ripe and the effort matures, this is then called "the time of the full moon."
>
> Master Torei Enji (1721–1792)[2]

Countless minds have been stretched by the notion that distinct steps occur along the spiritual path, steps that can even help to define it. The early Soto school in China developed a system of five "ranks," "modes," or "stages." Yet, among those who rejected them was the Japanese Soto master, Dogen, who objected to the way such artificial, intricate formulations invited mentalizing.

In the Rinzai Zen tradition of Master Hakuin and Torei Enji, the more advanced states of insight were viewed as only the *beginning*. True enough, kensho-satori-Being were considered to yield insights into the "Basic Principle." This "principle" was regarded as an underlying domain of nondifferentiation, Unity, equality, and "emptiness" (see chapter 85). Yet, only after this preliminary groundwork would the aspirant be prepared to enter "The Stage of Advanced Practice."[2] These distinctions are outlined in table 10.

Thus far in these pages, much of the emphasis on the Path of Zen has been on a kind of "subtraction." This means not trying to "gain" or "attain" something, but *letting go* of unfruitful layers of the overconditioned self (see chapter 60) [Z:579–584]. Engler's recent update of the early Indian Buddhist traditions also

Table 10
Beyond Mere Transitory States Lies the Stage of Advanced Practice

States of Kensho-Satori-Being (States of Insight-Wisdom)	*The Stage of Advanced Practice (After Wisdom, the "Matter Beyond")*
Insights involve unconditioning, nondifferentiation, Unity and equality	The Way of differentiation; maturation occurs through the rigorous route of "barrier" koans and interviews with an authentic teacher; this transmission proceeds "outside" the scriptures
Insights confer an increasing comprehension of the "Basic Principle" (noumenon) and of Emptiness.	Motivations evolve; behaviors are energized, and the trainee becomes more actualized toward effortless compassion
Archtypal Bodhisattva of Insight-wisdom: *Manjusuri*	Archtypal Bodhisattva of All-Pervading Beneficience: *Samantabhadra*

From V. Okuda, trans. *The Discourse on the Inexhaustible Lamp of the Zen School.* Zen Master Torei Enji. Commentary by Master Daibi of Unkan. Foreword by Myokyo-ni. London, Zen Centre, 1989.

reemphasizes "letting go." He summarizes four successive movements along the path toward enlightenment.[3]

During the first phase, the aspirant will let go of several delusions: the belief that the self has a separate and independent existence; the view that meditative practices cannot relieve anguish; and the delusion that good works and elaborate rituals—in themselves—can lead a person to awakening.

During the second and third phases, sense desires and various forms of ill will are first weakened and then extinguished.

Only during the fourth phase are the mental activities that cause suffering to oneself and to others finally extinguished. This means letting go of the conceits that compare oneself favorably with other persons. It also means dropping off all tendencies that had caused one (1) to dwell not in the here-and-now, but elsewhere in the past and future; (2) to resist the fact that all things are impermanent; (3) to avoid the fact that all attachments create suffering; (4) to be preoccupied with any other lingering self-referent notions.

Backsliding is inevitable during daily-life practice. No extinctions of self are this linear or this sequential. Moreover, in some respects, these four clusters are not subtractions unique to a spiritual path. They resemble two other kinds of changes a person might undergo. One is during psychotherapy. Far more common are the other changes in attitude that we develop incrementally during the little insights that come from confronting life's experiences[4] [Z:660–663]. First to be let go of are some unfruitful cognitive activities, the ones most accessible and easiest for us to modify. Much more difficult to let go of is our hunger for affective satisfactions and for the deeper yearnings that motivate us. Hardest of all to spot and pull out are our narcissistic, long-conditioned, investments in the psychic roots of the *I-Me-Mine.*

The basic reasons for important results are sometimes overlooked. Powerful affirmative impulses and energies are released in the process of getting rid of one's extra baggage of self. The person's more positive attributes seem to emerge in association with that greater clarity of awareness which finally focuses on priorities. The result is a simpler, more stable lifestyle. These changes begin to appear in the form of energized, skillful behaviors and more actualized, effortless forms of genuine compassion (see table 10).

Learning to "let go" of pejorative self-references can be of benefit whether the person meditates or not. Motor performances improve when one shifts into an automatic pilot mode [Z:665–677]. Consider the results from a simple task often used in the laboratory: selecting the one correct button to push when three other options are possible. After practicing these skills, normal subjects start to automate their motor sequences and become more skillful. Several things then happen. Error rates drop, reaction times become faster, and *fewer* fMRI signals arise in the left hippocampus and parahippocampal gyrus. In contrast, when normal subjects try "too hard" on a task, and process too many "top-down" instructions, their performance drops. Now under increased stress fMRI signals increase in their right lateral frontal region and in the thalamus on both sides.[5]

Zen is an agency of change. Could some long-range optimistic attitudes and behaviors reflect more efficient networking? In the next two chapters, we turn to a further discussion of how such affirmative actions relate to integrations of the whole personality [Z:668–677].

89

Cultivating Compassion, a Native Virtue

> Man's nature tends toward the good just as water tends to flow downwards.
>
> Mencius (371–289 B.C.E.)

> When another person's pain stirs compassion within me, then his weal and woe go straight to my heart, with exactly that same feeling, if not always to the same degree, as if it were otherwise my own. Consequently, an absolute difference between myself and him no longer exists.
>
> Arthur Schopenhauer (1788–1860)[1]

We can share in more than the pain and woe of other persons. We can also share in the positive expressions of their feelings of well-being. Similar feelings are now being studied worldwide. In Liverpool, India Morrison and colleagues were monitoring men and women, looking for the fMRI correlates of empathy. They found that signals increased in the right dorsal anterior cingulate region not only when their subjects felt pinprick pain themselves but also when their subjects just *watched* another person's fingers being pricked.[2] At some level, were the observers "in touch with", and "feeling" and "mirroring" the other person's pain?

On the other side of the ocean, 21 and 22 May 2001 were busy days and nights at the University of Wisconsin. Here, in 2001, Richard Davidson's team was studying the EEG and fMRI signals in Lama Öser's brain.[3] European by birth, the lama had become well trained for over 30 years in Tibetan Buddhist practices. By general agreement, he was also a "happy monk." Conditions were ideal: here was an articulate, exemplary subject, a monk who could consistently produce mental states that might yield reproducible data.

His task was to engage, repeatedly, in a series of six distinctive mental states. He played an active role in designing the experiments, and was very familiar with each state: (1) visualization (of a Tibetan deity); (2) one-pointed visual concentration on a spot; (3) devotion; (4) fearlessness (implying a certainty that there was nothing to gain or lose); (5) the open state (a letting go into a thought-free vastness); (6) love and compassion (for this, he used his teachers' kindness as a model, and engaged in an all-inclusive compassion with such intensity that it "soaked" his mind).

The six separate states were studied in the following manner. He began with 60 seconds "in," shifted into a neutral period of 60 seconds; then went back into another state for 60 seconds. This continued for a total of 5 minutes spent per state (later, he would engage in each state for 90 seconds).

His fMRI signals showed strong shifts distinctive of each state, consistent with changes in brain activities involving multiple networks.

Lama Öser then went down the hall where the same six states were then monitored in parallel EEG studies. There he was fitted with two different EEG caps. One was equipped with 128 sensors, the other with 256 sensors in different places. Source localization software helped to estimate the deeper origins of his brain wave activities.

During the sixth state of induced compassion, his EEG showed a marked shift toward gamma activity in the *left* middle frontal gyrus. This finding was consistent with previous research from this and other laboratories (see chapter 17). These earlier studies had revealed certain psychological correlates of left frontal lateralized EEG activity (see chapter 43). Among them were not only such positive emotions as happiness, enthusiasm, and joy but also feelings of high energy and alertness. In contrast, greater degrees of *right* prefrontal predominant activity were correlated with tendencies toward such distressing emotions as sadness, anxiety, and worry.

A few months earlier, Paul Ekman and Robert Levenson had monitored Lama Öser's responses with polygraphic techniques. On that occasion, his task was to view an unpleasant videotape. The tape showed a badly burned patient standing while physicians were peeling off strips of his burned skin. One can appreciate why research subjects usually respond to this unpleasant sight with feelings of disgust. Instead, the lama had a unique, compassionate response. In fact, his polygraph data showed that he was more relaxed during this viewing than even during his resting state.

Data such as these provide objective confirmation that, during an inclusive state of compassion, a highly trained, spiritually advanced monk can show distinctive changes in left frontal lobe activity and associated changes in the direction of relaxation involving heart rate, blood pressure, and perspiration. Furthermore, these changes can occur in association with compassionate responses that are voluntarily induced and with spontaneous responses of empathy during visually unpleasant circumstances.

Japanese Buddhists have a phrase that includes the level of compassion stemming from the insight of the identity between oneself and other beings. Self/other has evolved into self = other. The phrase is *dotai muen no jihi*.[4]

90

On "Moral Cognition"

> *Benevolence*: This organ lies in the upper and middle part of the frontal bone, disposes to compassion and active benevolence; and produces a desire for the happiness of others; and charitably to view their actions.
>
> F. Bridges, *A Manual of Phrenology* (1838)[1]

Two centuries ago, it was easy for Dr. Franz Gall (1757–1828) and Dr. J. Spurzheim (1776–1832) to localize various aspects of character and morality. Today, in what a few holdout skeptics might regard as a latter-day version of phrenology, a field of "moral cognition" has been developing. It is now bolstered by fMRI data, and in 2003 alone at least four articles reviewed this new topic area in the neurosciences.

"Moral emotions" hinge on the social context. They touch on our shoulds and oughts, our should nots and ought nots. They include the ways we feel guilty, blush with embarrassment, swell with pride, and grow green-eyed with jealousy.[2] "Virtually real" moral dilemmas can be created in the laboratory and monitored with neuroimaging methods. However, the human brain's redundant functions and inherent plasticity invite extreme caution if anyone tries to use laboratory data to predict how normal subjects or brain-lesioned patients will always behave in a social context out in the real world.

Our "moral cognitive" systems are widely distributed throughout the neuraxis. They do not arise only in the ventral-medial prefrontal and orbito-frontal cortex[3] (see chapter 43). Indeed, though the working model that Moll and colleagues propose for moral judgments and behaviors includes the frontalpolar and medial frontal regions, it could go on to involve almost all the regions cited in part III.[4]

This is not some new, multiple version of the old "bump" form of phrenology. Particular *combinations* of these widely distributed modules and networks enter into what we call "judgments." Any survey of (one's friends') decisions in a major election year reveals how often opinions are biased by ("their") personal, intuitive, quick, gut-level feelings and attitudes.[5] Why? Because many of these judgments had evolved in an early childhood milieu. There they were shaped by early authoritarian homegrown "shoulds" and "oughts" and by the general conditioning of our wider "culture" or lack thereof (see chapter 60). Our own reputation and character hinge on how this checkerboard of ingredients combines, reverses, and then plays out in consistent traits of behavior.

Carl Jung recognized that moral capacities evolve as people grow older. He spoke of maturity in terms of "individuation" [Z:135]. A deceptive word. It really meant a progressively more harmonious mode of development, *not* self-centered selfish behavior. It referred to that process of development which *unifies* both the person's *conscious and unconscious* modes of cognition and behavior.

Can long-range meditative training nurture our development toward this kind of maturity? (see chapter 79). Does the way it sponsors introspection and intuition serve to bring our unconscious attitudes up closer where we can actually *do* something about them?

91

Some Aspects of Maturity That Are Nurtured during Long-Range Meditative Training

If you wish to live, you must first attend your own funeral.

Katherine Mansfield (1888–1923)

Thus far, we have identified a major, innate developmental trajectory. Over the decades, it could serve to bring an increasingly lower-profile personal self into a more liberating accommodation with the *outside* world of people, things, and ideas (see chapter 79) [Z:50, 145].

Some conceptualizations view such a continuum from the standpoint of an emerging process of identity.[1] We can formulate the earliest stages as moving increasingly from the old selfish *I-Me-Mine* level of egocentric identity toward *You-Us-Ours* varieties of allocentric-ecocentric identification, then on toward successive identifications with all the other people in the world and beyond to include the entire universe.

The later openings into states of "Being" that include refined qualities of "Oneness" are relevant to these later varieties of expansive identification. A state of Being can enable a long-term meditator to deeply realize such an identification—such a unification—with the Universal at the level of direct experience (see chapter 87). Yet there remains one more accommodation that each self will be called upon to make.

Short Lives, Gray Hairs, and Vines That Break

Katherine Mansfield lived intensely, and wrote luminous short stories before her own life was cut short by tuberculosis when she was only 35. Our first gray hairs are subtle reminders of our own destination. The end of the wild strawberry season draws nearer; the vine will give way, no matter how hard we cling to it (see chapter 83).

Internal absorption involves a dearth of the physical self. Kensho arrives in a *death* of the psychic self. A meditator who has already tasted these prior dissolutions of the self may find it easier not only to face the inevitable with fewer concerns but also to feel a sense of being liberated into living out *this* life, *fully*, right into its final moments. Some fortunate persons discover that their sense of self does tend to drop out terminally. When Woody Allen once said, "I'm not afraid of dying; I just don't want to be around when it happens," he was perhaps being more accurate than he was aware of [Z:448–452].

Nature and nurture combine to mature each of us differently—in different ways, at different rates, and during different decades. That said, one observes that the long-term meditative path has an earthy pragmatic tendency. It tends to avoid getting swept up into exaggerated spiritual overtones or "cosmic" preoccupations. Instead, it seems to nurture a person's innate expressions of maturity in such everyday practical matters as

- confronting the reality of death, and making out one's will;
- letting go of longings and loathings, and renouncing negative habits;
- focusing attention on "just this" present moment;
- softening biased opinions and idealistic notions of perfection;
- extending ongoing patience and forgiveness to self and to others;
- realizing immanence: the quality of the sacred in simple, ordinary, everyday things;
- relying more on insights and introspective truths than on doctrines;
- radiating a playful flexibility and openness from a core of stability;

- accepting and reconciling life's opposites;
- expressing a sense of responsibility for others with kindness and selfless compassion;
- expressing a deep sense of gratitude for the gift of life and for all those who have eased its burdens.

* * *

I have been especially aware in these later decades of a spontaneous deep impulse to "count my blessings." Silent thanks occur as a matter of daily routine. It is of interest that a recent study found that a similar conscious positive focus on one's blessings was associated with a greater sense of well-being and optimism.[2]

Part IX

Pointing at Moonlight: Allusions and Illusions

The book of moonlight is
not written yet, nor half begun.

Wallace Stevens (1879–1955)

Pointing toward a Late Lunar Phase of Objective Vision

> The person who has had a mystical experience knows that all the symbolic expressions of it are faulty. The symbols don't render the experience, they suggest it. If you haven't had the experience, how can you know what it is?
>
> Joseph Campbell (1904–1987)[1]

Sensations are what we *feel;* thoughts are what we *think*. Yet, when we speak informally, we often use illusions and delusions interchangeably. In the neurosciences, a formal distinction separates sensory perceptions (which may slide into illusions) from thought-full ideations (which can harden into fixed delusions).

Visual illusions *change what we are already seeing out there*. They represent normal perceptual phenomena that have been slightly modified. Usually, this involves slight errors in visual processing in the back of the brain. Although visual illusions are brief misperceptions of real (*literal*) things, one does not dismiss their images as "imaginary." Instead, illusions invite scientific explanation, as do other facts of direct living experience.

In contrast, delusions are false beliefs. Their ideations linger and become rigid mental sets. In yet another category are hallucinations. Hallucinations are more unusual perceptions, ones that cannot be explained by any actual natural external sensory stimulus at that particular moment.

Figurative References

On the other hand, poetry and religion regularly employ many *figurative* images. Everyday we encounter their imaginative representations. They take familiar forms: allusions, similes, metaphors, and symbols.

Figurative references to the moon are commonplace throughout our ordinary literature and visual arts. That they seem almost "gravitational" is no accident. Daylight and moonlight are our two natural modes of illumination. No wonder our associations—and our moods—to each are as different as day and night. The way our emotions respond to some subtle kind of "pull" from the moon becomes especially interesting.

Within Zen Buddhism, both the moon and its silvery light took on special meaningful associations. As cultural symbols, each came to refer to sudden, deep, life-opening states of enlightenment. These "peak experiences" are profound states of "awakening" that can transform a person's subsequent behavior.

It is not difficult to appreciate why lunar lighting effects evoke poetic and other literary references. Let us say that it is a clear night in autumn. We are viewing a landscape bathed in moonlight. It takes on a cool silvery luster. The same scenery looks eerily different from the way it looked while it was being warmed by the golden glow of the sun. But why did moon symbolisms and figures of speech become so linked with Zen? Are we sure we know *every* possible historical reason, understand *all* the facts?

Part IX addresses such questions. Its chapters focus on the latest research findings that help explain some curious phenomena. Be prepared for essay themes that bridge disciplines in unusual ways. Dare we venture to examine cross-cultural issues closely? If not, all references to the moon could remain locked within the metaphors of fixed belief systems, forever estranged from neuroscience and from the living facts of direct personal experience.

The opening narrative reviews a confluence of rare events: a visually attuned neurologist undergoes an extraordinary *sequence* of experiences. As kensho's realizations unfold, a few deep feeling tones arise—a *mood*. Among its qualities are references vaguely reminiscent of what anyone might experience *secondarily* under the influence of moonlight on a clear night. But then, different visual events occur, very *late*, distinct from these "psychological" feelings. He *experiences visual perceptions that appear consistent with moonlight*. They are an actual, *primary visual illusion*. Not a metaphor, not a simile, not a figure of speech.

On the subsequent agenda are separate chapters that develop neuroscientific explanations for such independent, primary visual events, examine their associated psychic counterparts, and consider how each of these relate to longstanding cultural associations to moonlight.

Most figurative, cultural references that link the moon to Buddhist awakening are centuries-old legacies in verse form that celebrate Asian literary customs. Not so the closing example. It recalls a recent photograph, in stark black and white. It was still daylight when Ansel Adams snapped his shutter on this scene in 1941. Only later, in the darkroom, could Adams transform this negative into his now classic print: a moody nocturnal landscape seemingly infused by moonlight.

In years past, no reader ever had reason to think that enlightenment might be associated with *reduced* illumination. Nor did this writer. Who expects these two topics—light and dark—to be juxtaposed? Do conventional accounts in the West suggest that illumination can be *reduced* during major spiritual awakenings? No. What we recall is the blinding light that enveloped Saul of Tarsus on the road to Damascus. Similar accounts have led us to expect that "mental illumination" should be accompanied, if anything, by an increase in the quantity of light[2] [Z:376–379].

Not the following chapters. They will suggest that certain human brains have the potential to give rise not only to a moonlight *mood* but to the late, perceptual impression of a *darker*, "moonlight" phase. Why? One crucial part of the explanation will be a brief loss of *color* vision.

Does this seem counterintuitive? Were you perplexed by such a strange proposal. I once had the same expectations. Consider how puzzled I was when this visual paradox occurred.

93

A Contemporary "Taste of Kensho": Its Profile of Early and Late Phenomena

> A person's becoming enlightened is like the reflection of the moon in water. The moon does not get wet, nor is the water ruffled. . . . The entire moon and heavens are reflected in even a drop of dew in the grass . . .
>
> Master Dogen (1200–1253)[1]

Five attributes of the "moonlight phase" are noteworthy in the condensed account that will follow (Z:573–578). First, the timing: this "lunar phase" arrived *late*, evolved rapidly, faded quickly.

Second, the amount of illumination: it was obviously reduced. The subdued light that later pervaded this London scene resembled that dim nocturnal illumination we normally associate with moonlight. It was also diffuse; *no real moon was its visible source.* Nor was any moon image being hallucinated. No "blinding white light" occurred suddenly, as might happen in some other kinds of "peak" or "near-death" experiences.

Third, the lack of color: the late moonlight phase was colorless. Fourth, unusual highlights were superimposed. Fifth, the final sequence of other visual illusions: one quick shift into a negative afterimage; then, "distancing" and displacement.

The Path of Zen points in the direction of *insights* (see chapter 4). So, why would any serious student of Zen call attention to *late perceptual* phenomena? Because the five points cited above are clues. They can help direct us toward certain earlier physiological origins of kensho per se. Moreover, unless similar phenomena are openly analyzed, they seem likely to sow as much mystification in the future as they may have in centuries past.

* * *

A Condensed Contemporary Account

It happened at 9:00 A.M., on the second morning of a 2-day Zen retreat. Looking out at the London skyline beyond an empty train platform, I entered instantly into an alternate state of consciousness [Z:536–544, 589–621]. At once, every previous notion of having a physical and psychic self vanished. Viewing proceeded objectively, empty of all prior self-centered subjective notions of an *I-Me-Mine*.

Three new qualities instantly transfigured the previous view of this mundane station, its distant outdoor setting, and the open sky beyond. Absolute Reality, Intrinsic Rightness, and Ultimate Perfection infused everything seen.

At first, all the coloring of this pale blue-gray sky and of the rest of the urban scenery was *unchanged* from that a split second before. Nor did any visual details of this normally daylight scene appear to be more, or less, finer-grained than previously.

Next, as this anonymous, mirror-like, first phase deepened, it was permeated and overlaid by a second wave of fresh insights. These dissolved all the roots of time, of fear, and of the habitual inclination to act. The resulting experience became a seamless blend of Eternity, Absolute Fearlessness, the loss of every inclination to approach, and prolonged Deep Peace. This Immanent Reality of harmonious perfection was deeply comprehended wordlessly.

Only near the close of these two major prior overlapping phases of early insights did a late visual phase suddenly enter.[2] It arrived about the same time that the cool cavernous sense of visceral emptiness—empty of self, time, fear, and of the inclination to act—had plumbed its most unsentimental depths. So it was only then, *and for one fleeting moment*, that the anonymous witness observed this previous scenery "bathed in moonlight." This lunar phase shifted in, evolved, and then shifted out.

Let us be more specific: immediately before this late phase of lunar vision, while affirmative insights were transfiguring the entire scene, this same scenery had continued to register all its usual colors and details consistent with that morning's daylight. Suddenly, all those very same colors, forms, patterns, and shadings shifted into a *totally color-free and darker mode*.

Beneath this now-darkened sky, objects were rendered solely in subdued shades of black, white, and gray. Darker shadings still conveyed some impression of their original three-dimensional character.

This left a direct resulting impression: *moonlight*. Not an impression "*as if* it was moonlight." Moonlight registered as a soft, immediate, visual fact. It was accepted straightway, with no wondering about "why" it looked like moonlight.

During this late, colorless lunar phase, certain soft highlights within the scenery appeared enhanced, at least with respect to the even darker regions surrounding them.

Next, this nocturnal scene underwent a remarkable shift. Although it was still in the black-and-white mode, all of its previous light and dark patterns *reversed themselves*. Thus, it was all rendered, briefly, as one negative afterimage.

Finally, a partial sense of "i" began to return. Enough of a minute "i" to be vaguely aware that slight degrees of the original daylight coloring and illumination were now present. Only at this point did the entire "frame" then change that enclosed this faintly colored London scenery.

The perceptual frame shifted in two different ways*: (1) The entire scene (now faintly colored) was seen off at a *distance*. There it registered as being perhaps three times farther away than before. Even so, its overall dimensions appeared to have shrunk only slightly. (2) The entire scene's apparent subjective center of focus was *displaced*. Its new position was both slightly down and off to the left of where this diminutive "i" had the impression that his midline of awareness and its expected horizon was located.†

Which Phenomena Presented Themselves as Being Actually Seen, in Contrast to Their Only Feeling "Embodied," or Interpreted, or Intuited?

Suppose some reader, slightly baffled by all this, were now to press for an analogy. No oversimplified one would do. It does not suffice to suggest that this entire phase resembled the mere "insertion" of a "black-and-white filmstrip," as though it were an adequate substitute for the previous technicolor version of this same scene. Because any "spliced filmstrip" analogy might suggest that the witness had experienced only a single isolated change: say only some minor subtraction of those earliest steps of color processing, before the nuances of color vision had evolved further in his brain.

No. Because, in retrospect, the subject could identify *several different categories of events*. Some were *visual percepts of very different kinds*. Others were *embodied psychic events* that were embedded in the moonlight phase and its immediate aftermath. Each had entered consciousness at a particular time in a distinct sequence. They had also overlapped. In chapter 95 we organize these issues explicitly in table 11.

---

*Skeptical readers may wish reassurance. Can these observations be believed? The following information may help suggest why this "nocturnal, lunar" interval had registered so deeply on its anonymous observer. Colors had intrigued him since the age of 7, and he had always followed a visual imperative. As a sometime photographer in his 20s, he had developed, enlarged, and printed his own black-and-white negatives. Training in neurology taught him to take careful case histories. Neurologic diagnosis hinges on an accurate, detailed account of the sequences through which each patient's symptoms evolve. Still later, he would become a Sunday painter of landscapes in watercolors.

† This narrative tries to convey the way impressions presented themselves as literal facts of direct visual experience. (Paradoxes of the moment went unappreciated.) Accordingly, the words are not intended to communicate "as-if" similes, symbols, or the metaphors of literary imagination. Nor are they presented as an "as-it-were" aside.[3]

In retrospect, when the witness had returned to his former role as a neurologist, it would later become possible to interpret the delayed visual phenomena as visual illusions.

For now, we might still draw upon the theatre for an analogy, one more accurate than a filmstrip. Imagine that you are now seated indoors, a member of the audience. You have already been watching an ancient drama unfold on the stage. It seems to be drawn from Greek antiquity. As you look toward the stage, you find that the scenery for the play's next act has been designed to resemble a seascape. Above lies a big, blue daylight sky. Below you see a vast expanse of blue-green ocean stretching off to the faint line of the distant horizon.

A sunny glow (from rosy footlights and overhead lights) bathes this whole set in all the warm colors appropriate for daylight. Strangely, a deep pervasive sense of vacancy enters and coexists. It seems to relate to a lone rowboat on the perfectly calm surface of the sea. It lies empty, oarless, becalmed. You witness this warm/cool scene passively for a while, and then everything shifts. Each warm source of light suddenly switches off, silently. Now you see the same scenery, only it is nighttime. This pale white diffuse light is much cooler. Its source is uncertain, yet your immediate impression suggests moonlight, even though it seemed to flicker. Soon you sense the significance of that *empty* boat. It's been telling you that your hero—the one with whose actions you had so closely identified during all the earlier acts of the play—had indeed been lost at sea.

Later, long after you left the theatre, you might wonder about the paradox: you had been overcome by an unparalleled sense of deep peace, release, and clarity—even when you knew that your hero had died. Why had you felt no personal sense of loss? Later still, your curiosity might also have been piqued by some of those strange special effects. What had created the closing highlights? What did those strange light-dark reversals mean?

In order to clarify these seemingly paradoxical issues, the next chapter reviews the way our normal visual functions evolve.

94

How Our Brain Normally Perceives Light and Colors

> What meets the eye is the Way.
>
> Master Shih-t'ou Hsi Ch'ien (700–790)

> All cats are gray in the dark.
>
> Old Proverb

We met Master Shih-t'ou earlier, in chapter 76. He authored the verses in the Sandokai that reaffirmed One Reality. He spoke of light and dark, and of branching streams. Indeed, his own Soto Zen lineage branched out and flowed on so extensively that it continues down to the present day.[1]

It is now time to follow what he said "meets the eye" back into the brain, there to rediscover the simple explanation for why all cats *are* gray in the dark.

Rods, Cones, and the Earlier Visual Pathways

Each child bears witness to it: stars do "come out" at night. Today's schoolchildren also learn what else is involved. After it gets dark, the rod receptors in our retina can detect the light from these celestial objects. But first, these rods still need to adapt to darkness. Only then can we perceive the faint white lights coming from all the other stars off in our peripheral vision.

Cone receptors are different. Sensitive to all colors in daylight, the cones serve our keenest visual acuity in the center of our field of vision. Now for a key question: As their two pathways pass back from the eye into the brain, do these nocturnal and daylight functions still remain anatomically separate? For if rods and cones do follow separate paths, then our rod type of nighttime vision could still persist even though our color vision pathways had been blocked.

In very broad brushstrokes, this chapter will begin to answer the question. Later chapters illustrate why these answers are relevant to kensho. The simplified approach that follows is intended to meet this chapter's needs. It discusses our two familiar categories of rod and cone vision in terms of two separate "prototype visual paths." (It does so with the caveat that any such composite description greatly understates the complex ways they overlap.)

The Upper (Rod) Pathways That Contribute to "Where" Vision

From their rod receptors in the retina, most rod channels lead back to *large* nerve cells in the lateral geniculate nucleus[2] (see chapter 44). In primates, these big *magno*cellular (M) cells occupy the first two layers of the geniculate nucleus. M cells have *high contrast sensitivities*. This enables their visual signals to seem "brighter" in the very center of an image. These signals then "stand out" more than do others from zones off to the side.

The next relays carry rod channel impulses far back to the primary visual cortex (VI) in the occipital lobes[3] (BA 17) (see figure 7, chapter 40). Thereafter, many of their relevant messages abruptly change course. Their relays now leap forward (through the middle and superior temporal areas), to take an *upward* path into the parietal lobes.

This upward-directed stream contributes to our higher spatial functions (chapter 41). Such spatial functions provide us with refined 3D information about "where" some external item is located (see chapter 75).

However, these same upward relays also provide dynamic, actionable information. They help us decode *how* this external item is moving, *how* its shape is oriented with respect to other items out there in space, and *how* each of its positions relates back in ways that enable our hands and other parts of our own physical self to keep acting upon it.

The Lower (Cone) Pathways That Contribute to Color Vision

Relaying back from cone receptors in the retina, the "cone channels" reach much smaller cells in the lateral geniculate nucleus. These small cells are called *parvocellular* (P) neurons. In the geniculate, P cells occupy either layers 3 and 5, or 4 and 6. Even though their messages also lead back to the primary visual cortex (to separate zones of areas V1 and V2), many of their next cortical projections then pursue a *downward* course. This will lead them to several visual association regions. One in particular merits special attention.

In this region, many specialized nerve cells are not just highly sensitive to crude messages about visual wavelengths. They also help convert this raw sensory data into our more *conscious perceptions of color*. This specialized region is concentrated mainly in and near the fusiform gyrus (see figure 4, chapter 23). Extrasensitive to color, it lies hidden on the undersurface where the temporal and occipital lobes join. It seems prudent to refer to it here as the "V4 color complex."[4]

Note how far apart now are the two different main streams of the upper (rod) pathway and the lower (cone) pathway.

Subsequent Temporal Lobe Contributions to "What" Vision, to Our Sense of Psychic Selfhood, and to Our Notions of "When"

As we follow this lower stream of visual messages, we find it integrated into many other circuits farther forward within the rest of the temporal lobe. Remarkable pattern recognition functions arise within these templates. They help us identify "what" we are now looking at. Farther forward and medially, other intricate temporal lobe circuits do even more. They provide a matrix for our more intimate subjectivities. For example, in an instant, they start helping us resolve the answers to a second kind of "what" questions: *what* does this external object *mean to me*, personally, right now?

To answer the personal question, these networks must also have referred back, subconsciously, to a range of earlier, *time*-bound memories. (Had that object or event harmed me, *in the past*, or did it help me?) (See chapter 29.) In short, these lower networks not only quickly accessed their feature recognition systems (while noting the patterns of colors involved), they also consulted their storehouse of memories (see chapter 42). Instantly, there arrived a new kind of emotionally valanced, personal evaluation. This larger self-referent time frame now personified something quite subtle: our private, implicit sense of *"when."* And all this happened automatically.

The short paragraphs above condense volumes of highly technical information. Two qualifications must be added immediately to any such cavalier version of visual "streams." First, in their every operation, the two prototype paths engage in a myriad of to-and-fro interactions. They also consult in complex ways with multiple closely related regions (e.g., the thalamus, limbic, and paralimbic systems).

Second, as the "two" major visual streams continue to relay farther forward, they are constantly providing messages from the "bottom → up." These, the prefrontal cortex quickly processes in its usual executive "top-down" manner.[5]

How might such functions help us in our daily life? Suppose we are hungry, and happen to see a pile of round, red objects lying on a table. Instantly, we recognize *what* they are—a pile of apples and tomatoes, for example. Moreover, we are also poised to select one particular fruit in the back of this pile. It has the correct shape for an apple; its dark-red color means that it is ripe enough to eat; its relative position suggests that it is free to be grasped without dislodging the rest of the pile.

Colors Have Secondary Effects on Our Emotional Palate

If you put on blue-gray–tinted glasses, the scenery immediately appears more somber. Not only is it drained of color's familiar emotional overtones but sometimes its coolness also seems to be missing a few cognitive resonances. In these respects, putting on dark glasses is like shifting out of a daylight mode into a nocturnal mode. When you put on rose-colored glasses, the world certainly looks better.

Colors prompt secondary affective responses. Colors became linked with the ways various past experiences conditioned us. These old feeling tones infuse our everyday likes and dislikes. Even so, several color preferences seem common in the population at large. Some would generalize so far as to suggest that "extroverts like warm colors and introverts like cool colors." "Cool light at low levels makes things look eerie and unnatural." White is "bleak, emotionless, sterile."[6]

Moreover, color goes on subtly to influence our behavior. Some persons are more readily aroused by colors at the red end of the spectrum. In contrast, blue light tends to reduce a person's activities. Blue tones can calm crying infants, even infants who are not yet culturally conditioned.[7]

Sacks and Wasserman nicely sum up how very influential colors have finally become in the psychic lives of mature adults: "Color ... is taken to higher and higher levels, admixed inseparably with all our visual memories, images, desires, expectations, until it becomes an integral part of ourselves ... our life world."[8]

Clearly, color influences our outlook on life. Can you conceive of a process that first transforms one's whole outlook on life, then infuses a mood, and—much later—briefly wipes out color, *selectively*?

I couldn't either.

95

Significance of the Late "Moonlight" Phase within the Whole Profile of Kensho

The time when the moon appears is not necessarily night.

Master Dogen (1200–1253)[1]

Why did colors drop out during kensho's late "moonlight" phase? Is this a brief, temporary form of color blindness? Yes. But it is a rare kind of "color blindness." Not the one we are most familiar with. That kind affects cone receptors in the retina. It is chronic, congenital.

Rarely, however, a patient suddenly loses the conscious appreciation of colors after a localized brain infarct. This neurological disorder is called *cerebral achromatopsia*. It means that *brain* dysfunction, not retinal dysfunction, caused the patient to lose color vision. And if the major color-sensitive regions had been disabled on *both* sides of the brain, then *all* color vision would be lost in both the right and left fields of vision.

When, in the Total Profile of Kensho, Did the Colorless "Moonlight" Phase Arrive?

This colorless nocturne arrived *late* [Z:536–544]. Just *before* it arrived, it is important to emphasize the nature of an impression that was already there. It was a profound psychic vacancy. It had developed since the beginning of the first affirmations of Absolute Reality, Immanent Perfection, and Eternity. This vacancy reached cavernous proportions. It left the impression that the deepest roots of the *I-Me-Mine* were empty at their most visceral level. Chapters 97 and 98 explore the nature of this impression.

Here, it suffices to observe only that this tardy moonlight phase did not enter until *after* consciousness had first been totally drained of selfhood, of fear, of time, and of the impulse to act. Only then, finally, was visual perception suddenly drained of one special quality. *Of the last drop of color*. (See the top right quadrant of table 11.)

Table 11
A Succession of Earlier and Late Phenomena during a "Taste of Kensho"

	First Insight-Realizations			*The Late Visual Illusions*[a]			
	The Early Shift out of an Egocentric into an Allocentric Awareness			*The Late Shift toward the Phase of Visual Epiphenomena*			
				Phase of Moonlight Perception (Colors Lost, Light Dim)			
The succession of phases and topics	*A vacancy of I-Me-Mine; a deep impression of objectivity; as it progressed, it hinted at "moodlight"*	*A transfiguration,[b] perceived and felt as the objective reality and immanent perfection of all things as they really are (suchness)*	*A vacancy that dissolved all fear, and all sense of time into eternity*	*"Moonlight only"*	*Enhanced contrasts and soft "moon-glow" highlights*	*Negative afterimage*	*Final phase of visual distancing and displacement*
The first three major phases [Z:593–613]	*Reflection I*		*Reflection II*	*At end of reflection II*			*Start of reflection III*[c]
Relative duration of each, expressed as a percent of the total elapsed time (approximations)	*100 (Entered first, gathered momentum, and lasted throughout)*	*75 (Also entered first, then faded)*	*20 (Entered later during kensho, and lasted until the end)*	*2*	*1*	*1*	*1*
Usual sense of self (% of normal)	0	0	0	0	0	0	"i" (perhaps 3%)
Affirmative infusion	0	100	0	0	0	0	0
Visuoperceptual coloration (% of normal)	100	100	100	0	0	0	±25

[a]Think of the solid bar below the table as a condensed "timeline." Let it represent the apparent duration of the first insight-realizations of kensho per se. Note the elongated mound, superimposed. It represents the cool psychic vacancy and impression of "moodlight." Note that it began and was established long *before* the "moonlight" phase began. The slender extended bar at the end of the thickness suggests that the late visual epiphenomena occupied only the final 5% or so of all the events summarized in this table.

[b]Definition of *transfiguration*: that early inspirational infusion of sacramental/holy resonances which transforms the ordinary appearances and meanings of things.

[c]The sense of inexpressibility arrived late, just after this distancing and displacement faded.

Key Issues Raised in Contemporary Research by This Moonlight Nocturne

Master Dogen wrote that nighttime was not the only time that the "moon" of enlightenment might appear. Eight centuries ago, what did he really mean? We can't be sure. Dogen could tap into several levels of meaning in one line, simultaneously.

Today, we must ask a very pointed question of any contemporary observer (especially if he or she also happens to be a neurologist): How do you explain a late phase of "moonlight" *and* other final visual illusions, when they arrive at nine o'clock in the morning? Searching for possible answers, we find ourselves immediately out at the frontiers of the neurosciences, sifting the latest research.

Ten questions in this chapter serve as the preliminary agenda for our search. They address the nature and the mechanisms of visual illusions in general. They also provide a background for understanding the unusual perceptual phenomena of the first "moonlight only" phase (see table 11, fourth column from the right). Then, in subsequent chapters, we explore the implications of the next three epiphenomena: the exaggerated soft highlights, the late negative afterimage, and the final phase of visual distancing and displacement. (These illusions are summarized in the *the* three rightmost columns of table 11.)

1. Which physiological mechanisms underlie the *early* phases of insight during kensho? (starting at the left of table 11). Much still remains to be learned about this and other alternate states of consciousness (see chapter 86). Their elementary physiological themes might seem obvious: *excitation* and *inhibition* (see chapter 31). Yet a certain kind of inhibitory process can go on from there, to enhance excitation *secondarily* [Z:255, 462]. How does this occur? By inhibiting other local inhibitory mechanisms which previously had held excitation in check. *Disinhibition* is the term for this third mechanism.

   Let us start by commenting on two initial affirmative realizations—absolute reality and immanent perfection. Both affirmations merged in the form of one single meaningful comprehension: "suchness" (see chapter 82). *Suchness* is a Buddhist technical term (I would not appreciate its use until later). It serves as a very pale, temporary, shorthand substitute for the scope of an unparalleled, wordless insight. Suchness describes the unveiling, in one comprehensive flash, of all things directly, as *they* really are. Some think of this singular moment in terms of *reality realizing itself* [Z:549–553].

   A related term is *transfiguration*. It implies that the appearance of things is transformed, often to an exalted, spiritually sacred degree.

   What causes this extraordinary insight? How can the matrix of a person's ordinary conscious vision become so transfigured? Suppose we start with a simple postulate: perhaps an array of *net* excitatory processes converge in unusual ways and to unusual degrees; their confluence infuses atmospheres of salience into our normal interpretive functions.

Must the lofty, sacred resonances of suchness take place exclusively at "higher cortical" levels? No. Because this profoundly affirmative tone of the early insightful phase could also draw upon the person's more primitive networks and on functions that are basically intuitive. Noteworthy in this regard is the *wordless*ness of the insightful phase. Wordlessness suggests that deeper subcortical circuits are being drawn into novel configurations. Their intuitive functions could be far distant from the cortical circuits we engage when we construct our usual kinds of internal thought-language [Z:521–529]. Moreover, in order for salience to take over and transfigure the foreground, the mental field must drop out some ordinary "things" that had been there before and that had arisen at multiple levels, both conscious and unconscious.

2. Which systems that enter into kensho's initial shifts in consciousness could set the stage for its *late* changes in visual perception? Clearly, kensho's rapid onset, scope, and total impact represent a major *state* change in the brain. This is an immense shift of consciousness. It invites comparisons with the three other major conventional states that also shift us back and forth: waking, sleeping, and dreaming [Z:298–305].

   So, it is pertinent to ask: What kinds of mechanisms generate these other three states? Impulses rising mostly from the *brainstem* trigger many of their earliest sequences. These ascending excitations shift and reshape consciousness at successively higher thalamocortical levels. Both glutamate and acetylcholine systems are the prime movers for many of these ("positive") processes of fast excitatory transmission.

   But a major point cannot be emphasized enough: *subtractions* underlie many of kensho's early phenomena [Z:607, 611, 614, 657]. Which messenger systems had cut off all concepts and roots of my psychic self? Which had severed its prior notions of fear, of time, and of possessing a physical self-image? These ("negative") phenomena are predominately *inhibitory.*

   Kensho's early egocentric subtractions (and some of its late waves, as well) are most likely attributable to GABA, the brain's major fast inhibitory transmitter [Z:208–210]. They enable the conscious foreground, *and* the subconscious background to drop out their former preoccupations.

   However, the seven columns in table 11 also outline successive waves of phenomena. Kensho's initial events, major in amplitude, later trail off into a diminuendo. Could this extended profile mean that *different* messenger systems are in operation? Did they release their messengers at, or near, different receptor sites, some of whose responses occur more slowly? Receptors activated by biogenic amines are slightly "slower" sites. Slower still are the receptor sites for peptides, both opioid and nonopioid (see chapters 24, 34, 35, and 36).

Moreover, another wave of secondary metabolic consequences supervenes at many receptor sites. These changes reshape a nerve cell's excitability (see chapter 37). A novel candidate is nitric oxide, because this gas influences many remarkable processes, quickly or slowly, as tiny "puffs" diffuse out into the brain nearby (see chapters 68 and 69) [Z:407–413].

3. Having now surveyed this whole pattern of kensho's earliest insightful realizations, do any generalizations seem applicable to the very *late* phase of visual illusions? (see the right side of table 11).

   First, let us be very clear: Every conventional, orthodox Buddhist emphasis deserves to fall on kensho's initial aspects: its flashing insights (*prajna*) and its absolute selflessness (*anatta*). Both phenomena arrive early and impact profoundly. The condensed timeline at the bottom of table 11 illustrates that they also exerted their major influence throughout a relatively long period. Clinical neurology adheres to a similar principle. As a general rule, one assignes the greatest weight to the patient's *first* symptoms. These earliest phenomena are called the "focal signature." They point toward the primary, pivotal mechanisms.

   Then why would this witness/neurologist/author spend time on "postscript" phenomena? Aren't such late events epiphenomena? Yes. Won't they divert attention from the classic earlier themes of kensho? Yes, *but* these are what the witness *really experienced*. This is the way it *was*.

   So these delayed visual illusions are not some kind of grace note to be ignored or dismissed. They challenge us to provide contemporary answers in terms of psychophysiology. If we take at face value Shih-t'ou's statement that "What meets the eye is the Way," then this new millennium is poised to ask: What causes such delayed illusions? Who develops them?

   a. What does their delayed arrival signify? Does this time lag point toward the interval which separates the abrupt onset of the brain's fast *excitatory* transmitters from the delayed onset of its slower excitatory transmitters and their still slower second messengers? [Z:223–225]. Is $NO^{\cdot}$ implicated?
   b. Could the late illusions express a separate subset of *inhibitory* processes, the normal sequences of which simply evolve more slowly?
   c. Could some aspects of the later illusions represent a delayed inhibitory rebound, a late *secondary* response to the earlier primary excitatory processes (just cited in [a] above), whereas other aspects might reflect a late wave of rebound excitation released during a wave of *dis*inhibition?
   d. Could any of the three separate options just cited above (that pertain to late phenomena) also help us go back and identify some early major primary mechanisms, the ones which had first deleted selfhood from consciousness and had dissolved time into eternity?
   e. Do people predisposed to migraine have slightly different kensho experiences and associated perceptual illusions? (see chapter 73).

We now return to the issues on the original agenda.

4. At a time when vision would seem to have been drained only of color, why would the overall *amount* of lighting *also* appear suddenly to drop?

   Two potential mechanisms may have converged. The first serves as a reminder of a simple fact: it's our cone channels that contribute much of the *illumination* we normally register from any daylight scene. Why? Because cone messages convey *luminance, not just color.* Part of the explanation for this predominant cone contribution to luminance begins in our eye. The retina has eight times more small (P) ganglion cells in its cone pathway than it has large (M) ganglion cells in the rod pathway.[2] Therefore, when the impulse flow stops anywhere along this cone pathway it cuts down on how much "illumination" the person visualizes arising from the scene. Therefore, my impression of "dim nocturnal light" is consistent with a sudden block in the cone pathway.

   The second mechanism serves as another reminder: the rod pathway has an inherent limitation. Rods require many more minutes to adapt to darkness than we usually think. Remember how you had to grope for a seat when you left the sunlight and entered a dark theatre for a matinee? Your rod functions, bleached by daylight, were still down near baseline levels. The movie theatre seemed pitch-black at first. In fact, our rod functions take nearly *thirty* minutes of adaptation before they reach their peak nighttime sensitivity to light.

   Similar dual explanations could account for the "moonlight only" phenomena of the delayed lunar phase: visual functions abruptly deprived of their normal cone channel input; rod channel functions far from being fully adapted; a witness now left with the impression of viewing a dim "nighttime" scene (see table 11).

5. Why did many finer-grained details of the London scenery become submerged within a sea of darker tones? Cone channels add more than color and illumination. They also contribute sharp, fine-grained details to our normal vision in daylight. Rod channel circuits lack these high degrees of resolution. Indeed, *visual acuity drops fourfold* when only rod channels serve vision.[3]

   Could a similar loss of visual details (previously conferred by my usual cone channels) have contributed to my brief impression of a shift into "nighttime vision?" Probably. Such a drop in visual details would tend to confirm the illusion that this same London scene was being seen—less clearly now—during the kind of reduced light that seemed consistent with "nighttime."

6. Is inhibition of the major local, color-sensitive regions up in *cortex* per se the only explanation for such a sudden loss of color? The "V4 color complex" lies in the cortex of the fusiform gyrus and collateral sulcus (BA 37). This is hidden on the *undersurface* of the brain (see figure 4, chapter 23; figure 7, chapter 40).

Many case reports illustrate that patients lose their sense of color vision after lesions here.

Do such reports exclude a different potential site in the lateral geniculate nucleus, earlier along the cone pathway, and nearer to the retina?[4] No, because the small P cells of the geniculate are anatomically separate (as viewed with the aid of a microscope) from the large M cells. However, no local block limited to these P cells can explain kensho's other losses: of self, time, and fear. These are major experiential subtractions. They require substantial inhibitory deletions of functions elsewhere in the brain. Many of these distant modules are very far removed from any processes that might (theoretically) stop or otherwise jam the transmission of color messages down at the local geniculate level.

In contrast, the region of the V4 color complex—in and around the fusiform cortex—does lie close to relevant sites in the temporo-occipital cortex and farther on, sites where key categorizing and pattern-recognition functions reside.

7. What are some of the other vital functions linked to this inferior temporo-occipital region? We process more than colors here; we also begin to *recognize visual patterns and forms* (see chapter 42). An intense research interest is now focused on sorting out the many essential cognitive functions of the fusiform gyrus and its adjacent regions. Most such current research remains so technically complex as to fall outside our present scope. However, with regard to the phenomena of kensho, a brief survey of the way we recognize faces and bodies becomes pertinent. Indeed, recent research helps clarify how our brains bring a conscious sense of visual coherence to sensory data that are otherwise incongruous.[5]

   It now seems that our brains normally discriminate key information about faces not only in parts of the mid-fusiform gyrus just *in front of* the most color-responsive region but also selectively in the nearby *inferior* occipital region.[6] For example, some patients no longer recognize familiar faces even after small lesions occur in this general region. Their disorder is called *prosopagnosia*.

   Moreover, recent fMRI studies point to the importance of another nearby region of the visual association cortex. It lies out in the *lateral* part of the occipitotemporal region. There it is part of the so-called lateral occipital complex. This "body area" (especially on the *right* side) is specialized to respond *selectively* to visual images depicting human *bodies* and *body parts*. It serves normally as an initial processing step, helping us reduce an inchoate mass of environmental stimuli into simpler, coarse-grained shapes that will soon become the basis for further pattern recognition functions.[7]

   Kensho and satori briefly dissolve many similar discriminative, categorizing, and affective brain functions. It is plausible to attribute some of these subtractions to the dropping out of functions represented in these *inferior temporo-occipital and adjacent regions*. Inhibition of functions represented within this whole posterior temporal region could contribute both to kensho's striking *early* loss of certain prior cognitive distinctions and to the extent of the associated psychic deconditioning.

This is not to say, however, that this association cortex can only be inhibited (or enhanced) by mechanisms confined to the cortical level. The caveat in chapter 44 on the thalamus explains why.

8. Why did previous generations of clinicians attribute so many relevant visual illusions to the back of the brain, and especially to the junctions between the temporal, parietal, and occipital lobes? (BA: 37, 39, 40, and the posterior part of 22).

Current diagrams of the circuitry of this large region illustrate why. They reveal a vast mosaic of visual modules (now more than 32 and counting), linked by countless interactions that proceed in a feedforward, feedbackward, and horizontal manner. Maps depicting these linking connections are more intricate than diagrams of the Tokyo subway system.[8]

Over a century ago, Hughlings Jackson (1835–1911) analyzed visual illusions in the course of his pioneering neurologic studies. He concluded that they were "positive mental states."[9] Why did Jackson also believe that such episodic illusions were doubly "imperfect?" First, because he intuited an essential principle: some *prior* "negative" mental state had allowed them to be released; second, because his patients' visual symptoms were then manifested to degrees that exceeded normal.

Today, one stands in awe at Jackson's prescience. His bedside interpretations seem already to have suggested the possibility that some illusions (1) represented excessive, excitatory ("positive") mental states; and (2) had been released by prior inhibitory ("negative") processes. With respect to the first mechanisms of excess, one can envision today that some illusions could also be expressing a wave of secondary rebound excitatory phenomena (that were disinhibitory).

Critchley, who later reviewed additional case reports, was also an astute clinical neurologist. By 1955, it had become abundantly clear to him that a large "visuo-psychic association area" existed in the back of our brain. This region could also express "manifold visual phenomena of a most interesting and complex kind."[10]

Five decades ago, Critchley anticipated a major conclusion of part IX in this book. He carefully pointed out that such visual illusions were also often "met with in normal, though sensitive, aesthetic and introspective individuals." He appreciated that illusions were not caused only by focal diseases that damaged the structure of the brain.[11] Indeed, we considered in chapter 73 how the genetic and physiological aspects of such sensitivities might relate to migraine and we continue to examine this point in chapter 98.

The early neurological case reports cite several visual illusions pertinent to phases in the kensho narrative of chapter 93. The illusions are referable to sites more posterior within this intricate interlobar borderland of association cortex. They include:

a. An illusion of "distance." Objects "having the correct size may (still) seem to be . . . too far away."[12] This condition is sometimes called *teleopsia*, from the Greek *tele*, far off, distant.
b. An illusion of displacement. Things appear displaced to the opposite side of the environment with respect to the prior midline of the person's focus of awareness.[13]

9. What other pertinent illusions have been associated with sites farther forward in the temporal lobes themselves? These illusions involve visual and other forms of memory, feelings of reality, concepts of self, and concepts of time. For example, Williams regarded the normal middle and posterior temporal areas as "an extensive zone serving visual integration."[14]

   When Williams then summarized the clinical symptoms referable to *just* the "temporal" lobe, he cited an array of illusions. It is worth commenting again on two pertinent aspects of the first two pairs of symptoms listed below, (c) and (d) and (e) and (f): each pair hinges on the way time-related memory functions are interpreted; note that the diametrically *opposite* items in each pair lead to mutually exclusive conclusions (see chapter 83).

c. Simpler illusions of déjà vu; and of (d) jamais vu (already *seen* vs. never *seen* before) [Z:251–252]. These two illusions are referable to sites more anterior and medial in the temporal lobe.
e. More complex illusions of déjà vécu and of (f) jamais vécu (already *experienced*; vs. never before *experienced*). Subtly infusing the whole experience in the déjà vécu phenomenon are emotionally toned memories and deeper somatic/visceral resonances. Therefore, the person sees percepts changing not simply as isolated visual phenomena, but rather feels personally involved within a larger, much more organized and embodied, total *sensory-emotional experience*. (Vécu symptoms of this nature could resemble some normal "*mood*light" embodiments of our affective responses to actual moonlight, as well as similar deeper experiential impressions during kensho.) In contrast, jamais vécu is a major *dis*embodied feeling of *un*familiarity and even disenchantment within the total perceptual environment.

Many reports, including some voiced by my own patients, describe more elaborate experiences than are cited in the simpler examples of the two opposing pairs just above ([c] and [d] and [e] and [f]). This suggests that they draw on more complex networking systems. How do we judge what is *really* real? This would seem to involve the integrations among networks distributed both within and beyond the temporal lobe per se. Notice again that the person undergoes only one experience at a time, out of a potential pair that can manifest itself in either of two distinctly opposite directions:

g. The salient reality, significance, and novelty of the whole ongoing experience are greatly enhanced. This can evolve along an increasingly awesome scale leading to profound realizations.
h. Meanings associated with the current environment can disintegrate. This may reach such a degree that the experience becomes totally "unreal." This condition is called total *de*realization;

Still other elaborate states dissolve the sense of personal self and of time, again in ways that suggest inhibitory effects within networks that could extend beyond the temporal lobe:

i. The person's prior constructs and concepts of selfhood can vanish (along with all of selfhood's emotional and visceral attachments). This can reach degrees that are experienced as profound *de*personalization [Z:49].
j. Many concepts of time (past, present, future) can dissolve in ways experienced along a scale from timelessness to eternity (see chapter 84).[15]

10. How do different regions within the temporal lobe express themselves, especially during *discrete* electrical stimulations, or sometimes as the result of focal seizures that begin in the temporal lobe?

"Psychic" phenomena can develop when responsive sites in the temporal lobes of epileptic patients become overstimulated. This can occur either in the course of discrete brain stimulation techniques or during a spontaneous focal seizure. We next examine each category.

a. *The evidence from discrete electrical stimulations.* For our purposes in these pages, the most convincing evidence is derived from the kinds of pinpoint electrical stimulations used in the operating room. These preliminary steps help localize the site of the abnormal seizure focus. The neurosurgeon can then remove this focus with minimal damage to surrounding tissue.[16]

One crucial point about these discrete electrical excitations deserves emphasis: Patients report that their resulting experiential phenomena assume a "compelling immediacy."[17] Many of their percepts, now enhanced, penetrate the psyche with intimate personal resonances. As events, they become fully integrated into the patient's personality. They seem *actual* and in this sense "real." So at least *one aspect of our complex interpretation about real* reality *can arise from circuits that begin in the medial temporal region.*

Well-localized stimulations most frequently produce three kinds of phenomena: fear, visual illusions, and déjà vu illusions. They are often referred to as "positive" phenomena. (Jackson's interpretations would suggest that excitatory mechanisms were not their sole component.) An important point: the amygdala is the major source for eliciting both fear, visual illusions, and déjà vu illusions. It has the lowest threshold and is clearly the most sensitive site.

Yet, note that a *loss* of fear occurs in kensho. The simplest explanation for this loss is that parts of the amygdala or its connections are being inhibited (see chapter 27) [Z:608–609]. The *total* loss of fear during kensho suggests *bilateral inhibitions* within this network of fear.

Stimulating the hippocampus also causes psychic phenomena. Yet these symptoms begin only when afterdischarges have spread *beyond* the hippocampus to engage other sites, including the amygdala. Sites farther away in the temporal cortex (outside of these two anterior and medial locations) are much less responsive. Even so, some discrete stimulations can still be effective (especially on the right side). They can still produce various visual phenomena even when they are delivered to discrete cortical sites at points extending all the way from the temporo-occipital junction in the back up to the polar tip of the temporal lobe.[18]

When such symptoms take on a more complex experiential flavor, Gloor attributes this not to excitation alone, but to the "formation of a specifically patterned matrix of excited and inhibited neurons dispersed within widely distributed neuronal populations" of both the cortex and the limbic system. This sentence serves as a concise summary of the mechanisms underlying almost any experience, major or minor, that humans can undergo.

Seizures triggered by discrete, single-pulse, *intra*cranial stimuli seem to "ignite" by degrees. The *delayed* responses—the ones that start from 0.1 to 1.0 second *after* this electrical stimulus—best identify the most abnormally sensitive local site, the seizure focus which served to trigger most of that patient's own spontaneous seizures.[19]

Whether the phenomenon of a "sensed presence" during diffuse, artificial *extracranial* stimulation of the temporal lobe is equivalent to, or comparable with, other religious/spiritual experiences is a complex matter discussed elsewhere (see chapters 42 and 49).[20]

b. *The evidence from rare, spontaneous, temporal lobe seizure disorders*. Seizures are common in the population at large (estimates suggest around 1.7 cases per thousand). However, it is rare to find case reports of temporal lobe seizures, *fully documented by modern methods*, that begin with an aura of so-called ecstatic symptoms[21] [Z:405–407]. Physicians familiar with the classic core experiences of kensho-satori are not likely to confuse their expressions with true epileptic seizures [Z:405–407]. That epileptic seizures do differ from kensho both in their hallucinatory character and in their other features becomes evident from the following two case reports. These two reports, documented in journal articles, were published in 1988 and 1990. Symptoms in another patient have been cited briefly.[22]

The EEG focus of seizure activity in a 62-year-old woman was referable to her left anterior and middle temporal region. Her episodes were associated with visual hallucinations ("I saw my god!"; "A halo appeared around god"). Among her other words describing this experience were "joyous"; a "revelation"; "My mind, my whole being ... pervaded by a feeling of delight."[23]

In a 38-year-old man, a right anterior temporal lobe invasive tumor led to seizures. These began with feelings of irritation, then detachment. Next came a bright light. It seemed to be a source of knowledge and understanding, and was followed by the vague appearance of a young bearded man whom the patient assumed to be the Christ. Time expanded, the patient felt at ease with himself and his environment, and sensed an ineffable contentment and fulfillment.[24]

Chapter 93 surveyed the profile of an episode of kensho. Table 11 then called attention to its sequences. This chapter went on to pose an agenda of questions, and reviewed the variety of symptoms attributed to the temporal lobe *and* to its junction with the parietal and occipital cortex.

In the next chapter, we examine the delayed phenomena that occurred late in kensho—*after* the "moonlight only" phase. They are *not* seizures. They are illusions that illustrate three points: first, though the brain's physiological mechanisms might seem to be limited to excitation and inhibition, its repertoire of phenomena is phenomenal. Second, these phenomena vary remarkably, depending on which brain networks are involved. Third, they illustrate Critchley's point, that some visual illusions tend to occur in normal, visually "sensitive" individuals.

96

Significance of the Illusions at the Close of the Moonlight Phase

Penetrating the clouds to the sky beyond, even on a rainy night I see the moon.

Master Daito Kokushi (1282–1337)[1]

The doctrines which best repay critical examination are those which for the longest period have remained unquestioned.

Alfred North Whitehead (1861–1947)

The discussion in the previous chapter sounds like frank reductionism. If a reader were attached to a fixed belief system, then any attempt to associate kensho with visual illusions could also sound like heresy. Someone is likely to be offended. Why examine old belief systems at all?

Suppose you happened to be a person who had begun as a biologist-humanist, that you next wandered into the neurosciences, and that you then encountered Zen experience firsthand. Perhaps this might explain why you tried to make sense out of some of kensho's visual phenomena. And why our next agenda includes six questions with some answers.

Why were the soft highlights enhanced during the phase of moonlight perception?

Many local white-against-black contrasts appeared exaggerated. Blacks were darker, whites were lighter. No changes were so pronounced that they created an effect of glare. Inherent in rod pathways are distinctive properties that can also produce similar heightened contrast effects. For example, certain cells in the rod pathway are eight times more sensitive to light/dark contrasts than are cells of the cone pathway.[2] These high-contrast functions can become more obvious when all vision suddenly passes through rod channels alone.

The brain's center/surround mechanisms also enhance white-against-black contrast effects. Surround inhibitions and other related ("lateral") inhibitions are normal intrinsic properties of many different cell populations. These circuits extend from the retina far back into the occipital lobe (see chapters 31 and 94). Similar enhancements offer a plausible explanation for the softer highlights. Their presence along a wide variety of boundaries left the net impression that the London scenery was illuminated by a subtle kind of "moonglow."[3]

What can explain the brief, negative afterimage? (see table 11, at top right, in chapter 95).

The lunar interval terminated in this singular illusion. Recall that vision was still totally in its black-and-white mode. Suddenly it rendered this same entire scene as a *negative afterimage*.

What does such a (so-called) negative afterimage look like? It resembles what you see when you hold up an ordinary semitransparent photographic negative against an evenly lighted background. The overall effect is strange: white occupies each location where you would expect black to be in the final print; black occupies those other areas where you expect the final print to show white. Most details are there, but your whole mental set must shift 180 degrees to comprehend them.

Years later, when I began to analyze this negative image phase, I recalled how the early continental film directors had used this technique to infuse "otherworldly" qualities into dreamlike movie scenes (e.g. F. Murnau in *Nosferatu*, 1922).[4] Having searched in vain for clinical reports describing this curious light/dark negative shift, I would welcome correspondence concerning its mechanisms and occurrence.)

But that wasn't all. Quickly, this negative image reversed itself. It switched back to that immediately previous version, meaning that initial, contrast-enhanced, black-and-white rendition of the original scenery (see chapter 49).

Why did the negative image suddenly switch back to the positive black-and-white image?

A basic property of networks in the occipital and frontal cortex is that they strike a dynamic balance between being excited and being inhibited.[5] Recurrent interactions help to sponsor their reverberations. Any slight pause in these underlying recurrent processes—*by synaptic inhibition*—causes them to stop. In their simplest form, the abrupt reversals of perception that can then occur are described as resembling a kind of "network flip-flop." This switch from one mode to the other can occur several times a second. (I only saw one.)

Several aspects of such shifts are also consistent with the sparing of rod channel functions. Their distinctive fast-firing phasic attributes are in keeping with rapid shifts. Their intrinsic high-contrast sensitivities are also consistent with such light/dark reversals.[6]

Quick shifts also characterize the way other figure-ground illusions move in and out of our visual awareness. We return for one analogy to that familiar example so often pictured in psychology texts. In this ambiguous figure, sometimes we see two dark, inward-facing facial profiles; at other times the perceptual shift reveals the curving sides of that white vase in the center.

However, this London scene was different. It was a large complex mosaic of light/dark contrasts. Each detailed item of its entire pattern had been shifted back-and-forth in completely opposite directions. How can we explain such a totally orderly shift, one that reversed *all the contents* throughout a person's whole field of vision in a coherent manner? When pattern reversals involve details on so large a scale, it suggests that some global process(es) had been applied, simultaneously, at some supraordinate level of organization.[7] Where?

Solely to try out a first-order approximation of a final explanation, let us return to focus on that first moment of the "moonlight *only*" phase (see table 11, chapter 95). When my rod channel vision had first "framed" this extensive visual scene, where had its light/dark pattern been represented in my so-called mind's eye? Not at any one small spot, like a single frame on some 16 mm filmstrip. Rather within an intricate network of thalamic ↔ cortical and transcortical circuits.

Next, let us suppose that some "imperfect" out-of-phase oscillations had arrived. Say that these oscillations were so irregular that they disordered the firing rhythms within all these rod channel (black-and-white) networks. It wouldn't take much. Suppose, for example, that the reticular nucleus had briefly inserted a few cycles that were *over*inhibitory (see chapter 46). This brief dynamic "imbalance" could disrupt the usual *in*phase reverberations that the reticular nucleus normally uses to integrate the conscious functions of the first visual system (and perhaps to mesh them with the second visual system)[8] [Z:241].

How can the delayed phenomenon of "distancing" be explained?

Late in the London experience, the scenery seemed perhaps three times *farther* away than before. True, its overall dimensions seemed slightly smaller. Yet this reduction in size (micropsia) *did not seem commensurate in degree* with the impression of this much "depth." In retrospect, this brief paradoxical dissociation between distance and size appeared to represent the overlapping of two separate *visual perceptual phenomena*. No simple explanation, such as a feeling of being merely *emotionally* "distant" from the scene, suffices to account for this perceptual change.

Yet, even though the London scene seemed distanced, it had not actually been observed *in motion* on its way *back* there, as one normally perceives the action of a zoom lens while it "contracts" a scene. That is, the scene was not caught in the *act* of moving *back* toward that "distant" position in space. Nor was it "caught" in the next act which had then replaced it back in its conventional *forward* position.

This *lack of apparent motion* grabs our interest. It's like the dog that *didn't* bark in the Sherlock Holmes tale of "Silver Blaze" [Z:604]. Why no movement in the interim? Recent research indicates that the middle temporal region has more than one function. True, in the past, this V5 region was believed to help mediate only our dynamic perception of *moving* objects. However, some sites in this V5 region have been shown to confer a sense of depth perception. Specifically, these sites help primates perceive the *depth of stationary objects in space.*[9]

Therefore, the fact that a human subject could develop the visual impression of "distancing" per se, in the absence of motion back *to* "there" (and also to a degree out of proportion to the apparent reduction in size) lends support to the primate research data. It suggests that a person can arrive at this judgment of *static depth* as a separate, independent, function.

What factors normally enter into such higher-order *integrated* judgments about depth perception? We first need to extract information from multiple lower-order ("bottom-up") sources of data, including such factors as the *relative* size of objects; what we are led to expect based on perspective and experience; how much our two eyes converge or diverge, and so on.

Suppose, however, that a person's highest-order judgmental functions of depth perception have been engaged discretely, this time from the *top down*. The impression of "distancing" suggests that this person might then experience such a misjudgment of "depth" relatively independently of whatever other lower-order data might also be available.

Let us now return to regard this visual illusion of distancing from the perspective of what Hughlings Jackson believed were the causes of illusions. Then, distancing could serve to illustrate one more kind of high-level "imperfection." Today, one might regard this misperception as a brief *imbalance* between excitation and inhibition. Such a misjudgment of depth might be interpreted as the *net* result of an imbalance tipped more toward "positive" excitatory functions. In this instance, it could point to one small part of V5. This site might lateralize more to the middle temporo-occipital region, and be referable to the *right* side of the brain.

What caused the transient phenomenon of visual *displacement*?

The position of the *whole* London scene changed (again without its being observed to move en route). This late event occurred at about the same moment that two other functions first began to recover. One was the faintest sense of a subjective "i." The other was the partial return of the prior sense of colors (see table 11).

At this point, the whole field framed by visual experience was *doubly displaced* (in addition to its being substantially distanced, and rendered slightly smaller in size than before). Thus, the *entire* London scene appeared (a) displaced down below its expected horizontal position, and (b) miscentered slightly to the left of its expected (subjective) "midline."

Only on reflection, years later, did I begin to wonder along the following lines: could this late, partial renewal of the sense of "i"—given that it carried an implicit notion of a returning elementary, physical self-axis—have its correlate in the way this axial "i" could *center its attention*? It seemed plausible. For only if there had occurred some minimal recovery of the sense of a physical axis of self would it be possible to reestablish a "subjective midpoint of attention." And unless some vague subjective notion of a person's head, eyes, and trunk had returned, there would be no basis for recognizing that the "midpoint" of a visual frame had been displaced to an unnatural location.

The keyword in the previous paragraph is *attention* (see chapter 47). Why regard the two slight displacements of the scene as relatively minor misperceptions of attention? Because the other resources of attention were still being fully deployed to register all the many other details of the contents and their relationships throughout this distant scene. Moreover, the witness was then becoming aware that some faint coloration was returning within this large area of preserved attention.

On balance, these observations suggest that what was being misdirected was the *frame of attention* itself. When considered in the context of the other phenomena, this "imperfection" is consistent with a functional *imbalance* of attention. Consider for example, what happens to a person's attention when some slight *net over*activity occurs within the right posterior superior parietooccipital region. The frame of attention is directed *down and to the left** [Z:244–247]. In contrast, when localized brain damage *reduces* the normal activity of this upper parietooccipital region on the *right*, the patients cannot direct their full attention to items in the corresponding left lower quadrant of their visual fields.[10]

So brief an explanation needs to be qualified. The brain distributes attentive functions widely among various hierarchical levels beyond those in the frontal and parietal cortex [Z:274–286]. Physiological biases that operate normally farther down in the thalamus and in other subcortical regions can also "push," or "pull," attention downward and to the left. They, too, not only help *focus* our attention but turn its "frame" in different directions.

So the ways we normally direct our whole "frame" of attention—and the ways this frame can be *mis*directed—hinge on the *net balance* struck among multiple mechanisms at levels high and low. Each factor in such equations can exert a local effect that can finally summate to be either excitatory (+) or inhibitory (−).[11] And an imbalance of attention that arrives *late* is necessarily superimposed on whatever visuosensory association functions and *dys*functions happen to be available to the person at that particular moment.

Could the late illusions of displacement help clarify any functional locations underlying the earliest realizations?

Recall that these early comprehensive, global unifications conveyed an especially salient impression. In its meaningful "closure," all details of the visual field were integrated into one unified embrace. Where do such visual-perceptual integrative functions normally come from? Research into

*With your left eye closed, you can produce a similar "visual displacement" by pressing gently, through your right upper eyelid, on the right upper quadrant of your right eyeball. This will displace what you see with your right eye (only) down and to the left of where you expect it to be. Note that you can *see* the image move down to the left and back again by varying the degree of pressure. I saw no such movement.

their origins points toward one more of the junctional areas under discussion: the confluence between the uppermost visual association cortex and the adjacent posterior parietal lobe, lateralizing more to the *right* side.

To be more explicit, this general upper and posterior localization of many normal visual integrative functions correlates with the *net* results of those activations which would much *later* help displace attention in the opposite direction, namely, down and to the left [Z:601–602]. The two lines of evidence are converging on the back of the brain, on the right side.

Now, let us consider some potential sequences. Suppose several of these normal, coherent, physiological, integrative functions had first been *overactive* during the *early* sequences of kensho. These excessive right-sided parietooccipital activations might then have prompted a *secondary, opposing* inhibitory response. Still *later*, at the close, this might have been followed by a wave of rebound excitation on that right side that led to displacement[12] [Z:602–605] .

If that secondary inhibitory response (mentioned above) had also been excessive in degree and extent, it could then have gone on to block the color-sensitive functions referable to the V4 color complex on both sides, as well as other adjacent vital temporo-occipital associations. Do any visual clues raise the possibility that such an excessive and extensive inhibitory process might influence *both* inferior temporo-occipital regions? Perhaps cast in this role are the delayed visual illusions represented by the first two phases of "moonlight" perception. During then, colors dropped out and the light became dim (see table 11).

Inhibitory processes exert a powerful influence both on the frame of attention and on its contents. We have been referring above to their "net" results. Why? Because their interacting mechanisms are sometimes offsetting and always complex.[13]

This and the previous chapter have discussed a background of plausible explanations for such a delayed phase of moonlight perception during kensho. If the general concept of a "rods-in, cones-out" theory is valid, then why hasn't the Buddhist literature, long before this, made it clear that the *actual visual perception* of a colorless "moonlight" phase was linked with kensho?

Subsequent pages present circumstantial evidence suggesting that the Buddhist literature probably already has made such connections. However, it seems likely that relatively few persons in each century would have made any such link. Moreover, they would need to have set aside other contending options, both cultural and personal, before they could accept the data of their own eyesight.

Even if achromatopsia were to have occurred in only a few, why haven't these few committed themselves to an unequivocal formal recognition of an actual "moonlight" phase of kensho?

Zen isn't like this. Zen prefers to acknowledge by indirection and gesture. Zen tends to avoid speaking about kensho and satori, for many good reasons. Zen literature abounds in allusions. Shih-t'ou still reminds us that we'll always need to read between the lines to realize their deeper underlying principles (see chapter 76). And it also remains possible that an individual teacher might engage in outright rejection for other doctrinal, didactic, or personal reasons.

Keeping a variety of these cultural complications in mind, we turn in the next chapters to consider issues from the fields of psychology, psychophysiology, neurology, and linguistics that illuminate several kinds of associations between kensho and moonlight.

97

Some Cultural and Neural Origins of Moon Metaphors and Visual Symbols

In the mountain's deep places,
the moon of the mind resides in light serene;
Moon mirrors all things everywhere,
Mind mirrors moon . . . in satori now.

Saigyo (1118–1190)[1]

Pointing at the Moon in 1974

I had never spoken with a Zen master before. The two of us were meeting for the first time inside Ryoko-in, a subtemple of Daitokuji in Kyoto. Already in these early minutes, Kobori-Roshi was warning me about words:

"Don't be confused by abstractions or by the word definition of an object or of a person. This is like confusing one's finger with the moon. The word is like a finger; it only points in the direction of the real moon."

I did not understand this at first, but a few nights later, I found myself pointing at the real moon up high in the dark sky. Now, I could appreciate firsthand—informed by my own eyesight and the limited reach of my own finger—how huge was the gap between that actual moon and any words or symbols that might point merely in its direction. No essay in this book narrows such a gap; these paragraphs point only to some major misunderstandings the gap can create.

Cultural Metaphors, Similes, and Visual Symbols

To review: a metaphor implies that two categories are more directly identical than they really are in fact. We invent moon metaphors because we need them. Metaphors are our fundamental mode of communication. Indeed, "All language is highly metaphorical," and most of our "abstract terms are borrowed from physical objects or actions."[2]

We also need moon similes and moon symbols. A simile implies that two things or ideas are only similar, using the words *like* or *as*. A symbol is a sign (often one you can see). It stands for something else that exists independently and is much more complex.

Each of these devices creates problems when subjected to poetic, artistic, and personal license. We find it difficult to distinguish sensory reality from imaginative fiction. Too easily do we assume that every literary reference to moonlight *must* involve a metaphor or simile. We forget that metaphors, similes, and symbols are secondary, creative inventions that depend on the human brain. We use each device to create meaningful links between what we had already perceived first via our special senses, and what cognition then refashioned into concepts (no need to hammer home the point to illustrate the ways we "forge these associative links").

Buddhist iconography serves as an example. For centuries, artists have created distinctive, symbolic positions of the hand when they depict figures of the Buddha. These gestures are termed mudras. In the *abhayamudra*, artists depict the right palm facing outward, with the upright fingers extended. This gesture symbolizes the total fearlessness that is linked with selflessness in kensho.

A recent MEG study reveals what happens when we observe and recognize the meaning of different hand symbols. Our decodings activate several visual association systems. These regions, especially on the right side, are among these implicated in functions associated with different aspects of object recognition, "mirror" neuron responses, and social recognition. Three such locations activate simultaneously: the inferior temporo-occipital, superior temporal sulcus, and inferior parietal regions. The findings suggest that the superior temporal sulcus might act as an interface, helping to integrate the input ascending from the lower visual streams with that from its dorsal counterpart.[3]

Calligraphy is another art form that conveys much to Sino-Japanese expressions. In fluid, soft brushstrokes, Tesshu (1835–1888) once sketched *suigetsu*. Its two characters mean "water-moon."[4] They distill the essence of Zen: water receives the light of the moon directly. There is no pause for discrimination; the moon illuminates all things without discrimination. (chapter 99 will include passing references to symbols—to "moon circles" drawn with a brush, and to bright white circles.)

Buddhist Literary Metaphors and Similes in Haiku; Moodlight

Kobori-Roshi once said to me: "Zen is closest to poetry." Shelley (1792–1822) had expressed similar sentiments (in "A Defense of Poetry," the year before he died). "Poetry," said Shelley, "lifts the veil from the hidden beauty of the world." Let us turn first to poetry.

Two old poetry collections can help us lift the veil by illustrating the main issues. Henderson collected 378 haiku, representing major Japanese poets from the seventeenth to twentieth centuries.[5] Of these, 44 (12%) refer—in a relatively prosaic, seasonal manner—to the moon and its light. These 44 haiku exemplify the ordinary ways poets in every land use lunar metaphors and similes as literary devices to invite the reader's affective response (see chapter 54). These lunar poems invoke a *mood*. Therefore, let us introduce the term "*mood*light" to describe this mood that they happen to create. It will help establish an important distinction as we proceed.

A reader's internal moody response to the words of a haiku stimulus occurs secondarily. Don't let that fact obscure its deeper psychophysiological significance to the issues now under discussion. Because the underlying message of "moodlight" remains the same: certain constellations of nerve cells are being stimulated whether a person falls under the spell of the real moon up in the sky, or the spell of literary allusions to the moon, *or under that of an independent comparable, affective state that arises spontaneously inside the brain*. These neural configurations are signaling deep feeling tones, a *mood*.

Zen Poetry

Stryk and Ikemoto took a different tack.[6] First, they identified certain Japanese poets as Zen poets. Next, they went on to specify 88 "Zen poems." Not surprisingly, 14 of these 88 poems (16%) also mention the moon and its light, again in conventional ways. We have not learned anything so far, except that Japanese writers include figurative "moodlight" devices reasonably often in their poetry. And living in Kyoto helps one appreciate that this literary usage can resonate at different levels than does the "June-moon-spoon" varieties of ordinary rhyme with which we are familiar in the West. Not only do Buddhist monks engage in formal meditation during the waxing of the moon but in the Orient it is common to share in "moon viewing" with one's friends as a social occasion.

Next, however, the authors singled out 10 of the original group of 88 "Zen poems." Why did they designate only this subset as "satori poems" (*tokinoge*)? To be selected, each of the ten poems had to be composed shortly *after* this Zen poet himself had experienced kensho or satori. Three of these last 10 satori poems invoke the moon in clearly metaphoric imagery. Yet, in accord with Zen proscriptions that had prevailed for many centuries, not one of these three poems (from the fourteenth and fifteenth centuries) used the actual *ideograms* for kensho or satori (see chapter 81).

Quite apart from how rare an actual late moonlight illusion might be, the evidence thus far suggests three important points. On *literary* grounds alone, it could be very difficult to distinguish between

- a poet's *ordinary figurative "mood*light" allusions commonly used as a metaphoric device, as distinct from;
- a poet's specific reference to a "*mood*light quality of kensho, even if it were possible for the poet *separately* to identify and make an explicit statement about a
- *literal "moonlight"* image that had been directly experienced as a late perceptual illusion.

A plausible exception emerges in the work of the Buddhist poet-monk Saigyo (1118–1190). Why was Saigyo's longer poem (*waka*) selected to introduce this chapter? Returning to examine it, one observes that it makes a singular explicit reference to satori.[7] This Japanese word (found also by Professor LaFleur in the original text) suggests why such a monk might have been, in a sense, more "moonstruck" than his contemporaries. Moreover, examining these lines, one observes that Saigyo (who elsewhere often referred to the moon) does more than link satori with a serene lighting effect. He goes far beyond. He suggests the scope of a momentous, unifying experience. Moon and mind are not only *mirroring* each other, but everything everywhere in the world.

When Kobori-Roshi said "Zen is closest to poetry," he meant the way poetry plumbs deep intuitive levels. There it resonates far beyond the superficial levels of thought that yield our ordinary intellectual recognitions. It mirrors our deepest mirrors (see chapter 65).

Do the early Ch'an masters include certain code words in their verses and other written works? Crucial words that hint at other links between moodlight, moonlight, and kensho's key attributes? Yes, in a few instances (appendixes A and B include other examples from the Tang and Sung dynasties). The selections below are close to the essence of the taste of kensho in my experience. They are also relevant to Joseph Campbell's epigraph in chapter 92. Because once you have vanished—unexpectedly—into that cool, clear, eternal suchness and its serenity, you will not forget how its insights flashed in with no sense of mental friction. And after you have felt them viscerally, you will recognize the deep impressions made by this state even though the clues are mere words and metaphoric expressions pointing off in its general direction.

Early Ch'an References to the Arctic Quality of Kensho's Moodlight

Consider the familiar expression: "There's nothing new under the sun." The same might be said with reference to the moon. Hui Yung lived during the fourth to fifth century C.E. He was a Taoist monk-poet long before Ch'an developed in China. He chose a Taoist temple high in the mountains as the setting for his poem "Moon Sitting." Here among a few lamps in the glittering moonlight, his words describe the *unseasonable* arrival of a "heart of ice."[8] In Sino-Japanese, *shin* refers to one's heart-mind. Its usage reflects the ancients' understanding that *emotions infused our every cognition*. During most seasons of the year, the sudden entry of an ice-cold comprehension would strike unexpectedly.

Stark, moody psychic resonances of vacancy begin before—*and then coincide with*—the visual perception of moonlight (see table 11 and the timeline below it). Note how Ch'an Master Fa-yen Wen-i (885–958) first points to kensho's indescribability. Next he points to the way its several qualities take on an ongoing icy quality:

> Reason exhausted, concerns forgotten—
> how could this be adequately expressed?
> Wherever I go, the icy moonlight is there,
> falling just as it does on the
> valley ahead.[9]

Later, during the Literary Period (950–1260), two other Chinese masters would also comment on the chilly impress linked to this lunar aspect of kensho.[10] One spare line suffices to set this emotional temperature at a cool level. It comes from verses in the "Book of Serenity" by the twelfth-century master, T'ien-t'ung.

> Autumn's clear moon turns its frosty disc.

Master Wan-sung would later add his own prose commentary to this whole verse. He noted the way kensho's insights enter consciousness directly, as simple truths, free from any intervening thoughts, and stripped of the ordinary, sentimental emotions usually associated with shin.

> The clarity of unvarnished truth is "cold."
> It admits no sentimentality.
> The mind's eye accesses this mystery
> only when our stream of consciousness
> is free of clinging thoughts.

Other Aspects of Moodlight

The ancients recognized that there was a universal, unifying aspect of the moon and its light. Hsuan Chuih (665–713) was a student of the sixth Ch'an patriarch, Hui-neng. In a culture well aware that one moon entered the water everywhere, he likened this process to the way the whole Buddha-dharma entered into his very being when he became "at one with the Awakened One."[11]

The gutsy quality of Zen poetic expression contrasts with the vapid verses of court poetry during the same era. Although the earlier vigor of the Tang dynasty would wane, Master Fenyang (947–1024) helped catalyze the way Zen literature would continue during its so-called Literary Period. Once, when suddenly enlightened by his master's words, he was said to have prostrated himself, then to have arisen and exclaimed:

> The moon of empty worlds, reflected in
> ten thousand ancient pools, long-sought,
> is finally found.[12]

True, an insightful awakening is "long-sought." But why would Fenyang describe the mental field as "empty?" In large part because, as chapter 85 explains, this domain has lost all self-centered constructs, and is free from other deluded layers of psychic overconditioning.

Fenyang also became more explicit with regard to kensho's other qualities, saying:

> The original Buddha-nature of all living things is like the bright moon in the sky—it is only because it is covered by floating clouds that it cannot appear.[13]

As Braverman observes, Zen uses clouds as the metaphor for our delusions. Clouds are, of course, distinct from the moon (in a clear sky) which "stands for reality or enlightenment."[14]

Master Hongzhi (1091–1157) later expanded on similar themes:

> When you see into the source of reality, with no obstruction whatsoever, it is open and formless, like water in autumn, clear and bright, like the moon taking away the darkness of night.[15]

In his letters, Master Yanwu (1063–1135) explained that a "boatload of moonlight" would be associated with the process by which one got rid of delusions and attachments.[16]

The Visual Symbol of a Round Moon: Its Link with Every Aspect of Timelessness (Mid-Twelfth-Century China)

Kensho dissolves time. Lost into this awesome eternity are all concepts of that person's past, present, and future scenarios (see chapter 84). During the mid-twelfth century in China, Master Kuo-an Shih-yuan linked this total dissolution of time with the visual symbol of the full moon. A series of paintings made by different artists accompanied his own poems and written comments. They illustrated the potential milestones that some had conceptualized might lie along the spiritual Path.[17] By then, various artists' imaginations had created ten allegorical pictures. These artistic devices served to suggest the successive steps a Zen aspirant might take toward an advanced stage of enduring, ongoing enlightenment.

When does the moon appear? Not until the seventh of these so-called ox-herding pictures. Now the sky is indeed free of all clouds. In the foreground, we see the seeker viewing this full moon as it illuminates a nearby peak. Now, finally, the commentary describes him as enlightened.

In his poem that accompanies the seventh picture, Master Kuo-an says:

> The experience is like . . . the moon
> appearing from behind clouds, a serene
> light older than time.

What could be "older than time?" Only some kind of domain that continued innocent of every distinction human thoughts might make between past, present, and future. Here we find that moonlight is being linked with a state of serene consciousness. It has opened out at both ends. The resulting sense of eternity extends beyond beginning and end. Time has vanished as a concept.

A Fast-Forward Look

For purposes of illustration, we next shift forward into the twentieth century to examine the words and images of another master. The next chapter provides another visual reference to the powerful psychic resonances of *mood*light, and of how it enters into the larger process of creative transformation.

98

The Hernandez Connection: A Darkened Sky and Moonglow

> Mind like an autumn moon . . .
> Pure, transcendent, elegant.
> Beyond comparison with anything else.
> How could I possibly explain this to you?
>
> Old Chinese Poem[1]

> We all move on the fringes of eternity and are sometimes granted vistas through the fabric of illusion.
>
> Ansel Adams (1902–1984)[2]

Zen poets try to explain in words how kensho suddenly transformed their mental field of consciousness into an ineffable "autumn moon." Other writers invent allusive metaphors for literary effect. Ansel Adams had his darkroom. Here, he could recreate memorable vistas from his negatives. At his centenary in 2002, generations celebrated his birth, remembering the dramatic effects he brought into black-and-white photography.

It happened one late October afternoon in 1941, just after 4:00 P.M. Beneath the pale blue sky, Adams saw small houses huddling for shelter around a village church. In the church cemetery, the crosses "blazed a brilliant white" in the rays of that low-lying sun, off camera. The light was fading fast. He had time to snap his shutter on only one fugitive image.

Moonrise, Hernandez, New Mexico, 1941 would later become Adams's best-known photograph. But only the novel vista which he would long retain in his own mind made its transformed printings so memorable. Because with each print made from that single precious negative he was seeking to create an image at a very special level of reality. It needed to be, he said, "a romantic/emotional moment in time."[3]

To attain this level of reality, only one particular lighting effect could satisfy his aesthetic requirements; it had to be a timeless moment, frozen in *moonlight*. Why? Perhaps because Adams had experienced something similar two decades earlier. When writing about this earlier episode, he would refer to it as a "mood" on two occasions and its light was silvery.[4]

As he hurried that afternoon in 1941, one pivotal motif was already there—a small, pale moon did hang up in the pale sky. Thereafter, all efforts back in his darkroom would be pointed toward this moon. But all around it that day was a *daylight* sky. Could Adams later transform the whole image, create a nocturnal illusion of moon*rise*? Not unless his formidable technical skills could somehow transfigure all the elements in that scene. As he printed from his black-and-white negative, the next sequences would be crucial.

Adams, the musician, knew his tonal scales both by sight and sound. In his darkroom, that light gray sky would become black as midnight. Now the wan moon could emerge as a bright white orb, its edges sharply defined by their contrast against this new jet background.

Then the long low cloudbank became luminous beneath this full moon. So did the cold white snowfields on distant peaks. Stark white crosses, impaling the graves, heightened the sense of mortality. The afternoon landscape was transformed further into a lunar context by the suggestion of moon glow highlighting the low bush tops in the foreground. Each print now became a nocturnal vista, eerie, unearthly . . .

Adams had touched universal feeling tones. He had an alchemist's gift for recreating *a special mood* from strong black-and-white contrasts and unusual highlights. Solitary viewers, who contemplate a graveyard on a cold moonlit night, know the resonances of such a "moodlight." It *feels* like it looks.[5]

99

Other Ancient Fingers Pointing toward the Moon

> It's not difficult to see the reflections in a mirror, but can you take hold of the moon in the water? . . . One moon shines in the water everywhere; all the reflected moons are just that one moon. . . . People who are ignorant . . . mistake the pointing finger for the moon.
>
> Master Yung-chia (d. 713)[1]

Ansel Adams's *Moonrise* offers a contemporary example of the pervasive influence of "moodlight." Working in black-and-white photography, his moody scene still resonates in an eerie, universal way on each new generation of viewers. In earlier millennia, other creative persons worked in different media. They also were motivated to include the moon—and its reflections—in their works.

Yung-chia lived during the Tang dynasty. The epigraph above, attributed to him, helped crystallize the subsequent literary distinctions between one's pointing finger and the moon of enlightenment. Over the next centuries, a variety of other allusions would forge links between the moon and other qualities of kensho: its abrupt sense of psychic release, its "suchness," and even with those forms of enlightenment which developed gradually.

Comments about the Moon in the Tang Dynasty (618–907)

D. T. Suzuki translated the following lines about master Yueh-shan Wei-yen (745?–828?).

> One eve he climbed straight up the solitary peak; And, seeing the moon revealed in the clouds, what a hearty laugh he gave![2]

If one were to interpret this "seeing the moon," as referring to Yueh-shan's "peak experience," then his hearty laugh would be in keeping with many other similar accounts of sudden liberation. Because a profound sense of total mental and physical release occurs during kensho-satori. This emancipation is sometimes followed by a spontaneous outpouring of hearty laughter [Z:413–418].

Subtle Allusions during the Northern Sung Dynasty (960–1127)

Master Hsueh-tou Ch'ung-hsien (980–1052) may have been commenting on a relevant point: the obvious fact that colors do fade out when a scene is bathed in moonlight.[3] Referring to the flash of insight-wisdom he said:

> When the jewel staff strikes, heaven and earth lose their color . . . through this experience, all sage's eyes open.

The classic *Blue Cliff Record* includes many verses by this same Hsueh-tou. Among them is the line: "The Ancient crystal palace reflects the bright moon."[4] Of course, this reference to brightness need not imply the dazzling quality of light *perception* in and of itself. Instead, "bright" often hints at the crystal-clear *comprehension* that flashes in during kensho-satori. What about the word "Ancient?" In the context of moonlight, words like "Ancient" can allude to qualities even "older than time." They suggest the awesome sense of eternity associated with kensho (see chapter 84). (The epigraph in chapter 98 suggests that Ansel Adams had been graced by one such vista into eternity.)

Dogen's References to the Moon-in-Water in Thirteenth-Century Japan

Observe what happens, some night when you're alone before a calm pond mirroring the moon. Does that moon really "cast" its reflection? No. Reflections "happen," effortlessly. In Tesshu's ideograms for *suigetsu* (water-moon), neither moon nor water plays any *active* role.

An analogous process characterizes the way kensho's mental field "mirrors" such a moonlit world. Witnessing happens spontaneously. It proceeds directly, naturally, automatically. And because this mirror-like awareness lacks every self-centered trace of the *I-Me-Mine,* absolutely no sense of mental friction or other active effort is involved. Water-moon happens.

Zen Master Dogen Kigen (1200–1253) devoted an entire chapter to "The Moon" in his classic work, *Shobogenzo.* H.-J. Kim comments on how Dogen's wording, throughout this chapter presents the moon not only as "the perfection and purity of the enlightened mind" but also as that mind now being dynamically expressed in "radical freedom."[5] Dogen's own literary formulations are filled with creative wordplay. So in Kim we are fortunate to have a translator of considerable experience and depth of understanding.

Very early in this chapter, The Moon, Dogen began to draw a clear-cut distinction. In his second sentence, he quotes the Buddha's words about how the "true dharma-body ... like the empty sky ... manifests itself in various forms, like the moon in water." However, Dogen then maintains that the key to what the Buddha *really* meant resides in the "moon-in-water" phrase. He asserts that such a phrase presented the actual, nondual (ultimate) reality of moon-water itself—its essential "thusness/suchness." Dogen believed the Buddha did not truly intend "moon-in-water" to serve as a *simile* (even though the later translation above might happen to insert "like the" before "moon-in-water").

We are in the presence of a crucial distinction. The distinction is between secondhand, discursive "literary" Zen, and the Zen of direct experience. Compare the flavor of later Zen with the vigor of expression in early Zen (in chapter 97).

Kim observes that Dogen would never have set out to create an indirect, qualified literary image, a mere derivative which only "points to, represents, or approximates something other than itself." No, Dogen was rejecting the notion that this symbol was somehow "*re*-presenting" what it allegedly symbolized. Instead, in this passage, Dogen was contending that this "moon-in-water" phrase was the thing in itself, the *direct presentation* of the literal essence of the moon. One wonders why Dogen insisted on this very point. Had he (or someone he knew especially well) undergone this intimate visual experience during a state of kensho, either in the form of moodlight, or as a late illusion of moonlight?

Searching for explanations, we find Dogen confirming and amplifying similar constructs elsewhere. But note how the verses below, about an abandoned boat, go on to forge links between moonlight and other essential aspects of kensho. The themes go beyond those anticipated in chapter 93 and discussed in chapter 97. For these next lines do not just link moonlight and serenity with emptiness. They add one more telling association: they describe the state of grace experienced during kensho in terms of *a motionless null point. No sense of active push or pull* can exist. Why not? One reason is that this state has now become deconditioned. Gone is all that former self-driven, habit-energy invested in "doing."

Calm and serene in the moonlight,
Lo! A deserted boat on the water,
not tossed by the waves or drawn by the breeze,
bathed in the pale light of the moon.[6]

Dogen was not the only writer who emphasized how deep was kensho's feeling of emancipation, its profound sense of release from bondage into freedom.[7] In Kyoto, among a later generation of painter-poets, was Yosa Buson (1716–1783). The haiku form limited him to only a few terse words. But notice how Buson still specifies that great liberating release (*moksha*) from all "nets" and "snares" which is associated with the moon of enlightenment.

Escaped the nets,
escaped the snares—
moon on the water.[8]

A Single, Solitary Moon Enters Ink Painting in Fifteenth-Century Japan

You might think it would be easy to draw a moon: a simple circle, brushed in with ink on paper. But did you make the circumference round, or nearly so? Do its two ends join, more or less seamlessly?[9] And did the whole process flow, in one sweep of liberated brushplay? Or was your brushwork labored? [Z:669].

Freedom of action is one hallmark of sudden Zen enlightenment. Liberation expresses itself spontaneously. An astute observer notices it in the person's energized body language. Experienced Zen masters readily diagnose, on the spot, their trainees' novel body postures and facile behavioral responses. Thereafter, brush, ink, and paper can preserve, for posterity, the earlier evidence of such fluid behaviors.

Yoso Soi (1379–1458) was the twenty-sixth chief abbot of Daitoku-ji, that large Rinzai Zen temple where Kobori-Roshi introduced me to Zen. Yoso's painting still informs us that, on a date equivalent to 3 January 1455, his brush inscribed one of the earliest Japanese examples of a simple, solitary moon that serves as an isolated art form.[10] This kind of single moon-circle is called the *enso*.

What is being signified when an enlightened master's brush renders so austere a statement? After seven centuries, Yoso's brush still answers. There, next to that single moon, his original ideograms still reply:

Obvious. Obvious.

How apt! Indeed, the abrupt stroke of kensho-satori does render everything (doubly) "obvious." No other event clarifies things—as they *really* are—so directly, simply, and ultimately. It's enough to make you laugh.

Three centuries later would come another classic example of deceptively simple brushplay. Sengai Gibon (1751–1837) first stroked in the circle. He followed it next with a triangle, and finally with a square (Z:593). Some observers may be inclined to interpret this particular enso-like circle as symbolic of the original, timeless, already awakened, uncomplicated, universal Reality Principle of Infinite Potential (the Dharmakaya)[11] (see chapter 85). Buddhist teachings are in line with this elaborately simple interpretation.[12]

In the following poem by Kojiju (1121–1201) is the hint that in satori each human being is expressing the innate potential to comprehend such levels of ultimate reality.

> Once you realize that this flawless moon
> dwells deep and pure in each human heart,
> all dark nights dissolve into clear skies.[13]

Calligraphic Writing

Kobori-Roshi was an artist, potter, and calligrapher. Each time I visited him at Daitoku-ji in subsequent years, he presented me with a gift in his own fluid brushplay. During what turned out to be our last farewell, his final gift was a long poem, inscribed on a scroll [Z:513, 805]. A free translation reads:

> Sitting on a stone,
> a cloud materializes
> in the monk's garment.
> Only later will the moon appear
> in his jug of spring water.[14]

What could this mean? The first line describes an adverse situation. Anyone who meditates in the lotus position will experience some degree of leg, bottom, and back discomfort. (Not to mention the pain from trying to sit on a pointed stone during meditation, as young Bankei once did!) Prolonged aching pain elicits stress responses within the brain; these can contribute to the person's entering into a preliminary state of internal absorption. One's *physical* sense of having a self-centered image disappears during such an inturned state of intense absorption (see chapter 74).

How do these lines allude to such an apparent "absence" of the bodily self? A subtle clue: the "cloud" in the monk's garment. When the *physical* self-image disappears from inside the garment, any such "cloud" inside becomes more evident. And our clouds, as has been pointed out, are the delusions that keep standing in the way of our seeing clearly.

These first three lines reinforce facts known for millennia, and not only in the Orient: the absorptions remain superficial episodes. They lack the insightful, root-cutting transforming thrust of prajna.[15] Therefore, clouds do remain, signifying the burdensome delusions that still need to drop off.

The last two lines refer to the insight-wisdom of those much later, advanced states of kensho-satori. Only when the unfruitful *psychic* roots of self are cut is there the potential for a clear "moonlit" landscape to appear. This water-moon is free and clear from all obstructing clouds, for one brief moment.

The So-Called Great Death, as Distinct from Final Biological Death

"The Great Death" is one other phrase which became associated with that total voidness of self-in-the-world which occurs during kensho-satori.[16] Extinguished are both the self-centered core of the psyche and "all thoughts and conceptions" that this fictional self had once attached to the world outside. This vacancy of self is the major contributor to the impression of *mood*light that gathers momentum as kensho's sequences unfold (see table 11, chapter 95, and chapter 97). Let us attempt to describe it in words. *Moodlight is consistent with a person's affective response to being alone, detached, in a graveyard on a cool dark night lighted only by the moon.*

However, as a phrase, "great death" is still just another metaphor. The metaphor remains a figurative device. We would not confuse the term with actual neurological brain death or with a person's final *biological* death of both brain and body. On the other hand, the eighteenth-century Tibetan text next to be described does refer to phenomena of moonlight *and* moodlight during life's final moments.

Textual References to Moonlight and Emptiness during the Actual Final Death of the Brain

In the Dalai Lama's preface to this old text,[17] he notes that "Those who die within a virtuous attitude have a sense of passing from darkness into light, are free from anxiety and see pleasant appearances." Indeed, as the sequences of actual biological death evolve, many of the subject's prior conceptions are said to dissolve into "the mind of radiant white appearance." At this juncture, according to the older Tibetan literature, three distinct phenomena then converge: "the dawning of extreme clarity," of "light," and of "vacuity."

The *white* quality of this clear light takes on special attributes. It is "like a night sky pervaded by moonlight." Its clarity resembles that of the rain-rinsed atmosphere during the autumn months, when the "sky is free of defilement." As to the third phenomenon of vacuity, why is it also called "the empty?" Because it is devoid both of all the person's former conceptualizations *and* of the energy that had given rise to them. It is vacant of self.

This same old Tibetan text also refers much further back in time to Asanga. He was the Indian Buddhist monk who helped found the Yogachara school of Mahayana Buddhism in the fourth century. In his work "Actuality of the Levels," Asanga mentions that "night pervaded by moonlight" would appear during the intermediate (bardo) state after death. This explicit reference again suggests that a person can experience a "moonlight phase" as part of the complex psychophysiological processes which evolve during actual brain death.

Let us now briefly sum up the evidence of these centuries of ancient Asian literature (see chapters 97, 99, and appendix A).[18] Our reading of the evidence suggests that the early sages were keenly aware that extraordinary states of awakening transformed in great clarity a person's mental field. And the suggestion is that a few of these sages could have been pointing their fingers *beyond* an impression of "moodlight" toward an additional visual perception: a *darkened* scene, briefly "pervaded by moonlight," *late* in a selfless, deathlike state, or even in an actual terminal state.

Incremental Awakening, a "Hazy-Moon"

As Yoso Soi hinted, kensho's flashing insight makes doubly "obvious" a startling fact: one's previous mental landscape had been a laughably self-centered creation of pulp fiction. When that old deluded egocentric self drops out of the picture, all things finally reveal themselves. This is unveiled allocentric comprehension, things as THEY really are, a fresh, penetrating glimpse into the essence underlying all things.

A different timeline also exists. Kobori-Roshi explained that a "gradual enlightenment" occurs on the Path of Zen (see chapter 4). This is a slow process of maturation that evolves over decades, not during seconds or minutes (see chapters 88–91). Some use the "hazy moon" of enlightenment as a phrase to refer to the more advanced transformations of this slowly ripening incremental process.[19] It evolves in the course of daily-life practice, especially when the mindful, introspective path toward insight is conducted on a regular basis in a context that is both challenging and supportive [Z:125–129]. In an optimal monastic context, it is said that "When stones of various sizes are jostled together, they gradually wear themselves smooth."

Among those who referred to such a "hazy moon" of awakening was Daiun Harada-Roshi (1870–1961). The process was described in terms of an ongoing condition of consciousness, now grown so "ripe and pure" that the person would enter—but "in a hazy way"—into an approximation of "contact with the light of the essential world." Harada-Roshi believed that this deep understanding was useful in itself, but that if it did not further evolve it would remain at the level of a kind of "conceptual" or "proximate Zen." During our second interview in 1974,

Kobori-Roshi made it clear that he valued "both the gradual and the sudden types of enlightenment." Both are essential. No flash of prajna *in isolation* can ever constitute "enlightenment."

So, in reply to Seng-chao's ageless question in chapter 76, "Do you become a sage when you comprehend the myriad things *as* the self?," the short answer over the next sixteen centuries remains no! *Mu*.

It takes much more than one insightful state of "Oneness" to enter that *stage* of sage wisdom which is characterized by ongoing enlightened traits.[20] Not yet. Not yet.

100

People Differ in Their Response to Illusions: Psychological Considerations

> I myself believe that the evidence for God lies primarily in inner personal experiences.
>
> William James (1842–1910), *Pragmatism*

> Every great advance in natural knowledge has involved the absolute rejection of authority.
>
> Thomas H. Huxley (1825–1895)

Suppose someone does experience a late phase of moonlight perception. Might certain physiological and "psychological" factors interfere with their recognizing it, prevent them from remembering and acknowledging it? Let us list the more obvious factors.

1. Kensho's impressive insight-realizations strike early and last much longer. Their long, solid "timeline" simply overwhelms any late, furtive, visual images (see the bottom of table 11, chapter 95). The "moonlight only" phase lasts for perhaps only 2% of the total time. It not only lacks color, it shifts in and out quickly.
2. An arctic, visceral feeling accompanies kensho's early "death of selfhood." As it gains momentum, some of its feeling tones are reminiscent of the pervasive *mood* one feels out alone in an actual graveyard on a cold moonlit night. After kensho, second thoughts arrive: Did I really *see* this fleeing "moonlight" scene? Was it a *separate*, distinct, visuosensory perception? Two such incredible events strain credulity, the more so when they not only partially overlap in time but also when some of their resonances reinforce each other. When certain subjects are overcome by kensho, they may later find reason to forget or dismiss the earlier evidence of their senses.[1]

Not this witness. No cool psychic vacancy accounts for the observation that my color perception vanished. Moreover, the reduced illumination, highlights, contrast enhancements, distancing, and displacements are mutually reinforcing. They each line up to support one general thesis: rod channel functions continued; cone functions dropped out.

3. Zen emphasizes the essential primary, transforming role of *insights*. Zen doctrines downgrade sensory phenomena. No orthodox Zen master—in any century—has been programmed to acknowledge that a late phase of visual illusions might occur *after* the first phase of insights. This is to venture out toward a very slippery slope. It could open up unwelcome heretical possibilities, certain to offend someone.

Is that first awesome transfigured domain the "real" nondual Reality? Or is it an extraordinary mode of perception infused with a remarkable sense of significance? (see chapter 82). That second point of view carries humanist overtones. It could seem threatening to the larger cosmic perspective. Over a century ago, T. H. Huxley and others bore the brunt of major theological resistance to scientific explanations. The next chapter reviews recent contributions to such issues from this new millennium.

101

People Differ in Their Susceptibility to Illusions

At present, individuals are lost in the crowd.

John Stuart Mill (1806–1873)

Never follow the crowd.

Bernard Baruch (1870–1965)

Our two brains are different. Yours and mine vary genetically, biochemically, and physiologically. The "hard- and soft-wiring" in some brains seems more attuned to visual events: other persons seem more responsive within the auditory domain.[1]

Certain normal human subjects develop strong visual contrast illusions.[2] Their visual evoked potentials tend to be significantly higher. It also happens that their blood platelets show significantly lower activity of the enzyme monoamine oxidase B. However, it is not yet clear how lower oxidase B activity in blood platelets might correlate meaningfully with neurochemical events in the brain. Among the current weak leads[3] is evidence relating to serotonin, raising a remote possibility that increased serotonin functions might be reflected in visual contrast illusions (see chapter 24).

First, serotonin nerve cells do contain this same enzyme, monamine oxidase B, but only in certain of their mitochondria.[4] Second, the normal human parietotemporo-occipital region (a fertile source of perceptual illusions) does contain relatively high levels of one marker molecule that correlates with higher serotonin turnover[5] [Z:205–208].

Susceptibilities in Migraine That Can Overlap with States Arising on the Path of Zen

The phenomena of the migraine syndrome have clear implications both for the qualities and the amplitudes of many phenomena that can occur on the Path of Zen (see chapter 73). To consider a few more of the recent findings:

- Achromatopsia can occur during the *pre*headache prodrome of migraine.[6] Only one patient reported this loss of color vision in a group of 20 adult patients who had an assortment of neuropsychological symptoms. Micropsia (2 reports) and teleopsia (1 report) also occurred in this series.
- In a recent magnetoencephalographic (MEG) study of a migraine patient, a focal area of reduced gamma power (a 50% reduction) was evident early during the active phase of the aura. This area localized to the left inferior temporal lobe. This site is not too far removed from the V4 color complex region.[7] Interference with synchronized gamma oscillations is a plausible explanation for the colorless "moonlight only" phase (see table 11, chapter 95; chapters 44 and 96).
- Negative afterimage phenomena can continue to occur in a migraine patient, even after the primary visual cortex has been surgically removed.[8] This finding illustrates that other cortical and subcortical mechanisms can enter into negative afterimages (see chapter 96).
- Subjects susceptible to migraine often report that they are overly "sensitive to light," including during their headache-free periods. Controlled tests of twelve women (who had a family history of migraine) showed that they were "supersensitive" to light."[9] This excessive sensitivity penetrates deeply into the brain. Thirty minutes of exposure to light reduced their melatonin levels by some 54%, as compared with only 18% in their controls (see chapter 39).
- An explosion of information has occurred in the field of migraine genetics in the past year.[10] In certain families, the trend in the early data is toward genes that determine nerve cell excitabilities, because these genes code for proteins regulating ions, including calcium (see chapter 37).
- The clear-cut normal overlap between calcium, glutamate excitations, and nitric oxide—discussed in chapter 68—also extends in the direction of the spectrum of

phenomena included in the migraine syndrome (see chapter 73). Nitric oxide donors can precipitate migraine in susceptible persons. NO' donors can also precipitate a different head pain syndrome in patients who are already prone to have "cluster headaches."[11] Recent neuroimaging data in the migraine syndrome point toward midbrain regions as key early sites for triggering the symptoms. Data in the cluster headache patients point to a different early site in the hypothalamus.

However, NO' is synthesized in *many* brain regions. The endogenous release of this NO' is likely to be a factor superimposed on countless *localized* responses throughout the regions cited in part III. Generalized states of arousal are prone to develop during rigorous meditative retreats and will tend further to enhance these responses.

Given the range of functions that can respond to NO', one is led to suggest at least two plausible mechanisms for some sequences during kensho (see table 11): (1) the earlier phases of kensho could have generated sufficient calcium ions and glutamate to then release unusual local levels of nitric oxide; (2) this NO' then contributed to (at least) the late visual epiphenomena of a person whose preexisting visual sensitivities were heightened. Whether endogenous NO' itself serves as a "donor" in this manner, and in other relevant ways, is for future studies to determine.

Do subjects who have migraine present special opportunities for research? Yes, because the amplitudes of their excitatory *and* secondary inhibitory responses may be enhanced.[12] Table 12 further distinguishes two personally-witnessed states in which a "sensitivity" to visual phenomena played a distinctive role.

A careful weighing of an individual person's psychophysiological susceptibilities is a prerequisite not just for laboratory research. It is important with respect to the accuracy of other formal criteria. Zen masters are in positions of authority. They usually use reasonably exacting "quality-control" criteria to judge the authenticity and depth of enlightenment experiences. They quickly reject their student's report if certain details do not conform to the traditional doctrinal formulas that they happen to be familiar with.

On the other hand, they are likely to be more accepting if their student's report resembles their own previous experiences, which thereafter have a tendency to serve as their own internal standard of reference.[13]

The phrase, "Hildegard syndrome", was introduced in chapter 73 for several reasons. It points to the need to be fully aware of the personal background *and pertinent family* history of migraine if called upon to interpret any unusual immediate (primary) and more delayed (secondary) phenomena that arise during alternate states of consciousness.

Why has a late moonlight phase of kensho remained so relatively undocumented? Beyond the psychophysiological and cultural explanations discussed

Table 12
The Early Hallucination in Internal Absorption Differs from the Late Visual Illusions of Kensho

Attribute or Aspect	*Hallucinated Leaf at the Onset of Internal Absorption [Z:469–473]*	*Several Illusions Late in the Lunar Phase, at the Offset of Kensho*
Early or late position	An early herald of the hyperattentive state	A brief postscript that entered late during a state of insight-wisdom
Color saturation	Greatly enhanced	All color lost
Texture	Enhanced, both fine-grained and coarse-grained	Reduced details, seemingly consistent with a reduction of illumination
General state of awareness	Greatly enhanced with a sense of ambient space	Objective, clear, matter-of-fact, "realer than real"
Aesthetic response	Strong, to a vivid image	Passive during the lunar phase; distanced from the earlier phase of perfection, but still aware of it
Cortical correlates?	Heightened excitability, one focal point of which had probably enhanced the functions of the V4 color complex in and around the region of the right fusiform gyrus	A delayed, brief colorless phase: It points to inhibitory processes that had interrupted the usual synchronized oscillations that serve to convey the consciousness of color that is represented in the V4 color complex
Interpretation	A visual (hypnopompic) hallucination: It points to events during one particular transitional interval between sleeping and waking	A visual illusion of "moonlight": a basic misperception, to be distinguished from any separate and additional "mood" that can also be felt in association with moonlight
Relationship with any other states?	Similar vivid hallucinations can occur during normal sleep-related transitional states (e.g., during ascents from sleep into waking, or during descents into sleep)	The negative afterimage phase quickly shifted in and out; such shifts were reminiscent of the several "faded color snapshots" retrieved during an earlier, "tachistoscope" incident [Z:390–391]
Occurrence	Relatively common	Relatively rare delayed epiphenomena; potentially contributed to by some heightened responsitivities associated with an underlying tendency toward migraine
Reception	Promptly rejected by Japanese Zen master	Most Western Zen teachers declined to respond to a survey; further inquiries about "moonlight phase" dismissed as "barking up the wrong tree"

thus far, we need to consider the issue of rarity. The physiological "sensitivities" that Critchley referred to—which *so* often reflect a person's susceptibility to migraine—occur in a minority of the population. For example, migraine symptoms might occur—in clinically diagnosable form—in perhaps only one out of every eight men, and in perhaps only one out of every four women. Suppose that achromatopsia were to occur in only one out of twenty subjects whose migraine aura presents complex neuropsychological features.[14] Then by crude first approximations, a loss of color vision might occur as a diagnosable early pre-headache component in only 1 in 80 to 160 persons in the general population.

I do *not* suggest at this point that the achromatopsia of the "moonlight only" phase is simply equivalent to the early (prodromal) phase of the aura. Nor am I suggesting that a susceptibility to migraine is *the* single essential ingredient that causes the early insightful state of kensho and its "moodlight" quality, or its late moonlight and final phases. I *am* suggesting that the calcium-glutamate-nitric oxide interactions are likely to overlap, and to yield enhanced regional responses, in a few persons who happen both to be meditators *and* to have a low threshold for a variety of migraine symptoms. A few will also enter kensho.

There is no reason to think that the local discrete release of endogenous $NO^{\bullet}$ in certain key regions during kensho need mimic all the gross, headache-producing and other symptoms reported so far as the side-effects triggered by giving *exogenous* $NO^{\bullet}$ donors. Whether these donor molecules were inhaled or injected, they entered the systemic blood circulation of migraineurs and then affected the brain from without.

In this chapter lies a plea for this simple recognition: major variations exist among individuals in their amplitudes of *excitation and inhibition*. The broad spectrum we call "migraine" includes a host of more "sensitive" responses. These will influence both the primary, secondary, and delayed manifestations of phenomena experienced on the spiritual path. They can also shape the way extraordinary states of consciousness are later remembered, interpreted, accepted or rejected both by the subjects themselves, and by others to whom they are described.

102

Fourth Mondo

Why would a neurologist mix poetry, neuroscience, and Zen?

There's truth in what Kobori-Roshi emphasized: "Zen *is* closest to poetry." If you read between the lines of the old verses in these pages, you may find wordless hints that point toward the experiential core of kensho.

Why do you refer to the "moonlight only" phase of kensho? Where does it fit in with respect to the rest of kensho?

The dim light in this phase was colorless. It created the immediate impression of "moonlight." This moonlight phase arrived very late, only after the long prior insight phase of kensho.

Did you think it was really moonlight at that very moment?

No personal *I* was in there "thinking." At that instant, the scene simply registered as an immediate, soft visual image. It bore no familiar word label. Days later, "consistent with moonlight" seemed the best single, shorthand phrase to describe it.

So, was your first impression a simile?

What registered early was a direct impression. It was not an impression of thoughts that seemed to add up to be "like" moonlight. This immediate visual *illusion* was not an allusion, as are those ordinary kinds of similes or metaphors that someone invents later and uses for literary effect. Ever since then, my words keep attempting to convey that first impression. Later, in retrospect, it would become obvious that the "moonlight" interval was a misperception.

What do you think caused this moonlight phase?

A brief inhibitory process, one that disrupted the synchronized firing patterns of color-sensitive areas in and around the fusiform gyrus on both sides. This would block color vision selectively. The rod channel functions would be spared and would keep on rendering a black-and-white version of the same scene.

OK. So you first had the direct impression of moonlight. Is that local process, which just inhibited color vision, an intrinsic part of the kensho experience in general? Or is it likely to be restricted to certain individuals who are susceptible to migraine?

One function of this book is to raise this very question, get it out in the open, so that future generations can resolve this issue unambiguously.

Meanwhile, it's not just an either/or situation. Many inhibitory "subtractions" are already characteristic of kensho. For example, kensho is also empty of that person's prior functions of self, time, and fear, as well as of the inclinations to act and to approach. Moreover, we've seen that the ancient literature refers to the moon and its light in ways suggesting that a few kensho experiences might include an actual *colorless* phase—a true visual misperception.

Couldn't all those references to moonlight and to the moon in the earlier poetry and art be only literary metaphors and similes, or visual symbols?

Direct and circumstantial evidence indicates that most are indeed to be interpreted as ordinary, secondary allusions. A few seem not to be.

Why aren't they all allusory references?

A number of the examples cited suggest actual, direct visual phenomena. They seem closer to perceptual immediacy than are those later, willfully applied literary and artistic flourishes which are loose figments of creative imagination. Moreover, the accompanying verses appear to express the actual distinctive *insights, impressions, and psychic* resonances consistent with kensho-satori.

Why introduce the term "moodlight?" What does it try to describe?

It's there to sharpen the contrast between a mood and a perception, to help distinguish affect from sensation. "Moodlight" is a soft eerie *feeling*. It gathers momentum during the unparalleled vacancy when the psychic self drops out and the sense of eternity prevails. These awesome qualities contribute to the eerie, cool quality of kensho. This "other-worldly" aspect is reminiscent of how one might *feel* out in a cemetery, alone on a cool dark night, with only a full Autumn moon as the sole source of light.

What are the neural origins of this feeling of "moodlight?"

Most likely their cool emotional nuances reflect a widespread constellation of cortical and limbic sites, some activated, others inactivated. In sharp contrast, relatively few regions need to be inhibited to delete all color vision, so as to create the dim *perceptual* illusion of "*moon*light." This brief phase of moonlight and "moonglow highlights" arrived later.

So you're using two words, with a *d* and an *n*, to describe two distinct processes, which begin at different times?

Yes. The early one is a broadly affective, longer-lasting impression. It arises independently, internally. The second one is narrowly perceptual, brief, and late.

But, don't they overlap for part of the time?

Yes. This overlap of the earlier "moodlight" and later "moonlight" is certain to be confusing. Indeed, it may have contributed to the lack of general recognition that a late "moonlight" phase exists at all. If you spend some time looking into Ansel Adam's photograph, *Moonrise, Hernandez, New Mexico, 1941*, you may be able separately to identify the qualities of each of the two processes. Beyond a certain point, they tend to overlap.

The standard doctrine is that *all is metaphor*. You are cautioning that *all is* not *metaphor*. Isn't this an unorthodox distinction?

Yes. But this is a basic *biological* distinction. It is grounded in immediate perceptual experience, not on a literary concept that takes time to think about and is culture-bound. The distinction hinges on early and late physiological events. Event-related-potential studies show that they are separated by many milliseconds.

For example, impulses coding for perceptual illusions register first in the back of the brain. Only milliseconds later do such messages spread to networks farther forward. There, later still, after becoming accessible to thought forms, a swarm of associations transform them into figurative word images. Only much later, by an effort of some willful intent, can writers retrieve all these associations in forms that they can express as literary allusions.

Moods and perceptions are the neural settings out of which literary allusions arise later, finally to be elaborated into a variety of forms as similes, metaphors, and symbols. (Master Dogen, in his own way, was saying much the same about similes, centuries ago.)

Doesn't it complicate matters when you introduce the topic of migraine in the context of Zên?

Yes. However, nothing in that chapter on migraine asserts that the *insightful phenomena at the core* of states of awakening originate in the migraine syndrome. The known mechanisms of migraine do not govern, or explain, the striking qualities of the insights that flash in during the early, major, and relatively long phases of kensho. Nor would one consider that those brilliant, prodromal, excitatory scintillations that usher in a classic migraine aura are comparable with the late phenomenon of *reduced* illumination during the inhibitory "moonlight only" phase of kensho.

Migraine enters into our discussion on these pages for more subtle, modulatory reasons. One reason is that its protean manifestations affect many people, yet even now relatively few appreciate how diverse are all these *non*headache symptoms of migraine.

However, the many nonheadache phenomena do express underlying sensitivities, and tendencies toward excessive degrees of excitation and inhibition. When these physiological excesses are manifest in certain modules and networks, their expressions *can overlap with and become relevant to the basic phenomena of Zen experience.*

So?

Excitation and inhibition are *the* fundamental properties of nerve cells. This suggests that certain "sensitive" people, during their various states (of quickening, absorption, kensho-satori, and Being) could tend *also* to express—*again, to unusual degrees*—their underlying physiological susceptibilities. The modulating influence of migraine extends to *both* excitatory and inhibitory responses, increasing the amplitudes and the briskness of these responses, in either direction.

If color can drop out during a late phase near the close of kensho, doesn't this weaken the case that the sensory changes of internal absorption can always help distinguish it from kensho?

It defers the decision. First, one needs to specify the nature, extent, and timing of the sensory change. Next, identify which levels of sites are responsible. During internal absorption, all of vision and hearing are subtracted early. This suggests that inhibitory processes have blocked sensory messages from passing up through their two relay nuclei and other sensory nuclei *lower down* in the back of the thalamus.

However, this early major sensate loss contrasts sharply with kensho's moonlight phase during which color vision is lost *selectively and late*. Table 12 illustrates major differences between the two states. It also summarizes other evidence suggesting that kensho's mechanisms differ from those of internal absorption. For example, kensho subtracts certain associative processes and psychic functions more *selectively*. It does so at hierarchical levels that appear to involve higher order associations [Z:596, table 20].

Does a person need to have some underlying susceptibilities, say of the kinds associated with migraine, in order for a late, *moonlight only* phase to occur?

It might help. I think that the *potential* for a "moonlight only" phase is probably inherent in the state of kensho. Its loss of color is in keeping with the way kensho's basic mechanisms already seem to be disorganizing other higher association functions of the frontal, temporal, parietal, and occipital regions. One asks: could NO• promote some later illusions?

Yet this potential to develop further, to register deeply in awareness, and to last long enough to be *noticed*, may become fully evident only in certain persons. Suppose that such a person was a meditator who was already susceptible to some heightened responsivities linked with migraine. In this instance, a moonlight phase might assume an overt form and last longer. It's also possible that some prior visual aesthetic tendencies associated with migraine might be more attuned instantly to identify the "moonlight" quality of a brief interval of perception. The final minor epiphenomena of highlights and afterimages are consistent with the possibility that such a subject did have the kinds of visual sensitivities often associated with the migraine syndrome. A casual witness and nonmeditator might easily overlook such fleeting images.

How does this theory relate to any so-called Hildegard syndrome?

That was an expedient. Its sole purpose was to draw attention to a neglected, practical matter: a predisposition to migraine can modify the ways various states of consciousness present themselves to persons on the meditative path.

Do these observations have implications for contemporary Zen teachers and for those in other meditative traditions?

It depends on how open-minded they are and how informed they wish to be. Some may benefit from knowing how quickly raw, direct visual illusions register in the brain, long before writers or artists take up pen or brush to express their more refined, elaborate, allusive, products of literary and artistic imagination.

During these milliseconds, illusions *in themselves* are neither products of discursive thought, nor psychological symbols, nor do they have any spiritual significance. They are simple facts of visual experience. If students report a few strange illusory epiphenomena to their teachers, these descriptions do not negate the remaining core of a major experience that is otherwise authentic.

In Closing

Did you not know beforehand that all things must fade away?

Socho (1448–1532)[1]

It is said that the udumbara tree blooms and bears fruit only when a great being is born, once every three thousand years. The legend reminds many seekers: centuries might pass before the planet will again be graced by the next extraordinary Buddha. Meanwhile, can those original teachings of the previous historical Buddha, skillfully applied, help this fragile planet and its sentient beings survive until a successor arrives some five to six hundred years from now?

Let us hope so, and try to behave as though the previous and future Buddha were an actual living presence, walking with each of us on the Way.

It is a Path that follows the ancient Middle Way. Its traditions avoid extremes of behavior that lurk on either side. It is a *caring* path that expresses deeply ingrained biological instincts. Caregiving has never been solely in the province of the service professions. Its instinctual roots are innate and universal. We find that even the most insular of human beings is impelled to reach out beyond the boundary of self to care for a pet cat, turtle, or growing plant.

In the Path's simple tradition of bowing we find several expressions of life's fundamental unity and our endless gratitude for being alive every minute of it.

In the act of bowing we are surprised to discover a universal human gesture that can generate selflessness.

And the simple joining together of two opposing palms—gassho—signifies more than casual human behavior. It can reflect the way we learn to reconcile what seems to be good things and bad things in life—not just what others gave in acts of kindness, but those unkind events that will emerge as charitable in that greater scheme of things.

The neurosciences of the future can contribute to our understanding of this long spiritual Path. They can make it less mystifying and more accessible. Along the way, their respect will grow for the way the whole traditional process evolved in the past and how it can help to illuminate our understanding of neurobiology.

Appendix A

Other Links between the Moon and Enlightenment in the Old Zen Literature

> Nothing ever becomes real 'til it is experienced—even a proverb is no proverb to you 'til your life has illustrated it.
>
> John Keats (1795–1821)

> Moon talk by a poet who has not been in the moon is likely to be dull.
>
> Mark Twain (1835–1910)

The following samples illustrate additional ways that moon themes have entered into Zen literature for many centuries.

The Zenrin Kushu

In late fifteenth-century Japan several collections of Chinese classical sayings were gathered together representing the Tang and Sung dynasties. These collections would later grow to contain over six thousand entries. Students in some Zen centers were expected to select a particular saying appropriate for the theme of their own koan, then to present it to their roshi for his approval.

In 1981, Shigematsu's anthology included both a useful introduction to this practice and 1234 of the old sayings.[1] In English, only 17 (1.4%) contain the word "satori." One hundred six of the sayings (8.6%) mention the moon, but do so mostly in the ordinary literary manner. None that mention the moon also refer *explicitly* to kensho or satori using the appropriate Sino-Japanese ideogram for either word. However, to speak directly about kensho or satori during these earlier centuries might have been regarded as lacking the requisite subtlety.

On the other hand, several sayings that do refer to the moon also hint at the particular qualities implicit in kensho-satori that are the essence of enlightenment. For example, there are occasional hints that the Ultimate Reality is manifest both in an all-inclusive oneness *and* in the individuality of conventional phenomena:

> One moon appears in every pool;
> In every pool the one moon.
> (Saying 37)

> Moon above clouds;
> Always the same—

Valley moon, mountain moon
Different . . .
(Saying 95)

Other sayings citing the moon also convey kensho's surprising, dynamic, liberating sense of release:

The solitary moon shines:
Rivers, mountains silent.
Laughter rings out—
Heaven and earth surprised.
(Saying 328)

A recent addition is Victor Hori's recent anthology of the old classical sayings, entitled *Zen Sand*.[2] His list of index entries for "moon" extends for almost 8 cm. (3 inches). (Only the entries for the word "golden" exceed this length.) Included among the moon citations are these three:

I do not know into whose house the bright moonlight will fall.
I loaded my boat full of moonlight and came home.
In the still of the night the valley stream sounds close by; in the winter garden the moonlight is deeper still.

Earthy Reminders: An Impression of Moonlight Can Occur during the Daytime. Triggers Can Prompt Zen Enlightenment. This Awakening Is "Nothing Special"

While relieving himself in the toilet, Chang Chiu-Ch'en was still pondering his koan. Suddenly he heard a frog croak and was awakened, as evidenced by the following poem:

In a moonlit night on a spring day,
The croak of a frog
Pierces through the whole cosmos and turns it into a
single family.[3]

This concise description is remarkable for what it accomplishes. It confirms Dogen's early statement that moonlight does not necessarily occur at night. It attributes this episode of kensho to the springtime. This is in keeping with earlier suggestions by Richard Bucke that awakenings in the spring tend to be more common [Z:621]. It points to an auditory trigger, the frog's croak. It further suggests that striking degree of all-inclusive intimacy (within a "single family") which embraces the whole infinity of the cosmos.

Jijo's Zen master advised him to meditate single-mindedly, with no interruptions, for 7 days and nights. Being a monk both obedient and adaptable, Jijo was undaunted by a bout of dysentery. He continued to meditate single-mindedly even while sitting on a toilet bucket. On the seventh night, while in a secluded place, "he suddenly sensed the whole world like a snowy landscape under bright moonlight and felt as if the entire universe were too small to contain him." After a long time in this state, "he was startled [back] into self awareness on hearing a sound." He found that he was sweating profusely and that his dysentery had stopped.[4]

This account suggests a brighter degree of moonlight (on a "snowy landscape") than I had experienced. It also hints at an experiential paradox in which self/other boundaries are effaced in an unusual manner. An ordinary sound (not described as a trigger) seems to have brought him back later out of kensho into his prior, mindful state of consciousness.

Standard Metaphoric References to the Full Moon by Both Soto and Rinzai Zen Masters

Soto Master Yunmen (864–949) used the "fifteenth of the month" as a metaphor for that particular occasion when the waxing moon of a person's increasing awareness finally ripens into the "full moon" of enlightenment. However, he did not wish to mislead his listeners. He did not want them to think that any such episode of enlightenment was a "special" occasion. Instead—on each and every day of the month—he wanted them to stay closely focused on each present moment, on everyday events. This may explain why Yunmen immediately pointed out that "*every* day is a good day," a phrase that then entered into Zen lore.

Later, the Rinzai master Yuan-wu (1063–1135) addressed his own assembled monks. His remarks indicate the kinds of constraints that that then existed in China. These did not encourage open discussion of the full moon of enlightenment:

> Just on the fifteenth day are both sky and earth serene; equally clear, equally dark ... the ancients don't speak about this pivotal place, nor does this old monk open his mouth.[5]

Appendix B

On Wilderness Poetry during the Tang and Sung Periods

The moon became mind, and entered the heart.

The Aitareya Upanishad
(Hindu, eighth to sixth century B.C.E.)[1]

When Kobori-Roshi said: "Zen is closest to poetry," he knew how much Zen poetry dates back to old China, a land where mind and heart even share the same ideogram. The Chinese began their long tradition of rivers-and-mountains poetry (*Shan-shui*) as early as the fifth century.[2] In all literature, this tradition represents one of the earliest, longest-lasting, and most extensive literary engagements with the natural beauty of the wilderness. Moreover, many of its poets' aesthetic responses were well developed, either by their having undergone formal meditative training themselves or having been strongly influenced by Buddhism and Taoism. Ch'an practice thrived in the context of Nature, out of doors, not only on the cushion.

Spare language characterizes this rivers-and-mountains poetry. Its descriptive words evoke *tzu-jan*. The term refers to the sensibility that we and all things share in the cosmic creative force as it spontaneously generates being out of nonbeing (see chapter 85). In the West, the term *ex nihilo* suggests the great creative impulse that comes out of the void of nothingness.

In structure, this old poetry is not only bare but impersonal. The poets' ideograms exist in an open field. It is empty of the familiar grammar that we usually depend on to anchor our firm subjective sense of self at the epicenter of our experience. So these poems leave it up to a reader who can resonate with the call of wilderness to fill in the empty spaces.

One poem selected to be representative of this period is "In the Mountains, Asking the Moon."[3] The author, Po Chu-i (772–846), was "the quintessential Chinese poet," and nearly three thousand of his works have been preserved. In midcareer, as a government official, he became a devoted student of Ch'an Buddhism.

Po Chu-i was well known for the way he conveyed the interior sense of a mind that remained empty while it mirrored the wilderness landscape. Indeed, his original poem lacks words that refer explicitly to the human subject who witnesses this experience. The free translation rendered below chooses to describe him as a "poet," solely to bring these ancient verses to the reader in a more contemporary manner.

In his poem, Po Chu-i mentions the ancient northern capital city, Ch'ang-an. We are more familiar today with its modern version, the city called Xian. In olden times, Ch'ang-an was a remarkably cosmopolitan metropolis. Its sophisticated gridwork of bustling streets extended some five miles in diameter and was decorated by a garland of nearby imperial gardens and palaces.

Hermits and poets were at home in the many nearby mountains. Fifteen miles to the south was the Chungnan mountain range. Sixty miles to the east, the sacred mountain called Hua Shan rose to a height of 6552 ft. For millennia, its fathomless views have inspired countless Chinese poets and painters. Descriptions today tell us that it still remains famous for its "slender peaks of polished rock ornamented with sprays of pines" that rise up into the sky "like the delicate petals of a flower frozen in eternal bloom. Where ridges dip between its graceful summits, little temples perched in notches overlook precipices that drop into chasms of blue space."[4] No wonder Po Chu-i had retreated from his big, noisy capital city to seek solace in such mountains, bathed in the luster of moonlight.

In the Mountains, Asking the Moon
(Po Chu-i, freely translated[5])

Let a poet ask: Which doctrine remains with us always?
And the same Ch'ang-an moon always answers.

Its moonlight still goes on illuminating these mountains, just as clearly as it did on that night when the poet fled those city streets.

As this same moonlight lingers, it still helps him endure those desolate autumn hours of trying to sleep through nights that never end.

Should he ever return to this old homeland, it will welcome him back like family.

Even here, it's the friend who shares his walks beneath the pines, sits next to him on canyon ridge tops.

Among a thousand cliffs, and countless canyons this illumination abides with him everywhere.

Appendix C

Daio Kokushi "On Zen"

Daio Kokushi (1235–1309) traveled to China for his early training. He returned to Kamakura and Kyoto, bringing back a pure strict, traditional Rinzai style of Zen. Daito Kokushi was his dharma heir, and became the first abbot of Daitokuji, founded in 1324. The following lines, suggestive of the important influence Taoism had on Zen, are adapted from D. T. Suzuki's translation in *Manual of Zen Buddhism.*[1]

On Zen

A reality exists, even before heaven and earth;
It has no form, much less a name.
Eyes fail to see it. No voice has it for ears to hear.
To call it "Mind" or "Buddha" violates its nature.
For then it becomes like some visionary
flower in the air.

It is not "Mind" nor "Buddha."
It is absolute quiet, yet illuminating in
a mysterious way.
It allows itself to be perceived only
by the clear-eyed.
It is Dharma, truly beyond form and sound.
It is Tao, having nothing to do with words.

Once, wishing to entice the blind,
the Buddha playfully let words escape his golden
mouth. Ever since, heaven and earth have become full
of entangling briars. Oh my good worthy friends
gathered here, if you wish to hear the thunderous
voice of the Dharma, exhaust all your words,
empty all your thoughts.
For only then may you come to realize, at last,
this one essence.

Glossary

> Trying to understand from words is like washing a dirt clod in muddy water. But if you don't use words to gain understanding, it's like trying to fit a square peg in a round hole.
>
> Master Yuan-wu Keqin (1063–1135)[1]

acetylcholine (ACH) A fast neurotransmitter liberated at many brain synapses and at those peripheral cholinergic nerves which innervate muscles.

achronia Consciousness lacking a sense of time. A zero state of time.

affect In general use, it refers to the emotional. It also refers to the way we express emotion in observable behaviors.

agnosia A failure to recognize what is clearly perceived. Visual agnosia implies that an object, though seen, is not consciously recognized. But note that some other sensory avenue, such as touch, might still permit the person to identify this object.

agonist A drug which acts on specific receptors and mimics their natural response.

allusion An indirect reference. It *hints*, figuratively or symbolically. Allusions take many milliseconds longer than illusions. Moreover, their expressions later in the form of similes, or metaphors, or symbols can be long delayed.

alpha waves An electroencephalographic (EEG) pattern which has a frequency between 8 and 12 cycles per second (cps).

amino acids Most serve as the building blocks for proteins. Some, such as glutamic acid and aspartic acid, also function as excitatory neurotransmitters. Others, like glycine, act as inhibitory neurotransmitters.

amygdala The complex of nuclei, concentrated near the inner tip of each temporal lobe, which helps generate fear and other emotions.

antagonist A drug which blocks the usual response caused by an agonist.

ascending reticular activating system A network of nerve cells in the brainstem which sponsors arousal functions.

association cortex Regions of the neocortex which confer higher integrative functions. Especially well developed in primates, they have no direct sensorimotor function.

axon The fiber issuing from the nerve cell. It conducts nerve impulses out toward the terminals.

basal ganglia The paired deep nuclei on either side of the brain which integrate patterns of motor responses. They include the caudate, putamen, globus pallidus, and substantia nigra.

Being As used here, the term refers to an advanced alternate state which reaches silent levels of ultimate comprehension that elude all description.

beta-endorphin A large opioid peptide released in the deep midline regions of the brain.

beta waves Fast brain waves with an EEG frequency between 14 and 30 cps.

blindsight Responding to visual stimuli without being consciously able to "see" them, by using the second visual system which projects through the superior colliculus.

bodhisattva (Skt.) One who postpones reaching full enlightenment but remains dedicated to helping others become enlightened. A saintly person, or embodied principle skillfully applied.

brainstem The enlarged stalk which lies between the large forebrain and the long spinal cord. It consists of medulla, pons, and midbrain.

central nervous system The cerebrum, cerebellum, brainstem, and spinal cord.

cerebellum The brain structure lying behind the brainstem. It is especially involved in sensorimotor coordination and in balance.

cerebrum The major, forebrain enlargement of the central nervous system. It lies above the midbrain, and contains the outer layer of cortex, as well as deeper structures such as the basal ganglia, thalamus, and limbic system.

cholinergic A nerve cell or function which uses acetylcholine as its neurotransmitter.

circadian rhythms Biological rhythms which recur approximately every 24 hours.

coexistence The existence of both peptides and standard neurotransmitters within the same nerve cell. Both may be released when firing rates are high.

coherence A technical term indicating that the profile of EEG waves in one region resembles that in another. It suggests that both regions are yoked at deeper subcortical or transcortical levels.

colliculi The four bumps on the roof of the midbrain. The upper two are involved in visual reflexes; the lower two mediate auditory reflex functions.

conditioned reflex A basic reflex which has been so modified by past experience that it can now be prompted by a new, conditioned stimulus.

cortex The outer layer of gray matter covering the cerebrum and cerebellum.

delusion A false belief. It can persist despite facts to the contrary.

dendrites The branches at the receiving end of each nerve cell. They receive impulses and convey them down to the nerve cell body.

depolarization The reduction of the charged electrical potential across the nerve cell membrane. When this polarization is lost, the cell fires and generates a nerve impulse.

desynchronization The process of activating regions of the cerebrum. It is associated with arousal, rapid eye movement (REM) sleep (D sleep), and with low-voltage fast EEG activity. Recently it has been appreciated that some fast EEG waveforms are, in fact, synchronized, in which case this word is no longer appropriate.

disinhibition The release of a previously inhibited cell into increased firing, or a release of behavior. In either instance, a prior inhibitory brake is removed.

dopamine (DA) A biogenic amine and neuromessenger. Nerve cells located in the substantia nigra and ventral tegmental area of the midbrain release it at their distant terminals.

electrode A fine metal wire used to detect and transmit the faint traces of brain electrical activity. Stimulating electrodes are also used to deliver electrical stimuli to the brain.

electroencephalogram (EEG) The recording of the brain's waves of electrical activity. Electrodes are placed on the scalp, in the cortex (electrocorticogram), or even deeper in the brain (depth electrodes).

emotion A subjective feeling state.

endorphin See beta-endorphin.

enkephalins Small opioid peptides made by the brain, of two general types: leu-enkephalin and met-enkephalin.

enlightenment Awakening to the reality of the unity of all things. In Zen, also known as the states of kensho or satori.

evoked potential The amplified sum of local brain electrical activity that has been prompted by repeatedly delivering a stimulus at some distance away from the recording site.

excitatory neurotransmitter A neuromessenger which, when it activates its receptor on the next cell, causes that cell to become depolarized and to fire faster.

experiant The one experiencing, even though no sense of self remains at that moment. A term used here, not found in dictionaries.

extended amygdala A term applied to those nerve cells that extend from the central and medial nuclei of the amygdala to include the bed nucleus of the stria terminalis and the shell of the nucleus accumbens.

feeling The subjective experience during emotion.

frontal lobes The lobes which perform higher executive and associative functions. They lie in front of the sensorimotor cortex in the anterior portion of both cerebral hemispheres.

GABA (γ-aminobutyric acid) The major inhibitory neurotransmitter. It is released by many small interneurons, and by some larger nerve cells.

gamma waves Fast EEG waves with frequencies between 30 and 50 cps (or more). Increasingly recognized as a correlate of many excitatory, activating phenomena.

glutamate A major excitatory neurotransmitter. It is the amino acid precursor (glutamic acid) of GABA.

habituation The process by which a nerve cell, or the nervous system in general, reduces its responses after it receives single stimuli repeated with monotonous regularity.

hallucinations Sensory perceptions occurring when no appropriate external stimuli are present.

hippocampus A small region deep in each temporal lobe. It plays a major early role in laying down memory traces, including those that register a sense of "place."

hyperpolarization An increase in the charge of the original electrical potential across the nerve cell membrane. It makes it more difficult for the cell to fire.

hypothalamus The small, complex, centrally located region lying below the thalamus and above the pituitary gland. It integrates many vital brain and body functions crucial to survival: eating, drinking, blood pressure, etc.

illusion A misperception. It registers in milliseconds. We can then entertain it provisionally in our senses or in our imagination for much longer periods.

imagery A literal image is used in literature to provide a direct, factual sensory representation. A figurative image is used in literature. It changes the basic meaning of words, and translates meanings to a different level. In neurology, however, an image is a fact of personal visual experience. It is a distinct percept. An image may, or may not, be an accurate representation.

ineffability Inexpressibility; inability to communicate the essence of an experience.

inhibitory transmitter A neuromessenger which causes the next nerve cell to fire more slowly. It does so by acting on its receptor and causing the cell to become hyperpolarized. GABA is the major inhibitory transmitter.

insight-wisdom The major profound, insightful, comprehension of the essence of things, conferred by prajna.

kensho Seeing into the essence of things, insight-wisdom (Chin: *Chien-hsing*). It is regarded as the beginning of true training, a prelude to the depths of satori.

kinhin Walking meditation.

koan An enigmatic statement serving as a concentration device. Insight resolves it, not logical thought.

lateral geniculate nucleus The compact region at the base of the thalamus. It relays visual messages from the optic tracts back toward the visual cortex.

lesion A region of local damage to the nervous system. Lesions occur as a result of diseases, such as strokes, which destroy nerve cell bodies and axons. Experimental lesions are also produced by instruments such as a knife, by a local pulse of excess electrical current, or by chemical means, including excitotoxins.

limbic system A series of structures next to the midline on both sides of the brain linked by circuits which generate affective and instinctual responses. It includes the hypothalamus, hippocampus, cingulate gyrus, amygdala, and septal region. Allied regions now tend to be called "paralimbic."

limbic thalamus A term applied to three thalamic nuclei that have intimate connections with both the limbic system and the cortex: the medial dorsal, anterior, and lateral dorsal nuclei.

LSD (lysergic acid diethylamide) A hallucinogenic chemical derivative of lysergic acid. It has various other mental effects. Most reflect its major action on serotonin receptors in the brain.

meaning The quality conveyed when the brain links the raw perception of a item to its many related associations. Only certain meanings go on to assume major experiential import (salience).

medulla The lower part of the brainstem lying above the spinal cord. It mediates respiratory, cardiovascular, and other vital functions.

metaphor A figure of speech. It takes one particular name or descriptive phrase out of its original context, then transfers it elsewhere. It implies that two categories are more directly identical than would be accurate literally. A metaphor's tone expresses the general idea or subject matter. Its vehicle is the particular image chosen to convey this idea or subject.

midbrain The upper end of the brainstem.

migraine headaches vs. migraine syndrome Migraine headaches represent the clinical tip of the iceberg. They occur with, or without, a heralding aura, nausea, and vomiting. The migraine syndrome includes a wide variety of other phenomena. They represent the rest of the iceberg, and reflect additional psychophysiological sensitivities and responses. Many of these are subtle and are still being characterized.

mood The long-sustained, tidal, emotional feeling tone which markedly influences the way the person perceives the world. Its range extends from elated manic states to depression.

moodlight A term introduced in these pages because it contrasts with *moon*light. First, it refers to the ordinary kinds of transitory emotions that a person can feel, say, as a secondary response to actual *moon*light. In a different context, it also describes the extraordinary cool, eerie feeling that can occur during the deep vacancy of self in kensho. This feeling begins *before* the visual illusion of the "moonlight only" phase.

mysticism The ongoing practice of reestablishing, by the deepest of insights, one's direct relationship with the Ultimate Reality principle.

norepinephrine (NE) A biogenic amine neuromessenger. It is produced especially by the locus ceruleus in the brainstem. At most of its receptors, the first action of NE is predominantly inhibitory.

nucleus A very large collection of nerve cell bodies. They tend to be viewed as an anatomically distinct structure. (It has a second meaning. Each single nerve cell also contains a round nucleus which contains its DNA.)

occipital lobes* The lobes at the very back of the cerebrum. They mediate visual functions, and blend anteriorally into the parietal and temporal lobes.

optic nerves and tracts The pathways in the front part of the visual system. They convey impulses from the retina back to the two lateral geniculate nuclei.

paradoxical sleep (also known as desynchronized sleep, D sleep, or REM sleep) The activated sleep stage during which dreams and rapid eye movements can occur. One paradox is that the chin muscles and most other muscles along the long axis of the body are quiet.

paralimbic regions Those with strong affective responses and major connections with the limbic system. The term includes the insula, the orbitofrontal cortex, and sometimes the superior temporal gyrus.

parietal lobes Two lobes in the back half of the cerebrum. They are chiefly involved in integrating higher levels of sensory, multimodal, and attentional functions.

peptide A molecule composed of several, linked amino acids. Some peptides act as neuromessengers and as hormones.

phasic Pertaining to a brief period of increased nerve cell firing (as contrasted with sustained, tonic, discharges).

pituitary gland The "master" gland located below the hypothalamus and intimately connected with it. The pituitary gland regulates the internal environment of the body by releasing its hormones into the bloodstream.

pons The enlarged portion of the brainstem lying between the midbrain and the medulla.

prajna (Skt.; J: *hannya*) The flashing insight-wisdom of enlightenment.

proprioceptive The kinds of sensations entering from the muscles, joints, tendons, and vestibular system. These impulses contribute to one's sense of position and balance.

psychedelics "Mind-manifesting," psychoactive drugs such as LSD, psilocybin, and mescaline. They usually have prominent hallucinogenic effects.

rapid eye movement sleep (REM sleep) (also known as D sleep or paradoxical sleep) That stage of activated sleep when rapid eye movements and dreams occur.

receptor A large protein molecule embedded in the membrane of the cell. It is designed both to recognize the signal from only a certain specific transmitter, modulator, or hormone, and then to transduce its message into the cell.

reticular nucleus The thin outer layer of GABA nerve cells capping the thalamus. It plays a pivotal inhibitory role in thalamic functions and in thalamocortical interactions.

roshi Venerable teacher; the Japanese pronunciation (rōshî) of the name of the venerated Chinese teacher, Lao-tzu. Usually capitalized when it refers to a particular Zen teacher.

salience The leaping forth into meaning of the special quality which confers significant import.

samadhi (Skt.) An extraordinary alternate state of one-pointed absorption. The word has developed so many other meanings that it tends to imply merely a state.

satori The term frequently reserved for a deeper, more advanced state of insight-wisdom.

serotonin A biogenic amine. It is produced especially by cell bodies in the midline raphe system of the brainstem. Serotonin plays a predominantly inhibitory role. Its longer chemical name is 5-hydroxytryptamine, or 5-HT.

sesshin An intensive Zen meditative retreat lasting several days; literally, "to collect the mind."

simile A comparison that expresses similarities between things or ideas. It uses the words "like" or "as."

simultagnosia A patient's inability to grasp the whole scene, although its individual elements are perceived in isolation.

split brain A brain in which the corpus callosum has been divided surgically. But even after the other smaller (commissural) crossing fiber connections are also cut, the two hemispheres still communicate with each other via their lower "subcortical bridge."

state A temporary condition involving mentation, emotion, or behavior.

striatum Several nuclei of the basal ganglia which mediate motor functions. The caudate and putamen compose the dorsal striatum. The ventral striatum includes the nucleus accumbens.

substantia nigra The paired structures in the midbrain which are rich in dopamine cell bodies and which energize motor functions.

symbol A sign (often visible). It stands for something else that exists independently and is more complex.

synapse The specialized gap through which the terminals of one cell link with the dendrite, cell body, or terminal of the next cell. The nerve cell on the upstream side is called the *pre*synaptic cell. That on the other side of the gap is called the *post*synaptic cell. Neuromessengers leap quickly across the synaptic gap to activate their receptors on the opposite side. They are then taken back up again and recycled.

synchronization The process of bringing together regions of the cerebrum into regular, rhythmic patterns of firing activity. In the past, it has usually been associated with slower waveforms in the EEG, with drowsiness, and slowwave sleep (S sleep). More recently, however, fast activity has been recognized as also rhythmic and synchronized, as, for example, in gamma waves.

syncretism The reconciliation of conflicting opposites into a unity. The origins of the term trace to the way contending Cretan cities finally united into a larger federation.

tathagata (Skt.) A term originally referring to the Buddha, inferring one who has "thus gone" (through the entire Path). It implies a rare spiritually advanced person who appreciates all things as they really are, as a permanent ongoing condition.

temporal lobes The lobes lying deep to each temple. The term includes both the temporal lobe cortex and its deeper, limbic structures such as the parahippocampal gyrus, the hippocampal formation, and the amygdala.

thalamus The deeper nuclear structures positioned behind the basal ganglia and medial to them. They serve largely to integrate sensory and ever more refined messages at a subcortical level. They also become engaged in complex interactions with the cortex.

tonic Refers to a condition in which there is a sustained firing of nerve cells.

trait A distinctive, ongoing quality of attitude, character, or behavior. Traits are not usually thought of as subject to change. However, they can be transformed by a series of extraordinary, insightful alternate states superimposed on long-range meditative training.

transfiguration The transformation of the ordinary appearances of things by the infusion of sacramental/holy resonances of meaning.

ventral tegmental area A region near the midline in the front of the midbrain. It contains many dopamine cell bodies which project their axons forward through the mesolimbic DA system.

ventricles Spaces within the brain filled with fluid. They include the large, lateral ventricles within the two cerebral hemispheres; the third ventricle in the midline enclosed by the hypothalamus; and the fourth ventricle behind the brainstem. Its fluid drains from the third ventricle via the small aqueduct.

zazen Zen meditation in the sitting posture; from the Chinese, *tso-ch'an*.

Zen A form of Mahayana Buddhism which emphasizes a systematic approach to meditative training and spiritual growth. Its two major schools, Rinzai and Soto, were imported from China and developed in Japan during the twelfth and thirteenth centuries.

zendo The room used for formal Zen practice.

References and Notes

Preface

1. W. James. *The Varieties of Religious Experience*. New York, Longmans, Green, 1925.
2. H. Koenig, M. McCullogh, and D. Larson. *Handbook of Religion and Health*. Oxford, Oxford University Press, 2001.

By Way of Introduction

1. From Eisai's "Propagation of Zen for the Protection of the State." In W. DeBary, K. Keene, G. Tanabe, et al. *Sources of Japanese Tradition*, 2nd ed., vol. 1. New York, Columbia University Press, 2001, 315.
2. Readers curious about the author's other biases might wish to refer to the recent MIT Press edition of *Chase, Chance, and Creativity. The Lucky Art of Novelty*. Cambridge, MA, MIT Press, 2003.

Chapter 1 Is There Some Common Ground between Zen Experience and the Brain?

1. Leonardo, quoted in J. Cacioppo, L. Tassinary, and G. Berntson, eds. *Handbook of Psychophysiology*. Cambridge, UK, Cambridge University Press 2000, 20.
2. A. Lutz, J. Lachaux, J. Martinerie, et al. Guiding the study of brain dynamics by using first-person data: Synchrony patterns correlate with ongoing conscious states during a simple visual task. *Proceedings of the National Academy of Sciences U S A* 2002; 99:1586–1591.
3. J. Cacioppo, L. Tassinary, and G. Berntson. Psychophysiology science, 3–23. (Introduction in *Handbook of Psychophysiology*.)

Chapter 2 A Brief Outline of Zen History

1. H. Sigerist. Early Greek, Hindu, and Persian Medicine, vol. 2. In *A History of Medicine*. New York, Oxford University Press, 1961, 181–182.
2. Freely adapted from Edwin Arnold's *The Light of Asia*, cited by C. Humphreys, in *Buddhism*. Penguin, 1974, 33. The ridgepole is a roof's highest horizontal structural support. It holds the upper ends of the rafters. This theme of the shattered ridgepole is also referred to in the *Dhammapada*, verses 153–154. See J. Mascaro. *The Dhammapada. The Path of Perfection*. Aylesbury, UK, Penguin, 1986, 56–57; E. Conze, ed. *Buddhist Texts through the Ages*. Boston, Shambhala, 1990.

Chapter 3 Western Perspectives on Mystical Experiences

1. N. Kobori. *In The Spring I Come Back to My True Home* [In Japanese]. Kyoto, Japan, Institute for Zen Culture, c. 1996.
2. T. Maezumi. *Appreciate Your Life. The Essence of Zen Practice*. Boston, Shambhala, 2001, xi.
3. A. Hardy. *The Spiritual Nature of Man: A Study of Contemporary Religious Experience*. Oxford, Clarendon Press, 1979, 25–29.

Chapter 4 An Outline of the Path of Zen

1. T. Enji. *The Discourse on the Inexhaustible Lamp of the Zen School, trans. Yoko Okda*. London, Zen Center 1989, 120.
2. S. Suzuki. *Zen Mind, Beginner's Mind*. New York, Weatherhill, 1975. Already a classic. This seemingly "ordinary" Soto Zen master had an extraordinary personal influence on his students, as has this slim volume on generations of readers.

3. J. Kabat-Zinn. *Wherever You Go, There You Are. Mindfulness Meditation in Everyday Life*. New York, Hyperion, 1994. A popular book on how to practice meditation in daily life.
4. R. Aitken. *The Practice of Perfection. The Paramitas from a Zen Buddhist Perspective*. New York, Pantheon, 1994. A series of short essays by a senior, Japanese-trained, American Zen master.
5. T. Hirai. *Psychophysiology of Zen*. Tokyo. Igaku Shoin, 1974, 112.
6. J. Austin. Six points to ponder. *Journal of Consciousness Studies* 1999; 6:213–216.

Chapter 5 The Semantics of Self

1. A. Deikman. "I" = Awareness. *Journal of Consciousness Studies* 1996; 3:350–356.
2. A. Cohen and K. Wilber. The guru and the pandit: Breaking the rules. *What Is Enlightenment?* 2002; 22:30–49.

Chapter 6 Developing Our Conscious Levels of Self

1. B. Hoff. *The Tao of Pooh*. New York, Penguin, 1982, 146–147.
2. P. Zelazo. The development of conscious control in childhood. *Trends in Cognitive Sciences* 2004; 8:12–17.
3. J. Panksepp. The periconscious substrates of consciousness: Affective states and the evolutionary origins of the self. *Journal of Consciousness Studies* 1998; 5:566–582.
4. P. Zelazo and J. Sommerville. Levels of consciousness of the self in time. In *The Self In Time*, eds. C. Moore and K. Lemmon. Mahwah, NJ, Lawrence Erlbaum Associates, 2001, 229–252.

Chapter 7 Some ABCs of the I-Me-Mine

1. Consider the pale literary definitions of these three terms. "I" serves as a pronoun when it refers to the person who is speaking or writing. "I" is a noun when it refers to someone who is aware of possessing a personal individual identity, a self. "Me," on the other hand remains a pronoun, serving as the objective case of I. "Mine" is a personal pronoun indicating possession.
2. D. Galin. The concepts of "self," "person," and "I". In *Buddhism and Science. Breaking New Ground*, ed. B. Wallace. New York, Columbia University Press, 2003.

Chapter 8 Constructing Our Self, Inside and Outwardly

1. J.-D. Degos, A. Bachoud-Levi, A. Ergis, et al. Selective inability to point to extrapersonal targets after left posterior parietal lesions: An objectivization disorder? *Neurocase* 1997; 3:31–39. Patient 8 was an intelligent 58-year-old, right-handed man who had no right arm or leg weakness. The structural MRI scan showed that his underlying white matter was also infarcted. His self-referent symptoms resolved rapidly. This is a point in favor of their representing a disinhibitory phenomenon referable to the right side, and attributable to its being "released" by damage on the left side. All nine patients in this report could *name* the fingers of another person to whom the examiner was pointing. However, they could not *themselves* point to this other person's fingers. The animate nature of other living persons is a vital property. It needs further study in other patients who have the same problems aligning themselves to point at an external live target. Four of the nine patients who had allotopagnosia could not *point*—either with their hands, fingers, or eyes—at the requested target in the space outside of them. However, all nine could look correctly, and spontaneously, at the target.
2. J. Panksepp. The periconscious substrates of consciousness: Affective states and the evolutionary origins of the self. *Journal of Consciousness Studies* 1998; 5:566–582.

3. Chapter 41 speaks of an actively "embodied self-image." The phrase refers to normal spatial functions which take place at the self/other interface. It has no esoteric implications.
4. R. Saxe. A region of right posterior superior temporal sulcus responds to observed intentional actions. *Neuropsychologia* 2004; 42:1435–1446.
5. Self-referencing functions are not simple. Neither are the interpretations of their dysfunctions straightforward. In fact, many of the patients reported in Degos et al. (note 1) had a right visual field defect, aphasia, agraphia, finger agnosia (for named fingers), acalculia, right-left disorientation, and constructional apraxia. The last four make up the tetrad of Gerstmann's syndrome. These are the signs expected of lesions of the *left* angular gyrus, and the adjacent occipital association cortex.

Chapter 9 Two Interpreters: One Articulate, the Other Silent

1. M. Gazzaniga. The interpreter within: The glue of conscious experience. *Cerebrum* 1999; 1:68–78.
2. Ibid.

Chapter 10 Dissolving the Psychic Self and Its Veils of Interpretation

1. F. Cachin, I. Cahn, W. Feilchenfeldt, et al., eds. *Cézanne*. New York, Harry Abrams, 1996, 37–38. Young Paul Valery (1871–1945) overlapped this elder painter in the decades around the turn of that century.
2. A. Calder, A. Lawrence, and A. Young. Neuropsychology of fear and loathing. *Nature Reviews Neuroscience* 2001; 2:352–363.

Chapter 13 The Attentive Art of Meditation

1. S. Murphy. *One Bird, One Stone. 108 American Zen Stories*. New York, Renaissance/St. Martin's Press, 2002, 106.
2. B. Dunn, J. Hartigan, and W. Mikulas. Concentration and mindfulness meditations: Unique forms of consciousness? *Applied Psychophysiological Biofeedback* 1999; 24:147–165.
3. W. James. *The Principles of Psychology*. New York, Holt, 1890, chap. 4.
4. S. Lazar. Personal communication, 2 December 2004. A longitudinal study is awaited to replicate this finding.

Chapter 14 Just This

1. D. Chadwick. *Crooked Cucumber. The Life and Zen Teaching of Shunryu Suzuki*. New York, Broadway, 1999, 301.
2. Some potential options in the Japanese language might begin with *koko*. It stands for *this* place, *this* point, or for each *particular one* individually. *Kore* stands for *this*, or *this one*.
3. To keep the diagrams simple, no attempt has been made to make expiration stretch out into an extra prolonged line. Nor has the apparent volume of each breath been pictured as changing as meditation evolves into its deeper stages. However, the wavy line of awareness focused on the lower abdomen is shown becoming thicker. This is to suggest the fact that awareness becomes more focused into the tanden during later stages.
4. This is not easy. Our brain circuits already pay much more attention to sensations arising from the head than they do from the chest, and pay still less attention to sensations from the abdomen. This normal phenomenon is termed "rostral dominance."
5. Laboratory rats are also restless animals. Applying simple sensory deprivation techniques to their head can help quiet them. After the rat is anesthetized, one can clip off those long, sensitive facial whiskers along its muzzle. This removes one highly important source of stimulating input from its head. That rat is much less restless after it awakens. Whisker

sensations are no longer stimulating its brainstem via its large fifth cranial nerve. J. Austin, L.-G. Nygren, and K. Fuxe. A system for measuring the noradrenaline receptor contribution to the flexor reflex. *Medical Biology* 1976; 54:352–363.

Chapter 15 Meditative Attention: Accessing Deeper Avenues of Seeing and Hearing

1. T. Cleary. *Classics of Buddhism and Zen*, vol. 3. Boston, Shambhala, 2001, 457.
2. A. Braverman. *Mud and Water: A Collection of Talks by the Zen Master Bassui*. San Francisco, North Point Press, 1989, 46.
3. Thich Nhat Hanh. *Dharma Talk*. Presented September 1997, Santa Barbara, CA.
4. J. Loori. *The Eight Gates of Zen. A Program of Zen Training*. Boston, Shambhala, 2002, 106.
5. Braverman, *Mud and Water*, xv and xx. Braverman's commentaries make it clear that while Bassui may have been familiar with hearing as an avenue for his own awakening, he also appreciated the other sensory avenues.
6. Ibid., 101 (from the Suramgama Sutra).
7. Sheng-yen. Like a sound absorbing board—methods of practice using the ear. *Chan Magazine*, spring 2004, 12–14.
8. Braverman, *Mud and Water*, 45.
9. J. Snelling. *The Buddhist Handbook: A Complete Guide to Buddhist Schools, Teaching, Practice, and History*. Rochester, VT, Inner Traditions, 1991, 39.
10. R. Lane, P. Chua, and R. Dolan. Common effects of emotional valence, arousal, and attention on neural activation during visual processing of pictures. *Neuropsychologia* 1999; 37:989–997.
11. Studies of children and adults suggest that a drug like methylphenidate (Ritalin) can help patients who are accurately diagnosed with attention deficit hyperactivity disorder (ADHD) by enhancing their synaptic levels of dopamine.
12. J. Sweeney, C. Rosano, R. Berman, et al. Inhibitory control of attention declines more than working memory during normal aging. *Neurobiology of Aging* 2001; 22:39–47.

Chapter 16 Interpreting Synchronized Brain Waves

1. R. Davidson, D. Jackson, and C. Larson. Human electroencephalography. In *Handbook of Psychophysiology*, eds. J. Cacioppo, L. Tassinary, and G. Berntson. Cambridge, UK, Cambridge University Press 2000, 27–52.
2. K. Sasaki, T. Tsujimoto, S. Nishikawa, et al. Frontal mental theta wave recorded simultaneously with magnetoencephalography and electroencephalography. *Neuroscience Research* 1996; 26:79–81. A single EEG electrode reflects electrical activities from a wider cortical area than does a MEG sensor. In addition, the amplitude of EEG waves recorded at an electrode on one side of the scalp can be affected by the other currents generated obliquely over the opposite side of the brain. EEGs and MEGs also sample different populations. MEG detects mainly the horizontal component of magnetic dipoles, whereas the EEG picks up chiefly the signals of radial current dipoles. These radial signals are referable more to the excitatory postsynaptic dendritic potentials of cortical *gyri* at the surface than to potentials arising in the deeper sulci.
3. Davidson et al., Human electroencephalography. This reduction in localized alpha power becomes more evident when data from single leads are compared with other calculations representing a "whole-head" estimation of composite alpha power. This approach is most appropriate in adults because their absolute levels of power in the alpha band remain relatively stable. In children, the baseline alpha activities in prefrontal electrode sites are more variable.

4. Ibid. One way to compare the two sides is to derive an "asymmetry index." In practice, this is a useful formulation to the extent that alpha remains *inversely* associated with the degree of underlying brain activation in the waking EEG.

The index was set up so that the log of the alpha power on the left is *subtracted* from the log of the alpha power on the right. It follows that *positive* index numbers (which mean a relatively higher number on the *right*) will imply a relative preponderance of *left* activation over right. Note: This can make it more difficult to remember that a so-called *positive* affective style will tend to be associated with a relatively greater brain activation on the left side.

Of course, whenever researchers use ratios, they are obliged to look first into the individual numbers themselves. Consider the three physiologically different options in such a ratio. For example, does a *relatively* greater left-sided activation represent an *absolute* increase on the *left*? Or, is it caused instead by an absolute reduction in activation on the right side? Moreover, could such an asymmetrical ratio reflect, simultaneously, *both* an increased activation on the left *and* a reduced activation on the right?

5. Ibid.
6. R. Ishii, K. Shinosaki, S. Ukai, et al. Medial prefrontal cortex generates frontal midline theta rhythm. *NeuroReport* 1999; 10:675–679.
7. K. Sasaki, T. Tsujimoto, R. Matsuzaki, et al. Integrative functions of the human frontal association cortex studied with MEG. In *Integrative and Molecular Approach to Brain Function*, eds. M. Ito and Y. Miyashita. New York, Elsevier Science, 1996, 303–314. The corresponding subjective state is not described. Circumstantial evidence would suggest that perhaps the meditators were concentrating on some mental task.
8. L. Ward. Synchronous neural oscillations and cognitive processes. *Trends in Cognitive Sciences* 2003; 7:553–559.
9. J. Sarnthein, H. Petsche, P. Rappelsberger, et al. Synchronization between prefrontal and posterior association cortex during human working memory. *Proceedings of the National Academy of Sciences U S A* 1998; 95:7092–7096. (Gamma waves are cited here as ranging between 19 and 32 cps.)
10. L. Aftanas, N. Reva, A. Varlamov, et al. Analysis of evoked EEG synchronization and desynchronization in conditions of emotional activation in humans: temporal and topographic characteristics. *Neuroscience and Behavioral Physiology* 2004; 34:859–867.
11. J. White, M. Banks, R. Pearce, et al. Networks of interneurons with fast and slow γ-aminobutyric acid type A ($GABA_A$) kinetics provide substrate for mixed gamma-theta rhythm. *Proceedings of the National Academy of Sciences U S A* 2000; 97:8131–8133. Other studies in hippocampal slices confirm that gamma rhythms here might prove useful to synchronize relatively local activities. In contrast, synchronized *beta* rhythms might be useful to link transcortical regions (that are farther apart) into higher-level interactions. See N. Kopell, G. Ermentrout, M. Whittington, et al. Gamma rhythms and beta rhythms have different synchronization properties. *Proceedings of the National Academy of Sciences U S A* 2000; 97:1867–1872. For another view of how metabotropic glutamate receptors might contribute to generate gamma oscillations, see R. Traub, J. Jefferys, and M. Whittington. *Fast Oscillations in Cortical Circuits*. Cambridge, MA, MIT Press, 1999.
12. Davidson et al., Human electroencephalography.
13. H. Merica and R. Fortune. Spectral power time-courses of human sleep EEG reveal a striking discontinuity at ~18 Hz marking the division between NREM-specific and wake/REM-specific fast frequency activity. *Cerebral Cortex* 2005; 15:877–884 (note reference 9).
14. A. Salek-Haddadi, K. Friston, L. Lemieux, et al. Studying spontaneous EEG activity with fMRI. *Brain Research Reviews* 2003; 43:110–133.

15. H. Laufs, K. Krakow, P. Sterzer, et al. Electroencephalographic signatures of attentional and cognitive default modes in spontaneous brain activity fluctuations at rest. *Proceedings of the National Academy of Sciences U S A* 2003; 100:11053–11058.

16. E. Basar, C. Basar-Eroglu, S. Karakas, et al. Are cognitive processes manifested in event-related gamma, alpha, theta and delta oscillations in the EEG? *Neuroscience Letters* 1999; 259:165–168.

17. A. Sokolov, W. Lutzenberger, M. Pavlova, et al. Gamma-band MEG activity to coherent motion depends on task-driven attention. *NeuroReport* 1999; 10:1997–2000.

18. H. Parthasarathy. Mind rhythms. *New Scientist* 1999; 2210:28–31. The hypothesis is attributed to John Lisman and colleagues. A theoretical model simpler to explain suggests that during short-term working memory, gamma oscillations might become enhanced some six times a second at a theta frequency. (See L. Ward, reference 8, on page 555.) The central issue remains: What useful *functions* emerge from these myriad processes of excitation, inhibition, and disinhibition? The waveforms recorded are but indirect reflections of the rhythmic, dynamic flux of *these* basic underlying processes.

19. D. Lehmann, P. Faber, P. Achermann, et al. Brain sources of EEG gamma frequency during volitionally meditation-induced, altered states of consciousness, and experience of the self. *Psychiatry Research* 2001; 108:111–121. This beta-2 activity was measured at 18 to 21 cps.

20. A. Lutz, J. Lachaux, J. Martinerie, et al. Guiding the study of brain dynamics by using first-person data: Synchrony patterns correlate with ongoing conscious states during a simple visual task. *Proceedings of the National Academy of Sciences U S A* 2002; 99:1586–1591. First-person data had long been emphasized by Francisco Varela, who led this team before his untimely death. See note 32.

21. F. Aoki, E. Fetz, L. Shupe, et al. Increased gamma-range activity in human sensorimotor cortex during performance of visuomotor tasks. *Clinical Neurophysiology* 1999; 110:524–537.

22. M. Pastor, J. Artieda, J. Arbizu, et al. Activation of human cerebral and cerebellar cortex by auditory stimulation at 40 Hz. *Journal of Neuroscience* 2002; 22:10501–10506.

23. S. Andino, C. Michel, G. Thut, et al. Prediction of response speed by anticipatory high-frequency (gamma band) oscillations in the human brain. *Human Brain Mapping* 2005; 24:50–58. Anticipation enhances top-down attentional control.

24. J. Fell, G. Fernandez, P. Klaver, et al. Is synchronized neuronal gamma activity relevant for selective attention? *Brain Research Reviews* 2003; 42:265–272.

25. V. Goffaux, A. Mouraux, S. Desmet, et al. Human non-phase-locked gamma oscillations in experience-based perception of visual scenes. *Neuroscience Letters* 2004; 354:14–17.

26. J. Cantero, M. Atienza, J. Madsen, et al. Gamma EEG dynamics in neocortex and hippocampus during human wakefulness and sleep. *Neuroimage* 2004; 22:1271–1280.

27. C. Tallon-Baudry, O. Bertrand, M. Henaff, et al. Attention modulates gamma-band oscillations differently in the human lateral occipital cortex and fusiform gyrus. *Cerebral Cortex* 2005; 15:654–662.

28. G. Foffani, A. Priori, M. Egidi, et al. 300-Hz subthalamic oscillations in Parkinson's disease. *Brain* 2003; 126:2153–2163.

29. F. Grenier, I. Timofeev, and M. Steriade. Focal synchronization of ripples (80–200 Hz) in neocortex and their neuronal correlates. *Journal of Neurophysiology* 2001; 86:1884–1898.

30. M. Steriade, E. Jones, D. McCormick. *Thalamus*. Vol. 1, *Organization and Function*. Oxford, Elsevier Science, 1997.

31. A. Gamma, D. Lehmann, E. Frei, et al. Comparison of simultaneously recorded [$H_2{}^{15}O$]-PET and LORETA during cognitive and pharmacological activation. *Human Brain Mapping* 2004; 22:83–96.

32. F. Varela, J. Lachaus, E. Rodriguez, et al. The brainweb: Phase synchronization and large-scale integration. *Nature Reviews Neuroscience* 2001; 2:229–239.

Chapter 17 Some Gamma EEG and Heart Rate Changes *during* Meditation

1. T. Deshimaru. *The Zen Way to the Martial Arts*. New York, Arkana (Penguin), 1982, 3.
2. A. Lutz, L. Greischor, N. Rawlings, et al. Long-term meditators self-induce high amplitude gamma synchrony during mental practice. *Proceedings of the National Academy of Sciences U S A* 2004; 101:16369–16373. Muscle artifact can be a thorny problem. The methods used in this article to measure and reduce muscle artifact may interest other researchers who wish to study gamma activities.
3. Ibid.
4. R. Davidson and colleagues. *Transforming Affective Style*. Presented at the Mind and Life Summer Research Institute, June 25, 2004, Garrison, NY, Garrison Institute. (The midfrontal regions were BA 6 and BA 10.)
5. C.-K. Peng, J. Pietus, Y. Liu, et al. Exaggerated heart rate oscillations during meditation techniques. *International Journal of Cardiology* 1999; 70:101–107.
6. F. Travis. Autonomic and EEG patterns distinguish transcending from other experiences during Transcendental Meditation practice. *International Journal of Psychophysiology* 2001; 42:1–9.

Chapter 18 EEG and Heart Rate Changes *in Zen* Meditation

1. Kobori Nanrei Sohaku. Zen and the art of tea. *The Middle Way*, 1972; 46:148–152.
2. T. Hirai. *Psychophysiology of Zen*. Tokyo, Igaku Shoin, 1974, 64–65.
3. Ibid., 27–31. Because frontal midline theta activity can develop during mental concentration, it remains possible that some monks might have been concentrating on their breathing, on their koan, or on some related mental focus during some of this rhythmic theta activity.
4. Y. Kubota, W. Sato, M. Toichi, et al. Frontal midline theta rhythm is correlated with cardiac autonomic activities during the performance of an attention demanding meditation procedure. *Cognitive Brain Research* 2001; 11:281–287.
5. Ibid.
6. T. Murata, T. Takahashi, T. Hamada, et al. Individual trait anxiety levels characterizing the properties of Zen meditation. *Neuropsychobiology* 2004; 50:189–194.
7. F. Travis, J. Tecce, A. Arenander, et al. Patterns of EEG coherence, power, and contingent negative variation characterize the integration of transcendental and waking states. *Biological Psychology* 2002; 61:293–319.
8. L. Aftanas and S. Golocheikine. Non-linear dynamic complexity of the human EEG during meditation. *Neuroscience Letters* 2002; 330:143–146. Sahaja, in Sanskrit, means "natural."
9. L. Aftanas and S. Golocheikine. Human anterior and frontal midline theta and lower alpha reflect emotionally positive state and internalized attention: High-resolution EEG investigation of meditation. *Neuroscience Letters* 2001; 310:57–60.

Chapter 19 Delayed Physiological Responses *to* Meditation

1. C. MacLean, K. Walton, S. Wenneberg, et al. Effects of the Transcendental Meditation program on adaptive mechanisms: Changes in hormone levels and responses to stress after 4 months of practice. *Psychoneuroendocrinology* 1997; 22:277–295.
2. D. Goleman. *Destructive Emotions. How Can We Overcome Them?* New York, Bantam Dell 2003, 344. A commentary on the findings published in note 4 below.
3. MacLean et al., Effects of the Transcendental Meditation program.

4. R. Davidson, J. Kabat-Zinn, J. Schumacher, et al. Alterations in brain and immune function produced by mindfulness meditation. *Psychosomatic Medicine* 2003; 65:564–470.
5. K. Barrows and B. Jacobs. Mind-body medicine. An introduction and review of the literature. *Medical Clinics of North America* 2002; 86:11–31.
6. J. Kiecolt-Glaser, L. McGuire, T. Robles, et al. Psychoneuroimmunology and psychosomatic medicine: Back to the future. *Psychosomatic Medicine* 2002; 64:15–28.
7. J. Infante, P. Fernando, M. Martinez, et al. ACTH and β-endorphin in transcendental meditation. *Physiology and Behavior* 1998; 64:311–315.
8. MacLean et al., Effects of the Transcendental Meditation program. Note: The serial subtractions lasted for 6 minutes. The star tracing and hand grip tests lasted for 3.5 minutes each. As a result of attrition, the number of volunteer subjects dropped from 49 to 29. This qualifies a number of conclusions in the study.
9. R. Sudsuang, V. Chentanez, and K. Veluvan. Effect of Buddhist meditation on serum cortisol and total protein levels, blood pressure, pulse rate, lung volume and reaction time. *Physiology and Behavior* 1991; 50:543–548.
10. J. Infante, M. Torres-Avisbal, P. Pinel, et al. Catecholamine levels in practitioners of transcendental mediation technique. *Physiology and Behavior* 2001; 72:141–146.
11. Davidson et al., The authors note that the relatively small number of subjects in this study limits its statistical power. State and trait tests were used to assess positive and negative emotions, and were supplemented with the subjects' own self-report evaluations.

    Asymmetrical alpha activation was indexed with the aid of the "asymmetry score." The rationale for using alpha power as an inverse index for activation is discussed further in chapter 16, and in note 13, below.
12. Goleman, *Destructive Emotions*.
13. R. Benca, W. Obermeyer, C. Larson, et al. EEG alpha power and alpha power asymmetry in sleep and wakefulness. *Psychophysiology* 1999; 36:430–436.
14. Our body responds to an influenza vaccination not only with the activities of B cells (which produce antibodies) but also by involving our T helper cells in *their* interactions with B cells. Acute and chronic stress situations adversely affect the ways our hypothalamic-pituitary-adrenal axis and sympathetic nervous systems normally mediate these complex immune responses.
15. Goleman, *Destructive Emotions*, 345. These observations raised the possibility that certain meditators might have improved because their actual *daily-life* practice of mindfulness *while on the job* became more effective, even though they may also have reported that their attempts to meditate at home were less than ideal.
16. Davidson et al., ibid.
17. M. Rosenkranz, D. Jackson, K. Dalton, et al. Affective style and *in vivo* immune response: Neurobehavioral mechanisms. *Proceedings of the National Academy of Sciences U S A* 2003; 110:11148–11152.
18. R. Davidson, C. Coe, I. Dolski, et al. Individual differences in prefrontal activation asymmetry predict natural killer cell activity at rest and in response to challenge. *Brain, Behavior, and Immunity* 1999; 13:93–108. Cytokines (interleukin and interferon) normally activate natural killer cells. These killer cells then help dissolve malignant cells or cells infected by viruses.
19. L. Carlson, M. Speca, K. Patel, et al. Mindfulness-based stress reduction in relation to quality of life, mood, symptoms of stress, and immune parameters in breast and prostate cancer outpatients. *Psychosomatic Medicine* 2003; 65:571–581. Cytokine responses are complex, and are open to more than one interpretation. The lack of a nonmeditating control group limits

the inference that meditation was the sole mechanism for the improvements in these patients.

Chapter 20 Breathing In; Breathing Out

1. T. Hirai. *Psychophysiology of Zen*. Tokyo, Igaku Shoin, 1974, 69. Figures 68 a–c, on pages 68–69, depict the thoracic and abdominal breathing *movements* of a Zen monk who had practiced for 22 years. Before the period of meditation begins, his abdomen expands slightly before his thorax. During meditation, respirations slow from 17 to 4 a minute. Again, on the in-breath his abdomen expands just before his thorax. As meditation ends, the respiratory rate rebounds to 21 a minute. Future research needs to distinguish between: (1) expansion movements of the abdomen on the in-breath caused by passive relaxation of the abdominal wall, and (2) active *contractions* by several muscle groups. These are the intercostal muscles which expand the thorax, the diaphragm which adds further to inspiration, and the lower abdominal muscles. By compressing the abdomen, these lower muscles help expel air during the out-breath (expiration).
2. J. Feldman, G. Mitchell, and E. Nattie. Breathing: Rhythmicity, plasticity, chemosensitivity. *Annual Review of Neuroscience* 2003; 26:239–266.
3. P. Gray, W. Janczewski, N. Mellen, et al. Normal breathing requires preBotzinger complex neurokinin-1 receptor-expressing neurons. *Nature Neuroscience* 2001; 4:927–930. Rats develop nonrhythmic (ataxic) breathing when all 600 of these nerve cells are destroyed.
4. X. Shao and J. Feldman. Pharmacology of nicotinic receptors in preBotzinger complex that mediate modulation of respiratory pattern. *Journal of Neurophysiology* 2002; 88:1851–1858.
5. N. Chamberlin and C. Saper. A brainstem network mediating apneic reflexes in the rat. *Journal of Neuroscience* 1998; 18:6048–6056. This region between the two nuclei is sensitive to glutamate and has extensive connections.
6. Y. Bouin. *Effects of Meditation on Respiration and the Temporal Lobes: An Exploratory and Meta-analytic Study*. Lund, Sweden, Lund University Press, 2000.
7. W. Janczewski, H. Onimaru, I. Homma, et al. Opioid-resistant respiratory pathway from the preinspiratory neurones to abdominal muscles: In vivo and in vitro study in the newborn rat. *Journal of Physiology* 2002; 545:1017–1026.
8. R. Fried. Relaxation with biofeedback-assisted guided imagery: The importance of breathing rate as an index of hypoarousal. *Biofeedback and Self-Regulation* 1987; 12:273–279.
9. F. Plum and J. Posner. *The Diagnosis of Stupor and Coma*, 3rd edn. Philadelphia, F.A. Davis, 1980, 34–38.
10. J. Kesterson and N. Clinch. Metabolic rate, respiratory exchange ratio, and apneas during meditation. *American Journal of Physiology* 1989; 256:632–638.
11. S. Reilly and R. Trifunovic. Lateral parabrachial nucleus lesions in the rat: Aversive and appetitive gustatory conditioning. *Brain Research Bulletin* 2000; 52:269–278.
12. Chamberlin and Saper, A brainstem network.
13. D. Abbott, H. Opdam, R. Briellmann, et al. Brief breath holding may confound functional magnetic resonance imaging studies. *Human Brain Mapping* 2005; 24:284–290.
14. T. Deshimaru. *The Zen Way to the Martial Arts*. New York, Arkana (Penguin) 1982, 65.

Chapter 21 A Quest for No Answers: Koan, Huatou, Jakugo, Mondo

1. B. Glassman. Notes on koan study. In *On Zen Practice. Body, Breath, Mind*, eds. T. Maezumi and B. Glassman (rev. W. Nakao and J. Buksbazen). Boston, Wisdom, 2002, 83–87.
2. J. Snelling. *The Buddhist Handbook*. Rochester, VT, Inner Traditions, 1991, 14.

3. Nagarjuna was not only a legendary philosopher and a Buddhist but he took an active role in practical affairs during his tenure as a court counselor in the south of India.
4. T. Cleary. *Classics of Buddhism and Zen*, vol. 4. Boston, Shambhala, 2001, 232–236.
5. Glassman. Notes on koan study.
6. C. Sheng-yen, J. Crook, S. Child, et al. *Chan Comes West*. Elmhurst, NY, Dharma Drum Publications, 2002, 16–19.
7. K. Craft. *Eloquent Zen. Daito and Early Japanese Zen*. Honolulu, University of Hawaii Press, 1992.
8. V. Hori. *Zen Sand: The Book of Capping Phrases for Koan Practice*. Honolulu, University of Hawaii Press, 2003. This recent compilation of capping phrases is extracted from phrase books used in contemporary Japanese monastic training. The capping phrases in appendix A are from an earlier collection of the Zenrinkushu. They were chosen to illustrate how much certain old phrases can contribute to our understanding. Still, there are often substantial cultural gaps between the versions in Chinese, Japanese, and English. The student must wrestle with many ambiguities in an effort to get on the same wavelength as the teacher, especially when the two persons come from different historical and ethnic traditions.

Chapter 22 The Roshi

1. G. Seldes. *The Great Quotations*. New York, Pocket Books, 1967, 905.
2. M. Caplan. *Do You Need a Guru? Understanding the Student-Teacher Relationship in an Era of False Prophets*. London, Thorsons, 2002.
3. Adapted from Koji Hoashi's translation of one chapter in Nanrei Kobori, *In the Spring I Come Back to My True Home* [in Japanese]. Kyoto, Institute for Zen Culture, c. 1996. In his 20s, Shonen-Roshi was a student of Professor Ketaro Nishida (1870–1945) at Kyoto University. He then taught Japanese at a women's college. He became a Zen monk, full-time, when he was over 40 years old. He led a simple, austere lifestyle, like that of a Zen monk in the Tang dynasty.
4. I thank Jack Duffy-Roshi for bringing this home.
5. Only years later, did I learn, to my further embarrassment, that this kind of stick was a symbol of authority among Japanese roshis. In India, naive monkeys can be trapped by their longing for sweets. At first, the size of that hole in the tethered coconut is large enough to admit their empty hand. But the hole remains too small an exit as long as that hand keeps grasping for the sweets inside.
6. Red Pine. *The Zen Teaching of Bodhidharma*. San Francisco, CA. North Point Press, 1989. Two other all-inclusive ingredients were in this recommended practice: (3) not striving to seek anything; (4) consistently following the Dharma.

Chapter 23 Landmarks. Brain In Overview

1. C. Noback and R. Demarest. *The Human Nervous System. Basic Principles of Neurobiology*, 3rd edn. New York, McGraw-Hill, 1.

Chapter 24 Messenger Molecules: Some New Data

1. R. Miles. Diversity in inhibition. *Science* 2000; 287:244–246.
2. M. Picciotto, B. Caldarone, S. King, et al. Nicotinic receptors in the brain: Links between molecular biology and behavior. *Neuropsychopharmacology* 2000; 22:451–465.
3. J. Fallon, D. Keator, J. Mbogori, et al. Hostility differentiates the brain metabolic effects of nicotine. *Cognitive Brain Research* 2004; 18:142–148. Eighty-six high- and-low hostility subjects were studied. Psychological tests showed that the high-hostility subjects had higher ratings for anger, impatience, irritability, and nervousness.

4. S. Anagnostaras, G. Murphy, S. Mitchell, et al. Selective cognitive dysfunction in acetylcholine M(1) muscarinic receptor mutant mice. *Nature Neuroscience* 2003; 6:51–58. Their memory for tasks that involved matching-to-sample was normal or enhanced.
5. D. Lewis and S. Sesack. Dopamine systems in the primate brain. In *Handbook of Chemical Neuroanatomy*. Vol. 13, Pt. 1, *The Primate Nervous System*, eds. F. Bloom, A. Bjorklund, and T. Hokfelt. Amsterdam, Elsevier Science, 1997, 263–375.
6. K. Black, T. Hershey, J. Koller, et al. A possible substrate for dopamine-related changes in mood and behavior: Prefrontal and limbic effects of a D3-preferring dopamine agonist. *Proceedings of the National Academy of Sciences U S A* 2002; 99:17113–17118. The fact that the baboons were being ventilated with 70% nitrous oxide complicates the conclusions.
7. S. Bissiere, Y. Humeau, and A. Luthi. Dopamine gates LTP induction in lateral amygdala by suppressing feedforward inhibition. *Nature Neuroscience* 2003; 6:587–592. These studies were conducted in the mouse.
8. P. Tobler, C. Fiorillo, W. Schultz. Adaptive coding of reward value by dopamine neurons. *Science* 2005; 307:1642–1645.
9. A. Breier, L. Kestler, C. Adler, et al. Dopamine D_2 receptor density and personal detachment in healthy subjects. *American Journal of Psychiatry* 1998; 155:1440–1442. An early report in 1996 that the DA_4 receptor was associated with novelty seeking has not been confirmed.
10. N. Volkow, G. Wang, J. Fowler, et al. Evidence that methylphenidate enhances the saliency of a mathematical task by increasing dopamine in the human brain. *American Journal of Psychiatry* 2004; 161:1173–1180. Raclopride was the radiolabeled molecule.
11. M. Forray and K. Gysling. Role of noradrenergic projections to the bed nucleus of the stria terminalis in the regulation of the hypothalamic-pituitary-adrenal axis. *Brain Research Reviews* 2004; 47:146–160.
12. B. Waterhouse, H. Moises, and D. Woodward. Phasic activation of the locus coeruleus enhances responses of primary sensory cortical neurons to peripheral receptive field stimulation. *Brain Research* 1998; 790:33–44.
13. B. Strange, R. Hurlemann, and R. Dolan. An emotion-induced retrograde amnesia in humans is amygdala- and β-adrenergic-dependent. *Proceedings of the National Academy of Sciences U S A* 2003; 100:13626–13631. Propranolol, a beta NE antagonist, reversed this phenomenon. The phenomenon seems attributable to the amygdala, because a patient who had selective amygdala damage on both sides did not demonstrate it.
14. C. Berridge and B. Waterhouse. The locus coeruleus-noradrenergic system: Modulation of behavioral state and state-dependent cognitive processes. *Brain Research Review* 2003; 42:33–84.
15. J. Abrams, P. Johnson, J. Hollis, et al. Anatomic and functional topography of the dorsal raphe nucleus. *Annals of the New York Academy of Sciences* 2004; 10:46–57.
16. K. Varnas, C. Halldin, and H. Hall. Autoradiographic distribution of serotonin transporters and receptor subtypes in human brain. *Human Brain Mapping* 2004; 22:246–260.
17. J. Borg, B. Andree, H. Soderstrom, et al. The serotonin system and spiritual experiences. *American Journal of Psychiatry* 2003; 160:1965–1969.
18. F. Moresco, M. Dieci, A. Vita, et al. In vivo serotonin 5HT(2A) receptor binding and personality traits in healthy subjects: A positron emission tomography study. *Neuroimage* 2002; 17:1470–1478.
19. B. Ham, Y. Kim, M. Choi, et al. Serotonergic genes and personality traits in the Korean population. *Neuroscience Letters* 2004; 354:2–5.
20. F. White. Cocaine and the serotonin saga. *Nature* 1998; 393:118–119.

21. K. Zajicek, C. Price, S. Shoaf, et al. Seasonal variation in CSF 5-HIAA concentrations in male rhesus macaques. *Neuropsychopharmacology* 2000; 22:240–250.
22. A. Kemp, M. Gray, R. Silberstein, et al. Augmentation of serotonin enhances pleasant and suppresses unpleasant cortical electrophysiological responses to visual emotional stimuli in humans. *Neuroimage* 2004; 22:1084–1096.

Chapter 25 The Septal Region and the Nucleus Accumbens

1. M. Barrot, J. Olivier, L. Perrotti, et al. CREB activity in the nucleus accumbens shell controls gating of behavioral responses to emotional stimuli. *Proceedings of the National Academy of Sciences U S A* 2002; 99:11435–11440.
2. L. Heimer, J. de Olmos, G. Alheid, et al. The human basal forebrain. In *Handbook of Chemical Neuroanatomy*. Vol. 15, *The Primate Nervous System*, eds. F. Bloom, A. Bjorklund, and T. Hokfelt. Amsterdam, Elsevier Science, 1999, 57–226.
3. J. Parkinson, P. Willoughby, T. Robbins, et al. Disconnection of the anterior cingulate cortex and nucleus accumbens core impairs Pavlovian approach behavior: Further evidence for limbic cortical-ventral striatopallidal systems. *Behavioral Neuroscience* 2000; 114:42–63.
4. A. Phillips, S. Ahn, and J. Howland. Amygdalar control of the mesocorticolimbic dopamine system: Parallel pathways to motivated behavior. *Neuroscience and Biobehavioral Reviews* 2003; 27:543–554. These studies are in rats.
5. M. Jackson and B. Moghaddam. Amygdala regulation of nucleus accumbens dopamine output is governed by the prefrontal cortex. *Journal of Neuroscience* 2001; 21:676–681.
6. Barrot et al., CREB activity. Drugs of abuse activate CREB in the shell of the nucleus accumbens.
7. J. Ma, N. Ye, N. Lange, et al. Dynorphinergic GABA neurons are a target of both typical and atypical antipsychotic drugs in the nucleus accumbens shell, central amygdaloid nucleus and thalamic central medial nucleus. *Neuroscience* 2003; 121:991–998. These local GABA nerve cells also contain dynorphin.
8. G. Pagnoni, C. Zink, P. Montague, et al. Activity in human ventral striatum locked to errors of reward prediction. *Nature Neuroscience* 2002; 5:97–98.
9. J. Jensen, A. McIntosh, A. Crawley, et al. Direct activation of the ventral striatum in anticipation of aversive stimuli. *Neuron* 2003; 40:1251–1257.
10. C. Zink, G. Pagnoni, M. Martin, et al. Human striatal response to salient nonrewarding stimuli. *Journal of Neuroscience* 2003; 23:8092–8097.
11. F. Kjaer, C. Bertelsen, P. Piccini, et al. Increased dopamine tone during meditation-induced change of consciousness. *Cognitive Brain Research* 2002; 13:255–259.
12. S. Pappata, S. Dehaene, J. Poline, et al. In vivo detection of striatal dopamine release during reward: A PET study with [(11)C]raclopride and a single dynamic scan approach. *Neuroimage* 2002; 16:1015–1027.
13. T. Sheehan, R. Chambers, and D. Russell. Regulation of affect by the lateral septum: Implications for neuropsychiatry. *Brain Research Reviews* 2004; 46:71–117.

Chapter 26 The Wide Variety of Cingulate Gyrus Functions

1. P. Luu and M. Posner. Anterior cingulate cortex regulation of sympathetic activity [editorial]. *Brain* 2003; 126:2119–2120. This editorial comments on the difficulties involved in interpreting how the anterior cingulate regulates sympathetic activity. A recent fMRI report suggests that one of the reasons for the complexity of human responses is to be found in the way our prefrontal cortex normally helps us reduce anxiety. Threatening stimuli do strongly activate the anterior cingulate. However, subjects who begin with higher anxiety levels feel more anxiety when they await threats if, at the same time, their *lateral* prefrontal

cortex activity and their anterior cingulate activity are both reduced. The authors suggest that the frontal cortex contributes a useful degree of cognitive *control* that normally helps moderate anxiety. See S. Bishop, J. Duncan, M. Brett, et al. Prefrontal cortical function and anxiety: Controlling attention to threat-related stimuli. *Nature Neuroscience* 2004; 7:184–188.

2. B. Vogt, L. Vogt, E. Nimchinsky, et al. Primate cingulate cortex chemoarchitecture and its disruption in Alzheimer's disease. In *Handbook of Chemical Neuroanatomy*. Vol. 13, *The Primate Nervous System*, eds. F. Bloom, A. Bjorklund, and T. Hokfelt. Amsterdam, Elsevier Science, 1997, 455–528. Authorities differ on the way they number different regions of the cingulate. In part, this is because of the overlapping at the front end near the genu of the corpus callosum, and at the back end (the splenium) where the cingulate shades off into the retrosplenial cortex. Some human brains have two cingulate sulci. This contributes to the difficulties in defining cingulate boundaries.
3. J. Fan. Mapping the genetic variation of executive attention onto brain activity. *Proceedings of the National Academy of Sciences U S A* 2003; 100:7406–7411. The subjects' task was to specify whether a central arrow had its arrowhead pointing left or right. Two distracting arrows, above and below it, could have their arrowheads pointing in the same or opposite direction. On balance, the evidence suggests that the anterior cingulate monitors conflicting choices and interacts with the prefrontal cortex in engaging the appropriate degrees of attentional cognitive resources. See J. Kerns, J. Cohen, A. MacDonald, et al. Anterior cingulate conflict monitoring and adjustments in control. *Science* 2004; 303:1023–1026.
4. N. Eisenberger, M. Lieberman, and K. Williams. Does rejection hurt? An fMRI study of social exclusion. *Science* 2003; 302:290–292. During lesser degrees of self-reported distress, the right ventral prefrontal cortex also showed increased signals in the person who felt rejected. The authors suggested that the right ventral prefrontal cortex might reduce the amount of distress during social rejection by interfering with the activity of the anterior cingulate cortex (see also reference 2).
5. G. Winterer, C. Adams, D. Jones, et al. Volition to action—an event-related fMRI study. *Neuroimage* 2002; 17:851–858. Parallel studies showed that responses referable to this region occurred within 120 to 150 ms.
6. T. Luks, G. Simpson, R. Feiwell, et al. Evidence for anterior cingulate cortex involvement in monitoring preparatory attentional set. *Neuroimage* 2002; 17:792–802.
7. H. Critchley, R. Melmed, E. Featherstone, et al. Brain activity during biofeedback relaxation. A functional neuroimaging investigation. *Brain* 2001; 124:1003–1012. The subjects could see a simple red representation of a "thermometer." It served as their biofeedback signal for relaxation.
8. H. Critchley, C. Mathias, O. Josephs, et al. Human cingulate cortex and autonomic control: Converging neuroimaging and clinical evidence. *Brain* 2003; 126:2139–2152.
9. S. Matthews, M. Paulus, A. Simmons, et al. Functional subdivisions within anterior cingulate cortex and their relationship to autonomic nervous system function. *Neuroimage* 2004; 22:1151–1156. The task involved a counting version of the Stroop task, and presented congruent and incongruent choices. Ventral anterior cingulate signals correlated with high-frequency heart rate variations.
10. J. Schwartz. Obsessive-compulsive disorder. *Science and Medicine* 1997; March/April, 14–23.
11. A. Brody, M. Mandelkern, E. London, et al. Brain metabolic changes during cigarette craving. *Archives of General Psychiatry* 2002; 59:1162–1172.
12. M. Paulus, J. Feinstein, A. Simmons, et al. Anterior cingulate activation in high trait anxious subjects is related to altered error processing during decision making. *Biological Psychiatry* 2004; 55:1179–1187.

13. C. Holroyd, S. Nieuwenhuis, N. Yeung, et al. Dorsal anterior cingulate cortex shows fMRI response to internal and external error signals. *Nature Neuroscience* 2004; 7:497–498.
14. J. Allman, A. Hakem, K. Watson. Two phylogenetic specializations in the human brain. *Neuroscientist* 2002; 8:335–346. It would be of interest to determine the opioid receptor patterns on spindle-shaped and other nerve cell types in the anterior cingulate regions in view of the opioid and placebo responses reviewed in chapter 36.
15. I. Morrison, D. Lloyd, G. DiPellegrino, et al. Vicarious responses to pain in anterior cingulate cortex: Is empathy a multisensory issue? *Cognitive, Affective and Behavioral Neuroscience* 2004; 4:270–278.
16. R. Maddock, A. Garrett, and M. Buonocore. Posterior cingulate cortex activation by emotional words: fMRI evidence from a valence decision task. *Human Brain Mapping* 2003; 18:30–41. Note: Unpleasant words activated the right amygdala; pleasant words activated the left frontal pole.
17. M. Sugiura, N. Shah, K. Zilles, et al. Cortical representations of personally familiar objects and places: Functional organization of the human posterior cingulate cortex. *Journal of Cognitive Neuroscience* 2005; 17:183–198.
18. R. Maddock. The retrosplenial cortex and emotion: New insights from functional neuroimaging of the human brain. *Trends in Neurosciences* 1999; 22:310–316. The areas of controversy and the reply by Maddock are important to review. See *Trends in Neurosciences* 2000; 23(5):195–197.

Chapter 27 The Amygdala as a Gateway to Our Fears

1. D. Zald. The human amygdala and the emotional evaluation of sensory stimuli. *Brain Research Review* 2003; 41:88–123. The interested reader is referred both to this review article and to another recent review by J. McGaugh. The amygdala modulates the consolidation of memories of emotionally arousing experiences. *Annual Review of Neuroscience* 2004; 27:1–28.
2. M. Baxter and E. Murray. The amygdala and reward. *Neuroscience* 2002; 3:563–573. See also ibid., J. McGaugh, The amygdala.
3. N. Emery, J. Capitanio, W. Mason, et al. The effects of bilateral lesions of the amygdala on dyadic social interactions in rhesus monkeys (*Macaca mulatta*). *Behavioral Neuroscience* 2001; 115:515–544. Ibotenic acid creates excitotoxic lesions of local nerve cells while tending to spare axons from elsewhere (fibers of passage).
4. N. Kalin, C. Larson, S. Shelton, et al. Asymmetric frontal brain activity, cortisol, and behavior associated with fearful temperament in rhesus monkeys. *Behavioral Neuroscience* 1998; 112:286–292. Temperament was viewed in this study as a more complex attribute than a traitlike style of simple behavioral and emotional expression. Temperament was regarded as "a constellation of stable behavioral, emotional, and physiological characteristics."
5. N. Kalin, S. Shelton, R. Davidson, et al. The primate amygdala mediates acute fear but not the behavioral and physiological components of anxious temperament. *Journal of Neuroscience* 2001; 21:2067–2074. Even a 3-month-old monkey displays unconditioned freezing responses to a human intruder. The individual differences in this behavior remain stable thereafter. In one PET study, using a paradigm of paired electric shocks, fear conditioning in eight young women did not result in increased amygdala activity. See H. Fischer, J. Anderson, T. Furmark, et al. Fear conditioning and brain activity: A positron emission tomography study in humans. *Behavioral Neuroscience* 2000; 114:671–680.
6. C. Caldji, B. Tannebaum, S. Sharma, et al. Maternal care during infancy regulates the development of neural systems mediating the expression of fearfulness in the rat. *Proceedings of the National Academy of Sciences U S A* 1998; 95:5335–5340.

7. M. Jackson and B. Moghaddam. Amygdala regulation of nucleus accumbens dopamine output is governed by the prefrontal cortex. *Journal of Neuroscience* 2001; 27:676–681. Amygdala stimulation did cause an immediate rise in glutamate in the prefrontal cortex, a lesser rise in the nucleus accumbens, and behavioral arousal from sleep.
8. J. Repa, J. Muller, J. Apergis, et al. Two different lateral amygdala cell populations contribute to the initiation and storage of memory. *Neuroscience* 2001; 4:724–731. A caveat is in order with respect to the neuroanatomy of the human amygdala. An fMRI study of human responses to faces suggested that rapid habituation was more associated with signals from the ventromedial region of the amygdala. Surprisingly, at the anatomical level studied, this site would correspond more with the actual location of the *basolateral* complex of nuclei. In contrast, the subjects' more sustained responses to stimuli (which differed in their valences) were associated with signals from the more dorsolateral region. In fact, this lateral site would correspond more with the central nucleus. See C. Wright. Differential prefrontal cortex and amygdala habituation to repeatedly presented emotional stimuli. *NeuroReport* 2001; 12:379–383.
9. Zald, The human amygdala.
10. J. Austin. *Chase, Chance, and Creativity: The Lucky Art of Novelty*. Cambridge, MA, MIT Press, 2003, 132. Limbic system outflow through the hypothalamus and autonomic nervous system accounts for this "gooseflesh" (piloerection) response to music. Current PET scans do not provide sufficient resolution to detect highly discrete activation of the hypothalamus during unusually pleasant emotional stimuli. However, other evidence of the arousal response to music (increased heart rate and breathing rate) were cited by Zald in his table 3, p. 99. See note 1.
11. E. Phelps, M. Delgado, K. Nearing, et al. Extinction learning in humans: Role of the amygdala and vmPFC. *Neuron* 2004; 43:897–905; J. Gottfried and R. Dolan. Human orbitofrontal cortex mediates extinction learning while assessing conditioned representations of value. *Nature Neuroscience* 2004; 7:1144–1152.
12. T. Canli, H. Sivers, S. Whitfield, et al. Amygdala response to happy faces as a function of extraversion. *Science* 2002; 296:2191.
13. H. Fischer, M. Tillfors, T. Furmark, et al. Dispositional pessimism and amygdala activity: A PET study in healthy volunteers. *NeuroReport* 2001; 12:1635–1638.
14. R. Adolphs. Recognizing emotion from facial expressions: Psychological and neurological mechanisms. *Behavioral and Cognitive Neuroscience Reviews* 2002; 1:21–62. This article presents a critique of the extensive literature on this complex topic. For another recent critique of the social role of the amygdala at different times during the development and maturation of both humans and monkeys, see also D. Amaral, M. Bauman, J. Capitanio, et al. The amygdala: Is it an essential component of the neural network for social cognition? *Neuropsychologia* 2003; 41:517–522. Damage to the human amygdala prevents fearful faces from activating the fusiform gyrus and occipital cortex. See P. Vuilleumier, M. Richardson, J. Armony, et al. Distant influences of amygdala lesion on visual cortical activation during emotional face processing. *Nature Neuroscience* 2004; 7:1271–1278.
15. R. Dolan, J. Morris, and B. de Gelder. Crossmodal binding of fear in voice and face. *Proceedings of the National Academy of Sciences U S A* 2001; 98:10006–10010.
16. L. Cahill, R. Haier, N. White, et al. Sex-related difference in amygdala activity during emotionally influenced memory storage. *Neurobiology of Learning and Memory* 2001; 75:1–9.
17. T. Canli, J. Desmond, Z. Zhao, et al. Sex differences in the neural basis of emotional memories. *Proceedings of the National Academy of Sciences U S A* 2002; 98:10789–10794. The

women's left amygdala activations also correlated with their subsequent ability to remember (3 weeks later) the most emotionally arousing pictures.

18. W. Killgore, M. Oki, and D. Yurgelun-Todd. Sex-specific developmental changes in amygdala responses to affective faces. *NeuroReport* 2001; 12:427–433.
19. J. Morris and R. Dolan. Dissociable amygdala and orbitofrontal responses during reversal fear conditioning. *Neuroimage* 2004; 22:372–380. How do we judge what is *really* real? The frontal lobe may enter into some of our higher processing. PET studies show that the medial orbitofrontal cortex in its posterior part is activated during tasks that require normal subjects to sort out mental associations which pertain to ongoing reality. See A. Schnider, V. Treyer, and A. Buck. Selection of currently relevant memories by the human posterior medial orbitofrontal cortex. *Journal of Neuroscience* 2000; 20:5880–5884.
20. P. Shaw, E. Lawrence, C. Radbourne, et al. The impact of early and late damage to the human amygdala on "theory of mind" reasoning. *Brain* 2004; 127:1535–1548.
21. A. Anderson, K. Christoff, I. Stappen, et al. Dissociated neural representations of intensity and valence in human olfaction. *Nature Neuroscience* 2003; 6:196–202. Citral was the pleasant (fruity) odorant. Valeric acid was the unpleasant (rancid) odorant. Certain humans (e.g., professional wine tasters) have the capacity to use their orbitofrontal cortex to make subtle "judgments" of flavor and bouquet at very high levels of discriminating consciousness. One might expect that a rodent's remarkable survival skills would be built in at lower levels.
22. R. Adolphs and D. Tranel. Impaired judgments of sadness but not happiness following bilateral amygdala damage. *Journal of Cognitive Neuroscience* 2004; 16:453–462. These patients had chronic lesions. They viewed morphed faces. The expressions of sadness or happiness varied gradually from faint to pronounced. In *normal* subjects studied earlier by PET, their task was to imaginatively improvise sadness. Although this kind of self-generated sadness was carried to the point of tears it did not activate the amygdala. See H. Mayberg, M. Liotti, S. Brannan, et al. Reciprocal limbic-cortical function and negative mood: Converging PET findings in depression and normal sadness. *American Journal of Psychiatry* 1999; 156:675–681.
23. R. Davidson. Darwin and the neural bases of emotion and affective style. *Annals of the New York Academy of Sciences* 2003; 1000:316–336.
24. S. Schaefer, D. Jackson, R. Davidson, et al. Modulation of amygdalar activity by the conscious regulation of negative emotion. *Journal of Cognitive Neuroscience* 2002; 14:913–921.
25. V. Paquette, J. Levesque, B. Mensour, et al. "Change the mind and you change the brain": Effects of cognitive-behavioral therapy on the neural correlates of spider phobia. *Neuroimage* 2003; 18:401–409.
26. K. Ochsner, S. Bunge, J. Gross, et al. Rethinking feelings: An fMRI study of the cognitive regulation of emotion. *Journal of Cognitive Neuroscience* 2002; 14:1215–1229. Although increased activation did occur in the lateral and medial prefrontal regions, some of these signals may have reflected the extra cognitive effort involved in the task.
27. G. Holstege. Central nervous system control of ejaculation. *World Journal of Urology* 2005; 23:109–114.
28. A. Bechara, H. Damasio, A. Damasio, et al. Different contributions of the human amygdala and ventromedial prefrontal cortex to decision-making. *Journal of Neuroscience* 1999; 19:5473–5481.
29. A. Etkin, K. Klemenhagen, J. Dudman, et al. Individual differences in trait anxiety predict the response of the basolateral amygdala to unconsciously processed fearful faces. *Neuron* 2004; 44:1043–1055.

30. S. Shigematsu. *A Zen Forest. Sayings of the Masters*. New York, Weatherhill, 1981, no. 554. See also appendix A.

Chapter 28 Expanded Roles for the Insula

1. H. Critchley, S. Wiens, P. Rotshtein, et al. Neural systems supporting interoceptive awareness. *Nature Reviews Neuroscience* 2004; 7:189–195.
2. A. Craig. How do you feel? Interoception: The sense of the physiological condition of the body. *Nature Reviews Neuroscience* 2002; 3:655–666.
3. A. Calder, A. Lawrence, and A. Young. Neuropsychology of fear and loathing. *Nature Reviews Neuroscience* 2001; 2:352–363.
4. Ibid.
5. B. Wicker, C. Keysers, J. Plailly, et al. Both of us disgusted in my insula: The common neural basis of seeing and feeling disgust. *Neuron* 2003; 40:655–664. The anterior cingulate also participates to a lesser degree.
6. M. Heining, A. Young, G. Ioannou, et al. Disgusting smells activate human anterior insula and ventral striatum. *Annals of the New York Academy of Sciences* 2003; 1000:380–384. Pleasant odors (e.g., a banana) served as a control.
7. A. Damasio, T. Grabowski, A. Bechara, et al. Subcortical and cortical brain activity during the feeling of self-generated emotions. *Nature Neuroscience* 2000; 3:1049–1056. The emotions studied were happiness, sadness, anger, and fear. One awaits a similarly designed fMRI study in which respiratory responses are also monitored.
8. T. Singer, B. Seymour, J. O'Doherty, et al. Empathy for pain involves the affective but not sensory components of pain. *Science* 2004; 303:1157–1162.
9. C. Carr, M. Iacoboni, M. Dubeau, et al. Neural mechanisms of empathy in humans: A relay from neural systems for imitation to limbic areas. *Proceedings of the National Academy of Sciences U S A* 2003; 100:5497–5502.
10. S. Lazar, personal communication 2005. An area of cortex can become larger secondary to an increase in one or more of the following: Nerve cell bodies and processes, glial cells and processes, capillary blood vessels. See chapters 38 and 41.
11. A. Bartels and S. Zeki. The neural correlates of maternal and romantic love. *Neuroimage* 2004; 21:1155–1166.
12. S. Bense, P. Bartenstein, S. Lutz, et al. Three determinants of vestibular hemispheric dominance during caloric stimulation. *Annals of the New York Academy of Sciences* 2003; 1004:440–445.
13. Critchley et al., Neural systems. The HAMA and PANAS tests assessed anxiety rankings. Other cortical regions also supported the person's paying attention to interoceptive cues: the adjacent frontal operculum, the medial parietal lobe/precuneus, the supplementary motor region, and the anterior cingulate gyrus.
14. Craig. How do you feel? The posterior part of the ventral medial nucleus is abbreviated VMpo.
15. F. Netter. *The Ciba Collection of Medical Illustrations*. Vol. 1, *Nervous System*. Pt. I, *Anatomy and Physiology*. West Caldwell, NJ, Ciba, 1983, 70.
16. Critchley et al., Neural systems.
17. Craig. How do you feel? Figure 3 in this article indicates that each parabrachial ACH nucleus (the major cholinergic nucleus in the pons) also receives crossed sympathetic afferent input *plus* parasympathetic input from the solitary tract nucleus in the medulla. This nucleus then directs these dual messages to the basal subnucleus. In the course of further relays through the anterior insula, the afferent *sympathetic* activity then becomes

re-represented more in the *right* cerebral hemisphere. In contrast, afferent *parasympathetic* activity becomes referable more to the left hemisphere. To the degree that such lateralized generalizations remain valid in human beings, then we certainly need to know: How do these and other variations in our functional anatomy change the corresponding qualities of consciousness and temperaments of each of us individually?

18. Nuclei along the fast path in the thalamus include the ventroposterolateral nucleus (somesthetic messages from the body), ventral posteromedial nucleus (somesthetic messages from the head), and the lateral and medial geniculate nuclei (visual and auditory messages). See chapter 44.
19. A. Calder. Disgust discussed. *Annals of Neurology* 2003; 53:427–428.

Chapter 29 Remembrances and the Hippocampus

1. H. Geiger. Introduction to *The Farther Reaches of Human Nature*, ed. A. Maslow. New York, Viking Press, 1971, xvi.
2. A. Fisahn, F. Pike, E. Buhl, et al. Cholinergic induction of network oscillations at 40 Hz in the hippocampus in vitro. *Nature* 1998; 394:186–189.
3. P. Monfort, M. Munoz, E. Kosenko, et al. Long-term potentiation in hippocampus involves sequential activation of soluble guanylate cyclase, cGMP-dependent protein kinase, and cGMP-degrading phosphodiesterase. *Journal of Neuroscience* 2002; 22:10116–10122. Nitric-oxide, diffusing back across the synapse, further increases the release of glutamate.
4. K. Moore, R. Nicoll, and D. Schmitz. Adenosine gates synaptic plasticity at hippocampal mossy fiber synapses. *Proceedings of the National Academy of Sciences U S A* 2003; 100:14397–14402. Most of this adenosine arises during the sequences of membrane depolarization. Adenosine comes from the breakdown of adenosine triphosphate (ATP), after ATP has first been released from its complex with calcium ions.
5. M. Shapiro. Plasticity, hippocampal place cells, and cognitive maps. *Archives of Neurology* 2001; 58:874–881.
6. G. Quirk, R. Muller, J. Kubie, et al. The positional firing properties of medial entorhinal neurons: Description and comparison with hippocampal place cells. *Journal of Neuroscience* 1992; 12:1945–1963.
7. R. Hampson, T. Pons, T. Stanford, et al. Categorization in the monkey hippocampus: A possible mechanism for encoding information into memory. *Proceedings of the National Academy of Sciences U S A* 2004; 101:3184–3189.
8. P. Brasted, T. Bussey, E. Murray, et al. Role of the hippocampal system in associative learning beyond the spatial domain. *Brain* 2003; 126:1202–1223. These "nonspatial" functions could serve to register some ongoing events accurately both during internal absorption and in kensho, even though conventional spatial frames of reference had dropped out.
9. S. Li, W. Cullen, R. Anwyl, et al. Dopamine-dependent facilitation of LTP induction in hippocampal CA1 by exposure to spatial novelty. *Nature Neuroscience* 2003; 6:526–531.
10. H. Viola, M. Furman, L. Izquierdo, et al. Phosphorylated cAMP response element-binding protein as a molecular marker of memory processing in rat hippocampus: Effect of novelty. *Journal of Neuroscience* 2000; 20:RC112. See also chapter 37.
11. D. Genoux, U. Haditsch, M. Knobloch, et al. Protein phosphatase 1 is a molecular constraint on learning and memory. *Nature* 2002; 418:970–975.
12. R. Habib, A. McIntosh, M. Wheeler, et al. Memory encoding and hippocampally-based novelty/familiarity discrimination networks. *Neuropsychologia* 2003; 41:271–279.
13. P. Fries, G. Fernandez, and O. Jensen. When neurons form memories. *Trends in Neurosciences* 2003; 26:123–124.

14. L. Nyberg, P. Marklund, J. Persson, et al. Common prefrontal activations during working memory, episodic memory, and semantic memory. *Neuropsychologia* 2003; 41:371–177.
15. P. Bayley, J. Gold, R. Hopkins, et al. The neuroanatomy of remote memory. *Neuron* 2005; 46:799–810.
16. J. Luo and K. Niki. Function of hippocampus in "insight" of problem solving. *Hippocampus* 2003; 13:316–323. Of course, this high-resolution (3 tesla) fMRI study showed that multiple other activations were also present. These 8 seconds represented *the recognition of a previous word problem, now solved*. Thus, these 8 seconds were not monitoring the kind of spontaneously generated, insightful act of inspired problem-solving that corresponds with prajna.
17. P. Eriksson, E. Perfilieva, T. Bjork-Eriksson, et al. Neurogenesis in the adult human hippocampus. *Nature Medicine* 1998; 4:1313–1317. In adult monkeys, neurogenesis occurs both in the hippocampus and in the olfactory bulb. See D. Kornack and P. Rakic. Cell proliferation without neurogenesis in adult primate neocortex. *Science* 2001; 294:2127–2130.
18. Y. Tang, J. Nyengaard, D. De Groot, et al. Total regional and global number of synapses in the human brain neocortex. *Synapse* 2001; 41:258–273.
19. K. Taber, C. Wen, A. Khan, et al. The limbic thalamus. *Journal of Neuropsychiatry and Clinical Neurosciences* 2004; 16:127–132. Figure 6 also suggests that a lesser pathway may lead from the subiculum to the cingulate [Z:183].
20. R. Vertes, W. Hoover, and G. Di Prisco. Theta rhythm of the hippocampus: Subcortical control and functional significance. *Behavioral and Cognitive Neuroscience Reviews* 2004; 3:173–200.
21. R. Vertes, et al., ibid 2004.
22. S. Vann and J. Aggleton. The mammillary bodies: Two memory systems in one? *Nature Reviews Neuroscience* 2004; 5:35–44. Humans have relatively small lateral mammillary nuclei.
23. P. Sharp. Movement-related correlates of single cell activity in the medial mammillary nucleus of the rat during a pellet-chasing task. Journal of Neurophysiology 2005; 94:1020–1027. Most medial cells also tend to fire during movements in general.
24. F. Cacucci, C. Lever, T. Wills, et al. Theta-modulated place-by-direction cells in the hippocampal formation in the rat. *Journal of Neuroscience* 2004; 24:8265–8277. The firing rates of pure head-direction cells in the hippocampus are said not to vary with theta rhythms.
25. R. Vertes et al., ibid 2004. Back in the retrosplenial cortex, the head direction cells reside in the anterior part, whereas theta rhythm cells occur in the posterior part. There, their local discharges occur independently of the theta rhythms in the hippocampus.

Chapter 30 The Well-Concealed Hypothalamus

1. L. Squire, F. Bloom, S. McConnell, et al., eds. *Fundamental Neuroscience*, 2nd ed. San Diego, Academic Press, 2003, 897.
2. M. Chicurel. The sandman's secrets. *Nature* 2000; 407:554–556.
3. C. Saper, T. Chou, and T. Scammell. The sleep switch: Hypothalamic control of sleep and wakefulness. *Trends in Neurosciences* 2001; 24:720–725.
4. G. Petrovich, N. Canteras, and L. Swanson. Combinatorial amygdalar inputs to hippocampal domains and hypothalamic behavior systems. *Brain Research Reviews* 2001; 38:247–289.
5. J. Kiss, K. Kocsis, A. Csaki, et al. Metabotropic glutamate receptor in GHRH and β-endorphin neurones of the hypothalamic arcuate nucleus. *NeuroReport* 1997; 3703–3707.
6. J. Brown, J. Card, and B. Yates. Polysynaptic pathways from the vestibular nuclei to the lateral mammillary nucleus of the rat: Substrates for vestibular input to head direction cells. *Experimental Brain Research* 2005; 161:47–61.

7. D. Swaab. Neurobiology and neuropathology of the human hypothalamus. In *Handbook of Chemical Neuroanatomy*, eds. F. Bloom, A. Bjorklund, and T. Hokfelt. *The Primate Nervous System*. Vol. 13, Pt. 1, Amsterdam, Elsevier Science, 1997, 39–137.

Chapter 31 GABA Inhibits; Glutamate Excites

1. M. Steriade, E. Jones, and D. McCormick. *Thalamus*. Vol. 1, *Organization and Function*. Oxford, Elsevier Science, 1997, 491–513.
2. C. Saper, T. Chou, and T. Scammell. The sleep switch: Hypothalamic control of sleep and wakefulness. *Trends in Neurosciences* 2001; 24:720–725.
3. L. Nelson, T. Guo, J. Lu, et al. The sedative component of anesthesia is mediated by GABA(A) receptors in an endogenous sleep pathway. *Nature Neuroscience* 2002; 5:979–984.
4. J. Lee, E. Hahm, and B. Min. Roles of protein kinase A and C in the opioid potentiation of the $GABA_A$ response in rat periaqueductal gray neuron. *Neuropharmacology* 2003; 44:573–583.
5. A. Elias, S. Gulch, and A. Wilson. Ketosis with enhanced GABAergic tone promotes physiological changes in transcendental meditation. *Medical Hypotheses* 2000; 54:660–662.
6. S. Kuffler. Discharge patterns and functional organization of the mammalian retina. *Journal of Neurophysiolgy* 1953; 16:37–68. After Kuffler studied these distinctive center/surround responses of retinal ganglion cells, still other classes of ganglion cells were discovered which had various other functions.
7. H. Rodman, L. Pessoa, and L. Ungerleider. Visual perception of objects. In *Fundamental Neuroscience*, 2nd ed., eds. L. Squire, F. Bloom, and S. McConnell, et al. San Diego, Academic Press, 2003, 1201–1228.
8. S. Murray, D. Kersten, B. Olshausen, et al. Shape perception reduces activity in human primary visual cortex *Proceedings of the National Academy of Sciences USA* 2002; 99:15164–15169.
9. J. Trageser and A. Keller. Reducing the uncertainty: Gating of peripheral inputs by zona incerta. *Journal of Neuroscience* 2004; 24:8911–8915.
10. C. Cox and S. Sherman. Glutamate inhibits thalamic reticular neurons. *Journal of Neuroscience* 1999; 19:6694–6699.
11. S. Starkey. Melatonin and 5-hydroxytryptamine phase advance the rat circadian clock by activation of nitric oxide synthesis. *Neuroscience Letters* 1996; 211:199–2002.
12. M. Barbaccia, M. Serra, R. Purdy, et al. Stress and neuroactive steroids. In *Neurosteroids and Brain Function*, eds. G. Biggio and R. Purdy. San Diego, Academic Press, 2001, 243–272.
13. E. Tsvetkov, R. Shin, and V. Bolshakov. Glutamate uptake determines pathway specificity of long-term potentiation in the neural circuitry of fear conditioning. *Neuron* 2004; 41:139–151. Other effects of ketamine may be due to the release of dopamine. Likewise, memantine blocks serotonin-3 receptors and nicotinic ACH receptors to a minor degree.
14. P. Tariot, M. Farlow, G. Grossberg, et al. Memantine treatment in patients with moderate to severe Alzheimer disease already receiving donepezil. *Journal of the American Medical Association* 2004; 291:317–324.

Chapter 32 Stress Responses within the Brain

1. A. Dunn, A. Swiergiel, and V. Palamarchouk. Brain circuits involved in corticotropin-releasing factor–norepinephrine interactions during stress. *Annals of the New York Academy of Sciences* 2004; 1018:25–34.
2. J. Radulovic, A. Rühmann, T. Liepold, et al. Modulation of learning and anxiety of corticotrophin-releasing factor (CRF) and stress: Differential roles of CRF receptors 1 and 2. *Journal of Neuroscience* 1999; 19:5616–5625.

3. L. Takahashi. Role of CRF(1) and CRF(2) receptors in fear and anxiety. *Neuroscience Biobehavioral Reviews* 2001; 25:627–636.
4. C. Lowry, J. Rodda, S. Lightman, et al. Corticotropin-releasing factor increases in vitro firing rates of serotonergic neurons in the rat dorsal raphe nucleus: Evidence for activation of a topographically organized mesolimbocortical serotonergic system. *Journal of Neuroscience* 2000; 20:7728–7736.
5. K. Keay and R. Bandler. Parallel circuits mediating distinct emotional coping reactions to different types of stress. *Neuroscience Biobehavioral Reviews* 2001; 25:669–678.
6. Ibid.
7. R. De Oliveira, E. Del Bel, and R. Guimaraes. Effects of excitatory amino acids and nitric oxide on flight behavior elicited from the dorsolateral periaqueductal gray. *Neuroscience Biobehavioral Reviews* 2001; 25:679–685.
8. X. Cui, T. Lundeberg and L. Yu. Role of corticotrophin-releasing factor and its receptor in nociceptive modulation in the central nucleus of amygdala in rats. *Brain Research* 2004; 995:23–28. This result suggests that fibers from the central nucleus of the amygdala activate not only the midbrain central gray but also a descending inhibitory pathway, perhaps involving norepinephrine, which then inhibits pain perception.

   The brain uses other routes to organize escape and freezing responses. One is via the dorsal premammillary nucleus of the hypothalamus. See N. Canteras, E. Ribeiro-Barbosa, and E. Comoli. Tracing from the dorsal premammillary nucleus prosencephalic systems involved in the organization of innate fear responses. *Neuroscience Biobehavioral Reviews* 2001; 25:661–668.
9. M. Barbaccia, M. Serra, R. Purdy, et al. Stress and neuroactive steriods. In *Neurosteroids and Brain Function*, eds. G. Biggio and R. Purdy. San Diego, Academic Press, 2001, 243–272.

Chapter 33 Laid-Back Nurturing Promotes Laid-Back Limbic System Receptors

1. C. Caldji, B. Tannebaum, S. Sharma, et al. Maternal care during infancy regulates the development of neural systems mediating the expression of fearfulness in the rat. *Proceedings of the National Academy of Sciences U S A* 1998; 95:5335–5340.
2. Ibid.
3. D. Liu, J. Diorio, B. Tannenbaum, et al. Maternal care, hippocampal glucocorticoid receptors, and hypothalamic-pituitary-adrenal responses to stress. *Science* 1997; 277:1659–1662. Earlier observations had shown that—after humans had handled rat pups—their mothers then licked and groomed these pups much more. It turned out that certain rat mothers, on an individual basis, also happened to be especially solicitous and relaxed while nursing.
4. C. Caldji, D. Francis, S. Sharma, et al. The effects of early rearing environment on the development of $GABA_A$ and central benzodiazepine receptor levels and novelty-induced fearfulness in the rat. *Neuropsychopharmacology* 2000; 22:219–229.
5. Caldji et al., Maternal care during infancy. See also D. Francis and M. Meaney. Maternal care and the development of stress responses. *Current Opinion in Neurobiology* 1999; 9:128–134.
6. Liu et al., Maternal care, hippocampal glucocorticoid receptors. The rats' baseline hormonal levels of ACTH and corticosterone, before stress, were no different from controls.
7. Caldji et al., Maternal care during infancy. These later studies showed the adverse consequences of separating pups from their mothers. Separations caused increased fear-related responses and other delayed behavioral effects. As expected, these adverse maternal *deprivations* produced the opposite effects on relevant receptors: $GABA_A$ receptors were *reduced* in the medial prefrontal cortex, the locus ceruleus, and the nucleus of the solitary tract

[Z:229], in contrast to controls. Deprivation also caused other receptor levels to change in the opposite direction in both the central and lateral nuclei of the amygdala.

Chapter 34 Peptides in Social Affiliative Behaviors: Oxytocin and Vasopressin

1. L. Young. The neurobiology of social recognition, approach and avoidance. *Society of Biological Psychiatry* 2002; 15:18–26.
2. Ibid. See also C. Carter, L. Lederhendler, and B. Kirkpatrick, eds. *The Integrative Neurobiology of Affiliation. Annals of the New York Academy of Sciences* 1997; 807; C. Sandman, F. Strand, B. Beckwith, et al., eds. *Neuropeptides: Structure and function in biology and behavior. Annals of the New York Academy of Sciences* 1999; 897; T. Insel. Is social attachment an addictive disorder? *Physiology and Behavior* 2003; 79:351–357; and T. Lippert, A. Mueck, H. Seeger, et al. Effects of oxytocin outside pregnancy. *Hormone Research* 2003; 60:262–271.
3. S. Bealer and W. Crawley. Neurotransmitter interaction in release of intranuclear oxytocin in magnocellular nuclei of the hypothalamus. In *Neuropeptides: Structure and Function in Biology and Behavior*, ed. C. Sandman, F. Strand, B. Beckwith, et al. *Annals of the New York Academy of Sciences* 1999; 897:182–191.
4. M. Engelmann, P. Bull, C. Brown, et al. GABA selectively controls the secretory activity oxytocin neurons in the rat supraoptic nucleus. *European Journal of Neuroscience* 2004; 19:601–608; P. Bull, M. Ludwig, G. Blackburn-Munro, et al. The role of nitric oxide in morphine dependence and withdrawal excitation of rat oxytocin neurons. *European Journal of Neuroscience* 2003; 18:2545–2551.
5. K. Uvnas-Moberg. Physiological and endocrine effects of social contact. In *The Integrative Neurobiology of Affiliation*, eds. C. Carter, L. Lederhendler, and B. Kirkpatrick. *Annals of the New York Academy of Sciences* 1997; 807:146–163.
6. Young, Social recognition.
7. M. Lim, A. Murphy, and L. Young. Ventral striatopallidal oxytocin and vasopressin V1a receptors in the monogamous prairie vole (*Microtus ochrogaster*). *Journal of Comparative Neurology* 2004; 468:555–570.
8. Young, Social recognition. Montane voles have high levels of oxytocin receptors in their lateral septum.
9. Ibid.
10. S. Taylor, L. Klein, B. Lewis, et al. Biobehavioral responses to stress in females: Tend-and-befriend, not fight-or-flight. *Psychological Review* 2000; 107:411–429.
11. Ibid.
12. M. Kosfeld, M. Heinrichs, P. Zak, et al. Oxytocin increases trust in humans. *Nature* 2005; 435:673–676. Trust can be abused. Further studies are indicated to confirm these findings because they have obvious social implications.
13. Lim et al. Ventral striatopallidal oxytocin. Montane voles have many vasopressin receptors in the lateral septum.
14. Young, Social recognition. The males did groom themselves more.
15. Y. Liu, J. Curtis, and Z. Wang. Vasopressin in the lateral septum regulates pair bond formation in male prairie voles (*Microtus ochrogaster*). *Behavioral Neuroscience* 2001; 115:910–919. Whether vasopressin and oxytocin act concurrently or sequentially in the lateral septal nucleus remains to be determined.
16. Young, Social recognition.
17. I. Bielsky, S. Hu, K. Szegda, et al. Profound impairment in social recognition and reduction in anxiety-like behavior in vasopressin v1a receptor knockout mice. *Neuropsychopharmacology* 2004; 29:483–493.

18. D. Francis, L. Young, M. Meaney, et al. Naturally occurring differences in maternal care are associated with the expression of oxytocin and vasopressin (V1a) receptors: Gender differences. *Journal of Neuroendocrinology* 2002; 14:349–353.
19. Insel, Social attachment.
20. Young, Social recognition.
21. K. Uvnas-Moberg. Oxytocin may mediate the benefits of positive social interaction and emotions. *Psychoneuroendocrinology* 1998; 23:819–835.
22. E. Keverne, C. Nevison, and F. Martel. Early learning and the social bond. In *The Integrative Neurobiology of Affiliation*, eds. C. Carter, L. Lederhendler, and B. Kirkpatrick. *Annals of the New York Academy of Sciences* 1997; 807:329–339.

Chapter 35 Our Brain's Own Opioids

1. M. Narita, S. Ozaki, and T. Suzuki. Endomorphin-induced motivational effect: Differential mechanism of endomorphin-1 and endomorphin-2. *Japanese Journal of Pharmacology* 2002; 89:224–228. Mu receptors create secondary metabolic effects via G proteins.
2. A. Zangen, S. Ikemoto, J. Zadina, et al. Rewarding and psychomotor stimulant effects of endomorphin-1: Anteroposterior differences within the ventral tegmental area and lack of effect in nucleus accumbens. *Journal of Neuroscience* 2002; 22:7225–7233.
3. J. Zadina. Isolation and distribution of endomorphins in the central nervous system. *Japanese Journal of Pharmacology* 2002; 89:203–208.
4. Narita et al., Endomorphin-induced motivational effect.
5. S. Sakurada, T. Hayashi, and M. Yuhki. Differential antinociceptive effects induced by intrathecally-administered endomorphin-1 and endomorphin-2 in mice. *Japanese Journal of Pharmacology* 2002; 89:221–223.
6. R. Tao, S. Auerbach. Opioid receptor subtypes differentially modulate serotonin efflux in the rat central nervous system. *Journal of Pharmacology and Experimental Therapeutics* 2002; 302:549–556.
7. B. Roth, K. Baner, R. Westkaemper, et al. Salvinorin A: A potent naturally occurring non-nitrogenous κ opioid selective agonist. *Proceedings of the National Academy of Sciences U S A* 2002; 99:11937–11939.
8. E. Stogmann, A. Zimprich, C. Baumgartner, et al. A functional polymorphism in the prodynorphin gene promoter is associated with temporal lobe epilepsy. *Annals of Neurology* 2002; 51:260–263. For a full discussion of this controversial issue, see the comments by N. Tilgen and colleagues, and the reply by E. Stogmann et al. in *Annals of Neurology* 2003; 53:280–282.
9. Y. Hurd. Subjects with major depression or bipolar disorder show reduction of prodynorphin mRNA expression in discrete nuclei of the amygdaloid complex. *Molecular Psychiatry* 2002; 7:75–81.
10. T. Chou, C. Lee, J. Lu, et al. Orexin (hypocretin) neurons contain dynorphin. *Journal of Neuroscience* 2001; 21:RC168.
11. S. Mague, A. Pliakas, M. Todtenkopf, et al. Antidepressant-like effects of κ opioid receptor antagonists in the forced swim test in rats. *Journal of Pharmacology and Experimental Therapeutics* 2003; 305:323–330.
12. K. Ploj, E. Roman, and I. Nylander. Long-term effects of short and long periods of maternal separation on brain opioid peptide levels in male Wistar rats. *Neuropeptides* 2003; 37:149–156. Dynorphin undergoes some natural conversion to leu-enkephalin. The clinical significance of this is not clear. See M. Hallberg, F. Nyberg. Neuropeptide conversion to bioactive fragments—an important pathway in neuromodulation. *Current Protein and Peptide Science* 2003; 4:31–44.

13. R. Goody, K. Martin, S. Goebel, et al. Dynorphin *A* toxicity in striatal neurons via an alpha-amino-3-hydroxy-5-methylisoxazole-4-propionate/kainate receptor mechanism. *Neuroscience* 2003; 116:807–816.

Chapter 36 Opioids, Acupuncture, and the Placebo Response

1. P. Petrovic, E. Kalso, K. Petersson, et al. Placebo and opioid analgesia—imaging a shared neuronal network. *Science* 2002; 295:1737–1740. As the epigraph indicates, the authors do believe that "high placebo responders have a more efficient opioid system." The delivery of the drug differed from that in Wagner et al. (see note 15).
2. B. Pomeranz. Scientific research into acupuncture for the relief of pain. *Journal of Alternative and Complementary Medicine* 1996; 2:53–60; G. Ulett, S. Han, and J.-S. Han. Electroacupuncture: Mechanisms and clinical application. *Biological Psychiatry* 1998; 44:129–138.
3. Pomeranz, ibid., Scientific research.
4. T. Kaptchuk. Acupuncture: Theory, efficacy, and practice. *Annals of Internal Medicine* 2002; 136:374–383.
5. Ulett et al. Electroacupuncture. See also C. Huang, Y. Wang, J.-K. Chang, et al. Endomorphin and μ-opioid receptors in mouse brain mediate the analgesic effect induced by 2 Hz but not 100 Hz electroacupuncture stimulation. *Neuroscience Letters* 2000; 294:159–162. As Han notes (see note 6 below), the different stimulation parameters can be combined.
6. J.-S. Han. Acupuncture: Neuropeptide release produced by electrical stimulation of different frequencies. *Trends in Neurosciences* 2003; 26:17–22.
7. V. Panadow, N. Makris, J. Liu, et al. Effects of electroacupuncture versus manual acupuncture on the human brain as measured by fMRI. *Human Brain Mapping* 2005; 24:193–105. The stimulation site was at ST-36, below the knee.
8. M. Wu, J. Sheen, K. Chuang, et al. Neuronal specificity of acupuncture response: A fMRI study with electroacupuncture. *Neuroimage* 2002; 16:1028–1037. It is noteworthy that the sham application (at nontraditional meridian points) also activated various modules of the "pain matrix," but to lesser degrees.
9. D. Price and L. Soerensen. Endogenous opioid and non-opioid pathways as mediators of placebo analgesia, in *The Science of the Placebo. Toward an Interdisciplinary Research Agenda*, eds. H. Guess, A. Kleimman, J. Kusek, et al. London, BMJ Books, 2000; 183–206.
10. M. Amanzio and F. Benedetti. Neuropharmacological dissection of placebo analgesia: Expectation-activated opioid systems versus conditioning-activated specific subsystems. *Journal of Neuroscience* 1999; 19:484–494.
11. F. Beneditti, C. Arduino, and M. Amanzio. Somatotopic activation of opioid systems by target-directed expectations of analgesia. *Journal of Neuroscience* 1999; 19:3639–3648. Capsaicin is the burning irritant in red pepper.
12. K. Hui, J. Liu, N. Makris, et al. Acupuncture modulates the limbic system and subcortical gray structures of the human brain: Evidence from fMRI studies in normal subjects. *Human Brain Mapping* 2000; 9:13–25. Ordinary tactile stimulation at the same site as the acupuncture did not cause the decrease in the fMRI signal.
13. Petrovic et al., Placebo and opioid analgesia.
14. The data and interpretations in Beneditti et al. (see note 11) and Liberzon et al. (note 17) also need to be reconciled. Aside from that, it is to be noted that this lateral part of the *orbito*frontal cortex is far removed from the dorsolateral prefrontal cortex (Brodmann area 9). In this lateral orbitofrontal region, fMRI research indicates that emotion is so closely integrated with cognition that they "conjointly contribute to the control of thought and behavior." J. Gray, T. Braver, and M. Raichle. Integration of emotion and cognition in the lateral prefrontal cortex. *Proceedings of the National Academy of Sciences U S A* 2002; 99:4115–4120.

15. K. Wagner, F. Willoch, E. Kochs, et al. Dose-dependent regional cerebral blood flow changes during remifentanil infusion in humans. *Anesthesiology* 2001; 94:732–739. Opiate drugs have sedative effects. The drugs can also influence the way human subjects perceive colors [Z:213–223]. The authors did report that their subjects experienced levels of "sedation." Thus, an opioid-induced reduction in attention could be one explanation for the reduced activity in the inferior parietal region. However, one issue was not addressed. This issue is whether their subjects' *secondary* "psychological" responses to the perceived effects of the drug might have gone on further to influence their PET data. Nor was it reported what effect the drug had on the experience of color or on other relevant aspects of visual perception. Future neuroimaging studies could test whether such visual symptoms might be correlated with a reduction of activity in the left fusiform gyrus.

16. J. Zubieta, Y. Smith, J. Bueller, et al. Regional mu opioid receptor regulation of sensory and affective dimensions of pain. *Science* 2001; 293:311–314. The region of dorsolateral prefrontal cortex involved was Brodmann area 8/9, similar to the region described by Gray et al. (see note 14).

17. I. Liberzon, J. Zubieta, L. Fig, et al. μ-Opioid receptors and limbic responses to aversive emotional stimuli. *Proceedings of the National Academy of Sciences U S A* 2002; 99:7084–7089. The authors use the term "extended amygdala" for the extension of the amygdala under the sublenticular region of the substantia innominata. (The legends for figures 2 and 3 are reversed.) The authors are careful to point out that their "baseline" results on carfentanil binding might, in fact, be an index of how much local endogenous opioid release each individual subject had *already* exerted. The useful generalization that mu opioids decrease firing rates has an interesting exception in the hippocampus [Z:215].

18. R. Coghill, J. McHaffie, and Y.-F. Yen. Neural correlates of interindividual differences in the subjective experience of pain. *Proceedings of the National Academy of Sciences U S A* 2003; 100:8538–8542.

19. M. Sim and W. Tsoi. The effects of centrally acting drugs on the EEG correlates of meditation. *Biofeedback and Self-Regulation* 1992; 17:215–220. The particular form of meditation was called *su xi fa*.

20. J. Horgan. *Rational Mysticism*. New York, Houghton Mifflin 2003, 129.

21. R. Covenas, F. Martin, P. Salinas. A immunocytochemical mapping of methionine-enkephalin-Arg(6)-Gly(7)-Leu(8) in the human brainstem. *Neuroscience* 2004; 128:843–859.

22. J. Infante, F. Peran, M. Martinez, et al. ACTH and β-endorphin in transcendental meditation. *Physiology and Behavior* 1998; 64:311–315. The meditators' normal levels of blood cortisone indicate that (low) cortisone is not the explanation for their unusual 8:00 P.M. elevations of beta-endorphin and ACTH.

23. We need to know the degree to which peptides, released from the pituitary, might seep into the adjacent subarachnoid fluid near this gland, and not only enter into the bloodstream.

24. Stress responses (which release both peptides) could be less well developed in laboratory animals in which a rapid intravenous injection of potassium chloride is the cause of their sudden death from cardiac arrest. See J. Soleto, R. Perez, P. Guevara, et al. Changes in brain, plasma and cerebrospinal fluid contents of β-endorphin in dogs at the moment of death. *Neurological Research* 1995; 17:223–225. In contrast, when human patients die, some of their final moments can be both more prolonged and filled with considerable mental anguish.

25. During many, but not all. In humans, some terminal events are blissful. Protease inhibitors can protect peptide levels from being digested by tissue enzymes to some degree. These inhibitors were not added until after the dog brain tissue had already been homogenized. As one other potential explanation for the relatively minor elevation of beta-endorphin

in this report on dogs, the possible neural inhibitory effects of potassium chloride when it reaches the limbic system need further study.

A surge of opioids could be one factor contributing to several different phenomena during both the near-death experience, internal absorption, and kensho [Z:parts III, V, VI, and VII]. However, for the reasons given, this report by Soleto et al. of only a twofold (average) rise in beta-endorphin (and with great individual variation among dogs in the two groups) is insufficient evidence for or against this general hypothesis.

Chapter 37 Metabolic Cascades That Transform the Next Nerve Cell's Firing Responses

1. A. West, E. Griffith, and M. Greenberg. Regulation of transcription factors by neuronal activity. *Nature Reviews Neuroscience* 2002; 3:921–931. Greenberg reported his finding in 1986.
2. V. Pineda, J. Athos, H. Wang, et al. Removal of $G_{i\alpha 1}$ constraints on adenylyl cyclase in the hippocampus enhances LTP and impairs memory formation. *Neuron* 2004; 41:153–163.
3. West, Regulation of transcription. Most transcription factors operate through complex layers of mechanisms. Acronyms barely hint at the complexities. Thus, CREB is an acronym for a *c*yclic AMP *r*esponse *e*lement *b*inding protein. Often, after an early step that adds phosphate groups, the metabolic result can be reversed later by other steps, involving phosphatase enzymes, that remove these same phosphate groups.
4. F. Wei, C. Qiu, L. Liauw, et al. Calcium calmodulin–dependent protein kinase IV is required for fear memory. *Nature Reviews Neuroscience* 2002; 5:573–579.
5. S. Newton, J. Thome, T. Wallace, et al. Inhibition of cAMP response element–binding protein or dynorphin in the nucleus accumbens produces an antidepressant-like effect. *Journal of Neuroscience* 2002; 22:10883–10890.
6. West, Regulation of transcription.
7. Ibid. Studies of an inbred strain of mice confirm that DREAM acts normally to decrease dynorphin levels. Thus, when both parents *lack* this DREAM gene, their ("double knock-out") offspring show increased spinal levels of dynorphin A, an increase in its corresponding messenger RNA, and reduced pain sensitivity responses.
8. W. Gibbs. The unseen genome. Gems among the junk. *Scientific American* 2003; 289:47–53.

Chapter 38 Neurotrophins and Change

1. M. Chao. Neurotrophins and their receptors: A convergence point for many signaling pathways. *Nature Reviews Neuroscience* 2003; 4:299–309.
2. M. Kerschensteiner, C. Stadelmann, G. Dechant, et al. Neurotrophic cross-talk between the nervous and immune systems: Implications for neurological diseases. *Annals of Neurology* 2003; 53:292–304.
3. M. Egan, M. Kojima, J. Callicott, et al. The BDNF val66met polymorphism affects activity-dependent secretion of BDNF and human memory and hippocampal function. *Cell* 2003; 112:257–269.
4. Chao, Neurotrophins.
5. L. Mendell and V. Arvanian. Diversity of neurotrophin action in the postnatal spinal cord. *Brain Research Reviews* 2002; 40:230–239.

   Each year brings new insights into other intricacies of our pain pathways. What once was called "psychic pain" is no longer so easily explained away as being "all in the mind." Problems with transcultural communication are only one reason why gurus are so notoriously difficult to evaluate. Still, it may also be of parenthetical interest that one such "grandfather guru," named Ajja, suffered unusual excruciating physical pain at the beginning of his spiritual inquiry. The pain was referable to his chest, then to his entire body, and was relieved only after it had lasted for 6 months. See Who is Ajja? *What Is Enlightenment?* 2001 (fall/winter); 20:147–155, 218–219. Pains are also experienced during the "dark nights of depression" [Z:584–588]. Krishnamurti had a major transforming unitive experience at the age of 37. It was painful and he also complained of warmth. He called this "the process" and regarded it as akin to the awakening of Kundalini. See E. Blau. *Krishnamurti: 100 Years.* New York, Joost Effers, Stewart, Tabori, & Chang, 1995, 32–35.

6. I. Zagon, M. Verderame, and P. McLaughlin. The biology of the opioid growth factor receptor (OGFr). *Brain Research Reviews* 2002; 38:351–376.

Chapter 39 The Pineal and Melatonin

1. Descartes, quoted in R. Reiter and J. Robinson. *Melatonin.* New York, Bantam, 1995, p. 173.
2. G. Tooley, S. Armstrong, T. Norman, et al. Acute increases in night-time plasma melatonin levels following a period of meditation. *Biological Psychology* 2000; 53:69–78. Midnight was chosen because melatonin levels normally begin to peak between midnight and 4 A.M. The four pooled samples during the control period varied over a thirteen-fold range from 28 to 363 pg/mL. Comparably pooled samples varied in individual meditators over an almost tenfold range after meditation. This much individual variability makes it essential to study a large number of subjects in the future.
3. E. Solberg, A. Holen, O. Ekeberg, et al. The effects of long meditation on plasma melatonin and blood serotonin. *Medical Science Monitor* 2004; 10:96–101.
4. S. Fischer, R. Smolnik, M. Herms, et al. Melatonin acutely improves the neuroendocrine architecture of sleep in blind individuals. *Journal of Clinical Endocrinological Metabolism* 2003; 88:15–20. Melatonin induced the typical reduction of ACTH and cortisone associated with early sleep. During late sleep, both ACTH and cortisone showed the expected distinct rise.
5. J. Infante, F. Peran, M. Martinez, et al. ACTH and β-endorphin in Transcendental Meditation. *Physiology and Behavior* 1998; 64:311–315. Cortisol is expected to exert a negative feedback effect on the secretion of ACTH and beta-endorphin from the pituitary.
6. A. Carillo-Vico, A. Garcia-Perganeda, L. Naji, et al. Expression of membrane and nuclear melatonin receptor mRNA and protein in the mouse immune system. *Cellular and Molecular Life Sciences* 2003; 60:2272–2278.
7. M. Dubocovich, M. Rivera-Bermudez, M. Gerdin, et al. Molecular pharmacology, regulation and function of mammalian melatonin receptors. *Frontiers in Bioscience* 2003; 1:1093–1108.

Chapter 40 Cortical Anatomy by the Numbers

1. L. Garey ed. and trans. Introduction to, *Brodmann's Localization in the Cerebral Cortex.* London, Smith-Gordon, 1994.
2. C. Noback and R. Demarest, *The Human Nervous System: Basic Principles of Neurobiology,* 3rd ed., 1981, 486.

Chapter 41 Where Is It?—A Prelude to My Action. The Parietal Lobe

1. H. Ishibashi, S. Hihara, T. Heike, et al. Tool-use learning selectively induces expression of brain-derived neurotrophic factor, its receptor trkB, and neurotrophin 3 in the intraparietal multisensory cortex of monkeys. *Cognitive Brain Research* 2002; 14:3–9. Note that attention also enters into this learning task. Attention mechanisms are also represented in nearby parietal lobe regions.
2. M. Stark, H. Coslett, and E. Saffran. Impairment of an egocentric map of locations: Implications for perception and action. *Cognitive Neuropsychology* 1996; 13:481–523. This patient had

an atrophic, degenerative disorder. A brain tumor large enough to involve both superior parietal lobules would present a variety of local pressure effects that would interfere with this kind of careful evaluation of the clinical findings.

3. A. Iriki, M. Tanaka, S. Obayashi, et al. Self-images in the video monitor coded by monkey intraparietal neurons. *Neuroscience Research* 2001; 40:163–173.
4. J. Austin. *Chase, Chance, and Creativity. The Lucky Art of Novelty*. Cambridge, MA, MIT Press, 2003, 102–104.
5. Iriki et al., Self-images. Monkeys, like young children, don't immediately recognize their own individual self in a mirror or on a video screen. This they can learn. Higher primates, like chimpanzees, can do this instinctively.
6. Ishibashi et al., Tool-use learning. See also H. Ishibashi, S. Hihara, M. Takahashi, et al. Tool-use learning induces BDNF expression in a selective portion of monkey anterior parietal cortex. *Molecular Brain Research* 2002; 102:110–112.
7. S. Obayashi, T. Suhara, Y. Nagai, et al. Macaque prefrontal activity associated with extensive tool use. *NeuroReport* 2002; 13:2349–2354.
8. S. Lazar. Personal communication, 6 December 2004.
9. S. Potkin, G. Alva, D. Keator, et al. Brain metabolic effects of Neotrofin in patients with Alzheimer's disease. *Brain Research* 2002; 95:87–95. At present writing, the lack of placebo controls limits further interpretation of this preliminary study in human Alzheimer's disease.

Chapter 42 What Is It? The Temporal Lobe Pathway

1. The primary auditory cortex (BA 41) and the auditory association cortex (BA 42) are represented in the transverse temporal gyrus.
2. R. Saxe. A region of right posterior superior temporal sulcus responds to observed intentional actions. *Neuropsychologia* 2004; 42:1435–1446.
3. Receptors in the membranous labyrinth of the inner ear transmit these messages on up for further processing at higher levels.
4. B. Kirchhoff, A. Wagner, A. Maril, et al. Prefrontal-temporal circuitry for episodic encoding and subsequent memory. *Journal of Neuroscience* 2000; 20:6173–6180. The anterior inferior part of the frontal convexity is involved.
5. V. Goel and R. Dolan. The functional anatomy of humor: Segregating cognitive and affective components. *Nature Neuroscience* 2001; 4:237–238. Puns also activated the left inferior frontal gyrus (BA 44 and 45—a frontal region involved in processing the executive aspects of speech).
6. L. Tyler, E. Stamatakis, P. Bright, et al. Processing objects at different levels of specificity. *Journal of Cognitive Neuroscience* 2004; 16:351–362.
7. T. Bussey, L. Saksida, and E. Murray. Impairments in visual discrimination after perirhinal cortex lesions: Testing "declarative" vs. "perceptual-mnemonic" views of perirhinal cortex function. *European Journal of Neuroscience* 2003; 17:649–660.
8. M. Sabbagh, M. Moulson, and K. Harkness. Neural correlates of mental state decoding in human adults: An event-related potential study. *Journal of Cognitive Neuroscience* 2004; 16:415–426.
9. D. Williams. The structure of emotion reflected in epileptic experiences. *Brain* 1956; 79:29–67.
10. Seizures tend to recur, and to render nearby regions more excitable. This so-called kindling differs from normal long-term potentiation. It is the process by which, through repetition, the epileptiform electrical discharge propagates to sites elsewhere and enlists them in further discharges. ACH and glutamate induce it. GABA, thyrotropin-releasing hormone, and

norepinephrine inhibit it. The olfactory bulb and piriform cortex kindle more rapidly than does the amygdala. See T. Bolwig, J. Kragh, and O. Jorgensen. Hippocampal kindling: Some structure/activity relationships. In *The Temporal Lobes and the Limbic System*, eds. M. Trimble and T. Bolwig. Petersfield, UK, Wrightson Biomedical, 1992, 71–90.

11. E. Sowell, B. Peterson, P. Thompson, et al. Mapping cortical change across the human life span. *Nature Neuroscience* 2003; 6:309–315.
12. V. Ramachandran, W. Hirstein, K. Armel, et al. The neural basis of religious experience. *Society for Neuroscience Abstracts* 1998; 519.1.
13. W. Britton and R. Bootzin. Near-death experiences and the temporal lobe. *Psychological Science* 2004; 15:254–258.
14. A. Hardy. *The Spiritual Nature of Man: A Study of Contemporary Religious Experience*. Oxford, Clarendon Press, 1979, 25–29. In the (later) edited anthology of the Hardy survey, experiences of a "presence" could include not only God, angels, saints, and unnamed persons but also persons who had died. See M. Maxwell and V. Tschndin, eds. *Seeing the Invisible. Modern Religious and Other Transcendent Experiences*. Cambridge, UK, Arkana (Penguin), 1990.
15. J. Horgan. *Rational Mysticism. Dispatches from the Border between Science and Spirituality*. Boston, Houghton Mifflin, 2003, 91–105. It has not been clear what the composition of this control group is. It was the Canadian magazine *Maclean's* that first called this apparatus "The God Machine."
16. K. Mathiak, I. Hertrich, W. Kincses, et al. The right supratemporal plane hears the distance of objects: Neuromagnetic correlates of virtual reality. *NeuroReport* 2003; 14:307–311.
17. M. Persinger. *Neuropsychological Bases of God Beliefs*. New York, Praeger, 1987. Zen awakenings are not "God experiences" if that term must mean (1) "small microseizures" (2) that occur within just the temporal lobe (p. 111). True, Zen enlightenment experiences are "transient events" (p. 111–112). Some are obviously triggered physiologically by sensory events in a particular biochemical setting (see chapter 72). To describe this with the phrase, "biochemical crisis," would seem questionable. The range of phenomena during kensho-satori illustrate that, whatever mechanisms underlie such transient events, they are not restricted to the temporal lobe, as the term TLT (temporal lobe transients) would seem to indicate (p. x) [Z:589–621]. Nor are their core mechanisms "colored by conditioned images" (p. 137). Instead, the hallmark of Zen enlightenment is *de*conditioning. The Zen roshi is a skeptic. His is a "show me" attitude, the quality control for suggestible students who are all too easily misled by their superficial experiences into believing they have just become "enlightened."
18. M. Persinger, Ibid., 41.
19. M. Persinger. Experimental simulation of the god experience: Implications for religious beliefs and the future of the human species, in *Neurotheology, Brain, Science, Spirituality, Religious Experience* ed., R. Joseph. San Jose, CA, University Press, 2002, 267–284; P. Granqvist, M. Fredrikson, P. Unge, et al. Sensed presence and mystical experiences are predicted by suggestibility, not by the application of transcranial weak complex magnetic fields. *Neuroscience Letters* 2005; 379:1–6. In their discussion the Swedish authors noted that their "neutral" isolation chamber resembled a kind of sensory-deprivation chamber. They suggested that subjects whose basic personalities were open to unusual experiences would be the ones likely to have "more unusual experiences" when placed in such a setting.

Chapter 43 What Should I Do about It? The Frontal Lobes

1. H. Barbas. Proceedings of the human cerebral cortex: From gene to structure and function. *Brain Research Bulletin* 2000; 52:319–330.

2. J. Fuster. The prefrontal cortex of the primate: A synopsis. *Psychobiology* 2000; 28:125–131. The posterior parts of the orbital and medial cortex resemble both the limbic cortex and neocortex, and are sometimes called the paralimbic prefrontal cortex.
3. P. Fletcher, and R. Henson. Frontal lobes and human memory. Insights from functional neuroimaging. *Brain* 2001; 124:849–881.
4. P. Fletcher, J. Anderson, D. Shanks, et al. Responses of human frontal cortex to surprising events are predicted by formal associative learning theory. *Nature Neuroscience* 2001; 4:1043–1048. Damage to the dorsolateral frontal cortex on the right interferes most obviously with a patient's ability to appreciate the novel ingredients in humor and to express it with the appropriate emotional responses of laughter and smiling. See P. Shammi and D. Stuss. Humour appreciation: A role of the right frontal lobe. *Brain* 1999; 122:657–666. Lesions on the left that reduce patients' capacities for verbal abstraction will chiefly diminish their responses to verbal humor. Lesions on the right that interfere with their focusing of visual attention and search will interfere the most with those mental shifts involved in their "getting" the visual humor in a cartoon.
5. K. Daffner, M. Mesulam, L. Scinto, et al. The central role of the prefrontal cortex in directing attention to novel events. *Brain* 2000; 123:927–939. Normal subjects can also control—by degrees of intention—how long they choose to look at a stimulus using frontal lobe and brainstem gaze mechanisms.
6. F. Manes, B. Sahakian, L. Clark, et al. Decision-making processes following damage to the prefrontal cortex. *Brain* 2002; 125:614–639.
7. J. Hornak, J. Bramham, E. Rolls, et al. Changes in emotion after circumscribed surgical lesions of the orbitofrontal and cingulate cortices. *Brain* 2003; 126:1691–1712.
8. A. Aron, S Monsell, B. Sahakian, et al. A componential analysis of task-switching deficits associated with lesions of the left and right frontal cortex. *Brain* 2004; 127:1561–1573.
9. B. Kirchhoff, A. Wagner, A. Maril, et al. Prefrontal-temporal circuitry for episodic encoding and subsequent memory. *Journal of Neuroscience* 2000; 20:6173–6180.
10. R. Davidson. Thinking cross-culturally about emotions: A perspective from Western biobehavioral science. Paper presented September 14, 2003; in press 2006, in *Investigating the Mind: The Dalai Lama at MIT*, Harvard University Press.
11. J. Hornak, J. O'Doherty, J. Bramham, et al. Reward-related reversal learning after surgical excisions in orbito-frontal or dorsolateral prefrontal cortex in humans. *Journal of Cognitive Neuroscience* 2004; 16:463–478. See also L. Fellows and M. Farah. Ventromedial frontal cortex mediates affective shifting in humans: Evidence from a reversal paradigm. *Brain* 2003; 126:1830–1837. The authors note that orbitofrontal imaging by fMRI is sometimes difficult to evaluate for technical reasons.
12. G. Wang, N. Volkow, F. Telang, et al. Exposure to appetitive food stimuli markedly activates the human brain. *Neuroimage* 2004; 21:1790–1797.
13. D. Small, R. Zatorre, A. Dagher, et al. Changes in brain activity related to eating chocolate. *Brain* 2001; 124:1720–1733. Pleasant odors increased fMRI signals more in the right *medial* orbitofrontal gyrus; unpleasant odors increased signals more in the left *lateral* region. See A. Anderson, K. Christoff, I. Stappen, et al. Dissociated neural representations of intensity and valence in human olfaction. *Nature Neuroscience* 2003; 6:196–202. The posteromedial orbital cortex is activated in PET scans when normal subjects engage in tasks that distinguish ongoing real associations from associations not currently relevant. See A. Schnider, V. Treyer, and A. Buck. Selection of currently relevant memories by the human posterior medial orbitofrontal cortex. *Journal of Neuroscience* 2000; 20:5880–5884.
14. J. O'Doherty, H. Critchley, R. Deichmann, et al. Dissociating valence of outcome from behavioral control in human orbital and ventral prefrontal cortices. *Journal of Neuroscience*

2003; 23:7931–7939. The anterior insula was also implicated during punishing feedback situations.

15. B. Knutson, G. Fong, S. Bennett, et al. A region of mesial prefrontal cortex tracks monetarily rewarding outcomes: Characterization with rapid event-related fMRI. *Neuroimage* 2003; 18:263–272.

16. E. Ferstl and D. von Cramon. What does the frontomedian cortex contribute to language processing: Coherence or theory of mind? *Neuroimage* 2002; 17:1599–1612.

17. T. Shallice. Theory of mind and the prefrontal cortex. *Brain* 2001; 124:247–248. The position of the cingulate sulcus varies. This contributes to the difficulties in assigning precise anatomical boundaries in this medial region.

18. E. Koechlin, G. Corrado, P. Pietrini, et al. Dissociating the role of the medial and lateral anterior prefrontal cortex in human planning. *Proceedings of the National Academy of Sciences U S A* 2000; 97:7651–7656. The subjects held response buttons in their hands.

19. K. Christoff and J. Gabrieli. The frontopolar cortex and human cognition: Evidence for a rostrocaudal hierarchical organization within the human prefrontal cortex. *Psychobiology* 2000; 28:168–186.

20. J. Allman, A. Hakeem, and K. Watson. Two phylogenetic specializations in the human brain. *The Neuroscientist* 2002; 8:335–346.

21. P. Burgess, S. Scott, and C. Frith. The role of the rostral frontal cortex (area 10) in prospective memory: A lateral versus medial dissociation. *Neuropsychologia* 2003: 41:906–918.

22. M. Hunter, R. Green, I. Wilkinson, et al. Spatial and temporal dissociation in prefrontal cortex during action execution. *Neuroimage* 2004; 23:1186–1191.

23. Koechlin et al. Disassociating the role. These frontal signal increases occurred in association with those in the dorsolateral striatum.

24. P. Duus. *Topical Diagnosis in Neurology*. New York, Thieme-Stratton, 1983, 367–368.

25. G. Levine, S. Black, R. Cabeza, et al. Episodic memory and the self in a case of isolated retrograde amnesia. *Brain* 199; 121:1951–1973.

26. K. Vogeley, M. Kurthen, P. Falkai, et al. Essential functions of the human self model are implemented in the prefrontal cortex. *Consciousness and Cognition* 1999; 8:343–363. A subject's task, in a typical theory of mind experiment, is to model the knowledge, attitudes, beliefs, or intentions of another person.

27. J. Le Doux, J. Debiec, and H. Moss, eds. *The Self: From Soul to Brain. Annals of the New York Academy of Sciences* 2003; 1001.

28. Y. Nagai, H. Critchley, E. Featherstone, et al. Activity in ventromedial prefrontal cortex covaries with sympathetic skin conductance level: A physiological account of a "default mode" of brain function. *Neuroimaging* 2004; 22:243–251.

29. N. Fox, L. Schmidt, and H. Henderson. Developmental psychophysiology. In *Handbook of Psychophysiology*, eds. J. Cacioppo, L. Tassinary, and G. Berntson. Cambridge, MA, Cambridge University Press, 2000, 665–686.

30. Ibid.

31. J. Coan and J. Allen. Frontal EEG asymmetry and the behavioral activation and inhibition systems. *Psychophysiology* 2003; 40:106–114.

32. H. Markowitsch, M. Vandekerckhove, H. Lanfermann, et al. Engagement of lateral and medial prefrontal areas of the ecphory of sad and happy autobiographical memories. *Cortex* 2003; 39:643–665.

33. Kirchhoff et al., Prefrontal-temporal circuitry.

34. V. Goel and R. Dolan. The functional anatomy of humor: Segregating cognitive and affective components. *Nature Neuroscience* 2001; 4:237–238.

35. P. Derks, L. Gillikin, D. Bartolome-Rell, et al. Laughter and electroencephalographic activity. *Humor* 1997; 10:285–300. The authors conclude with a cogent statement emphasizing that the frontal lobes are one part of a much larger network: "Humor appreciation is a complex information processing task, incorporating mechanisms of pattern recognition, categorization, meaningful search, and emotionality."
36. D. Mobbs, M. Greicius, E. Abdel-Azim, et al. Humor modulates the mesolimbic reward centers. *Neuron* 2003; 40:1041–1048. This was a high-field (3 tesla) event-related functional fMRI study. Signals were slightly reduced in the right nucleus accumbens region when the cartoons were judged not to be funny.
37. Goel and Dolan, Functional anatomy.

Chapter 44 The Thalamus

1. K. Taber, C. Wen, A. Khan, et al. The limbic thalamus. *Journal of Neuropsychiatry and Clinical Neurosciences* 2004; 16:127–132. The sense of smell proceeds directly to the olfactory brain without first relaying in the thalamus.
2. A. DaSilva, D. Tuch, M. Wiegell, et al. A primer on diffusion tensor imaging of anatomical substructures. *Neurosurgical Focus* 2003; 15:1–4.
3. T. Behrens, H. Johansen-Berg, M. Woolrich, et al. Non-invasive mapping of connections between human thalamus and cortex using diffusion imaging. *Nature Neuroscience* 2003; 6:750–757. This imaging technique does not distinguish thalamo → cortical from cortico → thalamic connections.
4. M. Steriade, E. Jones, and D. McCormick, eds. *The Thalamus. Organization and Function*, vol. 1. Oxford, Elsevier Science, 1997, 46–48.
5. M. Webster, J. Bachevalier, and L. Ungerleider. Subcortical connections of inferior temporal areas TE and TEO in macaque monkeys. *Journal of Comparative Neurology* 1993; 335:73–91. In the monkey, reciprocal connections link areas TEO with the lateral, medial, and inferior nuclei of the pulvinar. In contrast, the most anterior temporal lobe area, TE, projects to only a limited degree to the medial dorsal nucleus of the thalamus, but it does go to the large cell portion.
6. C. Asanuma. Distributions of neuromodulatory inputs in the reticular and dorsal thalamic nuclei. In *The Thalamus, Experimental and Clinical Aspects*, vol. 2, eds. M. Steriade, E. Jones, and D. McCormick. Oxford, Elsevier Science, 1997, 93–153. See also Steriade et al., *The Thalamus*, vol. 1, 64.
7. Steriade et al., *The Thalamus*, vol. 1, 82.
8. *The Thalamus, Organization and Function*, vol. 1, eds. M. Steriade, E. Jones, and D. McCormick. Oxford, Elsevier Science, 1997, 755–779.
9. This anterior nucleus *can* be inhibited by the reticular nucleus in primates. This removes a restriction noted earlier in Zen and the Brain. There, I had suggested that the reticular nucleus would not be able to inhibit its actions. This restriction had been based on available data from the cat, an animal that lacks these functional reticular nucleus connections [Z:269–270]. See K. Kultas-Ilinski. Nucleus reticularis thalami input to the anterior thalamic nuclei in the monkey. *Neuroscience Letters* 1995; 186:25–28.
10. E. Jones. The thalamic matrix and thalamocortical synchrony. *Trends in Neurosciences* 2001; 24:595–601.
11. Taber et al., The limbic thalamus.
12. We need to understand all that the hypothalamus and the anterior nucleus contribute to consciousness. It is time for a detailed study of what this mammillary-thalamic tract contributes to primate behavior. Discrete, unilateral electrical stimulations are required. Discrete vascular lesions, limited to the tract, do not occur in humans [Z:183, 193, 260].

13. R. Vertes, N. Hoover, and G. DiPrisco. Theta rhythm of the hippocampus: Subcortical control and functional significance. *Behavioral and Cognitive Neuroscience Reviews* 2005; 3:173–200. We need more information in primates about the functional anatomy of the reuniens.
14. J. Taube. Head direction cells and the neurophysiological basis for a sense of direction. *Progress in Neurobiology* 1998; 55:225–256. How the various head directional cells in the anterior and lateral dorsal thalamus receive and relay all their requisite sensory input remains to be clarified in primates.
15. The *ventral* nuclei of the thalamus also relay important somatosensory and visceral information up to higher levels. These levels include the interoceptive "vestibular cortex" that is represented in the posterior insula (see chapter 28).
16. F. Javoy-Agid, B. Scatton, M. Ruberg, et al. Distribution of monoaminergic, cholinergic, and GABAergic markers in the human cerebral cortex. *Neuroscience* 1989; 29:251–259. Furthermore, in the monkey, the color-sensitive cortex also has low levels of cytochrome oxidase. Because this enzyme normally catalyzes the reactions of molecular oxygen (O_2) in mitochondria, the region could have some metabolic vulnerabilities worth studying.
17. A. Sillito and H. Jones. Functional organization influencing neurotransmission in the lateral geniculate nucleus. In *The Thalamus, Experimental and Clinical Aspects*, vol. 2, eds. M. Steriade, E. Jones, and D. McCormick. Oxford, England, Elsevier Science, 1997, 1–52.

Chapter 45 The Pulvinar

1. K. Grieve, C. Acuña, and J. Cudeiro. The primate pulvinar nuclei: Vision and action. *Trends in Neurosciences* 2000; 23:35–39.
2. P. Vuilleumier, J. Armony, J. Driver, et al. Distinct spatial frequency sensitivities for processing faces and emotional expressions. *Nature Neuroscience* 2003; 6:624–631. An fMRI study.
3. B. Liddell, K. Brown, A. Kemp, et al. A direct brainstem-amygdala-cortical "alarm" system for subliminal signals of fear. *Neuroimage* 2005; 24:235–243.
4. J. Coull, M. Jones, T. Egan, et al. Attentional effects of noradrenaline vary with arousal level: Selective activation of thalamic pulvinar in humans. *Neuroimage* 2004; 22:315–322. The noise suddenly arouses the subjects even though they had been heavily sedated by a norepinephrine alpha-2 receptor agonist. This result simply illustrates that reflex arousal functions employing major messengers (like ACH and glutamate) can override a sedation effect caused by autoreceptors that reduce norepinephrine tone.
5. K. Grieve et al., Primate pulvinar nuclei.
6. S. Shumikhina and S. Molotchnikoff. Pulvinar participates in synchronizing neural assemblies in the visual cortex, in cats. *Neuroscience Letters* 1999; 272:135–139.
7. In contrast, direct GABA inhibition of the first-order *sensory* relay nuclei down in the thalamus is proposed to be the pivotal mechanism responsible for the sensory blockade during internal absorption (see chapters 74 and 75) [Z:589–590].

Chapter 46 The Reticular Nucleus and its Extrareticular Allies

1. M. Steriade. The GABAergic reticular nucleus: A preferential target of corticothalamic projections. *Proceedings of the National Academy of Sciences U S A* 2001; 98:3625–3627.
2. R. Guillery and J. Harting. Structure and connections of the thalamic reticular nucleus: Advancing views over half a century. *Journal of Comparative Neurology* 2003; 463:360–371.
3. Steriade, GABAergic reticular nucleus.
4. D. Pinault. The thalamic reticular nucleus: Structure, function and concept. *Brain Research Reviews* 2004; 46:1–31. A review with 281 references.
5. S. Sherman. Tonic and burst firing: Dual modes of thalamocortical relay. *Trends in Neurosciences* 2001; 24:122–126.

6. Guillery and Harting, Structure and connections.
7. C. Brunia and G. Van Boxtel. Motor preparation. In *Handbook of Psychophysiology*, eds. J. Cacioppo, L. Tassinary, and G. Berntson. Cambridge, UK, Cambridge University Press, 2000, 507–532.
8. A. Gonzalez, C. Michel, G. Thut, et al. Prediction of response speed by anticipatory high-frequency (gamma band) oscillations in the human brain. *Human Brain Mapping* 2005; 24:50–58.
9. To begin to test this and related hypotheses, various components of the "readiness potential" could be examined in a longitudinal study.
10. Pinault, The thalamic reticular nucleus.
11. J. Mitrofanis. Some certainty for the "zone of uncertainty"? Exploring the function of the zona incerta. *Neuroscience* 2005; 130:1–15.
12. J. Trageser and A. Keller. Reducing the uncertainty: Gating of peripheral inputs by zona incerta. *Journal of Neuroscience* 2004; 24:8911–8915.
13. P. Bartho, T. Freund, and L. Acsady. Selective GABAergic innervation of thalamic nuclei from zona incerta. *European Journal of Neuroscience* 2002; 16:999–1014.
14. H. Bokor, S. Frere, M. Eyre, et al. Selective GABAergic control of higher-order thalamic relays. *Neuron* 2005; 45:929–940. The higher-order thalamic nuclei are sometimes termed the nonspecific nuclei. They receive the kinds of strong excitatory projections from layer 5 of the cortex that enable them to contribute to the higher functions involved in cognition, rewards, binding, discriminative attention and sensation.

Chapter 47 Higher Mechanisms of Attention

1. M. Corbetta, M. Kincade, and G. Shulman. Two neural systems of visual orienting and the pathophysiology of unilateral spatial neglect. *The Cognitive and Neural Basis of Spatial Neglect*, eds. H.-O. Karnath, A. Milner, and G. Valler. Oxford, Oxford University Press, 2002, 259–273.
2. M. Worden and J. Foxe. The dynamics of the spread of selective visual attention. *Proceedings of the National Academy of Sciences U S A* 2003; 100:11933–11935.
3. A. Milner and R. McIntosh. Perceptual and visuomotor processing in neglect. In *The Cognitive and Neural Basis of Spatial Neglect*, eds. H.-O. Karnath, A. Milner, and G. Valler. Oxford, Oxford University Press, 2002, 155–166.
4. N. Lawrence, T. Ross, R. Hoffmann, et al. Multiple neuronal networks mediate sustained attention. *Journal of Cognitive Neuroscience* 2003; 15:1028–1038.
5. S. Yantis, J. Schwarzbach, J. Serences, et al. Transient neural activity in human parietal cortex during spatial attention shifts. *Nature Reviews Neuroscience* 2002; 5:995–1002.
6. A. Nobre, J. Coull, P. Maquet, et al. Orienting attention to locations in perceptual versus mental representations. *Journal of Cognitive Neuroscience* 2004; 16:363–373.
7. M. Belmonte and D. Yurgelun-Todd. Anatomic dissociation of selective and suppressive processes in visual attention. *Neuroimage* 2003; 19:180–189.
8. Nobre et al., Orienting attention.
9. R. Compton, M. Banich, A. Mohanty, et al. Paying attention to emotion: An fMRI investigation of cognitive and emotional Stroop tasks. *Cognitive, Affective, and Behavioral Neuroscience* 2003; 3:81–96. The fMRI signals in the amygdala decreased when the subjects deliberately chose to ignore the distractions posed by negative emotional words.
10. Corbetta et al., Two neural systems.
11. Ibid.
12. K. Mathiak, I. Hertrich, W. Kincses, et al. The right supratemporal plane hears the distance of objects: Neuromagnetic correlates of virtual reality. *NeuroReport* 2003; 14:307–311.

13. P. Rainville, R. Hofauer, R. Paus, et al. Cerebral mechanisms of hypnotic induction and suggestion. *Journal of Cognitive Neuroscience* 1999; 11:110–125.
14. D. Spiegel. Negative and positive visual hypnotic hallucinations. Attending inside and out. *International Journal of Clinical and Experimental Hypnosis* 2003; 51:130–146. Suggesting "numbness" under hypnosis reduces the P300 component of the subject's evoked potential response to somatosensory stimulation.
15. A. Engle, P. Fries, and W. Singer. Dynamic predictions: Oscillations and synchrony in top-down processing. *Nature Reviews Neuroscience* 2001; 2:704–716.

Chapter 48 Ever-Present Awareness

1. F. Travis. The junction point model: A field model of waking, sleeping, and dreaming, relating dream witnessing, the waking/sleeping transition, and transcendental meditation in terms of a common psychophysiologic state. *Dreaming* 1994; 4:91–104. This is one imaginative, preliminary, theoretical approach to the daunting task of relating the EEG to meditation throughout a 24-hour period. It helps to recall how the EEG evolves during the normal drowsiness of subjects who are *not* meditators. Frontal alpha waves increase, the EEG slows, and occasional global bursts of theta activity develop. Do subjects who are experienced in transcendental meditation show similar findings? Yes, *during meditation, and these last for much longer periods* [Z:88–93]. There have been many technical advances since this 1994 report. These make it possible to test two of Travis's theories: (1) only the waves at one special frequency—7 to 9 cps ("theta/alpha activity")—were said to be the specific correlates of the transitional phases between normal waking, slow wave, and REM sleep; (2) these 7 to 9 cps waves were also said to be the specific correlates of some "underlying field" that human subjects can enhance by their long-term practice of meditation. Until these theories are tested with contemporary techniques, it remains questionable whether 7 to 9 cps EEG findings reminiscent of prolonged drowsiness provide a theoretical basis that (in its extensions) can hint at an "undifferentiated field."
2. K. Wilber. *One Taste. The Journals of Ken Wilber*. Boston, Shambhala, 1999.
3. B. Simini, G. Enlund, P. Samuelsson, and C. Lennmarken. Awareness during anesthesia: A prospective case study. *Lancet* 2000; 355:672–673.
4. M. Mahowald and C. Schenck. Dissociated states of wakefulness and sleep. *Neurology* 1992; 42(suppl. 6):44–52. Entering into this event-related potential equation are sensory threshold, level of awareness, and pattern recognition skills.
5. M. Wilenius-Emet, A. Revonsuo, and V. Ojanen. An electrophysiological correlate of human visual awareness. *Neuroscience Letters* 2004; 354:38–41.
6. Travis, The junction point model, 74.
7. Wilber, *One Taste*, 75–76.
8. C. Portas, K. Krakow, P. Allen, et al. Auditory processing across the sleep-wake cycle: Simultaneous EEG and fMRI monitoring in humans. *Neuron* 2000; 28:991–999. Neutral stimuli do not register as effectively as stimuli which have an affective significance.
9. M. Steriade. Coherent oscillations and short-term plasticity in corticothalamic networks. *Trends in Neurosciences* 1999; 22:337–344. The human somatosensory cortex develops very high-frequency oscillations (300–900 cps) as part of an evoked potential response when a peripheral nerve is stimulated. It remains to be proved that such bursts, produced artificially, can also serve as an index of a "floating focus of attention." Their potential relationship to the release of nitric oxide also remains to be clarified. See F. Klostermann, G. Nolte, and G. Curio. Independent short-term variability of spike-like (600 Hz) and postsynaptic (N20) cerebral SEP components. *NeuroReport* 2001; 12:349–352.

Chapter 49 Neuroimaging, EEG Tomography, Event-Related Potentials, and Caveats

1. A. Gamma, D. Lehmann, E. Frei, et al. Comparison of simultaneously recorded [$H_2{}^{15}O$]-PET and LORETA during cognitive and pharmacological activation. *Human Brain Mapping* 2004; 22:83–96.
2. A. Song, M. Woldorff, S. Gangstead, et al. Enhanced spatial localization of neuronal activation using simultaneous apparent-diffusion-coefficient and blood-oxygenation functional magnetic resonance imaging. *Neuroimage* 2002; 17:742–750.
3. A. Toga and J. Mazziota, eds. *Brain Mapping*, 2nd ed. San Diego, Academic Press 2002.
4. V. Walsh and A. Cowey. Transcranial magnetic stimulation and cognitive neuroscience. *Nature Reviews Neuroscience* 2000; 1:73–79; S. Anand and J. Hotson. Transcranial magnetic stimulation: Neurophysiological applications and safety. *Brain and Cognition* 2002; 50:366–368.
5. M. George, Z. Nahas, M. Molloy, et al. A controlled trial of daily left prefrontal cortex TMS for treating depression. *Society of Biological Psychiatry* 2000; 48:962–970.
6. R. Pascual-Marqui, M. Esslen, K. Kochi, et al. Functional imaging with low-resolution brain electromagnetic tomography (LORETA): A review. *Methods and Findings in Experimental and Clinical Pharmacology* 2002; 24(suppl. C):91–95. LORETA assumes that neighboring nerve cells are generating activity that will be most highly correlated. Its spatial resolution is low, in the order of 3 to 4 cm.
7. Gamma et al., PET and LORETA. Beta-2 activity showed some regional correlations.
8. M. Fabiani, G. Gratton, and M. Coles. Event-related brain potentials. In *Handbook of Psychophysiology*, eds. J. Cacioppo, L. Tassinary, and G. Berntson. Cambridge, UK, Cambridge University Press, 2000, 53–84. Responses to errors are visualized as waveforms that show "error-relative negativity."
9. D. Pizzagalli, L. Greischar, and R. Davidson. Spatio-temporal dynamics of brain mechanisms in aversive classical conditioning: High-density event-related potential and brain electrical tomography analyses. *Neuropsychologia* 2003; 41:184–194. The ERP data ware analyzed using LORETA-based techniques and an array of 128 scalp electrodes.
10. F. Di Russo, S. Pitzalis, G. Spitoni, et al. Identification of the neural sources of the pattern-reversal VEP. *Neuroimage* 2005; 24:874–886. Could such coarse-grained visual reversals be relayed earlier to the MT/V5 areas because their off/on characteristics are properties that resemble a "moving" stimulus? (see chapter 96).
11. H. Walach and E. Käseberg. Mind machines: A controlled study of the effects of electromagnetic and optic-acoustic stimulation on general well-being, electrodermal activity, and exceptional psychological experiences. *Behavioral Medicine* 1998; 24:107–114.
12. P. Granqvist, M. Fredrikson, P. Unge, et al. Sensed presence and mystical experiences are predicted by suggestibility, not by the application of transcranial weak complex magnetic fields. *Neuroscience Letters* 2005; 379:1–6. Interested readers will find aspects of the controversy starting to be aired on two websites: http://laurentian.ca/neurosci/News/Dec_news.htm, and http://www.innerworlds.50megs.com/granqvist-persinger.htm. The debate is likely to continue.
13. M. Persinger. Experimental simulation of the god experience: Implications for religious beliefs and the future of the human species, in *Neurotheology, Brain, Science, Spirituality, Religious Experience* ed., R. Joseph. San Jose, CA, University Press, 2002, 267–284. It is noted that the stimulation sites are said to be over the *temporoparietal* region, not the temporal lobe per se. This author describes the most common accompaniments of this sensed presence as "vibrations within the body, dream-like states, detachment of the self from the body, spinning, and either fear, aggression, or sexual arousal."

14. L. Standish, L. Johnson, L. Kozak, et al. Evidence of correlated functional magnetic resonance imaging signals between distant human brains. *Alternative Therapies* 2003; 9:121–125. An electromagnetic cage shielded the receiver from the control room.
15. L. Standish, L. Kozak, L. Johnson, et al. Electroencephalographic evidence of correlated event-related signals between the brains of spatially and sensory isolated human subjects. *Journal of Alternative and Complementary Medicine* 2004; 10:307–314. The subjects were separated by 10 meters in sound-attentuated rooms. Each receiver looked only at static checkerboard patterns. So, too, did each sender, during that sender's "off" condition. The one pair in whom the EEG effect was replicated (out of the four available for testing) also served as the subjects for the fMRI study in reference 14.

Chapter 50 Self/Other Frames of Reference: Laboratory Correlates?

1. M. Raichle and D. Gusnard. Appraising the brain's energy budget. *Proceedings of the National Academy of Sciences U S A* 2002; 99:10237–10239. The authors review data on the "oxygen extraction fraction" of the brain. This fraction represents the ratio between how much oxygen the brain *actually extracts and uses,* in contrast to how much oxygen happens to be delivered to it by the flow of blood. When do discrete brain regions reach their own baseline level of stabilization? When their ratios of oxygen supply to demand remain the same as the *average* ratios throughout the resting brain as a whole. With regard to the brain's "energy budget," a simple biochemical reaction reminds us how intimately linked are its two major modes of excitation and inhibition: glutamate is the immediate precursor of GABA (see chapter 31).
2. Ibid.
3. D. Gusnard and M. Raichle. Searching for a baseline: Functional imaging and the resting human brain. *Nature Reviews Neuroscience* 2001; 2:685–694. In PET and fMRI, activation reflects a brief local increase in blood flow not accompanied by a commensurate increase in oxygen consumption. Deactivation reflects the reverse. The visual association cortex (BA 19) was on the qualified early list of posterior and medial cortical regions. Later interpretations suggest that eye opening (which does increase blood flow in some of these extrastriate visual areas) is a condition closer to the physiological baseline.
4. N. Logothetis. The neural basis of the blood oxygen-level–dependent functional magnetic resonance imaging signal. *Philosophical Transactions of the Royal Society of London. Series B: Biological Sciences* 2002; 357:1003–1007; S. Kim. Progress in understanding functional imaging signals. *Proceedings of the National Academy of Sciences U S A* 2003; 100:3550–3552. Another recent model suggests that factors increasing cerebral blood flow (which also are an index of the generation of nerve action potentials) will also *increase* the amplitude of BOLD signals. In contrast, factors that increase cerebral oxygen metabolism (which also are an index of synaptic activity) will *reduce* the amplitude of BOLD signals. See V. Marcar and T. Loenneker. The BOLD response: A new look at an old riddle. *NeuroReport* 2004; 15:1997–2000.
5. D. Gusnard and M. Raichle. Functional imaging, neurophysiology and the resting state of the human brain. In *The Cognitive Neurosciences III,* ed. M. S. Gazzaniga. Cambridge, MA, MIT Press, 2004, 1267–1280. Our resting state can be defined in functional anatomical terms as a network of interrelated regions. How is this state being defined psychologically, in more provisional terms, in the laboratory? As a person who is awake, eyes *closed,* and has no constraints on cognition. Important point: this resting state is *not* the person's physiological baseline state, because it can be *reduced* even further during many different task activities.
6. Various neuroimaging studies suggest that the posterior cingulate gyrus, precuneus, and retrosplenial cortex also contribute to tasks that might be described as involving

"topographic cognition." This large topic is discussed in R. Parsons and T. Hartig. Environmental psychophysiology. In *Handbook of Psychophysiology*, eds. J. Cacioppo, L. Tassinary, and G. Berntson. Cambridge, UK, Cambridge University Press, 2000, 815–846. See also the discussions of the way we process space in chapter 75 and [Z:487–499].

7. B. Wicker, P. Ruby, J. Royet, et al. A relation between rest and the self in the brain? *Brain Research Reviews* 2003; 43:224–230.
8. K. McKiernan, J. Kaufman, J. Kucera-Thompson, et al. A parametric manipulation of factors affecting task-induced deactivation in functional neuroimaging. *Journal of Cognitive Neuroscience* 2003; 15:394–408.
9. A. Shmuel, E. Yacoub, J. Pfeuffer, et al. Sustained negative BOLD, blood flow and oxygen consumption response and its coupling to the positive response in the human brain. *Neuron* 2002; 36:1195–1210.
10. J. Chatton, L. Pellerin, and P. Magistretti. GABA uptake into astrocytes is not associated with significant metabolic cost: Implications for brain imaging of inhibitory transmission. *Proceedings of the National Academy of Sciences U S A* 2003; 100:12456–12461.
11. M. Hunter, R. Green, I. Wilkinson, et al. Spatial and temporal dissociation in prefrontal cortex during action execution. *Neuroimage* 2004; 23:1186–1191.
12. M. Vafaee, K. Ostergaard, N. Sunde, et al. Focal changes of oxygen consumption in cerebral cortex of patients with Parkinson's disease during subthalamic stimulation. *Neuroimage* 2004; 22:966–974.
13. H. Laufs, K. Krakow, P. Sterzer, et al. Electroencephalographic signatures of attentional and cognitive default modes in spontaneous brain activity fluctuations at rest. *Proceedings of the National Academy of Sciences U S A* 2003; 100:11053–11058.
14. D. Turk, T. Heatherton, C. Macrae, et al. Out of contact, out of mind. The distributed nature of the self. In *The Self: From Soul to Brain*, eds. J. LeDoux, J. Debiec, and H. Moss. New York, *Annals of the New York Academy of Sciences* 2003; 1001:65–78.
15. G. Viamontes, B. Beitman, C. Viamontes, et al. Neural circuits for self-awareness. Evolutionary origins and implementation in the human brain. In *Self-Awareness Deficits in Psychiatric Patients*, eds. B. Beitman and S. Nair. New York: Norton, 2004, 24–111.

Chapter 51 Moving Away from the Self: Embodied Teachings

1. S. Murphy. *One Bird, One Stone. 108 American Zen Stories*. New York, Renaissance/St. Martin's Press, 2003, 37.
2. M. Wexler. Voluntary head movement and allocentric perception of space. *Psychological Science* 2003; 14:340–346.
3. During 1981, three of the notes are dated 10/27, 11/17, and 11/25. Others, during 1982, are dated 3/3, 5/12, 7/4, 7/21, 7/23, and 7/27. To these entries I have added a few comments from my Zen teacher's recent letters in 2003, dated 7/25 and 7/28. This recent correspondence leaves unclarified the specific questions raised in my earlier letters of 2003. These asked when, where, and how she had learned that body movements could tend to dampen self-centered thoughts. Perhaps, as is typical of the style of Zen, her replies do not encourage a recipient to engage in further discursive, reductionistic thinking about this intriguing phenomenon.
4. M. Wexler, ibid. Three different experiments confirmed the observations.

Chapter 52 Neuroimaging Data from Different Studies of Self-Referent Functions

1. A. Reinders, E. Nijenhuis, A. Paans, et al. One brain, two selves. *Neuroimage* 2003; 20:2119–2125.

2. T. Kjaer, M. Nowak, and H. Lou. Reflective self-awareness and conscious states: PET evidence for a common midline parietofrontal core. *Neuroimage* 2002; 17:1080–1086. PET scans were performed three times, for 2 minutes, during each condition (for a total of 6 minutes each). It is easier to interpret a study like this one, because it does not require a subject to deliver a motor response (as discussed in chapter 51).
3. H. Lou, B. Luber, M. Crupain, et al. Parietal cortex and representation of the mental Self. *Proceedings of the National Academy of Science* 2004; 101:6827–6832. The effective stimulation had a latency of 160 ms.
4. T. Kircher, M. Brammer, E. Bullmore, et al. The neural correlates of intentional and incidental self processing. *Neuropsychologia* 2002; 40:683–692.
5. W. Kelley, C. Macrae, C. Wyland, et al. Finding the self? An event-related fMRI study. *Journal of Cognitive Neuroscience* 2002; 14:785–794. The president of the United States is liable to elicit more partisan emotional responses from U.S. citizens than the queen would elicit from her Danish subjects. This study was conducted in the spring of 2001 before several world events might have changed a participant's judgments about George W. Bush.
6. S. Johnson, L. Baxter, L. Wilder, et al. Neural correlates of self-reflection. *Brain* 2002; 125:1808–1814.
7. T. Schmitz, T. Kawahara-Baccus, and S. Johnson. Metacognitive evaluation, self-relevance, and the right prefrontal cortex. *Neuroimage* 2004; 22:941–947.
8. B. Wicker, P. Ruby, J. Royet, et al. A relation between rest and the self in the brain? *Brain Research* 2003; 43:224–230.
9. P. Fossati, S. Hevenor, M. Lepage, et al. Distributed self in episodic memory: Neural correlates of successful retrieval of self-encoded positive and negative personality traits. *Neuroimage* 2004; 22:1596–1604.
10. S. Platek, J. Keenan, G. Gallup, Jr., et al. Where am I? The neurological correlates of self and other. *Cognitive Brain Research* 2004; 19:114–122.
11. D. Lehmann, P. Faber, P. Achermann, et al. Brain sources of EEG gamma frequency during volitionally meditation-induced, altered states of consciousness, and experience of the self. *Psychiatry Research: Neuroimaging* 2001; 108:111–121. The amplitude of the "stronger" gamma activity was not reported. There was no evidence, however, that any gamma EEG activity arose from the same sources in the brain as did the beta-2 activity. Nor did the distribution of this beta-2 activity, measured at 19 to 21 cps, appear to represent a simple "technical harmonic" of the gamma activity.
12. Reinders et al., One brain, two selves. The study is based on 65 scans of 11 female patients. The actual content of the patient's mental field during the relived experience is unclear. The frontal lobe is "crowded" with postulated functions. Open to alternative interpretations would be any conclusion that such decreases are always a sign that a weakened, higher "executive" self is incapable of "subduing" or "coping with" such stressful memories (see chapter 50). The authors verified that when the patients were in their neutral personality state they processed the trauma-related memory script the same way as they did the neutral memory script.
13. D. Simeon, O. Guralnik, E. Hazlett, et al. Feeling unreal: A PET study of depersonalization disorder. *American Journal of Psychiatry* 2000; 157:1782–1788. BA 39 coincides with the angular gyrus. It would be a most delicate matter to enlist the interest of *acutely* depersonalized subjects in being studied under the kinds of claustrophobic conditions that are involved in fMRI research.
14. It remains to be clarified at which precise lower and higher levels all the mechanisms underlying such phenomena could be disorganized. See O. Blanke, T. Landis, L. Spinelli, et al.

Out-of-body experience and autoscopy of neurological origin. *Brain* 2004; 127:243–258; O. Blanke, C. Mohr, C. Michel, et al. Linking out-of-body experience and self processing to mental own-body imagery at the temporoparietal junction. *Journal of Neuroscience* 2005; 25:550–557; O. Blanke and S. Arzy. The out-of-body experience: disturbed self-processing at the temporo-parietal junction. *Neuroscientist* 2005; 11:16–24. Penfield and Ericsson reported an epileptic patient (G.A.) who experienced a quasi-vestibular impression of floating away when stimulated along the right posterior superior temporal gyrus or in one supramarginal gyrus site. See W. Penfield and T. Ericsson. *Epilepsy and Cerebral Localization* Springfield, Illinois. Charles C. Thomas. 1941.

15. P. Brotchie, M. Lee, D. Chen, et al. Head position modulates activity in the human parietal eye fields. *Neuroimage* 2003; 18:178–184. Head turning to the *right* produces a significantly greater increase in fMRI signals in the left intraparietal sulcus (and vice versa).
16. S. Gillihan and M. Farah. Is self special? A critical review of evidence from experimental psychology and cognitive neuroscience. *Psychological Bulletin* 2005; 131:76–97.
17. B. Postle and M. D'Esposito. Evaluating models of the topographical organization of working memory function in frontal cortex with event-related fMRI. *Psychobiology* 2000; 28:132–145.
18. J. Keenan, M. Wheeler, G. Gallup, et al. Self-recognition and the right prefrontal cortex. *Trends in Cognitive Sciences* 2000; 4:338–344. Note the difference between this right hemispheric lateralization for recognizing one's own face and the findings from split-brain research cited in chapter 50.
19. B. Miller, W. Seeley, P. Mychack, et al. Neuroanatomy of the self: Evidence from patients with frontotemporal dementia. *Neurology* 2001; 57:817–821.

Chapter 53 Imaging a Meditating Brain: A Commentary

1. H. Lou, T. Kjaer, L. Friberg, et al. A ^{15}O-H_2O PET study of meditation and the resting state of normal consciousness. *Human Brain Mapping* 1999; 7:98–105. This technique measures cerebral blood flow. The descriptions do not make clear how the 45-minute tape corresponds to the minutes allotted for each of the eight PET scans and for each of the four meditative stages. Yoga Nidra meditation does not mean sleep. It refers to a fully conscious state of relaxation.
2. S. Murphy. *One Bird, One Stone. 108 American Zen Stories*. New York, Renaissance/St. Martin's Press, 2002, 106.
3. H. Herzog, V. Lele, T. Kuwert, et al. Changed pattern of regional glucose metabolism during Yoga meditative relaxation. *Neuropsychobiology* 1990–1991; 23:182–187. This technique measures cerebral metabolism. The average metabolic increases in several frontal regions during meditation, (when expressed in percent) were +0.5% (inferior), +2.74% (intermediate), and +0.07 (superior). The average metabolic decreases in three posterior regions during meditation were −1.52% (temporo-occipital), −9.95% (occipital), and −6.3% (superior parietal).
4. T. Kjaer, C. Bertelsen, P. Piccini, et al. Increased dopamine tone during meditation-induced change of consciousness. *Cognitive Brain Research* 2002; 13:255–259. Chapter 24 discusses details of this recent report and what they might imply for the release of dopamine into the ventral striatum.
5. A. Newberg, A. Alavi, M. Baime, et al. The measurement of regional cerebral blood flow during the complex cognitive task of meditation: A preliminary SPECT study. *Psychiatry Research* 2001; 106:113–122. A labeled oxime (exametazine; HMPAO) was used to estimate blood flow. A recent subsequent SPECT report was based on three Franciscan nuns who engaged in a verbal prayer, repeating a phrase (internally) for some 50 minutes. As expected,

prefrontal and inferior parietal blood flow increased. The nuns' "subjective responses were impossible to quantify or analyze in a useful manner." The results were "preliminary" and "obviously severely limited by sample size." See A. Newberg, M. Pourdehnad, A. Alavi, et al. Cerebral blood flow during meditative prayer: Preliminary findings and methodological issues. *Perceptual and Motor Skills* 2003; 97:625–630.

6. The authors' words provide a general description. These are not as valuable as are actual first-person reports. This reader, without having more information, is left with the impression that the Tibetan-style meditators had entered their deliberately induced state more slowly, and at a relatively more superficial level, than has been described during the suddenly occurring, unexpected state of *deep* internal absorption [Z:508–510]. This particular category of deep internal absorption is a dramatic, relatively rare state (see chapter 74). It seems unlikely to be in the same category as that kind of induced "absorption" described in note 5. That kind was readily anticipated, and was produced in a research setting by meditators who had a long prior experience in techniques of visualization.
7. In 1988, the present writer (JHA) was the single subject of a 2-hour PET study while letting go of all thoughts and attending to the breathing movements of the lower abdomen [Z:281–286]. Under these conditions of meditative relaxation, the left thalamus and many right cortical regions at several levels were relatively more active metabolically than were their counterparts.

   We await multiple higher-resolution studies in multiple subjects in the future. With time, these may clarify the mechanisms operating not only within the thalamus but also along those major dynamic interfaces which the thalamus interposes between brainstem and cortex. Studies during transition periods could be especially informative.
8. G. Fink, H. Markowitsch, M. Reimkenmeier, et al. Cerebral representation of one's own past: Neural networks involved in autobiographical memory. *Journal of Neuroscience* 1996; 16:4275–4282.
9. Newberg et al., Regional cerebral blood flow, 119, 120.
10. A. Newberg and J. Iversen. The neural basis of the complex mental task of meditation: Neurotransmitter and neurochemical considerations. *Medical Hypotheses* 2003; 61:282–291. Table 1 indicates that the PET study of Herzog and colleagues (see note 3) measured cerebral blood flow (it measured cerebral metabolism). Figure 1 is an intricate "schematic overview" updating earlier theoretical models of meditation. A change is noted with reference to the earlier interpretation of the data reported in note 5. It is now being suggested that blood flow to the superior parietal lobule would be reduced when the reticular nucleus of the thalamus inhibits the lateral posterior nucleus.
11. S. Lazar, G. Bush, R. Gollub, et al. Functional brain mapping of the relaxation response and meditation. *NeuroReport* 2000; 11:1581–1585.
12. Lou et al., PET study of meditation.
13. Lazar et al., Functional brain mapping.
14. Newburg et al., Regional cerebral blood flow.
15. V. Torchilin. Neuroreceptor imaging in health and disease. In *Handbook of Targeted Delivery of Imaging Agents*, Boca Raton, FL, CRC Press, 1995, 553–573.
16. M. Koepp, R. Gunn, A. Lawrence, et al. Evidence for striatal dopamine release during a video game. *Nature* 1998; 393:266–268.
17. Torchilin, Neuroreceptor imaging.
18. V. Rowe. *Sea Creatures and Other Poems*. Overland Park, KS, Whirlybird Press, 1995, 28. Dr. Rowe is a neurologist and sleep medicine specialist.

Chapter 54 Words and Metaphors in Religious Traditions

1. J. Campbell (with Bill Moyers). *The Power of Myth*. New York, Doubleday, 1988, 56.
2. C. Phipps. Enlightenment unplugged. *What Is Enlightenment?* 2004; 24(February–April):87–92.
3. F. DiRusso, A. Martinez, M. Sereno, et al. Cortical sources of the early components of the visual evoked potential. *Human Brain Mapping* 2002; 15:95–111.
4. It would be a delusion if such a listener or reader were to remain attached to such a misinterpretation (to a fixed belief despite evidence to the contrary). The formal steps in neurological diagnosis can serve to postpone any such rush into language. They define two separate categories: illusions (based on sensory phenomena) and delusions (based on systems of belief).
5. R. Cytowic. *Synesthesia. A Union of the Senses*, 2nd ed. Cambridge, MA, MIT Press, 2002, 137 (see also 134–137, 142–144).
6. P. Grossenbacher and C. Lovelace. Mechanisms of synesthesia: Cognitive and physiological constraints. *Trends in Cognitive Sciences* 2001; 5:36–41.
7. J. Nunn, L. Gregory, M. Brammer, et al. Functional magnetic resonance imaging of synesthesia: Activation of V4/V8 by spoken words. *Nature Reviews Neuroscience* 2002; 5:371–375. Normal subjects who were overtrained on word-color associations did not produce enhanced signals in this V4/V8 region of the fusiform gyrus. fMRI may not always provide optimal images of the posterior part of the inferotemporal region, in which activation had been observed during one previous PET study of synesthesia.
8. N. Hadjikhani and P. Roland. Cross-modal transfer of information between the tactile and the visual representations in the human brain: A positron emission tomographic study. *Journal of Neuroscience* 1998; 18:1072–1084.
9. Cytowic, *Synesthesia*, 278, 279, 287, 290. In so-called lexical synesthesia, the subjects link ordinary words and numbers with very specific colors. For example, "2" is orange, but "two" is blue. See T. Palmeri, R. Blake, R. Marois, et al. The perceptual reality of synesthetic colors. *Proceedings of the National Academy of Sciences U S A* 2002; 99:4127–4131.

Chapter 55 Multiple Meanings of "Taste"

1. The TASTE website is www.issc-taste.org, or http://psychology.ucdavis.edu/tart/taste/
2. Various other accounts drawn from the Archives of the Religious Experience Research Centre in Lampeter, Wales, are included in their website: www.alisterhardytrust.org.UK.
3. K. Wilber. *A Brief History of Everything*, 2nd ed. Boston, Shambhala, 2000, 205–210.
4. Chokyi Nyima Rinpoche. The practice of thought-free wakefulness. *Shambhala Sun*, 2002 (November); 37–41, 103–106.
5. Thich Nhat Hanh. The practice of sangha. *Buddhadharma* 2002 (winter); 1(2):18–23, 62–65.
6. H. Inagaki. *A Dictionary of Japanese Buddhist Terms*. With supplement. Union City, CA, Heian International, 1998, 32. (I make no claim to accuracy in translating either Sino-Japanese or neuroscience jargon into simpler English.)
7. K. Wilber. *One Taste. The Journals of Ken Wilber*. Boston, Shambhala, 1999. To conserve space here, interested readers will find the page sources for the cited quotations already listed in Wilber's index under the entry, *one taste*.
8. "Just this" is a meaningful phrase, in common usage nowadays. I have used it as a temporary meditative device for nearly a decade (see chapter 14).
9. Wilber, *One Taste*, 55.

Chapter 56 Witnessing Awareness during Sleep (Continued)

1. F. Travis, J. Tecce, A. Arenander, et al. Patterns of EEG coherence, power, and contingent negative variation characterize the integration of transcendental and waking states. *Biological Psychology* 2002; 61:293–319.
2. R. Forman. *Mysticism, Mind, Consciousness.* Albany, State University of New York Press, 1999, 144, 142–143.
3. L. Mason, C. Alexander, F. Travis, et al. Electrophysiological correlates of higher states of consciousness during sleep in long-term practitioners of the transcendental meditation program. *Sleep* 1997; 20:102–110.
4. Travis et al., Patterns of EEG coherence. The subjects' tasks included pressing a key to stop a tone, and pressing a button in their right or left hand to signal whether a second two-digit number was larger or smaller than the first. Complex physiological models of "loop" dynamics are invoked to explain the data.

Chapter 57 Tilting the Emotional Set Point

1. M. Ricard, quoted in D. Goleman, ed. *Destructive Emotions. How Can We Overcome Them?* New York, Bantam Dell 2003, 76. Cf. *Hamlet,* 2.2: "There is nothing either good or bad, but thinking makes it so."
2. R. Davidson, J. Kabat-Zinn, J. Schumacher, et al. Alterations in brain and immune function produced by mindfulness meditation. *Psychosomatic Medicine,* 2003; 65:564–570.
3. R. Davidson. In *Destructive Emotions,* 338–346. The figure on p. 340 shows that this monk's score at these frontal F4–F3 electrode sites was the outlier, way off the curve, in relation to the 175 other subjects.
4. Goleman, *Destructive Emotions,* 341.

Chapter 58 The Roots of Our Emotions

1. A. Olendzki. Nibbida. *Buddhadharma* 2003; fall, 96.
2. P. Ekman, In D. Goleman, ed. *Destructive Emotions. How Can We Overcome Them?* New York, Bantam Dell 2003, 13–19.

Chapter 59 Attributing Different Emotions to Various Brain Regions

1. J. Panksepp. Emotions as natural kinds within in mammalian brain. In *Handbook of Emotions,* eds., M. Lewis and J. Haviland-Jones. New York, Guilford Press 2000, 137–156.
2. K. Heilman. The neurobiology of emotional experience. *Journal of Neuropsychiatry* 1997; 9:439–448.
3. J. Panksepp. The periconscious substrates of consciousness: Affective states and the evolutionary origins of the self. *Journal of Consciousness Studies* 1998; 5:566–582.
4. M. Bennett and P. Hacker. Emotion and cortical-subcortical function: Conceptual developments. *Progress in Neurobiology* 2005; 75:29–52.
5. J. Panksepp. *Affective Neural Science: The Foundations of Human and Animal Emotions.* New York, Oxford University Press 1998.
6. Panksepp, Emotions as natural kinds.
7. *Ibid.* Table 9.1 provides a summary.
8. M. Bradley. Emotion and motivation. In *Handbook of Psychophysiology,* eds. J. Cacioppo, L. Tassinary, and G. Berntson. Cambridge, UK, Cambridge University Press, 2000, 602–642.
9. Panksepp, *Affective Neural Science.*
10. J. Austin. *Chase, Chance, and Creativity. The Lucky Art of Novelty.* Cambridge, MA, MIT Press, 2003, 84–86, 118–125, 144–147.

11. F. Murphy, I. Nimmo-Smith, and A. Lawrence. Functional neuroanatomy of emotions: A meta-analysis. *Cognitive, Affective, and Behavioral Neuroscience* 2003; 3:207–233.
12. Bradley, Emotion and motivation.
13. G. Ahern, A. Herring, D. Labiner, et al. Affective self-report during the intracarotid sodium amobarbital test: Group differences. *Journal of the International Neuropsychological Society* 2000; 6:659–667. (See also chapter 96, note 13.)
14. E. Altenmuller, K. Schurmann, V. Lim, et al. Hits to the left, flops to the right: Different emotions during listening to music are reflected in cortical lateralisation patterns. *Neuropsychologia* 2002; 40:2242–2256.
15. S. Lewis, R. Thomas, M. Lanoue, et al. Visual processing of facial affect. *NeuroReport* 2003; 14:1841–1845.
16. R. Maddock, A. Garrett, and M. Buonocore. Posterior cingulate cortex activation by emotional words: fMRI evidence from a valence decision task. *Human Brain Mapping* 2003; 18:30–41.
17. G. Lee, K. Meador, D. Loring, et al. Neural substrates of emotion as revealed by functional magnetic resonance imaging. *Cognitive Behavior Neurology* 2004; 17:9–17.
18. L. Williams, K. Brown, P. Das, et al. The dynamics of cortico-amygdala and autonomic activity over the experimental time course of fear perception. *Cognitive Brain Research* 2004; 21:114–123. The subjects were 15 men and 7 women with a mean age of 28 years. Note that the conditions of this experiment prolonged the exposure to fearful stimuli.
19. In such an experiment, one might speculate that a viewer's left hemisphere could be more attentive to those subtle emotions displayed on the (opposite) left side of the subject's face in the picture. Left cerebellar signals also increased during the early and later responses.
20. T. Wager, K. Phan, I. Liberzon, et al. Valence, gender, and lateralization of functional brain anatomy in emotion: A meta-analysis of findings from neuroimaging. *Neuroimage* 2003; 19:513–531.
21. M. Piefke, P. Weiss, H. Markowitsch, et al. Gender differences in the functional neuroanatomy of emotional episodic autobiographical memory. *Human Brain Mapping* 2005; 24:313-324.
22. Y. Avnon, M. Nitzan, E. Sprecher, et al. Autonomic asymmetry in migraine: Augmented parasympathetic activation in left unilateral migraineurs. *Brain* 2004; 127:2099–2108.

Chapter 60 Conditioning: Learning and Unlearning

1. J. Mascaro. *The Dhammapada. The Path of Perfection*. New York, Viking-Penguin Books, 1973, 87(370). The *Dhammapada* includes 423 aphorisms, revered in the Theravada school of Buddhism. The collection may have begun as far back as the third century B.C.E.
2. J. Fernandez-Ruiz, J. Wang, T. Aigner, et al. Visual habit formation in monkeys with neurotoxic lesions of the ventrocaudal neostriatum. *Proceedings of the National Academy of Sciences U S A* 2001; 98:4196–4201.
3. M. Packard and B. Knowlton. Learning and memory functions of the basal ganglia. *Annual Review of Neuroscience* 2002; 25:563–593.
4. J. Medina, J. Repa, M. Mauk, et al. Parallels between cerebellum- and amygdala-dependent conditioning. *Nature Reviews Neuroscience* 2002; 3:122–1331.
5. R. Cardinal, J. Parkinson, J. Hall, et al. Emotion and motivation: The role of the amygdala, ventral striatum, and prefrontal cortex. *Neuroscience Biobehavior Review* 2002; 26:321–352.
6. K. Jugdahl, A. Berardi, W. Thompson, et al. Brain mechanisms in human conditioning: A PET blood flow study. *NeuroReport* 1995; 6:1723–1728. The interpretations of the mecha-

nisms underlying conditioning are based on estimates obtained by subtracting the regional blood flow during the habituation phase from that during the extinction phase.

7. C. Buchel, J. Morris, R. Dolan, et al. Brain systems mediating aversive conditioning: An event-related fMRI study. *Neuron* 1998; 20:947–957. The signals cited were in the rostrolateral part of the amygdala.
8. Jugdahl, Brain mechanisms in human conditioning.

Chapter 61 Addictions

1. E. Conze. *Buddhist Texts through the Ages*. Boston, Shambhala, 1990, 68.
2. J. Cami and M. Farre. Drug addiction. *New England Journal of Medicine* 2003; 349:975–986.
3. G. Koob. Neuroadaptive mechanisms of addiction: Studies on the extended amygdala. *European Neuropsychopharmacology* 2003; 13:442–452; G. Koob, P. Sanna, and F. Bloom. Neuroscience of addiction. *Neuron* 1998; 21:467–476.
4. Koob, Neuroadaptive mechanisms.
5. Cami and Farre, Drug addiction; Koob et al., Neuroscience of addiction. The DA nerve cells in the nigrostriatal system enter into the motoric aspects of behavior. The act of opening a pack of cigarettes and lighting up becomes a habitual behavior.
6. Koob, Neuroadaptive mechanisms.
7. O. Ben-Shahar, S. Ahmed, G. Koob, et al. The transition from controlled to compulsive drug use is associated with a loss of sensitization. *Brain Research* 2004; 995:46–54. Longer periods of cocaine withdrawal were said to produce similar results.
8. Cami and Farre, Drug addiction.
9. M. Abou-Saleh. Psychopharmacology of substance misuse and comorbid psychiatric disorders. *Acta Neuropsychiatrica* 2004; 16:19–25.
10. R. Elliott, K. Friston, and R. Dolan. Dissociable neural responses in human reward systems. *Journal of Neuroscience* 2000; 20:6159–6165.
11. Notably lacking were enhanced signals in the amygdala itself or other parts of the extended amygdala in the basal forebrain. The authors suggest one explanation: the animal studies (as reviewed in this chapter and its notes) reflect the potent pharmacological actions of *biologically* salient drugs. These results may not automatically generalize to the subtler ways in which abstract financial reinforcements, like dollar signs, can affect human brains.

Chapter 62 Being in Love

1. H. Fisher. *Why We Love. The Nature and Chemistry of Romantic Love*. New York, Henry Holt, 2004.
2. A. Bartels and S. Zeki. The neural correlates of maternal and romantic love. *Neuroimage* 2004; 21:1155–1166.
3. Fisher, *Why We Love*, xiii.
4. A. Bartels and S. Zeki. The neural basis of romantic love. *NeuroReport* 2000; 11:3829–3834. The average duration of being in love was 2.3 years.
5. Bartels and Zeki, The neural correlates.
6. Fisher, *Why We Love*.
7. Ibid., 241.
8. T. Brach. Making room for desire. *Tricycle* 2004; 13:71–73. See also the entire special section in this issue: "The Riddle of Desire," 58–87. The interested reader may find a different earlier perspective on the topic as a whole in a special issue of another publication: *What Is Enlightenment?* Special issue 13, spring/summer, 1998, entitled "What is the Relationship between Sex and Spirituality?"

9. Other neuromessengers would be contributing on more stressful retreats (see chapter 32). In Buddhist mythology, the daughters of Mara were said to have offered temptations to Siddhartha, which he declined.

Chapter 63 The Male Animal: Libido and Ex-libido

1. J. Thurber and E. Nugent. *The Male Animal*. New York, Random House. 1946, 130–131.
2. C. Roselli, S. Klosterman, and J. Resko. Anatomic relationships between aromatase and androgen receptor mRNA expression in the hypothalamus and amygdala of adult male cynomolgus monkeys. *Journal of Comparative Neurology* 2001; 439:208–223. Certain parts of the limbic system are more likely to respond to testosterone than others. The hypothalamus expresses high levels of mRNA for androgen receptors in its ventromedial, arcuate, periventricular, and medial preoptic nuclei. In the temporal lobe, the cortical amygdaloid nucleus and hippocampal pyramidal cells also have high densities of this messenger RNA for androgen receptors. See also R. Michael, H. Rees, and R. Bonsall. Sites in the male primate brain at which testosterone acts as an androgen. *Brain Research* 1989; 502:11–20. This study mentions sites where testosterone, after aromatization, is transformed to interact with estrogen receptors.
3. I. Savic, H. Berglund, and P. Lindstrom. Brain response to putative pheromones in homosexual men. *Proceedings of the National Academy of Sciences* 2005; 102:7356–7361. The meditation research could investigate gradations of the response by including male and female homosexuals. Current data suggest that male pherohormones activate the hypothalamus of gay men, whereas female pherohormones do not.
4. J. Goldstein, L. Seidman, N. Horton, et al. Normal sexual dimorphism of the adult human brain assessed by in vivo magnetic resonance imaging. *Cerebral Cortex*. 2001; 11:490–497. These structural MRI studies reveal neuroanatomical details.
5. S. Karama, A. Lecours, J. Leroux, et al. Areas of brain activation in males and females during viewing of erotic film excerpts. *Human Brain Mapping* 2002; 16:1–13.
6. Total androgen deprivation meant two things: (1) an intramuscular (depot) injection of leuprolide acetate: This synthetic compound is an analog of a pituitary hormone which normally acts to trigger the release of gonadotropin. In fact, the artifical molecule soon *stops* the release of this normal gonadotropin. Thereafter, this pituitary gonadotropin no longer stimulates the testis to produce testosterone (or the ovary to produce estrogen). As a result, serum testosterone falls to negligible levels within the first 30 days, and the drug continues to keep it low for the next 2 months. (2) The daily oral ingestion of bicalutamide 50 mg: This is a direct antiandrogen drug. It stops androgen receptors inside cells from responding to any testosterone that might reach them from the adrenal cortex or the testes. This total androgen blockade, followed by external (conformal) radiation and palladium seed implants, dropped my subsequent PSA levels to zero. There, fortunately, they have remained.
7. A. Bhikkhu. *Small Boat, Great Mountain. Theravadan Reflections on the Natural Great Perfection.* Redwood Valley, CA, Abhayagiri Monastic Foundation, 2003, 140–141.
8. Does such a "lack of wanting" occur because long-term meditators produce less pituitary gonadotropin and have lower testosterone levels? No very long-range longitudinal study seems to have resolved this issue. After 4 months of TM practice, the male meditators' testosterone levels were not significantly different from those levels in the active control group who had taken a comparable class in stress education. C. Maclean, K. Walton, S. Wenneberg, et al. Effects of the Transcendental Meditation program on adaptive mechanisms: Changes in hormonal levels and responses to stress after 4 months of practice. *Psychoneuroendocrinology* 1997; 22:277–295. A longitudinal study is indicated.

Chapter 64 Cracks in the Bowl: The Broken Seal

1. S. Shigematsu. *A Zen Forest. Sayings of the Masters*. New York, Weatherhill, 1981, no. 152.
2. The intent here is not to discredit the legitimate prescription of medication for valid replacement therapy. (Nor was the previous chapter designed to promote androgen deprivation drugs.) Still, given the steady erosion of standards in our media, comment seems overdue on the wider social implications of any three-page advertisement for this testosterone gel (manufactured in France).
3. N. Goldberg. Beyond betrayal. *Tricycle* 2005; 14:86–88.
4. H. Inagaki. *A Dictionary of Japanese Buddhist Terms*. Union City, CA, Heian International, 1988, 124.
5. P.-G. Go. *An Easy-Access Dictionary of 5000 Chinese Characters*. San Francisco, Simplex, 1995, S2.

Chapter 65 Empathies, Mirror Neurons, and Prolonged Affirmative Attitudes

1. H. Davis. Too early for a neuropsychology of empathy. *Behavioral and Brain Sciences* 2002; 25:32–33.
2. S. Preston and F. de Waal. Empathy: Its ultimate and proximate bases. *Behavioral and Brain Sciences* 2002; 25:1–20. Readers interested in empathy are referred both to the pages of this "target" article and to the next 51 pages. They include an open peer commentary, the authors' response, and 12 final pages of references.
3. G. Rizzolatti and L. Craighero. The mirror-neuron system. *Annual Reviews in Neuroscience* 2004; 27:169–192.
4. M. Iacoboni and G. Leuzi. Mirror neurons, the insula, and empathy. *Behavioral and Brain Sciences* 2002; 25:39–40.
5. P. Jacob and M. Jeannerod. The motor theory of social cognition: A critique. *Trends in Cognitive Science* 2005; 9:21–25.
6. S. Preston, 2002, ibid.
7. P. Jackson, A. Meltzoff, and J. Decety. How do we perceive the pain of others? A window into the neural processes involved in empathy. *Neuroimage* 2005; 24:771–779.
8. H. Walter, M. Adenzato, A. Ciaramidaro, et al. Understanding intentions in social interaction: The role of the anterior paracingulate cortex. *Journal of Cognitive Neuroscience* 2004; 16:1854–1863.
9. S. Shamay-Tsoory, R. Tomer, B. Berger, et al. Impaired "Affective Theory of Mind" is associated with right ventromedial prefrontal damage. *Cognitive and Behavioral Neurology* 2005; 18:55–67.
10. S. Preston, 2002, ibid.
11. *Shambhala Dictionary of Buddhism and Zen*. Boston, Shambhala, 1991, 143. In the past, most Zen schools have placed relatively little formal emphasis on the continuous metta practice of loving kindness.
12. D. Goleman, ed. *Destructive Emotions. How Can We Overcome Them?* New York, Bantam Dell, 2003, 1–27.

Chapter 66 Through What Steps Does Ordinary Insight Transform Consciousness?

1. J. Luo, K. Niki, and S. Phillips. The function of the anterior cingulate cortex (ACC) in the insightful solving of puzzles: The ACC is activated less when the structure of the puzzle is known. *Journal of Psychology in Chinese Societies* 2004; 5: no pages cited.
2. J. Luo and K. Niki. Function of hippocampus in "insight" of problem solving. *Hippocampus* 2003; 13:316–323.

3. J. Luo, K. Niki, and S. Phillips. Neural correlates of the "Aha! reaction." *NeuroReport* 2004; 15:2013–2017.
4. X.-Q. Mai, J. Luo, J.-H. Wu, et al. "Aha!" effects in a guessing riddle task: An event-related potential study. *Human Brain Mapping* 2004; 22:261–270. Fourteen subjects were monitored by a sixty-four-channel ERP technique while they processed a series of 120 Chinese riddles. A difficult riddle followed by a novel keyword provided data for the "Aha!" answer. A similar N2 component has been found in other tests of conflict detection, or error detection including the color conflict conditions inherent in the Stroop test.
5. Luo et al., The function of the anterior cingulate cortex.
6. J. Austin. *Chase, Chance, and Creativity. The Lucky Art of Novelty*. Cambridge, MA, MIT Press, 2003, 159–168.
7. V. Goel and O. Vartanian. Dissociating the roles of right ventral lateral and dorsal lateral prefrontal cortex in generation and maintenance of hypotheses in set-shift problems. *Cerebral Cortex* 2005; 15:1170–1177.

Chapter 68 The Remarkable Properties of Nitric Oxide

1. J. Cudeiro and C. Rivadulla. Sight and insight—on the physiological role of nitric oxide in the visual system. *Trends in Neurosciences* 1999; 22:110–115. In this and the following citations, the NO˙ being referred to is assumed to arise in normal nerve cells, not from altered glia or other cells.
2. J. Cudeiro, C. Rivadulla, R. Rodriguez, et al. Further observations on the role of nitric oxide in the feline lateral geniculate nucleus. *European Journal of Neuroscience* 1996; 8:144–152.
3. Y. Egberongre, S. Gentleman, P. Falkaj, et al. The distribution of nitric oxide synthase immunoreactivity in the human brain. *Journal of Neuroscience* 1994; 59:561–578. A caveat: The lack of nitric oxide synthase in the *human* thalamus and lateral geniculate nucleus suggests that certain local findings cited in Cudeiro et al. (note 2) might be applicable to NO˙ in humans only to the degree that NO˙ is released within these thalamic nuclei around nerve terminals that originate from cells elsewhere, not by local synthesis per se. We need more physiological data that reveal how effectively the ACH and serotonin nerve cells in the human brainstem release NO˙ from their terminal fibers.
4. G. DiGiovanni, G. Ferraro, P. Sardo, et al. Nitric oxide modulates striatal neuronal activity via soluble guanylyl cyclase: An in vivo microiontophoretic study in rats. *Synapse* 2003; 48:100–107; M. Silva, S. Rose, J. Hindmarsh, et al. Inhibition of neuronal nitric oxide synthase increases dopamine efflux from rat striatum. *Journal of Neural Transmission* 2003; 110:353–362.
5. G. Ahern, V. Klyachko and M. Jackson. cGMP and *S*-nitrosylation: Two routes for modulation of neuronal excitability by NO. *Trends in Neurosciences* 2002; 25:510–517.
6. N. Bryan, T. Rassaf, R. Maloney, et al. Cellular targets and mechanisms of nitros(yl)ation: An insight into their nature and kinetics in vivo. *Proceedings of the National Academy of Sciences U S A* 2004; 101:4308–4313. Nonetheless, the widely publicized effects of Viagra (Sildenafil citrate) and related compounds hinge on their ability to block one particular enzyme (PDE 5). This phosphodiesterase would otherwise act to destroy cGMP and to reduce the normal ability of cGMP to increase the local flow of blood into the corpus cavernosum.
7. Ahern et al., cGMP and *S*-nitrosylation, p. 511. These are the (BK) channels. Higher NO˙ levels cause "*inhibition* of the electrical activity" of those large-conductance, calcium ion–activated, potassium ion BK channels that are usually activated by calcium ions. See also M. Espey, K. Miranda, D. Thomas, et al. Chemical perspective on the interplay between

NO, reactive oxygen species, and reactive nitrogen oxide species. *Annals of the New York Academy of Sciences* 2002; 962:195–206. This article provides a further chemical perspective on NO• and related molecules.

8. D. Buerk, B. Ances, J. Greenberg, et al. Temporal dynamics of brain tissue nitric oxide during functional forepaw stimulation in rats. *Neuroimage* 2003; 18:1–9. The diameters at the electrode tip ranged between 5 and 10 microns, an appropriate size to measure a minute puff of NO•. The local field potentials are from a much greater area. The paw received an electrical stimulus.
9. J. Williams, S. Vincent, and R. Reiner. Nitric oxide production in rat thalamus changes with behavioral state, local depolarization, and brainstem stimulation. *Journal of Neuroscience* 1997; 17:420–427.
10. S. Fukami, I. Uchida, T. Mashimo, et al. Gamma subunit dependent modulation by nitric oxide (NO) in recombinant $GABA_A$ receptor. *NeuroReport* 1998; 9:1089–1093.
11. Y. Li, W. Zhang, and J. Stern. Nitric oxide inhibits the firing activity of hypothalamic paraventricular neurons that innervate the medulla oblongata: Role of GABA. *Journal of Neuroscience* 2003; 118:585–601. These studies are in mice.
12. Cudeiro et al., Further observations. The oxidized form of nitric oxide, NO^+, *reduces* glutamate transmission. It reacts with the thiol groups of the NMDA receptor and inhibits the influx of calcium ions.
13. Ahern et al., cGMP and *S*-nitrosylation, 511. See also V. Jevtovic-Todorovic, S. Todorovic, S. Mennerick, et al. Nitrous oxide (laughing gas) is an NMDA antagonist, neuroprotectant and neurotoxin. *Nature Medicine* 1998; 4:460–463. It is of interest that *nitrous* oxide (N_2O) can also block glutamate receptors of the NMDA type in a distinctive manner.
14. H. Lin, B. Kang, F. Wan, et al. Reciprocal regulation of nitric oxide and glutamate in the nucleus tractus solitarii of rats. *European Journal of Pharmacology* 2000; 407:83–89. In the brain as a whole, NO• production increases when the levels of its arginine precursor increase. Under these conditions, GABA levels also increase, apparently secondary to a decrease in GABA breakdown. See V. Paul and A. Jayakumar. A role of nitric oxide as an inhibitor of γ-aminobutyric acid transaminase in rat brain. *Brain Research Bulletin* 2000; 51:43–46.
15. A. West and A. Grace. The nitric–guanylyl cyclase signaling pathway modulates membrane activity states and electrophysiological properties of striatal medium spiny neurons recorded in vivo. *Journal of Neuroscience* 2004; 24:1924–1935.
16. M. Echeverry, F. Guimaraes, and E. Del Bel. Acute and delayed restraint stress-induced changes in nitric oxide producing neurons in limbic regions. *Journal of Neuroscience* 2004; 125:981–983. Rats become acutely stressed when they are subjected to restraint for 2 hours.
17. V. Grange-Messent, D. Raison, B. Dugas, et al. Noradrenaline up-regulates the neuronal and the inducible nitric oxide synthase isoforms in magnocellular neurons of rat brain slices. *Journal of Neuroscience Research* 2004; 78:683–690.
18. F. Qingling, L. Xin, Y. Chaowu, et al. The level of nitric oxide in the cortex correlates well with brain lateralization. *NeuroReport* 2004; 15:1465–1468. For example, higher NO• levels occur in the left cortex of right-pawed mice.
19. K. Meador, J. Allison, D. Loring, et al. Topography of somatosensory processing: Cerebral lateralization and focused attention. *Journal of the International Neuropsychological Society* 2002; 8:349–359.
20. This point is referred to in the notes to chapter 28 on the insula, discussing the review article by A. Craig. How do you feel? Interoception: The sense of the physiological condition of the body. *Nature Reviews Neuroscience* 2002; 3:655–666.

21. E. Heinzen, R. Booth, and G. Pollack. Neuronal nitric oxide modulates morphine antinociceptive tolerance by enhancing constitutive activity of the mu-opioid receptor. *Biochemical Pharmacology* 2005; 69:679–688.
22. A. Argiolas and M. Melis. The role of oxytocin and the paraventricular nucleus in the sexual behavior of male mammals. *Physiological Behavior* 2004; 83:309–317.
23. J. Kiss and E. Vizi. Nitric oxide: A novel link between synaptic and nonsynaptic transmission. *Trends in Neurosciences* 2001; 24:211–215.
24. Y. Itzhak, K. Anderson, and S. Ali. Differential response of nNOS knockout mice to MDMA ("Ecstasy")-and methamphetamine-induced psychomotor sensitization and neurotoxicity. *Annals of the New York Academy of Science* 2004; 1025:119–128.
25. D. Klamar, E. Palsson, K. Fejgin, et al. Activation of a nitric-oxide-sensitive cAMP pathway with phencyclidine: elevated hippocampal CAMP levels are temporally associated with deficits in prepulse inhibition. *Psychopharmacology* 2005; 179:479–488.
26. V. Dawson. Potent neuroprotectants linked to bifunctional inhibition. *Proceedings of the National Academy of Sciences U S A* 1999; 96:10557–10558.
27. U. Fass, K. Panicker, D. Personett, et al. Differential vulnerability of primary cultured cholinergic neurons to nitric oxide excess. *NeuroReport* 2000; 11:931–936.
28. M. Packer, Y. Stasiv, A. Benraiss, et al. Nitric oxide negatively regulates mammalian adult neurogenesis. *Proceedings of the National Academy of Sciences U S A* 2003; 100:9566–9571. The dentate gyrus of the hippocampus is included among these reductions.
29. B. Giasson, J. Duda, I. Murray, et al. Oxidative damage linked to neurodegeneration by selective α-synuclein nitration in synucleinopathy lesions. *Science* 2000; 290:985–989. Electron microscopy could be used to help detect whether a local excess of such nitrated residues might have occurred, and persisted, in the brain of certain sage meditation masters (like Master Hakuin) who had experienced multiple repeated prior episodes of kensho-satori [Z:655–659, 676].
30. H. Yun, M. Gonzalez-Zulueta, V. Dawson, et al. Nitric oxide mediates *N*-methyl-D-aspartate receptor–induced activation of $p21^{ras}$. *Proceedings of the National Academy of Sciences U S A* 1998; 95:5773–5778.
31. S. Leong, R. Ruan, and Z. Zhang. A critical assessment of the neurodestructive and neuroprotective effects of nitric oxide. *Annals of the New York Academy of Sciences* 2002; 962:161–181. The "Jekyll and Hyde" aspects of $NO^{\bullet}$ are reviewed and critiqued. See also A. Contestabile, B. Monti, A. Contestabile, et al. Brain nitric oxide and its dual role in neurodegeneration/neuroprotection: Understanding molecular mechanisms to devise drug approaches. *Current Medical Chemistry* 2003; 10:2147–2174.
32. A. Bahra, M. Matharu, C. Buchel, et al. Brainstem activation specific to migraine headache. *Lancet* 2001; 357:1016–1017.
33. H. Steinbusch, J. Divente, and S. Vincent, eds. Functional neuroanatomy of the nitric oxide system. In *Handbook of Chemical Neuroanatomy*, vol. 17, eds. A. Bjorklund and T. Hokfelt. Amsterdam, Elsevier Science, 2000.
34. N. Marsh and A. Marsh. A short history of nitroglycerine and nitric oxide in pharmacology and physiology. *Clinical Experiments in Pharmacological Physiology* 2000; 27:313–319.
35. This information is accessed from a website discussing the effects of "poppers." The name comes from the sound made when the capsules are crushed. Besides amyl nitrite, other alkyl nitrites include isobutyl nitrite and butyl nitrite.
36. T. Lowry. Psychosexual aspects of the volatile nitrites. *Journal of Psychoactive Drugs* 1982; 14:77–79. The yellow and purple visual side effects may be of retinal origin.
37. R. Cytowic. *Synesthesia. A Union of the Senses.* 2nd ed. Cambridge, MA, MIT Press, 2002, 137.

38. R. Mathew, W. Wilson, and S. Tant. Regional cerebral blood flow associated with amyl nitrite inhalation. *Brain Journal of Addiction* 1989; 84:293–299.
39. S. Afridi, H. Kaube, and P. Goadsby. Glyceryl trinitrate triggers premonitory symptoms in migraineurs. *Pain* 2004; 110:675–680. Twelve patients also described other typical prodromal symptoms. Does NO• enter into some late phases of kensho?
40. C. Juhasz, T. Zsombok, E. Modos, et al. NO-induced migraine attack: Strong increase in plasma calcitonin gene–related peptide (CGRP) concentration and negative correlation with platelet serotonin release. *Pain* 2003; 106:461–170.
41. C. Tassorelli, F. Blandini, R. Greco, et al. Nitroglycerin enhances cGMP expression in specific neuronal and cerebrovascular structures of the rat brain. *Journal of Chemical Neuroanatomy* 2004; 27:23–32.
42. M. Wang, J. Urenjak, E. Fedele, et al. Effects of phosphodiesterase inhibition on cortical spreading depression and associated changes in extracellular cyclic GMP. *Biochemical Pharmacology* 2004; 67:1619–1627.
43. D. Kim, Y. Moon, H. Kim, et al. Effect of Zen Meditation on serum nitric oxide activity and lipid peroxidation. *Progress in Neuro-Psychopharmacology & Biological Psychiatry* 2005; 29:331. Factors related to gender, diet, smoking, alcohol, exercise, drug intake were considered to be comparable in the two groups.

Chapter 69 The Nitrous Oxide Connection

1. R. Provine. *Laughter. A Scientific Investigation*. New York, Viking, 2000, 158.
2. Ibid., 158.
3. Y. Ohashi, T. Guo, R. Orii, et al. Brain stem opioidergic and GABAergic neurons mediate the antinociceptive effect of nitrous oxide in Fischer rats. *Anesthesiology* 2003; 99:947–954; M. Fujinaga and M. Maze. Neurobiology of nitrous oxide–induced antinociceptive effects. *Molecular Neurobiology* 2002; 25:167–189. Most pain relief during the abdominal constriction test used in this particular assay is referable to synapses down in the spinal cord, whereas beta-endorphin has been shown to be involved in pain relief at higher levels (see chapter 35).
4. F. Cahill, E. Ellenberger, J. Mueller, et al. Antagonism of nitrous oxide antinociception in mice by intrathecally administered antisera to endogenous opioid peptides. *Journal of Biomedical Science* 2000; 7:299–303. Technical factors might explain why the antisera to beta-endorphin are ineffective.
5. S. Sawamura, M. Obara, K. Takeda, et al. Corticotropin-releasing factor mediates the antinociceptive action of nitrous oxide in rats. *Anesthesiology* 2003; 99:708–715. These responses were assayed by using the tail-flick latency test. The "activity" of the paraventricular nucleus and locus ceruleus was assessed histochemically. The CRF antagonist was injected into the cerebral ventricle. From there it could flow down and gain access to the locus ceruleus in the brainstem (and the amygdala en route).
6. S. Mennerick, V. Jevtovic-Todorovic, S. Todorovic, et al. Effect of nitrous oxide on excitatory and inhibitory synaptic transmission in hippocampal cultures. *Journal of Neuroscience* 1998; 18:9716–9726. NMDA receptors are blocked on postsynaptic cells.
7. V. Jevtovic-Todorovic, D. Wozniak, N. Benshoff, et al. A comparative evaluation of the neurotoxic properties of ketamine and nitrous oxide. *Brain Research* 2001; 895:264–267.
8. V. Jevtovic-Todorovic, J. Beals, N. Benshoff, et al. Prolonged exposure to inhalational nitrous oxide kills neurons in adult rat brain. *Neuroscience* 2003; 122:609–616.
9. K. Kaiyala, T. Thiele, C. Watson, et al. Nitrous oxide–induced c-Fos expression in the rat brain. *Brain Research* 2003; 967:73–80. "Active" sites were assessed with c-Fos techniques.

10. T. Suzuki, K. Ueta, M. Sugimoto, et al. Nitrous oxide and xenon inhibit the human (alpha 7) 5 nicotinic acetylcholine receptor expressed in *Xenopus* oocyte. *Anesthesia Analgesia* 2003; 96:443–448. Other receptors remain to be tested.
11. F. Gyulai, L. Firestone, M. Mintun, et al. In vivo imaging of nitrous oxide–induced changes in cerebral activation during noxious heat stimuli. *Anesthesiology* 1997; 86:538–548. This slight degree of exposure to 20% N_2O sufficed to reduce the PET evidence of pain-induced activation in the right thalamus and right anterior cingulate gyrus. These sites afford alternative explanations for the relief from pain.
12. S. Li, Y. Ohgami, Y. Dai, et al. Antagonism of nitrous oxide–induced anxiolytic-like behavior in the mouse light/dark exploration procedure by pharmacologic disruption of endogenous nitric oxide function. *Psychopharmacology* 2003; 166:366–372. N_2O increases the activity of $NO^{\bullet}$ synthase in both the cerebellum and striatum. See also S. Li, Y. Dai, and R. Quock. Antisense knockdown of neuronal nitric oxide synthase antagonizes nitrous oxide–induced behavior. *Brain Research* 2003; 968:167–170. This inhibitor reduces $NO^{\bullet}$ synthase activity in the cerebellum and hippocampus.

Chapter 70 Self-Abuse by Drugs

1. A. Braverman. *Mud and Water. A Collection of Talks by the Zen Master Bassui.* San Francisco, North Point Press, 1989, xxiii.
2. S. Batchelor. In *Zig Zag Zen. Buddhism and Psychedelics.* San Francisco, Chronicle, 2002, 9.
3. B. Warner. *Hardcore Zen.* Somerville, MA, Wisdom, 2003, 172.
4. K. Thomas. Transpersonal experiences—a need for re-evaluation. *Network* 2003; 83:15–18; C. Bache. Is the sacred medicine path a legitimate spiritual path? *Network* 2003; 81:19–22; K. Thomas. Disbelieving "Sacred Medicine." *Network* 83:29–31.
5. S. McFarlane. Morals and society in Buddhism. In *Companion Encyclopedia of Asian Philosophy*, eds. B. Carr and I. Mahalimgam. McFarland, London, Routledge, 1997, 452–467.
6. R. Forte. *Entheogens and the Future of Religion.* San Francisco, Council on Spiritual Practices, 1997; A. Badiner. *Zig Zag Zen. Buddhism and Psychedelics.* San Francisco, Chronicle, 2002. Many essays in this book appeared in *Tricycle* 1996 (fall); 6:34–109. One very impressive chapter in this book is entitled "A Trip Not Taken" (pp. 143–148). The author, an alcoholic before 1981, openly reviews the reasons she decided *not* to take yage (ayahuasca).
7. J. Austin. *Chase, Chance, and Creativity. The Lucky Art of Novelty.* Cambridge, MA, MIT Press, 2003, 108.
8. R. Forte. A conversation with R. Gordon Wasson. In *Entheogens and the Future of Religion.* San Francisco, Council on Spiritual Practices, 1997, 67–94.
9. Badiner, *Zig Zag Zen.*
10. R. Doblin. Pahnke's "Good Friday Experiment": A long-term follow-up and methodological critique. *Journal of Transpersonal Psychology* 1991; 23:1–28.
11. J. Horgan. *Rational Mysticism. Dispatches from the Border between Science and Spirituality.* Boston, Houghton Mifflin, 2003, 25–29. Houston Smith was one of the five group leaders who also took psilocybin during the so-called Miracle of Marsh Chapel in Boston. He had to leave this Good Friday service briefly in order to chase and bring back the divinity student who had become acutely agitated and delusional.
12. H. Smith. *Cleansing the Doors of Perception. The Religious Significance of Entheogenic Plants and Chemicals.* New York, Tarcher/Putnam/Penguin, 2000. One current premise is that society now requires ways to "transcend" itself, and that this would imply the kind of religious freedom which must have access to drugs. When educated societies worldwide are all composed of Houston Smiths, when drugs are free from all serious side effects, and people do not abuse the privilege, then this might become a tenable proposition.

13. H. Smith. *Tricycle* 1996; 6:77.
14. R. Aitken, in The Roundtable, *Tricycle* 1996; 6:109.
15. P. Matthiessen. Shadow paths. In Badiner, *Zig Zag Zen*, 85–88.
16. E. Davis. The paisley gate. In Badiner, *Zig Zag Zen*, 151–163.
17. J. Barlow. Liberty and LSD. In Badiner, *Zig Zag Zen*, 175–177.
18. A. Smith and C. Tart. Cosmic consciousness experience and psychedelic experiences: A first person comparison. *Journal of Consciousness Studies* 1998; 1:97–107. His elation reached a stage of ecstasy. The enveloping light became too intense to see any objects whatsoever in his field of vision.
19. M. Maxwell and V. Teschudin, eds. *Seeing the Invisible*. Cambridge, UK, Arkana (Penguin), 1990, 49–51.
20. Smith, *Cleansing the Doors of Perception*.
21. Ibid., 12.
22. M. McDonald-Smith. On the front lines. *Tricycle* 1996 (fall); 6:67–71.

Chapter 71 How Do Certain Drugs "Alter" Consciousness?

1. N. Zinberg. The study of conscious states, problems and progress. In *Alternate States of Consciousness*, ed. N. Zinberg. New York, Free Press, 1977, 1–36. The problems continue, amid the progress.
2. R. de la Torre, M. Farre, P. Roset, et al. Human pharmacology of MDMA: Pharmacokinetics, metabolism, and disposition. *Therapeutic Drug Monitoring* 2004; 26:137–144. How the MDMA "rave" subculture might affect both the incidence of STD (sexually transmitted disease), and of fetal abnormalities remains to be determined.
3. M. Liechti and F. Vollenweider. Which neuroreceptors mediate the subjective effects of MDMA in humans? A summary of mechanistic studies. *Human Psychopharmacology and Clinical Experimentation* 2001; 16:589–598.
4. K. Bolla, U. McCann, and G. Ricaurte. Memory impairment in abstinent MDMA ("Ecstasy") users. *Neurology* 1998; 51:1532–1537. An earlier article about neurotoxicity in monkeys appeared in *Science* 297, 2260–2263 (September 27, 2002). That toxicity was due to methamphetamine, *not* MDMA. The retraction that appeared a year later in *Science* 301, 1479 (September 12, 2003) need not lull users into a false sense of security about the potential harmful effects of MDMA abuse in humans.
5. J. Halpern, H. Pope, A. Sherwood, et al. Residual neuropsychological effects of illicit 3,4-methylenedioxymethamphetamine (MDMA) in individuals with minimal exposure to other drugs. *Drug and Alcohol Dependence* 2004; 16:135–147. The study controlled for confounding variables.
6. E. Frei, A. Gamma, R. Pascual-Marqui, et al. Localization of MDMA-induced brain activity in healthy volunteers using low resolution brain electromagnetic tomography (LORETA). *Human Brain Mapping* 2001; 14:152–165.
7. L. Reneman, J. Booij, C. Majoie, et al. Investigating the potential neurotoxicity of Ecstasy (MDMA): An imaging approach. *Human Psychopharmacology* 2001; 16:579–588.
8. R. Buchert, R. Thomasius, F. Wilke, et al. A voxel-based PET investigation of the long-term effects of "Ecstasy" consumption on brain serotonin transporters. *American Journal of Psychiatry* 2004; 16:1181–1189; R. Buchert, R. Thomasius, B. Nebeling, et al. Long-term effects of "Ecstasy" use on serotonin transporters of the brain investigated by PET. *Journal of Nuclear Medicine* 2003; 44:375–184. The serotonin transporter molecule literally transports serotonin back to the presynaptic terminal from which it was released. When current serotonin reuptake inhibitors act, some serotonin keeps hanging around in the synapse and continues to excite its receptors on the next postsynaptic cell.

9. Buchert et al., Long-term effects of "Ecstasy."
10. A. Gamma, E. Frei, L. Dietrich, et al. Mood state and brain electric activity in Ecstasy users. *NeuroReport* 2000; 11:157–162.
11. M. Liechti, C. Baumann, A. Gamma, et al. Acute psychological effects of 3,4-methylenedioxymethamphetamine (MDMA, "Ecstasy") are attenuated by the serotonin uptake inhibitor citalopram. *Neuropsychopharmacology* 2000; 22:513–521. This drug can interfere with the way MDMA acts on the serotonin transporter.
12. Ibid.
13. J. Lyles and J. Cadet. Methylenedioxymethamphetamine (MDMA, Ecstasy) neurotoxicity: Cellular and molecular mechanisms. *Brain Research* 2003; 42:155–168.
14. K. Jansen. The ketamine model of the near-death experience. *Journal of Near-Death Studies* 1997; 16:5–26. Jansen's article is followed by a series of six interdisciplinary critiques and by Jansen's response, 79–95.
15. F. Vollenweider. Brain mechanisms of hallucinogens and entactogens. *Dialogues in Clinical Neuroscience* 2001; 3:265–279. This article reviews the serotonergic hallucinogens, the NMDA antagonists, and MDMA (119 references).
16. F. Vollenweider, K. Leenders, I. Oye, et al. Differential psychopathology and patterns of cerebral glucose utilization produced by (*S*)- and (*R*)-ketamine in healthy volunteers using positron emission tomography (PET). *European Neuropsychopharmacology* 1997; 7:25–38.
17. F. Vollenweider. Advances and pathophysiological models of hallucinogenic drug actions in humans: A preamble to schizophrenia research. *Pharmacopsychiatry* 1998; 31:92–103. See also Vollenweider (note 15).
18. F. Vollenweider, P. Vontobel, I. Oye, et al. Effects of (*S*)-ketamine on striatal dopamine: A [^{11}C]raclopride PET study of a model psychosis in humans. *Journal of Psychiatric Research* 2000; 34:35–43. The evidence of increased DA release is calculated from the reduced binding of this labeled DA agonist. [The (*S*)-ketamine dosage was 15 mg during the first 5 minutes; then 0.014 mg/kg per minute for 90 minutes.] In a recent fMRI study, normal subjects who developed dissociative symptoms on ketamine also performed a visual discrimination task. Their task performance did not differ significantly from that on the placebo. (Their ketamine dosage was 0.5 mg/kg over 45–60 minutes.) This report illustrates that fMRI and PET studies may yield different results. The reasons could be related to experimental design, as well as to differences in sensitivity. See K. Abel, M. Allin, K. Kucharska-Pietura, et al. Ketamine and fMRI BOLD signal: Distinguishing between effects mediated by change in blood flow versus change in cognitive state. *Human Brain Mapping* 2003; 18:135–145.
19. L. Iversen. Cannabis and the brain. *Brain* 2003; 126:1252–1270.
20. F. Grotenhermen. Pharmacology of cannabinoids. *Neurological Endocrinology Letters* 2004; 25:14–23. These receptors are normally activated by anandamide, a natural lipid neuromessenger. This *endocannabinoid* enters into a potent, long-lasting self-inhibition of small GABA interneurons in the cortex. The result alters the firing properties of cortical networks. See A. Bacci, J. Huguenard, and D. Prince. Long-lasting self-inhibition of neocortical interneurons mediated by endocannobinoids. *Nature* 2004; 431:312–316. Researchers are now testing various cannabinoid derivatives. These retain THC's many beneficial effects on pain, muscle relaxation, immunosuppression, stimulation of appetite, and so on. The goal is to find molecules that lack the psychoactive side effects which are clearly undesirable from the standpoint of safety (e.g., while the patient is driving an automobile).
21. M. Lynskey, A. Heath, K. Bucholz, et al. Escalation of drug use in early-onset cannabis users vs co-twin controls. *Journal of the American Medical Association* 2003; 289:427–433.

22. S. Lukas, J. Mendelson, and R. Benedikt. Electroencephalographic correlates of marihuana-induced euphoria. *Drug and Alcohol Dependence* 1995; 37:1331–1340. The subjects' eyes were closed.
23. S. Patel, B. Cravatt, and C. Hillard. Synergistic interactions between cannabinoids and environmental stress in the activation of the central amygdala. *Neuropsychopharmacology* 2005; 30:497–507.
24. M. Solinas, A. Zangen, N. Thiriet, et al. Beta-endorphin elevations in the ventral tegmental area regulate the discriminative effects of Delta-9-tetrahydrocannabinol. *European Journal of Neuroscience* 2004; 19:183–192.
25. C. Lupica, A. Riegel, and A. Hoffman. Marijuana and cannabinoid regulation of brain reward circuits. *British Journal of Pharmacology* 2004; 143:227–234.
26. A. Ilan, M. Smith, and A. Gevins. Effects of marijuana on neurophysiological signals of working and episodic memory. *Psychopharmacology* 2004; 176:214–222.
27. D. D'Souza, E. Perry, L. MacDougall, et al. The psychotomimetic effects of intravenous Delta-9-tetrahydrocannabinol in healthy individuals: Implications for psychosis. *Neuropsychopharmacology* 2004; 29:1558–1572.
28. Iversen, Cannabis and the brain. Multiple drug use and constitutional predispositions may have been contributing factors.
29. S. Smith, P. Fried, M. Hogan, et al. Effects of prenatal marijuana on response inhibition: An fMRI study of young adults. *Neurotoxicology and Teratology* 2004; 26:533–543. This result begs the genetic question: To what degree does this prenatal exposure reflect the capacities for frontal lobe impulse control of their mothers and fathers?

Chapter 72 Triggers

1. K. Kraft. *Eloquent Zen. Daito and Early Japanese Zen*. Honolulu, University of Hawaii Press, 1992, 1282–1338.
2. L. Williams, M. Brammer, D. Skerrett, et al. The Neural correlates of orienting: An integration of fMRI and skin conductance orienting. *NeuroReport* 2000; 11:3011–3015.
3. E. Kirino, A. Belger, P. Goldman-Rakic, et al. Prefrontal activation evoked by infrequent target and novel stimuli in a visual target detection task: An event-related functional magnetic resonance imaging study. *Journal of Neuroscience* 2000; 20:6612–6618.
4. C. Haenschel, T. Baldeweg, R. Croft, et al. Gamma and beta frequency oscillations in response to novel auditory stimuli: A comparison of human electroencephalogram (EEG) data with in vitro models. *Proceedings of the National Academy of Sciences U S A* 2000; 97:7645–7650.
5. J. Houston. The Psychenaut Program: An exploration into some human potentials. *Journal of Creative Behavior* 1973; 7:253–278.
6. O. Fasold, M. von Brevern, M. Kuhberg, et al. Human vestibular cortex as identified with caloric stimulation in functional magnetic resonance imaging. *Neuroimage* 2002; 17:1384–1393.
7. K. Meador, P. Ray, L. Day, et al. Physiology of somatosensory perception: Cerebral lateralization and extinction. Left-handed subjects showed no right/left asymmetry in sensory thresholds. *Neurology* 1998; 51:721–727. See also the discussion of the issues raised in this interesting paper, by B. Anderson and K. Heilman. Touching and timing consciousness. *Neurology* 1998; 51:666–668.
8. Readers will find a further discussion of these issues in *Neurology* 1998; 51: 927–928.

Chapter 73 The Extraordinary Scope of Migraine: "The Hildegard Syndrome"

1. D. Pietrobon and J. Striessnig. Neurobiology of migraine. *Nature Reviews Neuroscience* 2003; 4:386–398. Figure 2, page 388, depicts Lashley's version of his scintillating scotoma.

2. O. Sacks. *Migraine. Understanding a Common Disorder*. Berkeley, University of California Press, 1985, xii. The 84 case reports in Oliver Sacks's review illustrate the phenomenology of migraine.
3. Ibid., 57.
4. Ibid., 87–89.
5. Ibid., 102.
6. R. Evans, R. Lipton, and S. Silberstein. The prevalence of migraine in neurologists. *Neurology* 2003; 61:1271–1272. In his later letter to the editor about this article, Sacks described his personal history of "classical migraines" dating back to his childhood. He cited "the extraordinary phenomena of the aura (which for me included transient or partial achromatopsia, etc.)." O. Sacks. The prevalence of migraine in neurologists. *Neurology* 2004; 62:342.
7. Pietrobon and Striessnig, Neurobiology of migraine.
8. M. Russell, B. Rasmussen, P. Thorvaldsen, et al. Prevalence and sex-ratio of the subtypes of migraine. *International Journal of Epidemiology* 1995; 24:612–618.
9. K. Abe, N. Oda, R. Araki, et al. Macropsia, micropsia, and episodic illusions in Japanese adolescents. *Journal of the American Academy of Childhood and Adolescent Psychiatry* 1989; 28:493–496. Extrapolating from table 2 in this report, micropsia was reported by 15% of the boys and 9% of the girls (25/166 vs. 21/223). This micropsia was not further characterized as involving half-fields or full fields. Two other episodic illusions were reported: "slow motion illusion," and "fast motion illusion." The questionnaire used to survey these high-school students received some validation during an additional survey of older university students that was confirmed by follow-up interviews. Among these 409 older students, 4% of the males and 4% of the females had episodes of illusions. Migraine appeared to be the basis for the illusions in at least half (five of the ten) of these students.
10. L. Cohen, F. Gray, C. Meyrignac, et al. Selective deficit of visual size perception: Two cases of hemimicropsia. *Journal of Neurology, Neurosurgery, and Psychiatry* 1994; 57:73–78. The man was 50 years old and had migraine. The woman was 60. Their persistent (hemi)micropsia was caused by a cerebral infarction. It reduced the size of objects on the same side as the hemivisual field defect. The authors cite another postmortem report with the "unexpected" finding of a small retrosplenial hemorrhage.
11. R. de Silva. A diagnostic sign in migraine? *Journal of the Royal Society of Medicine* 2001; 94:286–287.
12. L. Battelli, K. Black, and S. Wray. Transcranial magnetic stimulation of visual area V5 in migraine. *Neurology* 2002; 58:1066–1069.
13. S. Hall, G. Barnes, P. Furlong, et al. Spatiotemporal imaging of cortical desynchronization in migraine visual aura: A magnetoencephalography case study. *Headache* 2004; 44:204–208. The gamma band activity was measured at 30 to 80 cps. It slowly returned to normal over a 16-minute period. Further documentations by MEG are awaited.
14. B. Fierro, R. Ricci, A. Piazza, et al. 1 Hz rTMS enhances extrastriate cortex activity in migraine: Evidence of a reduced inhibition? *Neurology* 2003; 61:1446–1448.
15. A. Shepherd, J. Palmer, and G. Davis. Increased visual after-effects in migraine following pattern adaptation extend to simultaneous tilt illusion. *Spatial Vision* 2002; 16:33–43.
16. Y. Petrov and A. Popple. Effects of negative afterimages in visual illusions. *Journal of the Optical Society of America A. Optics and Image Science* 2002; 19:1107–1111.
17. Pietrobon and Striessnig, Neurobiology of migraine.
18. M. Estevez and K. Gardner. Update on the genetics of migraine. *Journal of Human Genetics* 2004; 114:225–235. A. A. P. Leão studied this slowly spreading cortical depression experimentally in 1944. Lashley in 1941 had estimated the way the process slowly progressed over his own cortex, during his own migraine aura.

19. J. Juhasz, T. Zsombok, E. Modos, et al. NO-induced migraine attack: Strong increase in plasma calcitonin gene–related peptide (CGRP) concentration and negative correlation with platelet serotonin release. *Pain* 2004; 106:461–470. Botulism toxin injections are currently used in the prophylaxis of migraine. Perhaps some of their effects are related to the way this toxin can act on trigeminal ganglia nerve cells to decrease the amount of this CGRP peptide they release. See P. Durham, R. Cady, and R. Cady. Regulation of calcitonin gene–related peptide secretion from trigeminal nerve cells by botulinum toxin type A: Implications for migraine therapy. *Headache* 2004; 44:35–42.
20. S. Afridi, M. Matharu, L. Lee, et al. A PET study exploring the laterality of brainstem activation in migraine using glyceryl trinitrate. *Brain* 2005; 128:932–939.
21. Sacks, *Migraine,* 106–108. The unusual range of unusual symptoms associated with migraine emphasizes that only with due caution is a second diagnosis of "hysteria" to be entertained. For a recent discussion of the *lux vivens* and the life of this twelfth century Benedictive abbess, see A. Dreyer *Passionate Spirituality: Hildegard of Bingen and Hadewijch of Brabant.* New York, Paulist Press, 2005.
22. I conducted a preliminary written survey of the prevalence of a "moonlight phase" in 2002. A cover letter, a simplified questionnaire (with yes/no boxes to check), and a stamped self-addressed return envelope were mailed to 46 accomplished teachers worldwide, representing various schools of Soto, Rinzai, Tibetan, and Theravada Buddhism.

    Three questionnaires were filled out and returned. None indicated awareness of such a phenomenon. Three other letters came from Zen teachers, explaining that they chose *not* to respond. To them, not only was the survey pointless but the author was "barking up the wrong tree" (see table 12, chapter 101).
23. F. Wilkinson. Auras and other hallucinations: Windows on the visual brain. *Progress in Brain Research* 2004; 144:305–320.

Chapter 74 The Varieties of Absorption

1. The various phenomena of that 1974 episode are presented in another visual form in [Z:507, figure 17]. The reticular cap inhibits sensory relay nuclei [Z:590].
2. For example, the table does not specify the more generalized excitations rising up from the brainstem reticular activating system and relaying through its extensions. These would be contributing more diffusely to the excitation of local sites at several successive levels.
3. E. D'Aquili and A. Newburg. *The Mystical Mind. Probing the Biology of Religious Experience.* Minneapolis, Fortress Press, 1999, 91, 111, 115. It would far exceed the scope of this book to critique the highly speculative nature of others' theories. The interested reader is referred to the original writings themselves. For one recent theological critique, see I. Delio. Brain science and the biology of belief: A theological response. *Zygon* 2003; 38:573–785.
4. R. Forman. *Mysticism, Mind, Consciousness.* Albany, State University of New York Press, 1999, 21–24.
5. It would be helpful to have more details.
6. Sheng Yen. Dharma of teachings, dharma of mind. *Chan Magazine* 2005 (summer); 25:6–13. Such lengthy absorptions are rare. We await precise details and objective measurements in this millennium.
7. T. Fehr. The role of simplicity (effortlessness) as a prerequisite of the experience of Pure Consciousness—the non-dual state of Oneness: "Turiya," "Samadhi" in meditation. *Journal for Meditation and Meditation Research* 2002; 1:49–77. The term *Advaita* is derived from "A-dvaita" meaning "not two" (see part VII).
8. T. Fehr. From the vedas to the EEG: Characteristics of altered "higher" states of consciousness. *Journal for Meditation and Meditation Research* 2002; 1:82–83.

Chapter 75 Space

1. K. Heilman, R. Watson, and E. Valenstein. Spatial neglect. In *The Cognitive and Neural Basis of Spatial Neglect*, eds. H.-O. Karnath, A. Milner, and G. Vallar. Oxford, Oxford University Press, 2002, 3–30.
2. Karnath et al., *Spatial Neglect*. See note 1.
3. F. Previc. The neuropsychology of 3-D space. *Psychological Bulletin* 1998; 124:123–164. Elsewhere, our normal hidden capacity for sensate inferences is referred to as "unconscious circumspatial awareness" [Z:488]. The term "ambient vision" refers to the particular visual experience of witnessing unbounded space in every direction [Z:495–499].
4. A. Farne and E. Ladavas. Auditory peripersonal space in humans. *Journal of Cognitive Neuroscience* 2002; 14:1030–1043.
5. M. Behrmann and J. Geng. What is "left" when all is said and done? Spatial coding and hemispatial neglect. In *The Cognitive and Neural Basis of Spatial Neglect*, eds. H.-O. Karnath, A. Milner, and G. Vallar. Oxford, Oxford University Press, 2002, 85–100. Gravity contributes in covert ways to our visceral and visual frames of reference. Though the force of gravity might seem to "pull" from outside us, we still register its signals *preconsciously* inside us by virtue of (1) the otoliths in our vestibular system, and by other proprioceptive and tactile systems; and (2) the influence that gravity's vertical actions have on visual landmarks (e.g., we make use of the fact that tree trunks and walls stand at 90 degrees to the earth's surface).

   The right and left sides of an individual object out in space also seem to be coded allocentrically (with respect to the midline of this particular object). However, opinions differ, as Olson discusses (see note 6). Some interpret this evidence to suggest that the brain still maintains its usual covert egocentric attentional gradient while in the act of processing each such object out in object-centered space.
6. C. Olson. Brain representation of object-centered space in monkeys and humans. *Annual Review of Neuroscience* 2003; 26:331–354.
7. H. Rao, T. Zhou, Y. Zhuo, et al. Spatiotemporal activation of the two visual pathways in form discrimination and spatial location: A brain mapping study. *Human Brain Mapping* 2003; 18:79–89.
8. Behrmann and Geng, What is "left."

Chapter 76 Affirming One Reality: A Commentary on the Sandokai

1. D. Suzuki. In *The Awakening of Zen*, ed. C. Humphreys. Boulder, CO, Prajna Press, x. Suzuki responded after a minute-long pause. One can assume that the ancient Zen masters responded to questions instantly. Those persons close to D. T. Suzuki were familiar with his long silent moments. He would close his eyes, and no one could tell whether he was in deep meditation or fast asleep. These silent intervals were known as "doing a Suzuki."
2. *The Shambhala Dictionary of Buddhism and Zen*. Boston, Shambhala, 1991, 190. Both the original verse, and Shih-t'ou's other eighth-century writings are of special interest to historians. They influenced the much more elaborate metaphysical interpretations of similar themes that would be made later by his Ts'ao-tung (Jap. *Soto*) followers during the next and subsequent centuries.

   At Ch'ang-an (near present-day Xi'an), Seng-chao was a gifted, young disciple of Kumarajiva (344–413), his esteemed Indian teacher whose translation bureau was responsible for rendering important Indian Buddhist writings into Chinese. Even Kumarajiva acknowledged that to read the old sutras in translation was "like eating rice that someone else had already chewed."

3. N. Foster and J. Shoemaker. *The Roaring Stream: A New Zen Reader*. Hopewell, NJ, Ecco Press, 1996, cf. 38–43. The authors are to be congratulated on their succinct translation of the key phrase. To "comprehend the myriad things *as the self*" (implying that they *are* the self) is the essence of category III. This issue is discussed at length in chapter 78.
4. Sheng-yen, ed. *The Poetry of Enlightenment. Poems by Ancient Ch'an Masters*. Elmhurst, NY, Dharma Drum Publications, 1987, cf. 670.
5. J. Loori. *Two Arrows Meeting in Mid-Air. The Zen Koan*. Boston, Charles Tuttle, 1994, xi.
6. Sheng-yen, *The Poetry of Enlightenment*. Sheng-yen notes that Shih-t'ou chose the same title for his poem that a Taoist scholar and master had used for an earlier book.
7. T. Cleary. *Timeless Spring. A Soto Zen Anthology*. New York, Wheelwright Press, Weatherhill, 1980, cf. 36–39.
8. Foster and Shoemaker, *The Roaring Stream*.
9. S. Suzuki. *Branching Streams Flow in the Darkness. Zen Talks on the Sandokai*, eds. M. Weitsman and M. Wenger. Berkeley, University of California Press, 1999, cf. 20–21, 190–191.
10. B. Glassman. *Infinite Circle. Teachings in Zen*. Boston, Shambhala, 2002, cf. 77–78.
11. H. Dumoulin. *Zen Buddhism: A History*, vol. 1, *India and China*. New York, Macmillan, 1988, 229. Such a custom implied that we were ordinarily left in the dark about the noumenal domain. The reader, like myself, may wonder how often some old masters (including Dogen) might also have been alluding (covertly) to the "darkness" of the late lunar phase of kensho and to the impression that its "light" was like that of the moon.
12. Sheng-yen, *The Poetry of Enlightenment*.
13. This free translation is intended to serve only as a background for the particular themes in this book. The next chapters are relevant to the interpretations I choose to make in trying to resolve some inherent paradoxes and ambiguities in Shih-t'ou's verse. The interested reader is referred to notes 3, 4, 7, 9, and 10 for further discussions of various classic interpretations of the Sandokai.

Chapter 77 Varieties of "Oneness" and "Unity." Category I: A and B

1. I. Miura and R. Sasaki. *Zen Dust. The History of the Koan and Koan Study in Rinzai (Lin-Chi) Zen*. New York, Harcourt, Brace & World, 1966, 179–186, 296–300, 379–381, 415–418. Note 139 on p. 312 illustrates the "solid white circle" of such a fourth rank.
2. Worldwide, the circle is an ancient metaphysical and religious symbol in itself, apart from a specific reference to the moon. In China, it was often used (especially by the house of Kuei-Yang) during the Tang era of Ch'an. See T. Cleary, *Classics of Buddhism and Zen*, vol. 1. Boston, Shambhala, 2001, 278–283.
3. The importance of this distinction was openly discussed on 16 May 1998 with a senior author whose prior publications had suggested that meditators often entered a major, advanced unitive experience termed "Absolute Unitary Being." On this occasion, we readily came to agree that the vast majority of such meditative experiences were only states of absorption, not advanced states of genuine enlightenment.
4. A. Hardy. *The Spiritual Nature of Man: A Study of Contemporary Religious Experience*. Oxford, Clarendon Press, 1979, 25–29.
5. *Shambhala Dictionary of Buddhism and Zen*. Boston, Shambhala, 1991, 65. In short, "Oneness" or "Unity" means the insight of *one* reality, not two. It is not an insight that can be imagined. The words used in these pages describe the way events seemed *at that moment*. The reader, and the writer, understand that no such "realization" guarantees absolute Reality. "Suchness" was not a word I was aware of until later (see chapter 82). Capitals are used as a literary device to indicate the unusual quality of the experience. They have no esoteric significance.

6. This phase B realization of oneness fades with time. Repeated meditation might seem to bring it slightly closer, but not to a point that can approach or sustain the clarity of that one profound experience, during kensho, when samsara and nirvana become identical.

   A softer realization arrived slightly later. It entered directly, as does an intuition, and it lacked the "feel" that one associates with logical thought processes. This message was also clear, instantaneous, un-thought-out. It was the full appreciation of an obvious fact: *this experience cannot be described*. Not until weeks later would I associate this intuition with the term *ineffability* a word that had no real meaning for me prior to kensho [Z:515–516].

   Is kensho indescribable? These pages indicate that compulsive observers in the health sciences who are trained to take a careful case history, and who remain mindful, will persist in trying to describe its details. Even though their self has been "absent," a "witnessing awareness" (the experiant) still continues to register and remember. An analogy for readers who find this hard to believe would be the way the tape recorder on their telephone still goes on recording messages even after they have left the house.
7. A subsidiary logical thought became obvious in the interim: it was those intrusive veils of my egocentric self that had been obscuring and distorting the true view of "real Reality." These are the obscurations and distortions self-imposed by the "*I-Me-Mine*" (see figure 2, chapter 10).

Chapter 78 Varieties of "Oneness" and "Unity." Provisional Categories II and III

1. S. King. Awakening stories of Zen Buddhist women. In *Buddhism in Practice*, ed. D. Lopez Jr. Princeton, NJ, Princeton University Press, 1995, 513–524. The writer was 49 years old.
2. Note two risks that can arise in relation to the advanced state of insight in category II. The first risk is that its quasi-somatic component might be confused with a superficial external absorption, one whose shallow "mergings" had not yet completely shed all the physical layers of its body image.

   However, states in category II that develop in a calm, Buddhist meditative setting often arrive with a relatively clear sensorium in which vision is intact. In many Zen Buddhist retreats the mirrors are covered, as part of a whole process of deemphasizing the self. However, among the Western accounts cited in note 5 below is evidence indicating that an unusually stressful mental condition of intense mental anguish often precedes the more visionary and prophetic experiences.

   Second, this "quasi-somatic" component could also run the risk of being devalued because its externalized image might seem to take the form of an out-of-body experience or a benign hallucination. This latter term means only that it is an unusual sensate experience unexplained by any overt natural *external* stimulus at that time.
3. Note three risks related to category III. First, it is in the nature of a global existential insight to run the risk of being dismissed as merely "metaphysical" by someone uninformed, and to risk being overvalued by the person who experiences it. Neither extreme position is warranted, given the remarkable (if still underappreciated) potentials of the human brain. Third, the word "psychic" may be misunderstood to carry implications of supernatural powers, also unwarranted.
4. B. Warner. *Hardcore Zen*. Somerville, MA, Wisdom, 2003, 96–97. This contemporary example is chosen because the sentences clearly describe phenomena that represent a change in perception. The scope and depth of the accompanying release are, of course, known to their original author.
5. M. Maxwell and V. Tschudin, eds. *Seeing the Invisible. Modern Religious and Other Transcendent Experiences*. Cambridge, UK, Arkana, Penguin, 1990, 134. This edited anthology begins with the instructive caveat that these accounts are "of experiences, and therefore each is

totally unique, personal and completely subjective." This book distinguishes mystical experiences—characterized "by a sense of union"—from numinous experiences, characterized "by a sense of the presence of God." Most experiences arrived when the person was alone.

6. E. Kohler, C. Keysers, M. Umilta, et al. Hearing sounds, understanding actions: Action representation mirror neurons. *Science* 2002; 297:846–848.
7. C. Keysers, E. Kohler, M. Umilta, et al. Audiovisual mirror neurons and action recognition. *Experimental Brain Research* 2003; 153:628–636.
8. N. Ramnani and R. Miall. A system in the human brain for predicting the actions of others. *Nature Neuroscience* 2004; 7:85–90; V. Gallese. The roots of empathy: The shared manifold hypothesis and the neural basis of intersubjectivity. *Psychopathology* 2003; 36:171–180. The current data do not establish a perfect one-to-one correspondence between the sites in the brains of the two human subjects. However, the following hypothesis is plausible: When we *infer* that someone else is experiencing certain actions, sensations, or emotions, we too may develop somewhat *similar* neural configurations. At this moment, ours resemble the ones that *we* develop when *we* engage in this same motor behavior or feel the same sensations or emotions.
9. T. Shallice. "Theory of mind" and the prefrontal cortex. *Brain* 2001; 124:247–248.
10. R. Saxe and N. Kanwisher. People thinking about people. The role of the temporo-parietal junction in "theory of mind." *Neuroimage* 2003; 19:1835–1842.
11. By an interesting coincidence, this particular chant, by Zen Master Hakuin, does invoke the most advanced, inclusive levels of the Universal Oneness under discussion. Indeed, it begins with the line: "From the beginning, all beings are Buddha", and it ends with "This very body [is] the body of Buddha."
12. K. Tanahashi, ed. *Moon in a Dewdrop. Writings of Zen Master Dogen*. San Francisco, North Point Press, 1985, 70.
13. H.-J. Kim. *Flowers of Emptiness. Selections from Dogen's Shobogenzo. Studies in Asian Thought and Religion*, vol. 2. Lewiston/Queenstown, ON, Canada, Edwin Mellen Press, 1985, 52.
14. N. Waddell and M. Abe. *The Heart of Dogen's Shobogenzo*. Albany, State University of New York Press, 2002, 41. These authors interpret some of Dogen's next lines to suggest that the truth of the dharma is inseparable from oneself and is not to be found externally. In footnote number 10 on p. 41, they conclude that "When you are free from attachment to self and attachment to Dharma, [then] you receive the transmission of the Dharma." This is a process of "awakening to the Dharma inherent in oneself."
15. Ibid., 41.
16. J. Loori. *The Eight Gates of Zen. A Program of Zen Training*. Boston, Shambhala, 2002, 87.

Chapter 79 Varieties of "Oneness" and "Unity." Provisional Category IV

1. K. Tanahashi, ed. *Moon in a Dewdrop. Writings of Zen Master Dogen*. San Francisco, North Point Press, 1985, 69. If sensory boundaries between self and other become so blurred "that myriad things advance and experience themselves," and if "everything becomes one," then couldn't such an experience of oneness and unity be a kind of "global synesthesia." (see chapter 54 for a discussion of synesthesias.)
2. S. Bodian. The taboo of enlightenment. *Tricycle* 2004; 14:44–47, 108–111. An interview with Adyashanti, a.k.a. Steve Gray.
3. C. Phipps. No escape for the ego: An interview with venerable Master Sheng-yen. *What is Enlightenment?* 2000 (spring/summer); 17:50–58, 158–159, 162.
4. Sheng-yen. *Subtle Wisdom. Understanding Suffering, Cultivating Compassion through Ch'an Buddhism*. New York, Doubleday, 1999, 104–105.

5. Ibid. The path of the Bodhisattva outlined by Sheng-yen reserves full enlightenment for only a very rare advanced stage. Then such true wisdom comes "undetected and unannounced." Self-consciousness no longer exists, because now the truly "wise person has no special feeling of being wise." In short, the selfless, fully enlightened sage is liberated, having been released from all unfruitful attitudes of longing, loathing, fear, and attachment. Here the word "illusory" is being used in the ordinary sense of a person being deluded.
6. Phipps, No escape for the ego.
7. Sheng-yen, *Subtle Wisdom.* Sometimes nonmeditators experience states that include some degrees of self-in-oneness without having undergone long prior spiritual training. How can this be? Buddhist teachings envision these potential psychic circuits as being innate in everyone's brain. Formal meditative training and mindful introspection are viewed as serving to nurture and sponsor the development of natural capacities. And once the person's ethical nature had matured more fully in a monastic context, the added enlightenment experiences could go on to have more potent transforming effects on the personality. Moreover, when these fruitful effects are actualized in everyday life, they could tend to endure longer.
8. R. Saxe, S. Carey, and N. Kanwisher. Understanding other minds: Linking developmental psychology and functional neuroimaging. *Annual Review of Psychology* 2004; 55:87–124.
9. A. Calarge, N. Andreasen, and D. O'Leary. Visualizing how one brain understands another: A PET study of theory of mind. *American Journal of Psychiatry* 2003; 160:1954–1964. Included among the regions involved (mostly in the left hemisphere) are the medial and superior frontal cortex, the anterior and retrosplenial cingulate cortex, and the anterior temporal pole.
10. Sheng-yen, *Subtle Wisdom.*
11. Bodian, The taboo of enlightenment. The question that arose with the birdcall is reminiscent of that in the koan used by Zen Master Bassui: "Who is hearing this sound?" *Proprioceptive* is the general term referring to sensations of position arising from within the body. Kinesthetic implies a sense of movement of the body.
12. O. Blanke, T. Landis, L. Spinelli, et al. Out-of-body experience and autoscopy of neurological origin. *Brain* 2004; 127:243–258 (see also note 14, chapter 52). In out-of-body experiences, witnesses see their own body and the outside world from a location *other* than their habitual, grounded, egocentric perspective. For example, they may seem to be looking down at their own body from above. Neither autoscopy nor out-of-body projected experiences per se have spiritual significance. Note that in order for similar externalized visual phenomena to be included in the discussion of the category II qualities of "Oneness" in chapter 78, it would need to be assumed that they are accompanied by the other qualities that are characteristic of genuine deep states of insight, and are not simply shallow, isolated disorders of elementary perception and recognition.
13. A. Schnider, V. Treyer, and A. Buck. Selection of currently relevant memories by the human posterior medial orbitofrontal cortex. *Journal of Neuroscience* 2000; 20:5880–5884.

Chapter 80 Prajna: Insight-Wisdom

1. H. Inagaki. *A Dictionary of Japanese Buddhist Terms.* Union City, CA, Heian International, 1988, 249.
2. Sheng-yen. The sixth paramita: Wisdom. *Chan Magazine* 2003 (winter); 6. Other ideograms include brightness and absolute transparency and being completely at ease with no obstructions.
3. Inagaki, *A Dictionary of Japanese Buddhist Terms*, 288.

Chapter 81 Words for the Inexpressible

1. H. Inagaki. *A Dictionary of Japanese Buddhist Terms*. Union City, CA, Heian International, 1988, 249. *Satori* is defined simply as "enlightenment" in this dictionary. In a standard dictionary for the general reader, one can look in vain for entries for satori and kensho (e.g., *Kenkyusha's Japanese dictionary* [eighth edition] Tokyo, Kenkyusha, 1984). Yet one does find *kenosis*, a technical term useful in a Christian theological context. It means "to empty," and it implies the emptying of all of our egocentric tendencies. This "emptying" is an essential aspect of Zen.
2. S. Shigematsu. *A Zen Forest. Sayings of the Masters*. New York, Weatherhill, 1981.
3. Although this very first message of inexpressibility seemed almost "reflexive" at first, it would evolve into a more fully developed thought form much later.
4. Inagaki, *A Dictionary of Japanese Buddhist Terms*.
5. E. Wood. *Zen Dictionary*. Rutland, VT, Charles Tuttle, 1988, 154. Wood goes beyond Inagaki when he defines *kensho-godo* as the direct realization that one's basic nature is identical with the ultimate reality of the universe (and therefore amounts to satori). With regard to *Samyak sambuddhi*, *samyak* means "correct"; *sambodhi* means "complete knowing," "deep comprehension."
6. Shigematsu, *A Zen Forest*, 3. Zen's characteristic distaste for wordy discourse is embedded in the old descriptive phrase, "the sect which does not establish words" (*Furyu monji no shu*).

Chapter 82 Suchness and the Noumenon: An Allocentric Perspective

1. D. Suzuki. *Studies in Zen*. New York, Delta, 1955, 141–142.
2. S. Suzuki. *Zen Mind, Beginner's Mind*. New York, Weatherhill, 1975, 33, 66.
3. S. Schumacher and G. Woerner, eds. *The Encyclopedia of Eastern Philosophy and Religion*. Boston, Shambhala, 1994, 364.
4. P. Guyer and A. Wood, eds. and trans. *Critique of Pure Reason. Immanuel Kant*. Cambridge, UK, Cambridge University Press, 1998.
5. Kant, Quoted in Guyer and Wood, *Critique of Pure Reason*, 362–363.
6. E. Cassirer. *Kant's Life and Thought*. New Haven, CT, Yale University Press, 1981; P. Guyer, ed. *The Cambridge Companion to Kant*. Cambridge, UK, Cambridge University Press, 1991, 1–61. However, Kant's early extreme disaffection with metaphysics evolved after 1766. Soon, for example, in his dissertation of 1770, he would write that we could use our conceptual categories to develop a "paradigm" of "NOUMENAL PERFECTION [*sic*]." He viewed this positive noumenal paradigm as both equivalent to God in theory and to moral perfection in practice (see note 4, p. 39). Something caused Kant to shift his ground. What also fueled his remarkable continuing literary productivity? The underlying motivations for Kant's quest still await a satisfactory explanation.
7. Kant, Quoted in Guyer and Wood, *Critique of Pure Reason*, 168, 185.
8. P. Edwards, ed. *The Encyclopedia of Philosophy*. New York, vol. 4. Macmillan, 1967, 315.
9. Ibid., vol. 7, 327–332. Hegel also objected to the way Kant viewed the universe.
10. Ibid., vol. 6, 135–151; vol. 4, 96–98.
11. T. Nhat Hanh. *Living Buddha, Living Christ*. New York, Riverhead, 1995, 204. As discussed in chapter 76 and in appendix A, sages in ancient India and China had long before intuited concepts suggesting a harmonious, unified universe. In such a domain, each particular relative phenomenon was not to be viewed as totally walled off in one compartment from every absolute noumenal universality. Instead, everything existed in a vast, dynamically interfused domain. See also Chang Chung-Yuan, *Original Teaching of Chan Buddhism*. New York, Pantheon, 1969, 42–54.

12. Guyer and Wood, *Critique of Pure Reason.*
13. Cassirer, *Kant's Life and Thought*, 216–217, 250–266.
14. J. Austin. Consciousness evolves when the self dissolves. *Journal of Consciousness Studies*, 2000; 7:209–230.
15. *The Encyclopedia Americana. International Edition*, vol. 20. Danbury, CT, Grolier, 1997, 756.
16. Suchness includes not just the "Big Picture" in its "big frame," but also the details. Waddell and Abe interpret Dogen's "awakening to the Dharma inherent in oneself" as manifesting the "ultimate reality in which all things exist in their distinctive individuality and are at the same time identical in their manifestation of suchness." See N. Waddell and M. Abe. *The Heart of Dogen's Shobogenzo*. Albany, State University of New York Press, 2002, 39–45.
17. S. Suzuki, *Zen Mind, Beginner's Mind.*
18. Guyer and Wood, *Critique of Pure Reason*, chap. 4, The Transcendental Deduction of the Categories, 134–160. Kant's thought processes continually evolved. His handwritten marginal notes indicate that he was mulling over such critical matters between the years 1771 and 1777.

Chapter 83 The Construction of Time

1. D. Fish, P. Gloor, F. Quesney, et al. Clinical responses to electrical brain stimulation of the temporal and frontal lobes in patients with epilepsy. *Brain* 1993; 116:397–414.
2. R. Henson, M. Rugg, T. Shallice, et al. Recollection and familiarity in recognition memory: An event-related functional magnetic resonance imaging study. *Journal of Neuroscience* 1999; 19:3962–3972.
3. S. Perbal, N. Ehrle, S. Samson, et al. Time estimation in patients with right or left medial-temporal lobe resection. *NeuroReport* 2001; 5:939–942.
4. S. Pollman, R. Weidner, G. Humphreys, et al. Separating distractor rejection and target detection in posterior parietal cortex—an event related fMRI study of visual marking. *Neuroimage* 2003; 18:310–323.
5. V. Walsh. Time: The back-door of perception. *Trends in Cognitive Sciences* 2003; 7:335–338.
6. Ibid., 337.
7. M. Mimura, M. Kinsbourne, and M. O'Connor. Time estimation by patients with frontal lesions and by Korsakoff amnesics. *Journal of the International Neuropsychological Society* 2000; 6:517–528.
8. M. Suzuki, T. Fujii, T. Tsukiura, et al. Neural basis of temporal context memory: A functional MRI study. *Neuroimage* 2002; 17:1790–1796. Sequencing between two different lists requires more mental effort.
9. J. Halliwel, J. Perez-Mercader, and W. Zurek, eds., *Physical Origins of Time Asymmetry*. Cambridge, UK, Cambridge University Press, 1994. See also G. Whitrow, *What Is Time?* Oxford, Oxford University Press, 2003, for a general discussion of the many aspects of time.
10. N. Fortin, K. Agster, and H. Eichenbaum. Critical role of the hippocampus in memory for sequences of events. *Nature Reviews Neuroscience* 2002; 5:458–462. In these rats, hippocampal lesions cause a severe, selective loss of the ability to remember the sequence of a series of colors, but do not impair the capacity to recognize odors that had arrived recently.
11. A. Damasio. Remembering when. *Scientific American* 2002 (September); 68–73.
12. C. Morin, J. Guigot, R. Manai, et al. Impairment in clock-time estimation following right hemisphere ischemic damage. *Cognitive Brain Research* 2005; 22:305–307.
13. L. Nyberg, A. McIntosh, R. Cabeza, et al. General and specific brain regions involved in encoding and retrieval of events: What, where, and when. *Proceedings of the National Academy of Sciences U S A* 1996; 93:11280–11285. The tasks involved words that were presented visually.

14. N. Ross. *The World of Zen. An East-West Anthology*. New York, Vintage Books, 1960, 75. This old Zen tale was originally included in P. Reps and N. Senzaki. *Zen Flesh, Zen Bones: A Collection of Zen and Pre-Zen Writings*. Rutland, VT, Charles Tuttle, 1957.

Chapter 84 Disorders and Dissolutions of Time

1. K. Abe, N. Oda, R. Araki, et al. Macropsia, micropsia and episodic illusions in Japanese adolescents. *Journal of the American Academy of Child and Adolescent Psychiatry* 1989; 28:493–496. This article does not specify how many of these episodes were fast- or slow-motion illusions of time, as contrasted with the different kind of visual illusions that had increased the size of objects (macropsia) or had decreased them (micropsia).
2. Ibid.
3. P. Rapp and J. Bachevalier. Cognitive development and aging. In *Fundamental Neuroscience*, 2nd ed., eds. L. Squire, F. Bloom, S. McConnell, et al. San Diego, Academic Press, 2003, 1167–1200.
4. V. Hasse, L. Dinez, G. Wood, et al. The temporal structure of conscious mental states. *Journal of the Brazilian Association for the Advancement of Science* 1998; 50:153–158.
5. *Achronia* is definable as that zero quality within consciousness when all prior sense of time drops out. Its absence is appreciated afterward. The term could fit comfortably (both in these pages and in the index) next to achromia, a word found in some dictionaries to refer to the absence of color. Deeper experiences of achronia could occur in states of Ultimate Pure Being [Z:627–630].
6. This in itself is a remarkable preservation of the sequences that register in immediate memory. Prior training in mindful meditative practices could contribute.
7. N. Fortin, K. Agster, and H. Eichenbaum. Critical role of the hippocampus in memory for sequences of events. *Nature Neuroscience* 2002; 5:458–462.
8. B. Shanon. Altered temporality. *Journal of Consciousness Studies* 2001; 8:35–58. This citation is not an endorsement. The recipe for this brew includes the bark of a South American vine (it includes mild hallucinogens which block the action of monoamine oxidase), plus some shrub leaves. These leaves contain DMT (*N,N*-dimethyltriptamine), as well as various alkaloids such as harmaline and harmine. The article does confirm several of the observations that time dissolves into infinity in kensho, reported in the same journal (J. Austin. Consciousness evolves when the self dissolves. *Journal of Consciousness Studies* 2000; 7:209–230). Shanon makes a distinction between this particular ayahuasca drug state of "altered temporality" and a different kind of atemporality that includes a total stillness and a cessation. When this particular quality of silence and stasis occurs during a superficial experience on drugs, and when it is *not* coupled with major insightful meanings, then it might represent that preliminary change in the sense of time that can be experienced, without drugs, in internal absorption [Z:430].

Chapter 85 Emptiness

1. E. Conze, ed. Buddhist Texts through the Ages. Boston, Shambhala 1990, 91 (Samyutta-nikaya IV, 54). This is from the third collection of ancient sutras.
2. Ibid., 91 (Majjhima-nikaya I, 297–298). This is from the second collection of ancient sutras, said to date back to the first Buddhist Council around 480 B.C.E., shortly after Buddha died.
3. Ibid., 164. Sikshasamuccaya.
4. Ibid., 164. Sikshasamuccaya, 264 (Dharma Sangiti Sutra).
5. E. Conze, trans. *The Large Sutra of Perfect Wisdom*. Berkeley, University of California Press, 1975, 144–148.

6. F. Cook. *Hua-yen Buddhism. The Jewel Net of Indra.* University Park, Pennsylvania State University Press, 1981, 37–44.
7. Ibid., 38.
8. Ibid., 97.
9. S. Mitchell. *The Enlightened Mind. Anthology of Sacred Prose.* New York. Harper Perennial 1991; 59. The Madhyamika (Middle Way) school of Mahayana Buddhism stressed that liberation was also implicit in shunyata, not only the emptiness of the self.

Chapter 87 Problem Words: "Pure Consciousness"; "Being"; "Cosmic"

1. Edward Carpenter, Quoted in R. Bucke. *Cosmic Consciousness. A Study in the Evolution of the Human Mind.* Secaucus, NJ, Citadel Press, 1973, 202.
2. R. Forman, ed. *The Problem of Pure Consciousness: Mysticism and Philosophy.* New York, Oxford University Press, 1990.
3. J. Austin. Six points to ponder. *Journal of Consciousness Studies* 1999; 6(2–3):213–216.
4. G.-C. Chang. *The Practice of Zen.* New York, Harper, 1959, 204.
5. F. Travis and C. Pearson. Pure consciousness: Distinct phenomenological and physiological correlates of "consciousness itself." *International Journal of Neuroscience* 2000; 100:77–89. The relatively shallow nature of such "pure consciousness" events can be appreciated in the words chosen to describe the episodes: "the 'content' of pure consciousness is self-awareness."
6. Forman, *The Problem of Pure Consciousness*, 8.
7. Austin, Six points to ponder, 215.
8. R. Forman. What does mysticism have to teach us about consciousness? *Journal of Consciousness Studies* 1998; 5:185–201.
9. J. Shear and R. Jevning. Pure consciousness: Scientific exploration of meditation techniques. *Journal of Consciousness Studies* 1999; 6(2–3):189–209. Maharishi (cited on p. 193) considers this "easily experienced" state as "beyond all thinking and beyond all feeling." One can agree that arriving "as" the state of Being is likely to be more accurate than arriving "at" this state. Shear and Jevning go on to observe that "pure, qualityless consciousness" can also be accompanied by the "experience of what we can call 'pure positive affect' (pure bliss, joy, happiness, beauty, etc.)." In this case, the authors appear to be describing emotions commonly experienced during the absorptions, and in some quickenings. Kensho and satori also have a range of "qualities" within their experience of clarified consciousness [Z:542–544].
10. M. Heidegger. *The Question of Being,* trans. W. Kuluboch and J. Wilde. New York, Twayne, 1958, 33–109.
11. Edward Carpenter, Quoted in Bucke, *Cosmic Consciousness*, 201, 321, citing Carpenter's publication in 1892.
12. Ibid., 206.
13. T. Fehr. From the vedas to the EEG: Characteristics of altered "higher" states of consciousness. *Journal for Meditation and Meditation Research* 2002; 1:82–83. In Fehr's terminology, this so-called Cosmic Consciousness refers to more of an ongoing stage. It is said to be arrived at only by meditators who have practiced for many years. I prefer to discuss this kind of awareness as more of an "ever-present awareness" (see chapters 48, 55, and 56). Awareness is not wisdom, though the two may overlap. Therefore, I do not regard it as equivalent to the "sage wisdom" characteristic of the Stage of Ongoing Enlightened Traits. As Fehr notes, the laboratory correlates [of what I regard as an ever-present awareness] include a larger contingent negative variation in the ERP; greater degrees of theta-alpha EEG coherence when the eyes remain open; a tendency to experience "witnessing sleep," including higher theta/alpha power; and lesser degrees of muscle tone by EMG during deep sleep.

Chapter 88 Are There Levels and Sequences of "Nonattainment?"

1. T. Cleary. *Classics of Buddhism*, vol. 1. Boston, Shambhala, 2001, 394.
2. Y. Okuda, trans. *The Discourse on the Inexhaustible Lamp of the Zen School.* Zen Master Torei Enji. Commentary by Master Daibi of Unkan. Foreword by Myokyo-ni. London, Zen Centre, 1989, 499. Torei Enji (1721–1792) was a Dharma heir of Master Hakuin Ekaku (1686–1769).
3. J. Engler. Just as it is. *Tricycle* 2004; 13:53–57, 114–115.
4. Ibid.
5. P. Fletcher, O. Zafiris, C. Frith, et al. On the benefits of not trying: Brain activity and connectivity reflecting the interactions of explicit and implicit sequence learning. *Cerebral Cortex* 2005; 15:1002–1015.

Chapter 89 Cultivating Compassion, a Native Virtue

1. A. Shopenhauer. This epigraph is adapted from a translation cited in I. Morrison, D. Lloyd, G. diPellegrino, et al. Vicarious responses to pain in anterior cingulate cortex: Is empathy a multisensory issue? *Cognitive, Affective, and Behavioral Neuroscience* 2004; 4:270–278. Empathy is limited to the observer's *perceptive*, affective, imaginative side. We think of compassion as tending to accept some degree of responsibility for actively improving the situation [Z:648–653].
2. I. Morrison, et al., ibid. The video shows the pin coming in contact with the fingertips of another person who was not known to the subject. The authors relate the observer's anterior cingulate activation to the motivational-affective dimension of pain processing.
3. D. Goldman, ed. *Destructive Emotions. How Can We Overcome Them?* New York, Bantam Dell, 2003, 1–27.
4. H. Inagaki. *A Dictionary of Japanese Buddhist Terms. With Supplement.* Union City, CA, Heian International, 1988, 42. The phrase is said to include the realization of the nonsubstantiality of all living beings.

Chapter 90 On "Moral Cognition"

1. F. Bridges. *A Manual of Phrenology*. London, Tegg & Son, 1838, 24–25. (Ex libris, James Austin Jr.)
2. R. Adolphs. Cognitive neuroscience of human behavior. *Nature Reviews Neuroscience* 2003; 4:165–178.
3. W. Casebeer. Moral cognition and its neural constituents. *Nature Reviews Neuroscience* 2003; 4:840–845.
4. J. Moll, R. de Oliveira-Souza, and P. Eslinger. Morals and the human brain: A working model. *NeuroReport* 2003; 14:299–306. The bump of "benevolence" cited in the epigraph correlated with a high forehead, well in front of the bump of "veneration." It is only a coincidence that this posterior bump of veneration happens to lie in about the same position as the bigger midline enlargement (the ushnisha) which artists in an earlier millennium chose to imagine would be symbolic of the Buddha's expanded mental capacities [Z:687].
5. J. Greene. From neural "is" to moral "ought": What are the moral implications of neuroscientific moral psychology? *Nature Reviews Neuroscience* 2003, 846–849.

Chapter 91 Some Aspects of Maturity That Are Nurtured during Long-Range Meditative Training

1. A. Cohen and K. Miller. Following the grain of the kosmos. *What Is Enlightenment?* 2004 (May–July); no. 25, 44–52.

2. R. Emmons and M. McCullough. Counting blessings versus burdens: An experimental investigation of gratitude and subjective well-being in daily life. *Journal of Personality and Social Psychology* 2003; 84:377–389.

Chapter 92 Pointing toward a Late Lunar Phase of Objective Vision

1. J. Campbell (with Bill Moyers). *The Power of Myth*. New York, Doubleday, 1988, 61.
2. In fact, a bright enveloping light had once occurred while I was sleeping, but it was only an isolated quickening [Z:376–379].

Chapter 93 A Contemporary "Taste of Kensho": Its Profile of Early and Late Phenomena

1. F. Cook. *Sounds of Valley Streams. Enlightenment in Dogen's Zen*. Albany, State University of New York Press, 1989, 67.
2. The account of kensho in the earlier book (Z:536–544, 573–578, 589–621) described the "clear, cold moonlight-like quality" as "an internal fact of experience." It also specified that this was *not* a simile. I did not try then to analyze the details either of this phenomenon or of the other visual illusions. This was both for lack of space and for lack of information about what might have caused them.
3. P. Kapleau. *Zen: Dawn in the West*. Garden City, NY, Anchor/Doubleday, 1980, 148. The writer of that phrase—named "Roger"—had awakened at 2:00 A.M. on the morning after a Zen retreat. He then underwent an unusually extended "whole process" that "lasted for two hours." If it had begun as a variation on the theme of the absorptions, it later evolved into a state that was considered to be an "awakening" (the two states sometimes evolve in tandem [Z:617]). Early in this process, Roger had written of finding himself "in a vast, empty space, lit as it were by moonlight, with a feeling of just being at home." I appreciate the opportunity to have had a recent long, fruitful telephone conversation with Roger. On 26 March 2004, he verified that to the best of his recollection the quoted reference to moonlight was *not a visual sensory, perceptual, event* (i.e., it was *not* a visual illusion). Instead, he said he had used the word "moonlight" as an allusion. As an interesting sidelight, he described having the adult onset of migraine *aura* symptoms at the age of 54. Visual scintillations were prominent, but there was no nausea, vomiting, and never more than a minimal dull headache (see chapter 73).

Chapter 94 How Our Brain Normally Perceives Light and Colors

1. A. Ferguson. *Zen's Chinese Heritage. The Masters and Their Teachings*. Boston, Wisdom, 2000, 71–72.
2. M. Steriade, E. Jones, D. McCormick, et al. *Thalamus. Organization and Function*, vol 1. Oxford, Elsevier Science, 1997, 468–488.
3. C. Heywood and A. Cowey. Cerebral achromatopsia. In *Case Studies in the Neuropsychology of Vision*, ed. G. Humphreys. New York, Plenum, 1999, 17–39. Lesions of adjacent regions create other dysfunctions.
4. Expert researchers still differ in the ways they describe the location and extent of this region and interpret its functions. Recent designations speak in terms of V4, V4a, V4v and V4/V8. For this reason, the several related color-biased regions are referred to here with the provisional term, "V4 color complex." The interested reader is referred to the following articles for a further discussion: S. Zeki and L. Marini. Three cortical stages of colour processing in the human brain. *Brain* 1998; 121:1669–1685; N. Hadjikhani and R. Tootell. Projection of rods and cones within human visual cortex. *Human Brain Mapping* 2000; 9:55–63; A. Bartels and S. Zeki. The architecture of the colour centre in the human visual brain: New results

and a review. *European Journal of Neuroscience* 2000; 12:177–193; R. Tootell and N. Hadjikhani. Where is "dorsal V4" in human visual cortex? Retinotopic, topographic and functional evidence. *Cerebral Cortex* 2001; 11:298–311; K. Gegenfurtner. Cortical mechanisms of colour vision. *Nature Reviews Neuroscience* 2003; 4:563–572; R. Tootell, K. Nelissen, W. Vanduffel, et al. Search for color "center(s)" in macaque visual cortex. *Cerebral Cortex* 2004; 14:353–363; K. Gegenfurtner and D. Kiper. Color vision. *Annual Review of Neuroscience* 2003; 26:181–206. The last-named authors emphasize the important fact that color processing occurs widely, though the V4 region "has a high sensitivity to color relative to luminance."

5. I. Hasegawa and Y. Miyashita. Categorizing the world: Expert neurons look into key features. *Nature Reviews Neuroscience* 2002; 5:90–91.
6. F. Birren. *Color and Human Response*. New York, Van Nostrand Reinhold, 1978, 36, 119, 125.
7. F. Birren. *Color and Environment*. New York, Van Nostrand Reinhold, 1969, 15–20.
8. C. Riley. *Color Codes*. Hanover, NH, University Press of New England, 1995, 319–320. Riley's source for this quotation is Sacks and Wasserman's article in the *New York Review of Books*, 19 November 1987, 32.

Chapter 95 Significance of the Late "Moonlight" Phase within the Whole Profile of Kensho

1. K. Tanahashi, ed. *Moon in a Dewdrop. Writings of Zen Master Dogen*. San Francisco, North Point Press, 1985, 129.
2. W. Merigan and J. Munsell. How parallel are the primate visual pathways? *Annual Review of Neuroscience* 1993; 16:369–402.
3. W. Merigan, L. Katz, and J. Munsell. The effects of parvocellular lateral geniculate lesions on the acuity and contrast sensitivity of macaque monkeys. *Journal of Neuroscience* 1991; 11:994–1001. These localized excitotoxic lesions were made with ibotenic acid.
4. Merigan et al., Effects of parvocellular lateral geniculate lesions. A discrete inhibitory process in this nucleus might, in theory, spare its large rod pathway M cells in layers 1 and 2, even while it blocked its small P cells in lamellae 3, 4, 5, and 6 from relaying their color-related messages.
5. J. Cohen and F. Tong. The face of controversy. *Science* 2001; 293:2405–2407. This discussion focuses on the differences involved in two rival theories of face perception. One concept involves a single modular "face-selective area." The other involves a more distributed organization that draws on multiple "face-responsive areas."
6. N. Hadjikhani and B. de Gelder. Neural basis of prosopagnosia: An fMRI study. *Human Brain Mapping* 2002; 16:176–182.
7. P. Downing, Y. Jiang, M. Shuman, et al. A cortical area selective for visual processing of the human body. *Science* 2001; 293:2470–2473.
8. D. Van Essen and E. Deyoe. Concurrent processing in the primate visual cortex. In *The Cognitive Neurosciences*, ed. M. Gazzaniga. Cambridge, MA, MIT Press, 1995, 383–400.
9. J. Taylor, ed. *Selected Writings of John Hughlings Jackson*, vol. 2. London, Staples Press, 1958, 23–27.
10. M. Critchley. *The Parietal Lobes*. London, Arnold, 1955.
11. Ibid., 301.
12. D. Williams. Temporal lobe syndromes. In *Handbook of Clinical Neurology*, vol. 2, eds. P. Vinken and G. Bruyn. Amsterdam, North Holland, 1969, 700–724. My observations suggest that the degree of distancing may exceed the degree of micropsia at a time when the two separate phenomena happen to coincide.
13. Critchley, *The Parietal Lobes*, 300.
14. Williams, Temporal lobe syndromes.

15. J. Austin. Consciousness evolves when the self dissolves. *Journal of Consciousness Studies* 2000; 7:209–230. Items (g) through (j) are common in the responses to psychoactive drugs, and can shift rapidly from one to the other extreme (see chapter 71).

16. D. Fish, P. Gloor, F. Quesney, et al. Clinical responses to electrical brain stimulation of the temporal and frontal lobes in patients with epilepsy. *Brain* 1993; 116:397–414.

17. P. Gloor. Experiential phenomena of temporal lobe epilepsy. *Brain* 1990; 113:1673–1694.

18. Ibid.

19. A. Valentin, M. Anderson, G. Alarcon, et al. Responses to single pulse electrical stimulation identify epileptogenesis in the human brain in vivo. *Brain* 2002; 125:1709–1718.

20. John Horgan recently reviewed these issues in *Rational Mysticism. Dispatches from the Border between Science and Spirituality*. Boston, Houghton Mifflin, 2003, chap. 5, "The God Machine," 91–105. In the Hardy survey, 20% of the subjects reported a sense of "presence" as a phenomenon that was included in their religious experience.

21. J. Saver and J. Rabin. The neural substrates of religious experience. *Journal of Neuropsychiatry and Clinical Neurosciences* 1997; 9:498–510; H. Gastaut. New comments on the epilepsy of Fyodor Dostoevsky. *Epilepsia* 1984; 25:408–411.

22. V. Ramachandran and S. Blakeslee. *Phantoms in the Brain. Probing the Mysteries of the Human Mind*. New York, Morrow, 1998, 180–182. These pages present a brief informal account of a 32-year-old man who had many religious and philosophical preoccupations. His (epileptic) seizures started at the age of 8. They first began with a bright light. A few years later, several seizures "transformed his whole life." He experienced an unparalleled rapture, in which was a clear "apprehension of the divine—no categories, no boundaries, just a Oneness with the Creator."

23. H. Naito and N. Matsui. Temporal lobe epilepsy with ictal ecstatic state and interictal behavior of hypergraphia. *Journal of Nervous and Mental Disease* 1988; 176:123–124.

24. H. Morgan. Dostoevsky's epilepsy: A case report and comparison. *Surgical Neurology* 1990; 33:413–416.

Chapter 96 Significance of the Illusions at the Close of the Moonlight Phase

1. K. Kraft. *Eloquent Zen. Daito and Early Japanese Zen*. Honolulu, University of Hawaii Press, 1992, 187. Daito founded Daitokuji in Kyoto in 1326.

2. M. Steriade, E. Jones, and D. McCormick. *Thalamus. Organization and Function*, vol. 1. Oxford, Elsevier Science, 1997, 485.

3. Lateral inhibition and opposing center/surround effects can lead to localized enhancement of luminous contrasts along boundaries [Z:247–253]. White-against-black contrasts can be more obvious along the edges of larger objects. This particular distinction did not register on the witness in the brief time available. I thank Dr. Brian Dyre for the discussion that amplified this point.

4. The quick, negative afterimage phase represented a single "one-time-only" snapshot of an actual outdoor scene, rendered solely in black and white. However, several of its aspects were reminiscent of events during one earlier episode of visual "quickening" [Z:390–391]. This prior episode had presented not as one quick "negative snapshot," but as a whole (tachistoscopic) *series* of brief, positive images. Each scene recalled took the form of a visual memory. It represented an actual event in the past. Each old image, when briefly retrieved, had then entered my visual experience as a *faded* color print, not in full color. Moreover each faded image was comparable with a print I might have viewed—in *subdued light*—as I looked *down* at it while turning the pages of an old photograph album. All these images presented themselves as displaced *below* the expected horizontal line, though they were well centered.

On reflection, these qualities of reduced illumination and reduced coloring suggest that on that particular occasion also, all color pathways were not then fully engaged in rendering this sequence of memory "snapshots." The downward displacement of this series of images also suggested that some kind of poorly understood "coupling" may exist between one's frame of attention and this variety of projection of decolored images from memory stores.

5. Y. Shu, A. Hasenstaub, and D. McCormick. Turning on and off recurrent balanced cortical activity. *Nature* 2003; 423:288–293.
6. Steriade et al., *Thalamus*, 482–483, 486–488.
7. Such operations would need to be complex in order to create both (a) a brief, inhibitory reversal of each previously excited smaller region that had just served to mediate the image of "light," and (b) an equally coherent excitatory reversal of those previously inhibiting ("dark-inducing") functions served by the zones that had just surrounded them.
8. E. Jones. The thalamic matrix and thalamocortical synchrony. *Trends in Neurosciences* 2001; 24:595–601. The first system (for conscious perception) runs from the lateral geniculate to the visual cortex. The second visual system (for unconscious perception) runs from the superior colliculus through the pulvinar and into the posterior parietal lobe.
9. G. DeAngelis, B. Cumming, and W. Newsome. A new role for cortical area MT: The perception of stereoscopic depth. In *The New Cognitive Neurosciences,* 2nd ed., ed. M. Gazzaniga. Cambridge, MA, MIT Press, 2000, 305–314. The capacity of the witness to generate an illusion of "depth" is an additional confirmation (if one were needed) that this V5 part of his "rod pathway" was still functioning. V5 is located in the lateral part of the posterior temporo-occipital region and is considered to be one of those cortical modules on the upward-directed rod pathway.

   Recall that any simplified distinctions we set up earlier between "separate rod and cone" pathways are only provisional. The brain's many complex pathways provide ample opportunities for exceptions. One recent illustration suffices. Occipitotemporal lesions that are large enough to cause achromatopsia can still spare a pathway (one which also confers high-contrast color information) that does contribute to the way the patient continues to perceive motion. See P. Cavanagh, M.-A. Henaff, F. Michel, et al. Complete sparing of high-contrast color input to motion perception in cortical color blindness. *Nature Reviews Neuroscience* 1998; 1:242–247.
10. M. Mennemeier, E. Wertman, and K. Heilman. Neglect of near peripersonal space. *Brain* 1992; 115:37–50. Moreover, when normal subjects receive so much external magnetic stimulation that it "jams" the intricate functions of this region, their attention is disrupted within the corresponding left lower visual fields. See O. Bjoertomt, A. Cowey, and V. Walsh. Spatial neglect in near and far space investigated by repetitive transcranial magnetic stimulation. *Brain* 2002; 125:2012–2022.

    When the phrase "far space" is referred to (as in the reports just cited above), the actual task in the laboratory usually involves bisecting short lines that are still relatively "near" to the subject. Many useful conclusions can be drawn from line-bisection data tested at standard laboratory distances measured only in centimeters. However, they may not necessarily generalize to the long distances involved in an outdoor situation, as was the case with the London scenery that morning.
11. A. Barrett, R. Schwartz, R. Crucian, et al. Attentional grasp in far extrapersonal space after thalamic infarction. *Neuropsychologia* 2000; 38:778–784.
12. F. Grenier, I. Timofeev, and M. Steriade. Leading role of thalamic over cortical neurons during postinhibitory rebound excitation. *Proceedings of the National Academy of Sciences U S A*

1998; 95:13929–13934. It remains to be determined how much of the inhibition of color vision could occur at synapses precisely localized inside the temporo-occipital cortex per se, and how much could reflect other inhibitory effects mediated on thalamic ↔ cortical oscillations by the reticular nucleus of the thalamus (see chapter 44).

13. Each hemisphere directs covert inhibitory processes. These *negate* some attentional functions of its partner in the homologous region over on the opposite side. To illustrate: patients who have *right* posterior parietal damage show visual neglect of the environment off to their *left*. Some of their dysfunction reflects a *secondary* attentive *imbalance*. This bias is generated from the patients' intact (left) hemisphere. It is attributable to the way their right-sided lesion also damaged some of their usual inhibitory nerve cells on that right side. Normally, pathways from these cells cross over to the left side. There they serve to check the normal excitatory attentive mechanisms of the *left* parietal region. However, this left parietal region tends to overreact after it has been released from this normal tonic inhibitory influence. Now disinhibited, its functions are biased more to attend to events arising in the right side of the environment. This theory has been tested. See M. Oliveri, E. Bisiach, F. Frighina, et al. rTMS of the unaffected hemisphere transiently reduces contralesional visuospatial hemineglect. *Neurology* 2001; 57:1338–1340; C. Hilgetag, H. Theoret, and A. Pascual-Leone. Enhanced visual spatial attention ipsilateral to rTMS-induced "virtual lesions" of human parietal cortex. *Nature Neuroscience* 2001; 4:953–957.

Chapter 97 Some Cultural and Neural Origins of Moon Metaphors and Visual Symbols

1. W. LaFleur. *Awesome Nightfall: The Life, Times, and Poetry of Saigyo*. Boston, Wisdom, 2003, 130. I doubly thank Professor LaFleur: first, for personally verifying "satori"; second, for pointing out that, in the twelfth century, Japanese monks engaged in formal, extended meditation practice. This was in accord with the natural monthly cycle of the waxing and waning of the real moon, or with its symbolic representation (p. 66).
2. C. Holman. *Figures of speech*, vol. 11; *Imagery*, vol. 14. In the *Encyclopedia Americana, International Edition*. Danbury, CT, Grolier, 2000, 195–198, 796–797.
3. A. Nakamura, B. Maess, T. Knosche, et al. Cooperation of different neuronal systems during hand sign recognition. *Neuroimage* 2004; 23:25–34.
4. T. Terayama. *Zen Brushwork. Focusing the Mind with Calligraphy and Painting*. Tokyo, Kodansha International, 2003, 79.
5. H. Henderson. *An Introduction to Haiku*. Garden City, NY, Doubleday, 1958.
6. L. Stryk and T. Ikemoto. *Zen: Poems, Prayers, Sermons, Anecdotes, Interviews*, 2nd ed. Athens, OH, Swallow Press, Ohio University Press, 1981.
7. LaFleur, *Awesome Nightfall*.
8. S. Hamill and J. Seaton. *The Poetry of Zen*. Boston, Shambhala, 2004, 27.
9. N. Foster and J. Shoemaker. *The Roaring Stream. A New Zen Reader*. Hopewell, NJ, Ecco Press, 1996, 147.
10. T. Cleary. *Kensho. The Heart of Zen*. Boston, Shambhala, 1997, 92–93.
11. S. Hamill and J. Seaton, ibid., 29.
12. A. Ferguson. *Zen's Chinese Heritage. The Masters and Their Teachings*. Boston, Wisdom, 2000, 327–332.
13. A. Braverman, trans. *Mud and Water. A Collection of Talks by the Zen Master Bassui*. San Francisco, North Point Press, 1989, 126.
14. T. Cleary. *Zen Essence. The Science of Freedom*. Boston, Shambhala, 1989, 15 (Fenyang Shauchao).
15. T. Cleary. *Classics of Buddhism and Zen*, vol. 1. Boston, MA, Shambhala, 2001, 188 (Hung-chih Cheng-chueh). The same Hung-chih would also give this excellent advice with respect

to one's daily life practice: "Dig the pond, don't wait for the moonlight; when the pond is complete, the moonlight will naturally be there" (p. 329). He was in the Soto (T'sao-tung) lineage.

16. Cleary, *Classics of Buddhism and Zen*, 190. Getting rid of these delusions and attachments was described as "coming out of the weeds." Yuan-wu K'e-chin was in the Rinzai (Lin-chi) lineage.
17. S. Barnet and W. Burto. *Zen Ink Paintings*. Tokyo, Kodansha International, 1982, 82–85.

Chapter 98 The Hernandez Connection: A Darkened Sky and Moonglow

1. T. Kogetsu and E. Shimano. *Zen Words. Zen Calligraphy*. Printed in Kyoto, Japan, 1991, 68. This translation suggests that the original poem is attributable to Han Shan, a practicing Buddhist layman of the seventh or eighth century. He described his heart-mind (shin) as resembling the moon in autumn, as it was reflecting from the clear pure water of a pool. But he questioned what else could be said, because there was nothing to compare it with. See S. Hamill and J. Seaton. *The Poetry of Zen*. Boston, Shambhala, 2004, 32.
2. A. Adams. *An Autobiography*. Boston, Little Brown, 1985, 382. See also p. 273.
3. A. Adams. *Examples: The Making of 40 Photographs*. Boston, Little Brown, 1983, 40–43.
4. Adams was aiming for the particular photographic effect that "looks like it feels." One prior experience helped make the special quality of light so eloquent for Adams. It happened on a morning back in 1923, on a hike in the mountains. He observed that "the silver light" of the sun had "turned every blade of grass and every particle of sand into a luminous metallic splendor." (His phrase, "silver light" accurately describes this luminosity at high altitudes. It is reinforced by reflections from myriads of mica and silica particles. In this respect, that morning's ambient light resembled moonlight more than the golden light one usually associates with the sun. Parenthetically, the word luna referred to the silver used in alchemy.)

   Next, as he crunched along the ridge trail west of Mount Galen Clark, Adams was "suddenly arrested ... by an exceedingly pointed awareness of the light. The moment I paused, the full impact of the mood was upon me. I saw more clearly than I have ever seen before or since the minute detail of the grasses.... There are no words to convey the moods of those moments." From J. Szarkowski. *Ansel Adams at 100, Letters and Images*. Boston, Little Brown, 2001, 21–22.
5. Adams received more letters about this Hernandez photograph than from any of his other photographs. We can only wonder how much of its final, silvery moonlit theme could be attributable not just to the silver emulsion of that single 1941 negative but also to the earlier mood and mental image he had fixed in his own brain when he was on that ridge trail back in 1923. As for the darkness in the 1941 photograph, back in 1927 he had already used a red filter to revise the tonal relationships of Half-Dome in Yosemite to produce a sky darkened to black.

Chapter 99 Other Ancient Fingers Pointing toward the Moon

1. N. Foster and J. Shoemaker. *The Roaring Stream. A New Zen Reader*. Hopewell, NJ, Ecco Press, 1996, 22–32. (From "Song of Realizing the Way.")
2. D. T. Suzuki, Quoted in A. Watts. *The Spirit of Zen. A Way of Life, Work, and Art in the Far East*. Boston, Charles Tuttle, 1992, 80.
3. T. Cleary. *Zen Essence. The Science of Freedom*. Boston, Shambhala, 1989, 17 (Fenyang Shau-chao). Sino-Japanese uses the same ideogram for form and color. Material things that have form usually have color as well.
4. T. Cleary and J. Cleary. *The Blue Cliff Record*, vol. 2. Boulder, CO, Shambhala, 1977, 306–311 (case 43).

5. H.-J. Kim. *Flowers of Emptiness. Selections from Dogen's Shobogenzo. Studies on Asian Thought and Religion*, vol. 2. Lewiston/Queenston, ON, Canada, Edwin Mellen Press, 1985, 246–252.
6. M. Anesaki. *History of Japanese Religion*. Rutland, VT, Charles Tuttle, 1963, 208. (Anesaki's free translation is in accord with my experience.) Cf. the poem of "a small abandoned boat" in K. Tanahashi, ed. *Moon in a Dewdrop. Writings of Zen Master Dogen*. San Francisco, North Point Press, 1985, 215.
7. Of course, non-Buddhist poets also fall under the spell of the moon. They can invoke its presence in an oceanic context devoid of self (and possibly beyond time as well). One of Dogen's contemporaries was the great Sufi mystic and poet, Jelaluddin Rumi (1207–1273). Said Rumi: "I made a journey of the soul accompanied by the moon, until the secret of time was totally revealed. Heaven's nine spheres were in that moon. The vessel of my being had vanished in that sea." Here, the word "spheres" refers to all the higher cosmic wisdom implicit in that solar system of sun, moon, and major planets as they were then known. See K. Helminski. *Love Is a Stranger: Selected Lyric Poetry of Jelaluddin Rumi*. Boston, Shambhala, 2000, 76. See also note 15 below.
8. R. Hass. *The Essential Haiku. Versions of Basho, Buson, and Issa*. Hopewell, NJ, Ecco Press, 1994, 116. Master Kuo-an's earlier lines also spoke of breaking free from entangling nets and snares in his commentary on the seventh ox-herding picture, as noted in chapter 87.
9. D. Chadwick. *Crooked Cucumber. The Life and Zen Teaching of Shunryu Suzuki*. New York, Broadway, 1999, 279. An element of modesty may help determine whether the circle remains partially open or closed.
10. S. Barnet and W. Burto. *Zen Ink Paintings*. Tokyo, Kodansha International, 1982, 92–93; *The Shambhala Dictionary of Buddhism and Zen*. Boston, Shambhala, 1991, 229–230.
11. Ibid., *Shambhala Dictionary*, 229–230.
12. Early in his chapter on the moon, Dogen, too, referred to the "dharma-body of the Buddha" in this moon-circle context. When Dogen visited the Kuang-li temple in China in 1225, he saw a singular wall painting. It portrayed Nagarjuna not as a person like all the other early Indian patriarchs, but *as a round moon*. This symbolic version was in accord with an old legend from Indian Buddhism. It alleged that Nagarjuna was once said actually to have manifested absolute freedom, in the shape of a moon. Dogen cautioned (as he had once before in his chapter on the moon) against confusing any symbol of a mere artistic image with the genuine manifestations of enlightenment. See N. Waddell and M. Abe. *The Heart of Dogen's Shobogenzo*. Albany, State University of New York Press, 2002, 77–84.
13. K. Washburn, J. Major, and C. Fadiman, eds. *World Poetry. An Anthology of Verse from Antiquity to our Time*. New York, Norton, 1998, 504.
14. I would later come across a shorter version (with less explicit lines) in the translations of the Zenrin Kushu. See S. Shigematsu. *A Zen Forest. Sayings of the Masters*. New York, Weatherhill, 1981, 385.
15. As a sidelight of interest, the poet Rumi lived for many years in the city called Konya. Konya (in present-day Turkey) was in constant touch with many cultures and religions along the Silk Road all the way to China. Another of Rumi's poems has the title, "A World with No Boundaries." In its first two lines, the poem hints that a person's bodily (physical) self is the first to be lost (as in the absorptions). Only during a later shipwreck is the structure of the psychic self dismantled. Now the "time of union" can arrive (as in kensho-satori).

    When the wave of *Am I not*? struck,
    it wrecked the body's ship;
    When the ship wrecks again,
    it will be the time of union.

See K. Helminski, trans. *Love is a Stranger. Selected Lyric Poetry of Jelaluddin Rumi*. Boston, Shambhala, 2000, 62. See also note 7.

16. I. Miura and R. Sasaki. *Zen Dust. The History of the Koan and Koan Study in Rinzai (Lin-Chi) Zen*. New York, Harcourt, Brace & World, 1966, 179–186.
17. L. Rinbochay and J. Hopkins. *Death, Intermediate State and Rebirth in Tibetan Buddhism*. London, Rider, 1979. The multiple quotations are from pp. 9, 42, and 55. My thanks to Dr. Alan Wallace for kindly directing me to this reference.
18. Always remember that the evidence cited in these pages has passed through many hands as it found its way into our contemporary English translations.
19. H. Maezumi and B. Glassman. *The Hazy Moon of Enlightenment*. Los Angeles, Center Publications, 1977, 15–16.
20. Chapters 76–79 discuss Seng-chao and "Oneness."

Chapter 100 People Differ in Their Response to Illusions: Psychological Considerations

1. Alternatively, a witness who first writes about it inaccurately may later have an opportunity to reflect, to gather more data, and then to describe it correctly. When I first described kensho, I wrote that "a cool lunar perspective pervades this first phase" [Z:599]. Hindsight reminds me of the important distinctions: *a cool, clear mirror perspective* pervaded this first phase. "Moodlight" then gathered momentum. Perception did not become "lunar" until the end of reflection II, when all color dropped out.

Chapter 101 People Differ in Their Susceptibility to Illusions

1. Whether visual or auditory triggers for kensho correlate with such individual differences is unknown.
2. T. Magos. Correlation between platelet monoamine oxidase activity and the strength of a visual illusion. *Vision Research* 2002; 42:2031–2035. This report is also instructive in how readily it overlooks the possibility that migraine could influence the data. It leaves unstated how many of its 30 "healthy" subjects also had a history of migraine.
3. D. Holschneider, K. Chen, I. Seif, et al. Biochemical, behavioral, physiologic, and neurodevelopmental changes in mice deficient in monoamine oxidase A or B. *Brain Research Bulletin* 2001; 56:453–462. For decades, it has proved difficult to define the precise biological role(s) played by monoamine oxidase B. The enzyme preferentially breaks down phenylethylamine, not serotonin, dopamine, or norepinephrine. Increases in DA_2 receptors require further study.
4. R. Arai, N. Karasawa, K. Kurokawa, et al. Differential subcellular location of mitochondria in rat serotonin neurons depends on the presence and the absence of monoamine oxidase type B. *Neuroscience* 2002; 114:825–835. This mitochondrial B enzyme is in the dendrites and cell bodies of serotonin nerve cells, not out in the distant terminals.
5. F. Javoy-Agid, B. Scatton, M. Ruberg, et al. Distribution of monoaminergic, cholinergic, and GABAergic markers in the human cerebral cortex. *Neuroscience* 1989; 29:251–259. This serotonin metabolite is 5-hydroxyindoleacetic acid (5-HIAA).
6. A. Ardila and E. Sanchez. Neuropsychologic symptoms in the migraine syndrome. *Cephalalgia* 1988; 8:67–70.
7. S. Hall, G. Barnes, A. Hillebrand, et al. Spatiotemporal imaging of cortical desynchronization in migraine visual aura: A magnetoencephalography case study. *Headache* 2004; 44:204–208. This patient had a scintillating scotoma, without headache, twice a year.
8. L. Weiskrantz, A. Rao, I. Hondinott-Hill, et al. Brain potentials associated with conscious aftereffects induced by unseen stimuli in a blindsight subject. *Proceedings of the National*

Academy of Sciences U S A 2003; 100:10503–10505. Some of this patient's afterimages contain complementary colors.

9. B. Claustrat, J. Brun, C. Chiquet, et al. Melatonin secretion is supersensitive to light in migraine. *Cephalalgia* 2004; 24:128–133. The light was delivered starting at 12:30 A.M. Researchers should investigate why sunlight can trigger sneezing in some normals.
10. M. Estevez and K. Gardner. Update on the genetics of migraine. *Human Genetics* 2004; 114:225–235. A sodium, potassium–ATPase is included.
11. A. Cohen and P. Goadsby. Functional neuroimaging of primary headache disorders. *Current Neurology and Neuroscience Reports* 2004; 4:105–110.
12. A vivid hypnapompic hallucination of a leaf occurred very early during a personal experience of internal absorption [Z:470–473]. The quality and intensity of the colored leaf image could have been enhanced as early expressions of these heightened underlying visual sensitivities. Immediately after such a tendency toward excitability first manifested itself, this same underlying tendency toward heightened responses could also have mobilized secondary *inhibitory* responses—these also enhanced—from the reticular nucleus of the thalamus and from allied GABA systems [Z:469–506, 589–592].
13. In a formal interview, Kobori-Roshi immediately rejected the initial hypnapompic hallucination of the leaf referred to above. At a later informal interview, however, he was openly receptive to all other details of the episode of internal absorption, saying that he once had a similar experience [Z:472–473].
14. Ardila and Sanchez, Neuropsychologia symptoms. This study began with 200 subjects who had vascular headache. It then focused only on classic migraine patients who had unusual, *prodromal*, psychological symptoms. It remains for the future to test whether certain types of persons, already susceptible to migraine, might gravitate toward meditative training, and *persist* through its rigors. If so, then the percentages of persons susceptible to migraine among longer-term meditators might reach levels higher than in the general population. This would increase the percentages of meditators likely to manifest the so-called Hildegard syndrome.

In Closing

1. D. Keene. *Anthology of Japanese Literature*. New York, Grove Press, 1955, 316.

Appendix A Other Links between the Moon and Enlightenment in the Old Zen Literature

1. S. Shigesmatsu. *A Zen Forest. Sayings of the Masters*. New York, Weatherhill, 1981, 21.
2. V. Hori. *Zen Sand. The Book of Capping Phrases for Koan Practice*. Honolulu, University of Hawaii Press, 2003. The index entries are on p. 757, and the sample quotations are on pp. 282, 306, and 447.
3. J. Wu. *The Golden Age of Zen*, rev. ed. Taipei, Taiwan, United Publishing Center, 1975, 284.
4. T. Cleary. *Classics of Buddhism and Zen*, vol. 4. Boston, Shambhala, 2001, 643. Insufficient evidence is present to judge whether or not an illusion occurred that involved a distortion of size. A colorless phase of kensho could be unappreciated if it occurred at night when rod channel vision already predominated.
5. A. Ferguson. *Zen's Chinese Heritage*. Boston, Wisdom, 2000, cf. 426.

Appendix B On Wilderness Poetry during the Tang and Sung Periods

1. J. Cashford. *The Moon. Myth and Image*. New York, Four Walls, Eight Windows, 2003, 118.

2. D. Hinton. *Mountain Home. The Wilderness Poetry of Ancient China*. New York, Counterpoint, 2002. Special thanks to the author and publisher of this book from one who makes his home on a lesser mountain.
3. Ibid., 169.
4. E. Bernbaum. *Sacred Mountains of the World*. San Francisco, Sierra Club Books, 1990, 29.
5. Hinton, *Mountain Home*, 169. cf.

Appendix C Daio Kokushi "On Zen"

1. D. T. Suzuki. *Manual of Zen Buddhism*. New York, Grove Press, 1960, 145–146.

Glossary

1. A. Ferguson. *Zen's Chinese Heritage*. Boston, Wisdom, 2000, 428.

Source Notes

I wish to express my appreciation to the following authors, their copyright owners, and their publications for permission to reprint excerpts from their copyrighted works, as indicated here and so specified further in the reference pages:

Vernon D. Rowe, for his poem "MRI of a Poet's Brain," adapted from *Sea Creatures and Other Poems*, Overland Park, KS, 1995, 28. The Dana Press, 745 Fifth Avenue, Suite 900, New York, NY, for permission to reprint figures 2, 3, and 8, from "Your Self, Your Brain, and Zen". *Cerebrum* 2003; 5:47–66. McGraw-Hill, 2 Penn Plaza, New York, NY, for permission to reprint figures 16–7 and 16–8 from C. Noback and R. Demarest, *The Human Nervous System. Basic Principles of Neurobiology*, 3rd ed., 1981, 486.

James W. Austin and Bentley Smith for their assistance on figures 5 and 10.

In the interests of this shorter second book, readers are spared attributions for many epigraphs save for the following:

p. *vii*: D. Goleman, ed. *Destructive Emotions. How Can We Overcome Them?* New York, Bantam Dell, 2003.

p. *xiii*: G. Parrinder. *A Dictionary of Religious and Spiritual Quotations*. New York, Simon & Schuster, 1989.

Part II: S. Blackman. *Graceful Exits. How Great Beings Die*. New York, Weatherhill, 1997, 46.

Part V: F. Cook, trans. *The Record of Transmitting the Light. Zen Master Keizan's Denkoroku*. Boston, Wisdom, 2003, 174.

Part VI: Parrinder, *A Dictionary of Religious and Spiritual Quotations*, 93.

Part VII: D. Mitchell and J. Wiseman, eds. *The Gethsemani Encounter. A Dialogue on the Spiritual Life by Buddhists and Christian Monastics*. New York, Continuum, 1999, 260.

Part VIII: Kobori Nanrei Sohaku. Zen and the art of tea. *The Middle Way* 1972; 46:148–152.

Part IX: Wallace Stevens, The comedian as the letter C. III. 1. *Wallace Stevens. Collected Poetry and Prose*. New York, The Library of America, Penguin. 1997, 27.

Index